D0249413

Bali & Lombok

Ryan Ver Berkmoes, Lisa Steer-Guérard,
Jocelyn Harewood

Contents

North Bali (p233)
Central Mountains (p216)
West Bali (p251)
Ubud & Around (p138)
East Bali (p174)
DENPASAR (p79)
South Bali (p90)

Lombok (p266)

Destination Bali & Lombok

A religious procession brings the tourist-thronged streets of Kuta to a stop; a dancer displays trance-like artistry at an Ubud cultural pavilion; a diver is transfixed by an untouched reef; a surfer finds the perfect break; a walker rubs her eyes trying to cope with the lush green beauty of the surrounding rice paddies; a jaded tourist is charmed by an unexpected act of kindness by a local – all of these things are part of a typical day on Bali. A destination that rises far above a typical tropical island by virtue of its culture, scenery and people.

Where else will you find intricate offerings to the gods placed in serene little niches at world-class resorts? Or see a dance show with movements and music performed by a village dance troupe that has been perfecting their act for generations? Where else can you find sinuous ribbons of rice growing on green terraces wrapping around the hills, amid the myriad of palms and other lush growth?

Of course, Bali's many splendid beaches are a main draw, but it has so much more – from top restaurants and nightlife of South Bali to hidden villages, where travellers can escape the tourist hubbub and much of modern life. Or escape Bali altogether on neighbouring Lombok, which boasts its own unique culture and offers countless chances to get off the beaten track.

Together, Bali and Lombok offer travellers every kind of experience at every kind of budget. Perhaps their greatest appeal is that you can combine so many superb adventures in just one trip.

ALAIN EVRARD

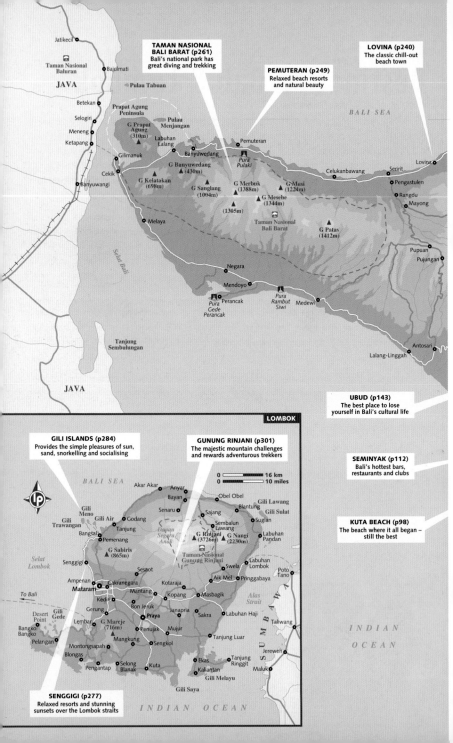

Jatikecil

Taman Nasional
Baluran

JAVA

Bajulmati

Betekan

Selogiri

Meneng

Ketapang

Pulau Tabuan

TAMAN NASIONAL
BALI BARAT (p261)
Bali's national park has
great diving and trekking

PEMUTERAN (p249)
Relaxed beach resorts
and natural beauty

LOVINA (p240)
The classic chill-out
beach town

BALI SEA

Prapat Agung
Peninsula

G Prapat
Agung
(310m)

Pulau
Menjangan

Labuhan
Lalang

Gilimanuk

Cekik

Banyuwangi

Banyuwedang

Pemuteran

Pura
Pulaki

Celukanbawang

Seririt

Lovina

Pengastulen

G Banyuwedang
(430m)

G Kelatakan
(698m)

G Merbuk
(1388m)

G Sanglang
(1004m)

G Musi
(1224m)

Rangdu

Mayong

G Mesehe
(1344m)

(1305m)

Taman Nasional
Bali Barat

G Patas
(1412m)

Pupuan

Pujungan

Melaya

Selat Bali

Negara

Mendoyo

Pura
Gede
Perancak

Perancak

Pura
Rambut
Siwi

Medewi

Tanjung
Sembulungan

Antosari

Lalang-Linggah

JAVA

UBUD (p143)
The best place to lose
yourself in Bali's cultural life

LOMBOK

GILI ISLANDS (p284)
Provides the simple pleasures of sun,
sand, snorkelling and socialising

GUNUNG RINJANI (p301)
The majestic mountain challenges
and rewards adventurous trekkers

SEMINYAK (p112)
Bali's hottest bars,
restaurants and clubs

BALI SEA

Akar Akar

Anyar

Bayan

Obel Obel

0   16 km
0   10 miles

KUTA BEACH (p98)
The beach where it all began –
still the best

Gili
Meno

Gili Air

Godang

Senaru

Sajang

Gili Lawang

Gili Sulat

Gili
Trawangan

Bangsal

Tanjung

Pemenang

Sembalun
Lawang

Sugian

Blantung

Labuhan
Pandan

Selat
Lombok

Danau
Segara
Anak

G Rinjani
(3726m)

G Nangi
(2230m)

G Sabiris
(865m)

Taman Nasional
Gunung Rinjani

Senggigi

Sesaot

Swela

Labuhan
Lombok

Ampenan

Cakranegara

Kotaraja

Aik Mel

Pringgabaya

Poto
Tano

Mataram

Mantang

Kopang

Masbagik

Alas
Strait

Kediri

Bon Jeruk

Gerung

Praya

Janapria

Sakra

Labuhan Haji

Desert
Point

Gili
Gede

Lembar

G Mareje
(716m)

Penujak

Mujur

Tanjung Luar

Taliwang

INDIAN

OCEAN

Bangko
Bangko

Pelangan

Mangkung

Sengkol

Jereweh

Montongsapah

Blongas

Pengantap

Selong
Blanak

Kuta

Ekas

Kaliantan

Tanjung
Ringgit

Maluk

Gili Melayu

Gili Saya

SENGGIGI (p277)
Relaxed resorts and stunning
sunsets over the Lombok straits

INDIAN   OCEAN

SUMBAWA

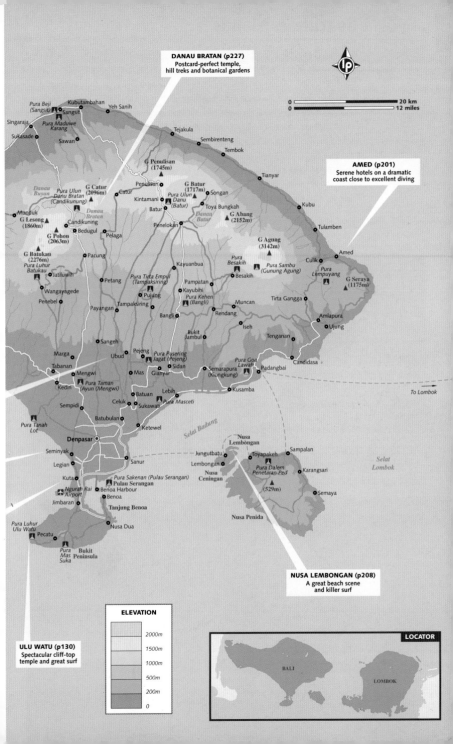

DANAU BRATAN (p227)
Postcard-perfect temple, hill treks and botanical gardens

AMED (p201)
Serene hotels on a dramatic coast close to excellent diving

NUSA LEMBONGAN (p208)
A great beach scene and killer surf

ULU WATU (p130)
Spectacular cliff-top temple and great surf

0 — 20 km
0 — 12 miles

Pura Beji (Sangsit)
Kubutambahan
Yeh Sanih
Sangsit
Singaraja
Pura Maduwe Karang
Sukasade
Sawan
Tejakula
Sembirenteng
Tembok
Tianyar
G Penulisan (1745m)
Penulisan
G Catur (2096m)
Catur
G Batur (1717m)
Kintamani
Pura Ulun Danu (Batur)
Songan
Kubu
Danau Buyan
Pura Ulun Danu Bratan (Candikunung)
Danau Bratan
Batur
Toya Bungkah
Danau Batur
Munduk
G Lesong (1860m)
Candikuning
Penelokan
G Abang (2152m)
Tulamben
Bedugul
Pelaga
G Pohon (2063m)
G Agung (3142m)
Amed
G Batukau (2276m)
Pacung
Kayuanbua
Pura Besakih
Pura Sambu (Gunung Agung)
Culik
Pura Luhur Batukau
Besakih
Pura Lempuyang
Jatiluwih
Petang
Pura Tirta Empul (Tampaksiring)
Pampatan
G Seraya (1175m)
Wangayagede
Pujung
Kayubihi
Penebel
Payangan
Tampaksiring
Pura Kehen (Bangli)
Muncan
Tirta Gangga
Bangli
Rendang
Iseh
Amlapura
Marga
Sangeh
Pejeng
Bukit Jambul
Tenganan
Ujung
Tabanan
Ubud
Pura Pusering Jagat (Pejeng)
Candidasa
Mengwi
Mas
Sidan
Gianyar
Semarapura (Klungkung)
Pura Goa Lawah
Padangbai
Kediri
Pura Taman Ayun (Mengwi)
Batuan
Lebih
Pura Masceti
Kusamba
To Lombok
Sempidi
Celuk
Sukawati
Batubulan
Ketewel
Selat Badung
Pura Tanah Lot
Denpasar
Nusa Lembongan
Seminyak
Sanur
Jungutbatu
Sampalan
Selat Lombok
Legian
Lembongan
Toyapakeh
Karangsari
Kuta
Pura Sakenan (Pulau Serangan)
Nusa Ceningan
Pura Dalem Penetaran Ped
Ngurah Rai Airport
Pulau Serangan
Benoa Harbour
(529m)
Semaya
Jimbaran
Benoa
Tanjung Benoa
Pura Luhur Ulu Watu
Pecatu
Nusa Dua
Nusa Penida
Pura Mas Suka
Bukit Peninsula

ELEVATION
2000m
1500m
1000m
500m
200m
0

LOCATOR
BALI
LOMBOK

Since tourism began on Bali, people have flocked to its many wonderful beaches. The best include **Kuta beach** (p98) for sunbathing, swimming and walking; **Sanur** (p119) for sun and moon rises over Nusa Penida; the many secluded beaches of the **Bukit Peninsula** (p127) and the rugged beaches north of Seminyak at places like **Canggu** (p118). Try the nearly deserted beaches of East Bali beyond Candidasa such as **Pasir Putih** (p198), the groovy scene at the beaches of **Nusa Lembongan** (p208), the classic chill-out beach town of **Lovina** (p240) and the snorkelling and diving joys of **Pemuteran** (p249). For stunning sunsets, head to **Senggigi** (p277) on Lombok.

Cast yourself adrift on Gili Air (p287), Lombok

BERNARD NAPTHINE

ANDREW LUBRAN

Enjoy crystal-clear waters at Gili Meno (p291), Lombok

Cast a line off a traditional Balinese fishing boat in Amed (p201)

PAUL BEINSSEN

Getting off the beach and into the water is the reason many people make the trip to Bali. The range of activities is superb; it includes vaunted locales like the low-key action at **Medewi** (p258), the classic laid-back charms of **Nusa Lembongan** (p208) and southwest Lombok's **Gili Nanggu** (p277) and **Gede** (p277). Under the waves, the diving and snorkelling is fabulous. Sites include the islets off **Candidasa** (p194), the coral reefs off **Amed** (p201), spectacular **Pulau Menjangan** (p263) and both challenging and rewarding **Nusa Penida** (p213).

RICHARD I'ANSON

Make some friends at Kuta Beach (p98)

ALAIN EVRARD

Catch a wave on the Bukit Peninsula (p127)

Dive into the deep at Tulamben (p206)

TIM ROCK

The beach may be fun but what really sets Bali apart as a destination is its amazing and captivating Hindu culture. From tiny offerings left outside your room to elaborate ceremonies involving hundreds, Balinese culture will pervade your trip. A great place to get grounded in the basics of the island's art, architecture, carvings and costumes is at Denpasar's **Museum Negeri Propinsi Bali** (p81). Other aspects of island culture you'll want to seek out are the huge cremations and the almost daily temple and religious processions, which often have a backdrop of traditional architecture.

Marvel at the beautiful dance performances at Ubud Palace (p148)

RICHARD I'ANSON

GREGORY ADAMS

Watch the battle between good and evil at a Barong dance (p41)

ERIC L WHEATER

Celebrate Balinese culture and leave a temple offering (p50)

Bali's culture is a fusion of both religion and the arts and just as the former is a principal part of everyday life, so to is the latter. Artists are integral to the culture and you will see their efforts everywhere. One of the best places for this is in the many villages in and around **Ubud** (p138), where traditional arts thrive. Many of these places bring together artisans skilled in one medium such as the jewellers of **Celuk** (p141), the many varied woodcarvers of **Mas** (p142) and **Tenganan** (p193) with its masters of 'double ikat' weaving. In addition you'll find painters almost everywhere. Over on Lombok, look for the handicraft villages around **Tetebatu** (p306).

Watch ikat weaving (p52) on Lombok

JULIET COOMBE

Admire stone-carvings in
Batubulan (p140)

LEE FOSTER

Purchase an original Pengosekan painting (p47)

JAMES LYON

Whatever your desires – and budget – you can find what you are looking for on Bali and Lombok. From cheap and mellow surfer scenes to luxurious and sybaritic retreats, there is literally something for everyone here. The many experiences possible includes hitting the latest bars, restaurants and clubs of **Seminyak** (p112), hanging around the laid-back traveller's scene on **Nusa Lembongan** (p208) and Lombok's **Gilis** (p284) or enjoying the beauty of one of **Pemuteran's** resorts (p249).

Tantalise all of your senses at the Ubud market (p146)

RICHARD I'ANSON

TONY WHEELER

Splash out and book a night at the Four Seasons Sayan (p162), Ubud

EDWARD AM SNIJDERS

Soak yourself in the hot springs at Air Panas Banjar (p248), Lovina

With religion playing such an important role in Balinese culture, it should be no surprise that temples and monuments dot the island. In fact, thanks to the ready availability of soft stone, these erections are often amazingly elaborate and detailed. Top sites you shouldn't miss include **Gunung Kawi** (p172), the home of ancient, strange stone statues, the sea temple of **Rambut Siwi** (p259) and its superb sunset silhouettes, the temples of **North Bali** (p233) with their 'Bali baroque' carvings and the spectacular cliff-top temple of **Pura Luhur Ulu Watu** (p130). On Lombok, look for temples and palaces of multiple faiths in and around **Mataram** (p268).

Take some time to reflect at Pura Ulun Danu Bratan (p229)

LEE FOSTER

JOHN BANAGAN

Immerse yourself in traditional Kamasan paintings decorating Kertha Gosa Palace (p179)

Visit the famous stone relief carving at Pura Maduwe Karang (p239)

ERIC L WHEATER

As if great beaches, amazing culture and vibrant nightlife aren't enough, Bali and Lombok are also simply beautiful places, where you can pause and soak up the splendour around you. Here's just a few ways to enjoy the islands: soaking up the superb sunsets from anywhere on the west coast, the verdant scenery of East and West Bali, hiking around the blue waters of **Lakes Buyan and Tamblingan** (p230), enjoying the superb views all the way to the North Bali coast from **Munduk** (p230) and trekking in **Taman Nasional Bali Barat** (p261). On Lombok, cruise the coastal road to **Bangsal** (p286) and enjoy the breathtaking mountainous scenery of the **Sembalun Valley** (p300). Its majestic mountain, **Gunung Rinjani** (p301), challenges and rewards trekkers.

JOHN BANAGAN

Wander between the palm trees, farm houses and rice paddies of Labuhan Lombok (p306)

Watch a procession through the rice fields near Tampaksiring (p172)

BILL WASSMAN

Hike around Danau Segara Anak and Gunung Baru, in the Gunung Rinjani region (p301)

JAMES LYON

Getting Started

One of the joys of Bali is that it takes very little to get started. You can land at the airport, find a place to stay in Kuta and be splashing in the waves in little more than an hour at almost any time of year. Although Lombok is not quite as easy, you can still pretty much find your way around with little advance preparation. Getting there is the biggest – but definitely not huge – challenge.

If Bali and Lombok reward the spontaneous traveller, they also reward the traveller who plans. On Bali especially, you can stay at exquisite places, experience unique aspects of the culture and tailor your trip to a remarkable degree with advance work. If you don't want to have any chance of an off day and truly want to maximise your fun, you can reap the rewards of forethought.

See p325 for Climate Charts

Whatever your travel style, you'll find that the real obstacles to independent travel in this part of the world are few. The islands are well used to travellers of all stripes, English is widely spoken and the people truly live up to the shopworn cliché of friendly.

WHEN TO GO

The best time to visit Bali, in terms of the weather, is during the dry season (April to September). The rest of the year is more humid, cloudier and has more rainstorms, but you can still enjoy a holiday.

There are also distinct tourist seasons that affect the picture. The European, American and Japanese summer holidays bring the biggest crowds – July, August and early September are busy. Accommodation can be very tight in these months and prices are higher. Many Australians arrive between Christmas and early January, when airfares to and from Australia are higher and flights can be booked solid. The school holidays in early April, late June to early July and late September also see more Australians, most of them on package tours to resort areas in southern Bali. Many Indonesians visit Bali around the end of December and during some Indonesian holidays. Outside these times Bali has surprisingly few tourists and there are empty rooms and restaurants everywhere.

DON'T LEAVE HOME WITHOUT...

- Double-checking the fast-changing visa situation (p339).
- Sunscreen, sunglasses and a hat to deflect the fierce equatorial sun.
- Ascertaining your country's travel advice for Indonesia (p329).
- A travel insurance policy covering you for any sticky situations.
- Earplugs for the endless repetitions of Bob Marley tunes at beach bars.
- Polishing up your breaststroke; pools and swimming beaches abound.
- Very comfortable but rugged walking shoes or sandals.
- Long trousers or a long skirt, and a collared shirt or blouse for visiting temples and sacred places.
- Warning others that you'll return tanned, rested and ready.
- That book you've been waiting to read.

Balinese festivals, holidays and special celebrations occur all the time, and most of them are not scheduled according to Western calendars, so don't worry too much about timing your visit to coincide with local events (see p330 and p332).

Just 8° south of the equator, Bali has a tropical climate – the average temperature hovers around 30°C (mid-80s°F) all year. Direct sun feels incredibly hot, especially in the middle of the day. In the wet season, from October through March, the humidity can be very high and oppressive. The almost daily tropical downpours come as a relief, then pass quickly, leaving flooded streets and renewed humidity.

There are marked variations across the island. The coast is hotter, but sea breezes can temper the heat. As you move inland you also move up, so the altitude works to keep things cool – at times it can get chilly up in the highlands, and a warm sweater or light jacket can be a good idea in mountain villages such as Kintamani and Candikuning. The northern slopes of Gunung Batur always seem to be wet and misty, while a few kilometres away, the east coast is nearly always dry and sunny.

Air-conditioning is not essential on Bali. A cool breeze always seems to spring up in the evening, especially by the sea, and the open bamboo windows, so common in Balinese architecture, make the most of the light breezes. Ubud is just high enough that sweltering daytime temperatures quickly fall off at night.

On Lombok, the west, where the main town and tourist areas are based, has a climate similar to South Bali but drier. The wet season, from late October to early May, is less extreme, with December, January and February the wettest months. In the dry season, from June to September, temperatures range from hot to scorching. At higher elevations it can get quite cold at night, so bring some extra layers of clothing. Clouds and mist usually envelop the slopes of Gunung Rinjani from early morning onwards, but the south coast is less humid and has clear skies almost every day. Travel is slightly less convenient during Ramadan, the Muslim fasting month (the ninth month in the Muslim calendar), especially in the traditional rural areas, but in the tourist areas there will be little difference in services.

COSTS & MONEY

On Bali, you can spend as much as you want – there are fabulous resorts where a room can be US$500 or more a night, where dinner can cost more than US$75 per person and you can be rejuvenated for US$100 an hour. At the other extreme, you can find decent budget rooms easily for 50,000Rp and enjoy a fresh meal from a *warung* (food stall) for about 10,000Rp. In short, Bali is a bargain for budget travellers, and offers excellent value for those seeking top-flight comforts.

In general, travellers who don't want air-con and hot water will discover they can get good rooms almost anywhere on Bali for under US$10. You can have an excellent three-course meal for US$6, including a large bottle of beer, at many tourist restaurants, while US$15 can get you a gourmet delight at some of the finest restaurants around. See Accommodation (p312) for a full discussion of what kind of bed your money will buy you on Bali and Lombok.

Transport is affordable – remember that Bali is a small island. Public minibuses, buses and *bemos* (small pick-up trucks) are the local form of public transport and they're very cheap – 15,000Rp will get you across the island. A rental motorcycle costs around US$4 per day and a small Suzuki jeep is about US$10 per day. You can charter a car *and* a driver for around US$15 to US$20 per day.

TOP FIVES

BEACHES

- **Kuta Beach** (p98) Cynics aside, this long, curved, wide stretch of sand boasts great surf that swimmers and surfers alike can enjoy. There's always a party scene, and locals and travellers mix and mingle.

- **Jimbaran Beach** (p127) Not as long as Kuta, but the smaller size suits its more quiet and intimate vibe. Great surf and lovely sand.

- **Pasir Putih** (p198) A little-known gem east of Candidasa, this crescent of palm-fringed white sand could be a postcard. Tremendous views of Nusa Penida and company across the water.

- **Nusa Lembongan** (p208) It's still the sixties at this long beach on the little island off East Bali. There's a great travellers' vibe, cheap places to crash and drink a beer, fabulous sunsets and darn good surfing and diving.

- **Gili Island Beaches** (p284) The beaches on these three islands are uniformly gorgeous with white sand, great snorkelling and a timeless mellow vibe.

FESTIVALS

Bali is filled with amazing religious events that will fascinate and transfix you. They occur throughout the year and are scheduled using calendars different from Western ones. See p330 for details. The following events follow an annual schedule and are each a worthy reason to hop on a plane.

- **Nyale Fishing Festival** February or March, Kuta (p310) Thousands of Sasak fishermen build bonfires on the beach at Lombok's Kuta while a myriad of rituals takes place.

- **Bali Art Festival of Buleleng** May or June, Singaraja (p237) Over one week dancers and musicians from some of the region's most renowned village troupes perform.

- **Bali Arts Festival** Mid-June to mid-July, Denpasar (p85) Denpasar hosts a month of cultural performances from the best groups on the island.

- **Kuta Karnival** Late September and early October, Kuta, Bali (p100) Parades, arts competitions, cultural shows, beach sports tournaments, kite-flying contests and more are part of this post-bombing celebration.

- **Ubud Writers & Readers Festival** October, Ubud (p156) Scores of writers and authors from around the world gather in a celebration of writing – especially that which touches on Bali.

SPECIAL PLACES

Travel is filled with moments where you stop, look around and with a sigh of contentment say, 'I'm so glad I'm here.' There's no shortage of places to do this on Bali and Lombok, but here's our favourite five. Now go find some of your own.

- **Beach at Canggu** (p118) The surf is wild and woolly, the beach wind-blown and it's all a little rough-edged. A perfect spot for getting away from the beach hordes elsewhere.

- **Taman Kertha Gosa** (p179) The remains of the old palace in Semarapura hint at the richness of royal life that once dominated Bali.

- **Views from Munduk** (p230) Walking the trails high in the hills, you can look down over coffee plantations, endless rice fields and groves of coconut palms right to the sea.

- **Sungai Ayung** (p151) This river valley west of Ubud near Sayan is surrounded by rice terraces which sinuously follow the flow of water. It's lush, there are bird calls aplenty and the paths are good. You want it to go on forever.

- **Gunung Rinjani** (p301) High on this volcano you can trek to Sembalun, nestled in a fertile valley. It's Shangri-la.

Nearly every museum, major temple or tourist site has an entry charge of about 3000/1500Rp per adult/child – it's a trifling amount. Government-run tourist attractions also charge an insurance premium of 100Rp to 300Rp on top of the admission price, which supposedly covers you against accident or injury while you're there; or maybe it just covers the management against you suing them. You may also have to pay another few thousand rupiah to rent a sarong and/or sash when you visit a temple (see Temple Etiquette, p38), and vehicle parking is usually around 500Rp to 1000Rp extra. If there is no fixed charge, a donation is sometimes requested – anything from 5000Rp to 10,000Rp is acceptable, but you may be encouraged to contribute a lot more. Commercial attractions, like the Taman Burung Bali Bird Park, are more expensive.

There are plenty of tours, water sports and other activities that cost anywhere from just a few dollars to more than US$50.

TRAVEL LITERATURE

Books about Bali are common. Visit one of the bookstores on the island and you will have many choices, with new works appearing monthly. Titles dealing with Lombok, however, are a rarity.

Bali: Paradise Rediscovered is an entertaining and upbeat look at 10 days of life on the island in 2003. A team of well-known photographers fanned out across Bali and managed to rise above the usual 'feel-good' genre.

Fragrant Rice by Janet De Neefe follows her from her time as a naive backpacker from Melbourne to her life today as a mother of a Balinese family. She brings her experience running the wonderful Casa Luna empire in Ubud to her chapters, which cherish local food.

A Patch of Paradise is Gaia Grant's search for 'real life on Bali'. Like many Westerners she was slowly drawn into the local culture and ultimately was transformed.

Bali Moon by Odyle Knight rounds out the subgenre of books about Western women who find more than an affordable holiday on Bali. The book will appeal to anyone who finds magic in crystals, as it recounts Knight's journey of spiritual discovery.

A House in Bali by Colin McPhee is the timeless classic about a Canadian who experienced Bali cultural and village life to the core in the 1930s.

Our Hotel in Bali by Louise Koke is another classic about Westerners on Bali in the 1930s. She and her husband Bob created the first-ever Kuta Beach hotel and had numerous delightful encounters along the way. It's a quick and fun read with lots of photos.

Gecko's Complaint is a morality tale told as an old Balinese children's fable. The recent Periplus edition is richly illustrated.

A Club of Small Men is a cute kid's book based on the Colin McPhee's 1930s children's orchestra.

INTERNET RESOURCES

Bali Discovery (www.balidiscovery.com) Although run by a tour company, this site is easily the best source for Bali news and features week in and week out. Excellent.

Bali Tourism Authority (www.balitourismauthority.net) The official site for the island's tourism department has good general information.

Bali & Beyond (www.baliandbeyond.co.id) The online edition of the tourist magazine has good features and provides a chronicle of what's new on the dining and entertainment fronts.

Lombok Network (www.lombok-network.com) Very comprehensive, this site brings together huge amounts of current information on the island.

Lonely Planet (www.lonelyplanet.com) Share knowledge and experiences with other travellers about islands which have been Lonely Planet favourites from the start.

Itineraries

CLASSIC ROUTES

TOTAL BALI

Two Weeks

Start your trip in **Seminyak** (p112), with the best places to go out for a meal, a drink or more. You'll want at least three days here to experience the wild charms of **Kuta Beach** (p98). Once you're sated on South Bali, head west, driving the back roads around **Tabanan** (p256) and **Kerambitan** (p257), where enormous bamboo trees hang over the roads and the rice terraces are some of the oldest on the island.

Continue west through **Taman Nasional Bali Barat** (p261), Bali's National Park. You can stop here but it's better to press on and settle in at **Pemuteran** (p249). From here you can snorkel or scuba the untouched reefs at **Pulau Menjangan** (p263). Driving east, stop at a few temples on the drier north side of the island. **Lovina** (p240) can be a stop for lunch or a day to enjoy its laid-back beach-town vibe. Either way, head up and over the string of volcanoes that are the heart – and soul – of the island.

Carry on through **Kintamani** (p218), where you'll be rewarded with vistas of Bali's big three: **Gunung Batur** (p220), **Gunung Abang** (p222) and the holiest of holies, **Gunung Agung** (p186). Coming back down on the wet side of the island, head straight to **Ubud** (p143), the spiritual centre of Bali. Nights of dance and culture are offset by days of walking through the serene countryside. Chill out on the beach for your final days on Bali. **Sanur** (p119) and the resorts of the **Bukit Peninsula** (p127) are good choices.

The best of everything on Bali comes together on this two-week trip of a lifetime. You'll bask on the best beaches, drown in a verdant sea of green rice paddies, let the aura of amazing temples flow over you like a warm bath and immerse yourself in Bali's incredible culture that makes it like no other island trip.

TROPICAL FEVER

Two Weeks

Don't stray far from the airport, as **Kuta** (p93) in all its glory is ten minutes away. Hit the bars and clubs after midnight and come back to earth on the beach by day. Maybe you can learn how to surf, or brush up on your skills. Eventually, head east to sober up and mellow out. **Sanur** (p119) inspires snoozes – get some on the sand here. When you're ready, get a boat from here or **Benoa Harbour** (p127) to **Nusa Lembongan** (p208). This little island still has the classic, simple charm of a rural beach town, with a string of hotels – from basic to comfy – lining the sands. It's a timeless travellers' scene with a backdrop of excellent surfing and splendid snorkelling and diving.

Return to Bali and press on to the beaches along the southeast coast. Try some of wild beaches around **Lebih** (p176), where the surf pounds the golden sand. When you get to **Padangbai** (p188), stop. This fun little port town is ideal to hang around in for a couple of days before you hop on a boat to Lombok, anchoring at **Lembar** (p276). Breeze through **Mataram** (p268) and plop down in **Senggigi** (p277), the heart of Lombok's beach scene. The coastline is lovely and gazing back towards Bali you'll already feel you've made a journey – less people visit Lombok than Bali.

Now it's time to push on to the ultimate reward for your island adventure: the **Gili Islands** (p284). Depart from buzzing **Bangsal** (p286) and find yourself cast adrift on three little bits of rock and sand surrounded by azure waters fringed with coral. These are the primo destination for scores of young travellers who revel in the party scene. You shouldn't just plunge in blind, however; set yourself a worthy goal to compare the joys of Gili Trawangan, Gili Meno and Gili Air – then pick your favourite.

If you're coming to Bali you must like islands. This itinerary gives you islands, beaches and more. As well as the numerous beaches on Bali, there's also the funky beach scene at Nusa Lembongan, the untrammelled sands of Lombok and the goofy joys of the Gili Islands. Here's how to live them all in one trip.

ROADS LESS TRAVELLED

LEAVING THE CROWDS BEHIND
One to Two Weeks

Start with a climb of **Gunung Batur** (p220), the 1717m peak in the volcanic caldera that still regularly erupts. The half-day treks up the hill are popular with hikers and the early morning views will give a panorama of things to come. The notorious local guiding agency should be viewed with a certain stoicism that's befitting of the sacred nature of the mountains. We suggest hiring a guide from one of the local agencies. From the volcanic sands atop Gunung Batur, you'll see the blue waters of **Danau Batur** (p218) and the nearby peaks of Gunung Abang and Gunung Agung.

Escape the day-trippers' trails and explore other parts of the mountains, including those where you can see cones forming, promising future volcanic events. Next, tackle **Gunung Agung** (p186), the spiritual centre of the island. Start early so you can reach the top and take in the views of Bali and other islands before the daily onslaught of clouds and mist.

Having climbed Bali's two most legendary peaks, head west to the little village of **Munduk** (p230), which looks down to the north coast and the sea beyond. Go on one of the myriad of walks in the area and enjoy waterfalls, truly tiny villages, wild fruit trees and the sinuous bands of rice paddies lining the hills like ribbons.

Finally, go all the way west and set yourself up for a trek in **Taman Nasional Bali Barat** (p261), the national park. You can quickly escape the development that pervades so much of Bali and plunge into dense tropical forest. Just hearing the chorus of birds is worth the jaunt, but if you're really blessed, you may see the fabled and rare Bali starling.

The great majority of visitors to Bali never get beyond the South Bali–Kuta conurbation – some don't even get up the hill to Ubud! On this trip, you'll definitely get up the hill; in fact you'll get up two, and then you'll work your way down to sea level through some back road villages and the national park.

FINDING BALI'S SPIRITUAL CENTRE   One to Two Weeks

Start at **Pura Luhur Ulu Watu** (p130) right at the southern tip of Bali. It's one of only nine directional temples, as well as a sea temple honouring the many gods in the waters right around the island. Head east to **Pura Mas Suka** (p131), with its remote outlook over the Indian Ocean. From here go north, following the sea temples of the west coast of South Bali – **Pura Petitinget** (p112) in Seminyak is a classic example. Time your visit to **Pura Tanah Lot** (p253) for the morning when crowds are few. One glimpse of its perfect location and you'll understand why the hordes descend for sunset.

Next, try to lose yourself in the hills above West Bali. Stroll around the wide moat protecting the 17th-century **Pura Taman Ayun** (p254) in Mengwi. Then there's more lush scenery to distract you while you travel east through the low hills, crossing innumerable streams and rivers – just the proliferation of water can't help but rejuvenate your spirits. In **Ubud** (p143), settle in for a few days at one of the amazing hotels and experience Balinese art and culture. It won't take long to see how beauty of the mind and spirit merge here.

Heading west of Bali, **Semarapura** (p179) was once the centre of Bali's most important kingdom. Learn how the Balinese held out against the Dutch among its fascinating palace ruins. Find your own spiritual centre in the verdant hills and valleys of East Bali. End your journey in **Amed** (p201), with its dramatic and contemplative ocean overlooks.

The first time you see one of the exquisite little temple offerings left by the side of a tiny shrine, you realise that Bali is like no other island you will visit. Spiritualism is the backbone of the culture and you'll soon see this manifested in numerous ways. This trip takes you to some of Bali's most spiritual places.

TAILORED TRIPS

SURFING SAFARI

You can have an endless summer in under a 100km radius on Bali. No matter the season, there's a break for you. Start where surfing in Asia was born, **Kuta Beach** (p98). Next head to the coast around **Canggu** (p118), where the water is wild and the beaches all but empty. For a classic scene there's **Medewi** (p258) further west, where people surf, sleep and then surf some more. Now, to head south for the incredible challenges of the many breaks around **Ulu Watu** (p130). Here you can find legendary surfing in an unadorned place that feels little-changed in decades. Just working your way through the more than half-dozen breaks will take days.

In the east at **Nusa Dua** (p131), the luxury hotels aren't the only things rising above the horizon – there's often great surf as well. North at **Sanur** (p119) you can pause to wax your board... but why bother? Get one of the boats out to **Nusa Lembongan** (p208) where you can get a room with a view of three legendary breaks for little more than the cost of good wax.

UNDERWATER ACTION

Everyone can see the surfer on top of Bali's waves, but underwater there's even more action. Follow the coast around Bali and you'll be rewarded with one legendary dive spot after another, all with great dive shops in nearby towns. **Pulau Menjangan** (p263) in the national park is renowned for its coral and has the best local diving. The nearby **Pemuteran** (p249) hotels define relaxation. Staying at these hotels is yet another reason why this is a good place to dive. **Lovina** (p240) is a good diving base, since you can reach many of Bali's best sites by day and still have time for one of the local night dives.

Down the east coast is **Tulamben** (p205), where scores of people explore the shattered hulk of a WWII freighter. A smaller wreck lurks off the shores of **Aas** (p202) near Amed. **Candidasa** (p194) is another good diving base; there are lots of local sites to explore and the fish life encompasses everything from sharks to sunfish.

The brass ring for your dives might just be in the distance offshore. **Nusa Penida** (p213) has scores of demanding dives to challenge experienced divers. The rewards are deep grottoes, drop-offs, and everything from mantas to turtles.

SPOIL ME

Kilometre for kilometre, Bali has about the greatest density of fabulous resorts anywhere. From incredible food to hedonistic spas, you can give yourself every sensation you deserve. Three great hotels – the flashy **Legian** (p114), the understated **Oberoi** (p114) and the **Sofitel Seminyak Bali** (p113) – are just north of Kuta in Seminyak. They set the standards for the clean, tropical look that has come to be known as 'Bali Style'.

Great places circle the Bukit Peninsula like a pearl necklace. The **Four Seasons** (p128) in Jimbaran pushes exclusivity while the **Ritz-Carlton** (p128) pushes posh. Across the peninsula, the **Westin Resort** (p133) and the **Conrad** (p136) are adding vitality to Nusa Dua and Tajung Benoa. At the Conrad you can plunge off your own patio into the vast pool which encircles the hotel.

Some of the most storeyed places can be found in the lush lands around Ubud. Along the Ayung Valley, another **Four Seasons** (p162) blends effortlessly with its surrounds. The **Amandari** (p162) and the **Alila** (p162) head the A-list going north along the valley. But top honours go to the **Begawan Giri** (p162), an exclusive compound of private villas which is regularly named one of the best five hotels in the world.

Along the east coast, you can be pampered at two excellent places with sweeping views of Nusa Penida: the **Alila** (p192) near Manggis and the nearby **Amankila** (p192).

LOMBOK: UNDISCOVERED PARADISE

Lombok's tourism ups and downs certainly haven't been to due to its inherent charms, of which there are many. Get a whiff of the colonial past in the faded port town of **Mataram** (p268), and sample the vibrancy of modern life in the thriving markets. **Senggigi beach** (p277) first attracted sun worshippers to its perfect swath of sand, in turn attracting resorts for the sun worshippers.

The eponymously named **Gili Islands** (p284) off the north coast are home to one of Asia's longest running travellers' scenes. Fun and frolic is fuelled by cheap beer that contrasts in colour with the turquoise waters.

Well off the beaten path, the south coast near Lombok's **Kuta** (p308) has stunning beaches and surfing which will reward the intrepid. The little-driven back roads of the interior will thrill the adventurous and curious, with tiny villages where you can leave your regular life far behind and learn about the amazing local handicrafts. Many of these roads lead up the flanks of **Gunung Rinjani** (p301), the volcanic peak which shelters the lush and remote **Sembalun Valley** (p300). Trekking from one village to the next on the rim can take days, but is one of the great walks.

The Authors

RYAN VER BERKMOES
Coordinating Author

Ryan Ver Berkmoes first visited Bali in 1993. On his visits since he has explored almost every corner of the island – along with side trips to Nusas Lembongan and Penida, and Lombok. Just when he thinks Bali holds no more surprises, he, for example, rounds a corner and is struck by the fabulous vistas from Munduk. Better yet, he simply never tires of the place, as an Australian family was bemused to see when he slapped his forehead during a Kecak dance in Ubud and explained: 'I love this.' Off island, Ryan lives in the San Francisco Bay Area and writes about travel for Lonely Planet and others. Ryan wrote the Bali chapters.

My Favourite Trip

I'd spend my days lazing on the beach and nights partying in Seminyak (p112). Sporting a fresh tan, I'd move up to Ubud (p143) where I'd get a room overlooking a rice paddy. I'd walk through the countryside and devour great novels. At night I'd work my way down the list of dance and cultural events posted at the Ubud Tourist Information office. The rest of the time, I'd wander the lush backroads of East and West Bali. You're transported out of the world as you know it and enveloped by vistas featuring shades of green you didn't know existed.

LISA STEER-GUÉRARD

Lisa's ventures into travel started with Indonesia where she trailed over many of the islands and got so hooked she did a degree in the country's cultures. Her fascination with all things Indonesian led to two very different dissertations – one was based on experiences with a Javanese *dukun* (traditional healer), the other, for more light relief, on the ubiquitous pop music, *dangdut*. While living in Java and Sumatra, Lisa also witnessed the political upheavals in '98, worked as a UN election observer, and finally became a travel writer. She currently lives in Paris, France, and writes mainly on Europe and Southeast Asia. Lisa wrote the Lombok chapter.

JOCELYN HAREWOOD

Jocelyn has been visiting Bali since the late 1970s, so of course her house is full of Balinese arts and crafts. In pride of place is a pen-and-ink jungle scene with a monkey grinning lasciviously. She bought it, half-finished, from a young man who was entertaining her children. To her, Bali is still the same glorious, chaotic, ornate place it has always been. The tourists streaming through for all these years have hardly left an imprint. Jocelyn wrote the Culture chapter.

CONTRIBUTING AUTHORS

Dr Trish Batchelor wrote the Health chapter. Trish is a general practitioner and travel medicine specialist who works at the CIWEC Clinic in Kathmandu, Nepal, as well as a medical advisor to the Travel Doctor New Zealand clinics. Trish teaches travel medicine through the University of Otago, and is interested in underwater and high-altitude medicine and in the impact of tourism on host countries. She has travelled extensively through Southeast and East Asia, and loves high-altitude trekking in the Himalayas.

Philip Goad wrote the Contemporary Hotel Design boxed text. Philip is Professor of Architecture at the University of Melbourne. An architectural historian and contemporary design critic, he is the author of *Architecture Bali: Birth of the Tropical Boutique Resort* and with Anoma Pieris is co-author of *New Directions in Tropical Asian Architecture* (2004).

Patrick Witton co-wrote the Food & Drink chapter. Patrick's interest in Indonesia was born out of necessity, when he found himself lost in a market in Java at the age of 12. He has since studied Indonesian both in Melbourne and Bandung, and wrote Lonely Planet's *Indonesian Phrasebook* and *World Food Indonesia*.

Snapshot

The Kuta bombings of October 2002 (see p96) did much more than just destroy hundreds of lives, they shattered an industry that had brought both wealth and problems to the island. During the boom years that were common from the mid-1980s onwards (with an occasional brief hiccup due to an economic crisis or other catastrophe) Bali got used to welcoming more and more visitors spending more and more money each year. Tourism spread from the budget bungalows of Kuta to almost every corner of the island. Upscale resorts appeared amid rice terraces that had otherwise been unchanged for centuries. People who had once faced lives of subsistence living could now look forward to earning wages – albeit low ones – and making plans for the future. The local Hindu culture found its majority status diluted by scores of new arrivals from Java and other islands who came seeking jobs and money.

After the bombs, the number of visitors dropped by more than half. For many Balinese, 2003 was a year of crisis as their once-secure futures, tied to tourism, were imperilled. Some businesses with outside investors kept staff on but tips that used to supplement incomes vanished. Harder hit were family-run lodgings, cafés and shops which had no outsiders to absorb the economic blow. Many feared destitution. Beyond money, many locals will agree that they simply missed the vibrancy provided by hundreds of new arrivals each week. Parts of the island that had grown used to bustle suddenly saw empty streets where children – and those darn dogs – could play with nary an interruption. (On Lombok, locals are all too familiar with this situation since the riots in 2000.)

Certainly, the first six months after the bombs were a time of shock. But then life slowly returned. What can be surprising as you tour the island is seeing the number of businesses – especially hotels – that used the downturn in business as an excuse to make improvements and build for the future. Less concrete, however, is a deeper change that has come to Bali which locals and expats will talk about in only the most careful terms. This centres on the concept that the bombings may have had the unforeseen side effect of helping Bali better prepare for the future. Nobody wants to hint that the blasts were anything but the most terrible of tragedies, but the pause in the years of go-go growth has given many a chance to take stock of what Bali has become. Questions about the environmental and cultural cost of unbridled tourism are being addressed more openly. Organised resistance to new resorts that would deplete the once-thought-inexhaustible waters surging in the hills around Ubud has emerged. Village councils have shown a new willingness to confront the less locally palatable aspects of tourism such as noise from clubs and unseemly behaviour on the beaches.

Whether these contemplative attitudes will persist as the numbers of visitors returns to the pre-bomb levels remains to be seen. For many on Bali, however, the years since 2002 have been a time to think about differing futures, even though the most common question heard is: 'Are people from your country coming back to Bali?'

FAST FACTS

Population Bali/Lombok:
3.1 million/3 million

Percentage of land used for rice production (Bali): 20%

Average monthly wage of a tourism worker: US$50-150

Average nightly rate in a luxury resort: US$250

Number of tourist arrivals on Bali (June, 2002): 130,563

Number of tourist arrivals on Bali (June, 2004): 131,707

Wet season: October to March

Dry season: April to September

Area: 5620 sq km, 140km by 80km

History

There are few traces of Stone Age people on Bali, although it's certain that the island was populated very early in prehistoric times – fossilised humanoid remains from neighbouring Java have been dated to as early as 250,000 years ago. The earliest human artefacts found on Bali are stone tools and earthenware vessels dug up near Cekik in western Bali, estimated to be 3000 years old. Discoveries continue, and you can see exhibits of bones that may be 4000 years old at the Museum Situs Purbakala Gilimanuk near Cekik. Artefacts indicate that the Bronze Age began on Bali before 300 BC.

Little is known of Bali during the period when Indian traders brought Hinduism to the Indonesian archipelago, although it is thought it was embraced on the island by the 7th century. The earliest written records are inscriptions on a stone pillar near Sanur, dating from around the 9th century AD; by that time Bali had already developed many similarities to the island you find today. Rice, for example, was grown with the help of a complex irrigation system, probably very like that employed now, and the Balinese had also begun to develop their rich cultural and artistic traditions.

If little is known about the earliest inhabitants of Bali, then even less is known about Lombok until about the 17th century. Early inhabitants are thought to have been Sasaks from a region encompassing today's India and Myanmar.

HINDU INFLUENCE

Java began to spread its influence into Bali during the reign of King Airlangga (1019–42), or perhaps even earlier. At the age of 16, when his uncle lost the throne, Airlangga fled into the forests of western Java. He gradually gained support, won back the kingdom once ruled by his uncle and went on to become one of Java's greatest kings. Airlangga's mother had moved to Bali and remarried shortly after his birth, so when he gained the throne there was an immediate link between Java and Bali. At this time the courtly Javanese language known as Kawi came into use among the royalty of Bali, and the rock-cut memorials seen at Gunung Kawi, near Tampaksiring, are a clear architectural link between Bali and 11th-century Java.

After Airlangga's death, Bali remained semi-independent until Kertanagara became king of the Singasari dynasty on Java two centuries later. Kertanagara conquered Bali in 1284, but the period of his greatest power lasted a mere eight years, until he was murdered and his kingdom collapsed. However, the great Majapahit dynasty was founded by his son, Vijaya (or Wiiaya). With Java in turmoil, Bali regained its autonomy, and the Pejeng dynasty, centred near modern-day Ubud, rose to great power. In 1343 the legendary Majapahit chief minister, Gajah Mada, defeated the Pejeng king Dalem Bedaulu and brought Bali back under Javanese influence.

Although Gajah Mada brought much of the Indonesian archipelago under Majapahit control, this was the furthest extent of their power.

7th Century	1292
Bali fully embraces Hinduism	Bail gains independence from Java with death of Kertanagara

On Bali, the 'capital' was moved to Gelgel, near modern Semarapura, around the late 14th century, and for the next two centuries this was the base for the 'king of Bali', the Dewa Agung. As Islam spread into Java, the Majapahit kingdom collapsed into disputing sultanates. The Gelgel dynasty on Bali, under Dalem Batur Enggong, extended its power eastwards to the neighbouring island of Lombok and even westwards across the strait to Java.

As the Majapahit kingdom fell apart, many of its intelligentsia, including the priest Nirartha, moved to Bali. Nirartha is credited with introducing many of the complexities of Balinese religion to the island, as well as establishing the chain of 'sea temples', which includes Pura Luhur Ulu Watu and Pura Tanah Lot. Artists, dancers, musicians and actors also fled to Bali at this time and the island experienced an explosion of cultural activity. The final great exodus to Bali took place in 1478.

DUTCH DEALINGS

The first Europeans to set foot on Bali itself were Dutch seamen in 1597. Setting a tradition that has prevailed to the present day, they fell in love with the island and when Cornelius de Houtman, the ship's captain, prepared to set sail from the island, several of his crew refused to come with him. At that time, Balinese prosperity and artistic activity, at least among the royalty, was at a peak, and the king who befriended de Houtman had 200 wives and a chariot pulled by two white buffaloes, not to mention a retinue of 50 dwarfs, whose bodies had been bent to resemble the handle of a *kris* (traditional dagger). By the early 1600s, the Dutch had established trade treaties with Javanese princes and controlled much of the spice trade, but they were interested in profit, not culture, and barely gave Bali a second glance.

In 1710 the 'capital' of the Gelgel kingdom was shifted to nearby Klungkung (now called Semarapura), but local discontent was growing; lesser rulers were breaking away, and the Dutch began to move in, using the old strategy of divide and conquer. In 1846 the Dutch used Balinese salvage claims over shipwrecks as a pretext to land military forces in northern Bali. Their cause was also aided by the various Balinese princes who had gained ruling interests in Lombok and thus were distracted from matters at home and also unaware that the wily Dutch would use Lombok against the Bali.

In 1894 the Dutch, the Balinese and the people of Lombok collided in battles that would set the course of history for the next several decades. See The Battle for Lombok p28.

With the north of Bali long under Dutch control and the conquest of Lombok successful, the south was never going to last long. Once again, it was disputes over the ransacking of wrecked ships that gave the Dutch an excuse to move in. In 1904, after a Chinese ship was wrecked off Sanur, Dutch demands that the *rajah* (lord or prince) of Badung pay 3000 silver dollars in damages were rejected, and in 1906 Dutch warships appeared at Sanur.

The Dutch forces landed despite Balinese opposition, and four days later had marched 5km to the outskirts of Denpasar. On 20 September

A Short History of Bali – Indonesia's Hindu Realm by Robert Pringle is a thoughtful analysis of Bali's history from the Bronze Age to the present, with excellent sections on the 2002 bombings and ongoing environmental woes caused by tourism and development.

DID YOU KNOW?

The 1815 eruption of Mt Tambora on Sumbawa to the east buried parts of Bali in a foot of ash, which later helped produce record rice crops.

1597	1894
Dutch first visit Bali	Dutch invade Lombok

THE BATTLE FOR LOMBOK

In 1894 the Dutch sent an army to back the Sasak people of eastern Lombok in a rebellion against the Balinese *rajah* (lord or prince) who controlled Lombok with the support of the western Sasak. The rajah quickly capitulated, but the Balinese crown prince decided to fight on.

The Dutch camp at the Mayura Water Palace was attacked late at night by a combined force of Balinese and western Sasak, forcing the Dutch to take shelter in a temple compound. The Balinese also attacked another Dutch camp further east at Mataram, and soon the entire Dutch army on Lombok was forced back to Ampenan where, according to one eyewitness, the soldiers 'were so nervous that they fired madly if so much as a leaf fell off a tree'. These battles resulted in enormous losses of men and arms for the Dutch.

Although the Balinese had won the first battles, they had begun to lose the war. They faced a continuing threat from the eastern Sasak, while the Dutch were soon supported with reinforcements from Java.

The Dutch attacked Mataram a month later, fighting street-to-street against Balinese and western Sasak soldiers and civilians. The Balinese crown prince was killed, and the Balinese retreated to Cakranegara (Cakra), where they had well-armed defensive positions. Cakra was attacked by a large combined force of Dutch and eastern Sasak. Rather than surrender, Balinese men, women and children opted for the suicidal *puputan* (a fight to the death) and were cut down by rifle and artillery fire. Their stronghold, the Mayura Water Palace, was largely destroyed.

The Balinese rajah and a small group of commanders fled to Sasari near Lingsar, and though the rajah surrendered, most of the Balinese held out. In late November 1894, the Dutch attacked Sasari and, again, a large number of Balinese chose the *puputan*. With the downfall of the dynasty, the local population abandoned its struggle against the Dutch. The conquest of Lombok, considered for decades, had taken the Dutch barely three months. The old rajah died in exile in Batavia (now Jakarta) in 1895.

1906 the Dutch mounted a naval bombardment on Denpasar and then began their final assault. The three princes of Badung realised that they were completely outnumbered and outgunned, and that defeat was inevitable. Surrender and exile, however, would have been the worst imaginable outcome, so they decided to take the honourable path of a suicidal *puputan* (a fight to the death). First the princes burned their palaces, and then, dressed in their finest jewellery and waving ceremonial golden kris, the rajah led the royalty and priests out to face the modern weapons of the Dutch.

The Dutch implored the Balinese to surrender rather than make their hopeless stand, but their pleas went unheeded and wave after wave of the Balinese nobility marched forward to their death. In all, nearly 4000 Balinese died. The Dutch then marched northwest towards Tabanan and took the rajah of Tabanan prisoner, but he also committed suicide rather than face the disgrace of exile.

The kingdoms of Karangasem and Gianyar had already capitulated to the Dutch and were allowed to retain some of their powers, but other kingdoms were defeated and their rulers exiled. Finally, in 1908 the rajah of Semarapura followed the lead of Badung, and once more the Dutch faced a *puputan*. As had happened at Cakranegara on Lombok, the beautiful palace at Semarapura, Taman Kertha Gosa, was largely destroyed.

1908	1936
Last Balinese kingdom falls to the Dutch	Two Americans build first hotel at Kuta Beach

With this last obstacle disposed of, all of Bali was under Dutch control and became part of the Dutch East Indies. There was little development of an exploitative plantation economy on Bali, and the common people noticed little difference between Dutch rule and rule under the rajahs. On Lombok, conditions were harder as new Dutch taxes took a toll on the populace.

WWII

In 1942 the Japanese invaded Bali at Sanur, but the Balinese could offer no resistance. The Japanese established headquarters in Denpasar and Singaraja (Buleleng district), and their occupation became increasingly harsh for the Balinese. When the Japanese left in August 1945 after their defeat in WWII, the island was suffering extreme poverty, but the occupation had fostered several paramilitary, nationalist and anticolonial organisations that were ready to fight the returning Dutch.

INDEPENDENCE

In August 1945, just days after the Japanese surrender, the Indonesian leader Soekarno proclaimed the nation's independence, but it took four years to convince the Dutch that they were not going to get their great colony back. In a virtual repeat of the *puputan* nearly 50 years earlier, a Balinese resistance group called Tentara Keamanan Rakyat (People's Security Force) was wiped out by the Dutch in the battle of Marga in

Bali and the Tourist Industry by David Shavit is a highly entertaining look at how tourism developed on Bali between the wars with the help of a menagerie of local and Western characters.

Bali – A Paradise Created by Adrian Vickers traces Balinese history and development by concentrating on the island's image in the West.

THE TOURIST INVASION

Beginning in the 1920s, the Dutch government realised that Bali's unique culture could be marketed internationally to the growing tourism industry. Relying heavily on images that emphasised the topless habits of Bali's women, Dutch marketing drew wealthy Western adventurers who landed in the north at today's Singaraja and were whisked about the island on rigid three-day itineraries that featured canned cultural shows at a government-run tourist hotel in Denpasar.

But even then some travellers arrived independently, often at the behest of the small colony of Western artists such as Walter Spies in Ubud (see p46 and p143). Two of these visitors were Robert Koke and Louise Garret, an unmarried American couple who had worked in Hollywood before landing in Bali in 1936 as part of a global adventure. Horrified at the stuffy strictures imposed by the Dutch tourism authorities, the pair (who were later married) built a couple of bungalows out of palm leaves and other local materials on the otherwise deserted beach at Kuta. Having recently been to Hawaii on a film shoot, Bob and Louise knew the possibilities of a good beach. As a few guests started to dribble in, Bob was also able to pass the time introducing local boys to surfing, which he had learned in Hawaii.

Word soon spread, however, and the Koke's were booked solid. Guests came for days, stayed for weeks and told their friends. The Dutch at first dismissed the Koke's Kuta Beach Hotel as 'dirty native huts', but soon realised that increased numbers of tourists were good for everyone. Other Westerners built their own thatched hotels, complete with the bungalows that were to become a Balinese cliché in the decades ahead. WWII wiped out tourism and the hotels (the Koke's barely escaped ahead of the Japanese), but once people began travelling again after the war, Bali's inherent appeal made its popularity a forgone conclusion. The introduction of jet travel, reasonably affordable tickets and dirt cheap accommodation on beautiful Kuta beach gave Bali an endless summer, which began in the 1960s.

1944	1946
Colin McPhee publishes *A House on Bali*, the enduring classic on Balinese culture	Battle at Marga leads to independence for Indonesia

western Bali (p255) on 20 November 1946. The Dutch finally recognised Indonesia's independence in 1949, but Indonesians celebrate 17 August 1945 as Independence Day.

At first, independence was not an easy path for Indonesia to follow, and Soekarno, an inspirational leader during the conflict with the Dutch, proved less adept at governing the nation in peacetime. Bali, Lombok and the rest of Indonesia's eastern islands were grouped together in the unwieldy province of Nusa Tenggara. In 1958 the central government recognised this folly and created three new governmental regions from the one, with Bali getting its own and Lombok becoming part of Nusa Tenggara Barat.

1965 COUP & BACKLASH

On 30 September 1965 an attempted coup – blamed on the Partai Komunis Indonesia (PKI, or Communist Party) – led to Soekarno's downfall. General Mohamed Soeharto emerged as the leading figure in the armed forces, displaying great military and political skill in suppressing the coup. The PKI was outlawed and a wave of anticommunist reprisals followed, which escalated into a wholesale massacre of suspected communists throughout the Indonesian archipelago.

On Bali, the events had an added local significance as the main national political organisations, the Partai Nasional Indonesia (PNI, or Nationalist Party) and PKI, crystallised existing differences between traditionalists, who wanted to maintain the old caste system, and radicals, who saw the caste system as repressive and who were urging land reform. After the failed coup, religious traditionalists on Bali led the witch-hunt for the 'godless communists'. The Chinese community was particularly victimised. Eventually the military stepped in to control the anticommunist purge, but no-one on Bali was untouched by the killings, estimated at between 50,000 and 100,000 out of a population of about two million. Many tens of thousands more died on Lombok.

SOEHARTO TAKES OVER

Following the failed coup in 1965 and its aftermath, Soeharto established himself as president and took control of the government, while Soekarno disappeared from the limelight. Under Soeharto's 'New Order' government, Indonesia looked to the West in foreign policy, and Western-educated economists set about balancing budgets, controlling inflation and attracting foreign investment.

Politically, Soeharto ensured that the Golkar party, with strong support from the army, became the dominant political force. Other political parties were banned or crippled by the disqualification of candidates and the disenfranchisement of voters. Regular elections maintained the appearance of a national democracy, but until 1999, Golkar won every election. This period was also marked by great economic development on Bali and later on Lombok as business interests took precedence over democracy.

SOEHARTO GOES BUST

In early 1997 Southeast Asia began to suffer a severe economic crisis, and within the year the Indonesian currency (the rupiah) had all but

1963	1965
Gunung Agung erupts, devastating East Bali	Political and religious violence on Bali and Lombok kills tens of thousands

collapsed and the economy was on the brink of bankruptcy. To help deal with the continuing economic crisis, Soeharto agreed to the International Monetary Fund's (IMF) demand to increase the government-subsidised price of electricity and petrol, resulting in immediate increases in the cost of public transport, rice and other food staples. Riots broke out across Indonesia and although Bali and Lombok were spared most of the violence, their tourism-dependent economies were battered.

Unable to cope with the escalating crisis, Soeharto resigned in 1998, after 32 years in power. His protégé, Dr Bacharuddin Jusuf Habibie, became president. Regarded as a Soeharto crony, he failed to tackle issues dogging Indonesia such as corruption or East Timor.

TERRORISTS, STRIFE & PEACE

In 1999, Indonesia's parliament met to elect a new president. The frontrunner was Megawati Sukarnoputri, whose party received the largest number of votes at the election. Megawati was enormously popular on Bali, partly because of family connections (her paternal grandmother was Balinese) and partly because her party was essentially secular (the mostly Hindu Balinese are very concerned about any growth in Muslim fundamentalism). However, Soeharto's party was still a force, and in a surprising development, Abdurrahman Wahid, head of Indonesia's largest Muslim organisation, emerged as president.

Outraged supporters of Megawati took to the streets of Java and Bali. On Bali, the demonstrations were more disruptive than violent – trees were felled to block the main Nusa Dua road, and government buildings were damaged in Denpasar and Singaraja. The election of Megawati as vice-president quickly defused the situation.

On Lombok, however, religious and political tensions spilled over in early 2000 when a sudden wave of attacks starting in Mataram burned Chinese-Christian businesses and homes across the island. The impact on tourism was immediate and severe, and the island is still trying to put this shameful episode behind it.

Wahid was a moderate, uncharismatic leader who made minor progress on issues like the economy but was less successful in tackling the ethnic, religious and regional conflicts that have plagued Indonesia. In July 2001, after a tense standoff, parliament gave the presidency to Megawati.

Indonesia's cultural wars continued and certainly played a role in the October 2002 bombings in Kuta. See The Bali Bombings, p96, for more on this tragedy which has had ramifications that many Balinese are still trying to both comprehend and understand. Besides the obvious enormous monetary loss (tourism immediately fell by more than half), the blasts fuelled the ever-present suspicions of the Hindu Balinese regarding Muslims (that the Muslim Javanese are trying to muscle in on the profitable Bali scene, and the Muslims from Indonesia are, in general, looking to show prejudice against the non-Muslim Balinese) and shattered the myth of isolation enjoyed by many locals.

Blessedly the elections of 2004 managed to dispel fears and were remarkably peaceful. Susilo Bambang Yudhoyono (popularly known as 'SBY') beat incumbent Megawati Sukarnoputri by garnering over 60% of the vote in the final round of balloting in September. A former general

DID YOU KNOW?

Ancient Goa Gajah near Ubud is literally evidence carved in rock of Hindu's place in Balinese culture in the 11th century.

Tragedy in Bali by Australian radio journalist Alan Atkinson details how his family vacation was shattered by the Kuta bombings. It's moving and also provides a good look at a typical contemporary Bali holiday, before the explosions.

1998	2000
Soeharto resigns as president although his family retains control of several Bali resorts	Religious riots on Lombok devastate tourism

---

BALI'S ROYAL LEGACY

Within Bali there are eight *kabupaten* (districts), which have their origins in the precolonial *rajahs'* (lords or princes) kingdoms, and were the basis of the Dutch administrative regencies. Denpasar was part of the Badung district until 1992, when the city, with Sanur and Tanjung Benoa, became a separate *kabupaten kota* (city district). Badung's administration is still mostly in Denpasar.

Each *kabupaten* is headed by a government official known as a *bupati*. The districts are then further divided into 51 subdistricts headed by a *camat;* then subdivided further into an official *desa,* or village (over 600 at last count), administered by a *perbekel;* and still further into an enormous number (about 3500) of *Banjar* and *dusun,* which are the local divisions of a village and which can yield enormous power. In 2004, the restaurants and bars of Jl Dhyana Pura in Seminyak (p71) were shut down for an entire busy weekend by the local *banjar* which didn't feel its concerns about noise were being properly addressed.

---

and government minister, he is known as something of an intellectual and an economist. All his experience will be needed in the latter area as goosing along Indonesia's sputtering economy is the biggest challenge. Obstacles include rampant corruption, uncertain legal processes and widespread ecological destruction. Still, SBY managed to garner strong support – even on Bali, a former Megawati stronghold – by his promises of strong and enlightened leadership.

Many books have been written about the terrorist attack on Bali. *Bali Blues* by Jeremy Allan tells of the struggle to survive in Kuta during the year following the terrorist attack that claimed over two hundred lives and drove away the foreign visitors who support the beach resort's economy. It's both highly personal and readable. *Who Did This to Our Bali* by Dewi Anggraeni is comprehensive in its coverage of the bombing and it is an excellent resource for understanding an event which you can't escape no matter where you are on the island.

2002	2004
Bombs in Kuta on October 22 killed over 300	Peaceful elections see Susilo Bambang Yudhoyono elected president

The Culture

REGIONAL IDENTITY

Balinese people are content. Ask a Balinese what heaven is like and the answer will be, 'Just like Bali'. They want to live in Bali, to be cremated in Bali when they die, and to reincarnate in Bali. Everything around them is seen as a wonderful rich resource: bamboo, vine, flowers and shells for their imaginative offerings; European perfumes; international CDs; brand-name clothing for rip-off copying. Even the tourist is a resource to be painted, oiled, massaged, manipulated, tattooed or plaited.

They have an amazingly active and organised village life – you simply can't be a faceless nonentity on Bali. Every activity – producing crops, preparing food, bargaining with tourists, keeping their youth employed – involves everybody. This involvement with the other people in their village extends to the tourists. To make you feel welcome, Balinese will go out of their way to chat to you. But they won't talk about the weather or even the football. They are interested in you, your home life and your personal relationships. Chatting in Bali can get awfully personal (see Small Talk, p50).

Balinese are known for their sense of fun, their joy of life, their ability to change a situation to suit changing needs. For example, legend relates how a group of Balinese farmers promised to sacrifice a pig if their harvest was good. As the bountiful harvest time approached, no pig could be found. Then they had an idea. The sacrifice had been promised after the harvest. If there was always new rice growing, the harvest would always be about to take place and no sacrifice would be necessary. Since then, farmers have always planted one field of rice before harvesting another.

Everybody loves children – visit Bali with your kids and you'll have a constant stream of young people making sure they enjoy every moment. Older children take care of the younger ones in their family or village. They're always seen carrying a child on their hips, all of them remarkably well-behaved and happy.

You can't get away from religion on Bali. There are temples in every village, shrines in every field, offerings made at every corner. The Balinese feel that their religion should be an enjoyable thing, for mortals as well as the gods. It's summed up well in their attitude to offerings – once the gods have eaten the 'essence' of the food, you've still got enough left over to be satisfied. See Offerings, p39.

The Balinese are a very proud, confident race, with a culture that extends throughout the generations. A culture they embrace with passion. After all, it's only a hundred years ago that 4000 Balinese nobility, dressed in their finest, walked out into the gunfire of the Dutch army, rather than become subjects (see p27).

DID YOU KNOW?
The Balinese love of beauty is seen in their own delightful home gardens which will have curved paths, a rich variety of plants and usually a water feature.

Island of Bali by Miguel Covarrubias, written in the 1930s, is still a fantastic introduction to the romance and seduction of the island and its culture.

LIFESTYLE

For the average rural Balinese, the working day is not long. Their expertise at growing rice leaves them free for lots of quality time to chat or prepare elaborate cultural events.

Life is concentrated in the villages under the tropical vegetation of palm, breadfruit, mango, papaya, and banana trees. In the centre of a village is an open meeting space, temples, the town market, perhaps a former prince's home, the *kulkul* (hollow tree-trunk drum used to sound a warning or call meetings) tower and quite likely a big Banyan

RICE

Rice cultivation has shaped the social landscape – the intricate organisation necessary for growing rice is a large factor in the strength of Bali's community life. Rice cultivation has also changed the environmental landscape – terraced rice fields trip down hillsides like steps for a giant, in shades of gold, brown and green.

There are three words for rice – *padi* is the growing rice plant (hence paddy fields); *beras* is the uncooked grain; and *nasi* is cooked rice, as in *nasi goreng* (fried rice) and *nasi putih* (plain rice). A rice field is called a *sawah*.

A harvested field with its left-over burnt rice stalks is soaked with water and repeatedly ploughed, often by two bullocks pulling a wooden plough. Once the field is muddy enough, a small corner is walled off and seedling rice is planted there. When it is a reasonable size it is replanted, shoot by shoot, in the larger field. While the rice matures there is time to practise the *gamelan* (traditional Balinese orchestral music), watch the dancers or do a little woodcarving. Finally, the whole village turns out for the harvest – a period of solid hard work. It's strictly men only planting the rice, but everybody takes part in harvesting it.

In 1969, new high-yield rice varieties were introduced. These can be harvested a month sooner than the traditional variety and are resistant to many diseases (see p69).

These new rice varieties have also upset traditional practices and customs. New rice falls easily from the stalk, so it must be threshed in the fields, not carried to the village. Husking is often done in mechanical mills, rather than by women pounding it in wooden troughs. Thus songs, rituals and festivals associated with old ways of harvesting and milling rice are dying out. Plus, everyone agrees that the new rice doesn't taste as good as *padi* Bali.

But progress is progress. New strains now account for more than 90% of rice, but small areas of *padi* Bali are still planted and harvested in traditional ways to placate the rice goddess, Dewi Sri, and there are still temples and offerings to her in every rice field.

DID YOU KNOW?

Farmers must join the local *subak* (rice growers' association). The *subak* ensures that water reaches all the paddies, so whoever's field is at the bottom usually volunteers to run it!

tree. The *banjar* (local division of a village consisting of all the married adult males) continues the strong community spirit by organising village festivals, marriage ceremonies, cremations and the local *gamelan* (traditional Balinese orchestra). The headquarters is the open-sided *bale banjar* (communal meeting place of a *banjar*) where you might see a gamelan practice, a meeting, food being prepared for a feast, or men preening their roosters for the next round of cockfights.

In Lombok, the culture is just as rich, but not as colourful or accessible as on Bali. The indigenous people, the Sasak, are predominantly Muslim, although some elements of ancient animist beliefs survive, and the Balinese and Buginese communities in Lombok add to the diversity.

Ceremonies & Rituals

Every stage of Balinese life, from conception to cremation, is marked by a series of ceremonies and rituals, which are the basis of their rich, varied and active cultural life.

BIRTH & CHILDHOOD

The first ceremony of Balinese life takes place when women reach the third month of pregnancy, with offerings to ensure the wellbeing of the baby. Soon after the birth, the afterbirth is buried with appropriate offerings. Twelve days later women are 'purified' through another ceremony. After 42 days, offerings are made for the baby's future.

Choosing a name is easy. Given names are the same for both sexes, and determined by birth order, representing the cyclic nature of things. The first child is called Wayan, Putu or Gede; the second is Made, Kadek or Nengah; the third is Nyoman or Komang; and the fourth is Ketut. Fifth, sixth, seventh and eighth children re-use the same set (Wayan, Made, Nyoman, Ketut).

A child goes through 13 celebrations, or *manusa yadnya*. At 105 days, the baby is welcomed to the family and its feet are allowed to touch the ground for the first time – ground is impure so babies are held until then. At 210 days (first Balinese year) the baby is spiritually blessed in the ancestral temple and there's a huge feast for the family and community.

Another important stage is the tooth-filing ceremony, when a priest symbolically files a teenager's (around 16 to 18 years) upper front teeth to produce a pleasing line. Crooked fangs are, after all, one of the chief distinguishing marks of evil spirits – just have a look at a Rangda mask!

Education begins with six years of primary school, then three years each of junior and senior high school, which leads to university. The majority of children complete primary school; literacy on Bali is higher than the national average. There are universities in Denpasar, Singaraja and on the Bukit Peninsula.

MARRIAGE

Every Balinese expects to marry at a young age. In general, marriages are not arranged, although there are strict rules that apply between the castes.

The respectable way to marry (*mapadik*) is when the family of the man visits the family of the woman and politely proposes. The Balinese, however, like their fun and often prefer marriage by elopement (*ngorod*). Nobody is too surprised when the young man spirits away his bride-to-be. The couple go into hiding and somehow the girl's parents, no matter how assiduously they search, never manage to find her.

Eventually the couple re-emerge, the marriage is officially recognised and everybody has had a lot of fun and games. Elopement has another advantage: apart from being exciting and mildly heroic, it's cheaper.

The local tourist website www.lombok-network .com also gives details of Lombok customs, and the arts and crafts of various areas.

DEATH & CREMATION

Often the last ceremony – the cremation, or *pitra yadna* – is the biggest, most amazing, spectacular, colourful, noisy and exciting event. It can take years to organise; so the body will have been temporarily buried. An auspicious day is chosen and many people may join in, sending their dead on their way at the same time. *Brahmanas* (high priests), however, must be cremated immediately.

The body is carried in a high, incredibly artistic multitiered tower made of bamboo, paper, tinsel, silk, cloth, mirrors, flowers and anything else colourful, on the shoulders of a group of men. The size of the tower depends on the importance of the deceased. The funeral of a *rajah* (lord or prince) or high priest may require hundreds of men to tote the tower.

Along the way, the group confuses the deceased's spirit so it cannot find its way back home. They shake the tower, run it around in circles, throw water at it and generally make the trip anything but a stately funeral crawl. Meanwhile, the priest halfway up the tower hangs on grimly, doing his best to soak bystanders with holy water. A gamelan sprints behind, providing an exciting musical accompaniment.

At the cremation ground, the body is transferred to a funeral sarcophagus which corresponds to their caste (see p38) – a black bull for a Brahmana, white bull for priests, winged lion for a Ksatriyasa, and elephant-fish for a Sudra. Finally, up it all goes in flames – funeral tower, sarcophagus and body. And where does your soul go after cremation? Why, to a heaven that is just like Bali!

Reality Check

There is a growing problem with drug use among Balinese youth, especially methamphetamines brought over from Java and sold cheaply to teenagers with access to cash raised from the tourism economy.

Local attitudes to sexuality differ to the Western misconceptions that still persist. For example, in rural areas people still bathe naked by the side of the road – this is not a show of exhibitionism, but a tradition; while bathing, they consider themselves invisible.

There are strict family, village and social taboos against premarital sex by the Balinese – the unmarried sex rate among Balinese women is 2% to 3%. Sex workers and willing companions looking for some cash or merchandise on the side, however, are common in tourist areas. These people – of both sexes – are usually from another island, with Java being the primary source. In a few cases they are from villages in the north and are counting on seeing nobody they know in the south.

An exciting resource on Bali is www.murnis.com. Track through to Culture to find explanations on everything from kids' names to what one wears to a ceremony, and the weaving of the garments.

POPULATION & MULTICULTURALISM

Bali is densely populated, with over 3.1 million people, who are almost all of Balinese Hindu religion. Other residents are from Java, Sumatra and Nusa Tenggara; the tourist industry is a magnet for people seeking jobs and business opportunities.

The Balinese people are predominantly of the Malay race; descendants of the groups that travelled southeast from China around 3000 BC. Before that, ethnic strands have been traced to the Australian Aborigine, India, Polynesia and Melanesia, and a diverse range of physical features from those groups can be seen in Bali's population.

Population control is a priority of the Indonesian government, and the family planning slogan *dua anak cukup* (two children is enough) is a recurring theme in roadside posters. It seems to be quite successful, as

---

AVOIDING OFFENCE

- Be aware and respectful of local sensibilities, and dress and act appropriately, especially in the rural villages and religious sites.

- Knees, shoulders and armpits should be covered. Shorts and singlet tops are not considered polite attire for men or women, although at beach resorts, where tourists are considered a little eccentric, they're fine. The rules are relaxing a little bit – an increasing number of younger Balinese now adopt the dress of visitors.

- Many women go topless on Bali's tourist beaches, but bring a bikini top for less touristy beaches (definitely if you're going to Lombok).

- Thongs (flip-flops) are acceptable in temples if you're otherwise well dressed, but if you are going to a government office, say to get a local driving licence, you need to look smarter.

- Take off your shoes before entering a mosque or someone's house.

- Don't touch anyone on the head, as it is regarded as the abode of the soul and is therefore sacred.

- Pass things with your right hand. To show more respect, pass something using both hands.

- Talking with your hands on your hips is a sign of contempt, anger or aggression – as displayed in traditional dance and opera.

- Handshaking is customary for both men and women on introduction and greeting.

- Beckon to someone with the hand extended and a downward waving motion. The Western method of beckoning is considered very rude.

COCKFIGHTS

Cockfights are a regular feature of temple ceremonies – a combination of sacrifice, sport and gambling. Men keep fighting cocks as prized pets, carefully grooming and preparing them for their brief moment of glory or defeat.

At the festival, the cocks are matched, a lethally sharp metal spur is tied to one leg, there's a crescendo of shouting and betting, the birds are pushed against each other to stir them up, then they're released and the feathers fly. It's usually over in seconds – a slash of the spur and one rooster is down and dying. After the bout, the successful gamblers collect their pay-offs and the winning owner gets to take the dead rooster home for his cooking pot. When travelling in rural Bali, you'll know there's a cockfight nearby when you see scores of vehicles and scooters parked near a temple but nobody in sight. The men are usually back behind the compound.

young families are not having the seven or nine children common two generations ago. Economic growth in Bali has been achieved by a huge expansion in the tourist industry. There have been dramatic improvements to roads, telecommunications, electricity and water supply, but also displacement of local populations to more lightly populated islands as part of the *transmigrasi* (transmigration) programme.

In Lombok, the majority of people live in and around the principal centres of Mataram, Praya and Selong. Almost 90% of the people are Sasak, with minority populations of Balinese, Chinese, Javanese and Arabs. The Sasak are assumed to have come from northwestern India or Myanmar (Burma), and the clothing the women wear today, long black sarongs called *lambung* and short-sleeved blouses with a V-neck, is very similar to that worn in those areas. The sarong is held by a 4m scarf called a *sabuk*, trimmed with brightly coloured stripes. Women wear very little jewellery and never any gold ornaments. Most Sasak people are Muslims, and many traditional beliefs are interwoven with Muslim ideology.

The Balinese of Lombok have retained their Hindu customs and traditions. They contributed to the emergence of Lombok's Wektu Telu religion, and Balinese temples, ceremonies and processions are a colourful part of western Lombok's cultural life.

Ethnic minorities in Bali include the Bali Aga, whose Hindu traditions predate the arrival of the Majapahit court in the 15th century. There are Chinese in the larger towns, Indian and Arab merchants in Denpasar, and some permanent Western visitors. The island is a model of religious tolerance, with two Christian villages, some Chinese temples, a Buddhist monastery and Javanese and other Muslim communities, particularly around the ports of Gilimanuk, Singaraja and Padangbai.

Ethnic minorities in Lombok include the Chinese who were coolies in the rice paddies. Later they set up their own businesses which were singled out in the riots of January 2000. The Arabs in Lombok are devout Muslims, well educated and relatively affluent. In the late 19th century, Buginese from south Sulawesi settled in coastal areas and their descendants still operate much of the fishing industry.

DID YOU KNOW?

Indonesia has a long tradition of *waria*, female impersonators who work as entertainers, hostesses or prostitutes. The term is a combination of *wanita* (female) and *pria* (male).

SOCIAL ORGANISATION

What defines the people of Bali is cultural rather than racial. Caste, however, determines roles in religious rituals and the language to be used in every social situation. This caste system derives from Hindu traditions on Java around 1350, and the colonial period entrenched a caste structure that suited Dutch interests.

Most Balinese belong to the common *sudra* caste. The rest belong to the *triwangsa* (three people) caste which is divided into: Brahmana, high priests with titles of Ida Bagus (male) and Ida Ayu (female); Ksatriyasa, merchants with titles of Cokodor (males) and Ana Ayung (females); and Wesia, the nobility with titles of Gusti Ngura or Dewa Gede (male), and Gusti Ayu or Dewa Ayu (female). Despite the titles, the importance of one's caste is diminishing, as status now comes more from education, economic success and community influence.

Caste differences in language is overcome by the use of 'polite' forms of Balinese, or the national Indonesian language (Bahasa Indonesia), itself a sign of status (for information on languages, see p369). In a traditional village, however, caste is still a central part of life, and absolutely essential to all religious practices.

MEDIA

Following the end of Soeharto's authoritarian rule, the press enjoyed a degree of freedom. However, it was short lived. The courts have allowed defamation suits to be filed by government officials and businesspeople against editors and reporters using the Criminal Code instead of the Press Law. A consequence of this, some claim, has been an increase in self-censorship by journalists.

The Tempo media group has been especially hit, with many lawsuits filed against it. It is claimed the Tempo weekly is among the few media that try to bring to light any irregularities involving state officials, business leaders and politicians.

Meanwhile, the influential *Jakarta Post* promotes a more humane civil society whilst serving the needs of its readers, both expatriate and Indonesian.

See p47 for more on television broadcasting in Bali.

The ancient Hindu swastika seen all over Bali is a symbol of harmony with the universe. The German Nazis used a version where the arms are always bent in a clock-wise direction.

RELIGION
Hinduism

Hinduism was the predominant religion in Indonesia (there are remarkable Hindu monuments on Java) until the great Hindu kingdom, the Majapahit, evacuated to Bali, taking their religion and its rituals, and also their art, literature, music and culture. The Balinese, rather than resist a new influence, simply adapted it for themselves. So Hindu beliefs were overlaid on their animist beliefs – hence the peculiar Balinese interpretation of Hinduism.

Balinese worship the trinity of Brahma, Shiva and Vishnu and they have a supreme god, Sanghyang Widi. The basic threesome is always alluded to, but never seen – a vacant shrine or empty throne tells all. Balinese temples come to life at the regular and colourful temple festivals; see p330.

TEMPLE ETIQUETTE

Foreigners can enter most temple complexes but you have to wear a sarong – long trousers or a skirt may be acceptable. You may also need a *selandong* (temple scarf) or sash to tie around your waist – some temples have these for hire (around 2000Rp, or a donation).

Priests should be shown respect, particularly at festivals. Don't put yourself higher than them, eg by climbing on a wall to take photos.

Usually there's a sign at temple entrances warning you to be respectful, and asking that women don't enter if menstruating. At this time women are thought to be *sebel* (ritually unclean), as are pregnant women and those who have recently given birth, or been recently bereaved.

> **OFFERINGS**
>
> Bali has very many honoured guests. These are not the tourists, although the Balinese welcome them warmly and look after them delightfully well. No, these guests are the gods, ancestors, spirits and demons that live in Bali. They are presented with offerings all through each day to show respect and gratitude, or perhaps to bribe a demon into being less mischievous.
>
> A gift to a higher being must look attractive, so each offering is a work of art. The basic form is fresh food arranged on a palm leaf and crowned with a palm leaf decoration, called a *sampian*, that holds betel and flowers. Once presented to the gods, it cannot be used again, so new offerings are made again and again each day.

A temple ritual involves major communal offerings, plus each family brings its own large and colourful offering in a spectacular procession. The betel on top of every offering symbolises the Hindu Trinity, as do the three basic colours used – red for Brahma, black or green for Wisnu, and white for Siwa. Conical shapes are models of the cosmic mountain and rice cookies represent plants, animals, people or buildings.

Islam

Islam is a minority religion on Bali; most are descendants of seafaring people from Sulawesi. Mosques are most often seen at seaports and fishing villages.

Peaceful Gujarati merchants brought Islam to Lombok via the Celebes (now Sulawesi) and Java in the 13th century. The traditions and rituals affect all aspects of daily life. Friday afternoon is the official time for worship, when all government offices and many businesses close. Muslim women do not have to wear veils, nor are they segregated or considered second-class citizens.

Wektu Telu

This unique religion originated in Bayan, in north Lombok. *Wektu* means 'result' in Sasak, while *telu* means 'three' and signifies the three religions that comprise Wektu Telu: Balinese Hinduism, Islam and animism. The tenet is that all important aspects of life are underpinned by a trinity. The Wektu Telu believe they have three main duties: to believe in Allah; avoid the temptations of the devil; and cooperate with, help and love other people.

The Wektu Telu have three days of fasting and prayer for Ramadan. They pray when and where they feel the need, so all public buildings have a prayer corner that faces Mecca. And they believe that everything that comes from Allah is good, therefore pork is good.

WOMEN IN BALI & LOMBOK

Social life on Bali is relatively free and easy and the roles of the sexes are strictly delineated. Running the household is very much the woman's task. The preparation of offerings is undertaken by every Balinese woman, with several generations working together so knowledge and skills are handed down to the young. Every household has a shrine or god-throne, and areas on the ground, such as at the compound entrance, where offerings for the demons and gods are placed. The ritual is not diminishing, but as women take up work in offices or hotels, production of ready-made offerings has grown as an industry (see Offerings, above).

The traditional position of women as preparers of food – and buyers and sellers – places them in a good position to take part in the tourist

See examples of some of the work by Bali's female artists that is on display or available for sale at www .seniwatigallery.com.

industry. A successful Balinese restaurant or shop is most likely to have been established by a woman.

In cultural activities the roles are also gender-based, but things are changing. Traditionally only men play the gamelan, but there is now a women's gamelan group in Peliatan, near Ubud. Painting and carving were once male pursuits, but women painters in particular are becoming more common. The Seniwati Gallery of Art by Women, in Ubud, supports women painters. Its permanent collection includes *Topeng Masks*, by Ni Wavan Warti; *Cilli, Goddess of Riches and Fertility*, by Muntiana Tedja; and *Legong Dancers*, by Sri Haryani.

ARTS

The richness of Bali's arts and crafts has its origin in the fertility of the land. The purest forms are the depictions of Dewi Sri, the rice goddess, intricately made from dried and folded strips of palm leaf to ensure that the fertility of the rice fields continues.

Until the tourist invasion, the acts of painting or carving were purely to decorate temples. Today, with galleries and craft shops everywhere, paintings are stacked up on their floors and you trip over stone- or woodcarvings. Much of this work is churned out quickly, but you will still find a great deal of beautiful work.

Balinese dance, music and *wayang kulit* (shadow puppetry) theatres are continually enriched by contemporary influences, yet are still laden with religious connotations to please the gods and goddesses.

See Bali Arts Festival, p85.

DID YOU KNOW?

British-born Mary Northmore founded Seniwati Gallery of Art by Women in Ubud, in 1991, the only gallery devoted to collecting, exhibiting, and promoting female artists.

Dance
BALI

You can catch a quality dance performance in Bali anywhere there's a festival or celebration, and you'll find all sorts of dances at hotels and restaurants in the tourist areas. To see good Balinese dance on a regular basis, you should stay near Ubud, where the tourist office has information and tickets. For a full programme, see p148 and p155.

Many tourist shows offer a smorgasbord of dances – a little Topeng, a taste of Legong and some Baris to round it off. Admission is generally 25,000Rp to 50,000Rp. Try to experience some dances in their entirety. Music, theatre and dance courses are available in Ubud, where private teachers advertise instruction in various Balinese instruments.

Balinese love a blend of seriousness and slapstick, and this shows in their dances. Some have a decidedly comic element, with clowns who convey the story and also act as a counterpoint to the staid, noble characters. Most dancers are not professionals. Dance is learned by performing, and carefully following the movements of an expert. It tends to be precise, jerky, shifting and jumpy, remarkably like Balinese music, with its abrupt changes of tempo and dramatic contrasts between silence and crashing noise. There's little of the soaring leaps or the smooth flowing movements of Western dance.

To the expert, every movement of wrist, hand and fingers is important; and facial expressions are carefully choreographed to convey the character of the dance. Watch the local children cheer the good characters and cringe back from the stage when the demons appear.

Kecak

Probably the best known of the dances, the Kecak has a 'choir' of men who provide the 'chak-a-chak-a-chak' accompaniment. In the 1930s, the modern Kecak developed in Bona, near Gianyar in eastern Bali, where the dance is still held regularly. It is also performed in the grounds of Pura Luhur Ulu Watu.

The Kecak tells a tale from the *Ramayana*, one of the great Hindu holy books, about Prince Rama and his Princess Sita. The evil Rawana, King of Lanka, lures Rama away with a golden deer (Lanka's equally evil prime minister, who has magically changed himself into a deer). Then, when the princess is alone, he pounces and carries her off to his hideaway.

Hanuman, the white monkey-god, tells Princess Sita that Rama is trying to rescue her and gives her Rama's ring. When Rama arrives he is met by the evil king's evil son, Megananda, who shoots an arrow which magically turns into a snake and ties Rama up. Fortunately, he is able to call upon a Garuda (mythical man-bird creature) who helps him escape. Finally, Sugriwa, the king of the monkeys, comes with his monkey army and, after a great battle, good wins out over evil and Rama and Sita return home.

Throughout the dance the chanting is superbly synchronised with an eerily exciting coordination. If you would like to see this dance, it is very easy to locate a performance in Ubud.

Barong & Rangda

This rivals the Kecak as Bali's most popular dance for tourists. Again it's a battle between good (the Barong) and bad (the Rangda). The Barong is a strange but good, mischievous and fun-loving shaggy dog-lion. The widow-witch Rangda is bad through and through.

The story goes; Barong Keket, the most holy of the Barong, is enjoying the acclaim of its supporters – a group of men with *kris* (traditional daggers). Then Rangda appears, her long tongue lolling, terrible fangs protruding from her mouth, human entrails draped around her neck, and pendulous parody breasts.

The Barong and Rangda duel, and the supporters draw their *kris* and rush in. The Rangda throws them into a trance that makes them stab themselves. But the Barong dramatically casts a spell that stops the kris from harming them. They rush back and forth, waving their *kris*, rolling on the ground, desperately trying to stab themselves. It's all a conspiracy to terrify tourists in the front row!

Finally, the Rangda retires and good has triumphed again. The entranced Barong supporters, however, still need to be sprinkled with holy water. Playing around with all that powerful magic, good and bad, is not to be taken lightly. A *pesmangku* (priest for temple rituals) must end the dancers' trance and a chicken must be sacrificed to propitiate the evil spirits.

Legong

This most graceful of Balinese dances is performed by young girls. It is important in Balinese culture that in old age a classic dancer will be remembered as a 'great legong'.

Richly illustrated, *The Art & Culture of Bali* by Urs Ramseyer is a comprehensive work on the foundations of Bali's complex and colourful artistic and cultural heritage.

Dancing Out of Bali, by John Coast, tells a personal adventure story of music and dancing in Bali, with all the charm of the Balinese people.

The first English translation of the 1922 bestseller, *Bali: People and Art* by Gregor Krause, is full of superb photographs of life and art on Bali. See what inspired the tourist boom of the 1930s. Available online at www.thailine.com/lotus /indonesia/indonesia.htm.

Peliatan's famous dance troupe, often seen in Ubud, is particularly noted for its Legong Keraton (Legong of the Palace). The very stylised and symbolic story involves two *legong* dancing in mirror image. They are dressed in gold brocade, their faces elaborately made up, their eyebrows plucked and repainted, and their hair decorated with frangipani. The dance relates how a king takes a maiden, Rangkesari, captive. When her brother comes to release her, Rangkesari begs the king to free her rather than go to war. The king refuses and on his way to the battle meets a bird with tiny golden wings bringing ill omens. He ignores the bird and continues on, meets Rangkesari's brother and is killed.

Sanghyang

These dances were developed to drive out evil spirits from a village – Sanghyang is a divine spirit who temporarily inhabits an entranced dancer. The Sanghyang Dedari is performed by two young girls who dance a dream-like version of the Legong, but with their eyes firmly shut. Male and female choirs provide a background chant until the dancers slump to the ground. A *pesmangku* blesses them with holy water and brings them out of the trance. The modern Kecak dance developed from the Sanghyang.

In the Sanghyang Jaran, a boy in a trance dances around and through a fire of coconut husks, riding a coconut palm 'hobby horse'. Variations of this are called Kecak Fire Dance (or Fire and Trance Dance for tourists) and are performed almost daily.

DID YOU KNOW?

Belgian artist, Adrien Jean Le Mayeur, married renowned *Legong* (classic Balinese dance) dancer Ni Polok when he was 55 and she was 15. His house of antique carvings became a museum.

Other Dances

The warrior dance, the Baris, is a male equivalent of the Legong – grace and femininity give way to energetic and warlike spirit. The Baris dancer must convey the thoughts and emotions of a warrior preparing for action, then meeting the enemy, showing his changing moods through facial expression and movement – chivalry, pride, anger, prowess and, finally, regret. It is one of the most complex of dances requiring great energy and skill.

The Ramayana ballet tells the familiar tale of Rama and Sita but with a gamelan gong accompaniment. It provides plenty of opportunity for improvisation and comic additions.

The giant puppet dances known as Barong Landung take place annually on the island of Pulau Serangan and a few other places in southern Bali. The legend relates how the demon Jero Gede Macaling popped over from Nusa Penida, disguised as a standing Barong, to cause havoc on Bali. A huge Barong puppet was made to scare him away. The dance, often highly comical, features two gigantic puppet figures – a horrific male image of black Jero Gede and his female sidekick, white Jero Luh.

In the Topeng, which means 'Pressed Against the Face', as with a mask, the dancers imitate the character represented by the mask. The Topeng Tua is a classic solo dance where the mask is that of an old man. In other dances there may be a small troupe who perform various characters. A full collection of Topeng masks may number 30 or 40. Mask dances require great expertise because the dancer cannot convey thoughts and meanings through facial expressions – the dance has to tell all.

Dance on Bali is not a static art form. The Oleg Tambulilingan was developed in the 1950s, originally as a solo female dance. Later, a male part was added and the dance now mimics the flirtations of two *tambulilingan* (bumblebees).

You may often see the Pendet being danced by women bringing offerings to a temple. One of the most popular comic dances is the Cupak, which tells of a greedy coward (Cupak) and his brave but hard-done-by younger brother, and their adventures while rescuing a beautiful princess.

Drama Gong is based on the same romantic themes as a Balinese soap opera – long and full of high drama.

LOMBOK

Lombok has dances found nowhere else in Indonesia, but they are not widely marketed. Performances are staged in some luxury hotels and in the village of Lenek, known for its dance traditions.

The Cupak Gerantang is based on one of the Panji stories, an extensive cycle of written and oral stories originating on Java in the 15th century. It's often performed at traditional celebrations.

Another version of a Panji story is the Kayak Sando, but here the dancers wear masks. It is only found in central and eastern Lombok. The Gandrung follows a theme of love and courtship. It is a social dance, usually performed outdoors, most commonly in Narmada, Lenek and Praya.

A war dance, the Oncer (also called *gendang beleq*), is performed by men and boys. It is a highly skilled and dramatic performance, with dancers playing a variety of unusual musical instruments for *adat* (tradition, customs and manners) festivals, in central and eastern Lombok. The Rudat is danced by pairs of men in black caps and jackets and black-and-white check sarongs, backed by singers, tambourines and cylindrical drums called *jidur*. The music, lyrics and costumes reveal both a mixture of Muslim and Sasak cultures.

The Tandak Gerok combines dance with music played on bamboo flutes and the bowed lute called a *rebab*, as well as singers imitating the sound of gamelan instruments. It is usually performed after harvesting or other hard labour.

Balinese Music by Michael Tenzer features photographs, a sonography and a guide to all types of gamelan, each with its own tradition, repertoire and social or religious context.

Music

BALI

Balinese music is based around an ensemble known as a gamelan, also called a *gong*. A *gong gede* (large orchestra) is the traditional form, with 35 to 40 musicians. The *gong kebyar* is the modern, popular form, and has up to 25 instruments. Although it sounds strange at first with its noisy, jangly percussion, it's exciting and enjoyable.

The prevalent voice is from the xylophone-like *gangsa,* which the player hits with a hammer dampening the sound just after it is struck. The tempo and nature of the music is controlled by the two *kendang* drums – one male and one female. Other instruments are the deep *trompong* drums, the small *kempli* gong and the *cengceng* cymbals used in faster pieces.

The pieces are learned by heart and passed down from father to son – there is little musical notation or recording, although some cassette tapes and the occasional CD are available. Look in music shops and department stores in the Kuta region. Traditionally a male occupation, a gamelan for women has been established in Ubud, and there are more ancient forms, such as the *gamelan selunding*, still occasionally played in Bali Aga villages like Tenganan, eastern Bali.

You can see instruments being made (usually to order) in Blahbatuh in eastern Bali and Sawan in northern Bali. Giant bamboo gamelan, with deep resonating tones, are made in Jembrana in western Bali.

Artists on Bali by Ruud Spruit is a well-illustrated description of the work of Nieuwenkamp, Bonnet, Spies, Hofker, Le Mayeur and Smit who studied and documented the culture and natural beauty of the island.

LOMBOK

The *genggong* uses a simple set of instruments, which includes a bamboo flute, a *rebab* and knockers. Seven musicians accompany their music with dance movements and stylised hand gestures.

Theatre

Music, dance and drama are closely related on Bali – Balinese dance has the three elements working together, as does *wayang kulit* which are drama performances with the sound effects and the puppets' movements an important part of the show. The *arja* is a dance-drama, comparable to Western opera.

WAYANG KULIT

Wayang Kulit has been Bali's cinema for centuries, but it is primarily a sacred matter. It has the sacred seriousness of classical Greek drama. (Indeed the word drama comes from the Greek *dromenon*, a religious ritual.) The word *wayang* means shadow and can refer to the puppets or the show. It may be derived from *hyang*, meaning ancestor or gods. Alternatively it may be from *bayan*, meaning shadow. *Kulit* means leather or hide.

Bali Behind the Seen – Recent Fiction from Bali, translated by Vern Cork and written by Balinese authors, conveys much of the tension between deeply rooted traditions and the irresistible pressure of modernisation.

Shadow puppet plays are more than entertainment, for the puppets are believed to have great spiritual power and the *dalang* (the puppet master and storyteller) is an almost mystical figure. A person of considerable skill and even greater endurance, he manipulates the puppets and tells the story while conducting the small gamelan orchestra, the *gender wayang,* and beating time with his chanting. Having run out of hands, he does this with a horn held with his toes!

The *dalang's* mystical powers are needed because the *wayang kulit*, like so much of Balinese drama, is about the eternal struggle between good and evil. Endurance is also required because a *wayang kulit* can last six or more hours, and the performances always start so late that the drama is only finally resolved as the sun peeps over the horizon.

The intricate lacy puppets are made of buffalo hide carefully cut with a sharp, chisel-like stylus and then painted. The figures are completely traditional – there is no deviation from the standard list of characters and their standardised appearance, so there's definitely no mistaking who's who.

The *dalang* sits behind a screen on which the shadows of the puppets are cast, usually by an oil lamp, which gives a romantic flickering light. Traditionally, women and children sit in front of the screen, while the men sit with the *dalang* and his assistants.

Goodies are arrayed to the right and baddies to the left. Characters include nobles, who speak in the high Javanese language Kawi, and common clowns, who speak in everyday Balinese. The *dalang* also has to be a linguist! When the four clowns (Delem and Sangut are the bad ones, Twalen and his son Merdah are the good ones) are on screen, there is much rushing back and forth, clouts on the head and comic insults. The noble characters are altogether more refined – they include the terrible Durga and the noble Bima. *Wayang kulit* stories are chiefly derived from the great Hindu epics, the *Mahabharata* and the *Ramayana*.

Puppets are made in the village of Puaya near Sukawati, south of Ubud, and in Peliatan, just east of Ubud, but they're easy to find in craft, antique and souvenir shops. Although performances are normally held at night, there are sometimes daytime temple performances, where the figures are manipulated without a screen.

ARJA

An *arja* drama is not unlike *wayang kulit* in its melodramatic plots, its offstage sound effects and its cast of easily identifiable goodies and baddies – represented by the refined *alus* and unrefined *kras*. It's performed outside, often with a curtain as a backdrop. Sometimes a small house is built on the stage, and set on fire at the climax of the story!

The story is told by clown characters who describe and explain all the actions of the nobles, so the dialogue uses both high and low Balinese. The plot is often just a small part of a longer story well known to the Balinese audience but very difficult for a foreigner to understand or appreciate.

Literature

The Balinese language has several forms, but only 'high Balinese' is a written language, and that is a form of Sanskrit used for religious purposes and to recount epics such as the *Ramayana* and the *Mahabharata*. Illustrated versions of these epics inscribed on *lontar* (specially prepared palm leaves) are Bali's earliest books. The poems and stories of the early Balinese courts, from the 11th to the 19th centuries, were written in Old Javanese or Middle Javanese, and were meant to be sung or recited rather than read. Even the most elaborate drama and dance performances had no real written scripts or choreography, at least until Westerners, like Colin McPhee, started to produce them in the 1930s.

In the colonial period, a few Indonesians began writing in Dutch, while Dutch scholars set about documenting traditional Balinese language and literature. Later, the use of Indo-Malay (called Bahasa Indonesia) became more widespread. One of the first Balinese writers to be published in that language was Anak Agung Pandji Tisna, from Singaraja in northern Bali. His second novel, *The Rape of Sukreni* (1936), adapted the features of Balinese drama – the conflict between good and evil, and the inevitability of karma. It was a popular and critical success. Most of the action takes place in a *warung* (food stall). An English translation is available at bookshops on Bali, and is highly recommended.

Most modern Balinese literature has been written in Bahasa Indonesia. Short stories are frequently published in newspapers and magazines, often for literary competitions. An important theme has been tradition versus change and modernisation, often elaborated as a tragic love story involving couples of different castes. Politics, money, tourism and relations with foreigners are also explored. Several anthologies translated into English are currently in print, some by Putu Oka Sukanta, one of Indonesia's most important authors of poetry, short fiction, and novels. Another novelist,

A fascinating indexed and illustrated list of books about art, culture and Balinese writers, dancers and musicians is available at www.ganeshabooks bali.com/bookstore.html

---

LONTAR BOOKS

The Gedong Kirtya Library has the world's largest collection of works that are inscribed on *lontar* (specially prepared palm leaves). Some 4000 historic Balinese manuscripts cover everything from literary to mythological and historical to religious themes. They are written in fine Sanskrit calligraphy, and some are elaborately decorated.

Lontar is made from the fan-shaped leaves of the *rontal* palm. The leaf is dried, soaked in water, cleaned, steamed, dried again, then flattened, dyed and eventually cut into strips. The strips are inscribed with words and pictures using a very sharp blade or point, then coated with a black stain which is wiped off – the black colour stays in the inscription. A hole in the middle of each *lontar* strip is threaded onto a string, with a carved bamboo 'cover' at each end to protect the 'pages', and the string is secured with a couple of pierced Chinese coins, or *kepeng*.

WESTERN VISITORS IN THE 1930s

When Gregor Krause's book *Bali: People and Art* was published in 1922, it was a bestseller. Krause had worked in Bangli as a doctor between 1912 and 1914 and his unique photographs of an uninhibited lifestyle in a lush, tropical environment caused an amazing tourist boom in the 1930s. Visitors included many talented individuals who helped rejuvenate many dormant Balinese arts, and played a great part in creating the image of Bali that exists today.

Walter Spies

German artist Walter Spies (1895–1942) first visited Bali in 1925 and moved there in 1927, establishing the image of Bali for Westerners that prevails today. Befriended by the important Sukawati family, he built a house at the confluence of two rivers at Campuan, west of Ubud. His home soon became a prime gathering point for those who followed. He involved himself in every aspect of Balinese art and culture and was an important influence on its renaissance.

In 1932 he became curator of the museum in Denpasar, and with Rudolf Bonnet and Cokorda Gede Agung Sukawati, their Balinese patron, he founded the Pita Maha artists' cooperative in 1936. He co-authored *Dance & Drama in Bali*, which was published in 1938, and recreated the Kecak (monkey) dance for the German film, *The Island of Demons*.

Rudolf Bonnet

Bonnet (1895–1978) was a Dutch artist whose work concentrated on the human form and everyday Balinese life. Many classical Balinese paintings with themes of markets and cockfights are indebted to Bonnet. He returned to Bali in the 1950s to plan the Museum Puri Lukisan in Ubud, and again in 1973 to help establish the museum's permanent collection.

Miguel Covarrubias

Island of Bali, written by this Mexican artist (1904–57), is still the classic introduction to the island and its culture. Covarrubias visited Bali twice in the early 1930s and was also involved in theatre design and printmaking.

Colin McPhee

Canadian musician Colin McPhee (1900–65) wrote *A House in Bali*. It was not published until 1944, but remains one of the best written accounts of Bali, and his tales of music and house building are often highly amusing. After WWII, McPhee played an important role in introducing Balinese music to the West, and encouraging *gamelan* (traditional Balinese orcestra) to visit the US.

K'tut Tantri & the Kokes

A woman of many aliases, K'tut Tantri breezed in from Hollywood in 1932 inspired by the film *Bali, the Last Paradise*. She dyed her red hair black (only demons have red hair) and was befriended by the prince of the Bangli kingdom.

She teamed up with Robert and Louise Koke to open the first hotel at Kuta Beach (the Kuta Beach Hotel) in 1936, which was an instant hit. After the war, however, only traces of the hotel's foundations remained. K'tut worked for the Indonesian Republicans in their postwar struggle against the Dutch. As Surabaya Sue, she broadcast from Surabaya in support of their cause. Her book, *Revolt in Paradise* (written as K'tut Tantri), was published in 1960.

In 1987 Louise Koke's long-forgotten story of Kuta Beach Hotel was published as *Our Hotel in Bali*, illustrated with her incisive sketches and her husband's photographs. Robert Koke, who learned to surf in Hawaii, introduced surfing to Bali.

Other Western Visitors

Others played their part in chronicling the period, such as writer Hickman Powell, whose book *The Last Paradise* was published in 1930, and German author Vicki Baum, whose book *A Tale from Bali*, a fictionalised account of the 1906 *puputan* (fight to the death), is still in print.

Oka Rusmini, is both Balinese and female, which makes her book *Tarian Bumi*, a story of generations of Balinese women, rather special.

It is striking how much has been published about Bali in the Western world, and (until recently) how little of it has been written by Balinese – it says a lot about the Western fascination with Bali. Indonesian journals regularly have articles about aspects of Bali – its geography, economy, history and so on. Many are written in English, but few are appealing to a general audience.

The **Lontar Foundation** (www.lontar.org) is a nonprofit organisation run by Indonesian writers and dedicated to getting at least 100 of the most important Indonesian books translated into English so that universities can offer courses in Indonesian literature.

Cinema & TV

Fewer films have been filmed in Bali than one would expect, so the establishment in April 2002 of the Bali Film Commission (BFC) was an effort to change this. The BFC promotes the advantages of filming in the country, both for the production and for a boom in tourism, as films showcase the beauty of their settings. It also plans to establish a foundation offering workshops in the different performing arts and technical fields, from costume design to scriptwriting.

Apart from providing a location and support base for expected box-office hits like *Almayer's Folly* and *Toute la Beaute' du Monde*, the BFC is collaborating with South East Film & Video Archive to restore recently discovered colour film footage from *Trance and Dance in Bali*, which documents the great cultural importance of Balinese dance and provides a unique glimpse into Bali of 1939. It is also providing research for a feature film entitled *Walter Spies of Bali*.

Domestic television boomed in Indonesia when the government loosened its shackles. Then, during the Asian economic crisis in 1998, when many countries closed their studios, Indonesia turned to producing local soap operas to keep the cameras rolling. Today, 10 national networks demand local programming, particularly *sinetron* (soap operas). The country's new Broadcast Act, passed in 2002, however, limits the rebroadcast of both foreign and domestic programmes with the official intent of controlling news, sports and music programmes which are deemed improper. TV stations must now add a few minutes delay before airing foreign news. The new Act also makes it easier to take a broadcaster to court or to shut down a station.

Painting

Balinese painting is probably the art form most influenced by Western ideas and demand. There are a relatively small number of creative original painters, and an enormous number of imitators. Originality is not considered as important in Bali as it is in the West. Even some renowned artists will simply draw the design, decide the colours and leave apprentices to apply the paint. Thus, shops are packed full of paintings in the popular styles – some of them are quite good, a few of them are really excellent. It's rare to see anything totally new.

Visit the Neka Art Museum and Museum Puri Lukisan in Ubud to see the best of Balinese art and some of the European influences that have shaped it. Visit commercial galleries like the Neka Gallery near Ubud and the Agung Rai Gallery to view high-quality work. If you buy a painting, consider taking a frame as well. These are often elaborately carved works of art in themselves.

DID YOU KNOW?

The Bali Film Commission has patented the term 'Baliwood'. Here's hoping it becomes as famous as Hollywood and Bollywood.

Long before the gorilla appears(!), you know *Road to Bali* is one of the lesser 'road' movies of Bob Hope and Bing Crosby. Few last long enough to see the pair vie for the affections of 'Balinese princess' Dorothy Lamour.

TOP FIVE FILMS

- *Goona Goona, An Authentic Melodrama* (1932) Such was the impact of this film and the beautiful women of Bali that the topless look was called 'goona goona'. The film includes the famous I Mario, creator of the Kebyar dance.

- *The Island of Demons* (1933) This still remains the classic film about Bali, with stunning photography. It tells a story of young lovers thwarted by greed and black magic. Walter Spies remodelled the Kecak dance for the film.

- *Trance and Dance in Bali* (1952) A famous film shot in the 1930s, it shows the Calon Arang dance and ritual with some extraordinary scenes of trance. In 1999 it was deemed 'culturally significant' and was preserved in the USA Film Registry.

- *Lempad of Bali* (1980) This includes the elaborate cremation rites for 116-year-old master-artist, I Gusti Nyoman Lempad, the development of his many artistic talents and the history of the island during his lifetime.

- *Kiss Kiss Ko* (2003) Shooting this Bollywood film almost entirely on Bali helped prove that Bali was safe again after the bombings of 2002, and that it provides the perfect backdrop for any production. It features the popular Indian band, Band of Boys, and some 600 local extras.

Find out about new films being produced, or what's on offer in Bali if you are looking for the perfect location for a film shoot, at www.balifilm.com.

Traditional paintings faithfully depicting religious and mythological symbolism were customarily for temple and palace decoration. After the 1930s, Western artists introduced the novel concept that paintings could also be artistic creations which could be sold for money. The range of themes, techniques, styles and materials expanded enormously.

A loose classification of styles is: classical, or Kamasan, named for the village of Kamasan near Semarapura; Ubud style, developed in the 1930s under the influence of the Pita Maha; Batuan, which started at the same time in a nearby village; Young Artists, begun postwar, in the 1960s, and influenced by Dutch artist Arie Smit; and finally, modern or 'academic', free in its creative topics, yet strongly and distinctively Balinese.

CLASSICAL PAINTING

There are three basic types of classical painting – *langse, iders-iders* and calendars. *Langse* are large decorative hangings for palaces or temples which display *wayang* figures, rich floral designs and flame-and-mountain motifs. *Iders-iders* are scroll paintings hung along the eaves of temples. Calendars are still used to set dates and predict the future: they include simple yellow calendars from Bedulu, near Ubud; more complex calendars from Semarapura and Kamasan; and large versions of the zodiacal and lunar calendar, especially the 210-day *wuku* calendar, which regulates the timing of Balinese festivals.

Langse paintings helped impart *adat* (tradition, customs and manners) to the ordinary people, as traditional dance and *wayang kulit* puppetry does. *Wayang* tradition can be seen in stylised human figures shown in profile; their symbolic gestures; refined divine and heroic characters and vulgar, crude evil ones. The paintings tell a story in a series of panels, rather like a comic strip, and often depict scenes from the *Ramayana* and *Mahabharata*. Other themes are the Kakawins poems, and indigenous Balinese folklore with its beliefs in demonic spirits – see the painted ceilings of the Kertha Gosa (Hall of Justice) in Semarapura.

The skill of the artist is apparent in the overall composition and sensitivity of the line work. The colouring is of secondary importance often left to the artist's children. Natural colours were once made from soot, clay and pigs' bones, and artists were strictly limited to set shades. Today, modern oils and acrylics are used, but the range of colours is still limited. A final burnishing gives an aged look, and these pictures are known as *lukisan antic* (antique paintings).

THE PITA MAHA

In the 1930s, with few commissions from temples, painting was virtually dying out. Bonnet and Spies (see p46), with their patron Cokorda Gede Agung Sukawati, formed the *Pita Maha* (literally 'Great Vitality') to encourage painting as an art form and to find a market. The group had more than 100 members at its peak in the 1930s.

The changes Bonnet and Spies inspired were revolutionary. Balinese artists started painting single scenes instead of narrative tales and using everyday life rather than romantic legends as their themes: the harvest, the market, cockfights, offerings at a temple or a cremation. These paintings were known as the Ubud style.

Batuan is a noted painting centre that came under the influence of the Pita Maha, but retained many features of classical painting. They depicted daily life, but included many scenes – a market, dance and rice harvest might all appear in a single work. The Batuan style is also noted for its inclusion of some very modern elements, such as sea scenes with the odd windsurfer.

Themes changed, and so did the actual way of painting. Modern paint and materials were used and stiff formal poses gave way to realistic 3D representations. More importantly, pictures were not just painted to cover a space in a palace or temple.

In one way, however, the style remained unchanged – Balinese paintings were packed with detail; a painted Balinese forest, for example, has branches, leaves and a whole zoo of creatures reaching out to fill every tiny space. You can see these glorious styles at the Museum Puri Lukisan in Ubud and, of course, in all the galleries and art shops.

The new artistic enthusiasm was interrupted by WWII and Indonesia's internal turmoil. New work degenerated into copies of the original spirits, with one exception: the development of the Young Artists' style.

THE YOUNG ARTISTS

Dutch painter Arie Smit was in Penestanan just outside Ubud in 1956, when he noticed a boy drawing in the dirt and wondered what he would produce if he had proper equipment. The story is told of how the lad's father would not allow him to take up painting until Smit offered to pay somebody else to watch the family's ducks.

Other 'young artists' soon joined that first pupil, I Nyoman Cakra, but Smit did not actively teach them. He simply provided equipment and encouragement, and unleashed what was clearly a strong natural talent. An engaging new 'naive' style developed, as typically Balinese rural scenes were painted in brilliant technicolour.

The style is today one of the staples of Balinese tourist art. It is also known as work by 'peasant painters'. I Nyoman Cakra still lives in Penestanan, still paints, and cheerfully admits that he owes it all to Smit.

OTHER STYLES

There are some other variants of the main Ubud and Young Artists' styles. The depiction of forests, flowers, butterflies, birds and other naturalistic themes, sometimes called Pengosekan style, became popular in the 1960s, but can probably be traced back to Henri Rousseau, who was a significant influence on Walter Spies. An interesting development is the

Pre-War Balinese Modernists 1928-1942: an additional page in art-history by F Haks et al. is a beautiful book on the work of some brilliant but long-neglected Balinese artists.

WOJ Nieuwenkamp: First European Artist in Bali by Bruce Carpenter is a fascinating depiction of Bali from 1904, when the Dutch artist Nieuwenkamp first arrived with a sketchpad and a bicycle.

SMALL TALK

You're asked where you're staying by a stranger? That's Balinese small talk. Give some vague reply like 'in a *losmen* (small Balinese hotel) run by a guy called Wayan'. You're asked if you're married? It's easiest to say you are *sudah kawin*, 'already married'. Where's your partner? A dead spouse is considered less of a tragedy than a divorced one. Do you want a boyfriend? It's definitely easier to be 'married' than single.

Are you a Christian? If you're an atheist it's better not to say so; the logic is that communists are atheists, and therefore if you're an atheist you must be a communist, or you may not subscribe to one of the state-sanctioned monotheistic religions.

Try not to get annoyed by the personal level of questions and ask some of your own to deflect attention from yourself. You'll learn interesting things about the local people.

---

depiction of underwater scenes, with colourful fish, coral gardens and sea creatures. Somewhere between the Pengosekan and Ubud styles are the miniature landscape paintings that are popular commercially.

The new techniques also resulted in radically new versions of Rangda, Barong, Hanuman and other figures from Balinese and Hindu mythology. Scenes from folk tales and stories appeared, featuring dancers, nymphs and love stories, with an understated erotic appeal.

A growing number of Balinese artists receive formal art training. Others are influenced by artists who visit Bali. Basically, any painting that does not depict a recognisably Balinese subject or style can be called 'academic', and is very likely by someone with formal training.

Crafts

Bali is a showroom for all the crafts of Indonesia. A typical tourist shop will sell puppets and batiks from Java, ikat garments from Sumba, Sumbawa and Flores, and textiles and woodcarvings from Bali, Lombok and Kalimantan. The *kris*, so important in a Balinese family, will often have been made in Java.

On Lombok, where there's never been much money, traditional handicrafts are practical items, skillfully made and beautifully finished. The finer examples of Lombok weaving, basketware and pottery are highly valued by collectors. Some traditional crafts have developed into small-scale industries and villages now specialise in them; handweaving in one, basketware in another, pottery in a third. Shops in Ampenan, Cakranegara and Senggigi have a good range of Lombok's finest arts and crafts, as do the local markets.

OFFERINGS & EPHEMERA

Traditionally, many of Bali's most elaborate crafts have been ceremonial offerings not intended to last: *baten tegeh* (decorated pyramids of fruit, rice cakes and flowers); rice-flour cookies modelled into tiny sculptures and even into entire scenes which have a deep symbolic significance; *lamak* (long woven palm-leaf strips used as decorations in festivals and celebrations); stylised female figures known as *cili*, which are representations of Dewi Sri; or intricately carved coconut-shell wall hangings. Marvel at the care and energy that goes into constructing huge funeral towers and exotic sarcophagi, all of which will go up in flames.

TEXTILES & WEAVING

The sarong is an attractive article of clothing, sheet or towel with a multitude of other uses. There are plain or printed cottons, more elegant batik designs, and expensive fabrics, like *endek* (elegant fabric, like *songket*, but the weft threads are predyed) and *songket* (silver or gold-threaded cloth, hand-woven using a floating weft technique), that are necessary for special occasions – it is a religious obligation to look one's best at a temple ceremony. Dress for these occasions is a simple shirt or blouse, a sarong and a *kain*, a separate length of cloth wound tightly around the hips, over the sarong.

Balinese Textiles by Hauser, Nabholz-Kartaschoff & Ramseyer is a large and lavishly illustrated guide detailing weaving styles and their significance.

For more formal occasions, the blouse is replaced by a length of *songket* wrapped around the chest, called a *kamben*. Any market, especially those in Denpasar will have a good range of textiles.

Batik

Traditional batik sarongs are hand-made in central Java. The dyeing process has been adapted by the Balinese to produce brightly coloured and patterned fabrics. Watch out for 'batik' fabric that has been screen printed. The colours will be washed out compared to real batik cloth, and the pattern is often only on one side (the dye should colour both sides).

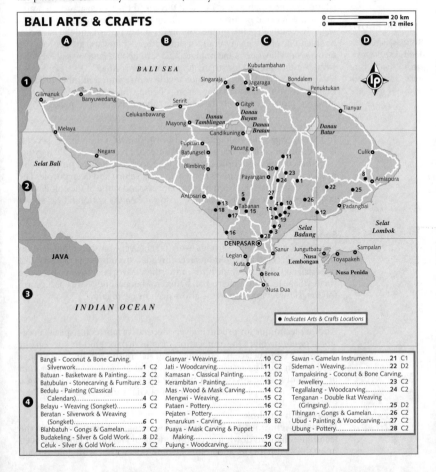

BALI ARTS & CRAFTS

• Indicates Arts & Crafts Locations

Bangli - Coconut & Bone Carving, Silverwork.....................................**1** C2	Gianyar - Weaving..........................**10** C2	Sawan - Gamelan Instruments.........**21** C1
Batuan - Basketware & Painting........**2** C2	Jati - Woodcarving.........................**11** C2	Sideman - Weaving.........................**22** D2
Batubulan - Stonecarving & Furniture.**3** C2	Kamasan - Classical Painting...........**12** D2	Tampaksiring - Coconut & Bone Carving, Jewellery.....................................**23** C2
Bedulu - Painting (Classical Calendars).....................................**4** C2	Kerambitan - Painting.....................**13** C2	Tegallalang - Woodcarving.............**24** C2
Belayu - Weaving (Songket).............**5** C2	Mas - Wood & Mask Carving............**14** C2	Tenganan - Double Ikat Weaving (Gringsing)................................**25** D2
Beratan - Silverwork & Weaving (Songket)......................................**6** C1	Mengwi - Weaving..........................**15** C2	Tihingan - Gongs & Gamelan...........**26** C2
Blahbatuh - Gongs & Gamelan..........**7** C2	Pataen - Pottery............................**16** C2	Ubud - Painting & Woodcarving......**27** C2
Budakeling - Silver & Gold Work.......**8** D2	Pejaten - Pottery...........................**17** C2	Ubung - Pottery.............................**28** C2
Celuk - Silver & Gold Work...............**9** C2	Penarukun - Carving.......................**18** B2	
	Puaya - Mask Carving & Puppet Making....................................**19** C2	
	Pujung - Woodcarving....................**20** C2	

AUSTRALIAN ARTIST

In 1968, one of Sydney's Charm School artists, Donald Friend, headed off to Bali. Rumours of his regal lifestyle and the beauty, culture and sensual atmosphere of his surroundings kept filtering back to his homeland and Bali became known as a place where sexuality was considered fluid and able to manifest itself in many forms. A new international set of expatriates and artists centred themselves around Sanur, where the vibe was low-key and discreet, and charged with sexual electricity. Arie Smit and Lempad became friends of Donald, who was collecting bronzes and cloth for his hotel, the Tanjung Sari. Donald was also working on his books, in particular *Bumbooziana*, an exotic, erotic, mind-blowing romp in exquisite line drawing, text and painting. His works were to explode the middle-class constrained ideas back in Australia, and open up a broader view of life for a new generation of Australian artists.

Ikat

In this complex process, the pattern is dyed into either the warp threads (those stretched on the loom), or weft threads (those woven across the warp) before the material is woven. The resulting pattern is geometric and slightly wavy. Its beauty depends on the complexity of the pattern and the harmonious blending of colours, typically of similar tone – blues and greens; reds and browns; or yellows, reds and oranges. Ikat sarongs and *kain* are not everyday wear, but they are not for strictly formal occasions either.

DID YOU KNOW?
Australian artist Donald Friend's hotel, Tanjung Sari, was regarded, in the 1960s, as one of the great hotels in the world.

Gianyar, in East Bali, is a major textile centre with a number of factories where you can watch ikat sarongs being woven on a hand-and-foot powered loom; a complete sarong takes about six hours to make.

Gringsing

In the Bali Aga village of Tenganan, in eastern Bali, a double ikat process is used, in which both warp and weft threads are predyed. Called *gringsing*, this complex and time-consuming process is practised nowhere else in Indonesia. Typical colours are red, brown, yellow and deep purple. The dyes used are obtained from natural sources, and some of the colours can take years to mix and age. The dyes also weaken the cotton fabric, so old examples of *gringsing* are extremely rare.

Songket

For *kamben*, *kain* and sarongs worn exclusively for ceremonial occasions, *songket* cloth has gold or silver threads woven into the tapestry-like material, and motifs include birds, butterflies, leaves and flowers. Belayu, a small village in southwestern Bali between Mengwi and Marga, is a centre for *songket* weaving. *Songket* is also woven near Singaraja.

Prada

Another technique for producing very decorative fabrics for special occasions, *prada* involves the application of gold leaf, or gold or silver paint or thread to the surface of a finished material. Motifs are similar to those used in *songket*. The result is not washable, so *prada* is reserved for *kain* or for decorative wraps on offerings and for temple umbrellas. For *prada*, have a look at shops in Sukawati, south of Gianyar.

Weaving in Lombok

Lombok is renowned for its traditional weaving on backstrap looms, the techniques handed down from mother to daughter. Each cloth is woven in established patterns and colours, some interwoven with gold thread.

Abstract flower and animal motifs sometimes decorate this exquisite cloth; look carefully to recognise forms like buffaloes, dragons, crocodiles and snakes. Several villages specialise in weaving cloth, while others concentrate on fine baskets and mats woven from rattan or grass. Factories you can visit around Cakranegara and Mataram produce weft ikat on old hand-and-foot-operated looms.

At Sukarara and Pringgasela they specialise in traditional ikat and *songket* weaving. Sarongs, Sasak belts and clothing edged with brightly coloured embroidery are sold in small shops.

WOODCARVING

A decorative craft, woodcarving was chiefly used for carved doors or columns; figures such as Garudas, or demons with a symbolic nature; minor functional objects, such as bottle tops; and the carved wooden masks used in Balinese dance. Yet, as with painting, it was the demand from outside that inspired new subjects and styles.

Ubud was a centre for the revolution in woodcarving. Some carvers started producing highly stylised figures. Others carved delightful animal figures, some realistic, some complete caricatures. More styles and trends developed: whole tree trunks carved into ghostly, intertwined 'totem poles', and curiously exaggerated and distorted figures.

Almost all carving is of local woods, including *belalu*, a quick-growing light wood, and the stronger fruit timbers such as jackfruit wood. Ebony from Sulawesi is also used. Sandalwood, with its delightful fragrance, is expensive, soft and used for some small, very detailed pieces.

Tegallalang and Jati, on the road north from Ubud to Batur, are noted woodcarving centres. Many workshops line the road east of Peliatan, near Ubud, to Goa Gajah (Elephant Cave). The route from Mas, through Peliatan, Petulu and up the scenic slope to Pujung is also a centre for family based workshops; listen for the tapping sound of the carvers' mallets.

Despite the emphasis on what sells, there's always something special, the technical skill is high and the Balinese sense of humour shines through – a frog clutching a leaf as an umbrella, or a weird demon on the side of a bell clasping his hands over his ears. It's difficult to separate traditional and foreign influences. The Balinese have always incorporated and adapted foreign themes in their work – religious figures based on Hindu mythology are very different to the equivalent carvings made in India.

In Lombok, carving usually decorates functional items, such as containers for tobacco and spices, and the handles of betel-nut crushers and knives. Materials include wood, horn and bone. A recent fashion is for primitive-style elongated masks, often decorated with inlaid shell pieces. Cakranegara, Sindu, Labuapi and Senanti are centres for carving.

Wooden articles lose moisture when moved to a drier environment. Avoid possible shrinkage by placing the carving in a plastic bag at home, then letting some air in for about one week every month for four months.

Mask Carving

A specialised form of woodcarving, only experts carve the masks used in theatre and dance performances, such as the Topeng dance. The mask maker must know the movements that each performer uses, so that the character can be shown by the mask.

Other masks, such as the Barong and Rangda, are brightly painted and decorated with real hair, enormous teeth and bulging eyes. Mas is

DID YOU KNOW?

Trees have a spiritual and religious significance in Bali. The Banyan is the holiest; creepers that drop from its branches take root, thus it is 'never-dying'.

recognised as the mask-carving centre of Bali, followed by the small village of Puaya, near Sukawati. The Museum Negeri Propinsi Bali in Denpasar has an extensive mask collection and is a great place to get an idea of different styles before buying anything.

STONE CARVING

Traditionally for the adornment of temples, sculpture hasn't been affected by foreign influences, mainly because your average stone statue isn't a convenient souvenir. Stone carving is also Bali's most durable art form. Though it is soon covered in moss, mould or lichen, it doesn't deteriorate in the humid atmosphere.

Stone carving appears in set places in temples. Door guardians are usually a protective personality like Arjuna. Above the main entrance, Kala's monstrous face often peers out, his hands reaching out beside his head to catch any evil spirits. The side walls of a *pura dalem* (temple of the dead) might feature sculpted panels that show the horrors that await evildoers in the afterlife.

www.balibagus.com has an index of where to buy arts and crafts in Bali and offers Internet shopping.

Even when decorating a modern building, stone carvers tend to stick to the tried and trusted – patterned friezes, floral decoration or bas-reliefs depicting scenes from the *Ramayana*. Nevertheless, modern trends can be seen and many sculptors are happy to work on non-traditional themes, like Japanese-style stone lanterns or McDonalds' characters outside its Kuta franchise.

Much of the local work is made from a soft, grey volcanic stone called *paras*. It's a little like pumice, and so soft it can be scratched with a fingernail. When newly worked, it can be mistaken for cast cement, but with age, the outer surface becomes tougher and darker. Soft sandstone is also used, and sometimes has attractive colouring. Because the stone is light it's possible to bring a friendly stone demon back in your airline baggage. A typical temple door guardian weighs around 10kg.

Batubulan, on the main highway from Denpasar to Ubud, is a major stone-carving centre. Stone figures from 25cm to 2m tall line both sides of the road, and stone carvers can be seen in action in the many workshops.

JEWELLERY

Bali is a major producer of jewellery and produces variations on currently fashionable designs. Very fine filigree work is a Balinese speciality, as is the use of tiny spots of silver to form a decorative texture – this is a very skilled technique, as the heat must be perfectly controlled to weld the delicate onto the underlying silver without damaging it. Balinese work is nearly always hand-made, rarely involving casting techniques. Most silver is imported, though some is mined near Singaraja in northern Bali.

Celuk has always been associated with silversmithing. To see the 'real' Celuk, visit family workshops about 1km east of the road. Other silverwork centres include Kamasan, near Semarapura in eastern Bali, and Beratan, south of Singaraja in northern Bali.

There's a wide range of earrings, bracelets and rings available, some using imported gemstones. Different design influences can be detected, from African patterning to the New Age preoccupation with dolphins and healing crystals.

You'll find many jewellery workshops in areas around Ubud. Tampaksiring, northeast of Ubud, has long been a centre for cheaper styles of fashion jewellery. Brightly painted, carved wooden earrings are popular and cheap.

KRIS

Often with an ornate, jewel-studded handle and sinister-looking wavy blade, the *kris* is the traditional and ceremonial dagger of Bali and Indonesia. A *kris* can be the most important of family heirlooms, a symbol of prestige and honour. It is supposed to have great spiritual power, sending out magical energy waves and thus requiring great care in its handling and use.

OTHER CRAFTS

To see potters at work, visit Pataen near Pura Tanah Lot, or Ubung and Kapal, north and west of Denpasar, respectively. Nearly all local pottery is made from low-fired terracotta. Most styles are very ornate, even functional items such as vases, flasks, ashtrays and lamp bases. Pejaten, near Tabanan, also has a number of workshops producing small ceramic figures and glazed ornamental roof tiles. Some excellent, contemporary glazed ceramics are produced in Jimbaran, south of Kuta.

Earthenware pots have been produced on Lombok for centuries. They are shaped by hand, coated with a slurry of clay or ash to enhance the finish, and fired in a simple kiln filled with burning rice stalks. Pots are often finished with a covering of woven cane for decoration and extra strength. Newer designs feature bright colours and elaborate decorations. Penujak, Banyumulek and Masbagik are some of the main pottery villages, or visit the Lombok Pottery Centre in Cakranegara.

Lombok is noted for its spiral-woven rattan basketware; bags made of *lontar* or split bamboo; small boxes made of woven grass; plaited rattan mats; and decorative boxes of palm leaves shaped like rice barns and decorated with shells. Beleka, Suradadi, Kotaraja and Loyok are noted for fine basketware, while Rungkang, about 1km east of Loyok, combines pottery and basketware. Sayang is known for palm-leaf boxes.

DID YOU KNOW?

Making a *kris* (traditional dagger) requires careful preparation, as it involves working with the forces of magic.

Architecture

Balinese architecture has a cosmic significance that is much more important than the physical materials, the construction or the decoration. Balinese sculpture and painting were once exclusively used as architectural decoration, and though temples are still heavily decorated, sculpture and painting have developed as separate art forms.

A village, a temple, a family compound, an individual structure and even a single part of the structure, must all conform to the Balinese concept of cosmic order. They consist of three parts that represent the three worlds of the cosmos – *swah* (the world of gods), *bhwah* (the world of humans) and *bhur* (the world of demons). They also represent a three-part division of a person: *utama* (the head), *madia* (the body) and *nista* (the legs). The units of measurement used in traditional buildings are directly based on the anatomical dimensions of the head of the household, ensuring harmony between the dwelling and those that live in it. Traditionally, the designer of the building is a combination architect-priest called an *undagi*.

The basic element of Balinese architecture is the *bale,* a rectangular, open-sided pavilion with a steeply pitched roof of thatch. Both a family compound and a temple will comprise of a number of separate *bale* for specific functions, all surrounded by a high wall. The size and proportions of the *bale*, the number of columns, and the position within the compound, are all determined according to tradition and the owner's caste status.

The focus of a community is a large pavilion, called the *bale banjar*, used for meetings, debates and *gamelan* (traditional Balinese orchestra) practice, among many other activities. You'll find that large, modern buildings such as restaurants and the lobby areas of resorts are often modelled on the larger *bale*, and they can be airy, spacious and very handsomely proportioned.

During the building process, the pavilions may get beyond a certain size, and traditional materials cannot be used. In these cases concrete is substituted for timber, and sometimes the roof is tiled rather than thatched. The fancier modern buildings like banks and hotels might also feature decorative carvings derived from traditional temple design. As a result of this, some regard the use of traditional features in modern buildings as pure kitsch, while others see it as a natural and appropriate development of modern Balinese style. Buildings with these features are sometimes described as Baliesque, Bali Baroque, or Bali Rococo if the decoration has become too excessive.

Visitors may be disappointed by Balinese *puri* (palaces), which prove to be neither large nor imposing. The *puri* are the traditional residences of the Balinese aristocracy, although now they may be used as top-end hotels or as regular family compounds. They prove unimposing, as a Balinese palace can never be built more than one storey high. This is because a Balinese noble could not possibly use a ground-floor room if the feet of people on an upper floor were walking above.

THE FAMILY COMPOUND

The Balinese house looks inward – the outside is simply a high wall. Inside there will be a garden and a separate small building or *bale* for each activity – one for cooking, one for washing and the toilet, and separate

Architecture of Bali by Made Wijaya is a lavish book detailing the personal observations and conclusions of the Australian-born Bali landscape designer. The vintage photos and illustrations are worth the price alone.

Bali Style by Rio Helmi and Barbara Walker is the coffee-table book that spawned enough imitations to crush a coffee table. First published in 1995, the book details the sort of clean and open-plan Bali design ethos that would become a cliché if it weren't simply so adaptable.

Architectural Conservation In Bali by Edo Budiharjo examines the case for conservation of architectural heritage on the island of Bali, an important issue at a time when modern forms are appearing everywhere.

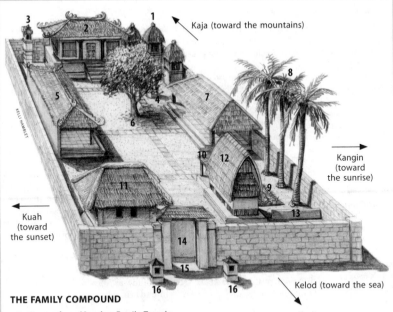

THE FAMILY COMPOUND

1 **Sanggah or Merajan** Family Temple
2 **Umah Meten** Sleeping pavilion for the family head
3 **Tugu** Shrine
4 **Pengijeng** Shrine
5 **Bale Tiang Sanga** Guest pavilion
6 **Natah** Courtyard with frangipani or hibiscus shade tree
7 **Bale Sakenam** Working & sleeping pavilion
8 **Fruit trees and coconut palms**
9 **Vegetable garden**
10 **Bale Sakepat** Sleeping pavilion for children
11 **Paon** Kitchen
12 **Lumbung** Rice barn
13 **Rice-threshing area**
14 **Aling Aling** Screen wall
15 **Candi Kurung** Gate with roof
16 **Apit Lawang or Pelinggah** Gate shrines

buildings for each 'bedroom'. In Bali's mild tropical climate people live outside, so the 'living room' and 'dining room' will be open veranda areas, looking out into the garden. The whole complex is oriented on the *kaja* (toward the mountians)–*kelod* (toward the sea) axis.

Many modern Balinese houses, particularly in Denpasar and the larger towns, are arranged much like houses in the west, but there are still a great number of traditional family compounds. For example, in Ubud, nearly every house will follow the same traditional walled design.

Analogous to the human body, there's a head (the family temple with its ancestral shrine), arms (the sleeping and living areas), legs and feet (the kitchen and rice storage building), and even an anus (the garbage

---

LOMBOK ARCHITECTURE

Lombok's architecture is governed by traditional laws and practices. Construction must begin on a propitious day, always with an odd-numbered date, and the building's frame must be completed on that day. It would be bad luck to leave any of the important structural work to the following day.

In a traditional Sasak village there are three types of buildings – *beruga* (the communal meeting hall), *bale tani* (family houses) and *lumbung* (rice barns). The *beruga* and the *bale tani* are both rectangular, with low walls and a steeply pitched thatched roof, although, of course, the *beruga* is much larger. The arrangement of rooms in a *bale tani* is also very standardised. There is a *serambi*an (open veranda) at the front and two rooms on two different levels inside – one for cooking and entertaining guests, the other for sleeping and storage.

Bali Modern, by the prolific pair of Gianni Francione and Luca Invernizzi Tettoni, takes a wide-ranging look at Balinese design today. It is good for going beyond resorts and looking at homes and other construction.

pit). There may be an area outside the house compound where fruit trees are grown or a pig may be kept. Usually the house is entered through a gateway backed by a small wall known as the *aling aling*. It serves a practical and a spiritual purpose, both preventing passers-by from seeing in and stopping evil spirits from entering. Evil spirits cannot easily turn corners so the *aling aling* stops them from simply scooting straight in through the gate!

There are several variations on the typical family compound, illustrated below. For example, the entrance is commonly on the *kuah*, or sunset side, rather than the *kelod* (sea end) side as shown, but *never* on the *kangin* (sunrise) or *kaja* (mountain end) side.

Introduction to Balinese Architecture, by Julian Davison and a host of others, provides a well-illustrated overview of everything from village and temple design to that found in houses.

TEMPLES

Every village on Bali has several temples, and every home has at least a simple house-temple. The Balinese word for temple is *pura*, from a Sanskrit word literally meaning 'a space surrounded by a wall'. Similar to a traditional Balinese home, a temple is walled in – so the shrines you see in rice fields or at 'magical' spots such as old trees are not real temples. Simple shrines or thrones often overlook crossroads, to protect passers-by.

All temples are built on a mountains–sea orientation, not north–south. The direction towards the mountains, *kaja*, is the end of the temple, where the holiest shrines are found. The temple's entrance is at the *kelod*. *Kangin* is more holy than the *kuah*, so many secondary shrines are on the *kangin* side. *Kaja* may be towards a particular mountain – Pura Besakih in eastern Bali is pointed directly towards Gunung Agung – or towards the mountains in general, which run east–west along the length of Bali.

Architecture Bali by Philip Goad and Patrick Bingham-Hall is a slim book that focuses on Balinese design as it has evolved in resort construction. The pictures may have you booking a holiday the minute you see them.

Temple Types

There are three basic temple types, found in most villages. The most important is the *pura puseh* (temple of origin), dedicated to the village founders and at the *kaja* end of the village. In the middle of the village is the *pura desa*, for the many spirits that protect the village community in daily life. At the *kelod* end of the village is the *pura dalem*, or temple of the dead. The graveyard is also here, and the temple may include representations of Durga, the terrible side of Shiva's wife Parvati. Both Shiva and Parvati have a creative and destructive side; their destructive powers are honoured in the *pura dalem*.

Other temples include those that are dedicated to the spirits of irrigated agriculture. Rice-growing is so important on Bali, and the division of water for irrigation is handled with the utmost care, that these *pura subak* or *pura ulun suwi* (temple of the rice-growers' association) can be

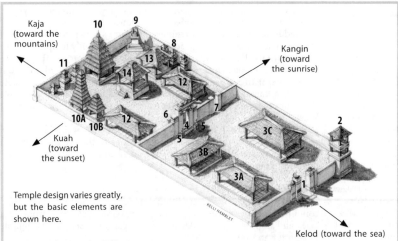

Kaja (toward the mountains)

Kangin (toward the sunrise)

Kuah (toward the sunset)

Temple design varies greatly, but the basic elements are shown here.

KELLI HAMBLET

Kelod (toward the sea)

TYPICAL TEMPLE DESIGN

1 **Candi Bentar** The intricately sculpted temple gateway, like a tower split down the middle and moved apart.

2 **Kulkul Tower** The warning-drum tower, from which a wooden split drum (kulkul) is sounded to announce events at the temple or warn of danger.

3 **Bale** A pavilion, usually open-sided, for temporary use or storage. May include a bale gong (3A), where the gamelan orchestra plays at festivals; a paon (3B) or temporary kitchen to prepare offerings; or a wantilan (3C), a stage for dances or cockfights.

4 **Kori Agung or Paduraksa** The gateway to the inner courtyard is an intricately sculpted stone tower. Entry is through a doorway reached by steps in the middle of the tower and left open during festivals.

5 **Raksa or Dwarapala** Statues of fierce guardian figures who protect the doorway and deter evil spirits. Above the door will be the equally fierce face of a bhoma, with hands outstretched against unwanted spirits.

6 **Aling Aling** If an evil spirit does get in, this low wall behind the entrance will keep it at bay, as evil spirits find it difficult to make right-angle turns.

7 **Side Gate (Betelan)** Most of the time (except during ceremonies) entry to the inner courtyard is through this side gate, which is always open.

8 **Small Shrines (Gedong)** These usually include shrines to Ngrurah Alit and Ngrurah Gede, who organise things and ensure the correct offerings are made.

9 **Padma Stone** Throne for the sun god Surya, placed in the most auspicious kaja-kangin corner. It rests on the badawang (world turtle), which is held by two naga (mythological serpents).

10 **Meru** A multiroofed shrine. Usually there is an 11-roofed meru (10A) to Sanghyang Widi, the supreme Balinese deity, and a three-roofed meru (10B) to the holy mountain Gunung Agung.

11 **Small Shrines (Gedong)** At the *kaja* (mountain) end of the courtyard, these may include a shrine to the sacred mountain Gunung Batur; a Maospahit shrine to honour Bali's original Hindu settlers (Majapahit); and a shrine to the taksu, who acts as an interpreter for the gods. (Trance dancers or mediums may be used to convey the gods' wishes.)

12 **Bale Piasan** Open pavilions used to display temple offerings.

13 **Gedong Pesimpangan** Stone building dedicated to the village founder or a local deity.

14 **Paruman or Pepelik** Open pavilion in the inner courtyard, where the gods are supposed to assemble to watch the ceremonies of a temple festival.

of considerable importance. Other temples may also honour dry-field agriculture, as well as the flooded rice paddies.

In addition to these 'local' temples, there are a lesser number of great temples. Each family worships its ancestors in the family temple, the clan worships in its clan temple and the village in the *pura puseh*. Above these are the state temples or temples of royalty, and often a kingdom would have three of these: a main state temple in the heartland of the state (like Pura Taman Ayun in Mengwi, western Bali); a mountain temple (like Pura Besakih, eastern Bali); and a sea temple (like Pura Luhur Ulu Watu, southern Bali).

Every house on Bali has its house temple, which is at the *kaja–kangin* corner of the courtyard. There will be shrines to the Hindu 'trinity' of Brahma, Shiva and Vishnu; to *taksu*, the divine intermediary; and to *tugu*, the lord of the ground.

Temple Design

Temple design follows a traditional formula. A temple compound contains a number of *gedong* (shrines) of varying sizes, made from solid brick and stone and heavily decorated with carvings. See Typical Temple Design for an example (p59).

Temple Decoration

Temples and their decoration are closely linked on Bali. A temple gateway is not just erected; every square centimetre of it is carved in sculptural relief and a diminishing series of demon faces is placed above it as protection. Even then, it's not complete without several stone statues to act as guardians.

The level of decoration varies. Sometimes a temple is built with minimal decoration in the hope that sculpture can be added when more funds are available. The sculpture can also deteriorate after a few years because much of the stone used is soft and the tropical climate ages it very rapidly (that centuries-old temple you're looking at may in fact be less than 10 years old!). Sculptures are restored or replaced as resources permit – it's not uncommon to see a temple with old carvings, which are barely discernible, next to newly finished work.

You'll find some of the most lavishly carved temples around Singaraja in northern Bali. The north-coast sandstone is very soft and easily carved, allowing local sculptors to give free rein to their imaginations; as a result, you'll find some delightfully whimsical scenes carved into a number of the temples.

Sculpture often appears in set places in Bali's temples. Door guardians – representations of legendary figures like Arjuna or other protective personalities – flank the steps to the gateway. Above the main entrance to a temple, Kala's monstrous face often peers out, sometimes a number of times – his hands reaching out beside his head to catch any evil spirits foolish enough to try to sneak in.

Elsewhere, other sculptures make regular appearances – the front of a *pura dalem* will often feature images of the witch Rangda and sculpted relief panels may show the horrors that await evil-doers in the afterlife.

Although overall temple architecture is similar in both northern and southern Bali, there are some important differences. The inner courtyards of southern temples usually house a number of *meru* (multiroofed shrines), together with other structures, whereas in the north, everything is grouped on a single pedestal. On the pedestal you'll find 'houses' for the deities to use on their earthly visits; they're also used to store religious relics.

MAJOR TEMPLES

Bali has thousands of temples, but some of the most important are listed here, and shown on the colour highlights map, pp4–5.

Directional Temples

Some temples are so important they are deemed to belong to the whole island rather than particular communities. There are nine *kahyangan jagat*, or directional temples.

- **Pura Besakih** (p183) In Besakih, East Bali
- **Pura Goa Lawah** (p182) Near Padangbai, East Bali
- **Pura Lempuyang** (p201) Near Tirta Gangga, East Bali
- **Pura Luhur Batukau** (p231) On Gunung Batukau, Central Mountains
- **Pura Luhur Ulu Watu** (p130) At Ulu Watu, South Bali
- **Pura Masceti** (p176) Near Gianyar, East Bali
- **Pura Sambu** (p186) Remotely located on Gunung Agung, East Bali
- **Pura Ulun Danu Bratan** (p229) In Candikuning (Danau Bratan), Central Mountains
- **Pura Ulun Danu** (p218) In Batur, Central Mountains

Most of these are well known and accessible, but some are rarely seen by visitors to Bali. Pura Masceti, on the coast south of Gianyar, is easily reached but seldom visited, and it's a stiff walk to remote Pura Lempuyang.

Sea Temples

The 16th-century Majapahit priest Nirartha founded a chain of temples to honour the sea gods. Each was intended to be within sight of the next, and several have dramatic locations on the south coast. From the west, they include the following.

- **Pura Gede Perancak** (p260) Where Nirartha first landed
- **Pura Rambut Siwi** (p259) On a wild stretch of the west coast
- **Pura Tanah Lot** (p253) The very popular island temple
- **Pura Luhur Ulu Watu** (p130) A spectacular cliff-top position (also one of the nine directional temples)
- **Pura Mas Suka** (p131) At the very south of the Bukit Peninsula
- **Pura Sakenan** (p126) On Pulau Serangan, southern Bali
- **Pura Pulaki** (p248) Near Pemuteran, in northern Bali

Other Important Temples

Some other temples have particular importance because of their location, spiritual function or architecture. They include the following.

- **Pura Beji** (p239) In Sangsit, northern Bali, it is dedicated to the goddess Dewi Sri, who looks after irrigated rice fields
- **Pura Dalem Penetaran Ped** (p213) On Nusa Penida, dedicated to the demon Jero Gede Macaling, and a place of pilgrimage for those seeking protection from evil
- **Pura Kehen** (p177) A fine hillside temple in Bangli, eastern Bali
- **Pura Maduwe Karang** (p239) An agricultural temple on the north coast, famous for its spirited bas-relief, including one of a bicycle rider
- **Pura Pusering Jagat** (p172) One of the famous temples at Pejeng, near Ubud, it has an enormous bronze drum
- **Pura Taman Ayun** (p254) The large and imposing state temple at Mengwi, northwest of Denpasar
- **Pura Tirta Empul** (p173) The beautiful temple at Tampaksiring, with springs and bathing pools at the source of Sungai Pakerisan, north of Ubud

CONTEMPORARY HOTEL DESIGN *by Philip Goad*

Intruding upon the serenity of Balinese cosmology and its seamless translation into the island's traditional architecture are tourists – interlopers, who, like Bali's many foreign visitors centuries ago, formed an intrinsic part of the island's myths and legends. Such legends describe tensions between the sacred and the profane, the high and the low, and it is these tensions that characterise boutique Bali hotels – the most accessible and significant examples of contemporary Balinese architecture. By their function, these hotels seem immediately alien to traditional Balinese culture. In all of them, however, despite obvious contradictions of commerce and privilege, there is the sincere attempt to define them as highly sophisticated architectures, albeit for hedonistic escape. These hotels are worth visiting because they heighten, even exaggerate, the sensation of being in Bali.

Hotels like the pioneering Oberoi in Legian by Australian architect Peter Muller, his pièces de resistance, the Amandari, Ubud, and the Lombok Oberoi as well as those designed by another Australian, Kerry Hill; the Amanusa, Nusa Dua and the Alila (formerly Serai), Candidasa employ the typical buildings and spaces of Bali: the walled house and garden compound and the village with its *bale* (an open-sided pavilion with a steeply pitched thatched roof), *bale agung* (village assembly hall), *bale banjar* (communal meeting place of a banjar; a house for meetings and gamelan practice) and *wantilan* (large bale pavilion used for meetings, performances and cockfights) structures. Yet such appropriation is not tokenistic. Much of the allure of these hotels is in the inclusion of traditional Balinese materials, crafts and construction techniques, as well as Balinese design principles that respect an archetypal approach to the world. Hence, a reflection on Balinese cosmology becomes an intrinsic part of each design. The inclusion of elaborate swimming pools and paradisaical garden designs by landscape architects like Made Wijaya and Ketut Marsa has added a further dimension to these free interpretations on tradition. Landscape has become one of the most powerful and seductive components of the Bali hotel experience, evidenced, for example, in the wonderful gardens of Bali's Four Seasons Resort at Jimbaran Bay.

Other designers have employed landscape but in a different way, drawing inspiration from the terracing of Bali's rural landscape or from water palaces like those as Tirta Gangga, Jungutan and Taman Ujung in East Bali. A feature of these sites are the bale kambang (water pavilions or 'floating palaces') that can also be found in the palaces of Klungkung and Karangasem, pavilions

Amandari Resort, Ubud
TONY WHEELER

where kings would meditate and commune with the gods. For hotel designers, such an analogy is extremely attractive. Thus a hotel like Amankila near Manggis in East Bali adopts a garden strategy, with a carefully structured landscape of lotus ponds and floating pavilions that step down an impossibly steep site.

Another attraction of these buildings is the notion of instant age, the ability of materials in Bali to weather quickly and provide 'pleasing decay'. Two Ubud hotels that epitomise this phenomenon are Ibah Luxury Villas and Begawan Giri. The latter is a private resort estate that comprises five uniquely styled residences designed by Malaysian-born architect Cheong Yew Kuan and where abstracted Balinese architectural principles are combined with exquisite craftsmanship.

By contrast, at Sayan near Ubud, John Heah of Heah & Company (London), has created a completely new image for the Balinese hotel. The Four Seasons Resort at Sayan is a striking piece of aerial sculpture, a huge elliptical lotus pond sitting above a base structure that appears like an eroded and romantic ruin set within a spectacular gorge landscape.

Many of these hotels go close to that boundary where the reproduction is more seductive than the original. And it has to be said that the hotel was never a traditional building form in Bali! Each hotel has been designed not to mimic but rather to facilitate a consciously artificial reading of the place. These buildings need to be seen for what they are: thoroughly convincing architectures of welcome. They are skilful and highly resolved exercises in appealing to the most profound wants in Western society's eyes – the pleasures of the threshold; the pleasures of the perception of an exotic 'other'; and the pleasures of simply being in another highly sensitised state, and in what better place than Bali, Island of the Gods.

Philip Good is Professor of Architecture at the University of Melbourne and author of Architecture Bali: Birth of the Tropical Boutique Resort.

Four Seasons Resort, Bali
TONY WHEELER

Environment

THE LAND

Bali is a small island, midway along the string of islands that makes up the Indonesian archipelago. It's adjacent to Java, the most heavily populated island, and immediately west of the chain of smaller islands comprising Nusa Tenggara.

The island is dramatically mountainous – the central mountain chain, a string of volcanoes, includes several peaks around 2000m. Gunung Agung, known as the 'Mother Mountain', is over 3000m high. South and north of the central mountains are Bali's agricultural lands. The southern region is a wide, gently sloping area, where most of Bali's abundant rice crop is grown. The northern coastal strip is narrower, rising rapidly into the foothills of the central range. It receives less rain, but coffee, copra, rice and cattle are farmed there.

Bali also has some arid, less-populated regions. These include the western mountain region, and the eastern and northeastern slopes of Gunung Agung. The Nusa Penida islands are dry, and cannot support intensive wet-rice agriculture. The Bukit Peninsula is similarly dry, but with the growth of tourism and other industries, it's becoming more populous.

The Malay Archipelago by Alfred Wallace is a natural history classic by the great 19th-century biogeographer, who postulated that the Lombok Strait was the dividing line between Asia and Australia. The book remains in print.

Bali is volcanically active and extremely fertile. The two go hand-in-hand because eruptions contribute to the land's exceptional fertility, and high mountains provide the dependable rainfall that irrigates Bali's complex and amazingly beautiful patchwork of rice terraces. Of course, the volcanoes are a hazard as well – Bali has endured disastrous eruptions in the past and no doubt will again in the future. Apart from the volcanic central range, there are the limestone plateaus that form the Bukit Peninsula, in the extreme south of Bali, and the island of Nusa Penida.

For hundreds of years, Bali has sustained a substantial population with intensive wet-rice cultivation, supported by an elaborate irrigation system that makes careful use of all the surface water. The rice fields are a complete ecological system, home for much more than just rice. In the early morning you'll often see the duck herders leading their flocks out for a day's paddle around a flooded rice field, and at night young boys head out with lights to trap tasty frogs and eels. Other crops are often grown on the levees between the fields, or planted as a rotation crop after several rice harvests.

As in Bali, Lombok's traditional economy has driven intensive wet-rice cultivation. The wooded slopes of Gunung Rinjani have provided timber while coconut palms also provided timber, as well as fibre and food. The land use has been environmentally sustainable for many years, and the island retains a natural beauty largely unspoiled by industry, overcrowding or overdevelopment. Some lessons have been learned from the more problematic tourist developments on Bali, and the slowdown in tourism has generally restrained the excesses of resort developers.

WILDLIFE

Birds of Bali by Victor Mason and Frank Jarvis is enhanced by lovely watercolour illustrations.

The island is geologically young, and virtually all its living things have migrated from elsewhere, so there's really no such thing as 'native' plants and animals. This is not hard to imagine in the heavily populated and extravagantly fertile south of Bali, where the orderly rice terraces are so intensively cultivated they look more like a work of sculpture than a natural landscape.

In fact, rice fields cover only about 20% of the island's surface area, and there is a great variety of other environmental zones: the dry scrub of the northwest, the extreme northeast and the southern peninsula; patches of dense jungle in the river valleys; forests of bamboo; and harsh volcanic regions that are barren rock and volcanic tuff at higher altitudes. Lombok is similar in all these respects.

Animals

Bali has lots and lots of lizards, and they come in all shapes and sizes. The small ones (onomatopoetically called *cecak*) that hang around light fittings in the evening, waiting for an unwary insect, are a familiar sight. Geckos are fairly large lizards, often heard but less often seen. The loud and regularly repeated two-part cry 'geck-oh' is a nightly background noise that visitors soon become accustomed to, and it is considered lucky if you hear the lizard call seven times.

Bats are quite common, and the little chipmunk-like Balinese squirrels are occasionally seen in the wild, although more often in cages.

Bali's only wilderness area, Taman Nasional Bali Barat (West Bali National Park) has a number of wild species, including grey and black monkeys (which you will also see around the hills in central Bali), *muncak* (mouse deer), squirrels and iguanas. Bali used to have tigers and, although there are periodic rumours of sightings in the remote northwest of the island, nobody has proof of seeing one for a long time.

There is a rich variety of coral, seaweed, fish and other marine life in the coastal waters. Much of it can be appreciated by snorkellers, but the larger marine animals are only likely to be seen while diving. Dolphins can be found right around the island and have unfortunately been made into an attraction off Lovina.

ENDANGERED SPECIES

Turtles are endangered, but can still be seen wild in the waters around Nusa Penida. Turtle numbers have declined greatly in Indonesian waters, and most tourists are well aware of the problem. Turtle-meat dishes have

DID YOU KNOW?

Bull races are a regular and traditional event in northern and western Bali, and are sometimes promoted as a tourist attraction. The animals seem to fare no worse than racehorses in Western countries.

THE WALLACE LINE

The 19th-century naturalist Sir Alfred Wallace (1822–1913) observed great differences in fauna between Bali and Lombok – as great as the differences between Africa and South America. In particular, there were no large mammals (elephants, rhinos, tigers etc) east of Bali, and very few carnivores. He postulated that during the ice ages, when sea levels were lower, animals could have moved by land from what is now mainland Asia all the way to Bali, but the deep Lombok Strait would always have been a barrier. Thus he drew a line between Bali and Lombok, which he believed marked the biological division between Asia and Australia.

Plant life does not display such a sharp division, but there is a gradual transition from predominantly Asian rainforest species to mostly Australian plants like eucalypts and acacias, which are better suited to long dry periods. This is associated with the lower rainfall as one moves east of Java. Environmental differences, including those in the natural vegetation, are now thought to provide a better explanation of the distribution of animal species than Wallace's theory about limits to their original migrations.

Modern biogeographers do recognise a distinction between Asian and Australian fauna, but the boundary between the regions is regarded as much fuzzier than Wallace's line. Nevertheless, this transitional zone between Asia and Australia is still called 'Walacea'.

SEA TURTLES

The green-sea turtle and hawksbill turtle both inhabit the waters around Bali and throughout Indonesia, and the species are supposedly protected by legislation that prohibits trade in all species of sea turtle. It's also illegal to export any products made from green-sea turtles from Indonesia, and in many countries including Australia, the USA, the UK and other EU countries it's illegal to import turtle products without a permit.

On Bali, however, green-sea turtle meat is a traditional and very popular delicacy, particularly for Balinese feasts. Bali is the site of the most intensive slaughter of green-sea turtles in the world – no reliable figures are available, although in 1999 it was estimated that more than 30,000 are killed annually. A more recent survey suggests that 4000 or more turtles are smuggled off the island annually as part of illegal trade.

The environmental group, **World Wide Fund for Nature** (www.wwf.or.id), campaigns to protect Indonesia's sea turtles from illegal trade and slaughter, and actively seeks to bring violations of international treaties to the attention of the government. The organisation appeals to travellers to Indonesia not to eat turtle meat or buy any sea-turtle products, including tortoiseshell items, stuffed turtles or turtle-leather goods. **ProFauna** (www.profauna.or.id) is an Indonesia-based non-profit that works to protect the environment. It has been active in promoting the plight of Bali's turtles, including having volunteers dress up like turtles and emerge from the sea.

Individuals and organisations are also involved in protecting the species, including Heinz von Holzen, the owner of Bumbu Bali restaurant in Tanjung Benoa, the Reef Seen Turtle Project at Reef Seen Aquatics in Pemuteran and Reefseekers Dive Centre & Turtle Nursery on Gili Air.

---

disappeared from tourist menus, and very few tortoiseshell souvenirs are sold. Unfortunately, turtle meat is still considered an important dish at Balinese ceremonial feasts. See Sea Turtles above.

Bali's other endangered species is the Bali starling, which has almost disappeared in the wild. Attempts are being made to reintroduce the birds to the Taman Nasional Bali Barat (p262). It is the only one of Bali's more than 300 species of birds that is native to the island.

Field Guide to the Birds of Java & Bali by John Mackinnon is probably the best field guide for bird-watchers on Bali.

INTRODUCED SPECIES

Bali is thick with domestic animals, including ones that wake you up in the morning and others that bark all through the night. Chickens and roosters are kept both for food purposes and as domestic pets. Cockfighting is a popular male activity and a man's fighting bird is his prized possession. Balinese pigs are related to wild boar, and look really gross, with their sway backs and sagging stomachs. They inhabit the family compound, cleaning up all the garbage and eventually end up spit-roasted at a feast – they taste a lot better than they look.

DID YOU KNOW?

Keeping birds has been a part of Indonesian culture for centuries. It's common to see caged songbirds warbling away, to the delight of owners and possible dismay of the birds.

Balinese cattle, by contrast, are delicate and graceful animals that seem more akin to deer than cows. Although the Balinese are Hindus, they do not generally treat cattle as holy animals, yet cows are rarely eaten or milked. They are, however, used to plough rice paddies and fields, and there is a major export market for Balinese cattle to Hong Kong and other parts of Asia.

Ducks are another everyday Balinese domestic animal and a regular dish at feasts. Ducks are kept in the family compound, and are put out to a convenient pond or flooded rice field to feed during the day. They follow a stick with a small flag tied to the end, and the stick is left planted in the field. As sunset approaches the ducks gather around the stick and wait to be led home again. The morning and evening duck parades are one of Bali's small delights.

GONE TO THE DOGS

For many people, the one off-note memory of their visit to Bali has been the hordes of mangy ill-tempered and ill-treated *anjing* (dogs). Why are there so many? Because for many Balinese they barely exist, inhabiting a lowly world of trash-eating and scavenging. Left to their own devices, the dogs keep reproducing and hanging around the fringes of society. Their reputation – and plight – is also not helped by the fact that many people consider them to be the embodiment of evil spirits. As if to confirm this, dogs are usually the first on the scene to scarf down offerings left for demons.

Plants
TREES

Nearly all of the island is cultivated, and only in the Taman Nasional Bali Barat are there traces of Bali's earliest plant life. Like most things on Bali, trees have a spiritual and religious significance, and you'll often see them decorated with scarves and black-and-white check cloths. The *waringin* (banyan) is the holiest Balinese tree and no important temple is complete without a stately one growing within its precincts. The banyan is an extensive, shady tree with an exotic feature: creepers that drop from its branches take root to propagate a new tree. Thus the banyan is said to be 'never-dying', since new offshoots can always take root. *Jepun* (frangipani trees), with their beautiful and sweet-smelling white flowers are also common in temples and family compounds.

Flowers of Bali and *Fruits of Bali* by Fred and Margaret Wiseman are nicely illustrated books that will tell you what you're admiring or eating.

Bali has monsoonal rather than tropical rainforests, so it lacks the valuable rainforest hardwoods that require rain year-round. The forestry department is experimenting with new varieties in plantations around Taman Nasional Bali Barat, but at the moment nearly all the wood used for carving is imported from Sumatra and Kalimantan.

A number of plants have great practical and economic significance. *Tiing* (bamboo) is grown in several varieties and is used for everything from satay sticks and string to rafters and gamelan resonators. The various types of palm provide coconuts, sugar, fuel and fibre.

DID YOU KNOW?

Cockfighting is a long-standing, popular and culturally important activity for Balinese men. Gambling – technically illegal – is a big part of the attraction. Cockfights are mercifully brief, and unquestionably cruel (see p37).

FLOWERS & GARDENS

Balinese gardens are a delight. The soil and climate can support a huge range of plants, and the Balinese love of beauty and the abundance of cheap labour means that every space can be landscaped. The style is generally informal, with curved paths, a rich variety of plants and usually a water feature.

You can find almost every type of flower on Bali, but some are seasonal and others are restricted to the cooler mountain areas. Many of the flowers will be familiar to visitors – hibiscus, bougainvillea, poinsettia, oleander, jasmine, water lily and aster are commonly seen in the southern tourist areas, while roses, begonias and hydrangeas are found mainly in the mountains. Less-familiar flowers include: Javanese *ixora (soka* or *angsoka)*, with round clusters of bright red-orange flowers; *champak* (or *cempaka)*, a very fragrant member of the magnolia family; flamboyant, the flower of the royal poinciana flame tree; *manori* (or *maduri)*, which has a number of traditional uses; and water convolvulus *(kangkung)*, the leaves of which are commonly used as a green vegetable. There are literally thousands of types of orchid.

DID YOU KNOW?

Besides providing the leaves for *lontar* books, *rontal* palms also supply the sap needed to make *tuac*, the brutal home-made palm beer that's been the basis for many a hangover.

Flowers can be seen everywhere – in gardens or just by the roadside. Flower fanciers should make a trip to the Danau Bratan area in the central mountains to see the Bali Botanical Gardens, or visit the plant nurseries along the road between Denpasar and Sanur.

RESPONSIBLE TRAVEL

The tourism industry, though largely dependent on an attractive environment, does have its negative effects. Although numbers dropped off after the 2002 bombings, visitor figures are on track to again average close to the 1.3 million tourists per year that were visiting Bali at the end of the 1990s. The most obvious environmental effect is the conversion of prime agricultural land to make way for hotels and other facilities, including several golf courses. Less obvious is the increased demand for water – with air-con, cleaning, showers, pools and gardens, a top-end hotel requires an average of over 570L of fresh water per day, per room. Much of this water is piped from the central mountains to southern Bali resort areas, sometimes depleting the water sources traditionally used for rice cultivation.

One obvious way to help out here is to minimise your use of water while you are in hotels. This might be a good time not to take the hotel up on its offer – if it has made one – to wash your towels and sheets every day, to save water. More ambitiously, you can stay in hotels that do *not* have pools or air-con. In most places the breeze really does cool things off at night and, as one hotel-keeper pointed out when asked if he had a pool; 'It's over there,' he said, pointing at the ocean.

Much of tourism's environmental impact has been indirect. For example, the huge increase in traffic on Bali is not principally caused by vehicles transporting tourists, but by the massive number of motorcycles and cars purchased with the income from tourism, and the increased use of buses, cars and trucks by a more affluent population. Denpasar has the worst traffic problem, but very few tourists. Still this might be good cause to weigh the flexibility and freedom of a car against adding one more car to the teeming roads.

Similarly, tourists probably have very little direct impact on the endangered turtle populations (no tourist restaurants offer turtle meat, and tortoiseshell souvenirs have virtually disappeared), but increasing numbers of affluent Balinese can afford turtle for ceremonial feasts.

Tourism has had little direct impact on the coastal and marine environment – those who come for diving, snorkelling and fishing actually make a strong case for conservation of coral reefs. The worst damage has resulted from digging up coral reefs for cement and building stone (some of it to make hotels of course), and by large projects such as the expansion of the airport and the abortive resort development on Pulau Serangan. This is not what either tourists or the tourist industry want, but the damage has been done.

One risk is the waste management problems caused by the ever-increasing number of water bottles sold to tourists on Bali. Many businesses simply burn discarded bottles, and chemicals carried in the smoke can drift along streets and into homes and hotels. In Ubud and other areas a few outlets provide filtered refills of water bottles for a price that's cheaper than buying a new bottle, in the hope that you'll buy fewer bottles during your stay. Stop by the **Pondok Pecak Library & Learning Centre** (Map pp146-7; ☎ 976194; Monkey Forest Rd, Ubud) to not only refill your water bottle but find out which other businesses offer this service.

If you would like information on ways you can help to protect Bali's environment, or would like to volunteer on Bali, see p341.

NATIONAL PARKS

The only national park on Bali is Taman Nasional Bali Barat (West Bali National Park). It covers 19,000 hectares at the western tip of Bali, plus a substantial area of coastal mangrove and the adjacent marine area, including some fine dive sites. It is also currently involved in the attempt to save the Bali starling (see p262).

The Taman Nasional Gunung Rinjani (Gunung Rinjani National Park), on Lombok covers 41,330 hectares and is the water-collector for most of the island. At 3726m, Gunung Rinjani is the second-highest volcanic peak in Indonesia. The four-day Rinjani Trek that traverses the national park starting with a climb to the crater rim, a side trip to the summit, a decent to the crater-lake, before re-ascending to the crater rim and down the mountain through lush forest, is considered one of the best treks in Southeast Asia.

ENVIRONMENTAL ISSUES

It's tempting to paint a picture of an ecologically sustainable island paradise, but it hasn't always been perfect. The periodic volcanic eruptions, which spread essential fertilising ash over much of the island, also cause death and destruction. Droughts, insect plagues and rats have, in the past, ravaged the rice crops and led to famine. The population has been kept at sustainable levels by high infant mortality and short life expectancy. On the other hand, deforestation is hardly an issue on Bali because most of the monsoonal rainforests were cleared long ago to make way for rice cultivation.

Since WWII, improvements in health and nutrition have resulted in increased life expectancy, and a bigger population has put pressure on limited resources. There has been some movement of Balinese people to other islands under the government's *transmigrasi* (transmigration) policy, but mainly it has been family planning that has kept population growth at manageable levels. Against this, Bali's tourist industry has actually attracted people to the island, and there is a rapid growth of urban areas that encroach onto agricultural land.

In order to increase agricultural output, new, high-yield rice varieties were introduced, but these resulted in new problems with insect, viral and fungal pests, and greater needs for irrigation water. The need for high output combined with ecological sustainability has created an ongoing environmental management problem. The new varieties, however, require more pesticides; this has caused the depletion of the frog and eel populations, which depend on the insects for survival.

There is very little manufacturing industry, so industrial pollution is not a big problem. The most pressing environmental problems on Bali today are water supply and sanitation, solid waste management (what to do with all those plastic bags and bottles?), traffic and vehicle emissions, and the protection of coastal and marine ecosystems.

DID YOU KNOW?

Mangoes are one of the leading cultivated trees on Bali. You'll see these green heavy hangers growing almost everywhere; in gardens, fields and by the side of the road.

DID YOU KNOW?

Bali Cares, a charity shop in Ubud, supports the work of numerous Bali charities, including IDEP (Indonesia Development of Education for Permaculture; www.idepfoundation.org), that deals with environmental issues.

Food & Drink

You will eat well on Bali: the dining possibilities are endless, the prices pleasantly low and the taste, aroma and presentation will more than satisfy. Ubud is the gourmet highlight of Bali, with a wonderful choice of Balinese, Indonesian, Asian, European and fusion cuisine. The Kuta area is not far behind, and there are excellent restaurants in Sanur, Candidasa and Lovina.

STAPLES & SPECIALTIES

Balinese specialities are often difficult to find as it's presumed that tourists won't like the spicier and unashamedly fleshy flavours. Even when specialities are dished up they are often tempered for foreign palates; ghoulies such as blood are omitted from dishes like *lawar* (salad of chopped coconut, garlic, chilli, along with pork or chicken meat and blood). More popular with visitors is *bebek betutu* (duck stuffed with spices, wrapped in banana leaves and coconut husks and cooked in a pit of embers). Other dishes that use banana leaves in the process are *tom* (duck, chicken or their livers cooked with spices in a banana leaf) and *pepes ayam* (spiced chicken cooked in banana leaf). The local version of satay, called *sate lilit*, is made with minced, spiced meat that's pressed onto skewers which are often sticks of lemon grass.

The grandest Balinese dish is *babi guling* (spit-roast pig), which is stuffed with chilli, turmeric, garlic and ginger, and the skin smothered in turmeric. This is a long and laborious dish made for special occasions, however there are restaurants that make one *babi guling* and serve it throughout the day. Gianyar is famous for its *babi guling*, as is Ubud.

Seafood restaurants literally abound. Few beaches don't have a sardine-like line of fishing boats and their labours bring forth fresh snapper, barracuda, prawns, lobster and more. You can find some excellent meals around the island and pick places with crowds. A restaurant with a long menu of seafood and few customers is not likely to be a good spot for a splurge on lobster. The seafood *warung* (food stalls) on the beach in Jimbaran are a good choice. Fresh fish is marinated in lime and garlic and roasted over a tray of burning coconut shells. The results can be excellent, but be sure to drive a good bargain first.

Of course with rice growing everywhere – in reality the fields cover only 20% of Bali but it seems like more – it plays a major role in the food.

DID YOU KNOW?

Beef is enjoyed widely on Bali, as the local form of Hinduism is the only one that allows the eating of cows.

DID YOU KNOW?

Every Balinese cook has their own variation of *base gede*, the basic spice mixture used in most dishes. Ingredients include shallots, garlic, chillis, coriander, turmeric, and the ginger-like *isen* and *laos*.

LOMBOK'S SPICY FLAVOURS

The Sasak people of Lombok are predominantly Muslim, so the porky plethora found on Bali gives way to a diet of fish, chicken, vegetables and rice. In fact rice here is of the finest quality, yet the drier climate means that sometimes only one crop can be produced a year. Lombok's stocky *lumbung* (rice barn) is a symbol of prosperity on the island and you'll see them everywhere, although they're used less for rice storage and more as an architectural style for tourist accommodation. The fact that *lombok* means 'chilli' in Indonesian makes sense, as Sasaks like their food spicy; *ayam Taliwang* (whole split chicken roasted over coconut husks served with a peanut, tomato chilli and lime dip) is one example. *Sares* is a dish made with chilli, coconut juice and banana-palm pith; sometimes it's mixed with chicken or meat. Three non-meat dishes are *kelor* (hot soup with vegetables), *serebuk* (vegetables mixed with grated coconut) and *timun urap* (sliced cucumber with grated coconut, onion and garlic).

It's served with almost every dish and every house has a fresh pot each morning that is scooped up throughout the day. Much of the rice grown now is a high-yield hybrid but traditional varieties are still valued. On Bali, look for *beras merah* (red rice), which is known for its astringent and nutty taste.

The Balinese make a wide range of rice-flour snacks, including *lak lak* (a small pancake with palm sugar and coconut) and *alam* (rice flour, sugar and pandan leaf cooked in a banana leaf cylinder). Rice flour is used for a range of cakes, many encompassing coconut and palm sugar.

Rice also figures in the sublime and sweet *bubuh injin*, a pudding made from black rice. Finally, watch for *jaja batun bedil*, the at-first-weird-but-soon-addictive dessert of tiny rice-cake globules in a rich, brown-sugar sauce.

It's almost worth making a trip to Bali just to sample the tropical fruit. If you've never gone beyond apples, oranges and bananas you've got some rare treats in store when you discover rambutans, mangosteens, *salaks* or *sirsaks*. Wander a market and you will be spoiled for choice. Among the more exotic and tasty items you are likely to find are: the lime-sized furry rambutans (sweet and creamy); small little lychees (juicy, sweet and non-acidic); enormous and knobby *nangkas* (jackfruit; chewy cross between pineapple and melon); *manggis* (mangosteen; cute little segments of soft, creamy fruit inside a brown shell); and the popular *mangga* (mango; meat that is sour to sweet depending on ripeness).

You will also see piles of more familar fruits such as oranges *(jeruk manis)* and other citrus fruits, melons and bananas *(pisang)* in at least a half dozen varieties, from finger-sized and green to yellow-brown behemouths.

DID YOU KNOW?

Those sweet and delicious pineapples sold by beach vendors come from plants imported to Bali from the US.

DRINKS
Nonalcoholic

Plastic bottles of drinking water are widely available. A 500mL bottle costs about 2500Rp; a 1.5L bottle is around 3000Rp at a supermarket or a local shop, but more in a tourist restaurant or hotel. Given the heat, you'll find you go through these quickly.

The usual brands of soft drinks are available. Fruit juice and UHT milk (flavoured if you like) are available in sealed cartons from supermarkets and most small shops.

Locally produced coffee is called *kopi* Bali. It is grown around volcanic areas near Kintamani, on the hills around Pupuan in central Bali, and along the north coast, not far from Singaraja. It's served strong, black and thick.

Possibly the greatest treat during a hot day is a glass of fresh fruit juice. The variations and ingredients are endless but range from simple squeezed fruit juice to frothy smoothies.

Alcoholic

Bir (beer) served cold in a bar or restaurant is a delight on a hot day. The most common brand of beer is Bintang, a crisp and refreshing lager. You'll probably soon come to enjoy it to the point that you'll start eyeing all those Bintang T-shirts for sale with genuine affection.

Local Balinese wine is more novelty than sensation. At better restaurants you can expect a long wine list with a myriad of good choices from Australia, France and further. Especially at bars catering to the sunset crowd, expect a plethora of mixed and specialty drinks. Don't expect

The Food of Bali by Heinz von Holzen and Lother Arsana brings to life everything from *cram cam* (clear chicken soup with shallots) to *bubuh injin* (black-rice pudding).

any surprises, although drinks made with fresh fruit juices and rum go down mighty easy.

Finally, a word on the local firewaters, *arak* and *brem*. The former is distilled from the sap of palm trees (often coconut) but in the east of Bali, from *rontal* (type of palm tree). The latter is a variation of this made from rice that's fittingly Balinese. Both have the subtlety of a hammer and are popular at clubs where people dance all night.

CELEBRATIONS

A complete Balinese feast is something local people would have only a couple of times a year, at a major religious or family occasion. A typical feast would include smoked duck, roast pork or Balinese *sate* (minced and spiced meat wrapped around a wide stick – quite different from the usual Indonesian satay). Vegetable dishes include items that Westerners think of as fruits – like papaya, *nangka* (jackfruit) and *blimbing* (starfruit). *Paku* is a form of fern and *ketela potton* is tapioca leaves, both prepared as tasty vegetables. *Anyang* (red onions) and *ketimun* (cucumber) will also feature. Then there might be Balinese-style *gado gado* (dish of steamed bean sprouts, various vegetables and a spicy peanut sauce) and *mie goreng* (fried noodles with vegetables and sometimes meat), and a dish of duck livers cooked in banana leaves and coconut.

DID YOU KNOW?

With thousands of temples across the island, there are scores of *odalans* (temple birthday celebrations) happening every day. Each features a vast feast.

Standard accompaniments include rice (white, red or both), *krupuk* (prawn crackers) and *brem* (Balinese rice wine). To finish there are desserts like *sumping*, a leaf-wrapped sticky-rice concoction with coconut, palm sugar and banana or jackfruit, as well as Balinese coffee.

WHERE TO EAT & DRINK

Ubud and Seminyak now vie for being known as serving the best food on Bali. For years, Ubud, by virtue of its restaurants' emphasis on freshness and creativity, was the undisputed champ. Seminyak has come on strong lately, however, and now boasts scores of excellent places, many of them along Jl Dhyana Pura and Jl Oberoi (enticingly known as 'Eat St'). At the best places in both towns, you can expect to find chefs fusing flavours from around the world and presenting the results on frequently changing menus. Other places specialise in cuisines from Japanese to Moroccan.

For a comprehensive and searchable list of Bali restaurants, go to www .balieats.com which stays abreast of the fast-changing dining scene.

You can find excellent meals elsewhere in Bali as well, with a few places in Kuta and Legian and many more around the Bukit Peninsula. Often you will enjoy an outstanding meal for much less than you would pay at home. At the very best and the newest hotels, expect to find a range of first-class cuisine, albeit at first-class prices.

The norm for most travellers as they explore Bali are innumerable restaurants that are minor variations on the same theme. Expect an open-air pavilion with tables and chairs and an unfailingly cheery waitstaff. The menu will be long and will feature all the Indonesian classics such as *nasi campur* (rice with a selection of meat and vegetable dishes on

---

TRAVEL YOUR TASTEBUDS

As well as providing rice, Bali's rice fields provide locals with eels and frogs. Dragonflies are another rice-field-dweller up for grabs – they're caught with sticky sticks and then roasted. On the north coast around Singaraja look for the vegetarian nightmare *siobak*, which is a concoction of minced pig's head, stomach, tongue and skin cooked with spices. To find these tasty dishes, look for street vendors selling something unfamiliar, and ask.

one plate) and various satays. There will be at least a smattering of stir-fried Chinese dishes too. Western tastes will be covered with the ubiquitous club sandwich, salads and probably cheeseburgers. Many will also include pizza (uniformly small and simple) and a few pastas. Even if the fare doesn't rise to the levels of the places with all the buzz, it's usually not bad. Ingredients are fresh and your food arrives quickly from the kitchen.

One thing you won't see at most restaurants popular with visitors is locals. Besides the obvious issue of affordability, Balinese have different styles of eating. Sitting down for a meal does not hold the same cultural significance as it does for most visitors. People like to eat snacks throughout the day, and when they're away from home, they go to a warung or cart (often called *kaki lima*, or 'five legs') parked along the side of the road, which often serve Javanese, Chinese or even Sumatran (ie Padang) food. *Kaki-lima* (roving vendors) are an essential part of the Indonesian culinary landscape; their carts usually consist of bench-top workspace, a portable stove and a glass display cabinet for ingredients and for advertising. The most common food they serve is *bakso*, a soup with noodles and meatballs; *bakso ayam* is chicken soup. *Nasi campur* is the most authentic Balinese-style dish served in a warung.

The great paradox of eating on Bali is that the cheaper the place, the tastier the food. The really inexpensive places are for the locals, and they serve the genuine Balinese article. At a street cart, for about 5000Rp, you can get a *nasi goreng* (fried rice) that is simply out of this world – hot and spicy, with fresh ingredients that are cooked while you wait. Of course, the trade-off is that you might have to sit on the curb to eat it, and the plate may not be as carefully washed as you would like.

VEGETARIANS & VEGANS

Although pure vegetarian restaurants are few, with the delightful Zula restaurants in Seminyak and Ubud being notable examples, vegetarians can do okay on Bali. First of all, most places have at least a few vegetarian dishes on the menu. Secondly, given that the food is mostly made fresh, you can easily ask that meat be left out of many dishes. *Nasi goreng* can be a mighty fine dish without the usual chicken.

WHINING & DINING

There are few specific allowances made for children in restaurants on Bali and Lombok, but that doesn't mean they won't receive a warm welcome. The locals love kids, and they are always a source of much fussing and attention. All but very few high-end places are so casual that kids will feel right at home. There's more than one stylish Seminyak restaurant that features scores of kids romping on the grass while their parents dine nearby. In fact, the major concerns for parents are the same as those anywhere: what happens if your child doesn't like the food? Where can you find treats they'll like? The average café on Bali and Lombok where tourists congregate has a menu most kids will gobble up: pizza, burgers and more. If, however, they really do want a genuine taste of home, most of the international fast food chains have outlets around South Bali. You won't need this book to find them either.

Finally, for very young children, if there is something essential they need to eat from home, bring it. South Bali has groceries with Western foods, especially from Australia, but the selection is limited at best.

See p323 for more details on travelling on Bali and Lombok with children.

DID YOU KNOW?

Keripik Ubi are crisps made from thinly sliced tapioca root. They're sweeter, crispier and even more addictive than potato chips.

DID YOU KNOW?

Every town of any size on Bali and Lombok will have a *pasar malam* (night market). Here after dark you can sample a vast range of fresh offerings from *warung* (food stalls) and carts.

DID YOU KNOW?

The sensual *kacang asin* (salted peanuts) which are served hot with a cold Bintang are mainly grown in East Bali.

HABITS & CUSTOMS

Lonely Planet's *World Food Indonesia* by Patrick Witton has the low-down on Balinese high feasts as well as details of the cuisine the islands are known for.

Although Bali does have its own cuisine, it's not readily adaptable to a restaurant menu. The everyday Balinese diet at home is a couple of meals and a few snacks of cold steamed rice, with some vegetables, some crunchy stuff like nuts or *krupuk* (prawn crackers), and a little chicken, pork or fish. The food is prepared in the morning and people help themselves throughout the day. Dedicated Balinese cuisine is reserved for the elaborate food offerings made to the gods and sumptuous feasts to celebrate important occasions.

That said, should you be invited to a Balinese home for a meal, it will be a great honour. You will be fêted, and end up sated, on scores of delicious dishes. Best of all, you can enjoy them with little concern for faux pas as the relaxed attitudes elsewhere extend to meals. Fingers, forks and spoons are the utensils of choice and you should employ them in any way that works for you. In fact, you will undoubtedly be bound more by strictures and etiquette from home than by the local norms.

Generally, mealtime on Bali is not an occasion to stand on ceremony – far from being bound by strict dos and don'ts, the first rule is to enjoy yourself. That's one of the reasons we love Bali!

COOKING COURSES

Dozens of detailed Balinese food recipes can be found at www .indochef.biz, a site run by renowned chef Heinz von Holzen. There are scores of illustrations guaranteed to have you drooling on your keyboard.

Several places offer cooking courses, with an emphasis on Balinese cuisine. These can be fun ways to spend a day, as you visit local markets and learn about the fresh ingredients essential to Balinese cuisine. You'll also meet fellow travellers with a shared interest (food!), and best of all, you get to eat the fruits of your labours.

Excellent courses can be found in Ubud, including one taught by Janet de Neefe (see Do-It-Yourself Gado Gado, below). In Tanjung Benoa, Heinz von Holzen's courses are also well-liked. In addition, many upmarket hotels offer courses in their large and well-equipped kitchens.

DO-IT-YOURSELF GADO GADO

If you enjoy authentic Balinese food, you'll love the cooking classes led by enthusiastic Australian, Janet de Neefe, who lives in Ubud with her Balinese husband. They live in and run Honeymoon Guesthouse, where the classes are held, as well as the local restaurants, Casa Luna and Indus.

Janet introduces participants to the smell and tastes of the raw forms of spices, roots, herbs, fruits and other ingredients of Balinese cooking. Colours and shapes that you might never have associated with turmeric or torch ginger can be touched and seen on the table in front of you. The uses and significance of each ingredient in cuisine, culture and family life are explained. You will learn about what makes Balinese food distinctive from Indonesian food, while you taste dishes at the various stages they go through to finish as chicken satay, *gado gado* (dish of steamed bean sprouts, various vegetables and a spicy peanut sauce), beans in coconut milk, jackfruit salad, *nasi kuning* (yellow rice made with tumeric), and so on.

You could even get involved by stir-frying a sacred-spice mix until it's fragrant, just before throwing some chicken in the wok to make the ceremonial dish *lawar buncis* (finely chopped string beans with chilli and seasoning), or by grinding just the right amount of chilli with a mortar and pestle to create the perfect *sambal* (chilli sauce or paste served as an accompaniment to most meals).

You'll sit at a table in Janet's family compound under the large roof of an open-sided *bale* (a rectangular open-sided pavilion with a steeply pitched roof of thatch) surrounded by the kids, friends and employees of the family, and your fellow travellers.

Best of all, the food you've watched being prepared and helped cook becomes lunch – a grand spread of eight to 10 dishes, all delicious in their colour, smell, freshness and authenticity.

See above for more details on the classes.

BALI & LOMBOK'S TOP FIVE

- **Bumbu Bali** (p136) Excellent Balinese food in Tanjung Benoa.
- **Kafé Batan Waru** (p164) Ubud's best has creative takes on Balinese cuisine.
- **Mozaic** (p166) Chef Chris Salans cooks super French fusion dishes in Ubud.
- **Gado Gado** (p115) A stylish fusion place with a magical location on Seminyak's beach.
- **Abdi Fantastik** (p290) Beachfront place with the best Sasak food, on Gili Air off Lombok.

EAT YOUR WORDS

Although you won't find the language barrier much of a true barrier at all, see the Language chapter (p369) for pronunciation guidelines.

Useful Phrases

Here are some handy phrases to help you enjoy a meal on Bali and Lombok.

I'm hungry.	*Saya lapar.*
Where's a ... ?	*... di mana?*
food stall	*warung*
night market	*pasar malam*
restaurant	*rumah makan*
Do you accept credit cards?	*Bisa bayar dengan kartu kredit?*
What's that?	*Apa itu?*
I'll try what they're having.	*Saya mau masakan seperti yang mereka pesan.*
Can I see the menu, please?	*Minta daftar makanan?*
Do you have a menu in English?	*Apakah ada daftar makanan dalam bahasa Inggeris?*
Not too spicy, please.	*Kurang pedas.*
Is that dish spicy?	*Apakah masakan itu pedas?*
I like it hot and spicy.	*Saya suka masakan pedas.*
Thank you, that was delicious.	*Enak sekali, terima kasih.*
The bill, please.	*Minta bon.*
Can you please bring me (some/more) ...?	*Bisa minta ... (lagi)?*
chilli sauce/relish	*sambal*
beer	*bir*
a napkin	*tisu*
pepper	*lada*
soy sauce	*kecap*
a spoon	*sendok*
tea (with sugar)	*teh manis*
tea (without sugar)	*teh pahit*
water	*air minum*
Do you have a highchair for the baby?	*Ada kursi khusus untuk bayi?*

VEGETARIAN PHRASES

I'm a vegetarian/eat only vegetables.	*Saya hanya makan sayuran.*
I don't eat ...	*Saya tidak suka makan ...*
chicken	*ayam*
eggs	*telur*
fish	*ikan*
meat	*daging*
milk and cheese	*susu dan keju*
pork	*daging babi*

poultry	*ayam*
seafood	*makanan laut*
Do you have any vegetarian dishes?	*Apakah ada makanan nabati?*
Does this dish have meat?	*Apakah masakan ini ada dagingnya?*
Can I get this without the meat?	*Bisa minta masakan ini tanpa daging?*

Menu Decoder

Almost every restaurant on Bali – from humbled to fabled – will have a few of these classic dishes on the menu. Some can be found throughout Indonesia, others are unique to Bali and/or Lombok.

ayam pelalah – shredded chicken with chillies and lime

ayam Taliwang – whole split chicken roasted over coconut husks served with a peanut, tomato chilli, lime dip (Lombok)

babi guling – spit-roast pig stuffed with chilli, turmeric, garlic and ginger and smothered in turmeric (Bali)

bakmi – rice-flour noodles, fried to make *bakmi goreng* or used in soup

bakmi goreng – rice-flour noodles, fried

bakso – meatball soup with noodles; also ba'so

bakso ayam – chicken soup with noodles and meatballs; a street-stall standard

base gede – basic spice mixture including shallots, garlic, chillies, coriander, turmeric and the ginger-like *isen* and *laos*

bebek betutu – duck stuffed with spices, wrapped in banana leaves and coconut husks and cooked in a pit of embers (Bali)

bubuh injin – black-rice pudding

bubur ketan hitam – black-rice porridge with coconut milk

cap cai – stir-fried vegetables (Chinese)

cram cam – clear chicken soup with shallots

es buah – variety of *es campur* in which a few different fruits are featured

es campur – sweet drink of coconut milk, fruit, jelly and shaved ice, often served in a bowl

fu yung hai – a sort of sweet-and-sour omelette

gado gado – dish of steamed bean sprouts, various vegetables and a spicy peanut sauce

ikan mujair – small, sweet lake fish

isen – ginger-like spice

krupuk – prawn crackers

laos – ginger-like spice

lawar – salad of chopped coconut, garlic and chilli with pork (or chicken) meat and blood (Bali)

mie goreng – fried noodles with vegetables and sometimes meat

nasi campur – rice with a selection of meat and vegetable dishes on one plate

nasi goreng – literally, fried rice; basic *nasi goreng* may be little more than fried rice with a few scraps of vegetable to give it some flavour, but sometimes it includes meat

nasi kuning – yellow rice made with tumeric

opor ayam – chicken in pepper and coconut curry

pelecing – sauce made with chilli, shrimp paste and tomato is used liberally to make vegetable or chicken dishes (Lombok)

pisang goreng – fried banana fritters; a popular street-side snack

pisang molen – banana wrapped in pastry and fried

rempeyek – peanuts cooked within rice-flour crackers

rendang – beef or buffalo coconut curry

rijsttafel – literally, rice table; a Dutch adaptation of an Indonesian banquet encompassing a wide variety of dishes

sate ayam – chicken satay

sate daging – beef satay

sate lilit – satay of minced, spiced meat pressed onto skewers (Bali)

sate pusut – skewered sausage-shaped mixture of grated coconut, meat and brown sugar (Lombok and Bali)

serombotan – salad of chilli, water cress, bean sprouts, long beans, coconut milk and flesh (Bali)
soto ayam – chicken soup
timbungan bi siap – sharp-tasting chicken soup with minced chicken, tamarind, sugar and starfruit leaves for a bitter touch (Bali)
timun urap – sliced cucumber with grated coconut, onion and garlic (Lombok)
tom – duck, chicken or their livers cooked with spices in a banana leaf (Bali)
urab – salad of boiled and diced long beans, coconut milk and flesh, chilli, shrimp paste, shallots, salt and garlic (Bali)
sate pelecing – fish satay with Balinese spices
pepesan babi guling – suckling pig slices wrapped in banana leaf

Glossary

These words will help you piece together what you need.

air	water
air botol	bottled water
anggur merah	wine, red
anggur putih	wine, white
arak	spirits distilled from palm sap or rice
asap	moked
ayam	chicken
ba'mi	rice-flour noodles; often bami
bakso	meatball soup with noodles; also ba'so
babi	pork
bakar	grilled over an open flame or hot coals; burn
bami	noodles, egg
bebek	duck
Bintang	brand of local beer
bir	beer
brem	type of arak, distilled from white and black rice (Bali)
bumbu	pice mixture, paste or sauce
dadar	omelette
daftar makanan	menu
daging	meat
daging sapi	beef
dingin	cold
garam	salt
goreng	fry
gula	sugar
ikan	fish
ikan danau	freshwater fish
jambu	guava
jeruk	orange; citrus fruit
kacang putih	peanut
kaki-lima	roving vendor
kare	curry
kentang	potato
kepiting	crab
kodok	frog
kopi	coffee
mangga	mango
manis	sweet
mie	noodles
mie kuah	noodle soup
nanas	pineapple
nangka	jackfruit

nasi	cooked rice
nasi putih	plain white rice
pahit	'bitter'; word meaning 'no sugar' in tea or coffee
panas	hot (temperature)
pedas	hot (spicy)
pisang	banana
rambutan	red fruit covered in hairy spines, containing sweet white flesh
rumah makan	restaurant; literally, 'eating place'
sambal	chilli sauce or paste; contains chillies, garlic or shallots and salt
sate	grilled meat on skewers; also spelled satay
sayur	vegetable
soto	soup
susu	milk
teh	tea
teh limon	tea, lemon
telur	egg
tuac	palm beer/wine
warung	food stall

Denpasar

CONTENTS

Bali's capital has been the focus of a lot of the island's growth and wealth over the last five decades, and now has much of the bustle and congestion of many fast-growing cities in Asia, without any of the first-world infrastructure. There are still tree-lined streets and some pleasant gardens, but the traffic, noise and pollution can make it difficult to enjoy. A limited range of accommodation is available, so most visitors find it convenient and much more enjoyable to stay in Kuta-Legian, Sanur or Ubud, and visit Denpasar as a day trip, if at all. Denpasar might not be a tropical paradise, but it's as much a part of 'the real Bali' as the rice paddies and cliff-top temples, and it's not touristy. This is the hub of the island for locals and you may find it a good place for a couple of hours' break if you are transferring on *bemos* (small pick-up trucks) around the island.

Many of Denpasar's residents are descended from immigrant groups, such as Bugis mercenaries (from Sulawesi) and Chinese, Arab and Indian traders. More recent immigrants, including civil servants, artisans, business people and labourers, have come from Java and all over Indonesia, attracted by the opportunities in the growing Balinese capital. Schools, factories and businesses are among the draws and much of the business infrastructure that supports Balinese tourism is based here. Non-Balinese tend to live in detached houses or small apartments, but the Balinese communities still maintain their traditions and family compounds, even as their villages are engulfed by an expanding conurbation. In fact, Denpasar's southern reaches have all but collided with the northern expansion from Seminyak and Kerobokan.

TOP FIVE

- Checking out the art, architecture, carvings and costumes from all corners of Bali at **Museum Negeri Propinsi Bali** (p81)
- Visiting Bali's state temple, **Pura Jagatnatha** (p84), which has some of the biggest festivals in all of Bali
- Watching the Balinese shop while the young flirt on Sundays at the **malls** (p87)
- Navigating the old **markets** (p87) with their myriad of goods
- Plunging into Indonesian language and culture at **Indonesia Australia Language Foundation** (p85)

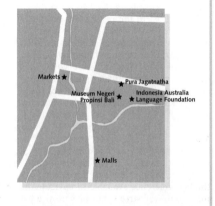

HISTORY

Denpasar, which means 'next to the market', was an important trading centre and the seat of local *rajahs* (lord or prince) before the colonial period. The Dutch gained control of northern Bali in the mid-19th century, but their takeover of the south didn't start until 1906. After the three Balinese princes destroyed their own palaces in Denpasar and made a suicidal last stand – a ritual *puputan* – the Dutch made Denpasar an important colonial centre. And as Bali's tourism industry expanded in the 1930s, most visitors stayed at one or two government hotels in the city of Denpasar.

The northern town of Singaraja remained the Dutch administrative capital, but a new airport was built in the south. This made Denpasar a strategic asset in WWII, and when the Japanese invaded, they used it as a springboard to attack Java. After the war the Dutch moved their headquarters to Denpasar, and in 1958, some years after Indonesian independence, the city became the official capital of the province of Bali. Formerly a part of the Badung district, Denpasar is now a self-governing municipality that includes Sanur and Benoa Harbour.

ORIENTATION

The main road, Jl Gunung Agung, starts at the western side of town. It changes to Jl Gajah Mada in the middle of town, then Jl Surapati and finally Jl Hayam Wuruk. This name changing is common in Denpasar, and can be confusing.

In contrast to the rest of Denpasar, the Renon area, southeast of the town centre, is laid out on a grand scale, with wide streets, large car parks and huge landscaped blocks of land. This is where you'll find the government offices, many of which are impressive and large structures, built with expansive budgets in modern Balinese style.

Maps

The map in this guidebook will be enough for most visitors. If you're driving, the Denpasar inset on the Periplus *Bali* map is the best reference available to navigate the many one-way streets, but be sure you get the 2004 or later edition.

INFORMATION

Emergency

Ambulance (☎ 227911) In an emergency, call ☎ 118.
Fire Brigade (☎ 225113) In an emergency, call ☎ 113.
Police Office (☎ 424346; Jl Pattimura) The place for any general problems.

Medical Services

Rumah Sakit Umum Propinsi Sanglah (RSUP Sanglah; ☎ 227911; Sanglah; ☼ 24hr) The city's general hospital has English-speaking staff and a casualty room. It's the best hospital on the island.

Money

All major Indonesian banks have offices in Denpasar, and most have ATMs. Several are on Jl Gajah Mada, near the corner of Jl Arjuna, and there are also plenty of ATMs in the shopping malls. The rates offered by the moneychangers along the northern end of Jl Diponegoro are better than the banks, but not as good as the moneychangers at Kuta or Sanur.

Post

Main post office (☎ 223565; Jl Panjaitan; ☼ 8am-8pm) Has poste restante service, but is inconveniently located in Renon.

Tourist Information

Denpasar tourist office (☎ 234569; Jl Surapati 7; ☼ 7.30am-3.30pm Mon-Thu, 8am-1pm Fri) Deals with tourism in the Denpasar municipality (including Sanur), but also has some information about the rest of Bali. It's not terribly helpful apart from handing out brochures, including the useful *Calendar of Events* booklet.
Tourist office (☼ 8am-2pm Mon-Thu, 8am-noon Fri) This far more helpful office is located at the Ubung Bus and Bemo Terminal.

SIGHTS

Museum Negeri Propinsi Bali

This **museum** (☎ 222680; adult/child 750/250Rp; ☼ 7.30am-3.30pm Sun-Thu, 7.30am-1pm Fri) was originally established in 1910 by a Dutch Resident who was concerned by the export of culturally significant artefacts from the island. Destroyed in a 1917 earthquake, it was rebuilt in the 1920s, but used mainly for storage until 1932. At that time, German artist Walter Spies and some Dutch officials revived the idea of collecting and preserving Balinese antiquities and cultural objects, and creating an ethnographic museum. Now it's quite well set up, and most displays

DENPASAR

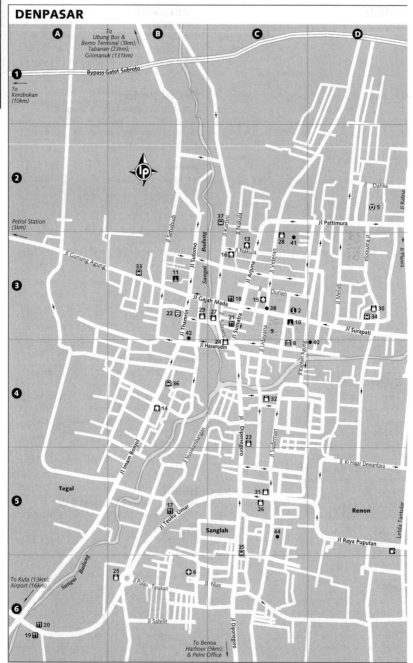

To
Ubung Bus &
Bemo Terminal (3km);
Tabanan (23km);
Gilimanuk (131km)

Bypass Gatot Subroto

To
Kerobokan
(10km)

Jl Dahlia

Jl Ratna

Petrol Station
(3km)

Jl Gunung Agung

Jl Setiabudi

Jl Sutomo

Sungai Badung

Jl Kartini

Jl Nakula

Jl Pattimura

Jl Kamboja

Jl Puwa

Jl Nakula

Jl Arjuna

Jl Veteran

Jl Melati

Jl Gajah Mada

Durian

Jl Thamrin

Sulawesi

Jl Sumatra

Jl Udayana

Jl Surapati

Jl Hasanudin

Jl Kapten Agung

Jl Imam Bonjol

Jl Nusakambangan

Jl Dipenegoro

Jl Sudirman

Jl Ki Hajar Dewantara

Tegal

Jl Teuku Umar

Renon

Sanglah

Jl Raya Puputan

Letda Tantular

To Kuta (13km);
Airport (16km)

Sungai Badung

Jl Pulau Tarakan

Jl Nias

Jl Satelit

Jl Diponegoro

To Benoa
Harbour (5km);
& Pelni Office

Jl 20

19

DENPASAR

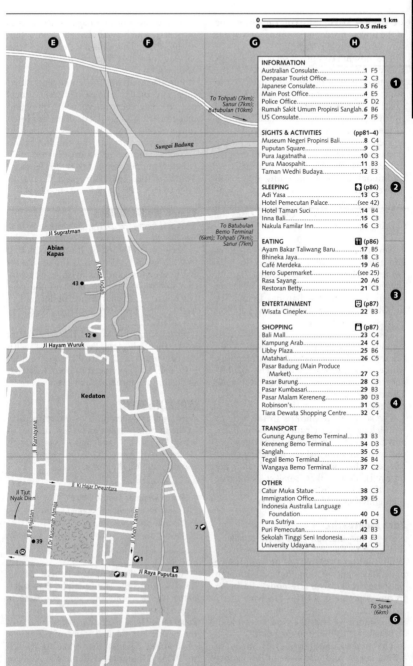

INFORMATION
Australian Consulate...........................**1** F5
Denpasar Tourist Office...................**2** C3
Japanese Consulate..........................**3** F6
Main Post Office...............................**4** E5
Police Office.......................................**5** D2
Rumah Sakit Umum Propinsi Sanglah.**6** B6
US Consulate.......................................**7** F5

SIGHTS & ACTIVITIES   (pp81–4)
Museum Negeri Propinsi Bali............**8** C4
Puputan Square.................................**9** C3
Pura Jagatnatha **10** C3
Pura Maospahit................................**11** B3
Taman Wedhi Budaya....................**12** E3

SLEEPING   🏠 (p86)
Adi Yasa **13** C3
Hotel Pemecutan Palace................(see 42)
Hotel Taman Suci.............................**14** B4
Inna Bali...**15** C3
Nakula Familar Inn..........................**16** C3

EATING   🍴 (p86)
Ayam Bakar Taliwang Baru.............**17** B5
Bhineka Jaya....................................**18** C3
Café Merdeka....................................**19** A6
Hero Supermarket...........................(see 25)
Rasa Sayang.....................................**20** A6
Restoran Betty..................................**21** C3

ENTERTAINMENT   🎭 (p87)
Wisata Cineplex...............................**22** B3

SHOPPING   🛍 (p87)
Bali Mall...**23** C4
Kampung Arab..................................**24** C4
Libby Plaza.......................................**25** B6
Matahari...**26** C5
Pasar Badung (Main Produce
   Market)..**27** C3
Pasar Burung....................................**28** C3
Pasar Kumbasari...............................**29** B3
Pasar Malam Kereneng.....................**30** D3
Robinson's...**31** C5
Tiara Dewata Shopping Centre........**32** C4

TRANSPORT
Gunung Agung Bemo Terminal........**33** B3
Kereneng Bemo Terminal.................**34** D3
Sanglah...**35** C5
Tegal Bemo Terminal.......................**36** B4
Wangaya Bemo Terminal..................**37** C2

OTHER
Catur Muka Statue **38** C3
Immigration Office...........................**39** E5
Indonesia Australia Language
   Foundation....................................**40** D4
Pura Sutriya **41** C3
Puri Pemecutan.................................**42** B3
Sekolah Tinggi Seni Indonesia.........**43** E3
University Udayana............................**44** C5

are labelled in English. You can climb one of the towers inside the grounds for a better view of the whole complex.

The museum comprises several buildings and pavilions, including examples of the architecture of both the *puri* (palace) and *pura* (temple), with features such as a *candi bentar* (split gateway) and a *kulkul* (warning drum) tower. The main building, to the back as you enter, has a collection of prehistoric pieces downstairs, including stone sarcophagi, and stone and bronze implements. Upstairs are examples of traditional artefacts, including items still in everyday use. Look for the fine wood-and-cane carrying cases for transporting fighting cocks, and tiny carrying cases for fighting crickets.

The northern pavilion is in the style of a Tabanan palace and houses dance costumes and masks, including a sinister Rangda (widow-witch), a healthy-looking Barong (mythical lion-dog creature) and a towering Barong Landung (tall Barong) figure. See the Glossary (p376) for further explanation of these mythical figures.

The central pavilion, with its spacious veranda, is like the palace pavilions of the Karangasem kingdom (based in Amlapura), where *rajahs* held audiences. The exhibits are related to Balinese religion, and include ceremonial objects, calendars and priests' clothing.

The southern pavilion is in the style of a Buleleng palace (from northern Bali), and has a varied collection of textiles (see p50 for more information, including *endek* (elegant fabric where the weft threads are predyed), double ikat, *songket* (silver- or gold-threaded cloth) and *prada* (cloth highlighted in gold and/or silver).

Pura Jagatnatha

Next to the museum, the **state temple** is dedicated to the supreme god, Sanghyang Widi. Built in 1953, part of its significance is its statement of monotheism. Although Balinese recognise many gods, the belief in one supreme god (who can have many manifestations) brings Balinese Hinduism into conformity with the first principle of Pancasila – the 'Belief in One God'.

The *padmasana* (shrine) is made of white coral, and consists of an empty throne (symbolic of heaven) on top of the

cosmic turtle and two *naga* (mythological serpents), which symbolise the foundation of the world. The walls are decorated with carvings of scenes from the *Ramayana* and *Mahabharata*.

Pura Jagatnatha is more frequently used than any other Balinese temples – local people come every afternoon to pray and make offerings – so it can often be closed to the public. Two major festivals are held here every month, during the full moon and new moon, and feature *wayang kulit* (shadow puppet plays). Ask at the Denpasar Tourist Office (p81) for exact details, or refer to its *Calendar of Events* booklet.

Taman Wedhi Budaya

This **arts centre** (☎ 222776; admission free; ☽ 8am-5pm Tue-Sun) is a sprawling complex in the eastern part of Denpasar. It was established in 1973 as an academy and showplace for Balinese culture, and has lavish architecture and not much else for most of the year (there are no regular dance performances here). The impressive-looking art gallery has a fair collection.

From mid-June to mid-July, the centre hosts the Bali Arts Festival (p85), with dances, music and craft displays from all over Bali. You may need to book tickets at the centre for more popular events.

WALKING TOUR

This walk includes most of the attractions in the middle of town and a few vestiges of when Denpasar – and Bali – was a much slower place. Allow extra time for visiting the museum or shopping.

Start: Denpasar Tourist Office
Finish: Tiara Dewata Shopping Centre
Distance: 3km
Time: 2-3hr

Starting at the Denpasar Tourist Office, head south to the state temple, **Pura Jagatnatha (1;** left), and the adjacent **Museum Negeri Propinsi Bali (2;** p81). Opposite is **Puputan Sq (3)**, a park that commemorates the heroic but suicidal stand of the *rajahs* of Badung against the invading Dutch in 1906. A monument depicts a Balinese family in heroic pose, brandishing the

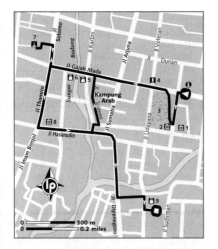

weapons that were so ineffective against the Dutch guns. The woman also has jewels in her left hand, as the women of the Badung court reputedly flung their jewellery at the Dutch soldiers to taunt them. The park is popular with locals at lunch time and with families near sunset.

Back on Jl Surapati is the towering **Catur Muka statue (4**; cnr Jl Surapati & Jl Veteran), which represents Batara Guru, Lord of the Four Directions. The four-faced, eight-armed figure keeps a close eye (or is it eight eyes?) on the traffic swirling around him. West of the statue the street is called Jl Gajah Mada (named after the 14th-century Majapahit prime minister). Follow it west, past banks, shops and restaurants to the bridge over the grubby Sungai Badung (Badung River). Just before the bridge, on the left, is the renovated **Pasar Badung (5)**, the main produce market. This is one of the better places to see the fertile fruit of Bali. On the left, just after the bridge, **Pasar Kumbasari (6)** is a handicraft and textiles market.

At the next main intersection, detour north up Jl Sutomo, and turn left along a small *gang* (lane) leading to the **Pura Maospahit (7)** temple. Established in the 14th century, at the time the Majapahit arrived from Java, the temple was damaged in a 1917 earthquake and has been heavily restored since. The oldest structures are at the back of the temple, but the most interesting features are the large statues of Garuda and the giant Batara Bayu.

Turn back, and continue south along Jl Thamrin, to the junction of Jl Hasanudin. On this corner is the **Puri Pemecutan (8)**, a palace destroyed during the 1906 invasion. It's now long since been rebuilt and has some hotel rooms for rent (see p86); you can look inside the compound but don't expect anything palatial.

Go east on Jl Hasanudin, then north onto Jl Sulawesi, and you'll be in the area of the gold shops, known as Kampung Arab for the many people there of Middle Eastern or Indian descent. Continue north past Pasar Badung market to return to Jl Gajah Mada.

Alternatively, go east on Jl Hasanudin and head south and then east past flower shops to **Tiara Dewata shopping centre (9)**, for refreshments at its food court.

COURSES

The best place for courses in Bahasa Indonesia is the **Indonesia Australia Language Foundation** (IALF; ☎ 221782; www.ialf.edu; Jl Kapten Agung 17), which has a language lab, library, and well-run four-week courses (A$840 for the language and cultural component, and an extra A$280 for a local homestay). Courses are available in six levels, from beginner to advanced.

Sekolah Tinggi Seni Indonesia (STSI; ☎ 227316; www.stsibali.ac.id), just off Jl Nusa Indah, is a government-run four-year college course for Balinese and Indonesian music, theatre, dance and art. Some of its courses may admit qualified visitors; contact the school in advance of your trip.

FESTIVALS & EVENTS

The annual **Bali Arts Festival** (www.baliartsfestival .com) is based at the Taman Wedhi Budaya arts centre (p84) in Denpasar, and lasts for about one month from mid-June to mid-July. It's a great time to be visiting Bali, and the festival is an easy way to see an enormous variety of traditional dance, music and crafts from all over the island. The productions of the *Ramayana* and *Mahabharata* ballets are grand, and the opening ceremony and parade in Denpasar are particularly colourful.

The festival is the main event of the year for the scores of village dance and musical groups. Competition is fierce with local pride on the line at each performance. To do well here sets a village on a good course for the year. Some events are held in a 6000-seat amphitheatre, a venue that allows you to realise the mass appeal of traditional Balinese culture. Overall, the festival provides an excellent way to experience local culture away from the artificial pomp of hotel shows. Tickets are usually available right before performances and schedules are widely available throughout South Bali and Ubud.

SLEEPING

Denpasar has several hotels, but it's hard to think of a compelling reason to stay here unless you want to be close to the bus stations or have some other business here. At times when many Indonesians travel (July, August, around Christmas and Idul Fitri – November/December), it may be wise to book a room.

Budget

Adi Yasa (☎ 222679; Jl Nakula 23B; s/d 25,000/40,000Rp) Budget travellers have crashed here since the 1970s. It's centrally located and friendly, but the nine rooms are very basic.

Nakula Familar Inn (☎ 226446; Jl Nakula 4; s/d 50,000/75,000Rp) Across the road and 100m west from the Adi Yasa, the eight rooms are decent (cold-water showers only) and clean, and all have a small balcony area. The traffic noise isn't too bad and there is a nice little enclave in the middle. Tegal–Kereneng bemos go along Jl Nakula.

Hotel Pemecutan Palace (☎ 423491; Jl Thamrin 2; s/d with air-con 70,000/80,000Rp; ❄) Don't let the name fool you: the simple rooms in the rebuilt Puri Pemecutan (the palace of a Badung rajah) are dilapidated and the staff at times asleep.

Mid-Range

Most mid-range places cater to Indonesian business travellers. There are no hotels in the top-end category.

Inna Bali (☎ 225681; fax 235347; Jl Veteran 3; s/d from 310,000/350,000Rp; ❄ 🐾) A government-owned hotel, the Inna Bali has simple gardens and retains a certain nostalgic charm from its early days as a Dutch outpost. Room interiors are standard, but many make up for this with deeply shaded verandas. The hotel is a good base for the Ogoh Ogoh parades that take place the day

before Nyepi (see Nyepi – The Day of Silence, p331), as they pass right by the front of the hotel.

Hotel Taman Suci (☎ 484445; www.tamansuci.com; Jl Imam Bonjol 45; r from 225,000Rp; ❄ 🖥) A good choice for business travellers, this modern, multifloor hotel insulates you from the hubbub outside from the minute you enter its air-con lobby.

EATING

Most places cater to local people and Indonesian visitors, so they offer a good selection of authentic food at reasonable prices. The cheapest places are *warung* (food stalls) at the bemo/bus terminals and the markets. At the Pasar Malam Kereneng (Kereneng Night Market) dozens of vendors dish up food till dawn. A number of places along Jl Teuku Umar cater to more affluent locals while all the shopping malls have food-court options as Balinese discover the 'joys' of fast food.

Ayam Bakar Taliwang Baru (☎ 263031; Jl Teuku Umar; mains 14,000-21,000Rp) Spicy Lombok-style chicken is the choice at this place, which is always full of locals.

Bhineka Jaya (☎ 224016; Jl Gajah Mada 80; coffee 3000Rp; ⏰ 9am-4pm) Home to Bali's Coffee Co, this storefront sells locally grown beans and makes a mean cup of coffee or espresso, which you can enjoy at the two tiny tables while watching the bustle of Denpasar's old main drag.

Rasa Sayang (☎ 262006; Jl Teuku Umar 243; mains 15,000-45,000Rp; ⏰ 11am-11pm; ❄) A classic Chinese seafood restaurant with an endless menu and tables fitted with white tablecloths.

Café Merdeka (☎ 244784; Jl Teuku Umar 240; baked goods from 500Rp) Delightful Balinese bakery with a wide range of sweet and savoury baked goods you choose yourself and can take away or enjoy at the outside tables.

Restoran Betty (Jl Sumatra 56; mains 7000-12,000Rp) This calm place (compared to the madness of the street outside) has a good range of juices and Indonesian dishes. On the menu is the delicious *sayur assam*, a thin soup of vegetables with tamarind and star fruit (4500Rp). Don't be put off by the antique plastic food models.

Hero Supermarket (Libby Plaza, Jl Teuku Umar) The place to stock up on those Indonesian spices and sauces.

ENTERTAINMENT

For bars and nightlife, join the locals and head to the beach towns. However, you might enjoy the raucous experience of an Indonesian cinema. **Wisata Cineplex** (☎ 424023; Jl Thamrin 21; tickets 10,000Rp) has five screens that show B-grade Indonesian and Western flicks (subtitled in Bahasa Indonesia).

SHOPPING

You'll find some craft shops along Jl Gajah Mada, and further west, on the corner with Jl Thamrin, but for most souvenirs you'll do better in the tourist areas. Other local goods can be found in the markets and at the large shopping malls south of the centre, which are all the rage with locals.

Markets

The Pasar Badung is busy in the morning and evening, and is a great place to browse and bargain. Jl Sulawesi, east of Pasar Badung, has many shops with batik, ikat and other fabrics; and in nearby Kampung Arab gold jewellery is sold by the ounce and can be made to order. On the opposite side of the river, Pasar Kumbasari has handicrafts, fabrics and costumes decorated with gold.

Further north on Jl Veteran, Pasar Burung is a bird market with hundreds of caged birds and small animals, such as guinea pigs, rabbits and monkeys, for sale. There are also wonderfully gaudy and colourful birdcages, as well as traditional wooden cages to purchase. You wonder how many endangered species are traded behind the scenes.

An impromptu dog market also operates directly opposite the bird market. (While you're here, have a look at the elaborate Pura Sutriya, just east of the market.)

Just north of Kereneng bus terminal, the busy Pasar Malam Kereneng (Jl Kamboja) sells mainly food and goods for the local community.

Shopping Centres

Western-style shopping centres are very fashionable. They sell a wide range of clothes, cosmetics, leather goods, sportswear, toys and baby things, all at marked prices that are quite inexpensive by international standards. The brand-name goods are genuine.

Most shopping centres have a food court with stalls serving Asian food, as well as international fast-food franchises. Some have video arcades for the kids and all offer plenty of parking (1000Rp).

Tiara Dewata Shopping Centre (Jl Udayan; **P**) A low-rise place with a good food court and a Dunkin' Donuts serving coffee and of course donuts.

Bali Mall (Jl Dipenegoro; **P**) Has the top-end Ramayana Department Store and an A&W restaurant.

Libby Plaza (Jl Teuku Umar; **P**) Has a huge Hero Supermarket, as well as the heretofore unknown franchise, Texas Chicken.

Matahari (Jl Teuku Umar; **P**) The main branch of the local department store, with numerous other stores in its mall as well as a Swenson's Ice Cream café.

Robinson's (Jl Teuku Umar or Jl Sudirman; **P**) The arch-competitor of Matahari has the same large selection of mid-range and top-end goods. A McDonald's restaurant lurks at the entrance.

GETTING THERE & AWAY

Denpasar is the hub of road transport on Bali – you'll find buses and minibuses bound for all corners of the island. The Transport chapter (p343) has details of transport between Bali and Lombok and other Indonesian islands.

Air

For information on getting to/from Denpasar from outside the region see p343.

Bemo

Denpasar is *the* hub for bemo transport and travel around Bali. The city has several terminals, so if you're travelling independently from one part of Bali to another, you'll often have to go via Denpasar, and transfer from one terminal to another. The terminals for transport around Bali are Ubung, Batubulan and Tegal, while the Gunung Agung, Kereneng, Sanglah and Wangaya terminals serve destinations in and around Denpasar. Each terminal has regular bemo connections to the other terminals in Denpasar for 4000Rp.

Bemos and minibuses cover shorter routes between towns and villages, while full-size buses are often used on longer, more heavily travelled routes. Buses are

DENPASAR

quicker and more comfortable, but they're less frequent.

UBUNG
Well north of the town, on the road to Gilimanuk, Ubung is the terminal for northern and western Bali. In the complex, there is a very helpful **tourist office** (8am-2pm Mon-Thu, 8am-noon Fri), which can provide help with fares and schedules.

Destination	Fare
Gilimanuk (for the ferry to Java)	20,000Rp
Kediri (for Tanah Lot)	4000Rp
Mengwi	4000Rp
Negara	9000Rp
Pancasari (for Danau Bratan)	7000Rp
Singaraja (via Pupuan or Bedugul)	11,000Rp
Tabanan	5000Rp

BATUBULAN
This terminal, a very inconvenient 6km northeast of Denpasar, is for destinations in eastern and central Bali. It can be hard for foreigners to get bemos at the local rate from Batubulan terminal. One ploy is to get tourists into a vehicle with no other passengers and start driving – the tourists then discover they have chartered the whole bemo to their destination at an enormous price. Try to arrive early at the terminal, when there are lots of locals coming and going, and get on a bemo with a group of them.

Destination	Fare
Amlapura	7000Rp
Bangli	4000Rp
Gianyar	6000Rp
Kintamani (via Tampaksiring)	6000Rp
Nusa Dua (via Sanur)	5000Rp
Padangbai (for the Lombok ferry)	5000Rp
Selat (via Semarapura & Amlapura)	12,000Rp
Semarapura	5000Rp
Singaraja (via Kintamani)	10,000Rp
Singaraja (via Semarapura & Amlapura)	14,000Rp
Tampaksiring (via Ubud)	5000Rp
Ubud	4000Rp

TEGAL
On the western side of town on Jl Iman Bonjol, Tegal is the terminal for Kuta and the Bukit Peninsula.

Destination	Fare
Airport	5000Rp
Jimbaran	7000Rp
Kuta	4000Rp
Legian	4000Rp
Nusa Dua/Bualu	7000Rp

GUNUNG AGUNG
This terminal, at the northwestern corner of town (look for orange bemos), is on Jl Gunung Agung, and has bemos to Kerobokan and Canggu (4000Rp).

KERENENG
East of the town centre, Kereneng has bemos to Sanur (4000Rp).

SANGLAH
On Jl Diponegoro, near the main hospital in the south of the city, Sanglah has bemos to Suwung and Benoa Harbour (5000Rp).

WANGAYA
From this tiny terminal near the river, bemos go up the middle of Bali – to Pelaga (6000Rp), via Sangeh.

Bus
The usual route to Java is a bus from Denpasar to Surabaya, which includes the short ferry trip across the Bali Strait. Other buses go as far as Yogyakarta and Jakarta, usually travelling overnight. There are also regular buses from Denpasar, via Padangbai and the ferry, to Mataram on Lombok. See p350 for details on these trips.

Book directly at offices in the Ubung terminal, 3km north of the city centre. To Surabaya or even Jakarta, you may get on a bus within an hour of arriving at Ubung, but at busy times you should buy your ticket at least one day ahead.

There are no tourist shuttle buses to/from Denpasar.

GETTING AROUND
To/From the Airport
Bali's Ngurah Rai airport is just south of Kuta (although it is referred to internationally as Denpasar). A taxi from the airport to Denpasar costs 40,000Rp. Bemos cost 5000Rp.

Bemo

The main form of public transport is the bemo – these small minibuses take various circuitous routes from and between the bus/bemo terminals. They line up for various destinations at each terminal, or you can hail them from anywhere along the main roads – look for the destination sign above the driver's window. The Tegal–Nusa Dua bemo (dark blue) is handy for Robinson's and Matahari department stores, and Renon; and the Kereneng–Ubung bemo (turquoise) travels along Jl Gajah Mada, past the museum and Denpasar Tourist Office, and turns north up Jl Veteran.

Car & Motorcycle

If you plan to hire a car or motorcycle one of the main problems is the one-way traffic restrictions, sometimes for only part of a street's length, which often change and are rarely marked on any maps. The traffic jams can be intense and parking can be difficult, so think twice about driving in Denpasar – take taxis or bemos or walk.

Taxi

As in South Bali, taxis prowl the streets of Denpasar looking for fares. As always, the blue cabs of **Bali Taxi** (☎ 701111) are the most reliable choice.

South Bali

CONTENTS

In Balinese terms, the mountains are always much more auspicious than the sea, but economically, the southern coastline is the most important and dynamic part of the island and the site of its major industry – tourism. If you're looking for a window on traditional Balinese village life, go elsewhere, but for a one-week sun, surf and sand holiday the area offers some of the best beaches, nightlife and shopping, and some outstanding restaurants, whether your tastes run from banana pancakes to fusion.

Kuta (and its southern sibling Tuban) is almost a cliché as a tourist centre, with its cheap surfer dives, narrow *gangs* (alleys) and rampant commercialism. This is the place where you can live on under US$20 a day and still have plenty left for many beers. Kuta's northern suburb, Legian, easily lives up to the stereotype as the place Australian surfers go after they've got a family and prefer a pool to the beach.

Still further north, Seminyak has emerged as the hottest destination on Bali with scores of trendy restaurants, clubs and posh resorts. What all of these places share is one magnificent beach, which bustles from sunrise to spectacular sunset. Whether you're surfing, swimming or just sunbathing, it's the best one on Bali.

To the east, Sanur is quiet, with a reef-protected shore, staid resorts and cafés and many a retired expat.

In the south, is the Bukit Peninsula. There are great surf breaks off the peninsula's west coast, as well as a smattering of world-class resorts. To the east, Nusa Dua is all that a planned luxury resort can be, in fact you may not even realise you're in Bali. To the north, Tanjung Benoa offers the same serene beach, but manages it with a spice of local flavour and accommodation that ranges from basic to luxurious.

Skipping the south won't mean you'll miss the real Bali but it will mean you'll miss the fun Bali.

TOP FIVE

- Sunbathing, swimming and walking at **Kuta Beach** (p98)
- Hitting the latest bars, restaurants and clubs of **Seminyak** (p117)
- Soaking up the superb sunsets from **Jimbaran Beach** (p127)
- Watching a full moon rise over Nusa Penida from **Sanur** (p119)
- Discovering **Bukit Peninsula's** (p127) cliff-top temples, killer surf, secluded beaches, water sports and luxury resorts

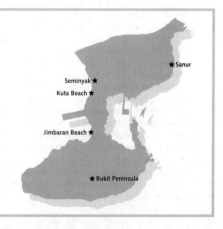

HISTORY

Following the bloody defeat of the three princes of the kingdom of Badung in 1906, the Dutch administration was relatively benign, and southern Bali was little affected until a fateful day in 1936 when Californians Bob and Louise Koke opened their idea of a little tropical resort on then deserted Kuta Beach. Sun, sand and somnolence in a thatched hut caught on, and except for a pause during WWII, the area has never looked back.

Mass tourism took off – or landed – in 1969, when Ngurah Rai international airport opened. The first planned tourist resort was conceived in the early 1970s, by 'experts' working for the UN and the World Bank. As luxury hotels were built at Nusa Dua, unplanned development raced ahead from Kuta to Legian. People made the most of their opportunities, and small-scale, low-budget businesses were set up with limited local resources.

At first, development was confined only to designated resort areas, such as Kuta, Sanur and Nusa Dua, but the boom of the 1990s saw tourism developments spreading north and south of Kuta, extending beyond Jimbaran Bay, and north of Nusa Dua to Tanjung Benoa, while real estate speculators grabbed prime coastal spots around the Bukit Peninsula and north along the beach from Seminyak.

The annual cycle of more visitors bringing more money was disrupted after the millennium by Indonesia's economic crisis, the fall-off of tourists after the 11 September 2001 attacks in the United States, upheavals in the Australian airline business, Avian flu (SARS virus) and a few other catastrophes. These paled, however, compared to the bombings of October 2002 (see The Bali Bombings, p96). South Bali's tourism collapsed, the community went into a state of shock and scores faced economic hardship. Within a year, however, the same factors that had made South Bali such a popular destination, again asserted themselves and visitors began returning.

KUTA REGION

☎ 0361

The Kuta region is overwhelmingly Bali's largest tourist resort. Most visitors come here sooner or later because it's close to the airport, has the best range of hotels, restaurants and tourist facilities and best of all, that unbeatable beach. Some find the area

---

STREET GANG WORRIES

A small lane or alley is known as a *gang*, and most of them lack signs or even names. Some are referred to by the name of a connecting street, eg Jl Padma Utara is the *gang* going north of Jl Padma. Many are too small for cars, although this doesn't stop some drivers trying.

Meanwhile some Kuta streets with names have more than one. Many streets are unofficially named after a well-known temple and/or business place, or according to the direction they head. In recent years there has been an attempt to impose official names on the streets, but the old, unofficial names are by far the most common usage – the only place you're likely to encounter the new (in brackets) names is on some new, small street signs, and on brochures for upmarket hotels. For example, the very popular Jl Dhyana Pura has an official name Jl Abimanyu that is seldom used.

In this guide, both old and new names are shown on the maps, but in the text, the old, commonly used names have been retained. For reference, here are the old and new names, from north to south.

Old/unofficial	New/official
Jl Oberoi	Jl Lasmana
Jl Dhyana Pura/ Jl Gado Gado	Jl Abimanyu
Jl Double Six	Jl Arjuna
Jl Pura Bagus Taruna/ Rum Jungle Rd	Jl Werkudara
Jl Padma	Jl Yudistra
Poppies Gang II	Jl Batu Bolong
Jl Pantai Kuta	Jl Pantai Banjar Pande Mas
Jl Kartika Plaza	Jl Dewi Sartika
Jl Segara	Jl Jenggala
Jl Satria	Jl Kediri

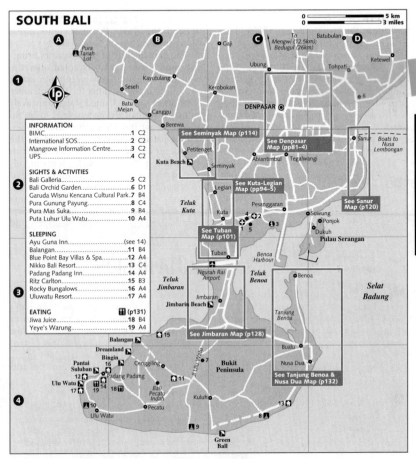

SOUTH BALI

```
0                    5 km
0                    3 miles
```

INFORMATION
BIMC...1 C2
International SOS..............................2 C2
Mangrove Information Centre........3 C2
UPS..4 C2

SIGHTS & ACTIVITIES
Bali Galleria.....................................5 C2
Bali Orchid Garden.........................6 D1
Garuda Wisnu Kencana Cultural Park..7 B4
Pura Gunung Payung......................8 C4
Pura Mas Suka.................................9 B4
Puta Luhur Ulu Watu....................10 A4

SLEEPING
Ayu Guna Inn.............................(see 14)
Balangan...11 B4
Blue Point Bay Villas & Spa............12 A4
Nikko Bali Resort...........................13 C4
Padang Padang Inn........................14 A4
Ritz Carlton....................................15 B3
Rocky Bungalows...........................16 A4
Uluwatu Resort..............................17 A4

EATING (p131)
Jiwa Juice.......................................18 B4
Yeye's Warung................................19 A4

SOUTH BALI

KUTA

It's easy to disparage Kuta for its rampant development, low-brow nightlife and crass commercialism, however the cosmopolitan mixture of beach-party hedonism and entrepreneurial energy can be exciting. It's not pretty, but it's not dull either, and the amazing growth is evidence that a lot of people find something to like in Kuta. Just south, Tuban shares the beach and is a slightly less frenetic area that fills in the land between Kuta and the airport. Legian, Kuta's north end, appeals to families and has more mid-range and top end surfside hotels.

Note too that ever as frantic as Kuta seems, a detour down a small *gang* (alley) can quickly transport you to a quiet and unhurried area.

overdeveloped and seedy, but if you have a taste for a busy surf scene, shopping and nightlife, you'll probably have a great time.

The *kelurahan* (local government area) of Kuta extends for nearly 8km along the beach and foreshore, and comprises four communities that have grown together.

North of Jl Melasti, Kuta merges into Legian, which has almost as many tourist businesses, and only slightly less traffic. Somewhere around Jl Arjuna/Double Six, Legian becomes Seminyak, which is less densely developed, but has some of the best restaurants and coolest nightspots, and great shopping. Somewhere along Jl Kartika Plaza, Kuta merges with Tuban, which has several beach resorts.

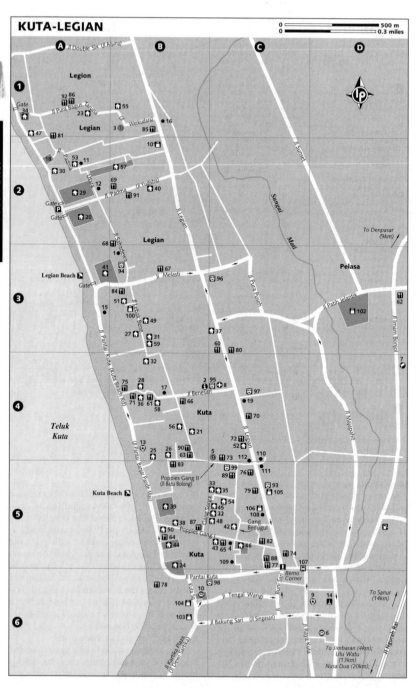

KUTA-LEGIAN

0 — 500 m
0 — 0.3 miles

SOUTH BALI

History

Mads Lange, a Danish copra trader and 19th-century adventurer, set up a successful trading enterprise near modern Kuta in 1839, and successfully mediated between local rajahs and the Dutch, who were encroaching from the north. His business soured in the 1850s, and he died suddenly, just as he was about to return to Denmark. His death may have been the result of poisoning possibly by potential competitors.

Bob and Louise Koke's Kuta Beach Hotel thrived in the late 1930s. The guests, mostly from Europe and the US, were housed in thatched bungalows built in an idealised Balinese style (the Dutch Resident called them 'filthy native huts'). After WWII, others built their own hotels along the beach, although most visitors were still wealthy travellers who arrived from abroad on ocean liners.

Kuta really began to change in the late 1960s, when it became known as a stop on the hippy trail between Australia and Europe. At first, most visitors stayed in Denpasar and made day trips to Kuta, but more accommodation opened and, by the early 1970s, Kuta had relaxed *losmen* (basic accommodation) in pretty gardens, friendly places to eat and a delightfully laid-back atmosphere. Surfers also arrived, enjoying the waves at Kuta and using it as a base to explore the rest of Bali's coastline. Enterprising Indonesians seized opportunities to profit from the tourist trade, often in partnership with foreigners seeking a pretext for staying longer.

Legian, the village to the north, sprang up as an alternative to Kuta in the mid-1970s. At first it was a totally separate development, but these days you can't tell where one ends and the other begins.

Although the physical effects of the 2002 bombings are negligible away from the immediate site, the toll taken manifests in

---

THE BALI BOMBINGS

On Saturday, 12 October, 2002, two bombs exploded on Kuta's bustling Jl Legian. The first blew out the front of Paddy's Bar. A few seconds later a far more powerful bomb obliterated the Sari Club. The blast and fireballs that followed destroyed or damaged neighbouring clubs, pubs, shops and houses.

Close to midnight on the busiest night of the week, the area was packed. More than 300 people from at least 23 countries were injured. The number dead, including those unaccounted for, reached over 200 although the exact number will probably never be known. Many injured Balinese made their way back to their villages where for lack of decent medical treatment they died.

Indonesian authorities eventually laid blame for the blasts on Jemaah Islamiyah, an Islamic terror group. Dozens have been arrested and many convicted of the Bali bombing and other terror acts throughout Indonesia. But even two years later, debate continued on the role other groups such as al-Qaida may have played in the attacks. Meanwhile the cases have bogged down in the Indonesian courts.

Beyond the human toll, the bombings were disastrous to Bali economically. For an economy based on tourism, the downturn of visitors – 50% in the first six months – was devastating. Scores of local people – who make perhaps US$100 a month in good times – were affected. So to was the Balinese sense of innocence. In a place where harmony is so valued, the bombings were an aberration that was very hard to understand. Many say the island was in a collective state of shock for the first year after the attack.

One year later, however, a ceremony to honour the victims was been described as profoundly moving by those who attended. At the same time a memorial (Map pp94-5) was unveiled across from the site of the Sari Club (Map pp94-5). Listing the names of the 202 known victims including 88 Australians and 35 Indonesians, it has an emotional effect on many who view it. Flower arrangements continue to arrive daily.

And there is simply the human will to get on with it. Businesses have been rebuilt (Paddy's has a new location south of the old one and has taken the unfortunate name Paddy's Reloaded) and old ones spiffed up. The Kuta Karnival (p100) started in 2003 under the name 'Celebration of Life, A Remembrance of Love'. It proved to be a cathartic and healing event and will be held annually.

Another local group of locals and people close to Bali have launched a campaign to get the site of the Sari Club turned into a **memorial park** (www.balipeacepark.com). Still, other groups, both on and off Bali, have used the bombings to promote charities to help the victims of the bombings and the Balinese in general.

---

other ways. Much of the new development and investment in South Bali has shifted to Seminyak. The situation was not helped by a massive World Bank project to install much needed storm drains in Kuta that left the streets looking like the fields of Flanders for 2004.

Orientation

Kuta is a disorienting place – it's flat, with few landmarks or signs, and the streets and alleys are crooked and often walled on one or both sides so it feels like a maze. Kuta has terrible traffic and walking is often the quickest way to get around, although scooters speeding down narrow *gangs* can cause peril.

Busy Jl Legian runs roughly parallel to the beach from Kuta north into Seminyak. At the southern end is Bemo Corner, a small roundabout at the junction with Jl Pantai Kuta (Kuta Beach Rd). This one-way street runs west from Bemo Corner then north along the beach to Jl Melasti. Together, these are the main roads although traffic and numerous one-way traffic restrictions will soon have you tearing at your hair.

Between Jl Legian and the beach is a tangle of narrow streets, tracks and alleys, with a hodgepodge of tiny hotels, souvenir stalls, *warung* (food stalls), bars, building construction sites and even a few coconut palms.

Most of the bigger shops, restaurants and low-rent nightspots are along Jl Legian and a few of the main streets that head towards the beach. There are also dozens and dozens of travel agents, souvenir shops, banks, moneychangers, motorcycle- and car-rental outlets, postal agencies, *wartels* (public telephone offices) and Internet cafés – all the needs of a holiday-maker are here.

MAPS
Besides the maps in this book, simple Kuta-area maps can be found in any of the scores of free tourist publications.

Information
BOOKSHOPS
Little used bookstores and exchanges can be found scattered along the *gangs* and roads, especially the Poppies.

Periplus Bookshop Matahari Department Store (Map pp94–5; ☎ 763988; Kuta Sq) On the 4th floor of this department store there is a good selection of books, magazines and newspapers. There is also a newsstand near the grocery section on the ground floor. Bali Galleria shopping centre (Map p93; ☎ 752670; Ngurah Rai By Pass) Has the largest selection of new books on Bali.

Sudani Bookshop (Map pp94–5; Jl Padma Utara) A book exchange near Sinar Indah losmen, which has a varied range of English titles, as well as travel guides. Sydney Sheldon never goes out of print here.

EMERGENCY
Police station (Map pp94–5; ☎ 751598; Jl Raya Kuta; ☺ 24hr) Next to the Badung Tourist Office.

Tourist police post (Map pp94–5; Jl Pantai Kuta; ☺ 24hr) Is a branch of the main police station in Denpasar. Right across from the beach, the officers – who have a gig that is sort of like a Balinese Baywatch – are very friendly and anxious to help although they are quite desperate for a telephone.

INTERNET ACCESS
There are scores of places to connect to the Internet in Kuta, Legian and Tuban. Most have fairly slow connections and charge about 200Rp to 300Rp a minute. The following two places have fast broadband connections and offer numerous computing services, including network connections for people with laptops, CD burners, digital camera downloads and more. Connection rates average 500Rp per minute, proving that you get what you pay for.

Bali@Cyber Café & Restaurant (Map pp94–5; ☎ 761326; Jl Pura Bagus Taruna; meals 20,000-30,000Rp) Has a full range of computer options as well as a good menu of snacks, meals and tasty smoothies.

Internet Outpost (Map pp94–5; ☎ 763392; Poppies Gang II) Has desks couches and cold drinks.

LAUNDRY
Most hotels, even top-end ones, do laundry for a comparatively low price. Back-street laundries are only marginally cheaper – about 1500Rp for jeans; 1000Rp for a shirt or shorts; 500Rp for underwear and – you have less recourse if something goes awry.

MEDICAL SERVICES
Apotek Bunda (Map pp94–5; ☎ 753920; Jl Sahadewa 11; ☺ 9am-10pm) A basic pharmacy with prescription drugs.

Legian Medical Clinic (Map pp94–5; ☎ 758503; Jl Benesari; ☺ on call 24hr) Has an ambulance and dental service. It's 200,000Rp for a consultation with an English-speaking Balinese doctor, or 300,000Rp for an emergency visit to your hotel room. It has a well-stocked pharmacy attached to the clinic.

MONEY
There are several banks along Jl Legian, at Kuta Sq and Jl Pantai Kuta. In addition, ATMs abound and can be found everywhere, including the ubiquitous Circle K and Mini Mart convenience stores.

The numerous 'authorised' moneychangers are faster, efficient, open long hours and offer better exchange rates. Rates can vary considerably, but be cautious, especially where the rates are markedly better than average – they may not have mentioned that they charge a commission or, judging by the number of readers' letters we've received, there may be a few that make their profit by adeptly short-changing their customers.

POST
Postal agencies, that can send but not receive mail, are dotted around the place (and indicated on the relevant maps).

There are several cargo agencies in the Kuta area. If you have bought bulky items, usually the store will have arrangements with shippers to handle things for you. For fast service, you can use one of the expensive international companies.

Main post office (Map pp94–5; Jl Selamet; ☺ 7am-2pm Mon-Thu, 7-11am Fri, 7am-1pm Sat) Is on a small road east of Jl Raya Kuta. It's small, efficient and has an easy, sort-it-yourself poste restante service. This post office is well practised in shipping large packages.

Postal agency (Map pp94–5; ☎ 761592; Kuta Sq; ☺ 10am-9pm) On the ground floor of the Matahari department store will mail packages.

UPS (Map p93; ☎ 766676; Jl Ngurah Rai Bypass; ☺ 9am-6pm Mon-Fri) Access to a worldwide service.

TELEPHONE

Wartels are concentrated in the main tourist areas, particularly along Jl Legian and along the main *gangs* between Jl Legian and the beach. Hours are generally from 7am to 9pm, but some are open later. In most places, you can make international calls and send faxes (shop around for international calls, as prices do vary), and arrange collect calls for a small fee.

TOURIST INFORMATION

Other places that advertise themselves as 'tourist information centres' are usually commercial travel agents, and some can be helpful, especially for booking tours, activities and transport.

Bali Tourist Office (Map pp94-5; ☎ 754090; Century Plaza building; Jl Benesari 7; ⏾ 8am-4pm Mon-Sat) Is responsible for the whole of the island. The friendly staff can answer specific local queries but have limited information about hotels and activities, and only a few brochures and maps to hand out.

Hanafi (Map pp94-5; ☎ 756454; www.hanafi.net; Poppies Gang I 77) The gay-friendly tour operator and guide operates from a small souvenir craft shop. He's a valuable source of information on the gay scene and can also organise tours for visitors.

TRAVEL AGENCIES

Many travel agents will arrange transport or car and motorcycle rental. They also sell tickets for tourist shuttle buses, Balinese dance performances, adventure activities and a variety of tours. Most will also change money and many can also book airline tickets.

The Poppies Gangs and Jl Benesari areas are good spots to hunt out travel agents.

Sumanindo Graha Wisata (Map pp94-5; ☎ 753425; Jl Padma Utara 2G) A reputable agent, can book and issue tickets for domestic and international airlines.

Dangers & Annoyances

Although the streets and *gangs* are usually quite safe, beware of a dubious gang linking Poppies Gang I with Jl Pantai Kuta. Scooter-born prostitutes (who may hassle single men late at night) consummate their business here.

HAWKERS

Occasional crackdowns mean that it's rare to find any food or souvenir carts in the Kuta tourist area, but street selling is common, especially on hassle street,

Jl Legian. The beach is not unbearable, although the upper part features souvenir sellers and licensed massage ladies. Closer to the water, you can sunbake on the sand in peace – you'll soon find where the invisible line is. Most annoying are the touts pelting you with cries of 'Transport?'.

SURF

The surf can be very dangerous, with a strong current on some tides, especially up north in Legian. Lifeguards patrol swimming areas of the beaches at Kuta and Legian, indicated by red-and-yellow flags. If they say the water is too rough or unsafe to swim in, they mean it.

THEFT

This is not a big problem, but visitors do lose things from unlocked hotel rooms or from the beach. Going into the water and leaving valuables on the beach is simply asking for trouble (in any country). Snatch thefts are rare. Valuable items can be left at your hotel reception.

WATER POLLUTION

The sea water around Kuta is quite commonly contaminated by run off from both built-up areas and surrounding farmland, especially after heavy rain.

Activities

From Kuta, you can easily go surfing, sailing, diving, fishing or rafting anywhere in the southern part of Bali, and be back for the start of happy hour at sunset.

Many of your activities in Kuta will centre on the superb **beach**. Hawkers will sell you sodas and beer, snacks and other treats. You can rent lounge chairs and umbrellas (negotiable at 10,000 to 20,000Rp) or just crash on the sand. You will see everyone from bronzed international youth strutting their stuff to local families trying to figure out how to get wet *and* preserve their modesty. When the tide is out the beach seems to stretch forever and you may be tempted to walk for many kilometres north or south. Sunsets are a time of gathering for just about everyone on South Bali. When conditions are right you can enjoy a fuchsia-coloured show that photos can't properly capture.

SURFING

The beach break called Halfway Kuta, off-shore near the Hotel Istana Rama, is the best place to learn surfing. More challenging breaks are on the shifting sandbars off Legian, around the end of Jl Padma; and also at Kuta Reef, 1km out to sea off Tuban Beach (see p319 for details on these surf breaks). Several shops on Jl Legian sell big-brand surf gear and surfboards. Smaller shops on the side streets hire out surfboards (for a negotiable 30,000Rp per day) and boogie boards, repair dings, sell new and used boards, and some can arrange transport to nearby surfing spots. **Redz** (Map pp94-5; ☎ 763980; redzsurf@iol.it; Jl Benesari) is a reputable operator for board rental.

Tubes Surf Bar & Restaurant (Map pp94-5; Poppies Gang II; 🕙 10-2am) is *the* surfers' hang-out. It shows surfing videos, and publishes a tide chart, which is widely circulated. Also keep an eye out for free surfing magazines such as *Magic Wave*.

Bali Surf School (Map pp114-5; ☎ 733666; Jl Double Six 7A; half-day lesson US$30) is one of the major surf schools with classes everyday. You can also get private lessons.

School of Surf (☎ 735858; www.schoolofsurf .com; half-day lesson US$39) holds a range of courses on the beach in Legian. Call for schedules and locations once on Bali. The school also offer custom tours to remote surf spots.

WATERBOM PARK

This popular **park** (Map p101; ☎ 755676; www .waterbom.com; Jl Kartika Plaza; adult/child/family US$18.50/9.50/50; 🕙 9.30am-6pm), south of Kuta, is set on 3.5 hectares of landscaped tropical parks and has assorted water slides, swimming pools, play areas, a supervised park for children under five years old, and a 'lazy river' ride. Other indulgences include 'The Pleasure Pool', a food court and bar, and the Mandara Spa (right). There are lifeguards and it's well supervised, but children under 12 years of age must be accompanied by an adult.

SWIMMING POOLS

Most hotels will allow nonguests to use their pool for a fee. The most impressive is the **aquatic playground** (Map pp94-5; ☎ 761869; Jl Pantai Kuta; adult/child/family 100,000/50,000/ 250,000Rp; 🕙 8am-9pm) at the Hard Rock Hotel where you could easily spend an entire day. The vast and sinuous pool features two water slides and a sandy beach island. There are lifeguards and if you need seclusion, you can rent private cabanas (100,000Rp).

MASSAGES, SPAS & SALONS

Professional masseurs, with licence numbers on their conical hats, offer massages on the beach. A realistic price is about 20,000Rp for a half-hour massage, or 40,000Rp for one hour, but you might have to bargain hard to get near this price if things are busy. Professional massages in your room or in a small massage establishment cost a negotiable 65,000Rp per hour. Most spas also offer facials, waxing and numerous indulgent services.

In the typically calm setting at **Jamu Spa** (Map pp94-5; ☎ 752520; www.jamutraditionalspa.com; Alam Kul Kul, Jl Pantai Kuta; traditional massage US$35; 🕙 9am-9pm) you can enjoy indoor massage rooms which open onto a pretty garden courtyard. If you've ever wanted to be a fruit salad here's your chance as you can have various treatments that involve tropical nuts, coconuts, papayas and more.

There are many **Mandara Spas** (www.mandara spa-asia.com) in top-end hotels including **Hotel Padma Bali** (Map pp94-5; ☎ 752111; Jl Padma 1; massages from US$30; 🕙 10am-8pm), where the divine spa is decorated with water features and impressive stone sculptural reliefs. Waterbom Park also has a Mandara Spa villa.

As stylish as its host hotel, the **Spa** (Map pp94-5; ☎ 751946; Bali Niksoma Beach Resort, Jl Padma Utara; traditional massage 270,000Rp; 🕙 9am-9pm) offers private suites where you can indulge in no end of pampering, from a Bali coffee scrub to Shiatsu.

The deliciously relaxed and ambient spa called **Spa at Mandira** (Map pp94-5; ☎ 765809; spame@dps.centrin.net.id; Bali Mandira Hotel, Jl Padma; Asian massage 264,000Rp; 🕙 10am-7pm) is redolent with Balinese style. The stone walled massage rooms are light-filled. Reflexology massage, body scrubs, Javanese *lulur* (body masks), manicures and pedicures are available. A romantic massage for two is 968,000Rp.

Run by stylish hipsters, **Kudo's** (Map pp94-5; Jl Legian; 🕙 10am-8pm) is a high-concept salon is *the* place to go for a new style. It's popular with brides before their Bali ceremony.

SOUTH BALI

Kuta for Children

Excepting the traffic, Kuta is a pretty good place for kids. With supervision – and sunscreen! – they can cavort on the beach for hours. Almost all the hotels and resorts above the beach-bum category have pools and many also offer kid's programmes.

Timezone video arcade (Map pp94-5; Jl Legian; ☺ 10am-10pm) has hundreds of screeching arcade games. Just south of the very kid-friendly Waterbom Park (p99) is **Le Speed Karts** (Map p101; ☎ 757850; Jl Kartika Plaza, Tuban; five-min ride 40,000Rp; ☺ 10am-7pm) where you can zip around a tiny track.

Tours

A vast range of tours all around Bali, from half-day to three-day tours can be booked through travel agents or hotels in Kuta. These tours are a quick and easy way to see a few sights if your time is limited, and you don't want to rent or charter a vehicle. See p356 for more information on the type of tours available.

Festivals & Events

The first **Kuta Karnival** (www.gokuta.com) was held in 2003 as way of celebrating life after the tragedy of 2002. Plans call for it to be an annual event held in late September and early October. Events include parades, arts competitions, cultural shows, beach sports tournaments, kite-flying contests and more. The event is already a hit and looks to expand each year.

Sleeping

Kuta, Legian and Tuban have hundreds of places for you to stay. The top-end hotels are along the beachfront, mid-range places are mostly on the bigger roads between Jl Legian and the beach, and the cheapest losmen are generally along the smaller lanes in between. Tuban and Legian have mostly mid-range and top-end hotels – the best places to find budget accommodation are Kuta and southern Legian.

With hotel names, be sceptical about words such as 'beach', 'sea view', 'cottage' and 'bungalows'. Places with 'beach' in their name may not be anywhere near the beach and a featureless, three-storey hotel block may rejoice in the name 'cottages'. Note that hotels on Jl Pantai Kuta are separated from the beach by a busy main road south of Jl Melasti. North of Jl Melasti the beach road is protected by gates which exclude almost all vehicle traffic, so hotels here have what is in effect a quiet, paved beachfront promenade.

Since the bombings in 2002 there has been a surprising amount of investment in Kuta accommodations by their owners. Many budget places now boast pools, while other places have had rooms remodelled and new amenities added – all usually without an increase in price.

BUDGET

The best budget accommodation is in a losmen with rooms facing a central garden. Look for a place that is far enough off the main roads to be quiet, but close enough so that getting to the beach, shops and restaurants is no problem. Many losmen still offer a simple breakfast.

Tuban

There's a scattering of cheap places on *gangs* east of Jl Kartika Plaza. They don't offer better value than budget places in Kuta and they are away from the action.

Puspa Ayu (Map p101; ☎ 756721; Gang Puspa Ayu; s/d 100/120Rp, with air-con 150/200Rp; ❷) The best of the bunch. All rooms have hot water here and while basic, are clean.

Kuta

Many of the cheap places are along the tiny alleys and lanes between Jl Legian and the beach in central Kuta. This is a good place to base yourself: it's quiet, but only a short walk from the beach, shops and nightlife. A few places on the eastern side of Jl Legian are close to the bars and restaurants, but can be noisy and a fair hike from the beach. Jl Benesari is a great place to stay, close to the beach and quieter than the Poppies Gangs.

Kedin's II (Map pp94-5; ☎ 763554; Gang Sorga; s/d 60,000/80,000Rp; ❷) One of the best budget choices, the 16 rooms here have hints of style and are set in some fine gardens that feature a good-sized pool.

Lima Satu Cottages (Map pp94-5; ☎ 754944; Gang Bedugul; s/d 100,000/150,000Rp; ❷ ❷) On a *gang* of cheapies off Poppies Gang I, the 11 rooms here are the best of the lot and quite comfortable.

Rita's House (Map pp94-5; ☎ 751760; s/d US$7.50/10) Since 1971 this cheap, clean, cramped and

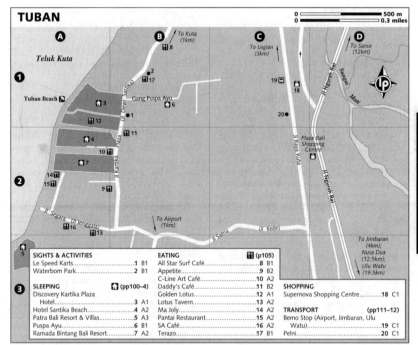

TUBAN

To Kuta (1km)
To Legian (3km)
To Sanur (12km)

Teluk Kuta

Tuban Beach

Gang Puspa Ayu

To Airport (1km)

Plaza Bali Shopping Centre

To Jimbaran (4km); Nusa Dua (12.5km); Ulu Watu (19.5km)

SIGHTS & ACTIVITIES			EATING	(p105)	
Le Speed Karts	1	B1	All Star Surf Café	8	B1
Waterbom Park	2	B1	Appetite	9	B2
			C-Line Art Café	10	A2
SLEEPING	(pp100–4)		Daddy's Café	11	B2
Discovery Kartika Plaza			Golden Lotus	12	A1
Hotel	3	A1	Lotus Tavern	13	A2
Hotel Santika Beach	4	A2	Ma Joly	14	A2
Patra Bali Resort & Villas	5	A3	Pantai Restaurant	15	A2
Puspa Ayu	6	B1	SA Café	16	A2
Ramada Bintang Bali Resort	7	A2	Terazo	17	B1

SHOPPING		
Supernova Shopping Centre	18	C1

TRANSPORT	(pp111–12)	
Bemo Stop (Airport, Jimbaran, Ulu Watu)	19	C1
Pelni	20	C1

cheerful inn just north of Poppies Gang I has been renting rooms to weary surfers and budget travellers. The showers are cold and the air is fan-driven.

Mimpi Bungalows (Map pp94-5; ☎ 751848; kumimpi@ yahoo.com.sg; off Gang Sorga; s/d 80,000/100,000Rp, with hot water & air-con 200,000/300,00Rp; 🖳 🖳) The cheapest rooms here are actually the best value. The gardens boast plenty of shade and privacy and the pool is good-sized.

Hotel Lusa (Map pp94-5; ☎ 753714; Jl Benesari; r 145,000-265,000Rp; 🖳 🖳) Older rooms here lack the flash of the rooms in a new block but they are the better value. All guests can enjoy the pool, café and the leafy grounds.

Masa Inn (Map pp94-5; ☎ 758507; www.masainn .com; Poppies Gang I; s/d 115,000/135,000Rp, with air-con 150,000/180,000Rp; 🖳 🖳) A friendly and central place, Masa Inn offers decent value. All rooms have hot water and the large pool is a popular hang-out.

Berlian Inn (Map pp94-5; ☎ 751501; off Poppies Gang I; s/d 50,000/60,000Rp, with hot water 90,000/100,000Rp) A cut above other budget places, the 24 rooms here are quiet and have ikat (cloth where a pattern is produced by dyeing the individual threads before weaving) bed-spreads and an unusual open-air bathroom design.

Komala Indah I (Map pp94-5; ☎ 753185; Jl Bene-sari; r 30,000-135,000Rp; 🖳) Not to be confuse with the losmen of the same name of Pop-pies Gang I, the range of rooms here is set around a pleasant garden. The cheapest rooms have squat toilets and twin beds only. Breakfast is included.

Bendesa (Map pp94-5; ☎ 751358; off Poppies Gang II; r 50,000-150,000Rp; 🖳) The clean and sim-ple rooms are quiet as the Bendesa is fairly isolated. The garden is spare but so are the prices. The cheapest rooms – all clean – have cold water and fan.

Taman Ayu II (Map pp94-5; ☎ 754376; fax 754640; off Poppies Gang II; r 35,000-65,000Rp, with air-con 70,000-100,000Rp; 🖳) The clean rooms here come with bamboo walls and most feature open-air bathrooms. Breakfast is included.

Legian

The streets are wider and the pace is less frenetic than just south in Kuta. Budget places tend to be larger as well.

SOUTH BALI

Su's Cottages II (Map pp94–5; ☎ 752127; fax 750372; Jl Pura Bagus Taruna; r 130,000Rp–160,000Rp; ✖ ⬛) The clean and bright rooms here feature rattan beds and open onto a deep-blue pool. Breakfast is included.

Legian Beach Bungalow (Map pp94–5; ☎ 751087; Jl Padma; s/d 70,000/80,000Rp; ⬛) The 16 rooms with cold water and fans are smallish, as is the pool. Beware of traffic noise, although the warm welcome may drown it out.

Senen Beach Inn (Map pp94–5; ☎ 755470; Gang Camplung Mas 25; s/d 50,000/60,000Rp) In a little *gang* near Jl Melasti, this low-key place is run by friendly young guys. Rooms have outdoor bathrooms and are set around a small garden. It's an atmospheric, quiet place to stay because there's a small furniture-making workshop in the same compound where you can watch stuff being made. It has a small café.

Sinar Indah (Map pp94–5; ☎ 755905; wayansuda@hotmail.com; Jl Padma Utara; s/d 80,000/100,000Rp, with air-con 125,000/150,000Rp; ✖) This standard, fairly basic losmen is handy to the beach. It offers plain, clean rooms which have hot water.

MID-RANGE
The bulk of accommodation in the Kuta area falls into the mid-range category. Quality varies widely, with some places offering quite a bit in terms of location, amenities and service, while others are more interested in simply taking your money. We honour the former while many tour groups find themselves stuck with the latter.

Tuban
There's mid-range accommodation away from the surf and in the back streets east of Jl Kartika Plaza, but the places are out of the way and not very convenient for the beach or the nightlife areas.

Risata Bali Resort (☎ 753340; www.risatabali.com; Jl Segara; r US$60–90; ✖ ⬛) The rooms here are pleasant and spacious. The resort is set around a pool in a colourful garden. It's a short walk to the beach.

Kuta
Most of these places are handy to the beach.

Un's Hotel (Map pp94–5; ☎ 757409; www.unshotel .com; Jl Benesari; s/d US$25/28, with air-con US$33/36; ✖ ⬛) Un's is one of those Kuta places that

somehow feels like a remote resort even though it is the heart of the action. It's a two-storey place with bougainvillea spilling over the balconies, which face a pool. The spacious rooms have solar hot water, antiques and open-air bathrooms.

Poppies Cottages I (Map pp94–5; ☎ 751059; www .poppies.net; Poppies Gang I; r US$65–80; ✖ ⬛ ⬛) This Kuta institution has a lush, green garden setting for its 20 thatch-roofed cottages which have outdoor sunken baths. The peaceful pool is surrounded by stone sculptures and water fountains and almost makes you forget you are in the heart of Kuta. Guests can use computers with broadband access.

Suji Bungalow (Map pp94–5; ☎ 765804; fax 752483; www.sujibglw.com; off Poppies Gang I; r US$19–29; ✖ ⬛) This fine, friendly place has a choice of bungalows and 47 rooms set in a shady, quiet garden around a pool. It's not flash but it's better than many similarly priced options. There's also a shady poolside café.

Kuta Lagoon Resort (Map pp94–5; ☎ 750888; www .kutalagoonresort.com; off Jl Legian; r 400,000Rp, with pool view 650,000Rp; ✖ ⬛) A long bamboo-lined path off Jl Legian isolates this property from the sights and smells of Jl Legian. The thatch-roofed hotel is in a bright white building set off by colourful hibiscus blooms. Rooms are lovely, although the standard ones face a wall. Those with pool views are a step away from the sinuous pool.

Hotel Camplung Mas (Map pp94–5; ☎ 751461; camplung@indo.net.id; Jl Melasti; s/d/tr 250,000/310,000/370,000Rp; ✖ ⬛) Balinese stone architecture highlights the 69 bungalows set in walled compounds – so if privacy is what you are after then this hotel is a good option. Even so, the rooms aren't really worth raving about so you're better off laying next to the lovely pool. Breakfast is included.

Hotel Puri Tanah Lot (Map pp94–5; ☎ 752281; tanalot@indo.net.id; Jl Lebak Bene; s/d with fan US$17/20, poolside with balcony & air-con US$35/40; ✖ ⬛) This comfy bungalow-style inn is quiet, but accessible to the beach and the action. The 57 stylish rooms are set around a pleasant garden. All have satellite TV.

Hotel Sayang Maha Mertha (Hotel Sayang Beach Lodging; Map pp94–5; ☎ /fax 751249; www.sayanghotel .com; off Jl Lebak Bene; r US$8–45; ✖ ⬛) The 56 rooms here range from basic with cold water to quite comfortable with a range of amenities like satellite TV. All are clean. It has a bar and is popular with surfers.

Sari Yasa Samudra Bungalows (Map pp94–5; ☎ 751562; fax 752948; Jl Pantai Kuta; s/d US$20/23, with air-con US$35/40; ✄ ▣) An excellent location directly opposite the beach makes this place fine value. It has pleasant bungalows set in lush gardens and the large pool has been renovated. Breakfast is included.

Kuta Seaview Cottages (Map pp94–5; ☎ 751961; www.kutaseaviewhotel.com; Jl Pantai Kuta; s/d US$80/90, cottages US$85/100; ✄ ▣) The 27 stylishly decorated cottages and 45 large rooms come complete with fresh flowers on the beds and a lovely garden setting. It's popular with a younger crowd and its azure pool is well-placed facing the ocean.

Hotel Sorga Kuta (Map pp94–5; ☎ 751897; sorga@idola.net.id; Banjar; r 68,000-184,000Rp; ✄ ▣) The 48 rooms here are squeezed into three-storey blocks, which in turn are squeezed on to the small site. A pool squeezes in as well. The cheaper cold water rooms are very good value. More money gets you air-con and satellite TV.

Bali Matahari Hotel (Map pp94–5; ☎ 763707; www.balimatahari.com; Jl Lebak Bene; r US$25-35; ✄ ▣) Just off Jl Melasti, the Matahari has contemporary architecture. Many of the 38 rooms, although small, are just by the pool. There's a posh restaurant and billiards area.

Rosani Hotel (Map pp94–5; ☎ 761042; rosani@dps.centrin.net.id; Jl Lebak Bene; r 200,000Rp; ✄ ▣) There's happy hour at the pool bar every night at this 36-room hotel. The brightly lit rooms have satellite TV.

Kuta Puri Bungalows (Map pp94–5; ☎ 751903; kuta_puri@hotmail.com; Poppies Gang I; s/d US$17/20, with air-con & hot water US$30-40/35-45; ✄ ▣) Guests at this popular place excuse a few rough edges for its convenient location and spacious gardens.

Simpang Inn (Map pp94–5; ☎ 761306; www.indo.com/hotels/simpanginn; Jl Legian 133; s/d US$22-46/27-60; ✄ ▣) Perfectly clean and functional, the Simpang is set around a pool. If you want to be close to the bars and nightlife it's ideal, and there's minimal traffic noise.

Legian

Hotel Puri Raja (Map pp94–5; ☎ 755902; www.puriraja.com; Jl Padma Utara; r US$75-110; ✄ ▣) Right on a great stretch of beach, the Puri Raja offers good value with its two, large circular pools and uncrowded grounds. Rooms have balconies or patios and include satellite TV. More money gets you up by the pools or beach.

Vilarisi Hotel (Map pp94–5; ☎ 768010; www.vilarisi.com; Gang Lebak Bena 15x; r US$30-75; ✄ ▣) A five-storey hotel in the heart of Legian, rooms here are comfortable and feature shady balconies with good views from the upper floors. It's worth stopping in just to see the unusual grotto-like walkway to the small pool. Outdoor tables at the café overlook the busy *gang* below. Staff are lovely.

Court Yard Hotel & Apartments (Map pp94–5; ☎ 750242; www.courtyard-bali.com; Jl Pura Bagus Taruna; r US$75, 1-/2-bedroom apt US$125/175; ✄ ▣) This sleek, contemporary two-storey hotel is designed so that all rooms face the pool. The rooms, decorated with abstract art, have a summery, airy ambience, and top-end facilities. The hotel's Hot Mango Bar is a cool little whitewashed place for a drink.

Three Brothers Inn (Map pp94–5; ☎ 751566; fax 756082; Jl Padma Utara; r US$20-45, with air-con US$30-32; ✄ ▣) Twisting banyan trees shade scores of brick bungalows holding 89 rooms in the Brothers' sprawling and shady grounds. The fan rooms are the best option, but all rooms are spacious, some have lovely outdoor bathrooms, and most have solar hot water. Some large rooms with fans are suitable for families and there's a pleasant poolside café.

Puri Tantra Beach Bungalows (Map pp94–5; ☎ 753195; puritantra@telkom.net; Jl Padma Utara 50X; s/d/f US$35/40/55) These six charming, traditional, fan-only cottages are a step back in time and make for a mellow retreat. All have outdoor bathrooms and are right by the beach.

TOP END

Getting a room on the Kuta Beach is one of Bali's great pleasures. Resorts in Tuban and Seminyak might have genuine beach frontage, but those in Kuta and some in Legian are separated from the beach by a busy main road.

Tuban

It's quieter here than Kuta but the action is a short walk north along the beach.

Discovery Kartika Plaza Hotel (Map p101; ☎ 751067; www.discoverykartikaplaza.com; Jl Kartika Plaza; r US$160-220, f US$250-300; ✗ ✄ ▯ ▣) The

SOUTH BALI

312 rooms at this large resort are pleasant and spacious. There are expansive gardens, a gigantic swimming pool and tennis courts. For real luxury, rent one of the private villas on the beach (units two to seven are best, with number four having a view up the surf to Seminyak and beyond).

Patra Bali Resort & Villas (Map p101; ☎ 751161; www.patra-jasa.com; Jl Ir H Juanada; r from US$150, villas from US$450; 🗷 🖵 🖭) Just beyond the south end of Tuban Beach, the Patra Bali combines contemporary flair with luxury. The grounds and pools are immaculate, the rooms well equipped and the location quiet. Some villas feature private pools.

Hotel Santika Beach (Map p101; ☎ 751267; http://santika.net; Jl Kartika Plaza; s/d/ste US$120/130/250; 🗷 🖭) The grassy and verdant grounds feature little surprises like a stimulating reflexology walk. Bungalows are secluded and have private gardens. Rooms have private balconies and suites feature ocean views.

Ramada Bintang Bali Resort (Map p101; ☎ 753292; www.bintang-bali-hotel.com; Jl Kartika Plaza; r US$145-285; 🗷 🗷 🖵 🖭) This group tour behemoth has over 400 rooms. It fronts a golden crescent of Tuban Beach and has a vast pool, tennis courts, health club, nightclub and more.

Kuta

Alam Kul Kul (Map pp94-5; ☎ 752520; www.alamresorts.com; Jl Pantai Kuta; r/villa US$125/250; 🗷 🖭) The Alam has a gorgeous setting among majestic, gnarled banyan trees. Rooms and villas have contemporary styling with lots of attention to detail, and there's a kids' daycare centre. The Jamu Spa is on-site (p99).

Hard Rock Hotel (Map pp94-5; ☎ 761869; www.hardrockhotels.com; Jl Pantai Kuta; r US$190-760; 🗷 🗷 🖵 🖭) The top spot in Kuta has over 400 themed rooms, which all feature appropriate memorabilia (as well as Hard Rock logos here, there and everywhere). It's totally formulaic and feels like a theme park (indeed the pool qualifies as one, see p99); the store selling the clichéd T-shirts isn't just a store, it's a 'megastore'. All rooms have an advanced music system and spa bath, and the hotel has a kids' club, spa, a gym and much more.

Mercure Kuta (Map pp94-5; ☎ 767411; www.accorhotels-asia.com; Jl Pantai Kuta; r US$90-140; 🗷 🖭) Part of the vast French lodging group, the

Mercure is a contemporary five-storey hotel with 129 rooms done up in Cubist style and featuring a lofty roof-top pool. The rooms facing the beach have some of the best views in Kuta proper and feature balconies.

Hotel Bounty (Map pp94-5; ☎ 753030; www.balibountygroup.com; Poppies Gang II; r US$90-160; 🗷 🖭) Two pools in leafy grounds are the draw here – one is quiet and low-key, while the other has a busy bar, loud dance music and plenty of lizards lounging in the sun. The 166 rooms are comfortable and fully equipped.

Harris Resort (Map pp94-5; ☎ 753875; www.harris-kuta-bali.com; Jl Pantai Kuta; r US$130; 🗷 🖵 🖭) Worth mentioning as it's 'new' and getting a lot of buzz, the Harris is really the back wing of the unremarkable Sahid Raya Hotel with a skin-deep renovation featuring a lot of orange paint. As one staffer cheerfully told us, the rooms are 'too small'. Most also lack patios or balconies.

Legian

Most of the top-end places in Legian are directly opposite the beach on stretches of road restricted to traffic. These tend to be relaxed places favoured by families.

Bali Niksoma Beach Resort (Map pp94-5; ☎ 751946; www.baliniksoma.com; Jl Padma Utara; r US$88-125, villa US$438; 🗷 🖭) The mannered and minimalist style here comes right from the pages of a design magazine. There are two multi-level pools, one of which seems to disappear into the ocean and horizon. The 58 rooms are exquisite and the villas sublime. There is a health club and a noteworthy spa (p99).

Jayakarta Hotel (Map pp94-5; ☎ 751433; www.jayakartahotelsresorts.com; Jl Pura Bagus; r US$140-180, ste US$200-350; 🗷 🖭) Looking for a large beach resort? The Jayakarta fits the bill nicely with beautiful palm-shaded grounds, large rooms, several pools and a good stretch of beach. Suites are good for families and all rooms have private patios or balconies.

Bali Mandira Hotel (Map pp94-5; ☎ 751381; www.balimandira.com; Jl Pantai Kuta; r US$130, cottage US$170; 🗷 🖵 🖭) Gardens filled with bird of paradise flowers set the tone at the Bali Mandira. Cottages have modern interiors, and the bathrooms are partly open-air. A dramatic pool at the peak of a stone ziggurat housing the spa offers uninterrupted ocean views. It also has a pleasant open-air beachfront café. Guests can use computers with broadband access. See p99 for information on the hotel's spa.

Legian Beach Hotel (Map pp94-5; ☎ 751711; www .legianbeachbali.com; Jl Melasti; r US$110, bungalows US$130-150, f US$160-170; 🖭 🖭) Thatched bungalows are set among lovely gardens of tall coconut palms. Rooms are comfortable, if a bit formulaic. The scenic pool area has fountains and a great view of the ocean from the swim-up bar. There's also a shallow pool for kids.

Hotel Padma Bali (Map pp94-5; ☎ 752111; www .hotelpadma.com; Jl Padma; r US$185-265, f US$245; 🖭 🖭) Guests are protected from the wilds of Kuta at this sprawling upmarket hotel. Grassy berms shelter the pool from what could be stunning beach views and regular souvenir shows are arranged to spare guests from venturing out onto the streets. Balinese artwork graces the tastefully decorated rooms. It has several restaurants and a branch of the well-regarded Mandara Spa (p99).

Eating

There's a profusion of places to eat around Kuta. Travellers and surfers cafés with their cheap menus of Indonesian standards, sandwiches and pizza are ubiquitous. Other forms of Asian fare can be found as well and there's numerous places serving fresh seafood, steaks and pasta. Places with interesting kitchens can be found along Jl Legian, the Poppies and towards the beach. There's really no shortage of choices.

If you're looking for the laid-back scene of a classic travellers café, wander the *gangs* and look for the crowds. Often what's busy one night will be quiet the next. For quick snacks and other victuals Circle K and Mini Mart convenience stores are everywhere and open 24 hours. Employees at the former are especially winsome.

TUBAN
The beachfront hotels all have numerous restaurants. In most cases the best feature for nonguests are the beachside cafés which are good for a tropical snack or a sunset drink.

Ma Joly (Map p101; ☎ 753708; Jl Pantai Segara; dishes 25,000-80,000Rp; 🕑 noon-11pm) A new upscale restaurant right on the beach, Ma Joly

has a good menu of seafood and pasta and a good wine list. A boutique hotel should open nearby by 2005.

Golden Lotus (Map p101; ☎ 752403; Jl Kartika Plaza; dishes 40,000-100,000Rp; 🕑 lunch & dinner; 🖭) People flock from all over South Bali for the lavish and creative Chinese cuisine at this refined restaurant in the otherwise unremarkable Bali Dynasty Hotel. The Peking duck is very popular.

Appetite (Map p101; ☎ 755815; Jl Kartika Plaza; dishes 27,000-60,000Rp; 🕑 dinner) Away from the road, the Appetite is a pleasant place in a pavilion featuring a grand piano and water fountains. Dishes span the gamut from steaks to seafood to Asian duck. The wine list is long.

Pantai Restaurant (Map p101; ☎ 753196; Jl Pantai Segara; dishes 28,000-55,000Rp) Let your toes feel the sand at the beachside tables in this simple seafood restaurant. It's a little ramshackle, but the food's fresh and good.

C-Line Art Café (Map p101; ☎ 751285; Jl Kartika Plaza 33; dishes 20,000-50,000Rp) Local art lines the walls and bougainvillea shades the tables. Breakfasts, pasta, Indo standards, seafood and more are on the menu. The banana smoothies have great appeal.

Terazo (Map p101; ☎ 759975; Jl Kartika Plaza; dishes 20,000-50,000Rp) Located next to Waterbom Park, Terazo has a long list of all the usual suspects but the surroundings – and the food – are a cut above the norm. Settle back into the comfy teak furniture and enjoy the friendly service.

Daddy's Café (Map p101; ☎ 762037; Jl Kartika Plaza; dishes 25,000-45,000Rp; 🕑 lunch & dinner) Greek fare like kebabs, moussaka, meze and other Mediterranean dishes are served at breezy 2nd-floor tables. Service is good and the food is an enjoyable change of pace.

Lotus Tavern (Map p101; ☎ 753797; Jl Segara; dishes 22,000-50,000Rp) The Tuban branch of the always reliable Bali-wide chain serves good quality Western and Asian cuisine plus pizza in a pleasant setting.

All Star Surf Café (Map p101; ☎ 757933; 2nd Flr, Kuta Ctr, Jl Kartika Plaza; dishes 20,000-56,000Rp; 🕑 7-1am) A large open-air restaurant cum bar has live bands and a menu of burgers, enchiladas and pizza. There's frequent drink specials.

SA Café (Map p101; Jl Segara; dishes 15,000-30,000Rp) A cheap option if you're staying at one of the resort hotels and need to get away. The menu has all the standards and you can check the Internet.

KUTA
On the Beach
Busy Jl Pantai Kuta keeps beachside businesses to a minimum in Kuta. Beach vendors are pretty much limited to drinks.

La Cabana (Map pp94-5; ☎ 766156; Jl Benesari at Jl Pantai Kuta; dishes 15,000-25,000Rp) A nice place on an otherwise barren strip, there are little fountains to cover the traffic noise and you have a clear view of sunsets. The menu has all the Kuta standards.

Circle K (Map pp94-5; Jl Pantai Kuta; sandwiches 14,000Rp; ☼ 24hr) This outlet of the cheerful chain has a deli counter where you can get freshly made salads and sandwiches. Quality is high and the prices are good. Picnic at one of the tables or scoot across to the beach.

Mentari (Map pp94-5; ☎ 715361; Natour Kuta Beach Hotel; dishes 15,000-50,000Rp; ☼ 10am-10pm) One of the few beachside options at the south end of Kuta Beach, Mentari serves up a long Indonesian and international menu. If you sit at the front tables, you'll get hassled by hawkers.

Central Kuta
Poppies Restaurant (Map pp94-5; ☎ 751059; Poppies Gang I; dishes 30,000-80,000Rp) Poppies was one of the first restaurants in Kuta (hence Poppies Gang I is named after it), and is popular for its lush garden setting and romantic atmosphere. Refined Balinese fare joins steaks and seafood on a menu that features many items made with local organic ingredients. You may need to book.

Un's Restaurant (Map pp94-5; ☎ 752607; south of Poppies Gang I; dishes 25,000-75,000Rp) At night little tea lights enliven the attractive gardens here and make for a lovely setting. Look for fusion offerings such as sesame-crusted tuna and grilled rack of lamb.

Made's Warung (Map pp94-5; ☎ 755297; Jl Pantai Kuta; dishes 18,000-90,000Rp) Longtime visitors debate whether longtime favourite Made's still 'has it', but service has definitely improved over recent years. What's certain is that the menu of Indonesian classics is prepared and served with more flair and care than the usual warung.

Fat Yogis (Map pp94-5; ☎ 751665; Poppies Gang I; dishes 10,000-37,000Rp) Good espresso joins the usual line-up of pizza and Indo classics at this popular travellers café.

Treehouse Café (Map pp94-5; ☎ 762755; Poppies Gang I; dishes 6000-50,000Rp, happy hour large Bintang 8000Rp) A low-key, relaxed place serving cheap juices and beers. On offer is also standard travellers fare from its international menu, such as tempeh burgers, complete with gherkin and fries.

Along Jl Legian
The possibilities of eating choices along Jl Legian seem endless, but avoid tables close to the busy street.

Ketupat (Map pp94-5; ☎ 754209; Jl Legian; dishes 25,000-120,000Rp) Hidden behind the Jonathan Gallery, Ketupat is a calm, serene oasis. The dining pavilions all centre on a strikingly blue pool. Dishes originate from across Indonesia, including Javanese curries, such as *nasi hijau harum* (fried rice with greens, shrimps and herbs). This is one of the best choices on Jl Legian.

Mini Restaurant (Map pp94-5; ☎ 751651; Jl Legian 77; dishes 20,000-70,000Rp; ☼ 11am-11pm) This place belies its name with maxi-sized portions and a plethora of often packed tables. Fresh seafood is grilled right up the front of the restaurant for the enjoyment and temptation of passers-by.

Kopi Pot (Map pp94-5; ☎ 752614; Jl Legian; dishes 22,000-40,000Rp) Shaded by trees, Kopi Pot is popular for its coffees, milk shakes and myriad of yummy desserts, as well as seafood, European and Indonesian main dishes. The upstairs dining area offers shelter if rain threatens the street-level outdoor tables.

Maccaroni (Map pp94-5; ☎ 754662; Jl Legian 52; dishes 20,000-90,000Rp; ☼ 9-1.30am) The trendy spot on Jl Legian, Maccaroni was designed by Giovanni, the designer responsible for other trendy joints such as Ku De Ta in Seminyak. There's dishes like eggs benedict at brunch and a long list of pastas and steaks through the day and night. The wine list is long. At night there's live music such as jazz or house.

Aroma's Café (Map pp94-5; ☎ 751003; Jl Legian; dishes 20,000-40,000Rp) A gentle garden setting encircled by water fountains makes a fine place to face the start of the day over the great juices, breakfasts and coffees. Other times the menu has good versions of Western and Indonesian classics.

SOUTH BALI

Nero Bar & Restaurant (Map pp94-5; ☎ 750756; Jl Legian; lunch 20,000-30,000Rp; dinner 40,000-70,000Rp; ✆ 10am-midnight) Nero has a slick, high-design interior. The international menu has a Mediterranean bent, while the many seafood choices include the very popular spaghetti with king prawns.

Kunti Japanese (Map pp94-5; ☎ 761454; Jl Legian 14; dishes 25,000-30,000Rp; ✆ noon-midnight) This little place has all the Japanese standards of udon, soba, tempura, sushi and sashimi, and all the right Japanese flavours.

On & Near Poppies Gang II

Kori Restaurant & Bar (Map pp94-5; ☎ 758605; Poppies Gang II; meals 15,000-80,000Rp) Kori wanders through a gorgeous assemblage of gardens and ponds. Popular with expats, it has a good selection of steaks, pasta, upscale Indonesian, burgers and more. You can have a secluded rendezvous in the flowerbedecked nooks out back. The drink list is long and includes many non-clichéd tropical drinks.

Balcony (Map pp94-5; ☎ 757409; Jl Benesari 16; dishes 17,000-90,000Rp) The Balcony has a breezy tropical design and sits above the hubbub below. The generous dishes are mostly Mediterranean – on offer are salads, skewers, tapas and paella. Happy hour runs between 5pm and 8pm.

Fresh (Map pp94-5; ☎ 752782; Jl Benesari 19; meals 10,000-20,000Rp; ✆ 10am-8pm) As its name implies, this cute little place offers fresh salads, juices and sandwiches on multi-grain rolls. Run by a pair of Australian women, it wraps around a small shrine.

Bali Corner (Map pp94-5; dishes 8000-15,000Rp) In the myriad of little lanes, this is one of the cheap travellers eateries with an indistinguishable menu. It serves up the usual range of Indonesian, Western and Chinese foods, and of course the perennial crowd pleaser, pizza.

Rainbow Café (Map pp94-5; ☎ 765730; Poppies Gang II 23; dishes 7000-17,500Rp) Anthropolgists studying the modern backpacker can research their thesis at this popular travellers café. Large comfy sofas make it a good place to watch life on the *gang*.

Warung Indonesia (Map pp94-5; dishes 5000-16,000Rp) This is one of several similar totally unpretentious cheapies on this lane serving up typical travellers fare. It's clean, has a genial mix of surfers and locals, and is popular at night.

Warung Wulon (Map pp94-5; dishes 6000-17,000Rp) Near Warung Indonesia, Wulon is dark and cool inside. The banana smoothies are great – cold, icy and very banana.

Komala Indah II Café (Map pp94-5; ☎ 754258; Jl Benesari; dishes 5000-17,000Rp) Over-amped surfers love this place as they can drop off their laundry next door and then absorb the load pounding music that included 'Motherfuckers from Hell' when we were there.

East of Kuta

Bali Bakery (Map pp94-5; ☎ 755149; Jl Imam Bonjol; meals 20,000-60,000Rp; ⊗) A classic Western bakery, there are fresh baguettes and much more daily. The chocolates are terrific. It also has a small café with a good menu of salads, sandwiches and steaks.

LEGIAN

Legian has some good restaurants which have good views of the surf in its seaside hotels. Elsewhere there are scores of places with a huge range of menus and atmospheres. Several places on Jl Melasti don't aspire to anything more than luring in jet-lagged tourists. We found the better choices.

Papa's Café (Map pp94-5; ☎ 755055; Alam Kul Kul, Jl Pantai Kuta; dishes 28,000-90,000Rp) Partake of some chilled *limoncello* (lemon-flavoured) liqueur or gelato while taking in the ocean views at this breezy Italian café. Or dine on simple meals of focaccia, antipasto and pizza, or more elaborate pasta and seafood dishes.

Parasol Restaurant (Map pp94-5; ☎ 751381; Bali Mandira Hotel, Jl Pantai Kuta; dishes 40,000-90,000Rp) Overlooking the beach, the Parasol has a good menu of Italian classics; pass by during the day and you can smell the garlic being added to the night's specials. Be sure to call to reserve an outdoor table for dinner.

Yut'z (☎ 765047; Jl Pura Bagus 52; 30,000-70,000Rp) An upscale and modern version of a Swiss and European restaurant, Yut'z overlooks the street and a small garden. Fruhstuck fanatics can get their fix here. Later in the day, the menu has a changing selection of specials from the creative kitchen.

Gosha Bar & Restaurant (Map pp94-5; ☎ 759880; Jl Melasti; dishes 20,000-85,000Rp) The scent of

THE AUTHOR'S CHOICE

Indo-National (Map pp94-5; ☎ 759883; Jl Sa-hadewa 13d; dishes 20,000-90,000Rp) Kerry and Milton Turner could make a success of a restaurant anywhere they chose to open. Happily for Bali travellers they're in Legian. Opened at the end of 2002, the Indo-National doesn't do anything radical with its menu, but what they serve is top quality and the portions will restore one's strength after a hard day of having fun. Many of the dishes – there are nightly specials – are seafood and the mixed platter (45,000Rp) is a feast. The décor is nonexistent but the welcome is effusive and genuine, the hosts and staff remember you after one visit and after a week you can feel like a longtime regular. The pristine kitchen ensures you'll be back with a smile on your face.

barbequed shrimp wafts through the airy bamboo interior here, where the focus is on charcoal-grilled seafood.

Restaurant Puri Bali Indah (Map pp94-5; ☎ 751644; Jl Melasti; dishes 12,000-60,000Rp) A good Chinese choice, this place has a typically epic menu of 174 items, with plenty of seafood options.

Joni Bar Restaurant (Map pp94-5; ☎ 751182; Jl Padma; dishes 17,000-46,000Rp) There's a party atmosphere around the large swimming pool. Put on a breaststroke performance for passers-by. The Tex-Mex meals and evening happy hour (6pm-9pm) are popular. Balinese dance performances are also held on Monday and Friday at 7.30pm. There's live music other nights.

Wayan & Friends (Map pp94-5; ☎ 761024; Jl Padma; dishes 9000-40,000Rp) Wayan and his pals have a relaxed place with batik tablecloths and low lighting. It has delicious vegetable juices, and gourmet sandwiches made from freshly baked baguettes, which you can customise. And there's a kids' menu.

Restoran Enak Glory (Map pp94-5; ☎ 751091; Jl Legian 445; Balinese buffet adult/child 45,000/22,000Rp) A long-standing place that's worth heading to on a Saturday night to try a Balinese buffet. There's a good seafood menu other nights.

Poco Loco (Map pp94-5; ☎ 756079; Jl Padma Utara; dishes 25,000-50,000Rp; ☾ dinner) Look for the calming pools streetside at this popu-lar, brightly decorated Mexican restaurant and bar, serving tasty food – the Tex-Mex chicken is a good choice.

Swiss Restaurant (Map pp94-5; ☎ 761511; Jl Pura Bagus Taruna; dishes 15,000-56,000Rp) Swiss favour-ites have been served up here since 1977 (long enough in any case for the décor to morph into a jarring collage of Swiss and Balinese design). Indonesian dishes are also on offer. Got a passport problem? Ba-li's consular agents have a sing-along here every Sunday night.

Entertainment

Around 6pm, the sunset at the beach is the big attraction, perhaps while enjoy-ing a drink at a café with a sea view. After a good dinner, many visitors are happy with another drink (or two) and a stroll in the cooler evening air. But a lot of people are on holiday and here to party, and in Kuta that means lots of drinking, danc-ing and late nights. The more sophisti-cated nightspots are mainly in Seminyak, where the ambience is decidedly hipper, and where many clubs don't get going until after 11pm.

Watching DVD movies at a bar with a crowd is a Kuta tradition and you'll find scores of places in and around Poppies Gang II. Look for signs during the day or follow your ears at night. Just don't expect any-thing that *ever* won an award at Cannes.

BARS & CLUBS

Most bars are free to enter, and often have special drink promotions and 'happy hours' between about 5pm and 8pm. During the low season, when tourist numbers are down, you might have to visit quite a few venues to find one with any life. A cover charge is a rarity. Ambience ranges from the low-down vibe of the surfer dives to the high-concept nightclubs with their long drink menus and hordes of prowling servers.

The high-concept clubs of Seminyak are most popular with gays and lesbians but in general you can find a mixed crowd pretty much anywhere in Kuta.

Tuban

All Star Surf Café (Map p101; ☎ 757933; 2nd fl, Kuta Ctr, Jl Kartika Plaza; ☾ 7-1am) After the diners have left it gets pretty raucous. Cheap drinks

Surfboards for hire, Kuta Beach (p98)

JOHN BANAGAN

Museum Negeri Propinsi Bali (p81)

LEE FOSTER

JERRY ALEXANDER

Fresh produce, Denpasar market (p86)

Offerings on the beach, Seminyak (p112)

Wave breaking off the Bukit Peninsula (p127)

Sunbathing on Kuta Beach (p98)

abound and after a few you can try their version of 'sumo wrestling' which is with and for dummies. There's also live music many nights and an adjoining dance club.

Kuta

Apache Reggae Bar (Map pp94-5; ☎ 761212; Jl Legian 146; 🕙 11pm-3am) One of the rowdier spots in Kuta, Apache jams in locals and visitors, many of whom are on the make. The music is highly variable but the *arak* (colourless distilled palm wine) flows very freely (often in huge plastic jugs) and there's a good chance you won't remember what you heard anyway the next day. An adjoining hall called Apache Surfers Bar offers top 40 music in similar conditions.

Bounty (Map pp94-5; ☎ 752529; Jl Legian; 🕙 10pm-6am) Set on a faux sailing boat, the Bounty is a vast open-air disco. Climb the blue-lit staircase and get down on the poop deck to hip hop, techno, house and anything else the DJs come up with. The compliant staff seem untroubled by outfits last seen on Gopher and Julie on the *Love Boat*. Drink specials feature *arak* and lots of it. Frequent foam parties.

Tubes Surf Bar & Restaurant (Map pp94-5; Poppies Gang II; 🕙 10-2am) A cavernous place that's deserted during the day, but attracts an enthusiastic crowd in the evening. The music is commercial and a long way from the bad cover bands found elsewhere. A kiosk opens in the evening with info on surf lessons and trips. Surfing videos and pool tables offer an alternative accompany to drinking, which you should note will net you a free stubbie holder for every five beers you knock back.

Putu Suartha (Map pp94-5; ☎ 0812 396 0982; off Jl Legian; dishes 7,000-15,000Rp; 🕙 4-11pm) Run by a French architect and antique collector and his Balinese family, this little chill-out place down a *gang* has an eclectic collection of chairs, couches and curios. There's a vast pile of Eurotrash CDs and a tiny gleaming kitchen that turns out some spectacular *mei goreng* (fried noodles with meat or vegetables).

Oscar's Pub (Map pp94-5; ☎ 755674; Jl Benesari; 🕙 noon-11pm) A low-key pub that has good drinks and a couple of tables outside is perfect for watching the hordes head to the clubs.

Suci Bar & Restaurant (Map pp94-5; ☎ 751330; Jl Pantai Kuta; dishes 7000-25,000Rp, cocktails 23,000-28,000Rp) A good people-watching spot that has been around forever. It has an impressive bar list and cocktails.

Hard Rock Café (Map pp94-5; ☎ 755661; Jl Pantai Kuta; trademark burgers 56,000Rp; 🕙 11-2am Sun-Thu, 11-3am Fri & Sat) A merchandising outlet disguised as a nightclub, the sprawling Hard Rock fronts the beach and is a magnet for local yuppies. It gets going after 11pm, when a (usually) slick band plays classic rock covers. It's also a venue for occasional overseas artists such as Deviate from the Philippines.

Peanuts (Map pp94-5; ☎ 754226; cnr Jl Legian & Jl Melasti; 🕙 11pm-late) There's a hint of desperation about Peanuts, which attracts gigolos of all persuasions and their suiters. *Arak* and 'Jungle Juice' feature big time at this place. It has a big outer bar with pool tables and loud live rock or reggae, and a large dance floor inside.

Legian

Legend (Map pp94-5; ☎ 755376; Jl Sahadewa; 🕙 3-11pm) A popular spot in the heart of Legian, the Legend draws crowds nightly for shows that include Elvis impersonators, drag queens and live music playing everything from pop to country.

BALINESE DANCE & MUSIC

The Ubud area is really the place to go for authentic dance and you'll see offers in many hotels from tour operators. But note that you'll not get back to Kuta until after 10pm with most of these. Expect to pay around US$20 each.

You can find some dance shows aimed square at tourists in Tuban. The **Discovery Kartika Plaza Hotel** (Map p101; ☎ 751067; Jl Kartika Plaza) and the **Ramada Bintang Bali Resort** (Map p101; ☎ 753292; Jl Kartika Plaza) have performances most nights. You usually need to watch the dance as part of a buffet dinner.

Shopping

Parts of the Kuta region are door-to-door shops and over the years these have steadily become more sophisticated. But there are still many simple stalls, where T-shirts, souvenirs and beachwear are the main lines, and where the price depends on your bargaining ability. Many of these stalls are crowded together in 'art markets' like the one near the beach end of Jl Bakung Sari or the one on Jl Melasti. The Poppies are pretty well lined with little shops.

The bigger, Western-style stores generally have higher quality goods at higher fixed prices. Don't be pressured into buying things during the first few days of your stay – shop around for quality and price first. Jl Legian is lined with shops and although there are exceptions, the quality generally gets better as you head north to Seminyak. The area around Kuta Sq is filled with brand-name shops although the tout count here is high. Ignore them unless your idea of a good investment is a time share condo.

ARTS & CRAFTS

Kuta shops sell arts and crafts from almost every part of the island, from Mas woodcarvings to Kamasan paintings to Gianyar textiles, and just about everything else in between. There are also many interesting pieces from other parts of Indonesia, some of questionable authenticity and value. There's a good selection of quality craft shops on Jl Legian, between Poppies Gang II and Jl Padma.

Apolina Gallery (Map pp94-5; ☎ 751334; Jl Lebak Bene, Legian; ☼ 10am-6pm) An offbeat place worth heading to and is run by a half dozen local artists. The paintings of artist Wahyoe Wijaya are on display, as well as all manner of items good, bad and profane. They are happy for you to stop by for a coffee and chat although sometimes you may have to hunt somebody out back.

BEACHWEAR & SURF SHOPS

A huge range of surf shops sell big-name surf gear – including brands such as Mambo, RipCurl, Quicksilver and Billabong – although the quality may not be as good as you'll find overseas, and is only marginally cheaper. Local names include Surfer Girl and Dreamland.

RipCurl (Map pp94-5; ☎ 765035; Kuta Sq) If everything in your luggage is tired and you want to make a splash, you can't go wrong in this big store with a huge range of beach clothes, water wear and surfboards.

Surfer Girl (Map pp94-5; ☎ 752693; Jl Legian 138) The winsome logo says it all about this vast funhouse for girls of all ages. Clothes, undies, gear, bikinis, you name it.

CLOTHING

The local fashion industry has diversified from beach gear to sportswear to fashion clothing. Most of the fashion shops are on or near Jl Legian. Kuta Sq has the most sophisticated group of shops – some selling brand-name clothing such as Mooks and Stussy.

From the intersection of Jl Padma and Jl Legian, north to Seminyak, you'll find some of the more interesting women's (and men's) clothing shops (far removed from the teen-girl hype of Surfer Girl), as well as interesting homewares shops (often the two are combined).

Milo's (Map pp94-5; ☎ 754081; Kuta Sq Block E) Milo is a legendary local designer who arrived from Italy three decades ago and made his fortune desgining and producing fine silk batik clothes. His shop has his exquisite merchandise on display across three floors. If cost is an issue, you might want to settle for just a scarf (2,000,000Rp).

Uluwatu (Map pp94-5; ☎ 751933; Jl Legian) There are numerous locations across South Bali. This is one of the largest and is an elegant shop for browsing through the collections of lace-accented linen and cotton clothing. The styles are simple and few tables wouldn't stand out with a set of Uluwatu table linens. The items are made in villages around Tabanan in West Bali.

Komodo (Map pp94-5; ☎ 761147; Jl Legian 427, Legian) A licensed store for the well-known fun and funky UK-label. It carries other lines as well and prices are a fraction of those on a British High St.

DEPARTMENT STORES & MALLS

Matahari department store (Map pp94-5; ☎ 757588; Kuta Sq; ☼ 9.30am-10pm) This store has fairly staid clothing, a floor full of souvenirs, jewellery, a supermarket and the recommended Periplus bookshop. You can find pretty much anything you might need here, including decent quality luggage should you need extra bags to haul home your loot.

Bali Galleria (Map p93; ☎ 758875; Jl Ngurah Rai) A large open-air Western-style mall that is busy with locals and tourists alike. There's numerous large stores and plenty of shops with well-known names (Body Shop, Marks & Spencer etc). The Matahari supermarket is popular with expats and long-term visitors, and the duty-free emporium is big with the bus-tour set.

Kuta Galleria (Map pp94-5; Jl Patih Jelantik) An enormous new open-air mall that aspires to be something out of West Hollywood – if it can get a few tenants. Until then all that's lacking from the bleak atmosphere are a couple of tumbleweeds. (There is a hardware store in the rear if your needs run towards plungers or duct tape.)

FURNITURE

On Jl Patih Jelantik between Jl Legian and Jl Pura Puseh there are scores of furniture shops manufacturing everything from instant 'antiques' to wooden Indians. However, a few make and sell teak outdoor furniture of very high quality at very low prices. A luxurious deck chair goes for about 200,000 to 250,000Rp. Most of the stores work with freight agencies and you can get eight of these chairs sent to Australia for about US$135.

Getting There & Away

BEMO

Public *bemos* (small vans) regularly travel between Kuta and the Tegal terminal in Denpasar – the fare should be 4000Rp. Most 'S' bemos go only to the terminal area in Kuta (on Jl Raya Kuta just east of Bemo Corner).

If you can't get a public bemo in the tourist area (some drivers don't stop for tourists), go to the terminal area on the street east of Bemo Corner. Southbound bemos go through Tuban, detour past the airport entrance, then continue south to Jimbaran and east to Nusa Dua. Northbound bemos go to Tegal terminal in Denpasar, where you can get another bemo to the appropriate Denpasar terminal for any other destination on Bali.

BUS

Public Bus

Travel agents in Kuta sell bus tickets to Java and Lombok that depart from Ubung terminal in Denpasar; you'll have to get yourself to Ubung. The tickets will be slightly more expensive than if you buy them at Ubung, but it's worth it to avoid a trip into Ubung and to be sure of a seat when you want to go. For public buses to anywhere else on Bali you will have to go first to the appropriate terminal in Denpasar, and pay your money there.

Tourist Shuttle Bus

Shuttle bus tickets are sold at most travel agents – buy them a day ahead, or call the company and pay when you check in.

Perama (Map pp94-5; ☎ 751551; www.peramatour .com; Jl Legian 39; ⏰ 7am-10pm) is the main shuttle bus operation, and will sometimes pick you up from your hotel for free (confirm this when making arrangements). Perama usually has at least one bus a day to its destinations. In busy seasons, there will be three or more to popular spots like Ubud.

Destination	Fare
Candidasa	30,000Rp
Lovina	50,000Rp
Padangbai	30,000Rp
Sanur	10,000Rp
Ubud	20,000Rp

There are bus-ferry-bus services to destinations in Lombok, including Mataram and Senggigi Beach (70,000Rp).

CAR & MOTORCYCLE

There are many car- and motorcycle-rental places, so prices are very competitive.

Getting Around

The hardest part about getting around the Kuta area is the traffic. Storm drain installation played havoc in 2004 and beyond. In any case traffic can be awful in the afternoon and evening, and anytime the vital streets like Jl Legian are closed for religious processions. In these cases you may just want to take to the beach. Darn.

TO/FROM THE AIRPORT

A taxi from the airport costs 20,000Rp to Tuban, 25,000Rp to Kuta and 30,000Rp to Legian. From Kuta *to* the airport, get a metered taxi for around 14,000Rp.

BEMO

Dark-blue bemos do a loop from Bemo Corner along and up Jl Pantai Kuta, along Jl Melasti, then up Jl Legian for a short while before returning down Jl Legian to Bemo Corner (about 3000Rp around the loop). Drivers can be reluctant to stop for tourists and, in any case, bemos are infrequent in the afternoon and nonexistent in the evening.

BICYCLE

Cycling is a good way to get around as Kuta is pretty flat – you can go up the narrowest *gang*, park anywhere and even push your bike the wrong way up a one-way street (though technically this is illegal). To find a bicycle, ask at your hotel. A bike shouldn't cost more than 20,000Rp per day. Check the bike carefully, and make sure you get a lock and key.

CHARTER TRANSPORT

It's easy to find a vehicle to charter – just walk down Jl Legian and you will be assailed with offers of 'transport', and in case you don't understand, the driver will effusively gesticulate the motions of driving a car.

Negotiate the fare before you get on board. You should be able to get from the middle of Kuta to the middle of Legian for around 6000Rp, but bargain hard. In any case a meter taxi will cost the same – or beat the traffic and walk.

A full-day, eight-hour charter should run to between 150,000Rp and 200,000Rp, but more if it's nonstop driving over a long distance. You can estimate a price for shorter trips on a proportional basis, but you'll have to bargain. The 'first price' for transport can be truly outrageous. Chartered vehicles should cost about the same as an equivalent trip in a metered taxi.

TAXI

Plenty of taxis work the Kuta area. Most use their meters and are quite cheap – 4000Rp flagfall plus 1000Rp per kilometre. Taxis are indispensable for getting around town at night, and they can be hired for longer trips anywhere in southern Bali, and even as far as Ubud. As always, the blue taxis of **Bali Taxi** (☏ 701111) are far and away the best bet.

SEMINYAK

Seminyak is the most exciting part of South Bali. It's the home of the best restaurants, bars and clubs. In fact new ones literally open every week. There's 'Eat St' (Jl Oberoi) which has had about 36 places to eat open in two years, and 'Eat and Drink St' (Jl Dhyana Pura), which is lined with new clubs and restaurants, as well as all sorts of spots scattered near the beach along Jl Kaya Aya.

The shopping along Jl Raya Seminyak is excellent as well.

All this creative energy is yours to enjoy, possibly from the luxury of one of the world-class hotels found along the water. Although all this fun comes at a price, Seminyak is an exciting place where half the fun is just finding out what's new.

Orientation

The southern border of Seminyak runs along Jl Double Six. The only road along the beach is down here, it passes several notable clubs and restaurants. Jl Raya Seminyak is the continuation of Jl Legian from Kuta. Jl Oberoi heads west to the resort of same name and meets Jl Kaya Aya which passes most of the resorts on the land side. See Street Gang Worries (p92) for information on street names in the Kuta region.

Seminyak shares many services with Kuta and Legian to the south.

Information
BOOKSHOPS

Bintang Supermarket (☏ 730552; Jl Raya Seminyak 17) There's a similar selection at the newsstand at this supermarket.

Periplus (☏ 734843; Made's Warung II, Jl Raya Seminyak) Has the usual good selection of art books and periodicals.

INTERNET ACCESS

Most of the hotels have broadband connections for guests. Cheap and slow Internet shops can be found along the main streets including Jl Dhyana Pura and Jl Oberoi.

MEDICAL SERVICES

Tiger Pharmacy (☏ 732621; Jl Raya Seminyak 19; ☺ 24hr) Has a full range of prescription medications.

MONEY

ATMs can be found along all the main roads.

POST

Postal agency (☏ 730552; Jl Raya Seminyak 17, Bintang Supermarket)

Sights

North of the string of hotels on Jl Kaya Aya, **Pura Petitenget** is an important temple and a scene of many ceremonies. It is one of a string of sea temples that stretches from

Pura Luhur Ulu Watu on the Bukit Peninsula and north to Tanah Lot in western Bali. It honours the visit of the a 16th-century priest.

Activities

Because of the limited road access, the beach in Seminyak tends to be less crowded than further south in Kuta. This also means that it is less patrolled and the water conditions are less monitored. The odds of encountering dangerous riptides and other hazards are ever present especially as you head north.

SPAS

Spa (☎ 730622; Legian Hotel, Jl Kaya Aya; ⏰ 10am-9pm) in the Legian Hotel is suitably lavish and clients can avail themselves of various private spa suites set among gardens.

Sicilia Spa (☎ 736292; www.siciliaspa.com; Jl Double Six; ⏰ 9am-9pm) has a pleasant set-up of open-air massage and treatment rooms. A back and shoulder massage starts at 45,000Rp.

NT Health & Beauty Spa (☎ 732226; Jl Dhyana Pura 6B; ⏰ 9am-10pm) offers a variety of services from simple haircuts (85,000Rp) to two-hour long treatments featuring exfoliations and other pleasures (190,000Rp).

BUNGY JUMPING

AJ Hackett Bungy (☎ 731144; Jl Arjuna; US$50; ⏰ 10am-7pm daily, 2-4am Fri & Sat), beside the beach in Legian, has a great view of the coast which means you can't see the hideous tower you're standing on (or bouncing from). It's located in the Double Six Club, which explains the late-night hours.

Sleeping

Seminyak isn't just about top-end hotels. There's a good bunch of cheaper places at the south and they're close to the beach. But if you're looking for the best places to stay in Bali, you'll find several here, including the Legian and the Oberoi, both of which regularly feature on lists of the best hotels in the world. Seminyak is also home to many villas available for holiday rental (see p313).

BUDGET

Blue Ocean (☎ 730289; fax 730590; r 100,000-120,000Rp, with air-con 150,000Rp; ✗) Right near the beach, the Blue Ocean is a clean and basic place

with hot water and pleasant outdoor bathrooms. Ask them about a pool and they have a good answer. Pointing at the ocean they say, 'We have a big one over there.'

MID-RANGE

Hotel Kumala (☎ 732186; www.indo.com/hotels/kumala; Jl Pura Bagus Taruna; r US$36-45; ✗ ✗) An attractive place convenient to both Legian and Seminyak, the Kumala has large rooms with teak furniture, modern bathrooms, and two pools in a garden filled with bamboo stands, frangipani and bougainvillea.

Resor Seminyak (☎ 730814; www.resorseminyak.com; Jl Kaya Aya; r from US$70; ✗ ✗) The grounds are spacious at this 60-room resort which is good value at its low end of prices. There's two pools and the poolside bar is lively until 11pm. The beachfront restaurant is attractive.

Puri Naga Sea Side Cottages (☎ 730761; puri naga@indosat.net.id; Jl Double Six; r 250,000-350,000Rp; ✗ ✗) Right at the beach end of Jl Double Six, this place has a small pool and pleasant rooms, with nice balcony views and amenities like fridges.

THE AUTHOR'S CHOICE

Sofitel Seminyak Bali (☎ 730730; www.theroyal-seminyak.com; Jl Dhyana Pura; r from US$200, villas from US$500; ✗ ✗ ✗ ✗) Like the paths around its beautiful gardens, the Sofitel has had a long and winding road since it opened in the 1980s. It first was part of Tokyo's fabled Imperial Hotel, then it was an independent property known as the Royal Seminyak. Finally management was assumed by Sofitel and it was renamed again in 2004. The management change has been all for the good because the underlying qualities of the hotel are superb. Its beachside location is ideal and it is close enough to the best clubs and restaurants on Jl Dhyana Pura to walk but far enough to escape the noise. The rooms have been redone in a smart contemporary style and the restaurants revamped. What really sets the property apart are the private walled units. The feel is like an old Balinese village, and in units like 116 or 117 the private pools and other pleasures mean you may never want to leave.

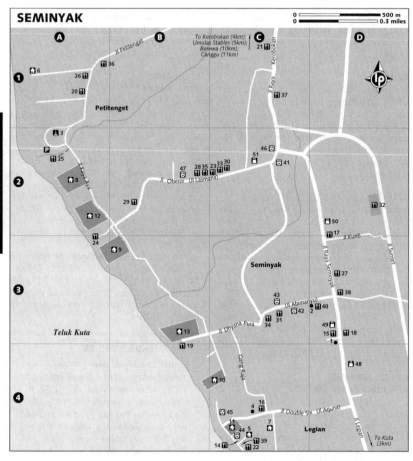

SEMINYAK

0 _____ 500 m
0 _____ 0.3 miles

TOP END

Oberoi (☎ 730361; www.oberoihotels.com; Jl Oberoi; r US$255-300, villas US$400-850; ✕ ✕ ☐ ✕) One of the world's top hotels, the Oberoi has been a refined beachside retreat since 1971. The architecture is understated, as is the service. But every detail is spot on, right down to the selection of fruit that graces your room. All accommodations here have private lanais and as you move up through the food chain additional features include private villas, ocean views and private, walled pools.

Legian (☎ 730622; www.ghmhotels.com; Jl Kaya Aya; ste from US$300, villa from US$600; ✕ ✕ ☐ ✕) The Legian is flashier than the Oberoi, with all rooms claiming to be suites, even if some

are just large rooms (called 'studios'). On a little bluff, the views are panoramic and the many personal services offered include the chance to enjoy gourmet dining at a table set up by the surf. Inside and out the design mixes traditional materials with contemporary flair.

Hotel Intan Bali (☎ 730777; www.intan-bali.com; r US$120-200; ✕ ✕) This once isolated four-star hotel is in a fast-growing part of Seminyak, but its beach still feels nearly private. The hotel has beautiful gardens, a spa, full sporting facilities and over 300 spacious rooms.

Pelangi Bali Hotel (☎ 730346; www.pelangibali .com; off Jl Dhyana Pura; r US$90; ✕ ✕) The beachfront access here is excellent but otherwise

SOUTH BALI

the site is cramped. Two blocks of decent and contemporary rooms dominate the space and even the pool feels cramped. If you can get a good discount, then consider this place.

Eating

Seminyak is spread out so you won't be walking among the many dining choices, rather you'll be choosing a neighbourhood first. Note that where indicated, some restaurants morph into clubs as the night wears on. Conversely some of the places listed under Bars & Clubs also do decent food. Think of it as fusion fun.

JL DOUBLE SIX

The places near the beach have a funky atmosphere and are more hip than similar joints in Kuta.

Benny's Café (☎ 731305; Jl Double Six; dishes 14,000-40,000Rp) With gorgeous ocean views and a comfortable, beach holiday atmosphere, Benny's is the classic beachside café. The menu has Indonesian and Western classics. The banana milkshakes are recommended.

Zanzibar (☎ 733529; Jl Double Six; dishes 20,000-45,000Rp) Sunset is prime time, but during the day you can enjoy the shade of the large trees overhead. The menu features vegetarian and pasta dishes with a dash of style. Breakfasts are good too.

Kafe Warna (☎ 737138; Jl Pantai Arjuna; dishes 11,000-40,000Rp; ☻ 11am-10pm) A shady, easy-going spot opposite the beach at the cusp of Legian and Seminyak, Kafe Warna offers Tex-Mex dishes as well as the usual

Indonesian suspects. The chicken fajitas are popular.

Café Lounge 69 (☎ 734610; Jl Double Six; dishes 15,000-35,000Rp; ☻ 9am-9pm) A coffee house with a vaguely Viennese feel (although these guys got the Austrians beat on the palm tree count), 69 has comfy seating for lounging with the piles of reading material. The menu includes sandwiches, organic salads, juices and more.

JL DHYANA PURA

Gado Gado (☎ 736966; Jl Dhyana Pura; mains 90,000-190,000Rp; ☻ lunch & dinner) This stylish place has a magical location on the beach. To the sounds of surf, enjoy the excellent service and the fine menu of Asian and Mediterranean fusion dishes like black sesame lobster tempura. Service is laid-back but professional. The bar is popular and refined.

Tu (☎ 734298; Jl Dhyana Pura 100; dishes 18,000-30,000Rp; ☻ food 7-11pm, bar 7pm-4am) This large club opens onto a huge patio. The real attraction here is the sublime and exquisitely presented cooking of Vietnamese chef Luu Bien Lan.

Santa Fe Bar & Grill (☎ 731147; Jl Dhyana Pura 11A; dishes 15,000-45,000Rp; ☻ 7-4am) The pizza and Southwest food here is popular and deservedly so. People can be found dining here at all hours, especially late when there's live music (mostly rock). Not surprisingly tequila is popular.

Zula Vegetarian Paradise (☎ 732723; Jl Dhyana Pura 5; dishes 15,000-40,000Rp; ☻ 8-4am) It's all vegetarian at this fun little place where you can get tofu cheese, a tofu spring roll, tofu cheesecake, not to mention a tofu-chick pea burger. The long list of juices includes the highly appropriate for Jl Dhyana Pura 'Liver Cleanser' special.

JL RAYA SEMINYAK

Café Moka (☎ 731424; Jl Raya Seminyak; dishes 15,000-40,000Rp; 🏠) Enjoy French-style baked goods at this fine bakery, which is popular for breakfast. Fresh deli cuisine like superb salads is served for lunch and dinner. The bulletin board is a window into the local expat community.

Warung Road Kill (☎ 736222; cnr Jl Raya Seminyak & Jl Dhyana Pura; meals 16,000Rp) Overlooking the busy intersection, the dubiously named warung serves spruced-up versions of traditional dishes (point and select from the display) at smart little tables.

Made's Warung II (☎ 732130; Jl Raya Seminyak; dishes 18,000-90,000Rp) This northern branch of the Kuta stand-by is set in an impressively designed courtyard area. The menu features well-prepared Indonesian- and Asian-style dishes, desserts and drinks. Seafood is a specialty. Shops line the periphery.

Deli (☎ 732893; Jl Raya Seminyak 22; lunches 10,000-17,000Rp) The deli counter is loaded with imported cheeses, meats and baked goods. At lunch you can get sandwiches and salads and eat them at the little tables out front.

Bintang Supermarket (☎ 730552; Jl Raya Seminyak 17) People in long-term accommodation like this ever-useful store. It's got a huge selection including tastes from home such as Tim Tams, as well as all manner of items from sundries to office gear.

JL OBEROI

Otherwise known as 'Eat St', the new name Jl Laksmana is catching on – although some use Lasmana.

La Lucciola (☎ 730838; Jl Oberoi; dishes 80,000-140,000Rp) A sleek beachside restaurant with good views across a lovely lawn and sand to the surf from the 2nd-floor tables. The bar downstairs is big with sunset watchers. The menu is modern Australian (a tasty melange of Mediterranean, Asian, seafood and more) and Italian (try the risotto).

Ku De Ta (☎ 736969; Jl Oberoi; dishes 140,000-200,000Rp; 🕒 7am-1pm) Restaurant? Bar? Way of life? Ku De Ta swarms with Bali's beautiful. Kids play in the stylish pool while adults ponder drinks in the cigar bar. Everyone ponders the gorgeous sunsets over the

beach. The menu is a creative fusion mix and the service is professional.

Paul's Place (☎ 736715; Jl Oberoi; dishes 40,000-80,000Rp; 🕒 9am-midnight) Part restaurant, part empire, Paul's place combines dining rooms, a spa, a clothing boutique and a housewares store in one complex bifurcated by a rice paddy. The menu encompasses Asian and grilled specialties. Service is tops and the wine list is long. It's all very chic.

Trattoria (☎ 737082; Jl Oberoi; mains 36,000-80,000Rp; 🕒 6pm-midnight) Dine on very authentic and very good Italian cuisine at tables inside or outside. The menu changes often but always features fresh pastas, grilled meats and seafood. Service is good and this place is highly recommended.

Rumours (☎ 738720; Jl Oberoi 100; mains 20,000-50,000Rp; 🕒 6pm-midnight) The arch-rival of Trattoria competes on price. The menu often features a really good tenderloin steak for a really cheap 25,000Rp. Other dishes range from salads to pasta to seafood. Drink prices are aggressive as well, Bintang 7000Rp! It's always crowded so be ready to wait.

Mykonos (☎ 733253; Jl Oberoi 52; dishes 15,000-45,000Rp; 🕒 5pm-midnight) The island food of Greece comes to the island of Bali at this wildly popular spot. All the classics are here from meze like tzatziki to various grilled souvlakis. Cheap wine fuels the fun.

Khaima (☎ 7423925; Jl Oberoi; dishes 40,000-65,000Rp; 🕒 lunch & dinner) Morocco comes to Bali at this romantic spot with an authentic kitchen. Tagines (stews cooked in an earthenware pot) are good as is the many forms of couscous. Kebabs are grilled over a fire. On weekends there's belly dancing by quick-study locals.

Tuesday Night Pizza Club (☎ 730614; Jl Oberoi; pizza 25,000-118,000Rp; 🕒 6pm-midnight) Pizzas come in four sizes at this simple joint and have a range of goofy names like Hawaii Five-O (ham and pineapple) and The Italian Job (mozzarella and tomato). And guess what? They deliver.

NORTHERN SEMINYAK

Waroeng Bonita (☎ 731918; Jl Petitenget; dishes 17,000-49,000Rp) Balinese dishes such as *ikan rica-rica* (fresh fish in a spicy green chilli sauce) are the specialties at this cute little place with tables under the trees.

Living Room (☎ 735735; Jl Petitenget; mains 80,000-100,000Rp; 🕒 11am-11pm) At night hundreds of candles twinkle on and about the scores of outdoor tables at this lacy fantasy of a restaurant. The menu is Asian with good Thai, Vietnamese and Balinese dishes.

Hu'u (☎ 736443; Jl Kaya Aya; mains 50,000-100,000Rp; ◷ 11-2am) Organic fusion fare is featured at this trendy place. There's steaks and seafood but also a good selection of vegetarian dishes. Local legend DJ Johny mixes jazz and house after 11pm weekends.

Seminyak Night Market (Jl Sunset) Gets going around 6pm and plenty of warung sell delicious *bakso* (meat balls) and *soto ayam* (chicken soup). Loud music plays and there's a real convivial atmosphere. Few travellers make it to the market's new location along Jl Sunset.

Warung Batavia (☎ 731641; Jl Raya Kerobokan; dishes 15,000-30,000Rp) This simple roadside place has a big choice of excellent, authentic Indonesian dishes.

Entertainment
BARS & CLUBS
Jl Double Six is named for the legendary club on the beach and this area remains a centre of 3am Kuta area club culture. Jl Dhyana Pura, however, has become the destination of choice for the trendy with what seems like a new place every week. Note that where indicated some of the places do good food in the evening while some of the places listed under Eating also do music.

Jl Double Six
The eponymous club is the big destination here. There's usually another raucous post-midnight club running just next door (although the name changes by the season).

Double Six Club (☎ 0812 462 7733; Jl Double Six; ◷ 1-6am) This veteran club got a massive upscale makeover in 2004 to better compete with the hot clubs on Jl Dhyana Pura. The swimming pool is still there, so's the bungy jump (save the crowd and *don't* have that extra drink before leaping into the void) and there's still top international DJs playing a hot mix of dance tunes. But now it's all done in a sleek open-air pavilion right out of *Wallpaper* magazine.

De Ja Vu (☎ 732777; Jl Double Six; ◷ 5pm-4am; ⚇) DJs are on duty from opening every night at this high-concept glass-fronted club with beachfront tables outside and frosty ones inside.

Jl Dhyana Pura
One of the joys of Jl Dhyana Pura is bouncing from place to place all night long. Many pure clubs snooze until after midnight.

Q-Bar (☎ 762361; Jl Dhyana Pura; ◷ 8pm-3am) This bright bar caters to gay clubbers but by no means exclusively. Rainbow lovers will rejoice; the music of choice is house. There's good views of the action – inside and out – from the upper floor.

Bali Globe (☎ 730328; Jl Dhyana Pura 9; ◷ 8pm-3am; ⚇) This two-level club is big on trance music. The upper level is good place to cool off and engage in running commentary on the clubbers passing by below.

Oxygen (☎ 730885; Jl Dhyana Pura; ◷ 9pm-4am) The glossy narrow bar downstairs is spare of colour and the staff outfits are spare of fabric. Upstairs DJs spin house and R&B.

Bush Telegraph Pub (☎ 732963; Jl Dhyana Pura 10XX; dishes 24,000-50,000Rp; ◷ 11-2am) The focus at this cavernous place is on sports television. This is the place to go if you'd rather, say, catch the latest in F1 action than find romance. You also can tuck into Australian steaks, hamburgers and general pub fare.

Jl Oberoi
Zappaz (☎ 7425534; Jl Oberoi; dishes 20,000-30,000Rp; ◷ 11am-midnight) Brit Norman Findlay tickles the ivories nightly at this great piano bar. What he lacks in talent he makes up for in his enthusiastic patter with the crowd. Happy hour is 6pm to 8pm. There's a short menu of café standards with some surprisingly good fried eggplant.

Aina Bar (☎ 730182; Jl Oberoi; ◷ 6pm-2am) Mellow rock is the music of choice at this intimate little open-fronted bar. Pull up a stool and chat up the bartender.

Warung Music (Jl Raya Kerobokan; ◷ music 10pm-2am) A cool spot for its varied line-up of nightly live music.

Shopping
In Seminyak, fashion shops are much more funkier than in Kuta. There are many interesting clothing stores on this stretch of Jl Raya Seminyak. North of Jl Dhyana Pura there are numerous shops selling artworks, housewares, furniture and other designer goods aimed at helping you create your own 'Bali Style'.

Designer's Corner (☎ 731658; Jl Raya Seminyak 29X) Has a collection of clothes from Jakarta designers. The most interesting collection is the menswear by Denny Kho; the other garments have their design base firmly rooted in Indonesian traditions.

CopyCat (☎ 735706; Jl Raya Seminyak 40) The place for trendy and comfortable casual women's cottons.

Randelli Gallery (Jl Raya Seminyak) Has works by contemporary Indonesian artists.

Salim Gallery (Jl Oberoi) A good-sized space which frequently has shows by noted local artists such as the luminous work of Martin Agam Sitepu.

Getting There & Around

Most transport information is the same as for Kuta. Metered taxis are easily hailed. A trip from the airport costs 35,000Rp, to the airport about half that. A taxi to the heart of Kuta will be about 8000Rp. You can beat the traffic and have a good stroll by walking the beach south. Legian is about 20 minutes.

NORTH OF SEMINYAK

☎ 0361

Even as Seminyak grows, the small towns to the north are growing as well. Kerobokan is where Seminyak was 10 years ago – on the cusp of major growth. Expats and land speculators are snatching up property here and in Canggu along the coast. Getting to most of the places listed is really only convenient with your own transport or by taxi. Think 20,000Rp or more from Kuta.

KEROBOKAN

Lots of interesting little places can be found here, a trend sure to continue. To get here from Kuta and points south, follow Jl Legian north, through its Jl Raya Seminyak phase until it becomes Jl Raya Kerobokan just north of Seminyak.

Umalas Stables (☎ 731402; www.balionhorse.com; Jl Lestari 9X), 5km north of Seminyak, has a stable of 30 horses and ponies, and offers one-hour rice field tours for US$30, and two-/three-hour beach rides for US$50/70. Lessons in beginner to advanced equestrian events such as dressage and showjumping can also be arranged.

For a romantic getaway, **Villa Seri** (☎ 730262; www.villaseri.com; Br Umalas Kauh; r US$55-65; ❋ ☒) is a great little hideaway. The rooms have

four-poster beds and lots of Indonesian touches, as well as spacious balcony areas, that come complete with TVs.

One of Bali's finest restaurants, **Kafe Warisan** (Map pp114-5; ☎ 731175; www.kafewarisan. com; Jl Raya Kerobokan; set dinner menus US$25-40; ❤ lunch & dinner) is in Kerobokan. The chef Nicolas Tourneville gives fine French cooking a Mediterranean flair. The tranquil setting looks out over rice paddies. The changing menu reflects what's in season locally (although the oysters – intrepid little fellas – fly in from France). For what you get it's very good value. This is where you come if you've got a hankering for a 3.2 million Rp bottle of French red.

Just past the jail off Jl Raya Kerobokan, **Warung Gossip** (☎ 0817 970 3209; Jl Pengubengan Kauh; meals 15,000-20,000Rp; ❤ lunch) quickly became wildly popular thanks to its top-notch versions of Balinese warung staples. Get a plate, tell the staff what you'd like and soon you'll be enjoying a fine lunch at one of the shady tables. The line-up of food changes daily. There's also a café area for more formal dining.

BEREWA

This greyish beach, secluded among stunning paddy fields, is 6km along the beach from Kuta (although by car it is closer to 15km). The turn-off is along the road heading west from Kerobokan. There are several decent cafés and warung in the village, about 200m from the beach.

Bolare Beach Bungalows (☎ 730258; www.bali -paradise.com/bolare; r US$48-68; ❋ ☒) has a great beachfront location, lush gardens and 20 renovated rooms, with open-air bathrooms. The hotel has a café and daily shuttle buses south to Kuta.

CANGGU

A popular surf spot with right- and left-hand breaks, Canggu is literally getting on the map. You'll spot quite a few satellite dishes poking above the rice paddies denoting the locations of lavish expat homes. Surfers congregate at beaches where various local roads hit the sand. There's usually a few unnamed warung a few metres from the beach. See p320 for details on these surf breaks.

Right at Canggu Beach, **Hotel Tugu Bali** (☎ 731701; www.tuguhotels.com; Jl Pantai Batu Bolong,

Desa Canggu; r US$300-550; ⚒ ☎) is a unique hotel backed by rice paddies. It blurs the boundaries between a museum and gallery, especially the Walter Spies and Le Mayeur Pavilions, where memorabilia from the artists' lives decorates the rooms. The stunning collection of antiques and artwork begins in the lobby and extends through the hotel. There's a spa and numerous customised dining options.

To get to Canggu, go west at Kerobokan and south at Kayutulang. Bemos leave from Gunung Agung terminal in Denpasar (4000Rp). Taxis from Kuta will run 30,000Rp or more.

BATU MEJAN

The next popular bit of beach northwest of Canggu Beach is Batu Mejan or Echo Beach. Besides the surfer's warung, there's the smart new **Beach House** (☎ 738471; Jl Pura Batu Mejan; dishes 5,000-40,000Rp), which faces the waves. It has a variety of couches and tables where you can hang out, watch the waves and enjoy the menu of breakfasts, sandwiches and salads.

SANUR

☎ 0361

Sanur is a slightly upmarket sea, sun and sand Bali holiday alternative to Kuta. The white-sand beach is sheltered by a reef. At low tide the beach is wide, but the water is shallow and you have to pick your way out over rocks and coral through knee-deep water. At high tide the swimming is fine, but the beach is narrow and almost nonexistent in places. At all times the reef is responsible for the greatest difference between Sanur and Kuta – the latter has surf for swimmers while the former doesn't. In fact the lethargic wave action at shore contributes to Sanur's nickname 'Snore'. Although this is also attributable to the area's status as a haven for expat retirees.

While not as frenetic as Kuta, Sanur is all about tourism. A walk on the delightful beachside walkway reveals plenty of vendors selling the same tat and brings you past numerous cafés. It's just calmer here, that's all. Offshore you'll see gnarled fishermen in woven bamboo hats standing in the shallows rod-fishing for a living and, at the northern end of the beach, elderly men convivially gather at sunrise and beyond for *meditasi* – swimming and baking in the black volcanic sand found only at that end of the beach.

Some parents prefer the beach at Sanur because its calmness makes it a good place for small children to play.

HISTORY

Inscriptions on a stone pillar found near modern Sanur tell of King Sri Kesari Varma, who came to Bali to teach Buddhism in AD 913.

Sanur was one of the places favoured by Westerners during their pre-war discovery of Bali. Artists Miguel Covarrubias, Adrien Jean Le Mayeur and Walter Spies, anthropologist Jane Belo and choreographer Katharane Mershon all spent time here. The first simple tourist bungalows appeared in Sanur in the 1940s and 1950s, and more artists, including Australian Donald Friend and Scotsman Ian Fairweather, made their homes in Sanur. This early popularity made Sanur a likely locale for Bali's first big tourist hotel, the Soekarno-era Inna Grand Bali Beach Hotel.

Over this period, Sanur was ruled by insightful priests and scholars, who recognised both the opportunities and the threats presented by the expanding tourism. Properly horrified at the high-rise Bali Beach Hotel, they imposed the famous rule that no building could be higher than a coconut palm. They also established village cooperatives that owned land and run tourist businesses, ensuring that a good share of the economic benefits remained in the community.

The priestly influence remains strong, and Sanur is one of the few communities still ruled by members of the Brahmana caste. It is known as a home of sorcerers and healers, and a centre for both black and white magic. The black-and-white chequered cloth known as *kain poleng*, which symbolises the balance of good and evil, is emblematic of Sanur.

ORIENTATION

Sanur stretches for about 5km along an east-facing coastline, with the lush and green landscaped grounds of resorts fronting right onto the sandy beach. The appalling Grand Bali Beach Hotel, located at the northern end of the strip, and fronts the best stretch of beach. West of the beach-front hotels is the noisy main drag, Jl Danau Tamblingan, with hotel entrances, oodles of tourist shops, restaurants and cafés.

Jl Ngurah Rai, commonly called Bypass Rd, skirts the western side of the resort area, and is the main link to Kuta and the airport.

INFORMATION
Bookshops
Other than a few used book exchanges in hotels which will allow you to complete your Danielle Steele collection, Sanur lacks a good bookshop.

Hardy's Supermarket (☎ 285806; Jl Danau Tamblingan 136; ⏰ 8am-10pm) Sells newspapers and magazines.

Emergency
Police station (☎ 288597; Bypass Rd)

Internet Access
Cyber cafés on Jl Danau Tamblingan can provide Internet access from about 400Rp to 500Rp per minute.

Sunshine Holiday (☎ 287376; Jl Danau Tamblingan 178; per min 400Rp; ⏰ 8am-10pm).

Medical Services
Dokter Paktek Umum (☎ 282678; Jl Danau Tamblingan 27) On call 24 hr and charges 100,000Rp per consultation.

Toko Bagus (☎ 286743; Jl Danau Tamblingan; ⏰ 10am-10pm) Doubles as a pharmacy and minimart.

Money
Moneychangers here have a dubious reputation. There are numerous ATMs along Jl Danau Tamblingan and several banks.

Post
There are convenient postal agencies on Jl Danau Tamblingan.

Post office (☎ 754012; Jl Danau Buyan; ⏰ 8am-7pm Mon-Sat) Located west of Jl Ngurah Rai.

Tourist Information
There's no tourist office in Sanur.

Mangrove Information Centre (Map p93; ☎ 726969; admission free; ⏰ 8am-4pm Mon-Thu, 8am-2pm Fri). West of Sanur are vast mangroves that stretch almost to Kuta. Learn about this vital yet abused

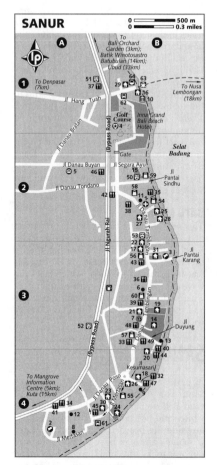

resource at the joint Indonesian-Japanese project. The centre studies ways to preserve the health of the mangroves which are vital to filtering much of the island's run-off. A 1.5km walk to the beach is sign-posted with information. Look for the signs 5km west of Sanur south of Bypass Rd.

Pusat Pendidikan Lingkungan Hidup (PPLH; ☎ 287314; www.pplhbali.or.id; Jl Danau Tamblingan 148) An environmental education centre working on sustainability issues, which has a small library. Money from the Hotel Santai (the home to PPLH) and the adjacent Café Tali Jiwa funds the centre (so eat up!).

SIGHTS
Museum Le Mayeur
The Belgian artist Adrien Jean Le Mayeur de Merpes (1880–1958) arrived in

SOUTH BALI

Bali in 1932. Three years later he met and married the beautiful Legong dancer Ni Polok when she was 15. They lived in this compound when Sanur was still a quiet fishing village. The main house must have been a delightful place then – a peaceful and elegant home filled with art and antiques right by the tranquil beach. After his death, Ni Polok lived in the house until she died in 1985. The house is an interesting example of Balinese-style architecture – notice the beautifully carved window shutters that recount the story of Rama and Sita from the Ramayana.

Some Le Mayeur paintings are displayed inside the **museum** (☎ 286201; adult/child 2000/1000Rp; ☼ 7.30am-3.30pm Sun-Thu, 7.30am-1pm Fri), with information in Indonesian and English. A free new guidebook in English is available and it is not only filled with useful information but has fantastic colour photos to boot. Some of Le Mayer's early works are interesting, Impressionist-style paintings from his travels in Africa, India, Italy, France and the South Pacific. Paintings from his early period on Bali are romantic depictions of Balinese daily life and beautiful Balinese women – often Ni Polok. The more recent works, from the 1950s, are in much better condition and show less signs of wear and tear, with the vibrant colours that later became popular with young Balinese artists. There are beautiful black-and-white photos of Ni Polok.

Bali Orchid Garden

Given Bali's weather and volcanic soil, no-one should be surprised that orchids grow very well. At this **garden** (Map p93; ☎ 466010; Jl Bypass Tohpati; admission US$5; ☼ 8am-6pm) you can see thousands of orchids in a variety of settings. Fans will love everything, others will enjoy the back areas which have a wild tropical feel. The gift shop sells orchid plants as well as books about the flowers. It's 3km north of Sanur along Jl Ngurah Rai just past the major intersection with the coast road, Jl Bypass Tohpati.

Stone Pillar

The pillar, behind Pura Belangjong, is Bali's oldest dated artefact and has ancient inscriptions recounting military victories of more than 1000 years ago. These inscriptions are in Sanskrit and are evidence of Hindu influence 300 years before the arrival of the Majapahit court.

ACTIVITIES
Surfing

Sanur's fickle breaks (tide conditions often don't produce waves) are off-shore along the reef. The best area is called **Sanur Reef**, a right break in front of the Inna Grand Bali Beach Hotel. Another good spot is known as the **Hyatt Reef**, in front of, you guessed it, the Bali Hyatt. However, this break is easily blown out, so only try this one on calm days. See p321 for details on these surf breaks.

Diving

The diving near Sanur is not great, but the reef has a good variety of fish and offers quite good snorkelling. Sanur is the best departure point for dive trips to Nusa Lembongan. A recommended local operator is **Global Aquatic Diving Center** (☎ 282434; www .globalaquatic.com; Jl Kesumasari No 9; local half-day trip €50), which is located right on the beach. Besides trips out to the Sanur Reef, which is known for its lion fish, Global can arrange trips throughout Bali.

Water Sports

Various water sports are offered at kiosks along the beach: close to Museum Le Mayeur; near Sanur Beach Market; and at **Surya Water Sports** (☎ 287956; Jl Duyung). Prices at all three places are similar, and are based on a minimum of two people. You can go parasailing (US$15 per go), jet-skiing (US$20, 15 minutes), water-skiing (US$20, 15 minutes), snorkelling by boat (US$25, two hours), windsurfing (US$25, one hour), or be towed on an inflatable banana (US$10, 15 minutes).

Three good surf breaks on the Sanur Reef need a big swell to work well, and they are only good in the wet season (October to March), when winds are offshore. Boats to Nusa Lembongan, another great surf spot, leave from the northern end of the beach.

Spas

Natural Spa (☎ 283677; Jl Danau Tamblingan 23; massage 400,000Rp; ☷ 9am-10pm) is a huge operation, which offers various massages, reflexology and body treatments, including an after-sun treatment.

SLEEPING

The best places are right on the beach, however, that doesn't mean they are any good. A few of the properties have been coasting for decades, while others offer wonderful experiences. Modest budgets will find fiscal succour on the non beach side of Jl Danau Tambligan, although overall Sanur is a top-end town.

In case you find yourself at the mercy of a travel agent, don't let them book you into either the Inna Grand Bali Beach Hotel or the Inna Sindhu Beach. Both are well past their prime.

Budget

Keke Homestay (☎ 287282; Jl Danau Tamblingan 96; s/d 60,000/75,000Rp) Set back a little from the noisy main road, Keke welcomes travellers with seven quiet, clean rooms. All have cold water and fans.

Watering Hole I (☎ 288289; wateringhole_sanur bali@yahoo.com; Jl Hang Tuah 37; r 60,000-125,000Rp, f 150,000Rp; ☷) In the northern part of Sanur, the Hole is a busy, friendly place, with 25 pleasant, clean rooms over a few storeys. The cheapest rooms have fan cooling; all have cold water only.

Watering Hole II (☎ 270545; wateringhole_ sanurbali@yahoo.com; Jl Mertasari; r 80,000-150,000Rp, f 200,000Rp; ☷ ☷) The southern branch of the Hole group has 14 rooms and a pool with a little waterfall. All rooms have hot water, the cheaper ones have fan cooling.

Jati Homestay (☎ 281730; www.balivision.com /hotels/jatihomestay; Jl Danau Tamblingan; r 150,000-200,000Rp) Situated in pretty grounds, Jati has 15 pleasant and clean rooms, with small but well-organised kitchen facilities and hot water.

Yulia 2 Homestay (☎ 287495; kf_billy@indo.net .id; Jl Danau Tamblingan; s/d 90,000/100,000Rp) Further south of Yulia 1 and on the beach side, Yulia 2 has seven clean, pleasant rooms in a somewhat cramped compound. All have hot water and fans.

Hotel Santai (☎ 287314; santai@indosat.net.id; Jl Danau Tamblingan 148; s/d 130,000/150,000Rp; ☷) The Santai has clean if somewhat dreary rooms facing a pool. But you can't argue with the price.

Mid-Range

Hotel Paneeda View (☎ 288425; www.paneedaview .com; Jl Danau Tamblingan 89; s/d US$40/45, bungalow US$60; ☷ ☷) Right on the beach, this hotel has three small pools and 55 rooms. Much attention to detail is devoted to the modern interiors, although none of the rooms have views, each has a patio. The Paneeda is good value.

Diwangkara Beach Hotel (☎ 288577; dhvbali@ indosat.net.id; Jl Hang Tuah 54; s/d from US$60/70; ☷ ☷) Facing the beach near the end of Jl Hang Tuah, this hotel is a tad old-fashioned (especially the pool), but the smaller bungalows are right by the beach.

Respati Bali (☎ 288427; brespati@indo.net.id; Jl Danau Tamblingan 33; s/d US$60/65; ☷ ☷) Despite its narrow site, the Respati's 16 contemporary bungalow-style rooms don't feel cramped. The beach frontage is a plus and the pool is decent-sized.

Tamu Kami Hotel Restaurant & Bar (☎ 282510; www.tamukami.com; Jl Danau Tamblingan 64X; r US$40-70; 🔀 🔄) There are 20 large, modern rooms and bungalows, finished with Indonesian touches, overlooking a swimming pool. The beach is a short walk.

Flashbacks (☎ 281682; www.flashbacks-chb.com; Jl Danau Tamblingan 106; r 120,000-135,000Rp; bungalows 250,000-320,000Rp; 🔀 🔄) With only six rooms, this is a lovely little place. The accommodation is inviting and has amenities such as satellite TV. The small pool is in a lush garden. The rooms share bathrooms.

Hotel Segara Agung (☎ 288446; www.segara agung.com; Jl Duyung 43; r/f US$20-35/50; 🔀 🔄) Down a quiet, unpaved residential street, the hotel is only a few minutes walk to the beach. The 17 rooms are clean and pleasant, staff are friendly and there's a big swimming pool.

Hotel Palm Gardens (☎ 287041; plmgrd@indosat .net.id; Jl Kesumasari 3; r/f US$60/$120; 🔀 🔄) Everything is peaceful here, from the 17 low-key rooms to the relaxed service. It's close to the beach and there is a nice medium-sized pool with a small waterfall.

Stana Puri Gopa Hotel (☎ 289948; www.puri gopabali.com; Jl Kesumasari 4; r US$30-45; 🔀 🔄) This 24-room hotel has traditional Balinese architecture, large bathrooms, and a small pool. It's a short walk to the beach, which you can see from some rooms.

Top End

Tandjung Sari (☎ 288441; www.tandjungsari.com; Jl Danau Tamblingan 29; bungalows US$150-265; 🔀 🔄) The mature trees along the shaded driveway set the gracious tone at this Sanur veteran which was one of the first Balinese bungalow hotels. Like a good tree it has flourished since its start in 1967; the 26 gorgeous traditional-style bungalows are superbly decorated with crafts and antiques. The staff is a delight. Highly recommended.

Bali Hyatt (☎ 281234; www.bali.resort.hyatt.com; Jl Danau Tamblingan; r US$90-350; 🔀 🔀 🔄 🔄) The gardens are an attraction themselves at this 390-room beachfront resort. Hibiscus, wild ginger, lotus and many more species can be found in profusion. Rooms are comfortable and the resort is regularly updated. Regency Club rooms come with free drinks

and food in a lovely pavilion. The two pools are vast, one has a waterfall-shrouded cave with what can best be described as a snogging nook.

Desa Segara (☎ 288407; segara1@denpasar.wasan tara.net.id; s/d US$65/75, bungalows US$130; 🔀 🔄) Two pools and beach access ensure fun at the Desa Segara. The 127 rooms come in a variety of flavours, from blocks to bungalows. At the bar, Le Pirate, you can debate the eternal question: What's a pirate always looking for even though it's right behind him? (Answer: his booty.)

Natah Bale Villas (☎ 287429; natah_balevilla@ yahoo.com; Jl Mertasari; villas US$110-210; 🔀 🔄) On a large stretch of land dotted with coconut palms, expect a modern, stylish fully furnished villa (there's five), including a versatile open-air kitchen. However, you have to walk to the beach.

Puri Santrian (☎ 288009; www.santrian.com; Jl Mertasari; r/f US$125-200/250-325; 🔀 🔄) Lush gardens, three good pools, a tennis court and beach frontage, as well as 184 comfortable, well-equipped rooms make this a good choice. Many rooms are in older-style bungalows.

EATING

There's great eating in Sanur at every budget level. Cheap warung and street food carts can be found around the Pasar Sindhu night market, at the beach end of Jl Segara Ayu, and along Jl Danau Poso, at the southern end of Sanur, beyond the resort area.

Jl Ngurah Rai

West of the main Sanur strip, the fast-moving bypass road Jl Ngurah Rai is ignored by most tourists, but several places are patronised by those in the know.

Kafe Wayang (☎ 287591; Komplek Sanur 12; dishes 25,000-70,000Rp; 🔀) Popular with expats and affluent locals. Traffic noise is blocked out in the cool interior, and menu offerings include sandwiches, pasta and contemporary Asian fare. A kids' menu is available. Live music gigs are held regularly.

Splash Bakery (☎ 288186; Jl Ngurah Rai; 🕙 8am-8pm) Makes a good selection of bread, cakes, pastries and pies. It has a small eat-in area.

Pala (☎ 283835; Jl Ngurah Rai 121; dishes 20,000-40,000Rp; 🕙 lunch & dinner Mon-Sat; 🔀) Its name means nutmeg and this refined spot exudes the same sort of careful taste. Retro French dishes are joined by creative versions of Indonesian classics. The wine list is lengthy.

Northern Sanur

There are numerous little cafés and warungs down by the beach.

Watering Hole (Agung & Sue) Restaurant (☎ 288289; Jl Hang Tuah; dishes 10,000-40,000Rp) Popular for Chinese, Indonesian and Western meals that are served at decent prices. This is a good traveller's hang-out at this end of town.

Kalimantan (☎ 289291; Jl Pantai Sindhu 11; dishes 15,000-55,000Rp) This relaxed place has a nice palm-tree shaded expanse with lots of tables where you can relax with one of the cheap drinks. The menu has Mexican and Indonesian classics and steaks.

Beach

The beach path offers restaurants, warung and bars where you can catch a meal, a drink or a sea breeze. There are several places near the end of each road that ends at the beach.

Benno's Corner Café (dishes 20,000-30,000Rp) Looks over the water and is good for snacks and drinks. Many places have sunset drinks specials (though the beach faces east, so you'll need to enjoy the reflected glow off Nuda Penida).

New Banjar Club (☎ 287359; near Jl Duyung; dishes 20,000-40,000Rp) A nice beachfront restaurant, look for a typical menu of pizza, pasta and Indo classics.

Sanur Bay (☎ 288153; Jl Duyung; 25,000-40,000Rp) Tables right on the sand allow for great views at this classic beachside seafood grill.

Stiff Chili (Jl Kesumasari; dishes 8,000-20,000Rp) Besides the evocative name, this beach side hut features good sandwiches and gelato.

Jl Danau Tamblingan

Telaga Naga (☎ 281234; Jl Danau Tamblingan 180; dishes 25,000-100,000Rp; ☺ dinner) Torches light the pathway to this jewel-like restaurant where bright red lanterns glow over the tables. Offerings on the Chinese Szechwan menu are gourmand, such as *abalone masak jamur hitan* (abalone with black mushrooms). Recommended.

Lotus Pond Restaurant (☎ 289398; Jl Danau Tamblingan 30; dishes 35,000-105,000Rp) The Sanur branch of the Lotus empire is in a high-thatched building surrounded by lotus ponds (of course). It serves pastas, wood-fired oven pizzas, seafood and Indonesian dishes. There's children's dancing and Legong (classic Balinese dance) some nights.

Alise's Restaurant (☎ 282510; Tamu Kami Hotel, Jl Danau Tamblingan 64X; dishes 20,000-60,000Rp; ☺ 7.30-10pm Sun, Tue, Thu & Fri) Alise's has a romantic, lantern-lit outdoor dining area by the pool and serves excellent European, Indonesian and Japanese dishes and delicious pasta. Good local musicians perform Balinese and Western music.

Village (☎ 285025; Jl Danau Tamblingan 66; dishes 25,000-55,000Rp; ☺ lunch & dinner) This airy and romantic Italian restaurant serves wood-fired oven pizzas as well as delicious pastas. There's real risotto as well.

Randy's Café Bar & Restaurant (☎ 288962; Jl Danau Tamblingan 17; dishes 12,000-30,000Rp) Randy's hypes its Canadian theme although the 'Canadian' items on the menu, like chicken fingers, will dishearten Cannuck gourmets. On offer are good sandwiches, veggie burgers and chocolate brownies with ice cream.

Retro Café & Gallery (☎ 282472; Jl Danau Tamblingan 126; dishes 25,000-45,000Rp) There's a relaxed back section here, well away from the traffic noise, with walls filled with paintings. The menu has all the classics.

Lumut (☎ 270009; Jl Danau Tamblingan; dishes 15,000-55,000Rp; ☺ 10am-10pm) This gracious 2nd-floor café is set back from the road. The menu has the usuals but the emphasis is on the fresh seafood. It's also good for a coffee or juice during the day.

Café Tali Jiwa (☎ 287314; Jl Danau Tamblingan 148; dishes 10,000-32,000Rp) In front of Hotel Santai, this wholesome place has an appetising choice of dishes, from icy smoothies to filling chickpea veggie burgers. Many of the ingredients are organic and the bread is properly brown and whole grains.

Apakabar (☎ 286365; Jl Danau Tamblingan 190; dishes 20,000-100,000Rp; ☺ lunch & dinner) The name at this place means 'how are you?' and you'll answer 'just fine' after one of their signature grilled seafood platters for two, which come loaded with lobster and other treats.

Café Batu Jimbar (☎ 287374; Jl Danau Tamblingan 152; dishes 25,000-35,000Rp) This local expat

RICHARD I'ANSON

TIM ROCK

Tropical red-ginger plant (p67)

Boats on Sanur Beach (p119)

Decorated boats, Jimbaran Bay (p127)

JAMES LYON

Selling sarongs on Kuta Beach (p98)

BERNARD NAPTHINE

RICHARD I'ANS

Beach bungalows on Sanur Beach (p119)

RICHARD I'ANS

Sunset bike ride along Kuta Beach (p98)

Beach restaurants at sunset, Jimbaran (p127)

ANDREW LUBRAN

meeting place (one of many) is sheltered by shady palm trees from the constant motorbike cacophony of the main drag. It serves fresh juices, soups, home-made pastas, curries and fresh-baked goods. The coffee is tops.

Billy's Kafe (☎ 287495; Yulia 2 Homestay, Jl Danau Tamblingan; dishes 8000-20,000Rp) Billy's is a nice place for a cheap breakfast. It also has sandwiches, but offerings are mostly simple Indonesian tastes, such as *soto ayam*.

For groceries and personal items, there's a good **Hardy's Supermarket** (☎ 285806; Jl Danau Tamblingan 136; ☺ 8am-10pm), which has all manner of local and imported food items and periodicals. There's also a typically cheerful **Circle K** (Jl Danau Tamblingan; ☺ 24hr). The **Pasar Sindhu night market** (off Jl Danau Tamblingan; ☺ 6am-midnight) sells fresh vegetables, dried fish, pungent spices and various household goods.

South Sanur
Abian Boga (☎ 287174; Jl Kesumasari 5; set menus 80,000-100,000Rp; ☺ dinner) This cavernous place with dowdy furniture is redeemed by its nightly Legong performances at 8.30pm. The menu is predominantly Chinese, with a few Western and Indonesian dishes thrown in.

Sari Laut (☎ 289151; dishes 12,500-25,000Rp) Among a cluster of warungs by the bemo stop offer cheap dining. Sari Laut is always full of locals.

Cat & Fiddle (☎ 270572; Jl Mertasari 2; dishes 25,000-50,000Rp; ☺ 11am-11pm) Owner Mark Wilson's background is in Blackpool catering, so Brits will get a taste of Blighty with the fish and chips here. This smallish place is an expat hang-out and is also home to the British Consulate (have a pint while you ponder your passport needs).

Bali International Cricket Club (☎ 270728; Jl Danau Poso 63; dishes 15,000-40,000Rp) The lawn here is suitably green and weed-free. The menu covers staples such as eggs and baked beans, and sausages and mash.

ENTERTAINMENT
Bars & Clubs
Many of Sanur's drinking establishments cater to retired expats and are thankfully air-conditioned. Several serve food. For a real Sanur experience, have a drink at one of the many little beach side bars (really just a few chairs and a cooler of drinks) that can

be found along the promenade. One nice spot, near the Hyatt, almost puts you right at the surf.

Bali International Sports Bar (☎ 288375; Jl Pantai Sindhu 13) Sports fans coming here will enjoy international sporting events, especially football and rugby, on a big screen TV.

Jazz Bar & Grille (☎ 285892; Komplek Sanur 15, Jl Ngurah Rai; dishes 35,000-75,000Rp; ☺ 10-2am; ☒) There's live jazz from Sunday to Thursday and pop on Friday and Saturday. The international menu features Mexican and Mediterranean dishes.

Kafe Wayang (☎ 287591; Komplek Sanur 12, Jl Ngurah Rai; ☒) There's Latin fusion on Friday and Saturday from 9pm. Bar snacks are available.

Koki Pub (☎ 287503; Jl Ngurah Rai 9; dishes 28,000-50,000Rp; ☺ 11-2.30am; ☒) Dark windows screen out the sun and mean that once inside, you could be in a pub anywhere. Expect to find pool tables, televised sporting events, beefy types at the bar, and a menu focusing on German cuisine and Foster's on tap.

Speakezy's (☎ 288825; Jl Danau Tamblingan 94; ☺ 4pm-1am) One of the few true bars on the strip, this place has a cheesy theme, lots of drink specials and cheap beer.

Balinese Dance & Music
Fortunately, Ubud is less than an hour up the road and you can easily catch a performance up there.

Bali Hyatt (☎ 281234; www.bali.resort.hyatt.com; Jl Danau Tamblingan) Has Balinese dance performances, often coupled with lavish buffet dinners.

Among restaurants worth checking for performances, try **Lotus Pond Restaurant** (☎ 289398; Jl Danau Tamblingan 30) and **Abian Boga** (☎ 287174; Jl Kesumasari 5).

SHOPPING
Arts & Crafts
Sanur is in easy reach of much of the good arts and crafts shopping around Ubud. Locally, there are several painting studio shops, with a wide selection of paintings on offer, on the main street and also around Jl Pantai Sindhu. Batik cloth is also easy to find and Sanur has a plenty of tailors on the main strip if you want something special made up.

Batik Winotosastro (☎ 462069; Jl Ngurah Rai 96, Tohpati) A huge place that stocks hand-wax processed batik fabrics and clothes, sourced from Gianyar.

Rare Angon (☎ 288962; Jl Danau Tamblingan 17) A gallery with works from 12 local artists. Many are often working right in the shop.

Clothing & Homewares

Meidy (☎ 282572; Jl Danau Tamblingan) A great little fashion shop stocked to the brim with very feminine funky gear.

Mama Leon (☎ 288044; Jl Danau Tamblingan 99A) An upmarket women's fashion shop specialising in cool, classic cuts and colours, where many of the designs feature embroidery.

Putih Pino (☎ 287889; Jl Danau Tamblingan) For homewares try Putih Pino that sells a range of natural textiles and knick-knacks in an inviting setting.

Sari Bumi (☎ 284101; Jl Danau Tamblingan 152) A range of ceramic homewares on sale from Jengalla Keramics in Jimbaran.

Souvenirs

For souvenirs, try the numerous shops on the main street, or one of the various 'art markets'. **Sanur Beach Market** (off Jl Segara Ayu) has a wide selection. **Pasar Sindhu Art Market** (off Jl Danau Tamblingan), the maze-like **Beach Market** (south of Jl Pantai Sindhu) and **Jaya Kesuma Art Market** (Jl Mertasani) have numerous stalls selling T-shirts, sarongs, woodcarvings and other dubious items.

GETTING THERE & AWAY
Bemo

The public bemo stops are at the southern end of Sanur on Jl Mertasari, and just outside the main entrance to the Inna Grand Bali Beach Hotel on Jl Hang Tuah. You can hail a bemo anywhere along Jl Danau Tamblingan and Jl Danau Poso.

Green bemos go along Jl Hang Tuah and up Jl Hayam Wuruk to the Kereneng terminal in Denpasar (4000Rp).

Boat

Public boats to Nusa Lembongan leave from the northern end of Sanur beach at 7.45am (35,000Rp, 1½ to two hours). This is the boat used by locals and you may have to share space with a chicken. The Perama tourist boat (more reliable) leaves at 10.30am (50,000Rp).

From Nusa Lembongan to Sanur, public boats leave Jungutbatu beach at 7.45am. The Perama boat to Sanur leaves at 8.30am and connects with a through service to Kuta (70,000Rp) and Ubud (75,000Rp).

For details about various other boats to Nusa Lembogan, see p212.

Tourist Shuttle Bus

The **Perama office** (☎ 285592, Jl Hang Tuah 39; ☺ 7am-10pm) is at Warung Pojok at the northern end of town. It runs shuttles to the following destinations, most only once daily.

Destination	Fare
Candidasa	30,000Rp
Kuta	10,000Rp
Lovina	50,000Rp
Padangbai	30,000Rp
Ubud	15,000Rp

GETTING AROUND

A prepaid taxi from the airport to Sanur costs 55,000Rp. Going to the airport from Sanur, a metered taxi will cost about half. Bemos go up and down Jl Danau Tamblingan and Jl Danau Poso for 2000Rp.

Sunshine Holiday (☎ 287376; Jl Danau Tamblingan 178; per day 25,000Rp; ☺ 8am-10pm) rents bicycles. Agencies along Jl Danau Tamblingan in Sanur rent cars and motorcycles. Almost every hotel can make recommendations.

Metered taxis can be flagged down in the street, or call **Bali Taxi** (☎ 701111).

SOUTH OF SANUR

PULAU SERANGAN

Only about 250m offshore, south of Sanur, Pulau Serangan (Turtle Island) is connected to the mainland by a causeway and bridge. This link, and a large area of landfill on the eastern and southern sides of the island, were part of a massive, abortive development project associated with Soeharto's infamous son Tommy. The earthworks obliterated the island's sandy beaches and other features. The island was named for the turtles that used to lay eggs here, but no beach means no turtles.

The island has two villages, Ponjok and Dukuh, and an important temple, **Pura**

Sakenan, just east of the causeway. Architecturally, the temple is insignificant, but it's one of the holiest on Bali, and major festivals attract huge crowds of devotees, especially during the Kuningan festival.

The only other reason to come here is for the irregular **surf break** at the southern end of the landfill area, where a row of warung has appeared to provide food, drinks and souvenirs (see p321 for details on surfing). The wide, unsealed road to the island branches off Jl Ngurah Rai just east of the Benoa Harbour turn-off – a booth at the end of the causeway collects a 1000Rp fee.

BENOA HARBOUR
Bali's main port is at the entrance of Teluk Benoa (Benoa Bay), the wide but shallow bay east of the airport runway. Benoa Harbour is on the northern side of the bay – a square of docks and port buildings on reclaimed land, linked to mainland Bali by a 2km causeway. It's referred to as Benoa port or Benoa Harbour to distinguish it from Benoa village, on the southern side of the bay.

Benoa Harbour is the port for tourist day-trip boats to Nusa Lembongan and for Pelni ships to other parts of Indonesia.

Visitors must pay a toll to go on the causeway (1000Rp per vehicle). Public bemos (5000Rp) leave from Sanglah terminal in Denpasar. A taxi from Kuta or Sanur should cost around 15,000Rp one way, plus the toll.

For more information on cruises to Nusa Lembongan from Benoa Harbour see p212.

BUKIT PENINSULA

☎ 0361
The southern peninsula is known as Bukit (*bukit* means 'hill' in Indonesian), but was known to the Dutch as Taffelhoek (Table Point). Once a reserve for royal hunting parties, and a place of banishment for undesirables, the Bukit Peninsula was sparsely inhabited. Its only significant site was Pura Luhur Ulu Watu, the spectacular 'sea temple' at the southwestern tip of the peninsula.

Over the last few decades, a university campus and a cement industry have been established, as well as hotel developments around Jimbaran, Tajung Benoa and the luxury tourist enclave at Nusa Dua. The western and southern coasts are magnificent, and have some lovely, isolated beaches and great surf (for details about Bukit Peninsula surf breaks, see p322).

JIMBARAN
South of Kuta and the airport, Teluk Jimbaran (Jimbaran Bay) is a superb crescent of white sand and blue sea, fronted by a long string of seafood warung, and ending at the southern end in a bushy headland, home to the Four Seasons Resort. The sunset towering over the horizon is what brings travellers to Jimbaran to feast on seafood grilled over coconut husks, fresh from the local fishing fleet.

Facilities are very limited. Jl Raya Uluwatu has a couple of small markets for supplies like water but for most things you will need to head to Kuta or Nusa Dua.

Sights & Activities
The temple, **Pura Ulun Siwi**, dates from the 18th century. The **Ganeesha Gallery** at the Four Seasons Resort has exhibitions by international artists and is worth a visit. You can reach it by walking south along the beach.

The **fish market** is well worth an early morning exploration, as it is one of the best in Bali.

Jimbaran is a good place to access the surf breaks off the airport. See p320 for details.

Sleeping
The Jimbaran area is home to South Bali's most luxurious resorts, as well as more modest accommodation.

BUDGET
Jimbaran Ocean Cottages (☎ 702253; info@kirakira -stay.com; Jl Pantai Jimbaran 3; r 150,000Rp, with air-con 200,000-250,000Rp; 🔀) Things are pretty tight here but you cannot beat the site across from the beach. All rooms have hot water and there is a nice café on the 2nd-floor with good views. Ask for weekly rates of US$100.

Villa Batu (☎ 703186; Jl Pemelisan Agung 21A; r 120,000-180,000Rp) Behind Café Layar, this simple place has small rooms with open-air cold-water bathrooms, but it's in a good spot.

SOUTH BALI

MID-RANGE

Udayana Eco Lodge (☎ 261204; www.ecolodges
indonesia.com; s/d US$45/50; ⚒ ⚏) Near Uday-
ana University, this lodge has grand views
over South Bali from its perch on a knoll in
70 hectares of bushland. The 15 rooms are
comfortable and there is an inviting common area with a fine library. Guests enjoy
services like free laundry.

Hotel Puri Bambu (☎ 701377; www.puribambu
.com; r US$55-90; ⚒ ⚏) This hotel is 200m
from the beach. It has rooms in three-storey
blocks around a pool; it also has character
and friendly staff.

TOP END

Four Seasons Resort (☎ 701010; www.fourseasons
.com; villas with/without ocean views US$675/575;
⚒ ⚒ ▣ ⚏) The fun begins in the lobby
with its view along the coast from the high
vantage point on a hillside. The 147 villas are designed in a traditional Balinese
manner complete with a carved entrance-
way, which opens onto an open-air dining
pavilion overlooking a plunge pool. The spa
is open to guests only.

Ritz Carlton (Map p93; ☎ 702222; www.ritzcarlton
.com; r US$270-400, villas US$310-750; ⚒ ⚒ ▣ ⚏)
The opulence here is hidden in vast private grounds and compound overlooking
the sea. Rooms are large but do not have
the intimate feel of the Four Seasons. With
290 rooms and 48 villas, this is the place for
people who want a large and lavish resort
setting. The Ritz maintains its own gorgeous beach.

Hotel Intercontinental Bali (☎ 701888; www
.bali.intercontinental.com; r US$240-260; ⚒ ⚒ ▣ ⚏)
With 425 rooms, the Intercontinental is a
vast place, but it's beautifully decorated
with fine Balinese arts and handicrafts.
The plethora of pools feed each other and
wander through the grounds. There is a
good kids' club and the crescent of beach
is tops.

Villa Balquisse (☎ 701695; www.balquisse.com; Jl
Ulu Watu 18X; r from US$90; ⚒ ⚏) An interna-
tionally lauded inn, this is a charming and
intimate little hideaway. Each light-filled
room has a four-poster bed, high bamboo
ceilings, an open-air bathroom and a small
outdoor lounging area. A relaxed open-air
living room sits at one end of the pool.

Pansea Puri Bali (☎ 701605; www.pansea.com; Jl
Yoga Perkanti; cottages US$199-235; ⚒ ⚏) Set on

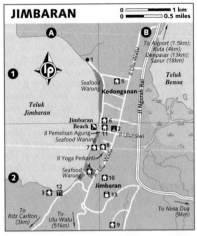

JIMBARAN

0 ———— 1 km
0 ———— 0.5 miles

To Airport (1.5km);
Kuta (4km);
Denpasar (13km);
Sanur (18km)

Teluk
Benoa

Seafood
Warung Kedongonan

Teluk
Jimbaran

Jimbaran
Beach
Jl Pemelisan Agung 11 Jl Ulunswi
Seafood Warung

Jl Yoga Perkanti

Seafood
Warung

Jimbaran

To Nusa Dua
(9km)

To
Ritz Carlton
(3km) To
Ulu Watu
(51km)

SIGHTS & ACTIVITIES	(p127)
Fish Market...	1 A1
Ganeesha Gallery................................	(see 3)
Pura Ulun Siwi.....................................	2 B2

SLEEPING	(pp127–8)
Four Seasons Resort............................	3 A2
Hotel Intercontinental Bali................	4 A2
Hotel Puri Bambu................................	5 B1
Jimbaran Ocean Cottages..................	6 B1
Pansea Puri Bali...................................	7 A2
Puri Kosala..	8 B2
Udayana Eco Lodge.............................	9 B2
Villa Balquisse....................................	10 B2
Villa Batu..	11 B2

EATING	(pp128–9)
PJ's..	12 A2

SHOPPING	(p129)
Janggala Keramik Bali.........................	13 B2

nice grounds complete with a figure-eight
pool that looks on to open ocean, cottages
here have private gardens, deeply shaded
patios and stylish room design.

Puri Kosala (☎ 701673; www.purikosala.com; Jl Yoga
Perkanti 2; villas US$140-180; ⚒ ⚏) With only six
comfortable cottages, this secluded resort
makes for a good getaway. It's close to the
beach and has a large pool.

Eating

The destination of many Kuta-area tourists, are Jimbaran's three groups of seafood warung do fresh barbecued seafood
every evening (and many are also open for
lunch). The simple open-sided shacks are
right by the beach and perfect for enjoying sea breezes and sunsets. Tables and
chairs are set up on the sand almost to the
water's edge. The usual deal is to select your

seafood fresh from an ice bucket and pay according to weight. Per 100g, expect to pay around 25,000Rp for live lobster, 13,000Rp to 20,000Rp for prawns, and 5000Rp for fish, squid and clams. Prices are open to negotiation and the accuracy of the scales is a joke among locals. However, the best places can combine garlic and lime marinade with a chilli and oil dousing during grilling for fabulous results.

The longest row of restaurants is at the northern end of the beach, south of the fish market. This is the area where you will be taken by a taxi if you don't otherwise specify. The middle area, however, is a better choice and is just south of Jl Penelisan Agung. The atmosphere is more relaxed and the operators less avaricious. The southernmost group beside Hotel International Bali is quietest and the least swamped by night-time hordes.

PJ's (☎ 701010; dishes 100,000-180,000Rp) In the Four Seasons this is the stand-out among the resort restaurants and bars. In an enviable position, PJ's smart open-air dining pavilion overlooks the beach, and is known for its Californian and Mexican dishes.

Shopping
Jenggala Keramik Bali (☎ 703310; Jl Uluwatu II; ☻ 9am-6pm) A modern warehouse with aircon showcasing slick and pricey homeware ceramics and a smattering of hand-painted pieces by local artists. There's also a viewing area where you can watch ceramic production. Ceramic courses are available for adults and children (US$10/50 for one/six sessions). There is also a pleasant café.

Getting There & Away
Public bemos from Tegal terminal in Denpasar go via Kuta to Jimbaran (7000Rp), and continue to Nusa Dua. They don't run after about 4pm, but plenty of taxis wait around the beachfront warung in the evening to take replete diners back to Kuta (about 20,000Rp), Sanur or wherever. However, at other times you – or your hotel – will need to call a cab.

CENTRAL BUKIT
Jl Ulu Watu goes south of Jimbaran, climbing 200m up the hill for which the peninsula is named, affording fine views back over the airport and southern Bali.

For years the only tourist facilities on the west coast of the Bukit were a few warung at the surf breaks, but in the late 1990s speculation ran rampant. A huge real-estate development, Bali Pecatu Indah, went bankrupt, leaving an imposing road network in empty fields, and making part of the coast almost inaccessible (the road network doesn't reach the coast). But one of the most grandiose tourist attractions ever conceived for Bali is still going ahead.

Sights
The centrepiece of **Garuda Wisnu Kencana Cultural Park** (GWK; ☎ 703603; admission 15,000Rp, parking 5000Rp; ☻ 8am-10pm) is the yet to be completed 66m-high statue of Garuda, to be erected on top of a shopping and gallery complex, for a total height of 146m. Touted as the biggest and highest statue in the world, it is to be surrounded by performance spaces, art galleries, a food court and an adventure playground.

Well that's the plan. So far the only completed part of a statue is the large bronze head. The shopping mall is done as are two restaurants, but they are mostly empty. At least the restaurants have good views over South Bali. What was promoted as a 10-year project is now called a '30-year project' and the US$200 million needed seems to be in short supply. Critics pan GWK for its potential to commercialise the Hindu religion and reduce Balinese culture to theme-park status.

As it stands – or doesn't – the deserted site is not worth going out of your way for except for the views.

Sleeping & Eating
Balangan (☎ 708080; Banjar Cenggiling 88; www.the balangan.com; villas US$350-575; ☒ ☒) Off the road to the west in Cenggiling, this is an isolated boutique hotel with three luxury villas, each with a private plunge pool and stunning, breezy views. There's also a spa and a restaurant serving fusion Asian.

WEST COAST
The west coast has some legendary surf breaks as well as the important Pura Luhur Ulu Watu.

The surf break at Padang Padang is the centre of development of late and boasts numerous small inns and warung that sell and rent surfboards, and provide food, drink, ding repairs or a massage – whatever you need most. It is the only good place to swim in the area. From its bluff, you get a good view of all the area surf breaks.

Coming from the east you will first encounter a gated parking area (car/motorcycle 2000/1000Rp) which is about a 400m walk from the water. Continuing on over a bridge, there is an older parking area (car/motorcycle 1000/500Rp) that is a hilly 200m from the water.

Sights & Activities
SURFING
To reach the surf break at **Balangan** you'll need your own transport – go all the way through the deserted development of Pecatu Indah, and at the gate on the far side, go right and follow the dirt track. Going left through Pecatu Indah should get you to **Dreamland**, another good surf break. Neither beach is good for swimming.

A paved road goes northwest towards **Padang Padang** from Pecatu village (turn right at the small temple), passing a small side road branching off to **Bingin**, a popular beach with savage surf and a renowned left break. **Impossibles** is nearby.

Ulu Watu, or Ulu's, is a legendary surf spot – the stuff of dreams and nightmares. It's about 1km south of Padang Padang and its legend is match closely by nearby **Pantai Suluban**. Since the early 1970s these breaks have drawn surfers from around the world. The left breaks seem to go on forever.

See p319 for details on these surf breaks.

PURA LUHUR ULU WATU
This **temple** (admission 3000Rp, including sarong & sash rental; parking 1000Rp; ☼ 8am-7pm) is one of several important temples to the spirits of the sea along the south coast of Bali. In the 11th century, the Javanese priest Empu Kuturan first established a temple here. The temple was added to by Nirartha, another Javanese priest who is known for the seafront temples at Tanah Lot, Rambut Siwi and Pura Sakenan. Nirartha retreated to Ulu Watu for his final days, when he attained *moksa* (freedom from earthly desires).

The temple is perched precipitously on the southwestern tip of the peninsula, atop sheer cliffs that drop straight into the pounding surf. You enter through an unusual arched gateway flanked by statues of Ganesha. Inside, the walls of coral bricks are covered with intricate carvings of Bali's mythological menagerie. The small inner temple is only open to Hindu worshippers.

The real attraction is the location – for a good angle, especially at sunset, walk around the clifftop to the left (south) of the temple. Watch out for monkeys, who – when not reproducing – like to snatch sunglasses and handbags, as well as hats and anything else within reach.

An enchanting **Kecak dance** (tickets 35,000Rp; ☼ 6-7pm) is held in the temple grounds at sunset. Although obviously set up for tourists, the gorgeous setting makes it one of the more delightful performances on the island.

Sleeping
There's a whole string of cheap and very basic surfing dives on the road near Padang Padang, many with shared bathrooms. Expect to pay about 50,000Rp for a room with cold water, a fan and a shared bath. Many surfers choose to stay in Kuta and make the under one-hour drive.

Uluwatu Resort (☎ 7420610; www.uluwaturesort .com; Jl Pantai Suluban; villas US$83-93; ✖ ✺) On the clifftop across the river from Padang Padang, this stylish place has impressive ocean views. It's laid-back and a good place to chill out.

Rocky Bungalows (☎ 0817 346 209; off Jl Ulu Watu; r 125,000Rp) This low-key place on the road to Padang Padang has 10 rooms with great water views from the balconies. It's a three-minute walk to the water.

Blue Point Bay Villas & Spa (☎ 7441077; www .bluepointbayvillas.com; Jl Labuansait; villas from US$230; ✖ ✺) A swanky new resort right above the Padang Padang break, it has a stunning pool to go with the stunning views. There's a high level of service and a good restaurant.

Padang Padang Inn (☎ 0812 391 3617; Jl Melasti 432; s/d 50,000/80,000Rp) A better than average surfer joint, this place has clean rooms with private bathrooms and a nice little café.

Ayu Guna Inn (☎ 0823 611 517; Jl Melasti 39X; bungalows 70,000Rp; ⓟ) Simple but pleasant *lumbung* (rice-barn style bungalows) are dotted among gardens and there's plenty of room for parking.

Eating

Most of the hotels and inns have restaurants and any beach where there's surfers will have a few warung selling necessities like beer, sandwiches and Indonesian staples. There are several cafés on the road from Pecatu.

Yeye's Warung (Jl Labuan Sait; dishes 18,000-25,000Rp) A gathering point away from the cliffs, there's an easy-going ambience, cheapish beers and tasty Western, Indonesian and vegetarian food. Nightly movies make it a gathering place.

Jiwa Juice (☎ 7424196; Jl Melasti; sandwiches 15,000-20,000Rp; ⊠) Jiwa means 'soul' and the juices and fresh, light food here are good for the same. There's also Internet access.

Getting There & Away

The best way to see the west coast is with your own vehicle or by chartering a taxi.

Public bemos to Ulu Watu are infrequent, and stop running by mid-afternoon. Some of the dark blue bemos from Kuta serve Jimbaran and Ulu Watu – it's best to catch one west of Tuban (on Jl Raya Kuta, outside the Supernova shopping centre) or Jimbaran (on Jl Ulu Watu).

You may see offers in Kuta or Sanur to see the sunset or the Kecak dance at the temple, these cost from about 80,000Rp and sometimes include a side trip to a beach or to Jimbaran.

SOUTH COAST

The south coast has high cliffs and big swells. From the west, look for a steep track down to the beach and the **Green Ball** surf break about 4km from the little village of Ulu Watu. Other roads lead down to the coast to small beaches and sea temples such as **Pura Mas Suka** and **Pura Gunung Payung**. The latter is near the unappealing Bali Cliffs Resort, a Soeharto-era relic. See p322 for details on the area surf breaks.

NUSA DUA

Nusa Dua translates literally as 'Two Islands' – the islands are actually small raised headlands, each with a little temple. Nusa Dua is better known as Bali's top-end beach resort enclave – a gilded ghetto of top end hotels. There are no independent developments, no hawkers, no warung, no traffic, no pollution and no noise. The drawback is the isolation from any sense of Balinese community life, in many ways, you could be at any international tropical beach resort the world over.

In fact the original purpose of the resort in the 1970s was just that: attract free-spending holiday-makers while keeping them isolated from the rest of the island in an area that was sparsely populated, dry and blessed with good beaches. At Nusa, Balinese 'culture' in the form of attenuated dances and other performances was brought in for the masses nightly. It all worked for a long time but nowadays, after the bombings of 2002, the place feels a bit forlorn. The huge resorts with their hundreds of rooms have been hard hit by the downturn in package travel – people not coming to Bali for anything Balinese but rather because they got a good deal. The Galleria Nusa Dua, once an enclave of exclusive shops, is mostly desolate, with a few dazed souls wandering around after being dropped off by the gaily painted shuttle buses.

But reality is on the march just outside the enclave gates. The village of Bualu is a burgeoning Balinese town, home to many of the hotel staff and an escape for visitors confined to Nusa hotels. It has shops with Asian prices and tourist restaurants that would not be out of place in Kuta. You'll see lots of warung Muslim (halal food) and makan Padang (Padang food) eateries too.

Orientation & Information

As a planned resort, Nusa Dua is very spread out. You enter the enclave through one of the big gateways, and inside there are expansive lawns, manicured gardens and sweeping driveways leading to the lobbies of large hotels. It can be surprisingly confusing to walk anywhere as streets curve this way and that.

In the middle of the resort, the **Galleria Nusa Dua** (☎ 7716625) shopping centre has some services, an ATM and a grocery amid the mostly shuttered shops.

Hotels provide Internet access for their guests, otherwise there's an **Internet shop** (Jl By Pass Nusa Dua, Jl Ngurah Rai; ⊠ 9am-10pm) at the Tragia Shopping Centre. Nearby is a **post office** (Jl Ngurah Rai).

All of the hotels have doctors on call.

TANJUNG BENOA & NUSA DUA

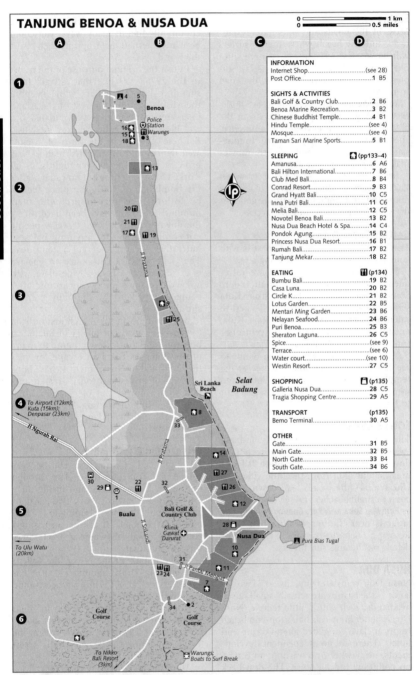

INFORMATION	
Internet Shop	(see 28)
Post Office	**1** B5

SIGHTS & ACTIVITIES	
Bali Golf & Country Club	**2** B6
Benoa Marine Recreation	**3** B2
Chinese Buddhist Temple	**4** B1
Hindu Temple	(see 4)
Mosque	(see 4)
Taman Sari Marine Sports	**5** B1

SLEEPING	(pp133–4)
Amanusa	**6** A6
Bali Hilton International	**7** B6
Club Med Bali	**8** B4
Conrad Resort	**9** B3
Grand Hyatt Bali	**10** C5
Inna Putri Bali	**11** C6
Melia Bali	**12** C5
Novotel Benoa Bali	**13** B2
Nusa Dua Beach Hotel & Spa	**14** C4
Pondok Agung	**15** B2
Princess Nusa Dua Resort	**16** B1
Rumah Bali	**17** B2
Tanjung Mekar	**18** B2

EATING	(p134)
Bumbu Bali	**19** B2
Casa Luna	**20** B2
Circle K	**21** B2
Lotus Garden	**22** B5
Mentari Ming Garden	**23** B6
Nelayan Seafood	**24** B6
Puri Benoa	**25** B3
Sheraton Laguna	**26** C5
Spice	(see 9)
Terrace	(see 6)
Water court	(see 10)
Westin Resort	**27** C5

SHOPPING	(p135)
Galleria Nusa Dua	**28** C5
Tragia Shopping Centre	**29** A5

TRANSPORT	(p135)
Bemo Terminal	**30** A5

OTHER	
Gate	**31** B5
Main Gate	**32** B5
North Gate	**33** B4
South Gate	**34** B6

Activities

BEACH PROMENADE

One of the nicest features of Nusa Dua is the 5km-long beach promenade that stretches the length of the resort and continues north along much of the beach in Tanjung Benoa as well. Not only is it a good stroll at any time but it also makes it easy to sample the pleasures of the other beachside resorts. The walk is paved for most of its length with a couple of exceptions: the Melia Bali Sol has cynically built a fence across the recently constructed walk for no good reason, forcing you out onto the sand and there is always the chance you'll be hassled by the security zealots at the Club Med.

SURFING & BEACHES

The reef-protected beach at Nusa Dua is shallow at low tide, and the wave action is pretty flacid. The surf breaks at Nusa Dua are way out on reefs to the north and south of the two 'islands'. They work best with a big swell during the wet season. **Sri Lanka** is a right-hander in front of Club Med. The so-called **Nusa Dua** breaks are peaks, reached by boat from the beach south of the Hilton – go past the golf course and turn left on a dirt road. See p321 for details on these surf breaks. Nonsurfers from all over southern Bali also flock to this pretty beach, which now has a dozen warung.

The beach between the two peaks behind the Galleria Nusa Dua is also nice and has a large shady and paved parking area that makes it a good stop for day-trippers, especially families who will enjoy the calm atmosphere.

GOLF

The **Bali Golf & Country Club** (☎ 771791; green fees US$142) is a top-flight 18-hole course with all the amenities one would expect from a course at a major resort. Designed by Nelson & Wright, it is the best links on Bali (and almost the *only* links on Bali).

Sleeping

The Nusa Dua hotels are similar in several ways: they are all big (although some are just plain huge) and they have long beachfronts. Each has several restaurants and bars, as well as various pools and other resort amenities. But what's most important is the details of these similarities, as that's where the real differences lie. Some hotels, like the Westin and Hyatt, have been investing heavily in their properties, adding in loads of amenities (such as the elaborate pools and day camps for kids) demanded by travellers today. Other properties seem little changed from when they were built during the heyday of the Soeharto era in the 1970s.

The listings below cover all eight Nusa resorts on the strip, from best down, plus a couple of options away from the strip. Note that this is especially the place to look for deals on the Web and other places, as the rack rates listed are often mere fantasy. Each hotel has a range of rooms – from relatively modest affairs with 'garden' views to palatial oceanfront suites.

Westin Resort (☎ 771906; www.westin.com/bali; r from US$220; ☒ ☒ ☐ ☒) There are 355 rooms on offer. Attached to a large convention centre, the Westin has an air-conditioned lobby (one of three on Bali) and vast public spaces. Formerly a Sheraton, it was comprehensively renovated and reopened in 2004 with the Nusa's best pools which feature waterfalls. The Kids Club has extensive activities and facilities. There's broadband and wi-fi access throughout the hotel.

Grand Hyatt Bali (☎ 771234; www.bali.grand.hyatt .com; r from US$220; ☒ ☒ ☐ ☒) Sort of a little city, the Hyatt has directional signs scattered across the grounds which have up to 21 arrows. Like any city, some neighbourhoods are better than others. Some in the West Village (there are four, the East and South Villages are best located) face the taxi parking lot. The river-like pool is huge and has a fun slide. The children's club will keep the little buggers busy for days. Finally, the salsa bar atop a grassy knoll is a fine place for a panoramic evening cocktail. The 750 rooms are slated for redecoration in 2005.

Sheraton Laguna (☎ 771327; www.starwood.com /bali; r from US$258; ☒ ☒ ☐ ☒) The lobby sets the tone for this 270-room resort: understated with a few royal touches accenting the comfortable rattan furniture. The swimming pools (called 'swimmable lagoons') are vast with sandy beaches, landscaped islands and cascading waterfalls.

Melia Bali Soli (☎ 771510; www.meliabali.com; r from US$190; ☒ ☐ ☒) The resort has recently redecorated its 489 rooms with a sleek look from out of the many Bali style books. The large, naturalistic pool is good and there is shade by the beach. Ten private villas feature plunge pools. Most nights there is a cabaret show with the plucky performers reworking the same theme.

Bali Hilton International (☎ 771102; www .hiltonindonesia.com; r from US$165; ✖ ✖ ▯ ▣) An enormous place with 537 rooms (although it feels bigger) in six-storey blocks, the Hilton can't help but be impersonal. The lagoons covering the grounds would be better if you could swim in them (the main pool is ho-hum). There's lots going on at the Wayan Made Kids Club.

Nusa Dua Beach Hotel & Spa (☎ 771210; www .nusaduahotel.com; r from US$150; ✖ ▯ ▣) The design of many of the 381 rooms has a curious preponderance of walls where there could be windows. There are two large angular pools but the children's club is not one of the better ones.

Inna Putri Bali (☎ 771020; www.putribali.com; r from US$140; ✖ ▯ ▣) The dirty fish tank in one of the cafés puts the 'd' in Putri at this 384-room resort which is much need of a shake-up. The pool is average at best and most of the guests are part of group tours, thus insuring a steady stream of captive clients.

Club Med Bali (☎ 771521; www.clubmed.com; 1-week all-inclusive from s/d US$950/1300; ✖ ▯ ▣) The Club Med would do a paranoid person proud with its extensive security procedures. We were quizzed by guards while still on the public promenade and when we entered the grounds we were put under the equivalent of Club Med house arrest. We weren't allowed to see the facilities for the supposed extensive activities, which is a pity as the resort peddles day passes for 280,000Rp but won't say what this includes.

Amanusa (☎ 772333; www.amanresorts.com; villas US$650-1300; ✖ ▯ ▣) Overlooking the golf course and beyond across the Badung Strait, the Amanusa is one of the finest hotels on Bali, with elegant, understated architecture, superb decorations, brilliant views and just 35 individual villas. Private cooking classes and pretty much anything else you'd like to do can be arranged. Guests can enjoy a private beach club.

Nikko Bali Resort (☎ 773377; www.nikkobali.com; r from US$180; ✖ ✖ ▯ ▣) About 3km south of the enclave, the Nikko with 390 rooms, is dramatically built down the side of a cliff facing the sea. Spanning several buildings and 16 floors, there's a whole complex of swimming pools plus a private cove with a white sandy beach and a spa.

Eating

Restaurants in the hotels are in abundance. Not surprisingly, the better hotels have the better restaurants.

South of the enclave, the various warung at the surfers' beach serve some very good and typically fresh local standards.

Along Jl Pantai Mengiat, just outside the gate, there are a string of open-air eateries offering an unpretentious alternative to Nusa Dua dining. None will win any culinary awards but they are fun and if you pause long enough in front of any, the staff will offer you escalating inducements to step inside. Most will come and get you and take you back to your hotel afterwards, although the walk is not bad.

Watercourt (☎ 771234; Grand Hyatt Bali; dishes 40,000-120,000Rp; ☽ dinner) Surrounded by ponds with lily pads, it is a romantic vision at night with its hundreds of candles and twinkling lights. The chef, Lother Arsana, prepares excellent traditional Balinese food.

Terrace (☎ 772333; Amanusa; dishes 80,000-200,000Rp; ☽ lunch & dinner) You'll be torn at this restaurant between looking at the sweeping view or the exquisite Thai cuisine from chef Marcel Huser (actually, you should spare a glance at your companion).

Nelayan Seafood (☎ 773534; Jl Pantai Mengiat; dishes 18,000-31,000Rp; ☽ dinner) Part of a local chain, this well-run place has steaks and seafood as well as *rijstaffel* (Dutch adaptation of an Indonesian banquet encompassing a wide variety of dishes).

Mentari Ming Garden (☎ 772125; Jl Pantai Mengiat; dishes 15,000-50,000Rp) The Indonesian food is the best choice at this super friendly mid-priced restaurant. The free drinks aren't bad.

Lotus Garden (☎ 773378; Jl Ngurah Rai; dishes 24,000-64,000Rp) One of the higher quality options, this Lotus Garden branch serves pasta, seafood and nicely presented Indonesian dishes.

Entertainment

Most of the hotels offer Kecak and Legong dances one or more nights. Hotel lounges also often have live music, from crooners crooning ballads to mellow rock bands.

The restaurant-bars along Jl Pratama in Tanjung Benoa can be lively at night.

Shopping

Galleria Nusa Dua (☎ 771662) This shopping centre once had 70-plus shops selling all manner of stuff. But the downturn in tourism has left the place rather embarrassingly empty. Although its problems are in some part also inherent to Nusa Dua's premise; the isolation from Balinese life means that it hasn't enjoyed the boom in local shoppers experienced by other island malls.

Tragia Shopping Centre (☎ 772170; Jl Ngurah Rai) Just outside the resort, Bualu village has some reasonably priced tourist shops, as well as this shopping centre which has a department store and supermarket with an entire floor devoted to souvenirs and several fast-food outlets and ATMs. A sign in the main store has the following unintentionally ominous message: 'After checking out from your hotel come spend your last hours with your friends at Tragia.'

Getting There & Away

The fixed taxi fare from the airport is 55,000Rp; a metered taxi *to* the airport will be much cheaper. Public bemos travel between Denpasar's Tegal terminal and the terminal at Bualu (7000Rp). From Bualu, it's at least 1km to the hotels. Bemos run less frequently from Denpasar's Batubulan terminal (5000Rp).

Getting Around

Find out what shuttle bus services your hotel provides before you start calling taxis. A free **shuttle bus** (☎ 771662; ⏰ 9am-10pm) connects all Nusa Dua and Tanjung Benoa resort hotels with the Galleria shopping centre about every hour.

TANJUNG BENOA

The peninsula of Tanjung Benoa extends about 4km north from Nusa Dua to Benoa village.

Like beaches at Sanur and Nusa Dua, those here are protected from waves by an off-shore reef. However, that has allowed a local beach activities industry to flourish in the placid waters. Overall Tanjung Benoa is a fairly sedate place, especially at night.

Orientation & Information

Restaurants and hotels are spread out along Jl Pratama, which runs the length of the peninsula. It may be one of the most perilous streets in South Bali for a stroll. From the Nusa Dua north gate north to the Conrad Hotel, there are no sidewalks and in many places nowhere to walk but on the narrow road, which also has blind curves. Fortunately, the delightful beach promenade is just steps away.

The police station is easy to find. Hotels have doctors on call. Other services can be found south in the Nusa Dua area.

Sights

Benoa is one of Bali's multi-denominational corners, with an interesting **Chinese Buddhist temple**, a **mosque** and a **Hindu temple** within 100m. It's an interesting little fishing town that makes for a good stroll.

Activities

Quite a few water-sports centres along Jl Pratama offer daytime diving, cruises, windsurfing, water-skiing etc. Check equipment and credentials before you sign up. Most have a thatched-roof bar and restaurant attached to their premises. Each morning convoys of buses arrive from all over South Bali bringing day-trippers to enjoy the calm waters and various activities. By 10am parasailers float over the water like a flock of storks looking for a place to land.

Established water sports operators include **Taman Sari Marine Sports** (☎ 772583) and **Benoa Marine Recreation** (BMR; ☎ 771757). As if by magic, all operators have similar prices for activities.

Diving costs US$70/90 for one or two dives around Tanjung Benoa, including equipment rental; US$110 for two dives in Tulamben; and about US$350 for a three-day Professional Association of Diving Instructors (PADI) open-water course. A minimum of two people is required for most dive trips and courses. **Snorkelling** trips include equipment and a boat ride to a reef (minimum two people) for US$20 per hour per person.

Other water sports include the very popular **parasailing** (per round US$20) and **jet-skiing** (per 15 min US$25). You'll need at least two people for **water-skiing** (per 15 min US$25) or **banana-boat rides** (per 15 min US$15), or **glass-bottomed boat**

THE AUTHOR'S CHOICE

Bumbu Bali (☎ 774502; Jl Pratama; dishes 45,000-60,000Rp; 🕑 lunch & dinner) One of the finest restaurants on the island, Bumbu Bali serves the best Balinese food you'll have during your visit. Long-time resident and cookbook author Heinz von Holzen, his wife Puji and a large staff of enthusiastic locals serve exquisitely flavoured dishes beautifully. Many diners opt for one of several set menus (155,000Rp). The *rijstaffel* shows the range of cooking in the kitchen from satays served on their own little coconut husk grill to the tender *be celeng base manis* (pork in sweet soya sauce) to the amazingly tasty and different *jaja batun bedil* (sticky dumpling rice in palm sugar) with a dozen more courses in between.

The frenetic von Holzen can be seen every-where during opening hours, one minute adjusting the artful presentation of a dish, the next checking the seasoning of another and stopping for a moment to help with a backlog of dishes. The staff takes these cues and is both skilled and engaging. The tables are set under the stars and in four small pavilions. The sound of frogs can be heard from the fish ponds. A complimentary van picks up and returns diners to area hotels. During high season be sure to book a day or more in advance.

Von Holzen also runs a cooking school on many days. It starts with a 6am visit to local markets to buy goods and finishes with lunch (US$65). Late risers who just wish to cook can join the class at 9am (US$55).

---

trips (per hr per person US$20), and a maximum of four in a **speedboat** (per hr US$90).

A three-hour **fishing** trip costs US$35-80 per person, depending on boat and party size, and time of day.

Sleeping

The big news in 2004 was the opening of the huge new Conrad Resort. It may or may not be the harbinger of more new developments to come.

BUDGET

A few places close to Benoa village offer no frills accommodation across the road from the beach.

Pondok Agung (☎ 771143; roland@eksadata.com; Jl Pratama; r 90,000-175,000Rp; 🌣) The cheery rooms in a large house-like building are good value here. Higher priced rooms come with air-con and TV.

Tanjung Mekar (☎ 772063; Jl Pratama; r 90,000Rp) Set in a little garden, this small guesthouse has four simple, pleasant rooms.

MID-RANGE

Puri Benoa (☎ 771634; www.puribenoabungalows .com; Jl Pratama; r from US$50; 🌣 🖳 🖳) With only 18 bungalow style rooms, the Puri Benoa feels a bit like a boutique hotel on the beach. Some of the décor has a vague 1970s feel but the outdoor bathrooms in the rooms are quite nice. This is a good value place for the beach.

Princess Nusa Dua Resort (☎ 771604; fax 771394; Jl Pratama; r US$35-65; 🌣 🖳) Step back 30 years in time at this old-style resort around a huge pool. The 54 rooms are large and spotless and the long-time owners and staff are real charmers.

TOP END

Besides the Conrad, there are several lesser resorts along the beach charging top-end prices. Some are time share properties renting out rooms, while others are used almost exclusively by people on package tours. The better choices follow.

Conrad Resort (☎ 778788; www.conradhotels.com; Jl Pratama; r from US$120; 🌣 🌣 🖳 🖳) This impressive new property from the luxury branch of the American Hilton chain combines Bali modern styling with a refreshing style that is best embodied in the staff uniforms: lightweight casual cottons. The 314 rooms have broadband Internet and are large and very comfortable. Some units have patios with steps down into the enormous pool, easing the morning dip. Bungalows have their own private lagoon and there is a large kids' club.

Novotel Benoa Bali (☎ 772239; www.novotelbali .com; Jl Pratama; r US$130-150, beachfront cabana US$250; 🌣 🖳) The Novotel straddles both sides of the busy road, so you know which side to get a room. Rooms and facilities are tasteful with whimsical touches like a huge pineapple sculpture. The pool could use expansion but the beach is tops.

Rumah Bali (☎ 771256; www.balifoods.com; Jl Pratama; f US$100, villas US$185-320; ⊠ ⊠) Rumah Bali is a luxurious interpretation of a Balinese village. Guests have large family rooms or individual villas (some with three bedrooms) with their own plunge pools. There's a 'village centre' with a warung serving up the same exquisite food you'll find across the street at the restaurant. Private butlers attend to every need, including watching the kids while the parents go out to play.

Eating & Drinking

Each hotel has several restaurants. There is also several tourist restaurants in or near Benoa. On the 'border' with Nusa Dua, some cheap warung cater to hotel guests and offer good value for money, while several busy local warung are clustered around the police station in town.

Spice (☎ 778788; Conrad Resort, Jl Pratama; dishes 80,000-200,000Rp; ⊙ dinner) Has a grand setting atop the hotel with tables inside and out. The entire staff here is female and they prepare a wonderful array of pan-Asian dishes.

Service is properly good and you can call for a long list of wines from the cellar.

Casa Luna (☎ 773845; Jl Pratama; dishes 30,000-120,000Rp) This establishment is one of the better choices. Tables sit under flower-laden frangipani trees and if you can't find something on the diverse menu (Indonesian, Chinese, Western, Seafood, Mexican, Italian…) it's because you're insisting on Mongolian.

Circle K (Jl Pratama; ⊙ 24hr) The ever reliable shop sells sundries and properly priced bottled water.

Getting There & Around

You can reach Bualu by public bemo from Kuta (4000Rp), then take one of the infrequent green bemos that shuttle up and down Jl Pratama (2000Rp) – after about 3pm bemos become really scarce on both routes. A metered taxi will be easier and quicker.

Taxis from the airport cost 60,000Rp. Bemos are infrequent on Jl Pratama, so taxis or walking along the beach are the main options.

Ubud & Around

UBUD & AROUND

Perched on the gentle slopes leading up towards the central mountains, Ubud is the other half of Bali's tourism duopoly. Unlike Kuta, however, Ubud maintains its identity as the centre of 'cultural tourism' on Bali.

It's not surprising that many people come to Ubud for a day or two and end up staying longer. There are a lot of expats here, drawn by the rich culture and myriad of activities. Besides the very popular dance and music shows, there are numerous courses on offer to become fully immersed in Balinese culture.

More consumptive pursuits are amply rewarded with some of the best food on the island. From fabled world-class resorts to surprisingly comfortable little family-run inns, there is an ample choice of hotels. Many places come complete with their own spas for hours or days of pampering packages.

Around Ubud are temples, ancient sites and whole villages producing handicrafts (albeit mostly for visitors). Although the growth of Ubud has engulfed several neighbouring villages, leading to an urban sprawl, parts of the surrounding countryside remain unspoiled with lush rice paddies and towering coconut trees. There are some delightful possibilities for walking and you'd be remiss if you didn't hit one of the local paths during your stay.

Although there's commercialism aplenty, Ubud and its surrounding villages are still *desa adat* – communities adhering to traditional custom – with a priestly caste and a local royal family. Although the arts, crafts, music and dances are important parts of the cultural tourism industry, they also serve to support the religious rituals and ceremonies that are integral to community life. The making of offerings and the preparations for ceremonies are almost continuous, and if you stay at simple accommodation in a traditional family compound, you'll notice that the family temple is as elaborately carved, painted and decorated as anything sold to tourists in a gallery or art market. So you may be looking through a gilded frame but in Ubud you can see into the heart of Bali.

UBUD & AROUND

TOP FIVE

- Experiencing Bali's elaborate cultural life in Ubud and surrounding **villages** (p170)
- Sampling the world-class cuisine of Bali's culinary capital, **Ubud** (p162)
- **Walking** (p152) through fabulous scenery
- Enhancing your health and beauty by indulging and soaking in some heavenly **spas** (p151)
- Exploring **Gunung Kawi** (p172), the home of ancient, strange stone statues

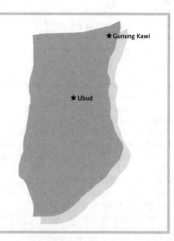

SOUTH BALI TO UBUD

☎ 0361

The road between South Bali and Ubud is lined with places making and selling handicrafts. Try not to be put off by the rampant development and commercialism – the craft villages are much more interesting when you stop and look. Many tourists shop along the route, sometimes by the busload, but much of the craftwork is actually done in small workshops and family compounds on quiet back roads. You may enjoy these places more after visiting Ubud, where you'll see some of the best Balinese arts and develop some appreciation of the styles and themes.

For serious shopping and real flexibility in exploring these villages, it's worth renting or chartering your own transport, so you can explore the back roads and carry your purchases without any hassles. If you decide to charter a vehicle, the driver may receive a commission from any place you spend your money – this can add 10% or more to the cost of purchases. Also, a driver may steer you to workshops or artisans that he favours, rather than those of most interest to you. From the Batubulan terminal (see p88), *bemos* (small pick-up trick) to Ubud stop at the craft villages along the main road.

BATUBULAN

The start of the road from South Bali is lined with outlets for stone sculptures – stone carving is the main craft of Batubulan (which means 'moonstone'), and workshops are found all along the road to Tegaltamu, with another batch further north around Silakarang. Batubulan is the source of the temple-gate guardians seen all over Bali. The stone used is a porous grey volcanic rock called *paras,* which resembles pumice; it's soft and surprisingly light.

The temples around Batubulan are, naturally, noted for their fine stonework. Just 200m to the east of the busy main road, **Pura Puseh** is worth a visit for its unusual decorations. The statues draw on ancient Hindu and Buddhist iconography and Balinese mythology; however, they are not old – many are based on illustrations from books on Javanese archaeology.

Batubulan is also a centre for making 'antiques', textiles and woodwork, and has numerous craft and antique shops. Several venues offer regular performances of traditional Barong (mythical lion-dog creature) and Rangda (widow-witch who represents evil in Balinese theatre and dance) dances, often during the day, and commonly included in tours from southern Bali.

TAMAN BURUNG BALI BIRD PARK & RIMBA REPTIL PARK

Just north of Tegaltama, the **bird park** (☎ 299352; adult/child US$7.50/3.80; ☻ 8am-6pm) boasts more than 1000 birds from over 250 species, including rare *cendrawasih* (birds of paradise) from Irian Jaya and highly endangered Bali starlings – many of which are housed in special walk-through aviaries. The 2 hectares of landscaped gardens feature a fine collection of tropical plants, and a couple of nonnative Komodo dragons.

Next door, **Rimba Reptil Park** (☎ 299344; adult/child US$7.50/3.80; ☻ 8am-6pm) has about 20 species of creatures from Indonesia and Africa, as well as turtles, crocodiles, a python and yet more Komodo dragons.

Both places are popular with kids. You can buy a combination ticket to both parks (adult/child US$14/7). Allow at least two hours for the bird park alone, which also has a good restaurant.

Many tours stop at the parks, or you can take a Batubulan–Ubud bemo, get off at the junction at Tegaltamu, and follow the signs north for about 600m. There is a large parking lot.

SINGAPADU

Singapadu is largely uncommercial and preserves a traditional appearance, with walled family compounds and shady trees. The area has a strong history of music and dance, specifically the *gong gede* (large orchestra) gamelan, the older, but smaller *gong saron* gamelan and the Barong dance. Local artisans specialise in producing masks for Topeng and Barong dances.

Singapadu's dancers now perform mostly at large venues in the tourist areas – there are no regular public performances. There are not many obvious places in the town to buy locally produced crafts, as most of the better products are sold directly to dance troupes or quality art shops. Ask around to find some of the workshops, but even at the source, the best quality masks will

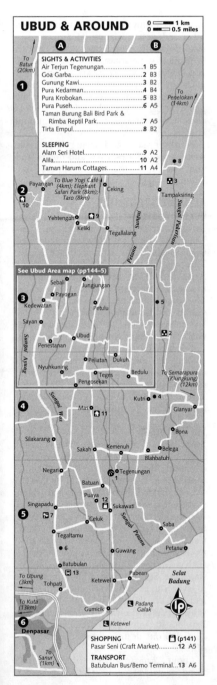

UBUD & AROUND

0 — 1 km
0 — 0.5 miles

SIGHTS & ACTIVITIES
Air Terjun Tegenungan.....................1 B5
Goa Garba.......................................2 B3
Gunung Kawi..................................3 B2
Pura Kedarman................................4 B4
Pura Krokoban.................................5 B3
Pura Puseh.....................................6 A5
Taman Burung Bali Bird Park &
  Rimba Reptil Park...........................7 A5
Tirta Empul.....................................8 B2

SLEEPING
Alam Seri Hotel...............................9 A2
Alila..10 A2
Taman Harum Cottages...................11 A4

SHOPPING   (p141)
Pasar Seni (Craft Market)...............12 A5

TRANSPORT
Batubulan Bus/Bemo Terminal...13 A6

still be quite expensive. If you are relying on public transport wait for a bemo at the junction at Tegaltamu.

CELUK

Celuk is the silver- and goldsmithing centre of Bali. The bigger showrooms are on the main road, and have marked prices that are quite high, although negotiation is possible. The variety and quality of the designs on display is not as good as those in the shops of Ubud, and the prices are no cheaper, except for commercial buyers.

Hundreds of silversmiths and goldsmiths work in their homes on the backstreets north of the main road. Most of these artisans are from *pande* families, members of a subcaste of blacksmiths whose knowledge of fire and metal has traditionally put them outside the usual caste hierarchy. Their small workshops are interesting to visit, and have the lowest prices, but they don't keep a large stock of finished work. They will make something to order if you bring a sample or sketch.

SUKAWATI & PUAYA

Once a royal capital, Sukawati is now known for a number of specialised crafts and for the daily **Pasar Seni**, a two-storey craft market where every type of quality craftwork and touristy trinket is on sale. One group of artisans, the *tukang prada*, make temple umbrellas, beautifully decorated with stencilled gold paint, which can be seen at roadside shops. The *tukang wadah* make cremation towers, which you're less likely to see. Other craft products include intricate patterned *lontar* (specially prepared palm leaves) baskets and wind chimes.

The craft market is on the western side of the main road – public bemos stop right outside. Across the road is the colourful morning produce market, which also sells sarongs and temple ceremony paraphernalia.

Sukawati is also renowned for its traditional dances and *wayang kulit* (shadow puppet) performances.

Puaya, about 1km northwest of Sukawati, specialises in high-quality leather shadow puppets and Topeng masks.

BATUAN

Batuan's recorded history goes back 1000 years, and in the 17th century its royal

UBUD & AROUND

family controlled most of southern Bali. The decline of its power is attributed to a priest's curse, which scattered the royal family to different parts of the island.

In the 1930s two local artists began experimenting with a new style of painting using black ink on white paper. Their dynamic drawings featured all sorts of scenes from daily life – markets, paddy fields, animals and people crowded onto each painting – while the black-and-white technique evoked the Balinese view of the supernatural.

Today, this distinct Batuan style of painting is noted for its inclusion of modern elements. Sea scenes often include a windsurfer, while tourists with video cameras or riding motorcycles pop up in the otherwise traditional Balinese scenery. There are good examples in galleries along, or just off, the main road in Batuan, and also in Ubud's Museum Puri Lukisan (p148).

Batuan is also noted for its traditional dance, and is a centre for carved wooden relief panels and screens. The ancient Gambuh dance is performed in Batuan's Pura Puseh every full moon.

MAS

Mas means 'gold' in Bahasa Indonesia, but woodcarving is the principal craft in this village. The great Majapahit priest Nirartha once lived here, and **Pura Taman Pule** is said to be built on the site of his home. During the three-day Kuningan festival (see p330), a performance of *wayang wong* (an older version of the Ramayana ballet) is held in the temple's courtyard.

Carving was a traditional art of the priestly Brahmana caste, and the skills are said to have been a gift of the gods. Historically, carving was limited to temple decorations, dance masks and musical instruments, but in the 1930s carvers began to depict people and animals in a naturalistic way, and the growth of tourism provided a market for woodcarving, which has become a major cottage industry.

Generally the carving for sale in Mas is priced quite high – you should see items for less elsewhere as you shop around. Although this is the place to come if you want something custom-made in sandalwood – just be prepared to pony up. Mas is also the centre of Bali's booming furniture industry, producing chairs, tables and reproduction

antiques, mainly from teak imported from other Indonesian islands. Along the main road in Mas are the **Taman Harum Cottages** (☎ 975567; www.tamanharumcottages.com; r from US$35, villas US$50-75; ❄ ☎). There are 17 rooms and villas – some are quite large and excellent value. By all means get one overlooking the paddy fields. It's behind a gallery, which is also a venue for a range of art and cultural courses (see p154).

North of Mas, woodcarving shops make way for art galleries, cafés and hotels, and you soon know that you're approaching Ubud.

ALTERNATIVE ROUTES
Via the Coast

An alternative route between Denpasar and Ubud goes through the coastal village of **Gumicik**, which has a broad, black beach. This bypasses the congested roads of Batubulan and Celuk, and is part of the new east coast road going via Lebih to Kusamba. The coast around here has some good wet-season surfing: **Padang Galak**, a right-hand beach break at low- to mid-tide; and **Ketewel**, a barrelling right-hander at high tide.

The beach at **Pabean** is a site for irregular religious purification ceremonies, and cremated ashes are ritually scattered here, near the mouth of the Sungai Wos (Wos River). Just north of Ketewel town, **Guwang** is another small woodcarving centre.

Via Blahbatuh

From Sakah, along the road between Batuan and Ubud, you can continue east for a few kilometres to the turn-off to Blahbatuh and continue to Ubud via Kutri and Bedulu.

In Blahbatuh, **Pura Gaduh** has a 1m-high stone head, said to be a portrait of Kebo Iwa, the legendary strongman and minister to the last king of the Bedulu kingdom. Gajah Mada – the Majapahit strongman – realised that he could not conquer Bedulu (Bali's strongest kingdom) while Kebo Iwa was there. So Gajah Mada lured him away to Java (with promises of women and song) and had him killed. The stone head possibly predates the Javanese influence on Bali, but the temple is a reconstruction of an earlier one destroyed in the earthquake of 1917.

About 2km southwest of Blahbatuh, along Sungai Petanu, is **Air Terjun Tegenungan**

THE STATUE OF KUTRI

This statue on the hilltop shrine at Kutri is thought to date from the 11th century and shows strong Indian influences.

One theory is that the image is of Airlangga's mother, Mahendradatta, who married King Udayana, Bali's 10th-century ruler. When her son succeeded to the throne she hatched a plot against him and unleashed *leyak* (evil spirits) upon his kingdom. She was defeated, but this led to the legend of Rangda, the widow-witch and ruler of evil spirits.

The temple at the base of the hill has images of Durga, and the body of a Barong, the mythical lion-dog creature, can be seen in one of the pavilions (the sacred head of the Barong is kept elsewhere).

(Tegenungan Waterfall; also known as Srog Srogan). Follow the signs from Kemenuh village for the best view of the falls, from the western side of the river.

KUTRI
North of Blahbatuh, Kutri has the interesting **Pura Kedarman** (also known as Pura Bukit Dharma). If you climb Bukit Dharma behind the temple, there's a panoramic **view** and a **hilltop shrine** (see above), with a stone statue of the six-armed goddess of death and destruction, Durga, killing a demon-possessed water buffalo.

BONA & BELEGA
On the back road between Blahbatuh and Gianyar, Bona is credited as the modern home of the Kecak dance; however, Kecak and other dances are no longer held here for tourists. Bona is also a basket-weaving centre and has many articles made from lontar leaves. Nearby, Belega is a centre for bamboo furniture production.

UBUD

☎ 0361

In addition to the cultural attractions outlined at the start of this chapter, Ubud also has charming accommodation for all budgets and some of the best food on Bali. It's just high enough to be cooler than the coast

during the evening and early morning and also during the wet season, but the days are just as steamy as the lowlands and its noticeably wetter. There's an amazing amount to see in and around Ubud. You need at least a few days to appreciate it properly, and Ubud is one of those places where days can become weeks and weeks become months, as the noticeable expatriate community demonstrates.

HISTORY
In the late 19th century, Cokorda Gede Sukawati established his branch of the Sukawati royal family in Ubud and began a series of alliances and confrontations with neighbouring kingdoms. In 1900, along with the kingdom of Gianyar, Ubud became (at its own request) a Dutch protectorate and, no longer troubled by local conflicts, was able to concentrate on its religious and cultural life.

The Cokorda's descendants encouraged Western artists and intellectuals to visit the area in the 1930s, most notably Walter Spies, Colin McPhee and Rudolf Bonnet (see Western Visitors in the 1930s, p46). They provided an enormous stimulus to local art, introduced new ideas and techniques, and began a process of displaying and promoting Balinese culture worldwide. As mass tourism arrived on Bali, Ubud became an attraction not for beaches or bars, but for the arts.

ORIENTATION
The once small village of Ubud has expanded to encompass its neighbours – Campuan,

UBUD IN...

One Day
Stroll the streets of Ubud, enjoying the galleries and sampling the fine cuisine. Try to get out on one of the short nearby walks through the verdant rice fields. Get to a dance performance in the centre.

Three Days
Take longer walks in the countryside, visit the art museums and attend dance performances not just in Ubud, but in the nearby villages.

UBUD AREA

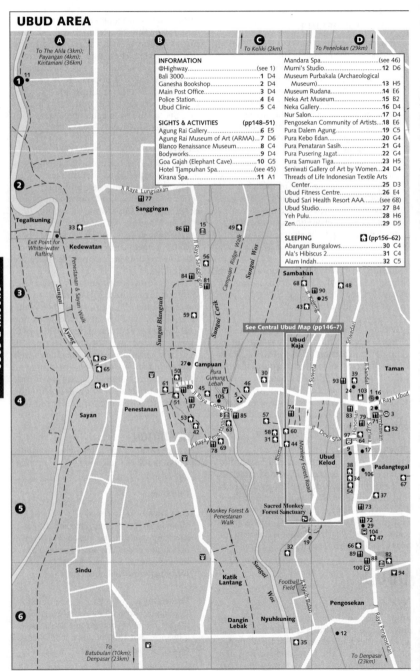

INFORMATION
@Highway..(see 1)
Bali 3000...1 D4
Ganesha Bookshop....................................2 D4
Main Post Office..3 D4
Police Station...4 E4
Ubud Clinic..5 C4

SIGHTS & ACTIVITIES   (pp148–51)
Agung Rai Gallery.......................................6 E5
Agung Rai Museum of Art (ARMA)...7 D6
Blanco Renaissance Museum.............8 C4
Bodyworks...9 D4
Goa Gajah (Elephant Cave)...............10 G5
Hotel Tjampuhan Spa...................(see 45)
Kirana Spa...11 A1

Mandara Spa.................................(see 46)
Murni's Studio..12 D6
Museum Purbakala (Archaeological
      Museum)...13 H5
Museum Rudana.....................................14 E6
Neka Art Museum..................................15 B2
Neka Gallery..16 D4
Nur Salon...17 D4
Pengosekan Community of Artists....18 E6
Pura Dalem Agung.................................19 C5
Pura Kebo Edan.....................................20 G4
Pura Penataran Sasih.............................21 G4
Pura Pusering Jagat...............................22 G4
Pura Samuan Tiga..................................23 H5
Seniwati Gallery of Art by Women...24 D4
Threads of Life Indonesian Textile Arts
      Center..25 D3
Ubud Fitness Centre..............................26 E4
Ubud Sari Health Resort AAA.........(see 68)
Ubud Studio..27 B4
Yeh Pulu...28 H6
Zen...29 D5

SLEEPING   (pp156–62)
Abangan Bungalows...............................30 C4
Ala's Hibiscus 2.......................................31 C4
Alam Indah..32 C5

0 — 500 m
0 — 0.3 miles

E **F** **G** **H**

To
Tegallalang (7km);
Pujung (10km);
Penelokan (29km)

Petulu

Heron
Roosting
Area

Amandari..............................33 A2
ARMA Resort.......................(see 82)
Artini Cottages II..................34 D5
Bali Spirit Hotel & Spa..........35 C6
Biang's................................36 E4
Biyukukung Villa...................37 D5
Candra Asri..........................38 D5
Eka's Homestay....................39 D4
Family Guest House...............40 E5
Four Seasons Resort..............41 A4
Gerebig Bungalows...............42 B4
Gusti's Garden Bungalows......43 C3
Homestay Rumah Roda.........(see 90)
Honeymoon Guesthouse........44 C4
Hotel Tjampuhan..................45 B4
Ibah Luxury Villas.................46 C4
Kajeng Bungalows................(see 43)
Kakiang Bungalows...............47 D5
Ketut's Place........................48 D3
Klub Kokos...........................49 C2
Kori Agung Bungalows..........50 B4
Kunang Kunang Guest House..(see 38)
Londo Bungalows II...............(see 50)
Londo Bungalows..................51 B4
Matahari Cottages.................52 D4

Melati Cottages....................53 B4
Nick's Homestay...................54 D5
Nyoman Astana's..................55 E6
Pita Maha.............................56 B3
Pondok Indah.......................57 C4
Pringga Juwita Water Garden
   Cottages...........................58 C4
Puri Raka Inn........................59 B3
Sama's Cottages...................60 C4
Santika Gardens...................(see 60)
Santra Putra.........................61 B4
Sayan Terrace......................62 A4
Sri Ratih Cottages.................63 C4
Suartha Pension....................64 D4
Tamam Bebek Villas..............65 A4
Tegal Sari............................66 D5
Tiing Gading Bungalows........67 D5
Ubud Sari Health Resort........68 C3
Villa Pagoda.........................(see 50)
Waka Padma.........................69 C4

EATING 🍴 (pp162–6)
Alon Alon.............................70 E4
Andalan Health Food Store.....71 D4
Bali Budda............................(see 71)
Barandi................................72 D5
Bebek Bengil 1......................73 D5
Café des Artistes...................74 C4
Coffee & Silver.....................75 E5
Delta Dewata Supermarket.....76 D5
Fly Café...............................77 B2
Gaja Biru.............................78 C4
Hanoman Juice Ja..................79 D4
Ibu Putih's Warung................80 B4
Indus Restaurant...................81 B3
Kakiang Bakery.....................(see 47)
Kokokan Club.......................82 D5

Masakan Padang...................83 D4
Mozaic.................................84 B3
Murni's Warung....................85 C4
Naughty Nuri's.....................86 B2
Pesto Café............................87 B4
Pizza Bagus..........................88 D5
Restaurant Lele Mas..............89 D5
Roda Restaurant...................90 D3
Village Café..........................91 E4
Warung Igelanca...................92 E4
Warung Taman......................93 E4

DRINKING 🍷 (pp166–7)
Café Exiles...........................94 D6

ENTERTAINMENT 🎭 (p167)
ARMA Open Stage................(see 82)
Jazz Café..............................95 E4
Oka Kartini...........................96 E4
Padangtegal Dance Stage.......97 D4
Peliatan Pura Dalem Puri........98 E5
Pura Dalem Puri....................99 E4
Wunderbar...........................100 D6

SHOPPING 🛍 (pp167–9)
Ashram................................101 E4
Kayan Gallery.......................102 E4
Moari...................................103 D4
Rudana Gallery.....................(see 14)
Tegun Galeri.........................(see 106)

TRANSPORT (p169)
Perama Terminal...................104 D5

OTHER
Bali Bird Walks.....................105 C4
Keep Walking Tours...............106 D5
Semara Tours.......................(see 9)

UBUD & AROUND

Kutuh
26 🍴 ⊙ 4
76

96 🏨 99
92
95 🏨 70 Tebesaya
101
102
36 🏨 91

40
75 Peliatan

98

6
6

Teges
18

55

14

Sala **Galiang**

Kelusu

21

22 **Pejeng**

20

13

Sungai
Pejeng & Bedulu Walk
Petanu

See Goa Gajah
(Elephant Cave)
Map (p171)

10

Jl Bedulu

Jl Raya Pengosekan

Jl Raya Tampaksiring

23 **Samuan
Tiga**

Bedulu

28

To
Gianyar
(9km)

To Denpasar (23km)

Penestanan, Padangtegal, Peliatan and Pengosekan are all part of what we see as Ubud today. The centre of town is the junction of Monkey Forest Rd and Jl Raya Ubud, where the bustling market and crowded bemo stops are found, as well as Ubud Palace and the main temple, Pura Desa Ubud. Monkey Forest Rd (officially Jl Wanara Wana, but always known by its unofficial name) runs south to Sacred Monkey Forest Sanctuary and is lined with shops, hotels and restaurants.

Jl Raya Ubud ('Ubud Main Rd' – often Jl Raya for short) is the main east–west road. In the east, a mix of cheap accommodation, idiosyncratic shops and little cafés gives Jl Goutama a feel of Ubud 20 years ago. West of Ubud, the road drops steeply down to the ravine at Campuan, where an old suspension bridge, next to the new one, hangs over the Sungai Wos. West of Campuan, the pretty village of Penestanan is famous for its painters and bead-work. East and south of Ubud proper, the 'villages' of Peliatan, Nyuhkuning and Pengosekan are known variously for painting, woodcarving and traditional dance. The latter has been the focus of recent development, with rice paddies giving way to new hotels. The area north of Ubud is less densely settled, with picturesque paddy fields interspersed with small villages, many of which specialise in a local craft.

Maps

The maps in this guidebook will be sufficient for most visitors, but if you want to explore the surrounding villages on foot or by bicycle, the best map to buy is the pocket-sized *Ubud* map published by Periplus.

INFORMATION

Along the main roads, you'll find most services you need. There are numerous travel agents and several *wartel* (public telephone offices).

Bookshops

Ubud is the best place for book shopping. Selections are wide and varied and you can get numerous books about Balinese art and culture. Many carry books by small and obscure publishers. Shops typically carry newspapers such as the *International Herald Tribune*.

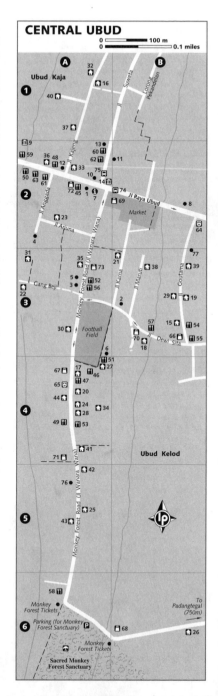

CENTRAL UBUD

Ary's Bookshop (Map pp146-7; ☎ 978203; Jl Raya Ubud) Good for art books and maps.

Cinta Bookshop (Map pp146-7; ☎ 973295; Jl Dewi Sita) Nice assortment of used novels and vintage books about Bali.

Ganesha Bookshop (Map pp144-5; ☎ 970320; www.ganeshabooksbali.com; Jl Raya Ubud) Ubud's best bookshop has an amazing amount of books jammed into the small space. Excellent selection of titles on Indonesian studies, travel, arts and music, fiction (including some used titles) and maps. Good recommendations and mail-order service as well.

Igna Bookshop (Map pp146-7; Monkey Forest Rd) Has a good selection of used books and current periodicals.

Neka Art Museum (Map pp144-5; ☎ 975074; Jl Raya Sanggingan) Has a particularly good range of art books.

Periplus (Map pp146-7; ☎ 975178; Monkey Forest Rd) A typically glossy branch of the Bali chain.

Pondok Pecak Library & Learning Centre (Map pp146-7; ☎ 976194; Monkey Forest Rd, on the far side of the football field) Regularly thins its collection and has some excellent fiction for sale.

Emergency

Police station (Map pp144-5; ☎ 975316; Jl Raya Andong; ☼ 24hr) Located on the eastern side of town at Andong.

Internet Access

Internet centres are common on the main streets; most have slow connections and charge 200Rp to 300Rp per minute. The following two neighbouring places are a cut above average with fast broadband connections and large screens.

@ Highway (Map pp144-5; ☎ 972107; Jl Raya Ubud; per min 500Rp; ☼ 24hr; ⧉) The choice for serious computing.

Bali 3000 (Map pp144-5; ☎ 978538; Jl Raya Ubud; per hr 16,000Rp; ☼ 8am-11pm; ⧉) Like a fashionable Internet café in Milan with a full range of computing services. Has a small café with good sandwiches, coffees and juices.

Libraries

Pondok Pecak Library & Learning Centre (Map pp146-7; ☎ 976194; Monkey Forest Rd, on the far side of the football field; ☼ 9am-5pm Mon-Sat, 1-5pm Sun) A relaxed place, which also has a children's book section. It charges a membership fees starting at 10,000Rp for five days' use. It has a small café and a pleasant reading area on the roof. See p155 for information on cultural courses.

Medical Services

See Health (p360) for details on international clinics and hospitals on Bali.

Ubud Clinic (Map pp144-5; ☎ 974911; Jl Raya Campuan 36; ☼ 24hr) Best medical centre in Ubud. Charges 150,000Rp for a clinical consultation, or 250,000Rp to 300,000Rp for a hotel visit (payment by credit card is possible).

Mua Pharmacy (Map pp146-7; ☎ 974674; Monkey Forest Rd; ☼ 8am-9pm)

Money

Ubud has numerous banks, ATMs and moneychangers along Jl Raya Ubud and

Monkey Forest Rd. ATMs can be found on most other main roads as well.

Post
Main post office (Map pp144-5; Jl Jembawan; ⏰ 8am-6pm) Has a sort-it-yourself poste restante system – address poste restante mail to Kantor Pos, Ubud 80571, Bali, Indonesia.

UPS (☎ 977161; Jl Hanoman 17; ⏰ 9am-5pm Mon-Fri, 9am-1pm Sat) Will ship parcels express worldwide.

Tourist Information
Ubud Tourist Information (Yaysan Bina Wisata; Map pp146-7; ☎ 973285; Jl Raya Ubud; ⏰ 8am-8pm) The one really useful tourist office on Bali. It has a good range of information and a notice board advertising current happenings and activities. The staff can answer most regional questions and have up-to-date information on ceremonies and traditional dances held in the region; dance tickets are sold here.

SIGHTS
Palaces & Temples
Ubud Palace and **Puri Saren Agung** (Map pp146-7; cnr Jl Raya Ubud & Jl Suweta) share space in the heart of Ubud. The compound has many ornate corners and was mostly built after the 1917 earthquake. Just north, **Pura Marajan Agung** (Map pp146-7; Jl Suweta), has one of the finest gates you'll find and is the private temple for Ubud's royal family. **Pura Desa Ubud** (Map pp146-7; Jl Raya Ubud) is the main temple for the Ubud community. Just a bit west is the very picturesque **Pura Taman Saraswati** (Ubud Water Palace; Map pp146-7; Jl Raya Ubud). Waters from the temple at the rear of the site feed the pond in the front which overflows with pretty lotus blossoms. There are carvings that honour Dewi Saraswati, the goddess of wisdom and the arts, who has clearly given her blessing to Ubud. There are weekly dance performances.

Museums
As well as numerous galleries where paintings are exhibited for sale, Ubud has several art museums.

MUSEUM PURI LUKISAN
The **Museum of Fine Arts** (☎ 975136; off Jl Raya Ubud; www.mpl-ubud.com; admission 20,000Rp; ⏰ 8am-5pm) displays fine examples of all schools of Balinese art. It was in Ubud that the modern Balinese art movement started; where artists first began to abandon purely

religious themes and court subjects for scenes of everyday life. Rudolf Bonnet was part of the Pita Maha artists' cooperative, and together with Cokorda Gede Agung Sukawati (a prince of Ubud's royal family) they helped to establish a permanent collection.

The pavilion straight ahead as you enter has a collection of early works from Ubud and the surrounding villages. These include examples of classical *wayang*-style paintings, fine ink drawings by I Gusti Nyoman Lempad and paintings by Pita Maha artists. The pavilion on the left as you enter has some colourful examples of the 'Young Artist' style of painting and a good selection of 'modern traditional' works. The pavilion on the right as you enter the grounds is used for temporary exhibitions, which change every month or so. Paintings are well displayed and labelled in English, and some of the artwork is often for sale. The museum has a good bookshop.

NEKA ART MUSEUM
Quite distinct from Neka Gallery, the **Neka Art Museum** (Map pp144-5; ☎ 975074; Jl Raya Sanggingan; adult/child 20,000Rp/free; ⏰ 9am-5pm) was opened in 1976, and is the creation of Suteja Neka, a private collector and dealer in Balinese art. It has an excellent and diverse collection and is the best place to learn about the development of painting on Bali.

The Balinese Painting Hall provides an overview of local painting, many influenced by *wayang kulit*. The Arie Smit Pavilion features Smit's works on the upper level, and examples of the Young Artist school, which he inspired, on the lower level. The Lempad Pavilion houses Bali's largest collection of works by I Gusti Nyoman Lempad.

The Contemporary Indonesian Art Hall has paintings by artists from other parts of Indonesia, many of whom have worked on Bali. The upper floor of the East–West Art Annexe is devoted to the work of foreign artists, such as Louise Koke, Miguel Covarrubias, Rudolf Bonnet, Han Snel, Donald Friend and Antonio Blanco.

The temporary exhibition hall has changing displays, while the Photography Archive Centre features black-and-white photography of Bali in the early 1930s and 1940s.

Any Ubud–Kintamani bemo will stop outside the museum.

AGUNG RAI MUSEUM OF ART (ARMA)

Founded by Agung Rai as a **museum, gallery and cultural centre** (Map pp144-5; ☎ 976659; Jl Raya Pengosekan; admission 20,000Rp; ⏲ 9am-6pm), the impressive ARMA is the only place on Bali to see works by the influential German artist Walter Spies. It also has work by 19th-century Javanese artist Raden Saleh. It exhibits classical Kamasan paintings, Batuan-style work from the 1930s and 1940s, and works by Lempad, Affandi, Sadali, Hofker, Bonnet and Le Mayeur. The collection is well labelled in English. Look for the enigmatic *Portrait of a Javanese Nobleman and his Wife* by Raden Saleh.

It's interesting to visit ARMA when local children practise **Balinese dancing** (⏲ 3-5pm Mon-Fri, 10.30am-noon Sun) and during **gamelan practise** (⏲ 5pm Tue, Thu & Sun). See p167 for details on regular Legong and Kecak (types of classic Balinese dance) dance performances. See p154 for details on the myriad of cultural courses offered here.

You can enter the museum grounds from the southern end of Jl Raya Pengosekan (there's parking near Kafe ARMA) or around the corner on Jl Pengosekan at the the Kafe ARMA. The Ubud–Gianyar bemo will drop you here.

THREADS OF LIFE INDONESIAN TEXTILE ARTS CENTER

This small, professional **textile gallery and educational studio** (Map pp144-5; ☎ 972187; Jl Kajeng 24; ⏲ 10am-6pm Mon-Sat) sponsors the production of naturally dyed, handmade ritual textiles, helping to recover skills in danger of being lost to modern dyeing and weaving methods. Commissioned pieces are displayed in the gallery, which has good explanatory material. It also runs regular textile appreciation courses (see p154) and has a good shop.

MUSEUM RUDANA

This large, imposing **museum** (Map pp144-5; ☎ 975779; admission 20,000Rp; ⏲ 8am-5pm) is run by local politician and art-lover Nyoman Rudana. The three floors contain interesting traditional paintings, including a calendar dated to the 1840s, some Lempad drawings, and more modern pieces. The museum is beside the Rudana Gallery, which has a large selection of paintings for sale.

BLANCO RENAISSANCE MUSEUM

Beside the Campuan bridge, a driveway leads to the superbly theatrical **Blanco Renaissance Museum** (Map pp144-5; ☎ 975502; Jl Raya Campuan; adult/child 20,000/10,000Rp; ⏲ 9am-5pm) and house of Antonio Blanco. He came to Bali from Spain via the Philippines. Blanco specialised in erotic art, illustrated poetry and playing the role of an eccentric, self-adulatory artist. He died on Bali in December 1999, and his flamboyant home is now a museum that is a fun place to visit.

Galleries

Ubud is dotted with galleries – every street and lane seems to have a place exhibiting artwork for sale. They vary enormously in the choice and quality of items on display. Several major galleries display a huge variety of work, generally of a very high quality, but at prices that are often similarly elevated. A few others in the surrounding villages, such as the **Pengosekan Community of Artists** (Map pp144-5; Jl Raya Pengosekan; ⏲ 10am-5pm) are also worth visiting.

Often you will find local artists in the most unusual places, including your place to stay! A good example is Nyoman Sudiarsa, a painter who has a studio on the grounds of his family's **Padma Accommodation** (see p157).

NEKA GALLERY

Operated by Suteja Neka, the **Neka Gallery** (Map pp144-5; ☎ 975034; Jl Raya Ubud; ⏲ 9am-5pm) is separate from the Neka Art Museum. It has an extensive selection from all the schools of Balinese art, as well as works by European residents such as the renowned Arie Smit.

SENIWATI GALLERY OF ART BY WOMEN

This **gallery** (Map pp144-5; ⏲ 975485; Jl Sriwedari 2B; ⏲ 9am-5pm Tue-Sun) exhibits works by over 70 Balinese, Indonesian and resident foreign women artists. The information on many of the artists makes for fascinating reading. The gallery and workshop aims to publicise Balinese women artists and to encourage the next generation. The works span all mediums and this place is an excellent example of the kinds of cultural and artistic organisations that can thrive in Ubud.

UBUD STUDIO

Founded by the contemporary American artist Symon, the **gallery/studio** (Map pp144-5;

☎ 974721; Jl Raya Campuan; 🕑 9am-6pm) is a spacious and airy place full of huge, colourful and exotic portraits. Symon's work ranges from the sub lime to the profane.

KOMANEKA ART GALLERY
Exhibiting works from established Balinese artists, the **gallery** (Map pp146-7; ☎ 976090; Monkey Forest Rd) is a good place to see high-profile art. The space is large and lofty, making a good place for viewing.

AGUNG RAI GALLERY
In Peliatan, the **gallery** (Map pp144-5; ☎ 975449; Jl Peliatan; 🕑 9am-6pm) is in a pretty compound and its collection covers the full range of Balinese styles. It works as a cooperative, with the work priced by the artist and the gallery adding a percentage.

RIO HELMI GALLERY
The man who has photographed many of those coffee-table books about Bali lives in Ubud and has a lovely **gallery** (Map pp146-7; ☎ 972304; Jl Suweta 5; 🕑 10am-8pm) where you can see examples of some of his works. Photos change often and aren't just of Bali but show Helmi's travels worldwide.

LEMPAD'S HOUSE
I Gusti Nyoman Lempad's **home** (Map pp146-7; Jl Raya Ubud; admission free; 🕑 daylight hours) is open to the public, but it's mainly used as a gallery for a group of artists, which includes Lempad's grandchildren. There are only a few of Lempad's own paintings and drawings here. The family compound itself is a good example of traditional Balinese architecture and layout – Lempad was also an architect and sculptor. The Puri Lukisan (p148) and Neka (p148) museums have more extensive collections of Lempad's drawings. You may or may not react well to the many caged critters.

MURNIASIH'S STUDIO
Murni (Gusti Kadek Murniasih) is one of Bali's most innovative contemporary artists. If you're down in Pengosekan, it's well worth dropping into her **studio** (Map pp144-5; ☎ 976453) to see what's on display.

Artists' Homes
The home of Walter Spies is now part of **Hotel Tjampuhan** (p162). Aficionados can stay in the 'Spies house' if they book well in advance. Dutch-born artist Han Snel lived in Ubud from the 1950s until his death in early 1999, and his family runs **Siti Bungalows** on Jl Kajeng (p159), where his work is exhibited in a gallery.

Music scholar Colin McPhee is well known thanks to his perennial favourite *A House in Bali*. Although the actual 1930s house is long gone, you can visit the riverside site (which shows up in photographs in the book) at the **Sayan Terrace** (p161). The location of McPhee's compound is about where the parking is located and continues down the hill. Longtime Sayan Terrace employee Wayan Ruma, whose mother was McPhee's cook, is good for a few stories.

Arie Smit (1916–) is the best-known and the longest surviving Western artist in Ubud. He worked in the Dutch colonial administration in the 1930s, was imprisoned during WWII, and came to Bali in 1956. In the 1960s, his influence sparked the Young Artists school of painting in Penestanan, earning him an enduring place in the history of Balinese art. His home is not open to the public.

Sacred Monkey Forest Sanctuary
This cool and dense swathe of jungle, officially called **Mandala Wisata Wanara Wana** (Map pp146-7; ☎ 971304; Monkey Forest Rd; adult/child 10,000/5000Rp; 🕑 8am-6pm), houses three holy temples. The sanctuary is inhabited by a band of grey-haired and greedy long-tailed Balinese macaques who are nothing like the innocent-looking doe-eyed monkeys on the brochures. They are ever vigilant for passing tourists who just might have peanuts and ripe bananas available for a quick hand-out. They can put on ferocious displays of temperament if you fail to come through with the goods and have been known to bite if provoked. Don't hand food directly to these creatures.

The interesting **Pura Dalem Agung** (Temple of the Dead; Map pp144-5) is in the forest, for this is the inauspicious *kelod* (direction away from the mountains and towards the sea) side of town. Look for the Rangda figures devouring children at the entrance to the inner temple.

You can enter through one of the three gates: at the southern end of Monkey Forest Rd; 100m further east, near the car park; or from the southern side, on the lane from Nyuhkuning.

Petulu

Every evening at around 6pm, thousands of big, white, water birds fly in to Petulu (Map pp144-5), squabbling over the prime perching places before settling into the trees beside the road, and becoming a minor tourist attraction. The herons, mainly Java pond herons, started their visits to Petulu in 1965 for no apparent reason. Villagers believe they bring good luck (as well as tourists), despite the smell and the mess. A few *warung* (food stalls) have been set up in the paddy fields, where you can have a drink while enjoying the spectacle. Walk quickly under the trees if the herons are already roosting – the copious droppings on the road will indicate if it's unwise to hang around.

A bemo from Ubud to Pujung will drop you off at the turn-off just south of Petulu (the trip should take about 10 to 15 minutes), but it's more convenient with your own transport. It would make a pleasant walk or bicycle ride on any of several routes north of Ubud, but if you stay for the herons you'll be heading back in the dark.

ACTIVITIES
Cycling

Many shops, agencies and hotels in central Ubud, especially on Monkey Forest Rd, rent mountain bikes. Out of the centre, you can have a nice walk to **Kememai Bike Rental** (☎ 977522; Jl Nyuh Bulan; per day 20,000Rp; ☽ 10am-6pm) and head south from there by bike.

In general, the land is dissected by rivers running south, so any east–west route will involve a lot of ups and downs as you cross the river valleys. North–south routes run between the rivers, and are much easier going, but can have heavy traffic. Some of the walking routes (p152) described are also suitable for cycling, especially southwest to Nyuhkuning and Penestanan, and southeast to Pejeng and Bedulu.

Rafting

The nearby Sungai Ayung is the most popular river on Bali for white-water rafting, so Ubud is a convenient base for rafting trips. A reputable operator, with reliable equipment and experienced guides is **Bali Adventure Tours** (☎ 721480; www.baliadventuretours.com) offering trips down Sungai Ayung from US$42 to US$66, and can combine rafting with a big choice of other outdoor activities.

Massage, Spas & Salons

Ubud has several salons and spas where you can seriously pamper yourself, as well as a gym – **Ubud Fitness Centre** (Map pp144-5; ☎ 974804; Jl Jero Gading; 1-day/week 40,000/100,000Rp; ☽ 8am-8pm) which offers weight training and aerobics.

Bodyworks (Map pp144-5; ☎ 975720; Jl Hanoman; 1hr massage 85,000Rp; ☽ 9am-9pm) is set in a traditional Balinese compound and treatment rooms are light-filled, although traffic noise competes with the gurgling fountains. A facial is 75,000Rp while a spice, salt, milk or seaweed bath costs from 125,000 to 150,000Rp.

Cendana Resort & Spa (Map pp146-7; ☎ 971927; Monkey Forest Rd; 1hr massage US$12; ☽ 9am-7pm) has a nice set up, including an open-air Jacuzzi and open-air rooms upstairs. The couples' massage room is particularly pleasant. One-day use of the hotel's pool, sauna and steam room is available for US$5. You can have a mud bath with your massage or milk bath with massage (both US$18) are all options. The spa also does colonic irrigation, which it euphemistically calls 'Total Tissue Cleansing'.

Kirana Spa (Map pp144-5; ☎ 976333; Kedewatan; 1hr treatment US$70; ☽ 9am-9pm) is set on a lengthy drive and you'll think you're going to an elegant hotel. Actually once you've made your way down through the myriad of levels to reception, you'll realise that it simply costs the same as an elegant hotel. The highest-end spa in Ubud, the Kirana is by Shiseido cosmetics. Treatments occur in private villas, the options are many and the staff are oh so gracious.

Komaneka Resort & Spa (Map pp146-7; ☎ 976090; Monkey Forest Rd; 1hr massage US$30; ☽ 9am-7pm) offers open-air treatments for singles and couples in lush surrounds. It has a wide variety of herbal baths and body scrubs.

Mandara Spa (Map pp144-5; ☎ 974466; Ibah Luxury Villas, off Jl Raya Campuan; 1hr massage US$45; ☽ 8am-8pm) has a very calm wooden interior and a Jacuzzi, as to be expected from this noted international chain. Treatments come with evocative names like Rhapsody, Harmony and Ultimate Indulgence.

Milano Salon (Map pp146-7; ☎ 973448; Monkey Forest Rd; 1hr massage 60,000Rp; ☒ 10am-9pm) offers facials and massages in a simple setting.

Nur Salon (Map pp144-5; ☎ 975352; Jl Hanoman 28; 1hr massage 83,000Rp; ☒ 9am-8pm) is in a traditional Balinese compound. It offers a long menu of spa and salon services including a traditional Javanese massage that takes two hours and starts with a body scrub (247,000Rp).

Hotel Tjampuhan Spa (Map pp144-5; ☎ 975368; Jl Raya Campuan; 1hr massage US$25; ☒ 9am-7pm) which is in a unique grotto setting, overlooking the river, and features organic carved stone reliefs. Use of the sauna and steam room is US$15 and a *mandi lulur* (body mask) is from US$35 to US$120.

Ubud Sari Health Resort (Map pp144-5; ☎ 974393; Jl Kajeng; 1hr massage US$15; ☒ 8am-8pm) is a spa and hotel in one. Besides a long list of one-day spa and salon services, there are a vast range of packages that combine a stay at the hotel with courses and therapies that stretch over many days. See p159 for details on the resort.

Zen (Map pp144-5; ☎ 970976; Jl Hanoman; 1hr massage 75,000Rp; ☒ 9am-8pm) has a good reputation. It offers body scrubs, 90-minute *mandi lulur* and massage treatments (90,000Rp).

WALKS AROUND UBUD

For information on guided walks see p155. The growth of Ubud has engulfed a number of nearby villages, although they have still managed to retain distinct identities. There are lots of interesting walks in the area, to surrounding villages or through the paddy fields. You'll frequently see artists at work in open rooms and on verandas, and the timeless tasks of rice cultivation continue alongside luxury villas.

In most places there are plenty of warung or small shops selling snack foods and drinks, but bring your own water anyway. Also bring a good hat, decent shoes and wet-weather gear for the afternoon showers; long pants are better for walking through thick vegetation.

It's good to start walks at daybreak, before it gets too hot. In the walks below, distances are approximate and are measured with the Ubud Palace as the start and end point. Walking times do not include any stops so you need to factor in your own eating, shopping and rest stops.

Monkey Forest & Penestanan

This walk features a good range of rice paddy and rural Ubud scenery.

Distance: 8km
Duration: 2hr

Take your time strolling through the Sacred Monkey Forest Sanctuary at the bottom of Monkey Forest Rd, then take the sealed road at the southwestern corner of the forest near the temple. Continue south on the lane to the village of **Nyuhkuning**, and turn west along the south end of the football field, then turn south down the narrow road. At the southern end of the village, turn right and follow the paved road across the bridge over Sungai Wos to Dangin Lebak (this busy road is the most unpleasant part of the trip but should only take around 15 minutes). Take the track to the right just after the large Bale Banjar Dangin Lebak (Dangin Lebak Community Hall). From here follow paths due north through the paddy fields, and veer left, westwards through the rice paddies to a paved road to reach **Katik Lantang**, where you join a paved road that continues north to **Penestanan**. Many artists live here, and you can stop at their homes/studios/galleries and see paintings for sale. Follow the paved road through the village, veering east, and go down through a deep cutting and back to Campuan and Ubud.

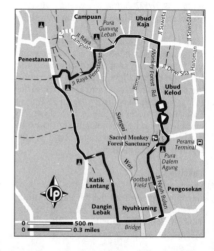

Campuan Ridge

This walk passes over the lush river valley of the Sungai Wos, offering views of Gunung Agung and glimpses of small village communities and rice fields.

> Distance: 7km
> Duration: 2hr

At the confluence of the Sungai Wos and Sungai Cerik is **Campuan**, which means 'Where Two Rivers Meet'. The walk leaves Jl Raya Campuan here at the Ibah Luxury Villas. Enter the hotel driveway and take the path to the left, where a walkway crosses the river to Pura Gunung Lebah. From there follow the concrete path north, climbing up onto the ridge between the two rivers. Fields of elephant grass, traditionally used for thatched roofs, slope away on either side.

Continuing north along the Campuan ridge past the Klub Kokos lodging (a convenient drink stop), the road improves as it passes through paddy fields and the small village of **Bangkiang Sidem**. On the outskirts of the village, an unsigned road heads west, which winds down to Sungai Cerik (the west branch of Sungai Wos), then climbs steeply up to **Payogan**. From here you can walk south to the main road, and continue along Jl Raya Sanggingan and on the centre of Ubud.

Penestanan & Sayan

The wonders of Sungai Ayung are the focus of this walk, where you will walk below the luxury hotels built to take advantage of this lush, tropical river valley.

> Distance: 6.5km
> Duration: 3hr

Just west of the Campuan bridge, past the Blanco Renaissance Museum, a steep uphill road, Jl Raya Penestanan, bends away to the left and winds across the forested gully of the Sungai Blangsuh to the artists village of Penestanan. West of Penestanan, take a small road north that curves around to **Sayan**, where the Sayan Terrace hotel is site of Colin McPhee's home in the 1930s, as chronicled in his book *A House in Bali*. The views overlooking the deep valley of the magnificent **Sungai Ayung** are superb. The best place to get down to the riverside is just north of Sayan Terrace – follow the increasingly more narrow tracks down.

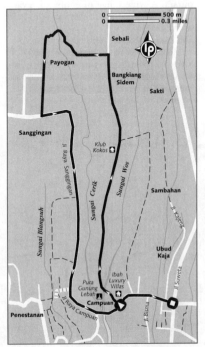

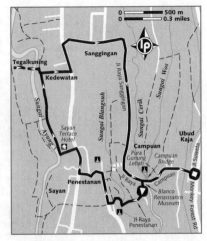

Following the at times rough trails north, along the eastern side of the Ayung, you traverse steep slopes, cross paddy fields and pass some irrigation canals and tunnels. After about 1.5km you'll reach the finishing point for many of the white-water rafting trips – a good but steep trail goes from there up to the main road at **Kedewatan**, where you can walk back to Ubud. Alternatively, cross the river on the nearby bridge and climb up to the very untouristy village of **Tegal Kuning** on the other side. There and back will add about 1km to your walk.

Pejeng & Bedulu

The temples of Pejeng and the archaeological sites of Bedulu (see p170) can be visited in a day's outing. As most of the attractions are on sealed roads, you can also go by bicycle. Looking at the map, you will see several places you can shorten the route if your energies wane. Also note that bemos to Ubud abound on Jl Bedulu.

> Distance: 10km
> Duration: 3hr

If you have the time and energy, do the entire loop by going to the far eastern end of Jl Raya Ubud, and taking the small road that continues east from there. It passes the garbage dump and descends steeply to cross the Sungai Petanu, then climbs to the village of Sala. Some back roads will take you east through Pejeng to the main road, where you turn south to pass several important temples and archaeological sites.

Keep walking south down through Bedulu to the carved cliffs of **Yeh Pulu**. From there follow Sungai Petanu upstream to **Goa Gajah** (Elephant Cave), but finding the right trail through the paddy fields can be tricky, don't hesitate to ask anyone you see. Follow the trail by Sungai Petanu back to the small road by the garbage dump – most of it is pretty, despite this landmark.

COURSES

Ubud is a very pleasant place to spend a few weeks developing your artistic or language skills, or learning about Balinese music, dance and cuisine. Two organisations, ARMA and the Pondok Pecak Library & Learning Centre offer a wide range of cultural courses.

Arts & Crafts

The Ubud area is the best place for art courses. A wide range of courses is available including batik, jewellery making and painting.

ARMA (Map pp144–5; ☎ 976659; www.armamuseum .com; Jl Raya Pengosekan; ☼ 9am-6pm) A cultural powerhouse offering classes in painting, woodcarving and batik. Other courses include Balinese history, Hinduism and architecture. Classes cost US$22 to US$50 depending on duration and materials used.

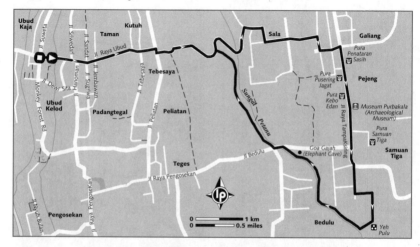

Nirvana Batik Course (Map pp146-7; ☎ 975415; Nirvana Pension & Gallery, Jl Goutama 10; ☼ classes 10am-3pm Mon, Wed & Sat) Nyoman Suradnya teaches the highly regarded batik courses here. One-day courses are $35, two-three-day courses are $30 per day, and four-five-day courses are $25 per day.

Pondok Pecak Library & Learning Centre (Map pp146-7; ☎ 976194; Monkey Forest Rd, on the far side of the football field; ☼ 9am-5pm Mon-Sat, 1-5pm Sun) Painting and mask carving classes are run here for tourists. Sessions cost from 50,000Rp for one hour. This is also a good place to find out about other courses being offered in the Ubud area.

Santra Putra (Map pp144-5; ☎ 977810; Penestan; classes per hr 50,000Rp) Intensive painting and drawing classes are run by abstract artist I Wayan Karja, whose studio is also onsite. Accommodation is also available, see p159.

Studio Perak (Map pp146-7; ☎ 0812 365 1809; Jl Goutama) This studio has a friendly atmosphere and it specialises in Balinese-style silversmithing courses. A three-hour/full-day lesson, where you'll make a finished piece, costs 100,000/120,000Rp.

Taman Harum Cottages (Map p141; ☎ 975567; www.tamanharumcottages.com; Mas; lessons per hr from US$10) The centre of Bali's woodcarving district, this place offers carving and painting courses. You can also learn how to make the temple offerings found just about everywhere. See p142 for details on accommodation.

Threads of Life Indonesian Textile Arts Center (Map pp144-5; ☎ 972187; www.threadsoflife.com; Jl Kajeng 24) Textile appreciation courses in the gallery and educational studio are run. There is a range of classes, including ones lasting eight days that involve extensive travel around Bali.

Cooking

Balinese Cooking Courses (Map pp144-5; ☎ 973283; www.casalunabali.com; Honeymoon Guesthouse, Jl Bisma) In Ubud, Bali's culinary capital, Janet de Neefe was a pioneer in creative cuisine. She runs regular cooking courses at her guesthouse. Well-recommended half-day courses (150,000Rp) are held five days per week and cover ingredients, cooking techniques and the cultural background of the Balinese kitchen. Excellent weekend gourmet tours are also held (200,00Rp).

Bumbu Bali Restaurant (Map pp146-7; ☎ 974217; Jl Suweta 2) offers a Balinese cooking course, with Indian cuisine also a possibility is offered here. Courses, which start at the local market, cost 120,000Rp for the first day and 80,000Rp thereafter.

Language
Pondok Pecak Library & Learning Centre (see above) offers inexpensive courses. Its notice board has ads for the private tutors

and teachers who provide courses on an ad hoc basis in both Bahasa Indonesia and the Balinese language.

Meditation & Spiritual Interests
ARMA (Map pp144-5; ☎ 976659; www.armamuseum.com; Jl Raya Pengosekan; ☼ 9am-6pm) has classes in Hindu and Balinese astrology.

Meditation Shop (Map pp146-7; ☎ 976206; Monkey Forest Rd), part of the Brahma Kumaris Society, offers silent meditation practice between 6pm and 7pm daily, and five-day meditation courses.

Ubud Sari Health Resort (Map pp144-5; ☎ 974393; Jl Kajeng; ☼ 8am-8pm) offers private guided meditation, as well as yoga classes.

Music & Dance
The most visitor-friendly courses are in Ubud, where private teachers advertise instruction in various Balinese/Indonesian instruments. A well-recommended teacher of Balinese music is **Eka's Homestay** (Map pp144-5; Wayan Pasek Sucipta; ☎ 970550; Jl Sriwedari 8) who charges 50,000Rp for one hour, or lower rates for longer lessons.

ARMA, Pondok Pecak Library & Learning Centre and Taman Harum Cottages have courses in Balinese dance and music (see left).

TOURS
Taking a tour or two is a good idea as many of the attractions around Ubud are quite difficult to reach by public transport, and finding your way around this part of Bali can be a challenge, even with your own vehicle.

All travel agencies in Ubud can arrange tours, but it's worth shopping around, as prices vary (eg check if entrance fees are included in the price). See p356 for general information.

Bali Bird Walks (Map pp144-5; ☎ 975009; US$33; ☼ 9am Tue, Fri, Sat & Sun) The legendary Victor Mason's walks depart from the restaurant building (in 2004 it was between operators) in Campuan (Map pp144-5). Most walks are actually guided by one of Victor's staff. The three-hour walk includes drinking water and lunch. Confirm that you'll receive your own set of binoculars.

Keep Walking Tours (Map pp144-5; ☎ 970581; Jl Hanoman) This organisation offers one- to seven-hour guided and themed walking tours around Ubud, including walks to rural villages and the herons at Petulu ranging from 50,000Rp to 275,000Rp. If the office is closed, you should seek information from Tegun Galeri next door.

Semara Tours (Map pp144-5; ☎ 975576; semara@indo
.net.id; Jl Hanoman 27A) Runs treks to Gunung Batur (per
person $US30; make sure they provide you with a torch),
as well as ones to Java.

Ubud Tourist Information (Yaysan Bina Wisata; Map
pp146-7; ☎ 973285; Jl Raya Ubud; ☺ 8am-8pm) Runs
interesting and affordable half- and full-day trips (75,000-
125,000Rp) to a huge range of places including Uluwatu,
Mengwi, Alas Kedaton and Tanah Lot, or Goa Gajah,
Pejeng, Gunung Kawi and Kintamani.

FESTIVALS & EVENTS
The Ubud area is one of the best places on
Bali to see the many religious and cultural
events celebrated on the island each year.
See p330 for details on the events.

The **Ubud Writers & Readers Festival** (www
.ubudwritersfestival.com) brings together scores of
writers and authors from around the world
in a celebration of writing – especially that
which touches on Bali. It is usually held in
October.

SLEEPING
Ubud has hundreds of places to stay.
Choices range from simple little *losmen*
(basic accommodation) to luxurious retreats that are among the best in the world.
Generally, Ubud accommodation offers
good value for money at any price level. A
simple, clean room within a family home
compound is the least expensive option.
The mid-range hotels generally offer swimming pools and other amenities, while the
top-end hotels are often perched on the
edges of the deep river valleys, with superb views and service. (Although some
very cheap places also boast amazing views
which urge you to curl up with a book and
contemplate.)

Addresses in Ubud can be imprecise –
but signage at the end of a road will often
list the names of all the places to stay. Away
from the main roads there are no street-
lights and it can be very difficult to find
your way after dark. If walking you will
definitely want a torch (flashlight).

Rentals
There are many houses you can rent or
share in the Ubud area. For information
about options, check the notice boards at
Pondok Pecak Library (see p147), Ubud
Tourist Information (see p148) and Casa
Luna restaurant (see p163). Also look in the

free *Bali Advertiser* broadsheet. For agencies, see p314.

Budget
Many inexpensive family lodgings are very
small, often with just two, three or four
rooms. They tend to operate in clusters so
you can easily look at a few before making
your choice.

CENTRAL UBUD
Monkey Forest Rd
This was the first place developed for tourists in Ubud and there are many good-value
places here.

Loka House (Map pp146-7; ☎ 973326; off Monkey
Forest Rd; s/d 90,000/100,000Rp) Across the football field from Monkey Forest Rd, Loka is
a peaceful place, where the two-storey main
building overlooks a small carp pond in the
garden. Rooms have hot water and fans.

Gayatri Bungalows 2 (Map pp146-7; ☎ 979129;
meggy292003@yahoo.com; off Monkey Forest Rd; r 150,000-
200,000Rp; 🏊) The 12 large rooms have hot
water and fans. It's a nice jaunt past rice
paddies.

Ubud Terrace Bungalows (Map pp146-7; ☎ 975690;
Monkey Forest Rd; r 100,000Rp; 🏊) There's good
value, as the basic rooms come with a pool
and hot water.

Nyuh Gading Accommodation (Map pp146-7;
☎ 973410; Monkey Forest Rd; s/d 50,000/70,000Rp) In
a quiet garden enclosure opposite the football field, this place has seven clean, simple
rooms. Ask for one with hot water.

Puri Muwa Bungalows (Map pp146-7; ☎ 976441;
Monkey Forest Rd; r 50,000-125,000Rp) Near the top

THE AUTHOR'S CHOICE

Oka Wati Hotel (Map pp146-7; ☎ 973386; www
.okawatihotel.com; off Monkey Forest Rd; r US$25-
55; 🏊) Opened in 1977, the Oki Wati is
an unassuming veteran with an old-Ubud
style. A three-minute walk from busy Ubud
streets and you're transported to an open-
air ideal. The 19 rooms have large verandas
where the oh so charming staff will deliver your choice of breakfast that always
includes a platter of fresh fruit. The décor
features vintage details like four-poster
beds. The pool is very large and the site is
surrounded by rice paddies and lush tropical foliage.

of Monkey Forest Rd in a thicket of basic of places, is this basic family-run place. It's reasonably quiet considering its location. Cheaper rooms are cold-water only.

Pramesti (Map pp146-7; ☎ 970843; uni_pramesti@hot mail.com; Monkey Forest Rd; s/d 70,000/80,000Rp) Pooh fans will find Winnie on many of the colourful bed linens here. The eight bungalow-style rooms have hot water and good porches for enjoying the simple garden.

Jungut Inn (Map pp146-7; ☎ 978237; Jl Arjuna; s/d 30,000/40,000Rp) The flag-bearer for value on thrift-seeker-friendly Jl Arjuna just off Monkey Forest Rd, Jungut is bare bones but also a good deal and near an atmospheric small temple.

Frog Pond Inn (Map pp146-7; Monkey Forest Rd; s/d 30,000/50,000Rp) It's quiet, ultra-basic, friendly and has open-air bathrooms with cold water.

Kubu Saren (Map pp146-7; ☎ 975704; Monkey Forest Rd; s/d 50,000/70,000Rp) It's the 1970s again in Ubud at this old-style simple place with seven bungalow rooms. You supply your own tie-dyed shirt.

Kubuku (Map pp146-7; ☎ 974742; Monkey Forest Rd; r 150,000-200,000Rp) Kubuku has a small vegetarian café with lounging *bales* (open-sided pavilion with a steeply pitched thatched roof). All six rooms have hot water, 2nd-floor ones add lovely paddy-field views.

East of Monkey Forest Rd
Small streets east of Monkey Forest Rd, including Jl Karna, have numerous, family-style homestays, which are secluded but still handy to the centre.

Sayong House (Map pp146-7; ☎ 973305; Jl Maruti; s/d 80,000/100,000Rp; ⊠) At the northern end of this deliciously quiet lane, Sayong has seven basic hot-water rooms, but there's a gorgeous pool in a private location across the lane from the rooms.

Gandra House (Map pp146-7; ☎ 976529; Jl Karna; s/d 40,000/50,000Rp) Modern bathrooms and spacious gardens are the highlights of this cold-water 10-room place. One of several on this street.

Jl Goutama
This charming street has several cheap, quiet and accessible places to stay.

Donald Homestay (Map pp146-7; ☎ 977156; Jl Gouta-ma; r 40,000-70,000Rp) The four rooms – some

with hot water – are in a nice back corner of the family compound. Chickens are running about, some shortly to be turned into satay.

Shana Homestay (Map pp146-7; ☎ 970481; Jl Goutama 7; r 40,000-60,000Rp) Basic cold-water rooms; some with private patios.

North of Jl Raya Ubud
Both Jl Kajeng and Jl Suweta, leading north from Jl Raya, offer an excellent choice of budget lodgings, some quite close to the centre of town.

Padma Accommodation (Map pp146-7; ☎ 977247; aswatama@hotmail.com; Jl Kajeng 13; r 120,000Rp) A very friendly place, Padma has only two adjoining, very private bungalows in a tropical garden. Rooms are decorated with local crafts and the modern outdoor bathroom has hot water. Nyoman Sudiarsa, a painter and family member, has a studio on the grounds.

Roja's Bungalows (Map pp146-7; ☎ 975107; Jl Ka-jeng 1; r 50,000-90,000Rp) One of the first places of several on Jl Kajeng, Roja's maintains a friendly atmosphere. Rooms are clean and well kept.

Arjana Accommodation (Map pp146-7; ☎ 975583; Jl Kajeng 6; s/d 30,000/50,000Rp) The good-value leader, bathrooms are outdoors in a mini-jungle, and the simple rooms are clean.

NORTH OF THE CENTRE
Things get quiet as you head north from Jl Raya Ubud, but note that some places are almost a kilometre to the north.

Kajeng Bungalows (Map pp144-5; ☎ 975018; Jl Kajeng; r 60,000-150,000Rp; ⊠) There's two big amenities here: a pool and a stunning setting overlooking a lush valley. The most expensive rooms have hot-water, tubs and the best views.

Gusti's Garden Bungalows (Map pp144-5; ☎ 973311; gustigarden@yahoo.com; Jl Kajeng 27; s/d 100,000/150,000Rp; ⊠) Gusti is another place with very good value: it opens onto a stunning garden, where rooms are perched overlooking a swimming pool with a café. Excellent valley views.

Homestay Rumah Roda (Map pp144-5; ☎ 975487; rumahroda@indo.net.id; Jl Kajeng 24; s/d 50,000/60,000Rp) Next door to the Threads of Life gallery, Rumah Roda is an ever friendly and understandably popular homestay. The five bungalows have hot water and there's a good breakfast.

EAST OF THE CENTRE

Jl Sriwedan

Eka's Homestay (Map pp144-5; ☎ 970550; Jl Sriwedari 8; s/d 40,000/50,000Rp) In a nice little family compound Eka's has basic cold-water rooms. It is the home of Wayan Pasek Sucipta, a teacher of Balinese music (see p155).

Jl Hanoman

East of central Ubud, but still conveniently located, this area has several budget lodgings along Jl Hanoman.

Suartha Pension (Map pp144-5; ☎ 974244; Jl Hanoman 17; r 100,000-150,000Rp) There's a charming, traditional family setting here. Ikat (dyed and woven cloth) and decorative features make for a welcoming setting. More expensive rooms have hot water.

Kunang Kunang Guest House (Map pp144-5; ☎ 976052; Jl Hanoman; r 90,000-160,000Rp) All nine rooms in this quiet retreat have hot water. More money buys you better rice paddy views from 2nd-floor rooms.

Candra Asri (Map pp144-5; ☎ 970517; Jl Hanoman 43; r 45,000-150,000Rp) Orchids dapple the attractive grounds here. The wide range of rooms add hot water as you climb the price scale. At the top – literally are 3rd-floor rooms with fine paddy views.

Nick's Homestay (Map pp144-5; ☎ 975526; nicksp@ indosat.net.id; Jl Hanoman; s/d 50,000/60,000Rp) Stroke the cockatoo as you check in at this nice place that likes pet birds. Seven hot-water rooms are set in spacious grounds with carp ponds.

Tebesaya

A little further east, this quiet village comprises little more than its main street, Jl Sukma, which runs between two streams.

Biangs (Map pp144-5; ☎ 976520; Jl Sukma 28; r 35,000-100,000Rp) In a little garden, Biangs has well-maintained rooms, with hot water. The lush views are more sweeping in the costlier rooms.

Family Guest House (Map pp144-5; ☎ 974054; Jl Sukma; familyhouse@telkom.net; r 66,000-99,000Rp) A gem, this popular place is set in a pleasant garden. The delightful staff serve up healthy breakfasts featuring brown bread. The 12 rooms have hot water and modern bathrooms.

SOUTH OF THE CENTRE

At the southeastern fringe of the Ubud area, the small community of Teges has a cluster of quiet, decent places.

Nyoman Astana's (Map pp144-5; ☎ 975661; off Jl Pengosekan; s/d 55,000/60,000Rp) Make your own fruit salad from the banana, papaya coconut and other trees growing in the lovely garden. The charming owner will explain these and other plants that include cocoa trees and orchids. The eight rooms are basic and clean.

WEST OF THE CENTRE

Jl Bisma

Mostly unpaved Jl Bisma goes south of Jl Raya Ubud, just west of the centre, and is handy to town.

Sama's Cottages (Map pp144-5; ☎ 973481; Jl Bisma; s/d 100,000/150,000Rp; 🏊) This lovely little hideaway is terraced down a hill. It also has a well-maintained pool in a private spot on the grounds.

Ala's Hibiscus 2 (Map pp144-5; ☎ /fax 970476; off Jl Bisma; r 150,000Rp) Smack bang in the middle of rice paddies, this good place is about 150m down a path off Jl Bisma. Rooms have exceptional views, hot water and mosquito nets and are decorated with local handicrafts.

Pondok Indah (Map pp144-5; ☎ 966323; off Jl Bisma; s/d 80,000/100,000Rp) Follow the coursing paddy waterways for 150m off the road to this quiet, peaceful place where the top-floor balconies look over paddy fields. All rooms have hot water.

Campuan & Penestanan

West of Ubud but still within walking distance, places in the paddy fields are pitched at those seeking low-priced, longer-term lodgings. Most will offer discounted weekly rates, and some bigger bungalows are quite economical if you can share with a group of people. Note that these places are a steep climb up a set of concrete stairs off Jl Raya Campuan.

Londo Bungalows (Map pp144-5; ☎ 976548; londo bungalows@hotmail.com; off Jl Raya Campuan; r 75,000-100,000Rp) It has two-storey bungalows with hot water and a carp pond fronting each room.

Londo Bungalows II (Map pp144-5; ☎ 976764; londobungalows@hotmail.com; off Jl Raya Campuan; bungalows 50,000Rp) It's ridiculously cheap. The three simple hot-water bungalows have gorgeous paddy views and morning views of Gunung Batukau.

Kori Agung Bungalows (Map pp144-5; ☎ 975166; well off Jl Raya Campuan; r US$15-20) This place has a lovely setting and nice double-storey bungalows with hot water. At night it's almost silent here (except for the dogs...).

Santra Putra (Map pp144-5; ☎ 977810; karjabali@yahoo.com; off Jl Raya Campuan; Penestan; r US$12-15) Run by internationally exhibited abstract artist I Wayan Karja whose studio/gallery is also onsite, this place has big, open airy rooms with hot water. Enjoy paddy field views from all vantage points. Intensive painting and drawing classes are offered by the artist, see p155.

Gerebig Bungalows (Map pp144-5; ☎ /fax 974582; well off Jl Raya Campuan; s/d 125,000/150,000Rp) Walking through rice paddies 150m south of Londo Bungalows rewards with wonderful views and good-value two-storey hot-water bungalows.

Mid-Range

Choices are many in this price range.

CENTRAL UBUD
Jl Raya Ubud

Look for a place on Ubud's main street that is protected from road noise.

Puri Saren Agung (Map pp146-7; ☎ 975057; fax 975137; Jl Raya Ubud; r US$50-65; ☒) Part of the Ubud royal family's old palace, this place is behind the courtyard where the regular dance performances are held. Accommodation is in traditional Balinese pavilions, with big verandas, four-poster beds, antique furnishings and hot water.

Puri Saraswati Bungalows (Map pp146-7; ☎ 975164; purisaraswati@yahoo.com; Jl Raya Ubud; r US$40-90; ☒ ☒) Recently redone, this 18-room place is very central and pleasant with lovely gardens and a friendly atmosphere. Rooms are well back from Jl Raya Ubud, so it's quiet. Cheaper rooms have fans.

Monkey Forest Rd

Cendana Resort & Spa (Map pp146-7; ☎ 973242; www.cendanaresort-spa.com; Monkey Forest Rd; r US$45-95; ☒ ☒) Rooms have TV and face a lone paddy field. Higher priced rooms have modern bathrooms and both face pools. The landscaping is superb, with the two pools appearing to cascade over the rice paddies. See p151 for details on the spa.

Lumbung Sari (Map pp146-7; ☎ 976396; www.lumbungsari.com; Monkey Forest Rd; r US$45-85; ☒ ☒) Lots of artwork decorates the walls of the rooms at the stylish Sari which has a nice

breakfast *bale* by the pool. The eight rooms have tubs but cheaper ones have fans.

Ubud Bungalows (Map pp146-7; ☎ 975537; w_widnyana@hotmail.com; Monkey Forest Rd; s/d 150,000/250,000Rp, with air-con 250,000/350,000Rp; ☒ ☒) Back from the road, it's pleasant here, with a pool, gardens and spacious rooms with hot water.

Sri Bungalows (Map pp146-7; ☎ 975394; sribungalows@hotmail.com; Monkey Forest Rd; r 250,000Rp; ☐ ☒) Some 50m off the bust street, this place has 16 bright bungalow-style rooms with hot water. The pool is large.

Jl Goutama

These three places have more style than the cheaper options on this street.

Nirvana Pension & Gallery (Map pp146-7; ☎ 975415; rodanet@denpasar.wasantara.net.id; Jl Goutama 10; r 150,000-275,000Rp) There's *alang alang* roofs, a plethora of paintings, ornate doorways and modern bathrooms with hot water here. Batik courses also take place here (see p155).

Agung Cottages (Map pp146-7; ☎ 975414; Jl Goutama; s/d 200,000/250,000Rp, villa 300,000Rp) This is a gem of a place. It has huge, spotless rooms with hot water, lovely gardens and friendly staff – local art hangs on the walls.

Dewangga Bungalows (Map pp146-7; ☎ 973302; www.dewangga-ubud.com; Jl Dewi Sita; r 150,000-400,000Rp) Close to Jl Goutama, rooms here – some very large – have a variety of wood and stone carvings, some playfully lurid. The grounds are large and decorated with colourful mosaic tiles.

North of Jl Raya Ubud

Pradha Guesthouse & Restaurant (Map pp146-7; ☎ 975122; www.pradhabali.com; Jl Kajeng 1; r US$75; ☒ ☒) Overlooking a deep lush pool and nice café, the Pradha has six pleasant rooms; traffic noise from Jl Raya Ubud is minimal.

Siti Bungalows (Map pp146-7; ☎ 975699; fax 975643; Jl Kajeng 3; bungalows US$30-60; ☒ ☒) Owned by the family of the late Han Snel, a well-known Ubud painter for many years, this quiet compound has eight bungalows and a small pool. Some rooms are perched right on the edge of the river gorge.

NORTH OF THE CENTRE

Ubud Sari Health Resort (Map pp144-5; ☎ 974393; www.ubudsari.com; Jl Kajeng; r US$25-45, villa US$45-75;

UBUD & AROUND

⊠ ⊠) There's charming accommodation and colonic irrigation for all guests here. See p151 for details on the spa. Daily health classes are held here and even the plants in the lunch gardens are labelled for their medicinal qualities. Week-long intensive health packages are available from US$1450.

Ketut's Place (Map pp144-5; ☎ 975304; www.indo .com/hotels/ketut-place; Jl Suweta 40; r 100,000-275,000Rp; ⊠ ⊠) The simply elegant rooms here range from simple with fans to deluxe versions with air-con and bathtub. All enjoy the stunning pool overlooking the river valley. The atmosphere here is restful; it's like entering your own compound. See p164 for details on the popular Balinese feasts.

Klub Kokos (Map pp144-5; ☎ 978270; www.klubkokos .com; s/d/f US$40/44/92; ⊠ ⊠) A beautiful 1.5km walk north in the small village of Bangkiang Sidem on the Campuan ridge, Klub Kokos is a secluded place with a big pool and spotless sizable rooms. It's reachable by car from the north, call for directions.

Abangan Bungalows (Map pp144-5; ☎ 975977; fax 975082; off Jl Raya Ubud; r US$20-30; ⊠ ⊠) Up a steep driveway, Abangan has a lovely setting, a pool and views of birds swooping around tree-tops by the river. Some of the 15 rooms have fans only.

EAST OF THE CENTRE

Artini Cottages II (Map pp144-5; ☎ 978424; artini@dps .centrin.net.id; Jl Hanoman; r US$35-45; ⊠ ⊠) In Padangtegal, Artini has a nice setting with paddy fields on two sides. The 26 tidy and comfortable rooms are in three-storey blocks around a large pool. It's a sociable and well-run place.

Matahari Cottages (Map pp144-5; ☎ 975459; www .matahariubud.com; Jl Jembawan; r US$25-60; ⊠) This wild place has flamboyant, themed rooms, including the 'Batavia Princess' and the 'Indian Pasha'. The Library is a vision out of a 1920s fantasy. The theme of the grounds is casual disarray. See p165 for details about the daily high tea.

Tiing Gading Bungalows (Map pp144-5; ☎ 973228; tiing@indosat.net.id; Jl Sukma; s/d US$40/45; ⊠ ⊠) Overlooking a rainforest valley, these bungalows have attractive views from its kidney-shaped pool and restaurant. Rooms are tastefully presented and surrounded by bamboo.

SOUTH OF THE CENTRE

Alam Indah (Map pp144-5; ☎ 974629; www.alamindah bali.com; Jl Nyuh Bulan; r US$50-65; ⊠ ⊠) Just south of the Monkey Forest in Nyuhkuning, this isolated and spacious 10-room resort has a good riverside location and rooms that are beautifully finished in natural materials. The Wos river valley views are tranquil.

Tegal Sari (Map pp144-5; ☎ 973318; www.tegalsari -ubud.com; Jl Raya Pengosekan; r 200,000-450,000Rp; ⊠ ⊠) Stylish and modern, the Tegal Sari is set among the rice paddies, in fact it's nearly awash in them. The 14 rooms have varying themes, the wooden one is as close as you can get to the rice without being a snail.

Kakiang Bungalows (Map pp144-5; ☎ 978984; www .kakiang.com; Jl Raya Pengosekan; r US$44-74; ⊠ ⊠) This modern place has 10 bungalows with a rural design but modern conveniences. All have nice verandas. The pool area is attractive and a study in cut stone. There's also a good bakery, see p165.

WEST OF THE CENTRE
Jl Bisma

Close to town, this area also manages some rural charm.

Honeymoon Guesthouse (Map pp144-5; ☎ 973283; www.casalunabali.com; Jl Bisma; r 150,000-400,000Rp; f 700,000Rp; ⊠) Run by the Casa Luna (p163) clan and set in a family compound, there's a high rate of return visitors so it's recommended to book ahead here. The 16 rooms have fans and tubs, more money gets you fridges and better views. The café is suitably tasty. See p155 for details about the cooking classes held here.

Campuan & Penestanan

Just west of the Campuan bridge, steep Jl Raya Penestanan branches off to the left, and climbs up and around to Penestanan.

Puri Raka Inn (Map pp144-5; ☎ 975213; puriraka@ yahoo.com; Jl Raya Sanggingan; s/d 300,000/400,000Rp; ⊠ ⊠) On the western side of the road in a paddy field, the inn has a soaring new public area and a wonderfully sited swimming pool. The 11 rooms are attractive.

Sri Ratih Cottages (Map pp144-5; ☎ 975638; sriratih@ dps.centrin.net.id; Jl Raya Penestanan; r US$15-35; ⊠ ⊠) There's a pool with a view of the lotus flower inspired roof of Antonio Blanco's house, spacious grounds and 26 clean, neat rooms with fridges here. Cheaper rooms have fans.

Melati Cottages (Map pp144-5; ☎ 974650; melati cottages@hotmail.com; off Jl Raya Penestanan; s/d/f US$25/35/45; 🔊) You can feel like a classic Ubud rice paddy duck as you stroll out to these traditional-style rooms set around a café by the pool. You can walk in from the north or south.

Villa Pagoda (Map pp144-5; ☎ 979265; well off Jl Raya Campuan; r US$65; ❌ 🔊) Next door to the budget Kori Agung Bungalows, Villa Pagoda feels like your own private retreat. It's luxurious and rooms have a kitchen and their own plunge pool set in carefully tended gardens.

Sayan & Ayung Valley

Sayan Terrace (Map pp144-5; ☎ 974384; www.sayanter raceresort.com; Jl Raya Sayan; r US$60-150; ❌ 🔊) With a million-dollar view of the Sungai Ayung Valley below and the tops of palm trees stretching west, the Sayan Terrace is a good place to relax. Rooms are large and open onto terraces and are best value at the lower end of the price range. This is the site of Colin McPhee's *A House in Bali*, see p150 for details.

Top End

At this price range you have your choice of prime properties in the area. The big decision: close to town or not. Look for views, expansive pools, rooms with architectural features such as marble and/or outdoor bathrooms and amenities including satellite TV, fridges, minibars and extensive room service.

CENTRAL UBUD

Ubud Village Hotel (Map pp146-7; ☎ 975571; www.indo .com/hotels/ubud_village; Monkey Forest Rd; r US$65-90; ❌ 🔊) Close to Ubud's urban action – such as it is, the Village features a big pool, lush garden and tasteful, fully equipped rooms. The hotel also has an impressive two-level restaurant and an open-air spa. Readers have praised the facilities.

Komaneka Resort & Spa (Map pp146-7; ☎ 976090; www.komaneka.com; Monkey Forest Rd; r US$165-250; ❌ 🔊) This 20-room resort exudes contemporary elegance. Rooms are beautifully decorated in rough-hewn furniture and feature sunken marble tubs, while the pool and minimalist style gardens are lovely. The Komaneka Art Gallery (p150) is at the front of the hotel. See p151 for details on the spa.

SOUTH OF THE CENTRE

ARMA Resort (Map pp144-5; ☎ 976659; www.armaresort .com; Jl Raya Pengosekan; r US$80-175, villas from US$375; ❌ 🔊) Plunge into culture at the accommodation part of the ARMA compound (see p149 for details about the excellent museum and p154 for details on the range of courses offered). The resort features fine views, imaginative architecture and attractive décor. Villas come with private pools.

Bali Spirit Hotel & Spa (Map pp144-5; ☎ 974013; www.balispirithotel.com; Nyuh Kuning Village; r US$95-145; ❌ 🔊) Overlooking the Wos Valley, the Bali Spirit has stylish rooms and stunning views. The 19 rooms tumble down the hillside and feature Balinese art works and antiques. The pool sits in a tropical bowl down by the rapids. There's complimentary car service to area locations.

Biyukukung Villa (Map pp144-5; ☎ 978976; www .biyukukung.net; Jl Sugriwa 89; r US$70-150; ❌ 🔊) Framed by coconut trees off Jl Hanoman, this lovely place has a pool that disappears into the rice paddies. The stylish two-storey rooms have magnificent views and satellite TV. Some have Jacuzzi tubs.

WEST OF THE CENTRE

Properties generally go from posh to posher as you near the fabled Ayung Valley.

Jl Bisma

Pringga Juwita Water Garden Cottages (Map pp144-5; ☎ 975734; www.thefibra.com; Jl Bisma; r US$57-150; ❌ 🔊) Quiet like the street, this 13-room resort has ponds and a swimming pool in one of the prettiest gardens in Ubud. The range of flowers and stoneworks are attractions themselves. There is a spa and extensive facilities.

Santika Gardens (Map pp144-5; ☎ 975443; santik@ indosat.net.id; Jl Bisma; d/ste/villa US$95/175/325; ❌ 🔊) A modern, very stylish boutique hotel, the Santika Gardens is a worthwhile retreat. The 17 rooms and villas have traditional *alang alang* ceilings and the balconies are draped in white bougainvillea. The mosaic-tiled pool is spectacular.

Campuan

Ibah Luxury Villas (Map pp144-5; ☎ 974466; www .ibahbali.com; off Jl Raya Campuan; ste US$210-315, villas US$430-500; ❌ 🔊) Overlooking the lush Wos Valley, the Ibah offers an elegant environment, Mandara Spa facilities (see p151), and spacious, stylish individual suites. The delightful garden is decorated with stone carvings, handcrafted pots and antique doors, and the swimming pool is set into the hillside beneath an ancient-looking stone wall.

Hotel Tjampuhan (Map pp144-5; ☎ 975368; www .indo.com/hotels/tjampuhan; Jl Raya Campuan; r US$70, with air-con US$115; ✗ ⚑) This venerable place, overlooks the confluence of Sungai Wos and Campuan. The influential German artist Walter Spies lived here in the 1930s, and his former home, which sleeps four people (US$175), is now part of the hotel. There are shared modern bungalows in the wonderful garden. The hillside swimming pool is especially delightful is in a splendid setting, with a verdant view in all directions. See p152 for details on the spa overlooking the rivers.

Waka Padma (Map pp144-5; ☎ 975719; www.waka experience.com; Jl Raya Penestanan; bungalows/villas US$115/165; ✗ ⚑) The 11 units are set in a walled compound that feels other-worldly. This isolation, coupled with the huge rooms, make this a good choice for families. Bathrooms are aquatic playgrounds with sunken tubs and outdoor tropical showers.

Sangginggan

Pita Maha (Map pp144-5; ☎ 974330; www.pitamaha-bali .com; Jl Raya Sanggingan; villas US$300-480; ✗ ⚑) Cascading down into the Sungai Valley, Pita Maha has no shortage of style in its spectacular balcony restaurant or its disappearing swimming pool. Each of the 24 elegant villas is in its own small private compound and higher rates mean better views.

Sayan & Ayung Valley

Two kilometres west of Ubud, the fast flowing Sungai Ayung has carved out a deep valley, its sides sculpted into terraced paddy fields or draped in thick rainforest. Overlooking this verdant valley are some of the most stylish, luxurious and expensive hotels on Bali.

Four Seasons Resort (Map pp144-5; ☎ 977577; www .fourseasons.com; ste US$450, villa from US$575; ✗ ✗ ⚑ ⚑) Set slightly into the valley, the curved open-air reception area is looks like a Cinerama screen of verdant Ubud landscape. Electric carts ferry guests around the well-spaced rooms and villas. Many have private pools and all share the same amazing views.

If you don't like green, consider a desert holiday. The many services include a spa.

Amandari (Map pp144-5; ☎ 975333; www.aman resorts.com; ste from US$650; ✗ ⚑ ⚑) In Kedewatan village, the Amandari is unquestionably classy with superb views over the paddies and down to the river – the main swimming pool seems to drop right over the edge. The 30 private pavilions have stone gateways and private gardens. They are spacious and exquisitely decorated. The best units have their own private swimming pool.

Taman Bebek Villas (Map pp144-5; ☎ 975385; tbv bali@indo.net.id; off Jl Raya Sayan; villas US$125-200; ✗ ⚑) Look for specials at this pleasantly old-fashioned place that shares owners with the mid-range Sayan Terrace. Simple Balinese furnishings and a beautifully located pool make it a pleasant place. The common area is a serene spot to idle away time.

NORTHWEST OF UBUD

Alila (Map p141; ☎ 975963; www.alilahotels.com; r US$240-260, villa US$450; ✗ ⚑) Near Payangan, the Alila offers great views and modern luxury amid rural tranquillity. Formerly the Chedi, it has a stunning ebony pool and renowned service. Many of the 56 rooms and eight villas are set back from the knoll, impeding valley views.

Begawan Giri (☎ 978888; www.begawan.com; ste US$495-2950; ✗ ⚑ ⚑) Well secluded in a remote location, is the most fabled hotel on Bali. Set amid 20 acres of riverside forest and paddy fields, the 22 unique suites are grouped into five 'residences', each with its own swimming pool, library, kitchen and butler. The design by Cheong Yew Kuan emphasises the natural surroundings and combines new and old materials from the archipelago.

EATING

Ubud's restaurants offer the most diverse and interesting food on the island. It's a good place to try authentic Balinese dishes, as well as a range of other Asian and international cuisine. The quintessential Ubud restaurant has fresh ingredients, a delightful ambience and an eclectic menu, with dishes fusing inspiration from around the world.

There's top dining in the top resorts in the Ayung Valley to the west, but you needn't stray far from town for a superb meal. Each area of Ubud has numerous restaurants of notes. There are also many inexpensive warung serving Indonesian and Chinese dishes. Many of the places listed under Drinking (p166) also serve food.

Central Ubud

JL RAYA UBUD

There's plenty to chose from on Ubud's main street.

Casa Luna (Map pp146-7; ☎ 977409; Jl Raya Ubud; dishes 9000-35,000Rp) One of Ubud's top choices has a creative international menu and a delicious range of bread, pastries, cakes and more from its well-known bakery. Crisp salads, homemade pasta and simple main courses are not to be missed. The owner, Janet de Neefe, runs regular Balinese cooking courses (see p155).

Ary's Warung (Map pp146-7; ☎ 978359; Jl Raya Ubud; mains 30,000-85,000Rp) Warung is something of a misnomer as crisp table linen, architectural food presentation, well-trained waiters and high prices won't be found in any other warung. The food is top-notch and a five course tasting from the changing menu costs 200,000Rp.

Zula (Map pp146-7; ☎ 972294; Jl Raya Ubud; dishes 15,000-25,000Rp) The twin 'vegetarian paradise' of the Seminyak original, Zula has all manner of healthy eats including falafel sandwiches, salads and juices. Tofu and brown rice figure prominently. The interior is done up in the shades of a salad.

Café Lotus (Map pp146-7; ☎ 975357; Jl Raya Ubud; dishes 26,000-55,000Rp) A leisurely meal at this Ubud classic overlooking the lotus pond is a relaxing option. The menu features Western and Indonesian fare that's well-prepared. For 50,000Rp you can book front-row seats for dance performances at Pura Taman Saraswati (Ubud Water Palace).

Ryoshi (Map pp146-7; ☎ 972192; Jl Raya Ubud; dishes 28,000-60,000Rp; ☽ 11am-midnight) The Ubud branch of the local chain of good Japanese restaurants is in new and attractive quarters.

Tino Supermarket (Map pp146-7; ☎ 975020; Jl Raya Ubud) Sells most grocery items, including newspapers and maps.

MONKEY FOREST RD

Lamak (☎ 974668; Monkey Forest Rd; dishes 40,000-155,000Rp; ☽ 11am-midnight) Step into the Balinese home you wished you lived in at this refined establishment. Mix and match small plates of Euro-Asian fusion food or go for mains like steak and seafood. The large kitchen is open and each day there are specials of Indonesian food that's not found on your average menu.

Ibu Rai (Map pp146-7; ☎ 975066; Monkey Forest Rd 72; dishes 15,000-30,000Rp) A small and attractive place, the fountains add to the cooling atmosphere on a sweltering day. It's a good stop for its juices and usual menu.

Bebek Bengil 2 (Map pp146-7; ☎ 978954; Monkey Forest Rd; dishes 18,000-50,000Rp; ☽ lunch & dinner) A branch of the long-established 'Dirty Duck Diner' on Jl Hanoman, Bebek Bengil 2 offers the same range of very tasty duck specialties in a rice field setting.

Bumbu Bali 2 (Map pp146-7; ☎ 976698; Monkey Forest Rd; dishes 15,000-45,000Rp) Unlike the varied Asian cuisine at the original a few hundred metres north, the menu here is almost entirely Balinese featuring items such as *lawar* (green bean salad), *bebek betutu* (smoked duck) and *sate lilit* (minced meat and grated coconut skewers). It's a large and attractive place.

Monkey Float (Map pp146-7; ☎ 0816 473 1997; Monkey Forest Rd; ice cream from 5000Rp; ☽ 10am-6pm) The monkeys at the nearby sanctuary get nothing but treats, so why shouldn't you? This shiny soda fountain has a long list of ice cream treats and juices.

Café Wayan & Bakery (Map pp146-7; ☎ 975447; Monkey Forest Rd; mains 20,000-50,000Rp) Another old Ubud favourite, Café Wayan stays popular because of its relaxed and pleasant garden-setting ambience and for its food such as the array of baked goods displayed up front. Sunday night Balinese buffets (105,000Rp) are especially popular.

Delta Mart (Map pp146-7; Monkey Forest Rd; ☽ 24hr) For self-caterers there are the local small chain of convenience stores useful for snacks and sundries. Among the many are two central locations.

EAST OF MONKEY FOREST RD

Deli Cat (Map pp146-7; ☎ 971284; off Monkey Forest Rd; dishes 12,000-30,000Rp) A character-filled place, Deli Cat is like a little tropical bodega. Wine – some delightfully cheap – is sold along with snacks and cheese and larger dishes like sandwiches and soups. Try the little grilled sausages outside at the tables right on the football field.

UBUD & AROUND

Tutmak Café (☎ 975754; Jl Dewi Sita; dishes 15,000-30,000Rp) The location here facing both Jl Dewi Sita and the football field makes this a breezy stop on a hot day. It's also a stylish one with several levels of seating. Break the banana shackles and have a blueberry shake or try one of the sandwiches, burgers, juices or coffees.

Gaia Warung (Jl Dewi Sita; dishes 10,000-25,000Rp) Tasty local roasted peanuts come with every beverage at this simple place with good veggie burgers, Indo standards and more. It's a good place for a pause during the day.

JL GOUTAMA

Fairway Café (Map pp146-7; ☎ 970810; cnr Jl Dewi Sita & Jl Goutama; dishes 8000-15,000Rp) Perched above the street, Fairway has a casual, easy-going atmosphere. Dishes are simple and include some Japanese favourites. Water refill is available and there's also a small Internet café. Sports fans enjoy the satellite TV.

Dewa Warung (Map pp146-7; Jl Goutama; dishes 4000-10,000Rp) You feel like you're in the country at this place with its shady position elevated above the street that shelters under a tin roof. Inexpensive offerings include tempeh curry with rice. Beers are cheap.

Toko Tako (Map pp146-7; Jl Goutama; tea 3,000Rp) A tiny outdoor Japanese teashop serving chai, coffee and juices. It's very sweet.

NORTH OF JL RAYA UBUD

Warung Ibu Oka (Map pp146-7; Jl Suweta; dishes 10,000Rp) Noontime crowds of locals opposite Ubud Palace are there for one thing: the eponymous Balinese-style roast piglet. Line up and find a place under the shelter for one of the best meal you'll have in Ubud. Order a *spesial* to get the best cut.

Bumbu Bali Restaurant (Map pp146-7; ☎ 974217; Jl Suweta 1; dishes 18,000-50,000Rp) Indian, Balinese and vegetarian influences combine at this excellent restaurant where many of its candle-lit tables face Ubud Palace. Dishes are inventive and the flavours complex. It also offers a cooking course (see p155).

Terazo (Map pp146-7; ☎ 978941; Jl Suweta; dishes 30,000-80,000Rp ☽ lunch & dinner) This stylish place serves brilliantly presented, eclectic Balinese fusion cuisine. The wine list is long and features numerous French, Italian and Australian choices. The austere interior is accented by vintage travel posters.

THE AUTHOR'S CHOICE

Kafé Batan Waru (Map pp146-7; ☎ 977528; Jl Dewi Sita; dishes 20,000-70,000Rp; ☽ 10am-midnight) One of Bali's best restaurants, Batan Waru serves consistently excellent Indonesian food. Tired of tired *mie gorengs* made from instant noodles? The version here is sublime, with noodles made fresh daily. Other dishes are more adventurous and the menu changes often. Western dishes include sandwiches and salads. The care and talent in the kitchen is apparent in the presentations and most of the ingredients are organic. Many dishes can be prepared vegetarian. Smoked duck *(bebek betutu)* and suckling pig *(babi guling)* can be ordered in advance. Tables out back have a gurgling stream running under the floor.

North of the Centre

Ketut's Place (Map pp144-5; ☎ 975304; Jl Suweta 40; feast 100,000Rp; ☽ Sun, Wed & Fri night) Ketut's famous traditional Balinese feast is an excellent introduction to Balinese life and customs. The range of dishes is amazing and the quality is tops. There's usually an interesting group, so it's very sociable. See p160 for details on accommodation.

Roda Restaurant (Map pp144-5; Jl Kajeng 24; dishes 6000-15,000Rp) Above Threads of Life Indonesian Textile Art Center, Roda is a pleasant little restaurant. It has good Indonesian dishes, including hard-to-find Balinese desserts, such as the Moorish *jaja Bali* (sticky rice, coconut, palm sugar and fruit steamed in banana leaves). Filtered water refills are also available (1000/1500Rp small/large). Roda also holds traditional meals (30,000Rp per person; minimum five people); book in advance.

East of the Centre

Warung Igelanca (Map pp144-5; ☎ 974153; Jl Raya Ubud; dishes 8000-15,000Rp) Noodle fans rejoice, this little streetside den has 'em in everything, from a Jakarta chicken noodle soup to North Sumatra fried rice noodles.

Masakan Padang (Map pp144-5; Jl Raya Ubud; dishes 6000-12,000Rp; ☽ noon-1am) This Padang-style eatery – where you choose from the plates on display – has some of the cheapest, tastiest eats in town. Food is fresh and much of it is spicy. There's another location just around the corner on Jl Hanoman.

Warung Taman (Map pp144-5; Jl Sriwedari; dishes 11,000-28,000Rp; ☎ lunch & dinner Mon-Sat) The woks are busy at this inviting little warung, which serves consistently good and ultra-fresh Indonesian and Chinese food. Rough-hewn tables and friendly staff make it a cheery choice.

Bali Buddha (Map pp144-5; ☎ 976324; Jl Jembawan 1; dishes 12,000-35,000Rp) Upstairs from Andalan Health Food Store (see below), Bali Buddha offers a full range of vegetarian *jamu* (health tonics), salads, tofu curries, savoury crepes, pizza and bagels, as well as gelato. It has a comfy lounging area and is candle-lit in the evening. The café also doubles as an exhibition space for local artists.

Matahari Cottages (Map pp144-5; ☎ 975459; Jl Jem-bawan; high tea 55,000Rp; ☎ 2-5pm) This flam-boyant inn serves extravagant high tea in open-air pavilions. See p160 for details on accommodation.

Andalan Health Food Store (Map pp144-5; ☎ 976324; Jl Jembawan 1) Sells fresh organic fruit and vegetables, other healthy foods such as muesli and olive oils, and home baked bagels, breads and cookies. Other items include cosmetics. Upstairs, Bali Buddha (above) serves a range of vegetarian dishes.

JL HANOMAN
Hanoman Juice Ja (Map pp144-5; ☎ 971056; Jl Hanoman 12; dishes 6000-18,000Rp) Cleanse your system at this simple café serving health juices, including wheat germ grass and ginseng shots. Solid items include bagels, salads and sandwiches.

Bebek Bengil 1 (Map pp144-5; Dirty Duck Diner; ☎ 975489; Jl Hanoman; dishes 18,000-50,000Rp; ☎ 10am-10pm) This sprawling place does a special line in crispy deep-fried duck dishes and has a delightful dining area. There's a branch off Monkey Forest Rd (p163).

TEBESAYA
Village Café (Map pp144-5; ☎ 973229; Rona Inn, Jl Sukma; dishes 7500-20,000Rp) Friendly staff serve up the usual suspects as well as extra-tasty juice concoctions, such as watermelon, carrot and apple juice. There's also Internet access.

Alon Alon (Map pp144-5; Jl Sukma; dishes 6000-10,000Rp; ☎ 3-10pm) An Ubud café for the 21st century, this cheery two-level place is bright, funky and colourful. Lots of little items on the menu from a range of coffees and juices to sandwiches and unusual items like pumpkin croquettes.

Coffee & Silver (Map pp144-5; ☎ 978228; Jl Sukma 45; dishes 20,000-70,000Rp; ☎ 10am-midnight) Tapas and more substantial items make up the menu at this comfortable and classy place. Snuggle back into a deep leather chair and enjoy dishes from salads to burgers to onion rings. Vintage photos of Ubud line the walls.

Delta Dewata Supermarket (Map pp144-5; ☎ 973049; Jl Raya Andong) Located on the east-ern side of town, this place gives you a Wal-Mart like shopping experience (vast arrange of goods) without the social guilt.

South of Ubud
Kokokan Club (Map pp144-5; ☎ 973495; Jl Raya Pen-gosekan; mains 35,000-55,000Rp; ☎ lunch & dinner) On the grounds of the ARMA Resort, this elegant restaurant serves superb Southern Thai and seafood dishes. *Hor mok goong* (prawns steamed in banana leaf) is as good as you'll find anywhere. The open-sided, upstairs dining area has a general air of understated elegance. Phone for transport.

Barandi (Map pp144-5; ☎ 975894; Jl Raya Pen-gosekan; lunch 25,000-37,000Rp, dinner 29,000-75,000Rp; ☎ lunch & dinner) The long black marble bar sets the tone at this excellent and contempo-rary two-level restaurant. The long wine list is matched to an interesting fusion menu. On Tuesday nights there's live Latin music; Friday there's jazz.

Restaurant Lele Mas (Map pp144-5; ☎ 972750; Jl Raya Pengosekan; dishes 20,000-50,000Rp) Following a sinuous path through lovely gardens brings you to this attractive 2nd-floor restaurant that looks out over rice paddies. The menu offers well-prepared renditions of local, Indonesian and Chinese standards.

Kakiang Bakery (Map pp144-5; ☎ 978984; Jl Raya Pengosekan; dishes 8000-20,000Rp; ☎) This mod-ern little café is a good place for a coffee, snack or sandwich.

Pizza Bagus (Map pp144-5; ☎ 978520; Jl Raya Pengosekan; dishes 18,000-30,000Rp) Ubud's best pizza bakes up with a crispy thin crust at this small place. Besides the long list of pizza options, there's pasta and sandwich. They deliver.

West of Ubud
The restaurants and cafés in this section are all pretty spread out.

UBUD & AROUND

JL BISMA

Café des Artistes (Map pp144–5; ☎ 972706; Jl Bisma 9X; dishes 22,000-86,000Rp; ☯ 10am-midnight) In a quiet and cultured perch up off Jl Raya Ubud, the popular Café des Artistes brings Belgian food to Ubud. But the menu strays into France and Indonesia as well, with a foray or two of other places for sandwiches and salads at lunch. Dinner mains show the care in the kitchen from the talented staff. Art by locals such as Theo Zantman is on display.

CAMPUAN

Restaurants here are strung out in a row near the bridge.

Murni's Warung (Map pp144–5; ☎ 975233; Jl Raya Campuan; dishes 16,000-47,000Rp) Since 1977, Murni's has been an Ubud favourite. The setting is beautiful and a four-level dining room overlooks the lush river valley. Indonesian dishes, curries and Western options are available. There's a cosy bar on the 2nd level down. One quibble: the gift shop gets bigger every year.

Indus Restaurant (Map pp144–5; ☎ 977684; Jl Raya Sanggingan; dishes 15,000-42,000Rp) Perched on a ridge above the Sungai Cerik Valley, this branch of the Casa Luna (see p163) empire is another top-class Ubud eatery. The creative menu changes often with the seasons and features Balinese fusion. The views are excellent.

Pesto Café (Map pp144–5; ☎ 975884; Jl Raya Campuan; dishes 17,000-23,000Rp) This cute little spot has good Italian and Mediterranean meals at good prices. The one curiosity is that pesto itself is not on the menu.

SANGGINGAN

Mozaic (Map pp144–5; ☎ 975768; Jl Raya Sanggingan; dishes 50,000-200,000Rp; ☯ lunch & dinner Tue-Sun) Chef Chris Salans has created a fine restaurant that brings excellent French fusion cuisine into a lush garden setting. One of Bali's finest, Mozaic is consistently popular for its high standards, putting it on par with top international restaurants. Tasting menus (190,000-240,000Rp) are available.

Naughty Nuri's (Map pp144–5; ☎ 977547; Jl Raya Sanggingan; dishes 15,000-50,000Rp) Martinis are the specialty here – you can get them to go. To give them something to wash it down with there's a menu of steaks, ribs and seafood. Thursday night grilled tuna specials are very popular.

Fly Café (Map pp144–5; ☎ 759049; Jl Raya Lungsiakan; 17,000-55,000Rp) Buzz in to this popular place with a stupid name for good meals of Western and Indonesian food. A good coffee bar and very comfortable wicker seats make it a good place for lounging especially after a walk into these parts.

PENESTANAN

Choices are limited if you're staying in Penestanan, although most of the hotels have a café.

Gajah Biru (Map pp144–5; ☎ 979085; Jl Raya Penestanan; dishes 40,000-55,000Rp; ☯ dinner) In a park-like setting, this lovely place offers a range of Indian curries and Thai classics.

Ibu Putih's Warung (Map pp144–5; ☎ 976146; off Jl Raya Campuan; dishes 6000-10,000Rp) This shady place on the stairs leading to Penestanan serves simple and excellent food from a varied menu. It has a friendly, family ambience and you may end up hanging out for a while.

SAYAN & AYUNG VALLEY

The top-end resorts have excellent restaurants that can make for a special night out from Ubud.

Ayung Terrace (Map pp144–5; ☎ 977577; Four Seasons Resort; dinner per person US$25-50) The same stunning view that makes the Four Seasons such a fine place to stay spreads out here for diners. Dining here during the day is casual. But at night the cuisine comes alive for dinner. Pan-Asian fusion is the theme, with menus changing almost nightly. Service and presentation are superb.

Restaurant (Map pp144–5; ☎ 975333; Amandari; dinner per person US$25-50) Thanks to the name you won't end up at the bar asking for food. A vision in teak, this place is perched over the valley below. The changing menu draws from Western and Asian influences. The wine selection befits a celebration.

DRINKING

No-one comes to Ubud for wild nightlife. A few bars do get quite lively around sunset and later into the night, but the venues certainly don't aspire to the extremes of beer-swilling debauchery and first-world hip clubs found in Kuta and Seminyak.

Bars close early in Ubud – around 1am – by local ordinance. Many places listed under Eating are also good just for a drink.

Nomad (Map pp146-7; ☎ 977169; Jl Raya Ubud; dishes 15,000-45,000Rp) There's a barbeque here daily and often a gamelan player as well. It's a good central spot for a drink, especially back in the dark corners.

Jazz Café (Map pp144-5; ☎ 976594; Jl Sukma; dishes 35,000-60,000Rp; ⏰ 5pm-midnight) An expat meeting place, Jazz Café has a relaxed atmosphere in a garden of coconut palms and ferns, good Asian fusion food and live music from Tuesday to Saturday from 7.30pm. The cocktail list is long. It provides free pick up and drop off around Ubud.

Putra Bar (Map pp146-7; Monkey Forest Rd; draught beer 12,000Rp) Ubud's rasta wannabes hang out at this dark place which features live reggae music from 9pm on Sunday, Tuesday, Wednesday and Friday, and video movies or sports telecasts on Marley-free evenings.

Ang Ka Sa (Map pp146-7; ☎ 977395; Jl Suweta; small/large Bintang 10,000/16,000Rp) This small, stylish bar-café, has papaya-coloured walls to go with papaya drinks on the menu.

Café Exiles (☎ 974812; Jl Raya Pengosekan; dishes 19,000-28,000Rp; ⏰ 11am-midnight) An open-air café-bar with a grassy outlook, Exiles pulls in a large crowd on Saturday nights, when there's live blues, jazz and rock music. The small menu is international and includes tapas. The name is a nod to its expat patrons.

Wunderbar (Map pp144-5; ☎ 978339; Jl Raya Pengosekan; dishes 23,000-52,000Rp; ⏰ 11-1am; 🗷) A vision in orange and blue like an Orangina bottle with an other-worldly glow thanks to lava lamps, Wunderbar boasts a pool table, satellite TVs for sports events and live jazz on Monday nights. A German chef cooks up a range of Euro-Asian dishes.

ENTERTAINMENT

The joy of Ubud – and what makes people stay weeks instead of days – is the cultural entertainment. This is where you can base yourself not only for the nightly array of performances, but also to keep up with news of scheduled events in surrounding villages.

If you're in the right place at the right time you may see dances performed in temple ceremonies for an essentially local audience. These dances are often quite long and not as accessible to the uninitiated. Dances performed for tourists are usually adapted and abbreviated to some extent to make them more enjoyable, but most are done with a high degree of skill and commitment, and usually have appreciative locals in the audience (or peering over the fence!). It's also common to combine the features of more than one traditional dance in a single performance.

In a week in Ubud, you can see Kecak, Legong and Barong dances, Mahabharata and Ramayana ballets, *wayang kulit* puppets and gamelan orchestras. The main venues are the **Ubud Palace** (Map pp146-7; Jl Raya Ubud), **Padangtegal Dance Stage** (Map pp144-5; Jl Hanoman), **Pura Dalem Puri** (Map pp144-5; Jl Raya Ubud), the **ARMA Open Stage** (Map pp144-5; ☎ 976659; Jl Raya Pengosekan), and **Peliatan Pura Dalem Puri** (Map pp144-5; Jl Peliatan). Other performances are in nearby towns like Batuan, Mawang and Kutuh.

You can also find shadow puppet shows – although these are greatly attenuated from traditional village performances that often last the entire night. Regular performances are held at **Oka Kartini** (Map pp144-5; ☎ 975193; Jl Raya Ubud; tickets 50,000Rp), which has bungalows and a gallery.

Ubud Tourist Information has performance information, and sells tickets (usually 50,000Rp). For performances outside Ubud, transport is usually included in the price. Tickets are also sold at many travel agencies and hotels, and by street-sellers who hang around outside Ubud Palace – all charge the same price as the tourist office.

Vendors sell drinks at the performances, which typically last about 90 minutes. Before the show, you might notice the musicians checking out the size of the crowd – ticket sales fund the troupes. Also watch for potential members of the next generation of performers: local children avidly watch from under the screens, behind stage and from a musician's lap or two.

One word to the wise about a problem unimaginable just a couple of years ago: turn off your cell phone! Nobody else wants to hear it.

SHOPPING

Ubud has a variety of art shops and galleries, and you can use Ubud as a base to explore craft and antique shops all the way down to Batubulan (see p140).

Arts & Crafts

You'll find paintings for sale everywhere. Check the gallery listings (p149) for recommendations. Prices in galleries range from almost cheap to stratospheric depending on the artist. Prices often are lower if you buy directly from the artist's workshop. Small landscape paintings with intricate wooden frames make great souvenirs – prices start from around 100,000Rp.

Small shops at Pasar Seni and by Monkey Forest Rd often have good woodcarvings, particularly masks. There are other good woodcarving places along Jl Bedulu east of Teges, and along the road between Nyuhkuning and the southern entrance to Monkey Forest Sanctuary.

Surrounding villages also specialise in different styles or subjects of masks. Along the road from Teges to Mas, look for masks and some of the most original carved pieces with natural wood finishes. North of Ubud, look for carved Garudas in Junjungan, and painted flowers and fruit in Tegallalang. Peliatan produces shadow puppets.

Tegun Galeri (Map pp144-5; ☎ 973361; Jl Hanoman 40) One of the better spots for unusual handicrafts and jewellery.

Moari (Map pp144-5; ☎ 977367; Jl Raya Ubud) New and restored Balinese musical instruments are sold here.

Clothes

For fashion and fabrics, the most interesting shops are found on Monkey Forest Rd, Jl Dewi Siti and Jl Hanoman. Many will make or alter to order.

Pasar Seni (Art Market; Map pp146-7; Jl Raya Ubud) Sells cheap sarongs for temple visits.

Zarong (Map pp146-7; ☎ 977601; Monkey Forest Rd) A slightly offbeat, hippy, chic fashion store. There's lots of cool cottons here that will be at home in any Balinese situation.

Tunjung (☎ 974078; Jl Hanoman 10) Great for kids' clothing. You'll find very sweet batik print outfits for newborns to 12-year-olds. Plus, there's even dolls clothes to fit Barbie and Ken in traditional Indonesian outfits!

Sisi (☎ 0818 349 225; Jl Goutama) A shop full of groovy fabric handbags by a Japanese designer.

Rascals (Map pp146-7; ☎ 461357; Jl Dewi Sita) You can gear up for your big splash at this store. Bathing suits range from next to nothing

to more strategic creations for those who'd rather hint than reveal.

Jewellery

Alamkara Monkey Forest Rd (Map pp146-7; ☎ 972213); Jl Dewi Sita (Map pp146-7; ☎ 971004) One of the best jewellery galleries in Ubud, if not Bali, where the craftsmanship is of a high standard. On display are unusual, but very wearable designs in gold and silver, featuring black pearls and gems. The work of foreign and local jewellers is on display.

Treasures – a Gallery of Gold Creations (Map pp146-7; ☎ 976697; Jl Raya Ubud) A posh place with expensive, gem encrusted gold jewellery by international artists.

Ashram (Map pp144-5; ☎ 0812 394 3354; Jl Sukma 1) A colourful, funky gallery of works by Jeli Lala, a foreign jeweller whose work is marked by a playful, naive style. It's a fun place to browse and you can pick up one of their free meditations.

Kayan Gallery (Map pp144-5; ☎ 980424; Jl Sukma 17) The distinctive work of Dutch jeweller Jan Van is on display, featuring black pearls, leather and silver chokers, and interestingly shaped rings.

Other Items

For concentrated souvenir shopping go to or streets such as Jl Hanoman and Monkey Forest Rd. Shops are stocked to the brim with baskets, textiles, paintings, mirrors, mosaics, bags, kites, drums, umbrellas – and much more.

Ubud's colourful produce market, adjacent to Pasar Seni starts early in the morning, but winds up by lunch time.

Places with DVDs of dubious origin have proliferated. Most also have large selections of CDs both legitimate and pirated.

Pasar Seni (Art Market; Map pp146-7; Jl Raya Ubud) Offers a wide range of souvenirs.

Ubud Music (Map pp146-7; ☎ 975362; Jl Raya Ubud) Has a huge music selection.

Threads of Life Indonesian Textile Arts Center (Map pp144-5; ☎ 972187; Jl Kajeng 24) Stocks exquisite handmade traditional fabrics. See p155 for information about the courses in weaving.

Bali Cares (☎ 981504; Jl Hanoman 44) This lovely shop sells goods to benefit several local charities, including Yayasan Bumi Sehat, a health and birthing centre, Eco-trainers, a community-based environment awareness group and VIBE (Volunteers & Interns for Balinese Education), which runs art and education courses for kids. Items range from wood-carvings made from sustainable woods to paintings, handicrafts and other items produced by local people. There's an adjoining small café and the shop is an excellent resource for information on charitable and non-profit groups.

Kertas Gingsir (☎ 973030; Jl Dewi Sita) Specialises in interesting paper handmade from banana, pineapple and taro plants. If you're a real fan, ask about factory visits.

Reincarnation Furniture (Map pp146-7; ☎ 978755; off Monkey Forest Rd) Restores old Balinese teak furniture. The results are worth a browse even if you doubt you'll have room in your carry-on for an ottoman.

Kites Centre (Map pp146-7; ☎ 970924; Monkey Forest Rd) There are colourful wind-born creations such as dragons and sailing ships. A sweet little small frog goes for 25,000Rp.

GETTING THERE & AWAY
Bemo
Ubud is served by two main bemo routes, but does not have a bemo terminal as such – bemos stop at one of two convenient points, north of the market in the centre of town, and nearby, at the southern end of Jl Suweta.

Brown bemos go to/from Batubulan terminal (4000Rp).

To get to most places in West and South Bali, you will first have to go to Denpasar and transfer, possibly between stations. See p87 for details.

Going north to Kintamani, get a brown bemo (7000Rp), from there you can connect to Singaraja, Lovina, and North Bali.

Small bemos travel between Ubud and Gianyar (4000Rp), where you can connect to points further east.

Taxi
There are very few taxis in Ubud – just a few that have brought in passengers from southern Bali and are hoping for a fare back. For private transport you'll need to arrange it with your hotel or negotiate with the many drives hanging around the centre.

Tourist Shuttle Bus
Perama (☎ 973316; Jl Hanoman; ☒ 9am-9pm) is the major tourist shuttle operator, but its terminal is inconveniently located in Padangtegal, to get to your final destination in Ubud will cost another 5000Rp.

Destination	Fare
Candidasa	30,000Rp
Kuta and airport	20,000Rp
Lovina	50,000Rp
Padangbai	30,000Rp
Sanur	15,000Rp

GETTING AROUND
To/From the Airport
Regular Perama tourist shuttle buses go to the airport from Ubud, while prepaid taxis from the airport to Ubud cost 115,000Rp. If you need a taxi, ask your hotel or a travel agent to arrange a vehicle one day ahead, or bargain with one of the ubiquitous transport touts. By bemo, go to Batubulan terminal in Denpasar, catch another bemo to Tegal terminal, and then another to the airport – it may be cheap, but it is slow and extremely inconvenient.

Bemo
Bemos don't directly link Ubud with nearby villages; you'll have to catch one going to Denpasar, Gianyar, Pujung or Kintamani and get off where you need to. Small bemos to Gianyar travel along eastern Jl Raya, down Jl Peliatan and east to Bedulu. To Pujung, bemos head east along Jl Raya and then north through Andong and past the turn-off to Petulu.

To Payangan, they travel west along Jl Raya, past Campuan and turn north at the junction after Sanggingan. Larger brown bemos to Batubulan terminal go east along Jl Raya and down Jl Hanoman.

Car & Motorcycle
A rented car or motorcycle is very convenient for getting around the outskirts of Ubud, visiting nearby attractions, and travelling further afield. Prices are quite competitive in Ubud, and you might avoid the horrors of driving around Kuta, Denpasar and other congested areas of southern Bali. The ubiquitous Suzuki Jimmy jeep costs about 80,000Rp per day with minimal insurance cover – a little bit less for a longer period. A bigger Toyota Kijang costs about

UBUD & AROUND

100,000Rp, and a motorcycle costs around 30,000Rp.

Numerous agencies on Monkey Forest Rd, Jl Hanoman and Jl Raya Ubud will happily arrange car rental.

AROUND UBUD

☎ 0361

The region east and north of Ubud has many of the most ancient monuments and relics on Bali. Some of them predate the Majapahit era and raise as-yet-unanswered questions about Bali's history. Others are more recent, and in other instances, newer structures have been built on and around the ancient remains. They're interesting to history and archaeology buffs, but not that spectacular to look at – with the exception of Gunung Kawi. Perhaps the best approach is to plan a whole day walking or cycling around the area, stopping at the places that interest you, but not treating any one as a destination in itself.

If you're travelling by public transport, start early and take a bemo to the Bedulu intersection southeast of Ubud, and another due north to Tirta Empul, about 15km from Ubud. From the temple of Tirta Empul, follow the path beside the river down to Gunung Kawi, then return to the main road and walk south for about 8km to Pejeng, or flag down a bemo going towards Gianyar.

BEDULU

Bedulu was once the capital of a great kingdom. The legendary Dalem Bedaulu (See the Legend of Dalem Bedaulu, below) ruled the Pejeng dynasty from here, and was the last Balinese king to withstand the onslaught of the powerful Majapahit from Java. He was defeated by Gajah Mada in 1343. The capital shifted several times after this, to Gelgel and then later to Semarapura (Klungkung). For a walking tour around this area see p154.

Sights
GOA GAJAH

Two kilometres southeast of Ubud on the road to Bedulu, a large car park and a few of souvenir shops indicate that you've reached a big tourist attraction – **Goa Gajah** (Elephant Cave; adult/child 4100/2100Rp, car parking 400Rp,

motorbike parking 300Rp; ☺ 8am-6pm). There were never any elephants on Bali; the cave probably takes its name from the nearby Sungai Petanu, which at one time was known as Elephant River, or perhaps because the face over the cave entrance might resemble an elephant.

The origins of the cave are uncertain – one tale relates that it was created by the fingernail of the legendary giant Kebo Iwa. It probably dates to the 11th century, and was certainly in existence during the Majapahit takeover of Bali. The cave was rediscovered by Dutch archaeologists in 1923, but the fountains and pool were not found until 1954.

The cave is carved into a rock face and you enter through the cavernous mouth of a demon. The gigantic fingertips pressed beside the face of the demon push back a riotous jungle of surrounding stone carvings.

Inside the T-shaped cave you can see fragmentary remains of the *lingam,* the phallic symbol of the Hindu god Shiva, and its female counterpart the *yoni,* plus a statue of Shiva's son, the elephant-headed god Ganesha. In the courtyard in front of the cave are two square bathing pools with water trickling into them from waterspouts held by six female figures. To the left of the cave entrance, in a small pavilion, is a statue of Hariti, surrounded by children. In Buddhist lore, Hariti was an evil woman who devoured children, but under the influence of Buddhism she reformed completely to become a protector of children and a symbol of fertility.

THE LEGEND OF DALEM BEDAULU

A legend relates how Dalem Bedaulu possessed magical powers that allowed him to have his head chopped off and then replaced. Performing this unique party trick one day, the servant entrusted with lopping off his head and then replacing it unfortunately dropped it in a river and, to his horror, watched it float away. Looking around in panic for a replacement he grabbed a pig, cut off its head and popped it upon the king's shoulders. Thereafter, the king was forced to sit on a high throne and forbade his subjects to look up at him; Bedaulu means 'he who changed heads'.

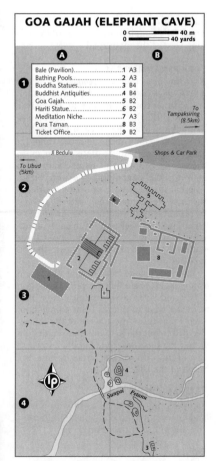

GOA GAJAH (ELEPHANT CAVE)

Bale (Pavilion)..........................1	A3
Bathing Pools.........................2	A3
Buddha Statues.......................3	B4
Buddhist Antiquities................4	B4
Goa Gajah.............................5	B2
Hariti Statue..........................6	B2
Meditation Niche....................7	A3
Pura Taman...........................8	B3
Ticket Office..........................9	B2

To Tampaksiring (8.5km)

Jl Bedulu

Shops & Car Park

To Ubud (5km)

Sungai Petanu

From Goa Gajah you can clamber down through the rice paddies to Sungai Petanu, where there are crumbling **rock carvings** of *stupas* (domes for housing Buddhist relics) on a cliff face, and a small **cave**.

Try to see it before 10am, when the big tourist buses start to arrive.

YEH PULU

This 25m-long **carved cliff face** (Map pp144-5; adult/child 4100/2100Rp) is believed to be a hermitage dating from the late 14th century. Apart from the figure of elephant-headed Ganesha, the son of Shiva, there are no obvious religious scenes here. The energetic frenzy includes various scenes of everyday life, although the position and movement of the figures suggests that it could be read from left to right as a story. One theory is that they are events from the life of Krishna, the Hindu god.

One of the first recognisable images is of a man carrying a shoulder pole with two jugs, possibly full of *tuak* (palm wine). He is following a woman whose jewellery suggests wealth and power. There's a whimsical figure peering round a doorway, who seems to have armour on his front and a weapon on his back. The thoughtful seated figure wears a turban, which suggests he is a priest.

The hunting scene starts with a horseman and a man throwing a spear. Another man seems to be thrusting a weapon into the mouth of a large beast, while a frog imitates him by disposing of a snake in the same manner. Above the frog, two figures kneel over a smoking pot, while to the right, two men carry off a slain animal on a pole. Then there's the depiction of the woman holding the horse's tail – is she begging the rider to stay or being dragged off as his captive?

The Ganesha figures of Yeh Pulu and Goa Gajah are quite similar, indicating a close relationship between them. You can walk between the sites, following small paths through the paddy fields, but you might need to pay a local kid to guide you. By car or bicycle, look for the signs to 'Relief Yeh Pulu' or 'Villa Yeh Pulu', east of Goa Gajah.

From the entrance, it's a pleasant 300m walk to Yeh Pulu.

PURA SAMUAN TIGA

The majestic **Pura Samuan Tiga** (Temple of the Meeting of the Three; Map pp144-5) is about 200m east of the Bedulu junction. The name is possibly a reference to the Hindu trinity, or it may refer to meetings held here in the early 11th century. Despite these early associations, all the temple buildings have been rebuilt since the 1917 earthquake. The imposing main gate was designed and built by I Gusti Nyoman Lempad, one of Bali's renowned artists and a native of Bedulu.

MUSEUM PURBAKALA

This archaeological **museum** (Map pp144-5; ☎ 942354; admission by donation; ☼ 8am-3pm Mon-Thu, 8am-12.30pm Fri) has a reasonable collection of artefacts from all over Bali, and most displays are in English. The exhibits in several small buildings include some of Bali's first pottery from near Gilimanuk, and sarcophagi dating from as early as 300 BC – some originating from Bangli are carved in the shape of a turtle, which has important cosmic associations in Balinese mythology. The museum is about 500m north of the Bedulu junction, and easy to reach by bemo or by bicycle.

Getting There & Away
About 3km east of Teges, the road from Ubud reaches a junction where you can turn south to Gianyar or north to Pejeng, Tampaksiring and Penelokan. Ubud-Gianyar bemos will drop you off at this junction, from where you can walk to the attractions. The road from Ubud is reasonably flat, so coming by bicycle is a good option.

PEJENG
Continuing up the road towards Tampaksiring you soon come to Pejeng and its famous temples. Like Bedulu, this was once an important seat of power, as it was the capital of the Pejeng kingdom, which fell to the Majapahit invaders in 1343.

Sights
PURA KEBO EDAN
Also called the **Crazy Buffalo Temple** (Map pp144-5), this is not an imposing structure, but it is famous for its 3m-high statue, known as the **Giant of Pejeng**, thought to be approximately 700 years old. Details are sketchy, but it may represent Bima, a hero of the *Mahabharata*, dancing on a dead body, as in a myth related to the Hindu Shiva cult. There is some conjecture about the giant's genitalia – it has either six small penises or one large one, and if that large thing is a penis, what are those interesting lumps and that big hole in the side?

PURA PUSERING JAGAT
The large **Pura Pusering Jagat** (Navel of the World Temple; Map pp144-5) is said to be the centre of the old Pejeng kingdom. Dating from 1329, this temple is visited by young couples who pray at the stone *lingam* and *yoni*. Further back is a large stone urn, with elaborate but worn carvings of gods and demons searching for the elixir of life in a depiction of the

Mahabharata tale 'Churning the Sea of Milk'. The temple is on a small track running west of the main road.

PURA PENATARAN SASIH
This was once the state **temple** (Map pp144-5; Jl Raya Tampaksiring) of the Pejeng kingdom. In the inner courtyard, high up in a pavilion and difficult to see, is the huge bronze drum known as the **Moon of Pejeng**. The hourglass-shaped drum is more than 2m long, the largest single-piece cast drum in the world. Estimates of its age vary from 1000 to 2000 years, and it is not certain whether it was made locally or imported – the intricate geometric decorations are said to resemble patterns from as far apart as Irian Jaya and Vietnam. Even in its in-accessible position, you can make out these patterns and the distinctive heart-shaped face designs.

Balinese legend relates that the drum came to earth as a fallen moon, landing in a tree and shining so brightly that it prevented a band of thieves from going about their unlawful purpose. One of the thieves decided to put the light out by urinating on it, but the moon exploded and fell to earth as a drum, with a crack across its base as a result of the fall.

TAMPAKSIRING
Tampaksiring is a small town with a large and important temple and the most impressive ancient monument on Bali.

Sights
GUNUNG KAWI
On the southern outskirts of town, a sign points east off the main road to Gunung Kawi and its **ancient monuments** (Map p141; adult/child 4100/2100Rp; ⊙ 7am-5pm). From the end of the access road, a steep, stone stairway leads down to the river, at one point making a cutting through an embankment of solid rock. There, in the bottom of this lush green valley, is one of Bali's oldest and largest ancient monuments.

Gunung Kawi consists of 10 rock-cut *candi* (shrines) – memorials cut out of the rock face in imitation of actual statues. They stand in 7m-high sheltered niches cut into the sheer cliff face. A solitary *candi* stands about a kilometre further down the valley to the south; this is reached by a trek

PAUL BEINSSEN

Shrines carved into rock, Gunung Kawi (p172)

EDWARD AM SNIJDERS

Monkey Forest Sanctuary (p150)

Dancer in traditional costume, Ubud Palace (p148)

GREGORY ADAMS

Stone carving on the road from
Denpasar to Ubud (p87)

PAUL BEINSSEN

RICHARD I'ANSC

Rice terraces, Ubud (p152)

GREGORY ADAMS

Condong dancer (p40)

through the rice paddies on the western side of the river.

Each *candi* is believed to be a memorial to a member of the 11th-century Balinese royalty, but little is known for certain. Legends relate that the whole group of memorials was carved out of the rock face in one hard-working night by the mighty fingernails of Kebo Iwa.

The five monuments on the eastern bank are probably dedicated to King Udayana, Queen Mahendradatta, their son Airlangga and his brothers Anak Wungsu and Marakata. While Airlangga ruled eastern Java, Anak Wungsu ruled Bali. The four monuments on the western side are, by this theory, to Anak Wungsu's chief concubines. Another theory is that the whole complex is dedicated to Anak Wungsu, his wives, concubines and, in the case of the remote 10th *candi*, to a royal minister.

TIRTA EMPUL
A well-signposted fork in the road north of Tampaksiring leads to the holy springs at **Tirta Empul** (Map p141; adult/child 4100/2100Rp; ☑ 8am-6pm), discovered in AD 962 and believed to have magical powers. The springs bubble up into a large, crystal-clear tank within the temple and gush out through waterspouts into a bathing pool – they're the main source of Sungai Pakerisan, the river that rushes by Gunung Kawi only 1km or so away. Next to the springs, **Pura Tirta Empul** is one of Bali's most important temples.

You'll need a sarong or long pants, and maybe a scarf. Come in the early morning or late afternoon to avoid the tourist buses. You can also use the clean, segregated and free public baths in the grounds.

OTHER SITES
There are other groups of *candi* and monks' cells in the area encompassed by the ancient Pejeng kingdom, notably **Pura Krobokan** and **Goa Garba**, but none so grand as Gunung Kawi. Between Gunung Kawi and Tirta Empul, **Pura Mengening** temple has a free-standing *candi*, similar in design to those at Gunung Kawi.

NORTH OF UBUD
The usual road from Ubud to Batur is through Tampaksiring, but there are other lesser roads up the gentle mountain slope. One of the most attractive goes north from Peliatan, past Petulu, and through Tegallalang and Pujung, to bring you out on the crater rim between Penelokan and Batur. It's a sealed road all the way. **Tegallalang**, **Jati** and **Pujung** are all noted woodcarving centres.

About 12km north of Ubud, **Bali Adventure Tours** (☎ 721480; www.baliadventuretours.com) runs the **Elephant Safari Park** (adult/child US$14/5.75, package incl elephant ride & transport adult/child US$68/47) in the cool, wet highlands of Taro. Although elephants are not native to Bali they are native to Indonesia and kids always enjoy this place.

A good lunch stop about 12km from Ubud, with picturesque paddy-field views is **Blue Yogi Cafe** (Map p141; ☎ 901368; dishes 15,000-40,000Rp; ☑ 8am-5pm). After lunch, walk things off with a stroll among the rice.

A smaller road goes north through **Keliki**, where you'll find **Alam Sari** (☎ 240308; www.alam sari.com; r US$100-250; ☒ ☒), a fine, small hotel in a wonderfully isolated location. There are 12 luxurious yet rustic rooms, a pool and a great view.

UBUD & AROUND

East Bali

EAST BALI

The eastern end of Bali is dominated by mighty Gunung Agung, known as the 'navel of the world' and Bali's 'Mother Mountain'. This towering 3142m-high volcano last erupted in 1963, causing a major disaster. Today, Gunung Agung is quiet, but the 'Mother Temple' of Pura Besakih, perched high on its slopes, attracts a steady stream of devotees, tourists and touts.

The traditional route east from South Bali goes through Gianyar and Semarapura (also known as Klungkung), and then close to the coast past Kusamba, the bat-infested temple of Pura Goa Lawah and the turn-off to Padangbai. A coast road to Kusamba saves time. Semarapura, with its royal legacy, is worth a detour.

From Padangbai, the port for the Lombok ferry, there are plenty of places to stay and lots of coast to explore. Candidasa is a quiet coastal town popular with travellers looking to simply relax. Further east are relatively untrammelled beaches.

An alternative route goes around the southern flank of Gunung Agung, with fine scenery and small villages. From Amlapura, another old kingdom capital, continue north past the rice fields of Tirta Gangga to reach the far east coast, a region with great diving and a relaxed seaside scene.

Throughout East Bali are many little roads traversing the island's verdant rice paddies. It's an orgasm of green. One of the great pleasures is simply wandering around the hills and valleys along small roads and soaking up the vistas. Late in the afternoon, you'll pass lines of people heading off to the streams and rivers to bathe. You can't really get lost – you're never far from a main road, and people are very happy to help with directions.

From much of East Bali you'll have views of three islands: Nusa Lembongan, Nusa Penida and Nusa Ceningan. The first is a popular escape for those who want a break from the South Bali bustle, while the other two are lightly visited. All offer superb diving.

EAST BALI

TOP FIVE

- Exploring **Gunung Agung** (p186) – a classic conical volcano

- Learning lurid legends at Semarapura's **Kertha Gosa** (p179)

- Diving around the islets off **Candidasa** (p194), coral reefs off **Amed** (p201) and WWII wreck off **Tulamben** (p205)

- Seeing sculpted rice terraces, rugged seascapes and superb sunrises

- Chilling out – or maybe catching a wave – on **Nusa Lembongan** (p208)

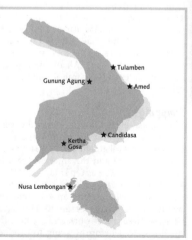

GIANYAR
☎ 0361
Gianyar is the affluent administrative capital and main market town of the Gianyar district, which also includes Ubud. It's on Bali's main eastern road, which carries heavy traffic between Denpasar and Padangbai. The town has a number of factories producing batik and ikat fabrics, and the palace of the surviving royal family, but it's of minimal interest to most visitors.

Sights
Puri Gianyar (Jl Ngurah Rai) dates from 1771, but was destroyed in a conflict with the neighbouring kingdom of Klungkung in the mid-1880s and rebuilt. Under threat from its aggressive neighbours, the Gianyar kingdom requested Dutch protection, and a 1900 agreement allowed Gianyar's ruling family to retain its status and its palace, though it lost all political power. The *puri* (palace) was damaged in the 1917 earthquake, but was restored soon after and appears little changed from the time the Dutch arrived. It's a fine example of traditional palace architecture, but tourists are not usually allowed inside. If you report to the guard inside the complex, you may be allowed a quick look around. Otherwise, you can see some of it through the gates.

Eating
People sometimes come to Gianyar to sample the market food, like *babi guling* (spit-roast pig) for which the town is noted. To try some, head straight to the stalls inside the open-air **food market** (🕑 11am-2pm) or try one of the small restaurants nearby in the main street, or the food stalls in the **main market** (🕑 6-9pm). All of these places line both sides of Jl Ngurah Rai in the very centre.

Shopping
There are a few textile factories at the western end of town on the main Ubud road, including **Tenun Ikat Setia Cili** (☎ 943409; Jl Astina Utara; 🕑 9am-5pm) and the adjacent **Cap Bakti** (Jl Astina Utara), as well as **Cap Togog** (☎ 943046; Jl Astina Utara 11; 🕑 8am-5pm). These places have showrooms where you can buy material by the metre, or have it tailored. You can at times see weavers at work and see how the thread is dyed before weaving to produce

the vibrantly patterned weft ikat, which is called *endek* on Bali. Prices are 40,000Rp to 60,000Rp per metre for cotton fabric, depending on how fine the weaving is – costs will rise if it contains silk. Handmade batik is also for sale here.

Getting There & Away
There are regular *bemos* (small pick-up trucks) between Batubulan terminal near Denpasar and Gianyar's main terminal (6000Rp), which is behind the main market. Bemos from Gianyar's main terminal also serve Semarapura (12,000Rp) and Amlapura (12,000Rp), and Sidan (4000Rp) and Bangli (4000Rp). Bemos to and from Ubud (4000Rp) use the bemo stop across the road from the market.

LEBIH & THE COAST
South of Gianyar, the coast is fringed by black-sand beaches and small coastal villages like Lebih, but you will need your own transport to get around. Sungai Pakerisan (Pakerisan River), which starts near Tampaksiring, reaches the sea near **Lebih**. Here, and at other coastal villages south of Gianyar, cremation formalities reach their conclusion when the ashes are consigned to the sea. Ritual purification ceremonies for temple artefacts are also held on these beaches. The impressive **Pura Segara** looks across the strait to Nusa Penida, home of Jero Gede Macaling – the temple helps protect Bali from his evil influence. The site is very quiet.

Further west is **Pura Masceti**, one of Bali's nine directional temples (p58). On the beach, the villagers have erected a huge and somewhat horrific swan in an attempt to create a tourist attraction.

One of the best beaches along this stretch of coast is just south of **Siyut** and 3km east of Lebih. With the extension of the coastal bypass road, access to the beaches has become easier. *Warung* (food stalls) and cafés are appearing along the little roads which lead to the pounding water. Swimming is generally dangerous. **Ketewel** and Lebih are good spots for surfing; see p320 for details.

SIDAN
Driving east from Gianyar you come to the turn-off to Bangli about 2km out of Peteluan. Follow this road for about 1km

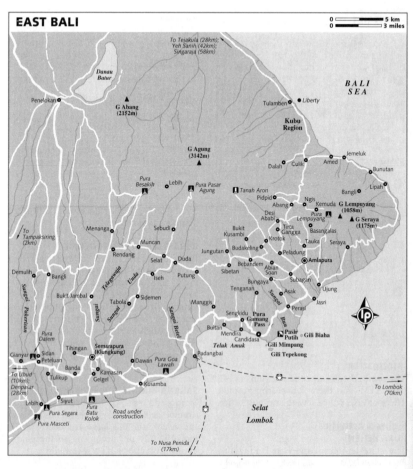

EAST BALI

To Tejakula (28km);
Yeh Sanih (42km);
Singaraja (58km)

Danau
Batur

Penelokan

G Abang
(2152m)

BALI
SEA

Tulamben • Liberty

Kubu
Region

G Agung
(3142m)

Jemeluk

Dalah   Culik   Amed

Bunutan

Pura
Besakih   Lebih   Pura Pasar
Agung

Tanah Aron

Pidpid

Lipah

Bangli

Abang   Ngis   Kemuda   G Lempuyang
(1058m)

Desi
Ababi

Pura
Lempuyang

G Seraya
(1175m)

To
Tampaksiring
(2km)

Menanga   Sebudi

Bukit
Kusambi

Tirta
Gangga   Basangalas

Muncan

Krotok   Tauka   Seraya

Rendang

Jungutan   Budakeling   Peladung

Amlapura

Demulih   Bangli

Selat   Duda

Bebandem

Abian
Soan

Bukit Jambal

Iseh   Putung

Sibetan

Subagan

To
Tampaksiring

Tabola   Sidemen

Bungaya   Asak

Tenganan

Ujung

Manggis

Sengkidu

Pura
Gamang
Pass

Perasi

Jasri

Butan

Mendira

Pasir
Putih   Gili Biaha

Pura
Dalem

Tihingan   Semarapura
(Klungkung)

Candidasa   Gili Mimpang

Teluk Amuk   Gili Tepekong

Gianyar   Sidan   Peteluan

Dawan   Pura Goa
Lawah

Padangbai

To Ubud
(10km);
Denpasar
(28km)

Banda   Kamasan

Tulikup   Gelgel

Kusamba

To Lombok
(70km)

Lebih

Siyut

Pura
Batu
Kolok

Road under
construction

Selat

Lombok

Pura Segara

Pura Masceti

To Nusa Penida
(17km)

0 ——— 5 km
0 ——— 3 miles

until you reach a sharp bend, where you'll find Sidan's **Pura Dalem**, a good example of a temple of the dead, with very fine carvings. Note the sculptures of Durga with children by the gate and the separate enclosure in one corner of the temple – this is dedicated to Merajapati, the guardian spirit of the dead.

BANGLI

☎ 0366

Halfway up the slope to Penelokan, Bangli, once the capital of a kingdom, is said to have the best climate on Bali.

It has an interesting temple, **Pura Kehen**, and the town makes for a good pit stop during a day of exploring.

History

Bangli dates from the early 13th century. In the Majapahit era it broke away from Gelgel to become a separate kingdom, even though it was landlocked, poor and involved in long-running conflicts with neighbouring states.

In 1849 Bangli made a treaty with the Dutch. The treaty gave Bangli control over the defeated north-coast kingdom of Buleleng, but Buleleng then rebelled and the Dutch imposed direct rule there. In 1909 the *rajah* (lord or prince) of Bangli chose to become a Dutch protectorate rather than face suicidal *puputan* (fight to the death) or complete conquest by the neighbouring kingdoms or the colonial power.

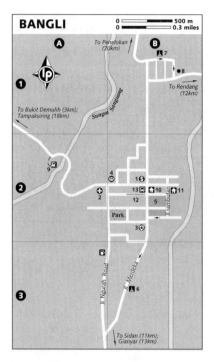

BANGLI

0 _____ 500 m
0 _____ 0.3 miles

To Penelokan
(20km)

To Rendang
(12km)

To Bukit Demulih (3km);
Tampaksiring (18km)

Sungai Sangsang

Jl Nguah Road

Merdeka

Jl Lambatu

Park

To Sidan (11km);
Gianyar (13km)

INFORMATION	
Bank BRI	1 B2
Hospital	2 A2
Police Station	3 B2
Post Office	4 B2

SIGHTS & ACTIVITIES	(p178)
Market	5 B2
Pura Dalem Penunggekan	6 B3
Pura Kehen	7 B1
Sasana Budaya Giri Kusuma	8 B1
Tirta Buana	9 A2

SLEEPING	⚑ (pp178-9)
Artha Sastra Inn	10 B2
Bangli Inn	11 B2

EATING	(pp178-9)
Pasar Malam (Night Market)	12 B2

TRANSPORT	(p179)
Bemo Terminal	13 B2

Sarong and/or sash rental costs 2000Rp (see Temple Etiquette, p38).

PURA DALEM PENUNGGEKAN
Just south of the centre, the exterior wall of this fascinating 'temple of the dead' features vivid relief carvings of wrong-doers getting their just desserts in the afterlife. One panel addresses the lurid fate of adulterers (men may find the viewing uncomfortable). Other panels portray sinners as monkeys, while another is a good representation of evil-doers begging to be spared the fires of hell.

SASANA BUDAYA GIRI KUSUMA
Supposedly a showplace for Balinese dance, drama, *gamelan* (Balinese orchestra) and the visual arts, this large arts centre rarely has anything on, according to the guard. This is a shame as it's a lovely site.

BUKIT DEMULIH
Three kilometres west of Bangli is the village of Demulih, and a hill called Bukit Demulih. If you can't find the sign pointing to it, ask local children to direct you. After a short climb to the top, you'll see a small temple and good views over South Bali.

On the way to Bukit Demulih, a steep side road leads down to **Tirta Buana**, a public swimming pool in a beautiful location deep in the valley.

Information
The compact and tidy centre has a Bank BRI with ATM, and there is a nearby hospital. There's also a police station and post office.

Sights & Activities
PURA KEHEN
The state temple of the Bangli kingdom, **Pura Kehen** (adult/child 2600/1000Rp; ⏰ 9am-5pm) is one of the finest temples in eastern Bali – it's a miniature version of Pura Besakih (p183). It is terraced up the hillside, with a flight of steps leading to the beautifully decorated entrance. The first courtyard has a huge banyan tree with a *kulkul* (warning drum) entwined in its branches. The Chinese porcelain plates were set into the walls as decoration, but most of the originals have been damaged or lost. The inner courtyard has an 11-roof *meru* (multiroofed shrine), and there are other shrines with thrones for the Hindu trinity – Brahma, Shiva and Vishnu (p38). The carvings are particularly intricate.

There's a counter opposite the temple entrance where you pay your admission.

Sleeping & Eating
A *pasar malam* (night market), on the street beside the bemo terminal, has some excellent warung, and you'll also find some in the market area during the day.

Artha Sastra Inn (☎ 91179; Jl Merdeka; s/d 30,000/45,000Rp) Still run by descendants of the last royal family, this bare-bones former royal residence is cheap and friendly.

Bangli Inn (☎ 91419; Jl Rambutan 1; s/d 80,000/ 100,000Rp) Somewhat modern, but just as friendly as the Artha Sastra, the cold-water rooms are clean and simple.

Getting There & Away

Bangli is easy to reach by bemo: it's on the main road between Denpasar's Batubulan terminal (4000Rp) and Kintamani (4000Rp), via Penelokan. Bemos also regularly leave Gianyar and go up the pretty, shaded road to Bangli, although it's often quicker to get a connection at the junction near Peteluan.

Tourist shuttle buses travelling between Ubud and Gunung Batur usually go via Tampaksiring and bypass Bangli.

SEMARAPURA (KLUNGKUNG)

☎ 0366

Semarapura was once the centre of Bali's most important kingdom, and a great artistic and cultural focal point. Today, the capital of Klungkung district, with its distinctly Chinese character, is a major public transport junction and has a chaotic market, Pasar Senggol. The town has been officially renamed Semarapura, but is still commonly called Klungkung. The Kertha Gosa complex is a must-see site and worth a detour from the coastal road. There are some fascinating attractions in the surrounding area, but accommodation is very limited. It's better to explore this area as a day trip from Ubud and South Bali or on the way to Candidasa and the east.

History

Successors to the Majapahit conquerors of Bali established themselves at Gelgel (just south of modern Semarapura) in around 1400, and the Gelgel dynasty strengthened with the growing Majapahit presence on Bali. During the 17th century, the successors of the Gelgel line established separate kingdoms and the dominance of the Gelgel court was lost. The court moved to Klungkung in 1710, but never regained a pre-eminent position.

In 1849 the rulers of Klungkung and Gianyar defeated a Dutch invasion force at

Kusamba. Before the Dutch could launch a counter attack, a force from Tabanan had arrived and the trader Mads Lange was able to broker a peace settlement.

For the next 50 years, the South Bali kingdoms squabbled, until the rajah of Gianyar persuaded the Dutch to support him. When the Dutch finally invaded the south, the king of Klungkung had a choice between a suicidal *puputan* (fight to the death), like the rajah of Denpasar, or an ignominious surrender, as Tabanan's rajah had done. He chose the former. In April 1908, as the Dutch surrounded his palace, the Dewa Agung and hundreds of his relatives and followers marched out to certain death from Dutch gunfire, or the blades of their own *kris* (traditional dagger). It was the last Balinese kingdom to succumb and the sacrifice is commemorated in the large Puputan Monument.

Information

The main street, Jl Diponegoro, has several banks with ATMs. The post office and *wartel* (public telephone office) are further west.

District tourist office (☎ 21448; ☼ 8am-2pm Mon-Fri) The small office is in the Museum Semarajaya building of Taman Kertha Gosa.

Police station (☎ 21115)

Sights

TAMAN KERTHA GOSA

When the Dewa Agung dynasty moved here in 1710, a new palace, the Semara Pura, was established. It was laid out as a large square, believed to be in the form of a mandala, with courtyards, gardens, pavilions and moats. The complex is sometimes referred to as Taman Gili (Island Garden). Most of the original palace and grounds were destroyed by Dutch attacks in 1908 – the Pemedal Agung, the gateway on the south side of the square, is all that remains of the palace itself (it's worth a close look to see the carvings). Two important buildings are preserved in a restored section of the grounds, and with a museum, they comprise the **Taman Kertha Gosa complex** (adult/child 5000/2000Rp, parking 1000Rp; ☼ 7am-5pm; **P**). Parking is easy, and the vendors are persistent.

Kertha Gosa

In the northeastern corner of the complex, the 'Hall of Justice' was effectively the

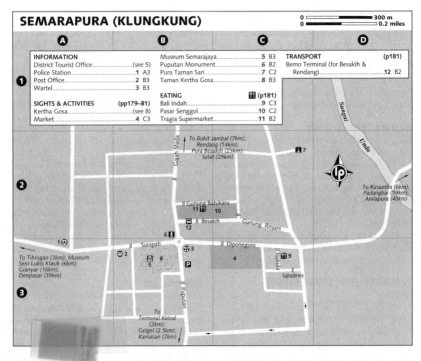

SEMARAPURA (KLUNGKUNG)

INFORMATION	
District Tourist Office	(see 5)
Police Station	1 A3
Post Office	2 B3
Wartel	3 B3

SIGHTS & ACTIVITIES	(pp179–81)
Kertha Gosa	(see 8)
Market	4 C3

Museum Semarajaya	5 B3
Puputan Monument	6 B2
Pura Taman Sari	7 C2
Taman Kertha Gosa	8 B3

EATING	(p181)
Bali Indah	9 C3
Pasar Senggol	10 C2
Tragia Supermarket	11 B2

TRANSPORT	(p181)
Bemo Terminal (for Besakih & Rendang)	12 B2

0 — 300 m
0 — 0.2 miles

To Bukit Jambal (7km);
Rendang (14km);
Pura Besakih (23km);
Selat (29km)

To Kusamba (6km);
Padangbai (19km);
Amlapura (40km)

Jl Gunung Batukaru

Jl Besakih — Gunung Rinjani

Surapati — Jl Diponegoro

Sahadewa

To Tihingan (3km); Museum
Seni Lukis Klasik (6km);
Gianyar (16km);
Denpasar (39km)

To
Terminal Kelod
(2km);
Gelgel (2.5km);
Kamasan (2km)

Gajah Mada

Jl Nakula

Jl Puputan

Sungai

Unda

---

supreme court of the Klungkung kingdom, where disputes and cases that could not be settled at the village level were eventually brought. This open-sided pavilion is a superb example of Klungkung architecture, and its ceiling is completely covered with fine paintings in the Klungkung style. The paintings, done on asbestos sheeting, were installed in the 1940s, replacing cloth paintings, which had deteriorated.

The rows of ceiling panels depict several different themes. The lowest level illustrates five tales from Bali's answer to the *Arabian Nights,* where a girl called Tantri spins a different yarn every night. The next two rows are scenes from Bima's travels in the afterlife, where he witnesses the torment of evil-doers. The gruesome tortures are shown clearly, but there are different interpretations of what punishment goes with what crime. (There's an authoritative explanation in *The Epic of Life – A Balinese Journey of the Soul* by Idanna Pucci, available for reference in the pavilion.) The fourth row of panels depicts the story of *Garuda's* (mythical man-bird creature)

search for the elixir of life, while the fifth row shows events on the Balinese astrological calendar. The next three rows return to the story of Bima, this time travelling in heaven, with doves and a lotus flower at the apex of the ceiling.

Bale Kambang

The ceiling of the beautiful 'Floating Pavilion' is painted in Klungkung style. Again, the different rows of paintings deal with various subjects. The first row is based on the astrological calendar, the second on the folk tale of Pan and Men Brayut and their 18 children, and the upper rows on the adventures of the hero Sutasona.

Museum Semarajaya

There are a few archaeological pieces and some quite interesting contemporary accounts of the 1908 *puputan* on display in this simple museum. There are old photos of the royalty, and displays in English as well. The rigours of salt production along the nearby coast are well documented (see Making Salt While the Sun Shines, p203).

MARKET

Semarapura's market is one of the best in East Bali. It's a vibrant hub of commerce and a meeting place for people of the region. You can easily spend an hour wandering about the warren of stalls as well as shops on nearby streets.

PURA TAMAN SARI

The quiet lawns and ponds around this temple make it a relaxing stop. The towering 11-roofed *meru* indicates that this was a temple built for royalty.

Eating

Snack stalls line the parking area.

Bali Indah (☎ 21056; Jl Nakula 1; dishes 10,000-17,000Rp) For a sit-down meal, try this one of two simple Chinese restaurants on the street.

Pasar Senggol (☺ 4pm-midnight) A night market, this is by far the best spot to eat if you're in town late. It's the usual flurry of woks, customers and noise.

Tragia supermarket (☎ 21997; Jl Gunung Batukaru) This has a large choice of groceries and sundries.

Getting There & Away

The best way to visit Semarapura is with your own transport.

Frequent bemos from Denpasar (Batubulan terminal) pass through Semarapura (5000Rp) on the way to Padangbai, Amlapura, Selat and Singaraja. They can be hailed from near the Puputan Monument.

Bemos heading north to Besakih (8000Rp) leave from the centre of Semarapura, a block northeast of Kertha Gosa. Most other bemos leave from the inconvenient Terminal Kelod, about 2km south of the city centre.

Perama shuttle buses between South Bali or Ubud and the east will stop in Semarapura on request, but as the coastal road was being finished when we visited, this may change.

AROUND SEMARAPURA (KLUNGKUNG)

Gelgel

Situated about 2.5km south of Semarapura, Gelgel was once the seat of Bali's most powerful dynasty. The town's decline started in 1710, when the court moved to present-day Semarapura, and finished when the Dutch bombarded the place in 1908.

Today the wide streets and the surviving temples are only faintly evocative of past grandeur. The **Pura Dasar** is not particularly attractive, but its vast courtyards are a real clue to its former importance, and festivals here attract large numbers of people from all over Bali.

A little to the east, the **Masjid Gelgel** is Bali's oldest mosque. It was established in the late 16th century for the benefit of Muslim missionaries from Java, unwilling to return home after failing to make any converts.

Kamasan

This quiet, traditional village is the place where the classical Kamasan painting style originated, and several artists still practise this art – you can see their workshops and small showrooms along the main street. The work is often a family affair, with one person inking the outlines, while another mixes the paints and yet another applies the colours. The paintings depict traditional stories or Balinese calendars, and although they are sold in souvenir shops all over Bali, the quality is better here. Look for smooth and distinct line-work, evenly applied colours and balance in the overall composition. The village is also home to families of *bokor* artisans, who produce the silver bowls used in traditional ceremonies.

To reach Kamasan, go about 2km south of Semarapura and look for the turn-off to the east.

Bukit Jambal

The road north of Semarapura climbs steeply into the hills, via Bukit Jambal, which is understandably popular for its magnificent views. There are several restaurants here that provide buffet lunches for tour groups. This road continues to Rendang and Pura Besakih.

Sungai Unda & Sungai Telagawaja

East of Semarapura, the main road crosses the dammed-up Sungai Unda. Further upstream, both the Unda and its tributary the Telagawaja are used for white-water rafting trips (see p151).

Tihingan

Tihingan has several workshops dedicated to producing gamelan instruments. Small foundries make the resonating bronze bars and bowl-shaped gongs, which are then carefully filed and polished until they produce the correct tone. Some pieces are on sale, but most of the instruments are produced for musical groups all over Bali. It's not really set up for tourists, but the workshops with signs out the front will receive visitors (albeit sometimes grudgingly); the work is usually done very early in the morning. From Semarapura, head west along Jl Diponegoro and look for the signs.

Museum Seni Lukis Klasik

Nyoman Gunarsa, one of the most respected and successful modern artists in Indonesia, established this **museum and arts centre** (☎ 0366-22255; adult/child 20,000Rp/free; ⏲ 9am-4pm) near his home village. The huge three-storey building exhibits an impressive variety of older pieces, including stone- and woodcarvings, architectural antiques, masks, ceramics and textiles. Many of the classical paintings are on bark paper and are some of the oldest surviving examples of this style. The top floor is devoted to Gunarsa's own work of colourful, semi-abstract depictions of traditional dancers and musicians.

There's a large performance space downstairs, and some fine examples of traditional architecture just outside.

The museum is about 6km west from Semarapura, near a bend on the road to Denpasar – look for the dummy policemen at the base of a large statue nearby.

The Coast

The coast south of Semarapura is striking, with seaside temples, black-sand beaches and pounding waves, but the sea is not suitable for swimming. The road was under construction when we visited, and until portions of it are complete, you need to take side tracks to the sea at places like Pura Batu Kolok. It's difficult without your own transport.

East of Semarapura, the main road crosses Sungai Unda, then swings south towards the sea. Lava from the 1963 eruption of Gunung Agung destroyed villages and cut the road, but the lava flows are now overgrown.

KUSAMBA

A side road leaves the main road and goes south to the fishing and salt-making village of Kusamba, where you will see lines of colourful fishing *prahu* (outriggers) lined up all along the beach. The fishing is usually done at night and the 'eyes' on the front of the boats help navigation through the darkness. The fish market in Kusamba is really excellent.

Local boats travel to the islands of Nusa Penida and Nusa Lembongan, which are clearly visible from Kusamba (but you can get faster and safer boats from Padangbai; see p191). Both east and west of Kusamba, there are small salt-making huts lined up in rows along the beach – see Making Salt While the Sun Shines on p203.

PURA GOA LAWAH

Three kilometres east of Kusamba is **Pura Goa Lawah** (Bat Cave Temple; admission 3000Rp, car park 1000Rp, sash rental 1000Rp; ⏲ 8am-6pm), which is one of nine directional temples on Bali. The cave in the cliff face is packed, crammed and jammed full of bats, and the complex is equally overcrowded with tour groups. There is a distinctly batty stench emanating from the cave, and the roofs of the temple shrines, which are in front of the cave, are liberally coated with bat droppings. Superficially, the temple is small and unimpressive, but it is very old and of great significance to the Balinese.

It is said that the cave leads all the way to Pura Besakih, some 19km away, but it's unlikely that you'd want to try this route. The bats provide sustenance for the legendary giant snake, the deity Naga Basuki, which is also believed to live in the cave.

SIDEMEN ROAD
☎ 0366

A less-travelled route to Pura Besakih goes northeast from Semarapura, via Sidemen and Iseh, to the Rendang–Amlapura road. The area offers marvellous paddy-field scenery, a delightful rural character and exciting views of Gunung Agung (when the clouds permit). The road is in good shape and regular bemos shuttle up and down from Semarapura.

Sidemen has a spectacular location and is a centre for culture and arts, particularly *endek* (ikat) cloth and *songket*, which is woven with threads of silver and gold. German artist Walter Spies lived in Iseh for some time from 1932 in order to escape the perpetual party of his own making in Ubud. Later, the Swiss painter, Theo Meier, nearly as famous as Spies for his influence on Balinese art, lived in the same house.

Sleeping & Eating

Near the centre of Sidemen, a small road heads west, signposted with the names of several places to stay. Views throughout the area are often spectacular, from terraced green hills to Gunung Agung.

Lihat Sawah (☎/fax 24183; r 100,000-150,000Rp; dishes 12,500-25,000Rp) Take the right fork in the road to this very friendly place with great gardens. All nine rooms (the cheapest have cold water) have views of the valley and mountain, and there's also an all-Indonesian restaurant.

Sacred Mountain Sanctuary (☎ 24330; sacred mt@indo.net.id; villas US$80-130, dishes 20,000-32,000Rp; 🏊) Close to the river, this remote and rusticated resort has a new-age vibe and a huge spring-fed swimming pool. The 19 bamboo villas have open-air bathrooms and many artistic touches. The resort has a restaurant that specialises in Thai and vegetarian cuisine and can arrange treks of Gunung Agung (US$55 for one, US$40 each for two or more), as well as a range of courses. Massage is also available.

Tanto Villa (☎ 0812 3950 271; r US$30-40) Views of the Luwah Valley are the appeal at this new place, which has four large rooms with hot water. Two upstairs have the best views of the surrounding chilli, bean and peanut fields.

Nirarta (Centre for Living Awareness; ☎ 24122; www.awareness-bali.com; Br Tabola; r US$25-60) Guests here enjoy programmes for personal and spiritual development, including meditation intensives and yoga. The comfortable bungalows have hot water and some are well suited to families and groups.

Pondok Wisata Sidemen (☎ 23009; s/d 200,000/ 400,000Rp) At the south end of Sideman, this place has clean, simple rooms with four-poster beds and great views. Accommodation includes a fine breakfast and dinner of traditional Balinese foods.

Patal Kikian (☎/fax 23005; villas US$35-55; 🏊) Several kilometres north of Sideman, look for a steep driveway on the eastern side of the road. This retreat has four spacious, stylishly furnished villas with vast verandas overlooking terraced hillsides to

Gunung Agung. For US$10 you can include all meals, which are served as private banquets on your own veranda. Rooms have hot water and there is a soaking pool.

PURA BESAKIH

Perched nearly 1000m up the side of Gunung Agung is Bali's most important temple, Pura Besakih. In fact, it is an extensive complex of 23 separate-but-related temples, with the largest and most important being Pura Penataran Agung. Unfortunately, many people find it a deeply disappointing experience due to the avarice of numerous local characters. See An Unholy Experience on p185 for the details, which may well help you to decide whether to skip it.

Besakih, as it is known, is most impressive during one of the frequent festivals, when hundreds, perhaps thousands, of gorgeously dressed devotees turn up with beautifully arranged offerings. The panoramic view and mountain backdrop are impressive too. A major disappointment for some is that tourists are usually barred from entering the temples.

History

The precise origins of Pura Besakih are not totally clear, but it almost certainly dates from prehistoric times. The stone bases of Pura Penataran Agung and several other temples resemble megalithic stepped pyramids, which date back at least 2000 years. There are legendary accounts of Sri Dangkyang Markendaya conducting meditation and ceremonies here in the 8th century AD, while stone inscriptions record a Hindu ritual on the site in AD 1007. There are some indications of Buddhist activity, but it was certainly used as a Hindu place of worship from 1284, when the first Javanese conquerors settled on Bali, and this is confirmed by accounts from the time of the Majapahit conquest in 1343. By the 15th century, Besakih had become a state temple of the Gelgel dynasty.

The central temple was added to over the years, and additional temples were built for specific family, occupational and regional groups. The complex was neglected during the colonial period, perhaps because of lack of royal patronage, and was virtually destroyed in the 1917 earthquake. The Dutch assisted with its reconstruction, and the

PURA BESAKIH COMPLEX

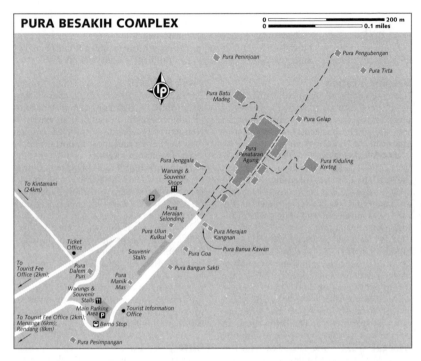

0   200 m
0   0.1 miles

Pura Peninjoan

Pura Pengubengan

Pura Tirta

Pura Batu Madeg

Pura Gelap

Pura Penataran Agung

Pura Jenggala

Pura Kiduling Kreteg

Warungs & Souvenir Shops

To Kintamani (24km)

Pura Merajan Selonding

Pura Ulun Kulkul

Pura Merajan Kangnan

Pura Banua Kawan

Ticket Office

Souvenir Stalls

Pura Goa

To Tourist Fee Office (2km);

Pura Dalem Puri

Pura Bangun Sakti

Pura Manik Mas

Warungs & Souvenir Stalls

Main Parking Area

Tourist Information Office

To Tourist Fee Office (2km); Menanga (6km); Rendang (8km)

Bemo Stop

Pura Pesimpangan

dependent rajahs were encouraged to support the maintenance of the temples.

Orientation

The main entrance is 2km south of the complex on the road from Menanga and the south. The fees are as follows: adult/child 7500/6000Rp, still camera 1000Rp, video camera 2500Rp and car park 1000Rp. The fact that you may well be charged for a video camera whether you have one or not gives you a taste of things to come.

About 200m past the ticket office, there is a fork in the road with a sign indicating Besakih to the right and Kintamani to the left. Go left because going to the right puts you in a large parking lot at the bottom of a hill some 300m from the complex. The walk up this shabby avenue, replete with smashed lights and crushed shrubs, is lined with souvenir shops, many of which are kaput. It also exposes you to the most touts.

Going left at the junction takes you up the hill and past the road to Kintamani, where there is a small ticket office (same

fees as the main office). There is a large parking lot near the end and another horde of touts and vendors, but from here you only have a 20m walk to the complex. Snack stands and warung are found along the approaches and at both parking lots.

Sights & Activities

PURA PENATARAN AGUNG

This is the central temple of the complex – in significance, if not exactly in position. It is built on six levels, terraced up the slope, with the entrance approached from below, up a flight of steps. This entrance is an imposing *candi bentar* (split gateway), and beyond it, the even more impressive *kori agung* is the gateway to the second courtyard.

Tourists are not permitted inside, so for the best view, climb the steps to the left of the main entrance and follow the path around the western side. From here, you can just see over the wall into the second courtyard (don't climb up on the wall), where the *padmasana* (temple shrine resembling a vacant chair) is. In most modern temples

AN UNHOLY EXPERIENCE

So intrusive are the scams and irritations faced by visitors to Besakih that many wish they had skipped the complex altogether. What follows are some of the ploys you should be aware of before a visit. We witnessed them all and numerous readers' letters confirm that this is a continuing problem. A recent effort by local authorities to clean up the situation has given guides who have gone through a training programme ID badges proclaiming their status as 'Official Guides'; how this will play out for visitors remains to be seen. Scepticism is a must.

■ Near the main parking area is a building labelled Tourist Information Office. Guides here may tell you that there is a festival that day (as there is for many days) and that your visit will be limited to a small area as shown on a worn map. Actually you may always walk among the temples but entrance inside is forbidden whether you are with a guide or not.

■ Guides – official or otherwise – may follow you if you refuse their services (the information office is best skipped) and demand you hire them. In the past there have been some good guides here who can add to your visit but they seem to be overshadowed by pushy ones whose services may be of dubious quality. Initial quotes of 30,000Rp will soon drop to 10,000Rp as you walk away.

■ It will require an endless repetition of 'no thank you' and 'please leave' to get the 'guides' to go away but this is essential as there have been reports of people giving in and allowing the guide to tag along without negotiating a price. Later they are intimidated into paying a fee of 200,000Rp or more.

■ Touts on scooters may follow you on your walk up the hill from the main parking area demanding that you pay 8000Rp for a ride. This is another good reason to use the parking lot close to the complex.

■ Once inside the complex, you may receive offers to 'come pray with me'. Visitors who seize on this chance to get into the forbidden temples can face demands of 50,000Rp or more.

It should be noted that guides or drivers who accompany you from other parts of Bali are generally not allowed in to the temples by the local 'guides'. If they attempt to intervene on your behalf after a scam, their vehicles may be attacked.

Overall the situation at Besakih is a real shame and does a huge disservice to this sacred site. Until authorities can rein in the excess of scams, visitors should think twice about a visit. At the minimum, the authorities should use some of the myriad of fees to clean up the disgusting amount of trash in the area.

this is a single throne for the supreme god, but Besakih stresses the Hindu trinity, and therefore it has a triple throne called *padmasana tiga,* or *padmasana trisakti,* with separate seats for Brahma, Vishnu and Shiva. This point is the spiritual centre of the temple, and indeed, of the whole Besakih complex.

Continuing on the footpath around the temple, you can see quite a few imposing *meru,* the multiroofed towers through which gods can descend to earth, but otherwise the temple is unspectacular. The upper courtyards are usually empty, even during festivals. One of the best views is from the path at the northeastern end, where you can look down past the many towers and over the temple to the sea.

OTHER TEMPLES

None of the other temples are striking, except when decorated for festivals, but each one has a particular significance, sometimes in conjunction with other temples. The *trimurti* (Hindu trinity) is represented by the combination of Pura Penataran Agung as Shiva, Pura Kiduling Kreteg as Brahma and Pura Batu Madeg as Vishnu. Just as each village on Bali has a *pura puseh* (temple of origin), *pura desa* (village temple) and *pura dalem* (temple of the dead), Pura Besakih has three temples that fulfil these roles for Bali as a whole – Pura Basukian, Pura Penataran Agung and Pura Dalem Puri, respectively.

The Balinese concept of *panca dewata,* which embodies a centre and four cardinal

EAST BALI

points, is represented by Pura Penataran Agung (the centre), Pura Kiduling Kreteg (south), Pura Batu Madeg (north), Pura Gelap (east) and Pura Ulun Kulkul (west). Each district of Bali is associated with a specific temple at Besakih, and the main temples of Bali are also represented by specific shrines here. Some temples are associated with families descended from the original Gelgel dynasty, and there are shrines and memorials going back many generations. Various craft guilds also have their own temples, notably the metal-workers, whose Pura Ratu Pande is built onto the side of the main temple.

FESTIVALS

Besakih is at its best when a festival is on, and with so many temples and gods represented here, there seems to be one every week or so. Ask at a tourist office anywhere on Bali, and try to identify which part of the Besakih complex will be the focus of attention. The founding of Besakih itself is celebrated at Bhatara Turun Kabeh around the full moon of the 10th lunar month (usually in March and April), when all the gods descend at once. The annual rites at Pura Dalem Puri, usually in January, attract thousands who make offerings for the dead. In addition, each individual temple has its own *odalan* (Balinese temple 'birthday festival'), held annually according to the 210-day *wuku* calendar.

Even more important are the great purification ceremonies of Panca Wali Krama, theoretically held every 10 years, and the Eka Dasa Rudra held every 100 years. In fact, the exact dates of these festivals are determined after long considerations by priests, and they have not been exactly regular. An Eka Dasa Rudra was held in 1963, but was disrupted by the disastrous eruption of Gunung Agung, and restaged successfully in 1979. The last Panca Wali Krama was in 1999.

Getting There & Away

Besakih is a *major* feature on any organised tour of eastern and northern Bali.

The best way to visit is with your own transportation, which allows you to explore the many gorgeous drives in the area.

You can visit by bemo from Semarapura (8000Rp) but from other parts of Bali this can make the outing an all-day affair. Be sure to ask the driver to take you to the temple entrance, not to the village about 1km from the temple complex. Make certain you leave the temple by 3pm if you want to return to either Semarapura or Denpasar by bemo.

GUNUNG AGUNG

Bali's highest and most revered mountain, Gunung Agung is an imposing peak seen from most of South and East Bali, although it's often obscured by cloud and mist. Many references give its height as 3142m, but some say it lost its top in the 1963 eruption and opinion varies as to the real height. The summit is an oval crater, about 700m across, with its highest point on the western edge above Besakih.

Climbing Gunung Agung

It's possible to climb Agung from various directions. The two shortest and most popular routes are from Pura Besakih, on the southwest side of the mountain, and from Pura Pasar Agung, on the southern slopes. The latter route goes to the lower edge of the crater rim (2900m), but you can't make your way from there around to the very highest point. You'll have great views south and east, but you won't be able to see central Bali. If you want to say you've been to the very top, climb from Besakih.

To have the best chance of seeing the view before the clouds form, get to the top before 8am, or preferably before sunrise at about 6am. You'll have to start at night, so plan your climb when there will be some moonlight (for religious reasons, many local guides don't want to do it on the night of the full moon, but a day before or after is okay). Take a strong torch (flashlight), extra batteries, plenty of water (2L per person), snack food, waterproof clothing and a warm jumper. The descent is especially hard on the feet, so you'll appreciate strong shoes or boots and manicured toenails.

You should take a guide for either route. Before you start, or early in the climb, the guide will stop at a shrine to make an offering and say some prayers. This is a holy mountain and you should show respect. Besides, you will want to have everything going for you.

It's best to climb during the dry season (April to September); July to September are

THE 1963 ERUPTION

The most disastrous volcanic eruption on Bali this century took place in 1963, when Gunung Agung blew its top in no uncertain manner at a time of considerable prophetic and political importance.

Eka Dasa Rudra, the greatest of all Balinese sacrifices and an event that takes place only every 100 years on the Balinese calendar, was to culminate on 8 March 1963. It had been well over 100 Balinese years since the last Eka Dasa Rudra, but there was dispute among the priests as to the correct and most favourable date.

Naturally, Pura Besakih was a focal point for the festival, but Gunung Agung was acting strangely as final preparations were made in late February. The date of the ceremony was looking decidedly unpropitious, but President Soekarno had already scheduled an international conference of travel agents to witness the great occasion as a highlight of their visit to the country, and he would not allow it to be postponed. By the time the sacrifices began, the mountain was glowing, belching smoke and ash, and rumbling ominously, but Gunung Agung contained itself until the travel agents had flown home.

On 17 March, Gunung Agung exploded. The catastrophic eruption killed more than 1000 people (some estimate 2000) and destroyed entire villages – 100,000 people lost their homes. Streams of lava and hot volcanic mud poured right down to the sea at several places, completely covering roads and isolating the eastern end of Bali for some time. The entire island was covered in ash and crops were wiped out everywhere.

Although Pura Besakih is high on the slopes of Gunung Agung, only about 6km from the crater, the temple suffered little damage from the eruption. In contrast, the inhabitants of the village of Lebih, also high up on Gunung Agung's slopes, were all but wiped out. Agung erupted again on 16 May, with serious loss of life, although not on the same scale as the March eruption.

the most reliable months. At other times, the paths can be slippery and dangerous, and you probably won't see anything of the view. Climbing Gunung Agung is not allowed when major religious events are being held at Pura Besakih, which generally includes most of April. No guide will take you up at these times, from either Besakih or Pura Pasar Agung, and there are horror stories about those who defied the ban and came to a sticky end on Gunung Agung.

GUIDES

Trips with guides on either of the following routes up Gunung Agung generally include breakfast and other meals and a place to stay, but be sure to confirm all details in advance. They can also arrange transportation.

Most of the places to stay in the region, including those around Sidemen and Tirta Gangga, will recommend guides for Gunung Agung climbs, but it's more convenient to start from a base nearer the mountain, and the local guides are more experienced.

Recommended guides:

Gung Bawa Trekking (☎ 0366-24379; gbtrekk@yahoo.com; Selat; per person from US$30) A reliable operation near the market.

Ketut Uriada (☎ 0812 3646 426; Muncan; per person US$40-50) It's easiest if you have your own car, but this experienced guide can arrange transport for an extra fee (look for his small sign on the road east of the village).

Nengan Kari (☎ 0366-23037; Jl Gunung Agung 5, Selat; per person 350,000Rp) This guide has received good reports.

FROM PURA BESAKIH

This climb is much tougher than from the south and is only for the very physically fit. For the best chance of a clear view before the clouds close in, you should start at midnight. Allow at least six hours for the climb, and four to five hours for the descent. The starting point is Pura Pengubengan, northeast of the main temple complex, but it's easy to get lost on the lower trails, so definitely hire a guide.

FROM PURA PASAR AGUNG

This route involves the least walking, because Pura Pasar Agung (Agung Market Temple) is high on the southern slopes of the mountain (around 1500m) and can be reached by a good road north from Selat. From the temple you can climb to the top in three or four hours, but it's a pretty demanding trek. With or without a guide, you must report to the police station at Selat before you start; if you don't have a guide the police will strongly encourage you to take one.

It is much better to stay the night near Muncan or Selat (see below) so that you can drive up early in the morning to Pura Pasar Agung. This temple has been greatly enlarged and improved, in part as a monument to the 1963 eruption that devastated this area.

Start climbing from the temple at around 3am. There are numerous trails through the pine forest but after an hour or so you'll climb above the tree line. Then you're climbing on solidified lava, which can be loose and broken in places, but a good guide will keep you on solid ground. At the top, you can gawk into the crater, watch the sun rise over Lombok and see the shadow of Agung in the morning haze over southern Bali.

Allow at least two hours to get back down to the temple. If you don't have a car waiting for you, walk down to Sebudi, from where there are public bemos down to Selat.

RENDANG TO AMLAPURA
☎ 0366

A scenic road goes around the southern slopes of Gunung Agung from Rendang to near Amlapura. It runs through some superb countryside, descending more or less gradually as it goes further east. If you have your own wheels, you'll find it very scenic, with some interesting places to stop. Water flows everywhere and you can easily exhaust your film, tape or memory card.

It's possible to take this road by public bemo, but very awkward. Starting from Semarapura, the bemo heads to Menanga, Rendang and Selat. From there you must either take a bemo to Duda and pick up a bemo for Amlapura, or pick one up that goes straight through from Selat.

Cyclists enjoy the route and find going east to be an easier ride.

Starting from the west, **Rendang** is an attractive town, easily reached via the very pretty, minor road from Bangli. Approximately 4km along a winding road, the old-fashioned village of **Muncan** has quaint shingle roofs.

East of Muncan, the road passes through some of the prettiest rice country on Bali

before reaching **Selat**, where you turn north for Pura Pasar Agung, the starting point for the easiest route up Gunung Agung.

Further on is **Duda**, where another scenic route branches southwest via Sidemen to Semarapura (see p182). Further east, a side road (about 800m) leads to **Putung**. This area is superb for hiking: there's an easy-to-follow track from Putung to **Manggis**, about 8km down the hill.

Continuing east, **Sibetan** is famous for growing *salak,* the delicious fruit with a curious 'snakeskin' covering – you can buy *salak* from roadside stalls. Nearby, a poorly signposted road leads north to Jungutan, with its **Tirta Telaga Tista** – a decorative pool and garden complex built for the water-loving old rajah of Karangasem.

The scenic road finishes at **Bebandem**, where there's a cattle market every three days, and plenty of other stuff for sale as well. Bebandem and several nearby villages are home to members of the traditional metal-workers caste, which includes silversmiths as well as blacksmiths.

Sleeping & Eating
Pondok Wisata Puri Agung (☎ 23037; s/d 100,000/ 150,000Rp) On the road between Selat and Duda, it has basic rooms and works with many of the local Gunung Agung guides.

Bukit Putung Resort (☎ 23039) In Putung, this resort has wonderful views down the southern slopes to the coast. It's a good stop for a snack or drink.

Homestay Lila (r 40,000-60,000Rp) In Abian Soan further east, this is family run with a friendly atmosphere and basic rooms. It's a good place to base yourself for walks around the area, and you can arrange a guide here (see p201 for information about the area). The homestay also organises trips to the Bebandem cattle market.

PADANGBAI
☎ 0363

On a perfect bay lined with colourful *prahu* and picturesque views of Nusa Penida, Padangbai is the port for Bali–Lombok ferries and passenger boats to Nusa Penida. A popular travellers' stop, offering excellent diving and snorkelling, and walks to nearby beaches, it has a relaxed ambience, added to by the main street's lazy traffic and the exuberance of local children swimming at the eastern end of the beach. The quiet is punctuated only by the blare of horns and the ripple of activity as ferries arrive and depart. You can easily laze away a few hours soaking up the scene at the cafés along Jl Segara or Jl Silayukti.

Information

Moneychangers at hotels and along Jl Pelabuhan offer rates slightly lower than in the South Bali tourist resorts – check the rates at **Bank BRI** (Jl Pelabuhan) first.

You can find Internet access at numerous places along the main streets such as Gang Segara and Jl Pelabuhan.

Dangers & Annoyances

Female travellers will notice a change in attitude towards women around the ferry terminal area. Expect a few snide remarks and unwanted stares.

Sights

With its protected bay, Padangbai has a good beach right in front. Others are nearby; walk southwest from the ferry terminal and follow the trail up the hill to idyllic **Bias Tugal**, also called Pantai Kecil (Little Beach), on the exposed coast outside the bay. Be careful in the water; it is subject to strong currents. There are a couple of daytime warung here.

On a headland at the northeast corner of the bay, a path uphill leads to three temples, including **Pura Silayukti**, where Empu Kuturan – who introduced the caste system to Bali in the 11th century – is said to have lived. On the other side of this headland is the small, light-sand **Blue Lagoon Beach**.

Activities
DIVING

There's some pretty good diving on the coral reefs around Padangbai, but the water can be a little cold and visibility is not always ideal. The most popular local dives are Blue Lagoon and Teluk Jepun (Jepun Bay), both in Teluk Amuk, the bay just east of Padangbai. There's a good variety of soft and hard corals and varied marine life, including sharks, turtles and wrasse, and a 40m wall at the Blue Lagoon.

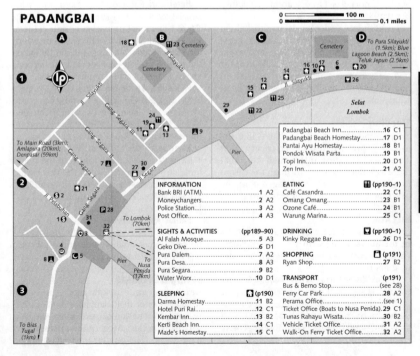

PADANGBAI

INFORMATION	
Bank BRI (ATM)	1 A2
Moneychangers	2 A2
Police Station	3 A2
Post Office	4 A3

SIGHTS & ACTIVITIES	(pp189–90)
Al Falah Mosque	5 A3
Geko Dive	6 D1
Pura Dalem	7 A2
Pura Desa	8 A3
Pura Segara	9 B2
Water Worx	10 D1

SLEEPING	(p190)
Darma Homestay	11 B2
Hotel Puri Rai	12 C1
Kembar Inn	13 B2
Kerti Beach Inn	14 C1
Made's Homestay	15 C1
Padangbai Beach Inn	16 C1
Padangbai Beach Homestay	17 D1
Pantai Ayu Homestay	18 B1
Pondok Wisata Parta	19 B1
Topi Inn	20 D1
Zen Inn	21 A2

EATING	(pp190–1)
Café Casandra	22 A2
Omang Omang	23 B1
Ozone Café	24 B1
Warung Marina	25 C1

DRINKING	(pp190–1)
Kinky Reggae Bar	26 D1

SHOPPING	(p191)
Ryan Shop	27 B2

TRANSPORT	(p191)
Bus & Bemo Stop	(see 28)
Ferry Car Park	28 A2
Perama Office	(see 1)
Ticket Office (Boats to Nusa Penida)	29 C1
Tunas Rahayu Wisata	30 B2
Vehicle Ticket Office	31 A2
Walk-On Ferry Ticket Office	32 A2

EAST BALI

Several good local outfits offer diving trips in the area, including to Gili Tepekong and Gili Biaha, and on to Tulamben and Nusa Penida. All dive prices are competitive, costing US$40 to US$70 for two boat dives, depending on the site. Courses range from Professional Association of Diving Instructors (PADI) open-water course (around US$280) to Dive Master. Dive instructors at the schools are German- and English-speakers.

Recommended operators:

Geko Dive (☎ 41516; www.gekodive.com; Jl Silayukti) The longest-established operator, it has a nice café across from the beach.

Water Worx (☎ 41220; www.waterworxbali.com; Jl Silayukti) Nearby, Water Worx is another good dive operator.

SNORKELLING

One of the best and most accessible walk-in snorkel sites is Blue Lagoon, which can be reached by walking east on Jl Silayukti and following the signs. Note that it is subject to strong currents when the tide is out. Other sites such as Teluk Jepun can be reached by local boat (or check with the dive operators to see if they have any room on their dive boats). Snorkel sets cost about 20,000Rp per day.

Local *jukung* (boats) offer snorkelling trips (bring your own snorkelling gear) around Padangbai (120,000Rp), and as far away as Nusa Lembongan (200,000Rp) for two passengers. These are advertised on boards around the village, or ask your hotel what's on offer.

Sleeping

Accommodation in Padangbai – like the town – is pretty laid-back. Prices are fairly cheap and it's pleasant enough here that there's no need to hurry through to or from Lombok if you want to hang out in the beach and cafés with other travellers.

VILLAGE

In the village, there are several tiny places in the alleys, some with a choice of small, cheap downstairs rooms or bigger, brighter upstairs rooms.

Pondok Wisata Parta (☎ 41475; off Gang Segara III; r 40,000-150,000Rp; honeymoon r 100,000Rp; 🔀) The pick of the rooms in this nice place is the 'honeymoon room', which has a harbour view and good breezes. The most expensive rooms have air-con.

Darma Homestay (☎ 41394; Gang Segara III; r 40,000-60,000Rp) Go for the private room on the top floor here; the breakfast buffet is a treat.

Kembar Inn (☎ /fax 41364; r 70,000-150,000Rp; 🔀) Readers have praised this friendly place where the more expensive rooms have air-con and hot water.

Zen Inn (☎ 41418; off Gang Segara I; r 40,000-70,000Rp) Closest to the ferry terminal, Zen's five rooms are eclectically designed and decorated, with a heavy emphasis on kitsch. There's a funky outdoor shower area.

JALAN SILAYUKTI

This little strip of simple beach places makes for a mellow hangout.

Padangbai Beach Homestay (☎ 081 2360 7946; s/d 95,000/125,000Rp, with air-con 250,000Rp; 🔀) The bungalows here are attractive, with open-air bathrooms, and set in a classic Balinese garden setting.

Topi Inn (☎ 41424; r 30,000Rp, f 150,000Rp) Sitting at the end of the bay in a serene location, Topi has pleasant rooms, including a spacious family room.

Hotel Puri Rai (☎ 41385; purirai_hotel@yahoo .com; Jl Silayukti 3; r 175,000Rp, with air-con 300,000Rp; 🔀 🖭) The most upmarket option in town, the Puri Rai has shady fan rooms in a double-storey stone building, pleasantly facing the pool. Some air-con rooms have harbour views; others overlook a parking area.

Padangbai Beach Inn (☎ 41417; Jl Silayukti; r 60,000-100,000Rp) Go with the bungalows and avoid the rice-barn style two-storey cottages, which have a bathroom downstairs and an oppressively hot, boxy bedroom upstairs.

Kerti Beach Inn (☎ 41391; Jl Silayukti; r 40,000-80,000Rp; 🖭) Go for the rooms in the pretty bungalows here rather than the rice barns.

Made's Homestay (☎ 41441; Jl Silayukti; s/d 35,000/60,000Rp; 🖭) Clean simple rooms and Internet access are the draws here.

Pantai Ayu Homestay (☎ 41396; Jl Silayukti; r 40,000-60,000Rp) Away from the beach, this homestay has small rooms and a pleasant restaurant with water views.

Eating & Drinking

Beach fare and backpackers' staples are what's on offer in Padangbai – lots of fresh seafood, Indonesian classics, pizza and, yes, banana pancakes. Most of the places to stay have a café. The beachfront restaurants on

Jl Segara and Jl Silayukti have similar menus and prices, harbour views during the day and cool breezes in the evening.

Warung Marina (Jl Silayukti; dishes 10,000-30,000Rp) One of several similar joints on this mellow strip and right on the water's edge, Marina has breezy views and serves tasty basic dishes and cheap beers.

Café Casandra (Jl Silayukti; dishes 8000-25,000Rp) A deliciously low-key place overlooking the water, it's ideal to kick back in the afternoon with a drink and soak up the sea breezes.

Omang Omang (Jl Silayukti; dishes 8000-20,000Rp) There's a dash of style here to go with the fish ponds and menu of seafood, Indo classics and sandwiches.

Ozone Café (☎ 41501; dishes 15,000-35,000Rp) This popular travellers' gathering spot has been spruced up with a new bakery and a full bar.

Kinky Reggae Bar Run by long-haired, guitar-toting local lads, this sets up on the eastern end of the beach in the late afternoon and is a fine spot for a sunset tipple. There are a few others like it on the sand here.

Shopping
Ryan Shop (☎ 41215; Jl Segara 38) With a name like this, how can you go wrong? It has a fair selection of second-hand paperbacks, some maps and a large aquarium.

Getting There & Away
BEMO
Padangbai is 2km south of the main Semarapura–Amlapura road. Bemos leave from the car park in front of the port; orange bemos go east through Candidasa to Amlapura (6000Rp); blue or white bemos go to Semarapura (7000Rp).

BUS
Several buses travel daily between Denpasar (Batubulan terminal) and Padangbai (8000Rp). These are theoretically timed to connect with ferries to Lombok, but don't depend on it. Buses also pass through Padangbai on the way to Surabaya (90,000Rp) and further west on Java. You can buy tickets at **Tunas Rahayu Wisata** (☎ 41287; Jl Segara; ☻ 7am-9pm).

TOURIST SHUTTLE BUS
Situated in a complex with Café Dona and Bank BRI, **Perama** (☎ 41419; Café Dona, Jl Pelabuhan; ☻ 7am-8pm) stops here on trips around the east coast. Services include Candidasa (10,000Rp), Kuta and the airport (30,000Rp), Lovina (80,000Rp), Sanur (30,000Rp) and Ubud (30,000Rp).

Tunas Rahayu Wisata (see left) operates daily minivans to Ubud for 20,000Rp, and to Sanur, Kuta and the airport for 25,000Rp.

BOAT
Lombok
Public ferries (adult/child 15,000/9350Rp) travel nonstop between Padangbai and Lembar (p276) all day. A one-way trip costs 36,400Rp for motorcycles and 258,700Rp for cars – go through the weighbridge at the west corner of the car park. Depending on conditions the trip can take three to five hours. Boats leave about every 90 minutes and food and drink is sold on board. Note that passenger tickets are sold near the pier.

Anyone who carries your luggage on or off the ferry will expect to be paid, so agree on the price first or carry your own stuff – the luggage porters here have a reputation (perhaps undeserved) for being aggressive. Expect more hassle at Lembar.

It's worth checking to see if the on-again, off-again Padangbai Express (55,000Rp, every two hours) to Lembar is running. Also note that you may still see reference to the Mabua Express, a service which ended years ago.

Perama has a 40-passenger boat (100,000Rp, four hours) which leaves at 9am for Senggigi, where you can get another boat to the Gilis (50,000Rp). Return trips are at 1pm. Snacks are sold on board.

Nusa Penida
On the beach just east of the car park you'll find the twin-engine fibreglass boats that run across the strait to Buyuk on Nusa Penida (25,000Rp, 45 minutes). The inconspicuous ticket office, open 7am to noon, is nearby. Boats leave at 9am – sometimes at 7am – and take one hour.

PADANGBAI TO CANDIDASA
☎ 0363
It's 11km along the main road from the Padangbai turn-off to the beach resort of Candidasa, and there are bemos or buses every few minutes. Between the two is an

attractive stretch of coast, which has some tourist development, and a large oil-storage depot in Teluk Amuk.

Buitan (Balina Beach) & Manggis

Balina Beach is the name bestowed on the small tourist development at the village of Buitan. It's an attractive area on a quiet coastal stretch, though the beach is being lost to erosion and what's left is black sand and stones. To find the turn-off, look for the small yellow sign 'Balina' from the main road. Nearby is the pretty village of Manggis.

SLEEPING & EATING

Amankila (☎ 41333; www.amankila.com; villa from US$650; ✕ ⌧ ⌧ ⌧) About 5.6km beyond the Padangbai turn-off and 500m past the road to Manggis, a discreetly marked side road leads to the exclusive Amankila. It features an isolated seaside location with views to Lombok and understated architecture – classically simple rectangular structures with thatched roofs and lots of natural wood and stone. The three main swimming pools step down into the sea, in matching shades of blue. The **'Beachclub' pool** (150,000Rp) is on a stretch of sand and is open to nonguests. It has a café and water sports. There are two restaurants at the Amankila. Both are open to nonguests but you'll need to book. The **Terrace** (lunch 80,000-190,000Rp) has varied fare ranging from an organic prawn salad to grilled tuna in a garlic and sesame crust, and the fine-dining **Restaurant** (mains 140,000-210,000Rp) has a mix of seafood, pasta and Balinese dishes.

Alila (☎ 41011; www.alilahotels.com; r US$180-210; ⌧ ⌧) This place has elegant, white, thatch-roofed buildings in spacious lawn gardens facing a beautiful stretch of secluded beach. The 55 rooms are very comfortable, with smart modern interiors; the best are the deluxe ones on the top floor with balconies. The restaurant features excellent nouvelle Balinese cuisine and you can be served in your room or at the beach. Activities include a kids' camp and adult cooking courses (from US$75 for half a day). There is a Mandara Spa on the grounds. In order to preserve the peace of guests, a gardener trims the vast lawn by hand.

Lumbung Damuh (☎ 41553; http://damuhbali.com; Jl Pantai; cottages 200,000-350,000Rp) This deliciously low-key place is right beside the water. There are only three *lumbung* (traditional rice barns) on the small site, and all are comfortable with outdoor bathrooms, inviting interiors and views.

There are several small cafés near Lumbung Damuh, including **Nyoman Café** (dishes 7000-20,000Rp).

Mendira & Sengkidu

Coming from the west, there are hotels and *losmen* (basic accommodation) off the main road at Mendira and Sengkidu, several kilometres before you reach Candidasa. Although the beach has suffered from erosion and somewhat unsightly sea walls have been constructed, it's a good place for a getaway if you have your own transport. All of the following are on small tracks between the main road and the water; look for signs.

SLEEPING & EATING

Candi Beach Cottage (☎ 41234; www.candibeachbali .com; r US$60-80, bungalow US$80-120; ⌧ ⌧) This delightfully low-key resort has two pools and lovely grounds. There are 32 rooms and 32 bungalows, all with satellite TV.

Amarta Beach Inn Bungalows (☎ 41230; r 75,000-120,000Rp) These 10 bungalows right on the sea are in a gorgeous location and are great value. The more expensive ones have hot water and spiffy new open-air bathrooms.

Pondok Pisang (☎ 41065; bananasbatik@yahoo .com; s 100,000-300,000Rp, d 100,000-350,000Rp) The name here means 'banana hut', and there's plenty of appeal. The six, spacious bungalows are widely spaced facing the sea. Each bungalow has a unique interior, including

---

THE AUTHOR'S CHOICE

Lotus Bungalows (☎ 41104; www.lotusbunga lows.com; r US$20-45; ⌧ ⌧ ⌧) The accommodation branch of the restaurant empire is a really nice place. There are 24 rooms (some with air-con, all with hot water) in bungalow-style units. Four (numbers one, two, 13 and 14) are right on the ocean, with the last being the top pick. The décor is bright and airy and there is a large pool. The restaurant lives up to Lotus standards with a good Italian and Indonesian menu.

mosaic-tiled bathrooms. Yoga intensives are held here at various times.

Homestay Dewi Utama (☎ 41053; r 75,000Rp) Looking for seclusion? Try this friendly little place with five clean, basic rooms.

There are a couple of cheap warung in the main street, including Bintang Restoran, part of Homestay Dewi Utama, but you'll probably end up eating at your hotel or another one nearby.

Tenganan

Tenganan is a village of Bali Aga people, the descendants of the original Balinese who inhabited Bali before the Majapahit arrival. The village is surrounded by a wall, and consists basically of two rows of identical houses stretching up the gentle slope of the hill. The Bali Aga are reputed to be exceptionally conservative and resistant to change, but even here the modern age has not been totally held at bay – a small forest of TV aerials sprouts from those oh-so-traditional houses. The most striking feature of Tenganan, however, is its exceptional neatness, with the hills providing a beautiful backdrop. As you enter the village you may be greeted by a guide who will take you on a tour of the village – and generally lead you back to their family compound to look at textiles and *lontar* (specially prepared palm leaves) strips. Unlike Besakih, however, there's no pressure to buy anything,

so you won't need your own armed guards. For more on *lontar* books, see p45.

A peculiar, old-fashioned version of the gamelan known as the *gamelan selunding* is still played here, and girls dance an equally ancient dance known as the Rejang. There are other Bali Aga villages nearby, including Tenganan Dauh Tenkad, 1.5km west off the Tenganan road, with a charming old-fashioned ambience, and several weaving workshops. At Asak, southeast of Tenganan, another ancient instrument, the *gamelan gambang,* is still played.

FESTIVALS

Tenganan is full of unusual customs, festivals and practices. At the month-long Usaba Sambah Festival, which usually starts in May or June, men fight with sticks wrapped in thorny pandanus leaves. At this same festival, small, hand-powered ferris wheels are brought out and the village girls are ceremonially twirled around.

EATING

Candi Bakery & Bistro (☎ 41883; Jl Tenganan; dishes 10,000-25,000Rp; ☺ 9am-8pm) About 50m up from the Tenganan turn-off, this is a real find. The tiny bakery specialises in delicious, authentic German pastries, cakes and croissants. Indonesian dishes and German schnitzel are also served.

SHOPPING

A magical cloth known as *kamben gringsing* is woven here – a person wearing it is said to be protected against black magic. Traditionally this is made using the 'double ikat' technique, in which both the warp and weft threads are 'resist dyed' before being woven. It's very time-consuming, and the pieces of double ikat available for sale are quite expensive (from about 600,000Rp). Other interesting textiles are sold here – some are handmade by local craftswomen, but much comes from other parts of Bali and Indonesia; in fact most of the traffic on the road is trucks bringing in goods to sell.

Many baskets from across the region, made from *ata* palm, are on sale. Another local craft is traditional Balinese calligraphy, with the script inscribed onto *lontar* palm strips, in the same way that the ancient *lontar* books were created. Most of these books are Balinese calendars or

---

THE LEGEND OF TENGANAN

There's a smelly legend about how the villagers of Tenganan came to acquire their land. The story relates how Dalem Bedaulu lost a valuable horse. When the villagers of Tenganan found the carcass, the king offered them a reward. They asked that they be given the land where the horse was found – that is, the entire area where the dead horse could be smelled.

The king sent a man with a keen nose who set off with the village chief and walked an enormous distance without ever managing to get away from the foul odour. Eventually accepting that enough was enough, the official headed back to Bedaulu, scratching his head. Once out of sight, the village chief pulled a large hunk of dead horse out from under his clothes.

depictions of the *Ramayana* (one of the great Hindu holy books). They cost 150,000Rp to 250,000Rp, depending on quality.

GETTING THERE & AWAY
Tenganan is 4km up a side road just west of Candidasa. At the turn-off where bemos stop, motorcycle riders offer *ojek* (motorcycle that carries pillion passengers) rides to the village for about 5000Rp. A nice option is to take an *ojek* up to Tenganan, and enjoy a shady downhill walk back to the main road.

CANDIDASA
☎ 0363

Until the 1970s, Candidasa was a just a quiet little fishing village, then beachside losmen and restaurants sprang up and suddenly it was *the* new beach place on Bali. As the facilities developed, the beach eroded – unthinkingly, offshore barrier-reef corals were harvested to produce lime for cement for the orgy of construction that took place – and by the late 1980s Candidasa was a beach resort with no beach.

Mining stopped in 1991 and concrete sea walls and groynes have limited the erosion, and now provide some sandy swimming spots, but it's not your typical, tropical stretch of golden-sand beach. Still, the relaxed seaside ambience and sweeping views from the hotels built right on the water appeal to a more mature crowd of visitors. Candidasa is a good base from which to explore the interior of East Bali and the east coast's famous diving and snorkelling sites. The downturn in visitors after 2002 has given the town back some of its sleepy character, although traffic along Jl Raya Candidasa, the major road linking East Bali, means daytime traffic can be tough. But there are secluded spots at the east end of town and the lotus-blossom-filled lagoon is a serene spot.

Information
The Candidasa **tourist office** (☎ 41204; Jl Raya Candidasa; ☽ 8am-2pm Mon-Sat) has more good cheer than useful brochures and maps.

Foto Asri (☎ 41098; Jl Raya Candidasa) sells groceries and sundries and has a postal agency. Several moneychangers are nearby, as is a Bank BNI ATM.

There are plenty of not-very-fast Internet options along Jl Raya Candidasa. A good

choice is the suitably amiable **Friendship Café & Internet** (☎ 41052; Jl Raya Candidasa; per min 400Rp).

Sights
Candidasa's temple, **Pura Candidasa** (admission by donation), is on the hillside across from the lagoon at the eastern end of the village strip. It has twin temples devoted to the male-female gods Shiva and Hariti.The fishing village, just beyond the lagoon, has colourful *prahu* drawn up on what's left of the beach. In the early morning you can watch the boats coasting in after a night's fishing. The owners canvass visitors for snorkelling trips to the reef and the nearby islets.

The main road east of Candidasa spirals up to **Pura Gamang Pass** (*gamang* means 'to get dizzy'), from where there are fine views down to the coast. If you follow the coastline from Candidasa towards Amlapura, a trail climbs up over the headland, with fine views over the rocky islets off the coast. Beyond this headland there's a long sweep of wide, exposed black-sand beach.

Apart from the Bali Aga village of Tenganan (p193), there are several traditional villages inland from Candidasa and attractive countryside for walking.

Ashram Gandhi Chandi (☎ 41108; Jl Raya Candidasa), a community by the lagoon, follows the pacifist teachings of Mahatma Gandhi. Guests are welcome to stay for short or extended periods, but are expected to participate in the life of the community, including waking early for daily yoga practice. Simple guest cottages are by the ocean, and payment is by donation.

Activities
Diving and snorkelling are popular activities in Candidasa. Gili Tepekong, which has a series of coral heads at the top of a sheer drop-off, is perhaps the best dive site. It offers the chance to see lots of fish, including some larger marine life. Other features include an underwater canyon, which can be dived in good conditions, but is always potentially hazardous. The currents here are strong and unpredictable, the water is cold and visibility is variable – it's recommended for experienced divers only.

Other dive sites are beside Gili Mimpang, further east at Gili Biaha, and Nusa Penida. A recommended dive operator is

Dive Lite (☎ 41660; www.divelite.com; Jl Raya Candidasa; 2 dives US$55-75), which dives Tulamben, Amed, Nusa Penida/Lembongan and Menjangan. A four-day PADI open water course is US$360. Snorkelling tours are US$25. Several other dive shops operate in Candidasa but standards vary, so choose carefully.

Hotels and shops along the main road rent snorkel sets for about 20,000Rp per day. For the best snorkelling, take a boat to offshore sites or to Gili Mimpang (a one-hour boat trip should cost about 70,000Rp to 100,000Rp for up to three people).

On shore, you can catch up on your beauty treatments at **Dewi Spa** (☎ 41042; Jl Raya Candidasa; ◷ 9am-7pm). A papaya scrub (87,500Rp) is a special service on offer – expect to be smeared all over with freshly pureed fruit.

Sleeping

Candidasa's main drag is well supplied with seaside accommodation, as well as restaurants and other tourist facilities. More relaxed, and only slightly less convenient, are the places east of the lagoon, hidden among the palm trees near the original fishing village.

BUDGET

Sekar Orchid Beach Bungalows (☎ 41086; bungalows 120,000-150,000Rp) The grounds here live up to the name with orchids growing in profusion. There's a small beach and the large rooms are very good value with nice views from the 2nd floor. The site is nicely isolated.

Bali Santi Bungalows (☎ 41611; bali_santi@hotmail.com; r 60,000-120,000Rp, with air-con 150,000Rp; ☒) Among the accommodation scattered in the palm trees west of the centre, Bali Santi is good value with 10 clean and comfortable rooms.

Puri Oka Cottages (☎ 41092; puri_oka@hotmail.com; r 100,000-250,000Rp; ☒ ☒) Hidden by a banana grove east of town, cheap rooms here are small, while the better ones have tasteful décor and water views. The pool is medium-sized, but at low tide there's a small beach out the front.

Kelapa Mas (☎ 41369; www.welcome.to/kelapamas; Jl Raya Candidasa; r 200,000-225,000Rp; ☒) This relaxing hideaway deserves its name – the grounds are filled with tall coconut palms.

Bamboo rooms with lounging verandas are set in lush gardens, with even a little sand lining the seashore. Some have views; others have hot water and air-con.

Seaside Cottages (☎ 41629; www.bali-seafront-bungalows.com; Jl Raya Candidasa; cottages 30,000-230,000Rp; ☒) There are lodging options galore at this clean and well-run place. Basic rooms have cold water and fan. As you move up the rate card you add hot water, air-con, open-air garden bathrooms and delightful views. The Temple Café (p197) here is a fun place.

Hotel Ida's (☎ 41096; jsidas1@aol.com; Jl Raya Candidasa; bungalows 80,000-100,000Rp) Set in a rambling seaside garden shaded by coconut trees, Ida's has thatched bungalows with open-air bathrooms. Rustic balcony furniture, including a day bed, makes relaxing a dream.

Rama Bungalows (☎ 41778; r from 35,000Rp) On a little road by the lotus-filled lagoon, this double-storey stone structure has a red temple design. Upstairs rooms have views of the lagoon, while downstairs rooms have open-air bathrooms.

MID-RANGE

Kubu Bali Bungalows (☎ 41532; info@kububali.com; s/d US$50/55, ste US$60-65; ☒ ☒) Behind Kubu Bali restaurant (p197) and up a lane, there are 20 beautifully finished individual bungalows. Streams, ponds and a swimming pool are landscaped into the steep hillside, with views over palm trees, the coast and the sea. You'll have to climb a bit to get to your room. There's also a café by the pool with wonderful views.

Ida Beach Village (☎ 41118; fax 41041; bungalow US$45-60; ☒ ☒) Accommodation ranges from Balinese rice-barn-style bungalows with private gardens to more modest cottages. The seaside swimming pool is a highlight. The location is very quiet.

Grand Natia (☎ 42007; hotelnatia@yahoo.com; Jl Raya Candidasa; r US$50-85; ☒ ☒) This hotel resembles a modern water palace – elegant pathways are lined with waterways teeming with carp. Each room has an open-air bathroom. The small pool drops away to a gorgeous ocean view, although the two 'ocean-view' rooms are not worth the extra sway.

Bali Shangrila Beach Club (☎ 41829; www.balishangrila.com; r US$30-75; ☒ ☒) This quiet place far from traffic is a good place for

EAST BALI

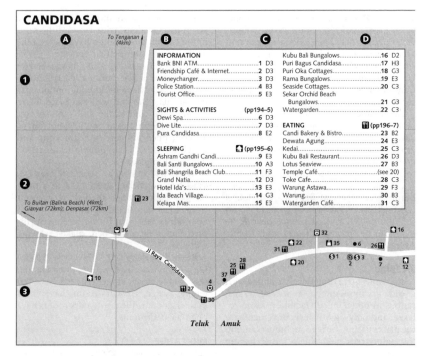

CANDIDASA

INFORMATION	
Bank BNI ATM	1 D3
Friendship Café & Internet	2 D3
Moneychanger	3 D3
Police Station	4 B3
Tourist Office	5 E3

SIGHTS & ACTIVITIES	(pp194–5)
Dewi Spa	6 D3
Dive Lite	7 D3
Pura Candidasa	8 E2

SLEEPING	(pp195–6)
Ashram Gandhi Candi	9 E3
Bali Santi Bungalows	10 A3
Bali Shangrila Beach Club	11 F3
Grand Natia	12 D3
Hotel Ida's	13 E3
Ida Beach Village	14 G3
Kelapa Mas	15 E3

Kubu Bali Bungalows	16 D2
Puri Bagus Candidasa	17 H3
Puri Oka Cottages	18 G3
Rama Bungalows	19 E3
Seaside Cottages	20 C3
Sekar Orchid Beach Bungalows	21 G3
Watergarden	22 C3

EATING	(pp196–7)
Candi Bakery & Bistro	23 B2
Dewata Agung	24 E3
Kedai	25 C3
Kubu Bali Restaurant	26 D3
Lotus Seaview	27 B3
Temple Café	(see 20)
Toke Cafe	28 C3
Warung Astawa	29 F3
Warung	30 B3
Watergarden Café	31 C3

To Tenganan (4km)

To Buitan (Balina Beach) (4km);
Gianyar (72km); Denpasar (72km)

Jl Raya Candidasa

Teluk Amuk

families. Rooms are very large and some have kitchens and DVD players. There's a small beach, a good pool and a games library available. The furniture is strangely plush.

TOP END

Watergarden (☎ 41540; www.watergardenhotel.com; Jl Raya Candidasa; r US$70-85, 2-bedroom ste US$160; ☒ ☒) A delightfully different place, the Watergarden lives up to its name with a swimming pool and fish-filled ponds that wind around the buildings and through the lovely garden. The design has a Japanese influence, and each room has a veranda projecting over the lily ponds. See p197 for details on the café.

Puri Bagus Candidasa (☎ 41131; www.bagus-discovery.com; r US$115-160; ☒ ☒) At the eastern end of the beach near an outcropping of outriggers, this handsome beachfront hotel is hidden away in the palm trees on grand grounds. A sandy beach area with cabanas is by the pool and restaurant. Rooms are pleasant, all with open-air bathrooms and air-con.

Eating

There's a good range of eating options in Candidasa. Many of the hotels have seafront restaurants and cafés that are lovely at lunch time and idyllic in the early evening.

Other restaurants are dotted along Jl Raya Candidasa, and the traffic noise can be particularly unpleasant, although it improves after dark. Among the cheapest and tastiest eateries are the warung and *kaki lima* (food carts) that spring up every evening (and to a lesser extent during the day) at the western end of town where the main road almost crashes into the sea. If you're staying at the eastern end of Candidasa, you can easily walk to the main road for meals (although the area is unlit at night) or try any of the warung clustered outside the hotels in the area – there are several.

Where noted, many of these places are also good for a drink.

Kedai (☎ 42020; Jl Raya Candidasa; mains 25,000-88,000Rp; ☽ lunch & dinner) Set in a stately open-air pavilion under a high conical thatched roof, Kedai is one of Candidasa's best restaurants. The service is excellent and the

EAST BALI

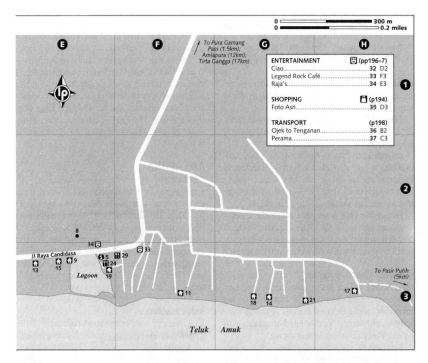

menu of Balinese specialties changes often.
The four-course tasting menu (95,000Rp)
is popular.

Lotus Seaview (☎ 41257; Jl Raya Candidasa; dishes
22,000-60,000Rp) This Lotus branch has a wonderful ocean outlook and a good Italian
and Indonesian menu. If you're just passing through, it's a good stop for lunch or
a refreshment.

Watergarden Café (☎ 41540; Jl Raya Candidasa;
dishes 15,000-40,000Rp) Overlooking a carp
pond, this stylish café somehow manages
to maintain a peaceful atmosphere amid the
traffic noise. The food is excellent, including Asian specialities, such as laksa, tempura and Thai dishes. Its breakfasts are also
good and everything comes with oodles of
fresh fruit.

Kubu Bali Restaurant (☎ 41532; Jl Raya Candidasa;
dishes 18,000-50,000Rp) This big stylish place has
an open kitchen out the front, where Indonesian and Chinese dishes are turned out
with great energy and panache. The seafood
is excellent.

Dewata Agung (☎ 41204; dishes 18,000-60,000Rp)
On the lagoon, the location adds serenity

to this reliable place with Indonesian and
seafood dishes. Many people come for the
Legong dance performances (see p198). It
offers free transport from as far away as
Sengkidu.

Toke Café (☎ 41991; Jl Raya Candidasa; dishes
20,000-30,000Rp) The open kitchen on the street
serves up some top seafood. It's got a nice
old bar and is a good place for a drink.

Temple Café (☎ 41629; Jl Raya Candidasa; dishes
15,000-30,000Rp) Travellers from around the
world can get a taste of home at this café
attached to the Seaside Cottages. The menu
has wraps, Vegemite, cabbage rolls, meat
pies and other mundane treats. The bar is
popular.

Warung Astawa (☎ 41363; Jl Raya Candidasa; dishes
15,000-30,000Rp) This simple place is popular
for its set-menu specials and congenial ambience – not to mention the happy hour.
Fresh squid prepared in many forms is the
speciality.

Entertainment
Many restaurants have happy hours with
cheap beer between 5pm and 8pm – look for

EAST BALI

the signs out the front. See the places noted on pp196–7 that are good for drinks.

Dewata Agung (☎ 41204; admission free; ⏱ 7.45pm) Presents free and unadorned Legong dances each night.

Raja's (☎ 42034; Jl Raya Candidasa) Shows movies at night, has pizza on the menu, tippling expats and blaring TVs.

Ciao (Jl Raya Candidasa; dishes 15,000-25,000Rp; ⏱ 5-11pm) Has an Italian menu and nightly movies.

Legend Rock Café (Jl Raya Candidasa; dishes 9000-24,000Rp) A bar that also serves Western and Indonesian meals, it has live music many nights each week. It's a well-mannered place, but as wild as things get in Candidasa.

Friendship Café & Internet (☎ 41052; Jl Candidasa; large Bintang 9500Rp) This Internet café is also a hangout for local musicians who play mellow guitar solos several nights a week.

Getting There & Away
Candidasa is on the main road between Amlapura and South Bali, but there's no terminal, so hail down bemos (buses probably won't stop). You'll need to change in either Padangbai or Semarapura.

Perama (☎ 41114; Jl Raya Candidasa; ⏱ 7am-7pm) is at the western end of the strip. There are tourist shuttle bus services to Kuta and the airport (30,000Rp), Lovina (80,000Rp), Padangbai (10,000Rp), Sanur (30,000Rp) and Ubud (30,000Rp).

Two or more people can charter a ride to Amed in the far east for 50,000Rp each.

Getting Around
Suzuki jeeps (about 80,000Rp per day), larger Toyota Kijangs (about 150,000Rp per day) and motorcycles (40,000Rp per day) can be rented from agencies along the main road. For exploring the nearby area, a chartered or rental vehicle is the best bet.

You can rent bikes at **Seaside Cottages** (☎ 41629; Jl Raya Candidasa; per day 25,000Rp).

AROUND CANDIDASA
Although Candidasa lacks good beaches, about 5km east is **Pasir Putih**, an idyllic white-sand beach. When you see a sign with 'Virgin Beach Club', turn off the main road and follow a paved track for about 1km to a bridge where locals will collect a fee (2000Rp). Another 1km brings you to a small temple which has good parking. You

can drive a further 600m directly to the beach but the road is a disaster and the walk instead is quite pretty.

The beach is almost a cliché: a long crescent of white sand backed by coconut trees. At one end cliffs provide shade; at the other is a little line of fishing boats. At times a stand sells drinks and most of the time visitors are few. The surf is often mellow; bring your own snorkelling gear to explore the waters.

AMLAPURA
☎ 0363
Amlapura is the capital of Karangasem district, and the main town and transport junction in eastern Bali. The smallest of Bali's district capitals, it's a tidy, multicultural place with Chinese shophouses, several mosques and confusing one-way streets. It's worth a stop to see Puri Agung Karangasem, but Tirta Gangga, 7km west, is a more picturesque, laid-back place to stay.

Information
The friendly staff at the **tourist office** (⏱ 21196; Jl Diponegoro; ⏱ 7am-3pm Mon-Thu, 7am-noon Fri) will be spellbound if any traveller walks in requesting information. Although, for best results you should have a distinct need for information. **Bank BRI** (Jl Gajah Mada) and **Bank Danamon** (Jl Gajah Mada) will change money and have ATMs. There is a **pharmacy** (Apotik; Jl Ngurah Rai 47) with a small hospital across the street.

Sights
Amlapura's three palaces, on Jl Teuk Umar, are decaying reminders of Karangasem's period as a kingdom at its most important when supported by Dutch colonial power in the late 19th and early 20th centuries.

Outside the **Puri Agung Karangasem** (Jl Teuku Umar; admission 3000Rp; ⏱ 8am-6pm), there is an impressive three-tiered entry gate and beautiful sculpted panels. After you pass through the entry courtyard, a left turn takes you to the main building, known as the Maskerdam (Amsterdam), because it was the Karangasem kingdom's acquiescence to Dutch rule that allowed it to hang on long after the demise of the other Balinese kingdoms. Inside you can see several rooms, including the royal bedroom and a living room with furniture that was a gift from the Dutch

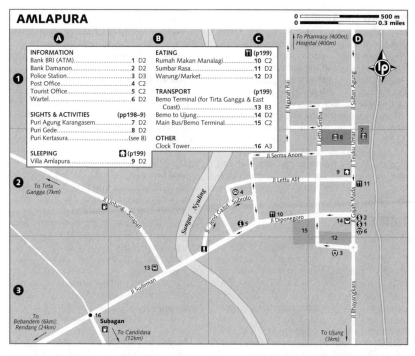

AMLAPURA

| | | 0 | 500 m |
| | | 0 | 0.3 miles |

INFORMATION
Bank BRI (ATM)..............................1 D2
Bank Damanon..............................2 D2
Police Station.................................3 D3
Post Office.....................................4 D2
Tourist Office.................................5 C2
Wartel...6 D2

SIGHTS & ACTIVITIES (pp198–9)
Puri Agung Karangasem..................7 D2
Puri Gede.......................................8 D2
Puri Kertasura............................(see 8)

SLEEPING (p199)
Villa Amlapura...............................9 D2

EATING (p199)
Rumah Makan Manalagi.................10 C2
Sumbar Rasa.................................11 D2
Warung/Market.............................12 D3

TRANSPORT (p199)
Bemo Terminal (for Tirta Gangga & East
  Coast)..13 B3
Bemo to Ujung.............................14 D2
Main Bus/Bemo Terminal................15 C2

OTHER
Clock Tower..................................16 A3

To Pharmacy (400m);
Hospital (400m)

Jl Ngurah Rai
Jl Sultan Agung
Jl Lettu Sintha
Jl Teuku Umar
Jl Serma Anom
Jl Lettu Alit
Jl Gajah Mada
Jl Jend Gatot Subroto
Sungai Nyuling
Jl Diponegoro
Jl Untung Surapati
To Tirta
Gangga (7km)
Jl Bhayangkara
Jl Sudirman
To
Bebandem (6km);
Rendang (24km)
Subagan
To Candidasa
(12km)
To Ujung
(3km)

---

royal family. The Maskerdam faces the ornately decorated Bale Pemandesan, which was used for royal tooth-filing ceremonies. Beyond this, surrounded by a pond, is the Bale Kambang, still used for family meetings and dance practice.

Across the street, **Puri Gede** (Jl Teuku Umar; admission free; 8am-6pm) is being extensively renovated. The rambling palace grounds feature many brick buildings dating from the Dutch colonial period. Look for stone and wood carvings from the 19th century. The Rangki has been returned to its glory and is surrounded by fish ponds. Look for the stern portrait of the late king AA Gede Putu; his wife still lives in one of the buildings.

The other royal palace building, **Puri Kertasura**, is not open to visitors.

Sleeping & Eating

Options are few in Amlapura; there are various warung around the market and the main bus/bemo terminal but there's more choice up the road in Tirta Gangga.

Villa Amlapura (☎ 23246; Jl Teuku Umar; r 100,000Rp) This is a funky place with a German owner

and four basic rooms. The good café has a simple menu.

Rumah Makan Manalagi (Jl Diponegoro; dishes 6000-20,000Rp) This place is always busy with locals due to its proximity to a mosque. On offer is *sate kambing* (goat satay) and other treats.

Sumbar Rasa (Jl Gajah Madah; dishes 5000-15,000Rp) This place is a good sit-down spot for a meal.

Getting There & Away

Amlapura is the major transport hub in East Bali. Buses regularly ply the main road to Batubulan terminal (7000Rp) in Denpasar, via Semarapura. Plenty of buses also go around the north coast to Singaraja (via Tirta Gangga, 6000Rp), Culik (the Amed turn-off) and Tulamben, leaving from the Tirta Gangga and East Coast bemo terminal southwest of town (you can hail these from outside Villa Amlapura).

If you are driving to Amed and beyond, fill up at the petrol station on the road to Tirta Gangga. It's the last one until Yeh Sanih in the north.

EAST BALI

AROUND AMLAPURA

Five kilometres south of Amlapura, **Taman Ujung** is a major complex that may leave you slack-jawed – and not with wonder. The last king of Karangasem completed the construction of a grand water palace here in 1921 which was extensively damaged by an earthquake in 1979. A tiny vestige of the old palace is surrounded by vast new ponds and terraces built for untold billions of rupiah. Today it is backed by a failed hotel and the wind-swept grounds are seldom trod by visitors. It's all rather depressing and you can see what you want from the road. Further on is the fishing village of **Ujung** on the coast.

TIRTA GANGGA

☎ 0363

The tiny village of Tirta Gangga (Water of the Ganges), high on a ridge with sublime views of rice paddies sprawling over the hills down to the sea, is a relaxing place to stop. The main attraction is the old water palace and guided treks through the gorgeous landscape (Good Karma or Genta Bali, right, are good places to find a guide). Facilities are limited. There are many interesting plant nurseries along the road.

Sights

Amlapura's water-loving rajah, after completing his lost masterpiece at Ujung, had another go at **Taman Tirta Gangga** (adult/child 3100/1600Rp; ☉ site 24hr, ticket office 6am-6pm). Originally built in 1948, the water palace was damaged in the 1963 eruption of Gunung Agung and again during the political events that rocked Indonesia two years later. The palace has several swimming pools and ornamental ponds, which serve as a fascinating reminder of the old days of the Balinese rajahs. 'Pool A' (adult/child 6000/4000Rp) is the cleanest and is in the top part of the complex. 'Pool B' (adult/child 4000Rp/free) is pond-like. Taman Tirta Gangga is a mellow place and has good views down to the ocean.

Sleeping & Eating

Most places to stay have cafés and there's another cluster by the sedate shops around the parking area.

Dhangin Taman (☎ 22059; r 35,000-70,000Rp, dishes 5000-8000Rp) Adjacent to the water palace, this fascinating place features elaborate tiled artworks in a garden. It has a range of simple rooms – the cheapest ones facing the rice paddies are the best – and a restaurant with tables overlooking the palace.

Tirta Ayu Homestay (☎ 22697; fax 21383; r 150,000-250,000Rp, villas 500,000Rp, dishes 10,000-25,000Rp; ☒) Right in the palace compound, this has three pleasant bungalows (cold water only) and three spacious villas with nice outdoor bathrooms. Free use of the palace swimming pool is included. A café overlooks the palace grounds.

Good Karma (☎ 22445; s/d 40,000/60,000Rp, dishes 10,000-16,000Rp) In the middle of a picturesque rice paddy, Good Karma has good vibes thanks to four very clean and pleasant bungalows. The restaurant serves excellent food in a comfortable setting; there are many vegetarian options.

Genta Bali (☎ 22436; dishes 10,000-12,000Rp) Across the road from the parking area, you can find a fine yoghurt drink here, as well as pasta and Indonesian food. It also has an impressive pudding list; everything on it is served with coconut milk, brown sugar and coconut.

Pondok Lembah Dukah (r 40,000-100,000Rp) Down the path to the right of Good Karma and past Dua Homestay, this simple place has only three bungalows and is a 300m walk, but worth it. Rooms are clean and simple, and have incredible views.

Puri Sawah Bungalows (☎ 21847; fax 21939; bungalows 100,000-250,000Rp, dishes 16,000-22,000Rp) Just up the road from the palace, Puri Sawah has comfortable and spacious rooms with great views, and larger, two-bedroom bungalows, which sleep six (with hot water). The restaurant has rice paddy views and serves Western and Indonesian food.

Ryoshi (☎ 081 2368 2791; dishes 10,000-35,000Rp; ☉ 10am-10pm) Literally an outpost of the Bali Japanese restaurant chain, it is about 500m past central Tirta Gangga and enjoys fabulous views of east Bali. The grilled seafood is good and you can dine under a canopy of frangipani.

Puri Prima (☎ /fax 21316; r 50,000-100,000Rp, dishes 10,000-16,000Rp) About 800m further on from Ryoshi, this offers outstanding views and nine pleasant rooms. It has a small restaurant. Staff can also organise trekking to Gunung Agung (600,000Rp for two people).

Pondok Batur Indah (☎ 22342; r 70,000-125,000Rp) Found in the village of Desi Ababi, on the hills above Tirta Gangga, it can be reached by a 10-minute walk that begins at the steps behind the water palace.

Getting There & Away

Regular bemos and minibuses pass through Tirta Gangga on routes north of Amlapura – they'll stop on request. Otherwise this is territory where you will need your own transport.

AROUND TIRTA GANGGA

The rice terraces around Tirta Gangga are some of the most beautiful on Bali. They sweep out from Tirta Gangga, almost like a sea surrounding an island. Back roads and walking paths take you to many picturesque traditional villages. Going to smaller, more remote villages, it's sensible and inexpensive to engage a guide – ask at your hotel or else contact the cafés Genta Bali or Good Karma, both in Tirta Gangga (see p200). Another good place to arrange treks is Homestay Lila in Abian Soan (p188). Guide prices are negotiable, at around 15,000Rp per person per hour for local treks, plus transport and food.

Throughout the area the *rontal* palms all look like new arrivals at army boot camp, as they are shorn of their leaves as fast as they grow them in order to meet the demand for inscribed *lontar* books.

Pura Lempuyang

This is one of Bali's nine directional temples, perched on a hilltop at 768m. To get here, turn south off the Amlapura–Tulamben road to Ngis (2km), a palm sugar and coffee-growing area, and follow the signs another 2km to Kemuda (ask for directions if the signs confuse you). From Kemuda, climb 1700 steps to Pura Lempuyang (allow at least two hours, one way). If you want to continue to the peaks of Lempuyang (1058m) or Seraya (1175m), you should take a guide.

Bukit Kusambi

This small hill has a big view – at sunrise Lombok's Gunung Rinjani throws a shadow on Gunung Agung. It is easy to reach from Abian Soan – look for the obvious large hill to the northwest, and follow the tiny canals

through the rice fields. On the western side of the hill, a set of steps leads to the top.

Budakeling & Krotok

Budakeling, home to several Buddhist communities, is on the back road to Bebandem, a few kilometres southeast of Tirta Gangga. It's a short drive, or a pleasant three-hour walk through rice fields, via Krotok, home of traditional blacksmiths and silversmiths.

Tanah Aron

This imposing monument to the post-WWII Dutch resistance is gloriously situated on the southeastern slopes of Gunung Agung. The road is quite good, or you can walk up and back in about six hours from Tirta Gangga.

AMED & THE FAR EAST COAST

☎ 0363

This once-remote stretch of coast, from Amed to Bali's far eastern tip, continues to develop as a resort area. The coastline is superb and still largely unspoilt, with views across to Lombok and behind to Gunung Agung. Hotels, restaurants, dive operators and other facilities are expanding as an increasing number of visitors come to enjoy the fine scenery, the relaxed atmosphere, and the excellent diving and snorkelling.

Amed itself has no standard tourist centre but is instead a series of small villages in scalloped inlets. It's the perfect hideaway if you want to simply stay put and never leave your village, apart from to swim or snorkel. If you're after a more dynamic holiday destination, head elsewhere.

Traditionally, this area has been quite poor, with thin soils, low rainfall and very limited infrastructure. Salt production is still carried out on the beach at Amed, and you'll see numerous rows of evaporating troughs in the dry season (or big stacks of them for the rest of the year). Villages further east rely on fishing, and colourful *jukung* line up on every available piece of beach. Inland, the steep hillsides are generally too dry for rice – corn, peanuts and vegetables are the main crops.

Orientation

In the rest of Bali, and to identify itself as a destination, this whole strip of coast is commonly called 'Amed' but, strictly speaking,

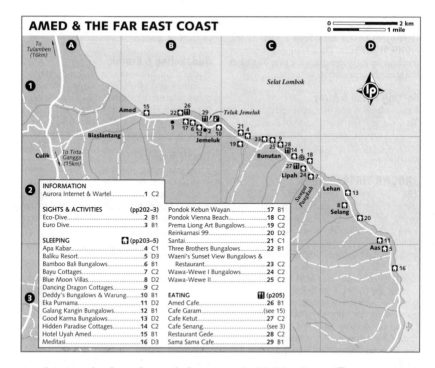

AMED & THE FAR EAST COAST

Amed is just the first of several *dusun* (small villages) set in a dramatic landscape of black-sand beaches, spread over 10km. Most development at first was around two bays, Jemeluk, which has cafés and a few shops, and Lipah, which has warung, shops and services. 'Progress' has marched onwards through Lehan, Selang and Aas. To really appreciate the coast, stop at the viewpoint at Jemeluk; besides the sweep of land, you can see fishing boats lined up like polychromatic sardines on the beach.

Information

There's no tourist office or post office, but you may be charged a tourist tax. Enforcement of a 3000Rp per person fee at a toll-booth on the outskirts of Amed is sporadic. When collected, the funds go in part to develop the infrastructure at the beaches. Public toilets are rumoured to be in the works.

Telephone services have not kept pace with development and land lines have only been strung a little past Lipah. **Aurora Internet & Wartel** (☎ 23519; Lipah; per min 500Rp; 🕙 8am-9pm) has dial-up Internet service.

Pondok Kebun Wayan (☎ 23473; east of Amed) changes US dollar travellers cheques and has a small market with groceries and sundries. There are moneychangers in Lipah but there are no ATMs or banks in the area.

Activities

DIVING & SNORKELLING

Snorkelling is excellent at several places along the coast. Jemeluk is a protected area where you can admire live coral and plentiful fish within 100m of the beach. There's a wreck of a Japanese fishing boat near Aas, offshore from Eka Purnama bungalows, and coral gardens and colourful marine life at Selang. Almost every hotel rents snorkelling equipment for about 20,000Rp per day.

Scuba diving is also excellent, with dive sites off Jemeluk, Lipah and Selang featuring coral slopes and drop-offs with soft and hard corals, and abundant fish. Some are accessible from the beach, while others require a short boat ride. The *Liberty* wreck at Tulamben (p206) is only a 20-minute drive away. The local operators have combined forces to organise beach clean-ups.

MAKING SALT WHILE THE SUN SHINES

In the volcanic areas and around the north-east coast between Amed, Yeh Sanih and Selang, as well as near Kusamba, you can see the thatched roofs of salt-making huts along the beach. Sand that has been satu-rated with sea water is collected from the beach, dried out and then taken inside a hut, where more sea water is strained through it to wash out the salt. This very salty water is then poured into a *palungan* (shallow trough), made of palm tree trunks split in half. Hundreds of these troughs are lined up in rows along the beaches during the salt-making season, and as the hot sun evaporates the water, the almost-dry salt is scraped out and put in baskets. The salt is used mainly for processing dried fish, not as table salt.

It's a laborious process, yielding a meagre income in the dry season and none at all in the wet season when rain stops production. Tourists who stop, look and take photos should consider leaving a small donation. You can learn more about the process at the Museum Semarajaya in Semarapura (p180) and at Hotel Uyah Amed (see right) and Café Garam east of Amed (p205).

Eco-dive (☎ 081 658 1935; www.ecodivebali.com; Jemeluk; dives from US$45) This has similar services and prices as Euro Dive, as well as very simple accommodation for clients.

Euro Dive (☎ 23469; www.eurodivebali.com; east of Amed; dives from US$45) A PADI resort, Euro Dive is a well-recommended operation that dives around Amed, Tulamben and Gili Selang. An open-water diving course costs US$310. Snorkelling equipment is available for rent.

TREKKING

Quite a few trails go inland from the coast, up the slopes of Gunung Seraya (1175m) and to some little-visited villages. The coun-tryside is sparsely vegetated and most trails are well defined, so you won't need a guide for shorter walks – if you get lost, just fol-low a ridge top back down to the coast road. Allow a good three hours to get to the top of Seraya, starting from the rocky ridge just east of Jemeluk Bay, near Prem Liong Art Bungalows (see p204). To reach the top for

sunrise you'll need to start in the dark, so a guide is probably a good idea – ask at your hotel. A fair rate is around 15,000Rp to 20,000Rp per hour for an English-speaking guide.

Sleeping

The Amed area is very spread out, so take this into consideration when choosing ac-commodation. If you want to venture to restaurants beyond your hotel's own, for example, you'll have to either walk or pay for transport.

You will also have to make the choice be-tween places in the little beachside villages or places on the sunny and dry headlands connecting the inlets. The former puts you right on the sand and offers a small amount of life while the latter gives you broad, sweeping vistas and isolation.

Accommodation can be found in every price category; almost every place has a res-taurant or café.

EAST OF AMED VILLAGE

Hotel Uyah Amed (☎ 23462; r 250,000-320,000Rp; 🏊) This upmarket place features four-poster beds set in creative interiors. Some units have views of the water; from all you can see the saltworks. The hotel makes the most of this by offering fascinating and free salt-making demonstrations (see Making Salt While the Sun Shines, left).

Three Brothers Bungalows (☎ 23472; r 70,000-120,000Rp, dishes 10,000-25,000Rp) The boys have popular and basic beachfront accommo-dation, plus an adjoining café with a few tables right on the sand.

Pondok Kebun Wayan (☎ 23473; www.amedcafe .com; r €8-40; 🏊 🏊) This Amed empire fea-tures a range of rooms mostly across from the beach. The most expensive have views and amenities like air-con while the cheap-est are small huts on the beach. The good café (see p205) is separate from the lodg-ing area.

JEMELUK

Santai (☎ 23487; www.santaibali.com; r US$55-95, dishes 18,000-52,000Rp; 🏊 🏊) This gorgeous top-end option has a lovely ambience. Rooms have four-poster beds, timber floors, open-air bathrooms and big comfy balcony sofas. A snaking swimming pool, fringed by purple bougainvillea, adds to the atmosphere. The

EAST BALI

restaurant faces the beach and specialises in seafood, Mediterranean and Indonesian cuisine.

Prema Liong Art Bungalows (☎ 23486; www .bali-amed.com; r 150,000-350,000Rp, dishes 11,000-30,000Rp) Given the name, the hippyish feel here shouldn't really surprise you. Javanese-style two-storey bungalows are terraced up the hillside. The cold-water, open-air bathrooms are lush and almost double as a garden, while the balconies have comfy cushions and day beds. Rooms are ideal for families or groups. The restaurant focuses on Balinese dishes and pizza.

Apa Kabar (☎ 23492; www.apakabarvillas.com; bungalows US$75-95, villas US$125-150, dishes 25,000-40,000Rp; 🏊 🍴) Right in front of fishing boats on the beach, Apa Kabar has stylish and spacious villas overlooking a swimming pool. Some bungalows have ocean views. Like Prema Liong, the restaurant serves classic Balinese dishes and pizza.

Bamboo Bali Bungalows (☎ 23478; s/d 30,000/40,000Rp, with air-con 50,000/60,000Rp; 🏊) On a hillside looking across a field to the water, this place is good value. There is a small pool and simple rooms, all with hot water and open-air bathrooms.

Galang Kangin Bungalows (s/d 45,000/75,000Rp) One of several cheap places, it has clean, basic rooms.

Deddy's Bungalows & Warung (☎ 23510; warung_deddys@hotmail.com; s/d 35,000/50,000Rp) On the hillside above the bay, Deddy's has three clean, pleasant rooms.

Waeni's Sunset View Bungalows & Restaurant (☎ 23515; madesani@hotmail.com; r 70,000-100,000Rp, dishes 14,000-30,000Rp) Readers have enjoyed Waeni's and its unusual rustic stone cottages with gorgeous views of the mountains behind, and the bay below. The restaurant is the perfect place to stop for a drink and watch the eponymous sunset.

Dancing Dragon Cottages (☎ 23521; www.danc ingdragoncottages.com; US$45-90; 🏊 🍴) Although billed as a 'Feng Shui Boutique Hotel', this is only true when the owners stage infrequent seminars on the subject. The large bungalows have comfortable rooms high on the headlands. Make certain that your 'ocean-view room' really has an ocean view.

Wawa-Wewe II (☎ 23521; r 80,000-150,000Rp, dishes 18,000-23,000Rp; 🏊) On the headlands, this nice and peaceful place offers cold-water villas. You can use the pool at the neighbouring Dancing Dragon Cottages. The simple little restaurant overlooks cows and the ocean.

LIPAH

Bayu Cottages (☎ 23495; www.bayucottages.com; r 200,000Rp, dishes 10,000-30,000Rp; 🏊 🍴) One of the best values on Bali, Bayu has rooms with balconies overlooking the coast from the knoll. There's a small pool and many amenities including open-air bathrooms. The café has a long and varied menu.

Wawa-Wewe I Bungalows (☎ 23506; rodanet@ depasar.wasantara.net.id; s/d 60,000/80,000Rp) Run by self-styled hipsters, the first Wawa-Wewe has simple rooms equipped with outdoor bathrooms.

Hidden Paradise Cottages (☎ 23514; www.hidden paradise-bali.com; cottages with fan/air-con US$40/50; 🏊 🍴) These simply decorated rooms have patios and open-air bathrooms with hot water. The pool is the classic kidney shape.

Pondok Vienna Beach (☎ 23494; www.members .aon.at/viennabeach; r US$30; 🍴) This Amed-area pioneer has lush, mature gardens and a nice pool. Rooms have hot water and are set on a nice boat-free part of the beach.

SELANG

Blue Moon Villas (☎ 0817 4738 100; www.bluemoon villa.com; r US$55-70, villa US$120-185; 🏊 🍴) On a knoll across the road from the cliffs, Blue Moon is a small and upmarket place, complete with a stylish little pool. The five rooms have lovely open-air stone bathrooms. The café **Komang John's** (dishes 20,000-30,000Rp), serves pizza and sandwiches, as well as Indonesian favourites. The local peanuts that come with cocktails are addictive.

Eka Purnama (☎ 0868 1212 1685; www.eka-pur nama.com; r 100,000-150,000Rp, dishes 17,000-25,000Rp) This gorgeous, cold-water only place is set high on a hill. The balconies, complete with hammocks, have pure ocean views. It also has a pleasant restaurant.

Good Karma Bungalows (r US$9-25, dishes 8000-22,000Rp) With a fittingly longhaired, guru-esque owner resident, it's no surprise that you hear a lot of 'dude!' and 'hey man' here. A range of rooms in thatch-roofed bungalows, all with cold-water, open-air bathrooms, is on offer, including bungalows that sleep up to four. The bungalows and peaceful restaurant overlook a black-sand beach crowded with *jukung*.

Fishing boat off Candidasa Beach (p194)

Coconuts drying by the road,
Candidasa (p194)

Pura Besakih (p183)

Rice terraces, Penulisan (p224)

TIM ROCK

GREGORY ADA

Stone carving of Boma, guardian of temples (p54)

Gunung Batur and Danau Batur (p218)

MICHAEL

Reinkarnasi 99 (s/d 90,000/150,000Rp) The owner of Good Karma Bungalows also has this similar place, 1km closer to Aas.

AAS
Meditasi (fax 22166; s/d 130,000/150,000Rp, dishes 10,000-25,000Rp) Rooms are close to good swimming at this chilled-out place where the bamboo bungalows have dreamy balconies overlooking the beach. There's also an open-air café by the water and good snorkelling nearby.

Baliku Resort (☎ 0817 4756 411; balidodo@yahoo.com; villa US$50; ☻) Set on a bluff overlooking Aas beach, this place has three family villas outfitted in marble and teak. The **Pavillion** (dishes 30,000-60,000Rp) restaurant is inviting and has a good menu of seafood and pasta.

Eating
Many of the hotels listed also have places for a meal or a sunset drink.

Amed Café (☎ 23473; east of Amed; dishes 15,000-40,000Rp) Set on a relaxed stretch of beach, this refined café has an extensive seafood menu, as well as the usual Chinese and Indonesian dishes.

Café Garam (☎ 23462; east of Amed; dishes 14,000-40,000Rp) There's a polished ambience here with pool tables and a menu of Thai and Indo food plus live Genjek music at 8pm on Wednesday and Saturday. The café also has a small exhibition on salt-making, and local salt is on sale (see Making Salt While the Sun Shines, p203).

Cafe Senang (East of Amed; dishes 6000-15,000Rp) At Euro Dive, this small, sleek bar/café is popular with travellers.

Sama Sama Cafe (Jemeluk; dishes 15,000-30,000Rp) Prawns, barracuda, mackerel and other fish almost jump from the boats onto the grill at this four-table beachside joint.

Restaurant Gede (☎ 23517; Bunutan; dishes 16,000-33,000Rp) The huge menu focuses on Chinese dishes, with a few Balinese dishes as well. Artwork by the owner decorates the walls.

Cafe Ketut (Lipah; dishes 7000-15,000Rp) A dash of style here goes well with the burgers and Indo classics. It's a good stop for lunch during the day.

Getting There & Around
Most people drive here via the main highway from Amlapura and Culik. The spectacular road going all the way around the headlands has been improved; it's possible to do the journey as a circle, with the foreknowledge that conditions between Ujung and Aas are twisting and narrow.

All the places east of Culik can be difficult to reach by public transport. Minibuses and bemos from Singaraja and Amlapura pass through Culik, the turnoff for Amed. Infrequent public bemos go from Culik to Amed (3.5km), and some continue to Seraya until 1pm. A public bemo should cost around 5000Rp from Culik to Lipah.

You can also charter transport from Culik for a negotiable 30,000Rp or so. Alternatively, if you're travelling light, you can get an *ojek* from Culik to as far as Aas for about 5000Rp to 10,000Rp (also negotiable). When negotiating, be careful to specify which hotel you wish to go to – if you agree on a price to 'Amed', you may be taken only to Amed village.

Perama (p198) offers charter touristbus services from Candidasa; the cost is 50,000Rp each for a minimum of two people. From Lovina (p247), it is 75,000Rp.

Many hotels rent bicycles, including **Hidden Paradise Cottages** (☎ 23514; Lipah; per day 25,000Rp).

KUBU REGION
Driving along the main road you will pass through vast old lava flows from Gunung Agung down to the sea. The landscape is strewn with lava, boulders and is nothing like the lush rice paddies elsewhere.

TULAMBEN
☎ 0363
The big attraction here is the wreck of the US cargo ship *Liberty* – among the best and most popular dive sites on Bali. Other great dive sites are nearby, and even snorkellers can easily swim out and enjoy the wreck and the coral. Tulamben's beachfront is quite different from other beach resorts – heavy, black, round boulders and pebbles make it unappealing for sunbathers or casual swimmers.

Orientation & Information
The town is a quiet place, and is essentially built around the wreck – the hotels, all with restaurants, and many with dive shops, are

spread along a 3km stretch either side of the main road.

You can change cash at a few signposted places at the eastern end of the main road, otherwise services are sparse.

For Internet access, try **Tulamben Wreck Divers Resort** (☎ 23400; per hr 500Rp).

Activities
DIVING & SNORKELLING
The wreck of the *Liberty* is about 50m directly offshore from Puri Madha Bungalows (there's also a shady car park here; 1000Rp). Swim straight out and you'll see the stern rearing up from the depths, heavily encrusted with coral, and swarming with dozens of species of colourful fish – and with scuba divers most of the day. The ship is more than 100m long, but the hull is broken into sections and it's easy for divers to get inside. The bow is in quite good shape, the midships region is badly mangled and the stern is almost intact – the best parts are between 15m and 30m deep. You will want at least two dives to really explore the wreck.

Many divers commute to Tulamben from Candidasa, Lovina or even the South Bali resorts, and the wreck can get quite crowded between 11am and 4pm, with dozens of divers there at a time. It's better, and cheaper, to get yourself to Tulamben, stay the night and do your dives early in the day, or perhaps between noon and 2pm, when many visiting divers take a lunch break. Amed is also a convenient base for Tulamben dives.

Most hotels have their own diving centre, and some will give a discount on accommodation if you dive with their centre, but not all of them can be recommended for inexperienced divers.

THE WRECK OF THE LIBERTY

In January 1942 the US Navy cargo ship USAT *Liberty* was torpedoed by a Japanese submarine near Lombok. Taken in tow, it was beached at Tulamben so that its cargo of rubber and railway parts could be saved. The Japanese invasion prevented this and the ship sat on the beach until the 1963 eruption of Gunung Agung broke it in two and left it just off the shoreline, much to the delight of scores of divers.

Expect to pay as little as US$20/35 for one/two dives at Tulamben, and a little more for a night dive or dives around Amed.

Most hotels and dive centres rent out snorkelling gear for a negotiable 20,000Rp.

Reputable dive operations:

Deep Blue Studio (☎ 22919; www.subaqua.cz) This Czech-run organisation charges US$200 for a dive course.
Tauch Terminal (☎ 0361-730200; www.tauch-terminal .com) This also has a hotel (see below). A four-day PADI open-water certificate course costs US$380.

Sleeping & Eating
At high tide, none of the places situated on the water have much rocky beach at all, but the waves are dramatic. Look for signs along the main road for the following places; most of them have their own dive operations.

Tauch Terminal Resort (☎ 0361-730200; www .tauch-terminal.com; r US$40-80, dishes US$3-6; 🛏 🔊) Down a side road, this is the pick of Tulamben accommodation. Rooms have spacious terraces and the cheaper ones in bungalows are actually more atmospheric. There is an idyllic waterfront pool, beach bar and restaurant. Italian, Indonesian and German dishes are on offer.

Mimpi Resort (☎ 21642; www.mimpi.com; r US$80-150, dishes 20,000-55,000Rp; 🛏 🔊) Designed by Australian architects and overlooking a picturesque stretch of waterfront, Mimpi has a range of 30 stylish bungalows with outdoor bathrooms, and an alluring pool, dive centre and spa. It also has a restaurant.

Bali Coral Bungalows (☎ /fax 22909; r 90,000Rp, with air-con 150,000Rp, dishes 10,000-25,000Rp; 🛏 🔊) Nine pleasant, clean bungalows with modern bathrooms cluster here, some with sea views. The restaurant has Indonesian and German items.

Matahari Tulamben Resort (☎ 22916; matahari tulamben@hotmail.com; r 75,000-200,000Rp, dishes 8000-15,000Rp; 🛏 🔊) On a long, narrow site, this small place has pleasant rooms ranging from those with cold-water bathrooms to swankier ones with hot water and air-con. There's a restaurant on the water.

Puri Madha Bungalows (☎ 22921; r 60,000Rp) This is the first hotel you approach from the west; it faces the wreck and the day-use parking area. There are nine small, clean cold-water rooms on the water.

Deep Blue Studio (☎ 22919; www.subaqua.cz; r US$10; 🔊) On the inland side of the road, the clean rooms have roof-top balcony views. The pool is small.

Puri Aries (☎ 23402; r 40,000-50,000Rp) Also on the inland side of the road, there are eight small, clean cold-water bungalows in a really lush, green garden setting.

Getting There & Away

Plenty of buses and bemos travel between Amlapura and Singaraja and will stop anywhere along the Tulamben road, but they're infrequent after 2pm. Expect to pay 6000Rp to 8000Rp to either town.

Perama (p188) offers charter tourist-bus services from Candidasa; it costs 50,000Rp each for a minimum of two people. From Lovina (p247), it is 75,000Rp.

TULAMBEN TO YEH SANIH

North of Tulamben, the road continues to skirt the slopes of Gunung Agung, with frequent evidence of lava flows from the 1963 eruption. Further around, the outer crater of Gunung Batur slopes steeply down to the sea. The rainfall is low and you can generally count on sunny weather. The scenery is very stark in the dry season and it's thinly populated. The route has regular public transport, but it's easier to make stops and detours with your own vehicle.

At Les, a road goes inland to lovely **Air Terjun Yeh Mampeh** (Yeh Mampeh Waterfall), said to be one of Bali's highest. Look for a large sign on the main road and then turn inland for 2km. Walk the last 2.5km or so on an obvious path by the stream. A 2000Rp donation is requested; there's no need for a guide.

The next main town is **Tejakula**, famous for its stream-fed public bathing area, said to have been built for washing horses, and often called the horse bath. The renovated bathing areas (separate for men and women) are behind walls topped by rows of elaborately decorated arches, and are regarded as a sacred area. The baths are 100m inland on a narrow road with lots of small shops – it's a quaint village, with some finely carved *kulkul* towers. Take a stroll above the baths, past irrigation channels flowing in all directions.

At Pacung, about 10km before Yeh Sanih, you can turn inland to **Sembiran**, which is believed to be a Bali Aga village,

although it doesn't promote itself as such. The most striking thing about the place is its hillside location and brilliant coastal views.

Sleeping

Alam Anda (☎ 0361-750444; www.alamanda.de; r €32, bungalow €53, villa €105, dishes €3-8; 🕃 🔳) Near Sambirenteng, this is a delightful resort on the beach, with a fine coral reef just offshore. It boasts its own diving centre, a pretty pool and nine very attractive bungalows in a spacious garden setting. Designed by the German architect owner, Alam Anda has a lush tropical feel. The waterfront restaurant has daily buffets and fresh seafood.

NUSA LEMBONGAN & ISLANDS

One of three islands just off the southern coast of East Bali, Nusa Lembongan is overshadowed by its much larger sibling Nusa Penida, but it is first and foremost in terms of traveller popularity thanks to its enjoyable beach scene and great diving, and because it's the destination of choice for aquatic sports day trips.

Nusa Lembongan, Nusa Penida and tiny Nusa Ceningan together are an administrative region within the Klungkung district. Nusa Lembongan is easily reached from Bali. The island of Nusa Penida has several villages, but is right off the tourist track and has few facilities for visitors, while Nusa Ceningan is very sparsely populated. The waters around the three islands have some of the best dive spots in Indonesia.

Lembongan is a wonderful place, where surfers and nonsurfers alike can get away from the relative chaos of southern Bali. Low-budget bungalows are ideal for extended stays by the seaside, while more upmarket hotels offer comfort and quiet. For an even shorter visit, take a comfortable cruise boat, stopping to snorkel or bask on a beach, or do a more specialised diving or surf trip.

It's been a poor region for many years and there has been some transmigration from here to other parts of Indonesia. Thin soils and a lack of fresh water do not permit the cultivation of rice, but other crops such as maize, cassava and beans are staples grown here. The main cash crop, however, is seaweed (see Seaweed Sundae p209).

NUSA LEMBONGAN
☎ 0366

The most developed island for tourism is the delightfully laid-back Nusa Lembongan, which is free of cars, motorcycle noise and hassles. It has a local population of about 7000 people, mostly living in two small villages, Jungutbatu and Lembongan. Many of the locals are involved in the seaweed industry and tourism is a secondary source of income.

Orientation

Most surfers, divers and budget travellers stay at Jungutbatu beach in the island's northwest, while more upmarket accommodation is further south, around Mushroom Bay, where many of the day-trip cruise boats stop.

About 4km southwest along the sealed road from Jungutbatu is Lembongan village, the island's other town. Leaving Jungutbatu you climb up a knoll that offers a wonderful view back over the beach. You can go right around the island, following the rough track that eventually comes back to Jungutbatu, but the roads are steep for cyclists and walkers.

There's no jetty at Jungutbatu – the boats usually beach in the shallows by the village. The Perama boat stops outside Mandara Beach Bungalows, while the public shuttle boat stops further south. The south end of the beach – where the Island Explorer boats land – is the one part that is truly filthy.

Information

There's no tourist office, but your hotel should be able to answer most questions. **Bank BPD** (☽ 8am-3pm Mon-Thu, 8am-1pm Fri) can exchange travellers cheques and cash; although it's advisable to bring sufficient cash with you, as rates are very poor. There is no ATM or post office. **Mainsky Inn** (☎ 0361-283065) operates a wartel and has Internet access. Small markets can be found on the main street with the bank.

Electricity operates only for certain hours (3pm to 8am Monday to Saturday and all day Sunday), but the better hotels have their own generators.

Any of the hotels can refer you to the local doctor in Jungutbatu village, although the consultation fee is a pricey 250,000Rp. The nurse's clinic in the village, opposite the path to Ketut's Bungalows, is a better option for simple problems.

Ketut's Bungalows (☎ 0366-24487) rents bicycles for 25,000Rp per day, surfboards for 30,000Rp to 40,000Rp per day, snorkelling

---

DIVING THE ISLANDS

There are great diving possibilities around the islands, from shallow and sheltered reefs, mainly on the northern side of Lembongan and Penida, to very demanding drift dives in the channel between Penida and the other two islands. Vigilant locals have protected their waters from dynamite bombing by renegade fishing boats, so the reefs are mostly still intact. The best local dive operation, based at Nusa Lembongan, is **World Diving** (☎ 081 2390 0686; www.world-diving .com), which runs trips to 18 different dive sites.

If you arrange a dive trip from Candidasa or South Bali, stick with the most reputable operators, as conditions here can be tricky and local knowledge is essential. A particular attraction is the large marine animals, including turtles, sharks and manta rays. The large (3m fin to fin) and unusual *mola mola* (sunfish) is sometimes seen around the islands between July and September, while manta rays are often seen south of Nusa Penida.

The best dive sites include Blue Corner and Jackfish Point off Nusa Lembongan and Ceningan Point at the tip of that island. The channel between Ceningan and Penida is renowned for drift diving but it is essential that you have a good operator who can judge fast-changing currents and other conditions. Upswells can bring cold water from the open ocean to sites such as Ceningan Wall. This is one of the world's deepest natural channels and attracts all manner and sizes of fish.

Sites close to Nusa Penida include Big Rock, Crystal Bay, SD, Pura Ped and Manta Point. Of these, Crystal Bay, SD and Pura Ped are suitable for novice divers and are good for snorkelling.

gear for 20,000Rp to 30,000Rp per day, and motorbikes for 30,000Rp per hour.

Sights

JUNGUTBATU

The beach here, a mostly lovely arc of white sand with clear blue water, has superb views across to Gunung Agung on Bali. The village itself is pleasant, with quiet lanes, no cars and a couple of temples, including **Pura Segara** and its enormous banyan tree.

MUSHROOM BAY

This gorgeous little bay, unofficially named for the mushroom corals offshore, has a perfect crescent of white-sand beach. During the day, the tranquillity may be disturbed by banana-boat rides or parasailing. In the morning and the evening, it's delightful.

The most pleasant way to get here from Jungutbatu is to walk along the trail that starts from the southern end of the main beach and follows the coastline for a kilometre or so, past a couple of little beaches. Alternatively, get a boat from Jungutbatu (or ask the skipper of the boat from Sanur to drop you at Mushroom Bay before they go on to Jungutbatu).

DREAM BEACH

Down a little track, this 150m crescent of white sand has pounding surf and a cute little café.

Activities

For a smorgasbord of activities, visit **Ketut's Bungalows** (☎ 24487) which rents bicycles for 25,000Rp per day, surfboards for 30,000Rp to 40,000Rp per day, snorkelling gear for 20,000Rp to 30,000Rp per day, and motorbikes for 30,000Rp per hour.

SURFING

Surfing here is best in the dry season (April to September), when the winds come from the southeast. It's definitely not for beginners, and can be dangerous even for experts. There are three main breaks on the reef, all aptly named. From north to south are Shipwreck, Lacerations and Playground. Depending on where you are staying, you can paddle directly out to whichever of the three is closest; for others it's better to hire a boat. Prices are negotiable – from about 10,000Rp for a one-way trip, and around

---

SEAWEED SUNDAE

The next time you enjoy some creamy ice cream, you might thank the seaweed growers of Nusa Lembongan and Nusa Penida. Carrageenan is an emulsifying agent that is used to thicken ice cream as well as cheese and many other products. It is also used as a fat substitute in 'diet' foods (just look for it on the endless ingredients label). In nature it turns seawater into a gel which gives seaweed its structure.

On Lembongan 85% of the population work at farming seaweed for carrageenan (as opposed to 5% in tourism) and it is the major industry. Although returns are OK, the work is very intensive and time-consuming. Women are the main labourers.

As you walk around the villages you'll see – and smell – vast areas used for drying the seaweed. Looking down into the water, you'll see the patchwork of cultivated seaweed plots. Small pieces of a marine algae (*Eucheuma*) are attached to strings that are stretched between bamboo poles – these underwater fences can be seen off many of the beaches, and especially in the shallows between Lembongan and Ceningan. Growth is so fast that new shoots can be harvested every 45 days. This region is especially good for production as the waters are shallow and rich in nutrients. The dried red and green seaweed is exported around the world for final processing.

100,000Rp waiting time. A fourth break – Racecourses – sometimes emerges south of Shipwreck.

The surf can be crowded here even when the island isn't – charter boats from Bali sometimes bring groups of surfers for day trips from the mainland, or as part of a longer surfing trip between Bali and Sumbawa. For day trips to Nusa Lembongan boats can be chartered from Sanur Beach for a minimum of 500,000Rp. See p318 for more information.

DIVING

The excellent **World Diving** (☎ 081 2390 0686; www.world-diving.com), based at Pondok Baruna on Jungutbatu Beach, has full PADI Resort status. It offers a full range of courses, including five-day PADI open-water courses

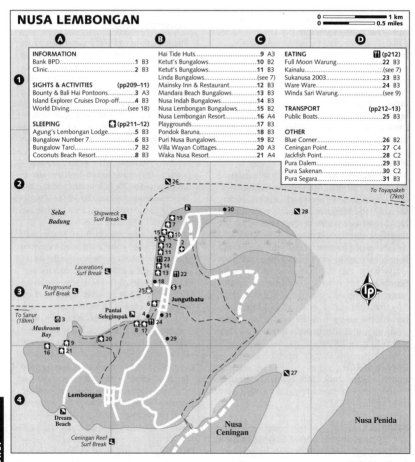

NUSA LEMBONGAN

0 ━━━━━ 1 km
0 ━━━━━ 0.5 miles

INFORMATION	
Bank BPD..**1** B3	
Clinic...**2** B3	
SIGHTS & ACTIVITIES (pp209–11)	
Bounty & Bali Hai Pontoons.............**3** A3	
Island Explorer Cruises Drop-off......**4** B3	
World Diving...............................(see 18)	
SLEEPING ⌂ (pp211–12)	
Agung's Lembongan Lodge...............**5** B3	
Bungalow Number 7.........................**6** B3	
Bungalow Tarci.................................**7** B2	
Coconuts Beach Resort.....................**8** B3	

Hai Tide Huts.....................................**9** A3	
Ketut's Bungalows..........................**10** B2	
Ketut's Bungalows..........................**11** B3	
Linda Bungalows...........................(see 7)	
Mainsky Inn & Restaurant...............**12** B3	
Mandara Beach Bungalows.............**13** B3	
Nusa Indah Bungalows....................**14** B3	
Nusa Lembongan Bungalows...........**15** B2	
Nusa Lembongan Resort..................**16** A4	
Pondok Baruna................................**17** B3	
Puri Nusa Bungalows......................**18** B3	
Villa Wayan Cottages......................**20** A3	
Waka Nusa Resort...........................**21** A4	

EATING 🍴 (p212)	
Full Moon Warung...........................**22** B3	
Kainalu..(see 7)	
Sukanusa 2003................................**23** B3	
Ware Ware.......................................**24** B3	
Winda Sari Warung.......................(see 9)	
TRANSPORT (pp212–13)	
Public Boats....................................**25** B3	
OTHER	
Blue Corner......................................**26** B2	
Ceningan Point................................**27** C4	
Jackfish Point..................................**28** C2	
Pura Dalem......................................**29** B3	
Pura Sakenan...................................**30** C2	
Pura Segara.....................................**31** B3	

for US$345, and dive trips for US$30 per dive to sites around all three islands. There are a few other dive operators based at Jungutbatu that operate from various hotels. See Diving the Islands, p208 for details on the area's dive sites.

SNORKELLING
There's good snorkelling just off the Bali Hai and Bounty pontoons off Jungutbatu Beach, as well as in areas off the north coast of the island. You can charter a boat from 30,000Rp to 50,000Rp per hour, depending on demand, distance and the number of passengers; for more information ask at your hotel. Snorkelling gear can be rented for 20,000Rp to 30,000Rp per day. World

Diving (see p209) allows snorkellers to join dive trips and charges 60,000Rp for a four-hour trip.

There's good drift snorkelling along the mangrove-filled channel west of Cenigan Point between Lembongan and Ceningan.

CRUISES
A number of cruise boats offer day trips to Nusa Lembongan from Benoa Harbour in South Bali. Trips include hotel transfer from South Bali, basic water sports, snorkelling, banana-boat rides and a buffet lunch. Most of the companies listed have overnight accommodation at Mushroom Bay on Nusa Lembongan if you are interested in extending your stay. Note that with

hotel transfers, the following day trips can make for a very long day.

Bali Hai (☎ 0361-720331; www.balihaicruises.com) This has an ugly offshore pontoon for snorkelling and water play. Reef cruises cost US$85/42.50 per adult/child, and catamaran cruises are US$85/57. Cruises depart Benoa Harbour at 9am and return at 4.30pm.

Bounty Cruises (☎ 0361-726666; www.balibounty group.com) This group has an offshore pontoon only slightly less ugly than Bali Hai and offers similar cruises for US$85/42.50 per adult/child, although the trip also includes a village tour on Lembongan. Cruises on a huge yellow boat depart at 9am and return at 4.30pm.

Island Explorer Cruises (☎ 0361-728088; www.bali -activities.com; per person US$49) This has three ways to get to Lembongan, which all get you back to Bali around 5pm: relaxing and slow-sailing catamaran (8.30am), party boat (8.30am) and fast boat (10.30am). The latter two maximise your time in the water at Lembongan, although the buffet lunch at the outfit's Coconuts Beach Resort can keep you from swimming for hours.

Sleeping
JUNGUTBATU

Most places to stay in Jungutbatu are basic. Most of the following places have beachfront restaurants serving typical travellers' fare. The strip of beachfront joints is going through the classic Bali development cycle: each year more rooms are added and old ones are spruced up. Unless noted otherwise, amenities are limited to cold water and fans.

Budget

Pondok Baruna (☎ 0812 3900 686; www.world-diving .com; s/d 65,000/95,000Rp, dishes 10,000-18,000Rp) Run by World Diving, this is one of the best places to stay. Staff are friendly, rooms are pleasant and porches face the ocean. The restaurant serves good meals.

Bungalow Number 7 (☎ 24497; r 50,000-100,000Rp, dishes 7000-20,000Rp) This good, clean and friendly place has 14 rooms, with two on the beach with great views. The grounds are attractive and it is a little apart from the rest of the strip. It has a beachfront restaurant serving simple but good dishes.

Mainsky Inn (☎ 24481; s/d 40,000/60,000Rp; 🖳) There's a popular café here and 26 hot-water rooms in bungalows and larger blocks going back from the beach.

Nusa Lembongan Bungalows (☎ 24484; nusa lembongan@hotmail.com; bungalows 50,000 to 150,000Rp) Of the five nice units here, the front one is a duplex with great views from the 2nd-floor

patio. Covered relaxation areas along the beach inspire daytime languor.

Bungalow Tarci (☎ 24494; r 100,000Rp) The upstairs units in front have excellent views of the water. This is a good place to organise surfing trips.

Ketut's Bungalows (☎ 24487; r 50,000-300,000Rp) The 12 rooms span the gamut from humble to modest. More expensive ones come with hot water, fridges and enormous beds. Upstairs rooms get good breezes and views of the ocean from the balconies. It's a scenic place where the small sandy area out the front fills with lounging travellers by day.

Linda Bungalows (☎ 24495; r 70,000-90,000Rp) Of the 12 rooms, only the one in front has an ocean view, but it is a good one. It's a very clean place.

Nusa Indah Bungalows (☎ 24480; r 50,000-100,000Rp) A pleasant and growing beachfront place with four newer bungalows and eight older rooms.

Agung's Lembongan Lodge (☎ 24483; s/d 30,000/40,000Rp, beachfront bungalow 100,000Rp, dishes 6000-15,000Rp) The simple rooms are mostly in colourful rice-barn style bungalows. The restaurant has hanging bird cages, ocean views and a much nicer atmosphere than many others.

Manadara Beach Bungalows (☎ 24470; www .mandara-lembongan.com; r 120,000-160,000Rp) Eight large rooms are set around a popular café. This stretch of beach is nice and there's a nascent garden away from the water.

Puri Nusa Bungalows (☎ 24482; r 50,000-70,000Rp) Set back from the beach, the 17 rooms are clean and comfortable. Room two has excellent views.

Mid-Range

Playgrounds (☎ 0817 4748 427; www.playground slembongan.com; r 250,000-350,000Rp; 🗶 🖳) On a hillside, Playgrounds' six rooms have good views, satellite TV and fridges. The cheaper rooms don't have air-con but do have better views from their long porch. The owner is from Brisbane and can talk about local surfing all day. There's also an adjoining private house for 600,000Rp a night.

Coconuts Beach Resort (☎ 0361-728088; www .bali-activities.com; d US$66, with air-con US$86; 🗶 🖳) South of the village, Coconuts has unusual, spacious, circular bungalows staggered up the hillside overlooking a lovely pool and the sea. It's part of Island Explorer Cruises.

MUSHROOM BAY

Nusa Lembongan Resort (☎ 0361-725864; www
.nusa-lembongan.com; villas from US$160, lunch 50,000Rp,
dinner 55,000-90,000Rp; 🍽 🍸) Twelve secluded
and stylish villas overlooking a gorgeous
sweep of ocean are the draw here. The resort has a smart restaurant; it's possible to
dine on six courses at ocean-side private
pavilions, or you can arrange picnics.

Hai Tide Huts (☎ 0361-720331; www.balihaicruises
.com; hut from US$69; 🍸) The Bali Hai Beach
Club has these small but well-finished rice-
barn thatched bungalows, albeit without
private bathrooms – you'll have to head
over to the bathroom block. Still, it's a relaxed place looking onto a clear stretch of
beach, and there's a flash swimming pool.
Packages are available.

Waka Nusa Resort (☎ 0361-723629; www.waka
experience.com; bungalows from US$90) This pretty
little place has 10 thatch-roofed bungalows
set in sandy grounds. The beachside restaurant and bar is delightfully located under
coconut palms. Ask about using the Waka
Louka (see right) sailing boat to transfer
from Bali.

Villa Wayan Cottages (Chelegimbai; ☎ 0361-
287431; r US$47-72) Just north of Mushroom
Bay, near another delightful little bay
called Pantai Selegimpak, Villa Wayan
Cottages has a few, varied and unusually
decorated rooms; some are suitable for
families or groups.

Eating

JUNGUTBATU

Many of the places listed under Sleeping
also have cafés and restaurants. The usual
menu of Indonesian and Western dishes
is omnipresent. There are some delightful
warung on the path to Pura Sakenan.

Full Moon Warung (8000-18,000Rp) A popular
dinner spot, Full Moon has four tables on
the sand away from the beach. The menu
is Balinese and the red snapper is very
popular.

Ware Ware (dishes 20,000-40,000Rp) Perched on
a hill, every table here has fabulous views of
the beach, water and Bali. The sunset happy
hours are a must.

Sukanusa 2003 (dishes 15,000-30,000Rp) This
pleasant café-bar is right on the sand and is
a good sunset spot.

Kainalu (dishes 14,000-28,000) Spread over two
levels right on the sand, it has a pool table,

serves up pizza, pasta and seafood and has
chairs for sunbathing.

MUSHROOM BAY

Winda Sari Warung (dishes 10,000-30,000Rp) Near
the Bali Hai Beach Club, this fun warung
has a good spot overlooking the fishing
boats at Mushroom Bay.

Getting There & Away

Getting to or from Nusa Lembongan offers
numerous choices. In descending order of
comfort are the Island Explorer boats used
by day-trippers, the Perama boat and the
public boats. Getting between the boats and
shore and getting around once on land is
not especially easy, so this is the time to
travel very light.

SANUR & SOUTH BALI

Public boats to Nusa Lembongan leave
from the northern end of Sanur beach
at 7.45am (35,000Rp, 1½ to two hours).
This is the boat used by locals and you
may have to share space with a chicken.
The Perama tourist boat (which is more
reliable) leaves at 10.30am (50,000Rp, 1½
hours). The ride is often rough and you're
likely to get wet.

From Nusa Lembongan to Sanur, public
boats leave Jungutbatu beach at 7.45am.
The Perama boat to Sanur leaves at 8.30am
and connects with a through service to
Kuta (70,000Rp) and Ubud (75,000Rp).

BENOA HARBOUR

There is space on **Bounty Cruises'** (☎ 0361-
726666; www.balibountygroup.com; one-way US$15)
huge yellow boat for people needing to
transfer to Nusa Lembongan (1½ hours).
Boats depart Benoa Harbour at 9am and
return at 3pm.

Island Explorer Cruises (☎ 0361-728088; www
.bali-activities.com; each way US$22) has three ways
to get to Lembongan.

Day trips to the island on **Waka Louka's**
(☎ 0361-723629; www.wakaexperience.com; per person
US$69) 23m sailing catamaran are leisurely,
and the service on board is good. Guests
enjoy the facilities of the Waka Nusa Resort
(see left). Check schedules in advance.

Quicksilver (☎ 0361-7425161; www.quicksilver-bali
.com) runs day cruises from Benoa Harbour
to its water-sports pontoon off Toyapakeh
for US$70/35 per adult/child. The fare

includes hotel transfers, a buffet lunch, snorkelling and a village walking tour. Options such as cycling tours are possible. Book at travel agents or online.

For more information on day trips to the island, see p210.

NUSA PENIDA
Boats take locals between Jungutbatu and Toyapakeh between 5.30am and 6am for 7000Rp. Otherwise, charter a boat for 200,000Rp one way.

Getting Around
The island is fairly small and you can easily walk around it in a few hours; however, the roads across the middle of the island are quite steep. Bicycles and scooters are widely available for rent.

NUSA PENIDA
☎ 0366
The island of Nusa Penida is a limestone plateau with white-sand beaches on its north coast, and views over the water to the volcanoes on Bali. The beaches are not good for swimming as most of the shallows are filled with bamboo frames used for seaweed farming. The south coast has limestone cliffs dropping straight down to the sea and a row of offshore islets – it's rugged and spectacular scenery. The interior is hilly, with sparse-looking crops and old-fashioned villages. The rainfall is low, and in *Caban* which water is stored for the dry season.

The population of around 47,000 people is predominantly Hindu, although there are some Muslims in Toyapakeh. The culture is distinct from that of Bali: the language is an old form of Balinese no longer heard on the mainland, and there is also local dance, architecture and craft, including a unique type of red ikat weaving. Nusa Penida was once used as a place of banishment for criminals and other undesirables from the kingdom of Klungkung, and still has a somewhat sinister reputation.

Sampalan
Sampalan, the main town on Penida, is quiet and pleasant, with a market, schools and shops strung out along the curving coast road. The market area, where the bemos congregate, is in the middle of town.

PENIDA'S DEMON

Nusa Penida is the legendary home of Jero Gede Macaling, the demon who inspired the Barong Landung dance. Many Balinese believe the island is a place of enchantment and *angker* (evil power) – paradoxically, this is an attraction. Although few foreigners visit, thousands of Balinese come every year for religious observances aimed at placating the evil spirits.

The island has a number of interesting temples dedicated to Jero Gede Macaling, including Pura Dalem Penetaran Ped, near Toyapakeh. It houses a shrine, which is a source of power for practitioners of black magic, and a place of pilgrimage for those seeking protection from sickness and evil.

SLEEPING & EATING
Made's Homestay (☎ 29609, 0818 345 204; s/d 60,000/75,000Rp) A friendly place with small, clean rooms and a pleasant garden. Breakfast is included. A small side road between the market and the harbour leads here.

Bungalow Pemda (☎ 21448, 23580; r 25,000-100,000Rp) Opposite the police station, a few-hundred metres east of the market, is the government rest-house, which has four good-value renovated rooms with hot water. The older rooms are basic.

There are a few warung and cafés along the main road and around the market.

Toyapakeh
If you come by boat from Lembongan, you'll probably be dropped at the beach at Toyapakeh, a pretty town with lots of shady trees. The beach has clean white sand, clear blue water, a neat line of boats, and Gunung Agung as a backdrop. Step up from the beach and you're at the road head, where bemos can take you to Ped or Sampalan (1000Rp). Few travellers stay here, but if you do, **Losmen Terang** (s/d 40,000/45,000Rp) is near the beach. There is no electricity.

Around the Island
A trip around the island, following the north and east coasts, and crossing the hilly interior, can be completed in a few hours by motorcycle. You could spend much longer, lingering at the temples and the small villages, and walking to less accessible areas,

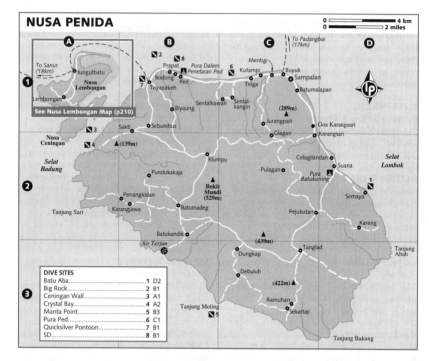

NUSA PENIDA

0 ___ 4 km
0 ___ 2 miles

To Sanur (18km)
To Padangbai (17km)

Jungutbatu
Nusa Lembongan
Lembongan
See Nusa Lembongan Map (p210)

2
8
Prapat
Pura Dalem Penetaran Ped
6
Mentigi
Kutampi
Buyuk
Sampalan
Bodong
Ped
Telga
Batumalapan
Toyapakeh
Biyaung
Sentalkawan
Sental-kangin
(289m)
Jurangpait
Goa Karangsari
Karangsari
Sakti
Sebunibus
Glagan
Nusa Ceningan
3
4
▲(139m)
Klumpu
Celagilandan
Suana
Selat Lombok
Selat Badung
Pundukakaja
Pulagan
Pura Batukuning
Penangkidan
Bukit Mundi (529m)
Semaya
1
Tanjung Sari
Karangjawa
Batumadeg
Pejukutan
Karang
Batukandik
(439m)
Tanglad
Tanjung Abah
Air Terjun
Dungkap
Debuluh
(422m)▲
Ramuhan
Tanjung Moling
5
Sekartaji
Tanjung Bakung

DIVE SITES

Batu Aba...1	D2
Big Rock..2	B1
Ceningan Wall...................................3	A1
Crystal Bay.......................................4	A2
Manta Point......................................5	B3
Pura Ped..6	C1
Quicksilver Pontoon..........................7	B1
SD..8	B1

but there's no accommodation outside the two main towns. The following description goes clockwise from Sampalan.

The coastal road from Sampalan curves and dips past bays with rows of fishing boats and offshore seaweed gardens. After about 6km, just before the village of Karangsari, steps go up on the right side of the road to the narrow entrance of **Goa Karangsari** caves. There are usually people who can provide a lantern and guide you through the cave for a small negotiable fee of around 20,000Rp each. The limestone cave is over 15m tall in some sections. It extends more than 200m through the hill and emerges on the other side to overlook a verdant valley.

Continue south past a naval station and several charming **temples** to Suana. Here the main road swings inland and climbs up into the hills, while a very rough side track goes southeast, past more interesting temples to **Semaya**, a fishing village with a sheltered beach and one of Bali's best dive sites offshore.

About 9km southwest of Suana, **Tanglad** is a very old-fashioned village and a centre for traditional weaving. Rough roads south and east lead to isolated parts of the coast.

A scenic ridge-top road goes northwest from Tanglad. At Batukandik, a rough road leads to a spectacular **air terjun** (waterfall). Limestone cliffs drop hundreds of feet into the sea, with offshore rock pinnacles surrounded by crashing surf. At the base of these cliffs, underground streams discharge fresh water into the sea – a pipeline has been made to bring the water up to the top. You can follow the pipeline down the cliff face on an alarmingly exposed metal stairway. From it, you can see the remains of rickety old wooden scaffolding – women used to clamber down this and return with large pots of water on their heads.

Back on the main road, continue to Batumadeg, past **Bukit Mundi** (the highest point on the island at 529m), through Klumpu to Sakti, which has traditional stone buildings. Return to the north coast at Toyapakeh.

The important temple of **Pura Dalem Penetaran Ped** is near the beach at Ped, a few kilometres east of Toyapakeh. It houses a shrine for the demon Jero Gede Macaling (see Penida's Demon, p213). The temple structure is crude, which gives it an appropriately sinister ambience. From there, the road is straight and flat back to Sampalan.

Getting There & Away
The strait between Nusa Penida and southern Bali is very deep and subject to heavy swells – if there is a strong tide, boats often have to wait. You may also have to wait a while for the public boat to fill up with passengers. Boats to and from Kusamba are not recommended.

PADANGBAI
On the beach just east of the car park in Padangbai, you'll find the twin-engine fibreglass boats that run across the strait to Buyuk on Nusa Penida (25,000Rp, 45 minutes). The inconspicuous **ticket office** (7am-noon) is nearby. Boats leave at 9am, sometimes at 7am, and take one hour.

NUSA LEMBONGAN
There is a public boat connection (5000Rp, 20 minutes) between Toyapakeh and Jungutbatu (Nusa Lembongan) between 5am and 6am. Ask at your hotel or on the beach. Alternatively, charter a whole boat between the two islands for a negotiable 200,000Rp.

Getting Around
Bemos regularly travel along the sealed road between Toyapakeh and Sampalan, and sometimes on to Suana and up to Klumpu, but beyond these areas the roads are rough or nonexistent and transport is limited. You should be able to charter your own bemo or private vehicle with driver for about 60,00Rp to 80,000Rp.

You may also be able to negotiate an *ojek* for about 20,000Rp per hour. If you really want to explore, bring a mountain bike and camping equipment from the mainland (but remember, Nusa Penida is hilly). Alternatively, plan to do some serious hiking, but come well prepared.

NUSA CENINGAN
There is a narrow suspension bridge crossing the lagoon between Nusa Lembongan and Nusa Ceningan, which makes it quite easy to explore the network of tracks on foot or by bicycle – not that there is much to see. The lagoon is filled with frames for seaweed farming and there's also a fishing village and several small agricultural plots. Although the island is quite hilly, if you're up for it, you'll get glimpses of great scenery as you wander or cycle around the rough tracks.

There's also a break off Nusa Ceningan, the middle island of the group, but it's very exposed and only surfable when it's too small for the other breaks.

Central Mountains

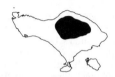

Most of Bali's mountains are volcanoes – some are dormant, some are definitely active. The mountains divide the gentle sweep of fertile rice land to the south from the narrower strip to the north. In East Bali, there is a small clump of mountains right at the end of the island, beyond Amlapura. Then there's the mighty volcano Gunung Agung (3142m), the island's 'Mother Mountain'. Northwest of Gunung Agung is the stark and spectacular caldera that contains the volcanic cone of Gunung Batur (1717m), Danau Batur and numerous smaller craters.

Further west, in the Danau Bratan area, lush vegetation covers another complex of volcanic craters, these ones long, dormant and interspersed with several lakes. A string of smaller mountains stretches off to the sparsely inhabited western region. Small, uncrowded roads cross Bali's steep central and western regions, through little-visited villages.

The popular round trip to the north coast crosses the mountains by one route (eg via Gunung Batur) and returns by another (from Singaraja via Bedugul), thus covering the most interesting parts of the central mountain region. You can do the circuit easily in either direction, and while getting to more remote areas by public transport is a little tricky, it's not impossible.

Trekking to the peak of Gunung Batur to watch the sunrise is popular, but there are many other possibilities around the central mountains and lakes. The area around the village of Munduk and Danau Tamblingan and Danau Buyan is growing in popularity and provides a bucolic alternative to the at times over-heated tourism scene around Danau Batur.

TOP FIVE

- Exploring the vast double caldera, crater lake, lava flows, hot springs and smoking cones of **Gunung Batur** (p218)
- Enjoying the beauty of the mountains while hiking around **Danau Buyan** (p230) and **Danau Tamblingan** (p230)
- Contemplating **Pura Ulun Danu Bratan** (p229) – a truly beautiful, meditative temple
- Exploring Bali's back country of winding roads and walking tracks through superb scenery and rural villages
- Hiking through and enjoying the superb views of lush valleys all the way to the North Bali coast from the region around **Munduk** (p230)

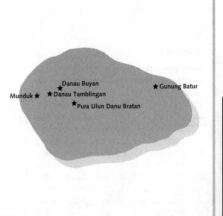

Danau Buyan

Munduk ★ ★ Danau Tamblingan

★ Gunung Batur

★ Pura Ulun Danu Bratan

CENTRAL MOUNTAINS

GUNUNG BATUR AREA

☎ 0366

This area is like a giant dish, with the bottom half covered with water and a set of volcanic cones growing in the middle. The road around the southwestern rim of the Gunung Batur dish is one of Bali's most important north–south routes and has one of Bali's most spectacular vistas. Most overnight visitors stay in the villages around the shores of Danau Batur, and plan an early start to climb the volcano.

ORIENTATION

The villages around the crater rim have grown together in a continuous, untidy strip. The main village is Kintamani, though the whole area is often referred to by that name. Kintamani itself is a dreary place where the locals never look quite warm enough. Coming from the south, the first village is Penelokan, where tour-group busloads stop to gasp at the view, eat a buffet lunch and be hassled by souvenir sellers.

Entry Tickets

If you arrive by private vehicle, you'll be stopped at ticket offices at either Penelokan or Kubupenelokan; to save any hassle, you should stop and buy a ticket. Entry is 3000/1500Rp per adult/child, plus 100Rp insurance, and 1000Rp for a car or 200Rp for motorcycle. Bicycles are free (and should be, given the climb needed to get here). This ticket is for the whole Gunung Batur area; you shouldn't be charged any more down

at the lakeside. Keep the tickets if you drive back and forth around the crater rim, or you may have to pay again and again. The entry ticket should be included in any organised tour. If you're passing through on a public bus or *bemo* (small pick-up truck) you don't have to pay anything.

INFORMATION

There's a *wartel* (public telephone office) just near the turn-off down to the lake at Penelokan, and several postal agencies along the Kintamani road.

Money

You can change money only at Bank PDB in Kintamani, and at a number of nearby stalls in Penelokan. The best idea is to stock up with cash before leaving the coastal tourist regions or Ubud.

Tourist Information

The **Tourist Information Office** (Yayasa Bintang Danu; ☎ 51370, 0813 3879 4894; Penelokan; ☺ 10am-3pm) has some information about local transport fares, trekking routes and homestays. You can also call or otherwise report complaints about price gouging and other problems to the office, although the efficacy of any remedies is untested.

ACTIVITIES
Trekking

The climb to see the sunrise from Gunung Batur is still the most popular trek, even with the high fees charged by, not to mention the dodgy reputation of, the HPPGB; see p219.

TREKKING AGENCIES

Even reputable and highly competent adventure tour operators from elsewhere on Bali cannot take their customers up Gunung Batur without paying the HPPGB and using one of their guides, so these tours are relatively expensive.

Trekking agencies in Toya Bungkah must also use guides from HPPGB for Gunung Batur treks, but they *may* be able to help you to get a full group together, and ensure that you get one of the better guides from the HPPGB. Alternatively, they can arrange other treks in the area, to Gunung Abang or the outer rim of the crater, or to other mountains such as Gunung Agung. All

---

WARNING

The Gunung Batur area has a reputation as a money-grubbing place. Keep an eye on your gear and don't leave any valuables in your car, especially at the start of any trail up the volcano. Also be wary of touts on motorcycles who will attempt to steer you to a hotel of *their* choice as you descend into the Danau Batur area from the village of Penelokan. Guide services are controlled by the HPPGB (Mount Batur Tour Guides Association; see p219). Finally, some of the vendors in the area can be highly aggressive and irritating.

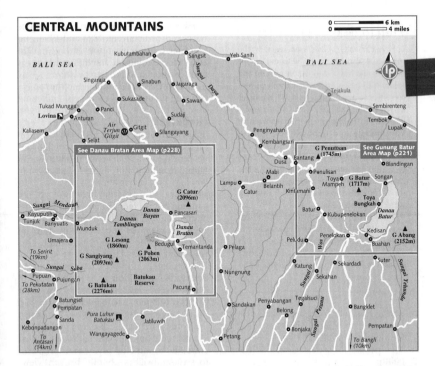

of the agencies listed here can get you up Gunung Batur for rates from about US$20; fees are negotiable. They also offer many more complex itineraries as well.

Arlina's Trekking Agency (Map p225; ☎ 51165; Arlina's Bungalows, Toya Bungkah) Offers a range of treks.

Hotel Astra Dana (☎ 52091; Kedisan) Another recommended place.

Hotel Miranda (☎ 52022; Jl Raya Kintamani, Kintamani) One of the few agencies that will take solo climbers.

Hotel Segara (☎ 51136; hotelsegara@plasa.com; Kedisan) Popular with larger groups.

Jero Wijaya Tourist Service (Map p225; ☎ 0366-51249; jero_wijaya@hotmail.com; Lakeside Cottages, Toya Bungkah) Well-regarded, offers treks up Gunung Agung (US$75) and in Taman Nasional Bali Barat (US$90).

HPPGB

The notorious **HPPGB** (☎ 52362; Toya Bungkah office ☼ 5am-9pm; Pura Jati office ☼ 3am-noon) has a monopoly on guided climbs up Gunung Batur. HPPGB requires that all trekking agencies hire at least one of its guides for trips up the mountain. In addition the HPPGB has developed an unsavoury reputation for intimidation in requiring climbers to use its guides. Reported tactics have ranged from dire warnings given to people who inquired at its offices to outright physical threats against people attempting to climb without a guide. There have also been reports of guides stationing themselves outside of hotels to intercept climbers.

The HPPGB, however, is claiming to be reformed. An HPPGB Official, Nyoman Sudiartha, claims that hikers wishing to ascend Gunung Batur without a guide will not be hassled. Further, he promises that the hard-sell tactics used by the guides will be curtailed. It's probably a good idea to seek advice from other travellers and check reports on the Thorn Tree (www.lonely planet.com) for the latest on this situation.

What seems clear is that HPPGB is determined to defend its turf and that readers should carefully consider whether the climb is worth the hassle. Certainly some of the HPPGB guides are better than others. Meanwhile the bad publicity and general downturn in visitors has forced the group to lower its rates. It is now quoting the

WHEN TO TREK

The volcanically active area west of the main peak can be deadly, with explosions of steam and hot lava, unstable ground and sulphurous gases. To find out about current conditions, ask at the trekking agencies in Toya Bungkah (p224), or alternatively look at the website of the **Directorate of Volcanology and Geographical Hazard Mitigation** (www.vsi.esdm.go.id).

The active areas are sometimes closed to visitors for safety reasons – if this is the case, don't try it alone, and don't pay extra for an extended main crater trek that you won't be able to do.

Think twice about trekking in the wet season (October to March), because the trails can be muddy and slippery, and clouds often block the views. Note that monsoonal rains often cause landslides in some mountain areas.

following fees, which are about half off the rates posted on a large signboard in the Toya Bungkah office. The rates cover up to four people. Breakfast is an additional 50,000Rp.

Trek	Duration	Cost
Batur Sunrise	4am-8am	150,000Rp
Gunung Batur Main Crater	4am-10am	200,000Rp

HPPGB also offers guides for many more treks in the region.

EQUIPMENT

If you're climbing before sunrise, take a torch (flashlight) or be absolutely sure that your guide provides you with one. You'll need good strong footwear, a hat, a jumper and drinking water.

GUNUNG BATUR

Vulcanologists describe Gunung Batur as a 'double caldera', ie, one crater inside another. The outer crater is an oval about 14km long, with its western rim about 1500m above sea level. The inner crater is a classic volcano-shaped peak that reaches 1717m. Activity over the last decade has spawned several smaller cones on its western flank, unimaginatively named Batur I,

II, III and IV. More than 20 minor eruptions were recorded between 1824 and 1994, and there were major eruptions in 1917, 1926 and 1963. Geological activity and tremors have continued to occur regularly.

Ideally, trekkers should get to the top for sunrise (about 6am), before mist and cloud obscure the view. It's a magnificent sight, though hardly a wilderness experience – it's not uncommon to have 100 people on top for sunrise in the tourist season. It's not necessary to be at the top for sunrise – a halfway point is fine. If you start at 5am, you'll avoid the crowds.

Guides will provide breakfast on the summit for a fee (50,000Rp), and this often includes the novelty of cooking an egg or banana in the steaming holes at the top of the volcano (although this isn't recommended for hygiene reasons). Unfortunately, the practice results in an accumulation of litter around the summit. There are several refreshment stops along the way, and people with buckets full of cold drinks. Agree on a price before they open the bottle – they can ask over 10,000Rp for a small soft drink. Some small *warung* (food stalls) at the top offer pricey tea, coffee and toasted sandwiches – but the brilliant views are free. (Check where the water comes from for the coffee and tea.)

From Toya Bungkah

The basic trek is to start climbing from Toya Bungkah at about 3am, reach the summit for sunrise, and possibly walk right around the main cone, then return to Toya Bungkah. The route is pretty straightforward – walk out of the village towards Kedisan and turn right just after the car park. There are a few separate paths at first but they all rejoin sooner or later – just keep going uphill, tending southwest and then west. After about 30 minutes you'll be on a ridge with quite a well-defined track; keep going up. It gets pretty steep towards the top and it can be hard walking over the loose volcanic sand – climbing up three steps and sliding back two. Allow about two hours to reach the top, which is at the northern edge of the inner crater.

Climbers have reported that they have easily made this journey without a HPPGB guide, although it shouldn't be tried while dark. The major obstacle is actually avoiding

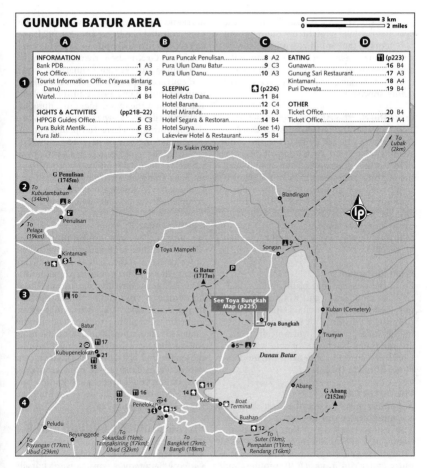

GUNUNG BATUR AREA

INFORMATION		
Bank PDB	1	A3
Post Office	2	A3
Tourist Information Office (Yayasa Bintang Danu)	3	B4
Wartel	4	B4

SIGHTS & ACTIVITIES	(pp218–22)	
HPPGB Guides Office	5	C3
Pura Bukit Mentik	6	B3
Pura Jati	7	C3

Pura Puncak Penulisan	8	A2
Pura Ulun Danu Batur	9	C3
Pura Ulun Danu	10	A3

SLEEPING	(p226)	
Hotel Astra Dana	11	B4
Hotel Baruna	12	C4
Hotel Miranda	13	A3
Hotel Segara & Restoran	14	B4
Hotel Surya	(see 14)	
Lakeview Hotel & Restaurant	15	B4

EATING	(p223)	
Gunawan	16	B4
Gunung Sari Restaurant	17	A3
Kintamani	18	A4
Puri Dewata	19	B4

OTHER		
Ticket Office	20	B4
Ticket Office	21	A4

any hassle from the guides themselves (see p219).

You can follow the rim to the western side, with a view of the area of the most recent volcanic activity, continue to the southern edge, and then return to Toya Bungkah by the route you climbed up. Alternatively, descend on a more southerly route through the lava field to Pura Jati, and walk (or get a bemo) along the road back to Toya Bungkah.

Longer trips go around the new volcanic cones southwest of the summit. This has the most exciting volcanic activity, with smoking craters, bright-yellow sulphur deposits, and steep slopes of fine black sand. If the activity is *too* exciting, the area may be closed for trekking, though the summit can still be okay. The most satisfying round trip is to climb Gunung Batur from Toya Bungkah, follow the inner crater rim around to the west, then go south through the area of the most recent volcanic activity, descend to the east, and traverse through the lava field to Pura Jati.

Climbing up Gunung Batur, spending a reasonable time on the top and then strolling back down takes four or five hours; for the longer treks around the newer cones, allow around eight hours.

From Pura Jati

If you stay at Kedisan rather than Toya Bungkah, you might want to start at Pura

CENTRAL MOUNTAINS

Jati. The shortest trek is basically across the lava fields, then straight up (allow about two hours to the top). If you want to see the newer cones west of the peak (assuming the area is safe to visit), go to the summit first – don't go walking around the active area before sunrise.

From the Northeast
The easiest route is from the northeast – that's if you can get transport to the trail-head at 4am. From Toya Bungkah take the road northeast towards Songan and take the left fork after about 3.5km. Follow this small road for another 1.7km to a badly signposted track on the left – this climbs another kilometre or so to a parking area. From here, the walking track is easy to follow to the top, and should take less than an hour.

From Kintamani
From the western edge of the outer crater, trails go from Batur and Kintamani down into the main crater, then up Gunung Batur from the west side. This route passes close to the rather exciting volcanically active area and may be closed for safety reasons. Check the current status with the guide at Hotel Miranda (p223).

THE OUTER CRATER
A popular place to see the sunrise is on the outer crater rim northeast of Songan. You'll need transport to Pura Ulun Danu Batur, near the northern end of the lake. From there you can climb to the top of the outer crater rim in under 30 minutes, and see Bali's northeast coast, about 5km away. At sunrise, the silhouette of Lombok looms

> **WARNING**
>
> The parking area is not secure, so don't leave anything of value in your car, or even a helmet with your motorcycle. There's a risk of damage to your vehicle if you don't use an official guide, and no guarantee of its safety even if you do. The best way to do this route is probably to engage one of the HPPGB guides, and ask him to arrange transport (for an extra cost) to the trailhead, climb to the top, then walk back by the southeastern trail to Toya Bungkah.

across the water, and the first rays strike the great volcanoes of Batur and Agung. If you can reconnoitre this route in daylight, you'll be able to do it without a guide.

Trails follow the outer rim to the north and south, and provide delightful trekking, with the sea on one side, and the lake and volcanoes on the other. The Toya Bungkah trekking agents know many minor trails that can bring you back to the lakeside.

Another option is an easy downhill stroll to the coast road at Lupak, from where you can take public transport back to Toya Bungkah via Kubutambahan and Penelokan. If you start early, you could complete this round trip in a single day.

GUNUNG ABANG
It's possible to hike up Gunung Abang (2152m), at the southeastern edge of the outer crater. It's the highest point on the crater, though the potentially panoramic view is largely obscured by forest. Go as far southeast around the rim as possible by road and, where the road swings south, look for the walking trail that continues eastwards and upwards. Beyond Gunung Abang there are little-used trails around the crater and beside the lake that can get you down to Trunyan or right around to Songan, but you'll need a good guide – talk to the trekking agents in Toya Bungkah (p219) or Kedisan (p225).

VILLAGES AROUND GUNUNG BATUR
☎ 0366
There are several small villages around Gunung Batur where you can base yourself. You'll need to choose between a lakeside setting with the mountains looming above (p224) or a ridge setting with views out over the lake below and beyond.

GETTING THERE & AROUND
The two main routes to Penelokan from the south, via Bangli and Tampaksiring, meet just before Penelokan, and are both good roads. You can also take the rougher road to and from Rendang via Menanga, which turns off a few kilometres east of Penelokan and goes on to Semarapura. In clear weather, you'll have fine views of Gunung Agung. The other roads are okay and offer off-beat views, but have little public transport.

You can also get to Penelokan from the north coast – the road climbs steeply from Kubutambahan, near Yeh Sanih, and has regular public transport. For information on entry tickets, see p218.

Bemo & Bus

From the Batubulan terminal in Denpasar, bemos regularly go to Kintamani via various routes, including Ubud and Payangan, Bangli, or Tampaksiring (6000Rp). They also run between Denpasar (Batubulan) and Singaraja via Kintamani and Penelokan (10,000Rp).

Orange bemos regularly shuttle back and forth around the crater rim, between Penelokan and Kintamani (6000Rp for tourists). To Penulisan, try to flag down a minibus going to Singaraja. Public bemos from Penelokan to the lakeside villages go mostly in the morning (tourist price is about 5000Rp to Toya Bungkah). Later in the day, you may have to charter transport (30,000Rp or more).

Tourist Shuttle Bus

Perama (see p169) will run charter mini-buses to the Penelokan–Kintamani ridge area from Ubud (50,000Rp per person, minimum two people).

Ojeks

An *ojek* (motorcycle that carries paying pillion passengers) can be an easy way to get around if you don't have much luggage. Fares are negotiable, but from Penelokan try to not pay more than 6000Rp to Kedisan, 7000Rp to Buahan or 12,000Rp to Toya Bungkah.

Penelokan

Penelokan means 'Place to Look' – and you will be gobsmacked by the view across to Gunung Batur and down to the lake at the bottom of the crater. Apart from the view (check out the large lava flow on Gunung Batur), there's not much here – a large hotel, several ugly monolithic restaurants peering over the crater and numerous desperate souvenir sellers. For other services in the village, see p218.

Right on the edge of the crater and with a brilliant view of the lake, **Lakeview Hotel & Restaurant** (☎ 51394; www.indo.com/hotels /lakeview; r US$35-57, buffet lunch 61,000Rp) has comfortable rooms with superb views. The more expensive ones feature amenities such as satellite TV. The restaurant here is the best choice on the rim, with modern, stylish décor. Tables outside are especially nice. Beware of souvenir sellers in the parking lot.

The road around the rim has several monstrous, overpriced restaurants geared to busloads of tour groups, including Gunawan, Puri Dewata and Kintamani. They all have fine views, and provide buffet-style lunches from 60,000Rp to 80,000Rp or more. Most will have a relatively expensive à la carte alternative if you ask. Dotted among these restaurants are some decent warung with similar views and meals for about 20,000Rp.

Batur & Kintamani

The villages of Batur and Kintamani now virtually run together and have minimal charm. Kintamani is famed for its large and colourful market held every three days. It starts early and by 11am it's all over. For other services in the village, see p218.

The original village of Batur was in the crater, but was wiped out by a violent eruption in 1917. It killed thousands of people and destroyed more than 60,000 homes before the lava flow stopped at the entrance to the village's main temple.

Taking this as a good omen, the village was rebuilt, but Gunung Batur erupted again in 1926. This time, the lava flow covered everything except for the loftiest temple shrine. Fortunately, the Dutch administration anticipated the eruption and had evacuated the village (partly by force), so very few lives were lost. The village was relocated up on the crater rim, and the surviving shrine was also moved up there and placed in the new temple, **Pura Ulun Danu** (sarong & sash rental 1000Rp, admission dona-tion 2000Rp). Spiritually, Gunung Batur is the second most important mountain on Bali (only Gunung Agung outranks it) so this temple is of considerable importance.

The **Hotel Miranda** (☎ 52022; Jl Raya Kintamani, Kintamani; s/d 25,000/50,000Rp) is the only reliable accommodation here. The six rooms are clean and very basic with squat toilets. It has good food and a congenial open fire at night. The informative owner can also act as a trekking guide (see p219).

CENTRAL MOUNTAINS

Penulisan

The road gradually climbs along the crater rim beyond Kintamani, and is often shrouded in clouds, mist or rain. Penulisan is where the road bends sharply and heads down towards the north coast. A viewpoint about 400m south of the Blandingan road junction offers an amazing view over three mountains: Gunung Batur, Gunung Abang and Gunung Agung. If you're coming from the north, this is where you'll first see what all the tourism fuss is about. On clear days you'll note some volcanic cones on Batur which portend geologic events to come.

Near the road junction, several steep flights of steps lead to Bali's highest temple, **Pura Puncak Penulisan** (1745m). Inside the highest courtyard are rows of old statues and fragments of sculptures in the open *bale* (pavilions). Some of the sculptures date back to the 11th century. The temple views are superb: facing north you can see over the rice terraces clear to the Singaraja coast (weather permitting).

With your own transport you can continue further around the crater rim for a gr█████ ██ █e northern side of Gunung Ba███ ██ █ while, the road leaves the rid██ ██ ██escends towards the north coast – you'll get glimpses of brilliant coastal scenery through the tall trees, but the road doesn't go all the way down.

VILLAGES AROUND DANAU BATUR

☎ 0366

The little villages around Danau Batur have a crisp lakeside setting and views up to the surrounding peaks. There's a lot of fish-farming here and the air is redolent with the smell of onions from the many farms.

A hairpin-bend road winds its way down from Penelokan to the shore of Danau Batur. At the lakeside you can go left along the good road that winds its way through lava fields to Toya Bungkah, the usual base for climbing Gunung Batur.

The road gets rougher as it continues around to Songan, under the northeastern rim of the crater, and an even rougher side road goes around to the north side of Gunung Batur, via Toya Mampeh. This round-the-volcano road is interesting, as it passes through a huge layer of solidified black lava from the 1974 eruption, but it now carries a huge number of large trucks hauling sand and gravel, making it hazardous and unpleasant. If you want to risk it, go clockwise around the crater, and at least you won't be meeting the trucks head-on.

Alternatively, go east around the lakeside, through Kedisan and Buahan. Another option is a boat trip across the lake to the ancient village of Trunyan and its alfresco cemetery at Kuban.

Toya Bungkah

The main tourist centre is Toya Bungkah (also known as Tirta), with its hot springs (*tirta* and *toya* both mean 'water'). Toya Bungkah is a scruffy little village, but many travellers stay here so they can climb Gunung Batur early in the morning – most of them leave quickly afterwards.

INFORMATION

The infamous **HPPGB** (☎ 52362; Toya Bungkah office ✆ 5am-9pm; Pura Jati office ✆ 3am-noon) guide agency has offices in Toya Bungkah and nearby at Pura Jati (see p219).

ACTIVITIES

Hot springs bubble out in a couple of spots, and have long been used for bathing pools. Beside the lake, with a wonderful mountain backdrop, **Tirta Sanjiwani Hot Springs Complex** (☎ 51204; adult/child US$5/2.50; ✆ 8am-8pm) has lovely gardens near the lake. Entry includes use of the cold-water pool (20°C) and hot spa (40°C).

SLEEPING

The main road through town is used by large gravel trucks day and night, so try to get rooms at the back of hotels. There are plenty of small, cheap *losmen* (basic accommodation), but only a few are worth recommending. Unless noted, hotels only have cold water, which can be a boon for waking up for a sunset climb.

Lakeside Cottages (☎ 51249; jero_wijaya@hotmail .com; r US$8-35, dishes 9000-14,000Rp; 🖳) At the end of the track on the water's edge, this is definitely one of the better places. The cheapest of the 11 rooms have cold water only; the top-end ones feature hot water and satellite TV. See p219 for details of the hotel's Jero Wijaya Tourist Service trekking guides.

Under the Volcano I (☎ 51166; s/d/tr 30,000/40,000/ 50,000Rp, dishes 12,000-20,000Rp) All seven large rooms here are around a small garden. The restaurant serves the local speciality *ikan mujair* (see below).

Under the Volcano II (☎ 52508; r with/without hot water 40,000/70,000Rp) Up off the water, the six rooms here are spotless.

Under the Volcano III (☎ 081 3386 0081; r 60,000Rp) With a lovely, quiet lakeside location opposite vegetable plots, this inn has clean and pretty rooms; go for room one right on the water. All of the 'Volcanoes' are owned by the same cheery clan.

Hotel Puri Bening Hayato (☎ 51234; www.indo .com/hotels/puribeninghayato; bungalow US$20-35, r US$45-80, dishes 12,000-24,000Rp) An incongruously modern three-storey place, it has a few quaint water-view bungalows and oversized wannabe 'deluxe' rooms all with hot water and lake views. The hotel has a restaurant, which is cool and quiet inside.

Arlina's Bungalows (☎ 51165; s/d 40,000/60,000Rp, with hot water 60,000/75,000Rp) Clean, comfortable, friendly and above the average standard. See p219 for details on the trekking service here.

EATING

Small, sweet lake fish known as *ikan mujair* are the delicious local speciality. The dish is barbecued to a crisp with onion, garlic and bamboo sprouts, making the bones crunchy and edible. Most of the hotels have restaurants; Arlina's and Under the Volcano I are worth seeking out, as is Lakeside Cottages. Its restaurant is worth trying for home-style Japanese dishes, such as *oyako-don* (rice topped with egg and chicken).

Volcano Breeze (☎ 51824; dishes 10,000-18,000Rp) A delightful and sociable travellers' café, well away from the constant truck noise. Fresh lake fish in many forms is the speciality here.

GETTING THERE & AROUND

Bemos between Toya Bungkah and Penelokan go mostly in the morning (4000Rp). Later you may have to charter transport (30,000Rp or more). *Ojeks* from Penelokan cost 12,000Rp.

Songan

Two kilometres around the lake from Toya Bungkah, Songan is a large and interesting village with market gardens extending to the lake's edge. At lakeside road end is **Pura Ulun Danu Batur**, under the edge of the crater rim.

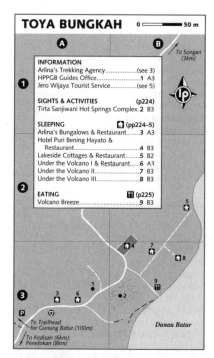

TOYA BUNGKAH   0 — 50 m

INFORMATION
Arlina's Trekking Agency..................(see 3)
HPPGB Guides Office...........................1 A3
Jero Wijaya Tourist Service...............(see 5)

SIGHTS & ACTIVITIES   (p224)
Tirta Sanjiwani Hot Springs Complex.2 B3

SLEEPING   (pp224–5)
Arlina's Bungalows & Restaurant........3 A3
Hotel Puri Bening Hayato &
    Restaurant.......................................4 B3
Lakeside Cottages & Restaurant........5 B2
Under the Volcano I & Restaurant.....6 A3
Under the Volcano II...........................7 B3
Under the Volcano III..........................8 B3

EATING   (p225)
Volcano Breeze...................................9 B3

To Songan (3km)

Danau Batur

To Trailhead for Gunung Batur (100m)
To Kedisan (6km); Penelokan (8km)

Toya Mampeh

A turn-off in Songan takes you on a rough but passable road around the crater floor. Much of the area is very fertile, with bright patches of market garden and quite strange landforms. On the northwestern side of the volcano, Toya Mampeh village (also called Yeh Mampeh) is surrounded by a vast field of chunky black lava – a legacy of the 1974 eruption.

Further on, **Pura Bukit Mentik** was completely surrounded by molten lava from this eruption, but the temple itself, and its really impressive banyan tree, were quite untouched – it's called the 'Lucky Temple'. The enjoyment is constantly shattered, however, by a continuous procession of trucks hauling out volcanic gravel and sand.

Kedisan & Buahan

The villages around the southern end of the lake have a few places available to stay in a fairly isolated setting. Buahan is a pleasant 15-minute stroll from Kedisan, and has market gardens going right down to the lakeshore.

CENTRAL MOUNTAINS

Beware of the motorcycle touts who will follow you down the hill from Penelokan trying out various guide and hotel scams. Local hotels ask that you call ahead and reserve so that they can have your name on record and thus avoid paying a bounty to the touts.

SLEEPING & EATING

Hotel Surya (Map p221; ☎ 51139; www.indo.com/hotels /surya; r 40,000-100,000Rp, dishes 7000-12,000Rp) Right at the bottom of the road from Penelokan, the Surya has a big range of decent rooms – the more expensive have views, hot water and bathtubs. Its restaurant, in a nice elevated position, has a better view than some of the expensive tourist restaurants in Penelokan. Free pick-up is offered from Ubud and Semarapura.

Hotel Astra Dana (Map p221; ☎ 52091; r 40,000-70,000Rp) The more expensive of the 12 rooms have hot water and views to the lake across onion and cabbage fields. This is the home of the always delightful Dizzy, local guide extraordinaire. See p219 for details on the trekking service here.

Hotel Segara & Restoran (Map p221; ☎ 51136; hotelsegara@plasa.com; r 60,000-100,000Rp; 🖳) Next door to Hotel Surya, Segara has bungalows set around a courtyard. The more expensive rooms have hot water. It's clean and comfortable enough for a night. The restaurant is a good place to sample the local fish. See p219 for details on the trekking service here.

Hotel Baruna (Map p221; ☎ 51221; r 50,000Rp) Out past the edge of Buahan, the Baruna offers a remote lake experience. It has a lovely outlook and offers basic, clean rooms.

Trunyan & Kuban

The village of Trunyan is squeezed between the lake and the outer crater rim. It is inhabited by Bali Aga people, descendants of the original Balinese who inhabited Bali before the Majapahit arrival. Trunyan is not a welcoming place, unlike Tenganan, the other well-known Bali Aga village in eastern Bali.

Trunyan is famous for the **Pura Pancering Jagat**, with its 4m-high statue of the village's guardian spirit, but tourists are not allowed to go inside. There are also several traditional Bali Aga-style dwellings, and a large banyan tree, said to be over

1100 years old. Touts and guides want large tips for brief and barely comprehensible commentaries, and solicit large 'offerings' at the temple or the graves – 2000Rp is sufficient.

A little beyond Trunyan, and accessible only by boat (there's no path) is the **cemetery** at Kuban. The people of Trunyan do not cremate or bury their dead – they lie them out in bamboo cages to decompose, although strangely there is no stench. A collection of skulls and bones lies on a stone platform. This is a tourist trap for those with macabre tastes.

GETTING THERE & AWAY

Getting across the lake from Kedisan to Trunyan was once one of Bali's great rip-offs. After negotiating a sky-high price, your boatman would then want to renegotiate halfway across. It got so bad that the government took over and set the prices, although you should be ever-vigilant should old habits return.

Boats leave from a jetty near the middle of Kedisan, where there is a ticket office and a secure car park (1000Rp) with a few pushy vendors. Tourists are not allowed to catch the public boat. The price for a four-hour round trip – Kedisan–Trunyan–Kuban–Toya Bungkah–Kedisan – depends on the number of passengers, with a maximum of seven (one/two/seven people costs 196,700/199,500/213,000Rp). Try to go before 10am, when the water is calmest and Gunung Batur is most photogenic.

If you want to do it on the cheap, don't consider hiring a canoe and paddling yourself – the lake is bigger than it looks from the shore and it can get rough. An alternative is to follow the footpath around the lake to Trunyan, an easy one- or two-hour walk (the walk will be the best part of the trip). From Trunyan, you may be able to negotiate a boat to the cemetery, Toya Bungkah or Kedisan, but it won't be cheap.

PELAGA

☎ 0362

A scenic road heads north from Ubud, via Sangeh and Petang, and continues through the pretty village of Pelaga to finish near Penulisan at the northwestern edge of Gunung Batur's outer crater. The road is sealed, little trafficked, and would make a fine cycling trip. Pelaga has great possibilities for trekking in the surrounding countryside.

There are bemos up this road all the way from Wangaya terminal in Denpasar (6000Rp), via Sangeh, but it's best with your own transport. With some directions, you could walk the 8km from Bedugul (near Danau Gratan) to Pelaga.

DANAU BRATAN AREA

Approaching from the south, you gradually leave the rice terraces behind and ascend into the cool, often misty mountain country around Danau Bratan. Candikuning is the main village in the area, and has an important and picturesque temple. Bedugul is at the south end of the lake, with the most touristy attractions. About 4km north of the lake, Pancasari has the local market, the main bemo terminal and a golf course. Danau Buyan and Danau Tamblingan are pristine lakes northwest of Danau Bratan which offer good trekking possibilities. Beyond this are some interesting villages. To the south and west there are other beautiful highland areas, little visited by tourists.

While the choice of accommodation near the lake is limited, much of the area is geared towards domestic, not foreign, tourists. On Sunday and public holidays, the lakeside can be crowded with courting couples on motorcycles and Kijangs bursting with day-tripping families.

Wherever you go, you are likely to see the delightfully sweet local strawberries on offer.

BEDUGUL
☎ 0368
The name Bedugul is sometimes used to refer to the whole lakeside area, but strictly speaking, Bedugul is just the first place you reach at the top of the hill when coming up from South Bali. At the large billboard, take a right turn to the southern edge of the lake, where a harmless tourist trap awaits.

Activities
TAMAN REKREASI BEDUGUL
Lakeside eateries, a souvenir market and a selection of water sports – parasailing,

water- and jet-skiing plus speedboats – are the features at this tacky and noisy **recreation park** (☎ 21197; admission 3300Rp, parking 1500Rp; **P**), which attracts many tour buses filled with locals.

TREKKING
From the water sports area, a trail around the south side of the lake goes to the mundane **Goa Jepang** (Japanese Cave), which was dug during WWII. From there, a difficult path ascends to the top of Gunung Catur (2096m), where the old **Pura Puncak Mangu** temple is popular with monkeys. Allow about four hours to go up and back from Taman Rekreasi Bedugul.

Sleeping & Eating
The Bedugul area can make a good place for a break in exploring the highlands. Upmarket hotels on the slope south of Bedugul offer outstanding views to the east and west.

Strawberry Hill (Bukit Stroberi; ☎ 21265; r 50,000Rp, dishes 10,000-18,000Rp) Opposite the Taman Rekreasi turn-off, this cosy place has 10 basic rooms with hot water – a fine budget choice. The excellent restaurant has polished floorboards and on a clear day you can see Kuta. On offer are dishes such as burgers and *soto ayam* (chicken soup). There's also a good bar.

Bedugul Hotel & Restaurant (☎ 0361-226593; r 250,000Rp, dishes 13,000-40,000Rp) Located on the grounds of Taman Rekreasi Bedugul above the lake, the hotel has clean, modern but charmless rooms, some with views. The restaurant has tables overlooking the lake.

Pacung Mountain Resort (☎ 21038; r US$90-200, buffet lunch 65,000Rp, à la carte 20,000-80,000Rp; ☒) Well down the road from the ridge, this resort is built on a steep terraced slope overlooking an exquisite valley carved with rice fields and early morning views of Gunung Batukau. It is a quiet and tasteful option. There is a bar-restaurant, with gorgeous views, which serves a buffet lunch (noon to 3pm) or à la carte (all day). It's worth stopping just to have a drink.

Pacung Indah (☎ 21020; r 190,000-750,000Rp, buffet lunch 55,000Rp, à la carte 18,000-50,000Rp; ☒) Across the street from the Pacung Mountain Resort, this hotel has views almost as good and the rooms are a cut above the average and all include a private courtyard. It also

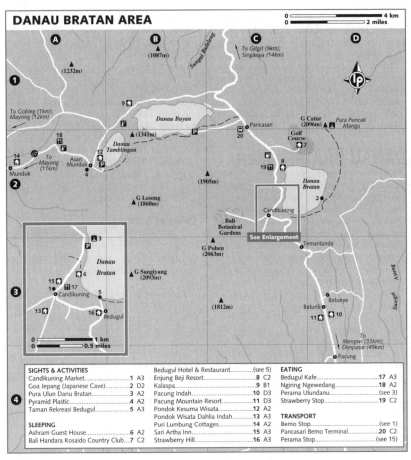

DANAU BRATAN AREA

0 — 4 km
0 — 2 miles

SIGHTS & ACTIVITIES		
Candikuning Market	1	A3
Goa Jepang (Japanese Cave)	2	D2
Pura Ulun Danu Bratan	3	A2
Pyramid Plastic	4	A2
Taman Rekreasi Bedugul	5	A3

SLEEPING		
Ashram Guest House	6	A2
Bali Handara Kosaido Country Club	7	C2

Bedugul Hotel & Restaurant	(see 5)	
Enjung Beji Resort	8	C2
Kalaspa	9	B1
Pacung Indah	10	D3
Pacung Mountain Resort	11	D3
Pondok Kesuma Wisata	12	A2
Pondok Wisata Dahlia Indah	13	A3
Puri Lumbung Cottages	14	A2
Sari Artha Inn	15	A3
Strawberry Hill	16	A3

EATING		
Bedugul Kafe	17	A3
Ngiring Ngewedang	18	A2
Perama Ulundanu	(see 3)	
Strawberry Stop	19	C2

TRANSPORT		
Bemo Stop	(see 1)	
Pancasari Bemo Terminal	20	C2
Perama Stop	(see 15)	

serves a buffet lunch (from noon to 3pm) or à la carte options such as pizza.

Getting There & Away

Any minibus or bemo between South Bali and Singaraja will stop at Bedugul on request (see p229 for details).

CANDIKUNING

☎ 0368

Spread out along the western side of the lake, Candikuning is the horticultural focus of central Bali. Its daily market was once the main supplier of vegetables, fruit and flowers for the southern hotels, but now its patrons are mostly tourists with a smattering of locals shopping for herbs, spices and potted plants. There's a wartel beside the market, and several moneychangers.

Sights & Activities

BALI BOTANICAL GARDENS

A recent change in management has turned the **Bali Botanical Gardens** (Kebun Raya Eka Karya Bali; ☎ 21273; admission 3500Rp, car parking 1500Rp; ☼ 8am-6pm; P) into a showplace. Established in 1959 as a branch of the national botanical gardens at Bogor, near Jakarta, they cover over 154 hectares on the lower slopes of Gunung Pohen. The gardens boast an extensive collection of trees and flowers, including wild orchids. Some plants are labelled with their botanical names, and the booklet *Six Self Guided Walks in the Bali*

Botanical Gardens, sold at the ticket office for 20,000Rp, is helpful.

Coming north from Bedugul, at a junction conspicuously marked with a large, phallic corncob sculpture, a small side road goes 600m west to the gardens. Although normally cool, shady, scenic and uncrowded, on Sunday and public holidays they're very popular with Balinese families. Cars can be taken into the park for an extra 6000Rp.

PURA ULUN DANU BRATAN

A few kilometres north of the market, this very important Hindu-Buddhist **temple** (adult/child 3300/1800Rp, parking 2000Rp; tickets 8.30am-6pm, site 24hr) was founded in the 17th century. It is dedicated to Dewi Danu, the goddess of the waters, and is actually built on small islands, which means it is completely surrounded by the lake. Both pilgrimages and ceremonies are held here to ensure that there is a supply of water for farmers all over Bali.

It is truly beautiful, with classical Hindu thatch-roofed *meru* (multiroofed shrines) reflected in the water and silhouetted against the often cloudy mountain backdrop – one of the most common photographic images of Bali. A large banyan tree shades the entrance, and you walk through manicured gardens and past an impressive Buddhist stupa to reach the lakeside.

An unfortunate aspect is the small animal zoo, left of the main entrance, where tourists are encouraged to be photographed alongside snakes, bats and iguanas, all of which appear to be kept in less than humane conditions.

If you are feeling hungry, **Perama Ulundanu** (21191; dishes 15,000-30,000Rp; 9am-5pm) in the grounds has a pleasant outdoor terrace and the usual Indonesian and Western standards.

WATER SPORTS

At the temple gardens, you can hire a four-passenger speedboat with a driver (60,000Rp per 15 minutes), a five-person boat with boat-man (70,000Rp per 30 minutes), or a two-person pedal boat (35,000Rp per 30 minutes). Canoes rented from the lakeside near the Ashram Guest House should cost a negotiable 90,000Rp for half a day.

For an almost surreal experience, take a quiet paddle across the lake and see Pura Ulun Danu Bratan at sunrise – arrange it with a boatman the night before.

Sleeping

Enjung Beji Resort (21490; fax 21022; cottages 350,000-500,000Rp) Just north of the temple and overlooking the lake, this 23-room place is a peaceful, pleasant option. The superior cottages are excellent quality and have outdoor showers and sunken baths.

Pondok Wisata Dahlia Indah (21233; r 50,000Rp) In the village, along a lane near the road to the botanical gardens, this is a decent budget option with comfortable, clean, hot-water rooms.

Ashram Guest House (21450; fax 21101; r 40,000-120,000Rp) The rooms here are utilitarian and the staff were indifferent the day we visited, but it overlooks the lake. It has a range of rooms and prices starting with shared bathroom and no hot water, more for a private bathroom, more still for hot water, and top price for everything, plus a view of the lake.

Sari Artha Inn (21011; r 50,000Rp) Close to the market and lacking views, this place has basic hot-water rooms and is conveniently located at the Perama stop.

Eating

Food stalls at Candikuning market offer cheap eats, and there are food carts further north at the car park overlooking the lake. At the entrance to Pura Ulun Danu Bratan are several Padang warung, and a restaurant on the grounds.

There are several roadside restaurants catering to Indonesian day-trippers, offering really good Indonesian food at very reasonable prices.

Bedugul Kafe (0813 3867 2677; dishes 15,000-30,000Rp; 8am-7pm) Stop here for a lake view, barbecued fish and cold beer.

Strawberry Stop (21060; dishes 6000-15,000Rp, strawberry wine 65,000Rp; 8am-6pm) North of Candikuning, Strawberry Stop makes good use of locally grown strawberries in milk shakes, juices and pancakes. Jaffles and other simple snacks and dishes are also available.

Getting There & Away

Danau Bratan is beside a main north–south road, so it's easy to reach from South Bali or Singaraja.

BEMO & BUS

The main bemo terminal is a few kilometres further north at Pancasari, but most mini-buses and bemos will stop along the main road in Bedugul and Candikuning. There are frequent connections from Denpasar's Ubung terminal (7000Rp) and Singaraja's Sukasada terminal (7000Rp). For Gunung Batur, you have to connect through Singaraja.

The big, fast through buses to and from Singaraja may not stop anywhere in the Danau Bratan area – if they do the fare is the same as for a cross-Bali trip.

TOURIST SHUTTLE BUS

Perama shuttle buses are by far the easiest way to get to the area from Kuta (30,000Rp), Sanur (30,000Rp), Ubud (30,000Rp) or Lovina (30,000Rp) – check schedules in advance. The Perama stop is at Sari Artha Inn (see p229) in Candikuning, but the driver should drop you off anywhere between Bedugul and Pancasari.

PANCASARI

The broad, green valley northwest of Danau Bratan is actually the crater of an extinct volcano. In the middle of the valley, on the main road, Pancasari is a non-tourist town with a bustling market and the main terminal for public bemos.

Just south of Pancasari, you will see the entrance to **Bali Handara Kosaido Country Club** (☎ 22646; www.indo.com/hotels/balihandara; r US$100-150, greens fee US$100, dishes 32,000-100,000Rp), a superbly situated, top-flight 18-hole golf course which offers comfortable accommodation in the sterile atmosphere of a grand 1970s resort. The restaurant has typically gorgeous views and serves both Japanese and international cuisine.

DANAU BUYAN & DANAU TAMBLINGAN

Also northwest of Danau Bratan are two more lakes, Danau Buyan and Danau Tamblingan – neither has been heavily developed for tourism, which is an advantage. There are several tiny villages and abandoned temples along the shores of both lakes, and although the frequently swampy ground makes it unpleasant in parts to explore, this is still a good place for taking a walk.

Sights & Activities

Danau Buyan (admission 2000Rp, parking 1000Rp; P) has parking right on the lake, a delightful 1.5km drive off the main road. The entire area is home to market gardens growing produce such as strawberries.

A 4km **hiking** trail goes around the southern side of Danau Buyan from the parking lot, then over the saddle to Danau Tamblingan, and on to Asan Munduk. It combines forest and lake views.

Danau Tamblingan (adult/child 3000/15000Rp, parking 1000Rp; P) also has a parking lot at the end of the road from the village of Asan Munduk. The lake is a 400m walk and this is where you can catch the trail to Danau Buyan. If you have a driver, you could walk this path in one direction and be met at the other end. There's usually a couple of guides hanging around the parking lot (you don't need them for the lake path) who will take you up and around **Gunung Lesong** (300,000Rp for six hours).

Sleeping

Pondok Kesuma Wisata (r 200,000Rp, dishes 8000-20,000Rp) A cute little guesthouse with hot-water rooms and a nice café just up from the Danau Tamblingan parking lot.

MUNDUK & AROUND
☎ 0362

Heading north from Pancasari, the main road climbs steeply up the rim of the old volcanic crater. It's worth stopping to enjoy the views back over the valley and lakes – watch out for the typically ill-behaved monkeys on the road. Turning right at the top will take you on a scenic descent to the coastal town of Singaraja, via the Gitgit waterfalls (see p239). Taking a sharp left turn, you follow a ridge-top road with Danau Buyan on one side and a slope to the sea on the other; coffee is a big crop in the area.

This road reaches a T-junction where you'll see a strange, decaying pyramid about 4m high. This is the **Pyramid Plastic**. It's made of melted down plastic waste, partly as a statement about the environmental problems plastic has caused on Bali (although its present state undercuts the argument that plastic is a permanent blight).

If you turn left at this junction, a trail leads to near Danau Tamblingan, among forest and market gardens. Turning right takes you along beautiful winding roads to the main village of Munduk. Watch for superb panoramas of North Bali and the ocean. About 2km west of Munduk look for signs indicating parking for a 15m waterfall near the road.

There's archaeological evidence of a developed community in the Munduk region between the 10th and 14th centuries, and accounts of the first Majapahit emissaries visiting the area. When the Dutch took control of North Bali in the 1890s, they experimented with commercial crops, establishing plantations for coffee, vanilla, cloves and cocoa. Quite a few Dutch buildings are still intact along the road in Munduk and further west, and the mountain scenery is sublime.

Almost everything is at an elevation of at least 1000m. Numerous trails are suitable for two-hour or much longer **treks** to coffee plantations, rice paddies, four waterfalls, villages, and around both Danau Tamblingan and Danau Buyan. You will be able to arrange a guide through your lodgings.

Sleeping & Eating

Puri Lumbung Cottages (☎ 92810; www.balihotels .com/north/purilumbung.php; cottage s/d US$65/73, cottage f US$92-149, dishes 15,000-24,000Rp) This great hotel has bright two-storey cottages that have stunning views (units three, eight, 10 and 11 have the best views) all the way down to the coast from their upstairs balconies. Rice grows right outside each unit. Fifteen trekking options and a range of courses, including dance and cooking, are offered. The hotel's restaurant, Warung Kopi Bali, has a great outlook onto the lush valleys and also serves great food, including the local dish *timbungan bi siap* (clear chicken soup with sliced cassava and fried shallots). The hotel is on the right-hand side of the road as you enter Munduk from Bedugul.

Guru Ratna (☎ 92182; s/d 100,000/150,000Rp, dishes 12,500Rp) The cheapest place in town has comfortable cold-water rooms in an old Dutch house. The restaurant here does good meals.

Kalaspa (☎ 082 636 1034; 3-day/2-night complete package US$760) On the road to Munduk and with mountain views to the sea, Kalaspa has luxurious two-room cottages, featuring private courtyards and bathrooms with garden views. It also has its own spa, yoga room and restaurant.

Ngiring Ngewedang (☎ 082 836 5146; dishes 15,000-40,000Rp; 🕙 10am-4pm) This coffee house 5km east of Munduk has views of the ocean when it's not clouded over. The café sells its own brand of coffee and staff will also take you through the coffee-production process.

Meme Surung and **Mekel Ragi** (☎ 92811; r 175,000Rp) are atmospheric old Dutch houses right next to each other and run by the same owner. The former has excellent views down the valleys.

Getting There & Away

Bemos leave Ubung terminal in Denpasar for Munduk frequently (16,000Rp); alternatively head to Singaraja and take a bemo from there (10,000Rp). Morning bemos from Candikuning also stop in Munduk (12,000Rp). If you're driving to or from the north coast, a decent road west of Munduk goes through a number of picturesque villages to Mayong, then down to the sea at Seririt.

GUNUNG BATUKAU & AROUND

West of the Mengwi–Bedugul–Singaraja road rises Gunung Batukau (2276m), the 'Coconut-shell Mountain'. This is the third of Bali's three major mountains and the holy peak of the island's western end.

For an alternative route to Pura Luhur Batukau, turn off the Mengwi–Singaraja road south of Pacung, and follow the rough road to Senganankaninan. From there, an even rougher road goes in a westerly direction to Wangayagede, via Jatiluwih. The name Jatiluwih means 'Truly Marvellous', and the view truly is – it takes in a huge chunk of South Bali.

Sights & Activities

If you want to climb Gunung Batukau, you'll need a guide, as there are many false trails. You'll also need to be very fit – it's an arduous climb. From Pura Luhur Batuku, a guide will cost a negotiable 500,000Rp. It takes about five or six hours to the top, and four hours to get down, through quite thick forest. If you want to get to the top before the mist rolls in, you'll need to spend a night near the summit, so bring a tent.

On the slopes of Gunung Batukau, **Pura Luhur Batukau** was the state temple when

Tabanan was an independent kingdom. It has a seven-roofed *meru* dedicated to Maha Dewa, the mountain's guardian spirit, as well as shrines for Bratan, Buyan and Tamblingan lakes. It's surrounded by forest, and often damp and misty. Sarongs can be rented and a donation to the temple is requested. Rules against pregnant or menstruating women entering the grounds are enforced (unlike most other temples, which waive these rules).

There are several routes to the temple. The easiest way is to follow the road north from Tabanan to Wangayagede, the last village before the temple.

Sleeping

Past the village of Wangayagede and signposted to the left off the main Pura Luhur Batukau road, **Prana Dewi Mountain Resort** (☎ 732032; www.balipranaresort.com; bungalows US$40-55, dishes 15,000-35,000Rp) is set amongst rice paddies and a snaking carp-filled stream. The rustic, beautifully furnished bungalows have thick slab timber floors and floor to ceiling views. Yoga and meditation classes are offerred. The restaurant, surrounded by low, terraced red-rice fields and a bamboo forest, has a closed, lush vista. Most of the vegetables, tempeh and rice is produced organically at the resort.

North Bali

CONTENTS

North Bali, the district of Buleleng, makes an interesting contrast with the south of the island. The Lovina beaches are popular with travellers looking for low-key fun, offering good-value places to stay and eat, but nothing like the chaos of the Kuta region. Many travellers coming from Java go straight from Gilimanuk to the north coast, rather than taking the south-coast road to South Bali. In the west, Pemuteran is peaceful and offers some very nice beaches and resorts.

The north coast has been subject to European influence for a long time. Having first encountered Balinese troops on Java in the 18th century, the Dutch became the main purchasers of Balinese slaves – many of whom served in the Dutch East India Company armies.

Various Balinese kings provided the Dutch with soldiers, but in the 1840s, disputes over shipwreck salvage, together with fears that other European powers might establish themselves on Bali, prompted the Dutch to make treaties with a number of the Balinese rajahs. However, the treaties proved ineffective, the plundering continued apace, and disputes arose with Buleleng's rajah.

During 1845 the rajahs of Buleleng and Karangasem formed an alliance, possibly to conquer other Balinese states or, equally possibly, to resist the Dutch. The Dutch attacked Buleleng and Karangasem in 1846, 1848 and 1849, seizing control of North Bali on the third attempt.

Until the airport in South Bali became the main means of arrival on Bali after World War II, most visitors arrived on steamships at Singaraja – it's where all the pre-war travel books started. Some writers complained it was too commercial and preferred South Bali because it was less developed.

Buleleng has a strong artistic and cultural tradition. Its dance troupes are highly regarded and a number of dance styles have originated here, including Janger. Gold- and silverwork, weaving, pottery, instrument-making and temple design all show distinctive local styles.

TOP FIVE

- Enjoying the beauty of the land and sea at one of **Pemuteran's** (p249) resorts

- Relaxing at **Lovina** (p240) – the north's mellow version of Kuta

- Discovering the temple at **Jagaraga** (p239) with its 'Bali baroque' carvings featuring bicycles and biplanes

- Diving and snorkelling at the north's many great sites

- Soaking in **Air Panas Banjar** (p248) – a natural spa of hot springs in a lush rainforest setting

YEH SANIH

☎ 0362

About 15km east of Singaraja, Yeh Sanih (also called Air Sanih) is a hassle-free seaside spot with a few guesthouses on the black-sand beachfront (albeit with a retaining wall). It's named for its freshwater springs **Air Sanih** (adult/child 2000/1000Rp; ⊙ 8am-6pm), which are channelled into large swimming pools before flowing into the sea. The pools are particularly picturesque at sunset, when throngs of locals bathe under heavily blooming frangipani trees.

Pura Ponjok Batu has a commanding location between the sea and the road, some 7km east of Yeh Sanih. It has some very fine limestone carvings in the central temple area.

A surprise in the area is **Art Zoo** (⊙ 8am-6pm), 5.7km east of Yeh Sanih on the Singaraja road. The American artist Symon (who also has a gallery in Ubud, see p149) has a gallery bursting with vibrant, exotic and often homoerotic paintings and sculpture. You can chat up his models.

Sleeping & Eating

Cilik's Beach Garden (☎ 26561; www.ciliksbeachgarden .com; s/d €35/50, villas €50-115, dishes 20,000-40,000Rp; 🖳) Coming here is like visiting your rich friends. These villas, 1km east of Yeh Sanih, are large and have vast private gardens. Other accommodation is in beautifully furnished *lumbung* (rice barn with a round roof) set in a delightful garden facing the ocean. A host of other services are available, including tours and dance performances. Meals are served in a pavilion.

Pondok Sembiran (☎ 0868 1210 3677; r 200,000-300,000Rp; 🍴🖳) There are two facilities here, one with a pool 20m from the beach and one right on the beach. The pleasant bungalows are large, good for families and have kitchens and hot water. The hotel is off the main road in Sembiran, 8.3km east of Yeh Sanih.

Puri Bagus Ponjok Batu (☎ 21430; dishes 15,000-30,000Rp) This lovely spot 6.8km east of Yeh Sanih is next to Pura Ponjok Batu and overlooks the water. It offers a big range of grilled seafood and Balinese dishes. Tables are well-spaced in pavilions.

Archipelago Restaurant (dishes 9000-18,000Rp) Across from Air Sanih and up a flight of stairs, Archipelago has an interesting menu of Indonesian and Western options. Tables are under an imposing *bale* (an open-sided pavilion) with good views.

Getting There & Away

Yeh Sanih is on the main road along the north coast. Frequent *bemos* (small pick-up trucks) and buses from Singaraja stop outside the springs (5000Rp).

If you are driving the coast road to Amed and beyond, be sure to fill up at the petrol station just east of Yeh Sanih as there is not another until almost Amlapura.

SINGARAJA

☎ 0362

With a population of over 100,000 people, Singaraja (which means 'Lion King') is Bali's second-largest city, but is far more low-key than Denpasar. With its tree-lined streets, Dutch colonial buildings and charmingly decrepit waterfront area, north of Jl Erlangga, it's worth wandering around for a few hours, but most people prefer to stay in nearby Yeh Sanih or Lovina.

Singaraja was the centre of Dutch power on Bali and remained the administrative centre for the Lesser Sunda Islands (Bali through to Timor) until 1953. It is one of the few places on Bali where there are visible traces of the Dutch period, but there are also Chinese and Muslim influences. Today Singaraja is a major educational and cultural centre, and its two university campuses provide the city with a substantial, and sometimes vocal, student population.

The 'suburb' of Beratan, to the south of Singaraja, is the silverwork centre of northern Bali. You'll find a few traditional pieces, such as *cucuk* (gold headpieces) on display, but it mostly has uninspiring tourist jewellery. A few workshops in and around Singaraja produce hand-woven sarongs – especially *songket*, cloth woven with silver or gold threads.

Orientation

The main commercial areas are in the northeastern part of town, south of the harbour. Most hotels, restaurants and bus company offices are found along Jl Jen Achmed Yani. The traffic does a few complicated one-way loops around town, but it's easy enough to get around on foot or by bemo.

NORTH BALI

NORTH BALI

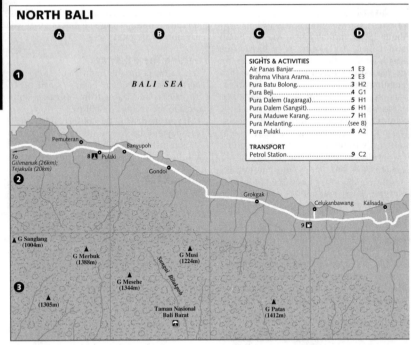

SIGHTS & ACTIVITIES
Air Panas Banjar..................................1 E3
Brahma Vihara Arama.....................2 E3
Pura Batu Bolong..............................3 H2
Pura Beji..4 G1
Pura Dalem (Jagaraga)....................5 H1
Pura Dalem (Sangsit)......................6 H1
Pura Maduwe Karang.....................7 H1
Pura Melanting...........................(see 8)
Pura Pulaki..8 A2

TRANSPORT
Petrol Station...................................9 C2

Information

EMERGENCY
Police station (☎ 41510; Jl Pramuka)

INTERNET ACCESS & TELEPHONE
There are several wartels along the main streets and there is Internet access at the rear of the post office (per hour 6000Rp).

MEDICAL SERVICES
RSUP Hospital (☎ 22046; Jl Ngurah Rai; ☽ 24hr)
Singaraja's hospital is the largest in northern Bali.

MONEY
There are numerous banks that will change money and have ATMs.
Bank BCA (Jl Jen Achmed Yani)
Bank Danamon (Jl Jen Achmed Yani)

POST OFFICE
Post office (Jl Imam Bonjol)

TOURIST INFORMATION
Diparda (☎ 25141 ext 22; cnr Jl Veteran & Jl Gajah Mada; ☽ 7.30am-3.30pm Mon-Fri) The tourist office loves visitors. Ask about dance and other cultural events.

Sights & Activities

OLD HARBOUR & WATERFRONT
The conspicuous **Yudha Mandala Tama monument** commemorates a freedom fighter killed by gunfire from a Dutch warship early in the struggle for independence. Close by, there's the colourful Chinese temple **Ling Gwan Kiong**. There a few old canals here as well and you can still get a little feel of the old colonial port here.

GEDONG KIRTYA LIBRARY & MUSEUM
This small historical **library** (☎ 22645; admission 5000Rp; ☽ 8am-4pm Mon-Thu, 8am-1pm Fri, 8am-noon Sat & Sun) was established in 1928 by Dutch colonialists and named after the Sanskrit word 'to try'. It has a collection of *lontar* (dried palm leaves) books (see p45), as well as some even older written works, in the form of inscribed copper plates called *prasasti*. Dutch publications, dating back to 1901, may interest students of the colonial period.

The nearby **museum** (donation 5000Rp; ☽ 7am-3pm) recalls the life of the last Radja (rajah) of Buleleng, Pandji Tisna, who is credited with developing Lovina's tourism. Among

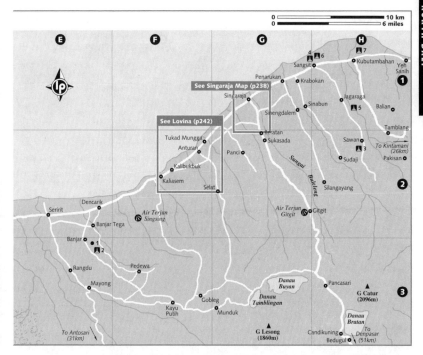

the items here is the Royal (brand) type-writer he used during his career as a travel writer (obviously, the rajah was a smart guy) before his death in 1978.

PURA JAGAT NATHA
Singaraja's main temple, the largest in northern Bali, is not usually open to foreigners. You can appreciate its size and admire the carved stone decorations from the outside.

Festivals & Events
Every May or June, Singaraja is host to the **Bali Art Festival of Buleleng**. Over one week dancers and musicians from some of the region's most renowned village troupes, such as those of Jagaraga, perform. Consult with the Diparda tourist office (see p236) for details.

Sleeping & Eating
There are slim accommodation pickings in Singaraja, and there's no real reason to stay here. It's just a short drive from Lovina.

Hotel Wijaya (☎ 21915; fax 25817; Jl Sudiman 74; s/d with fan 45,000/50,000Rp, with air-con 100,000/110,000Rp;

☒) This is the most comfortable place in town, although economy fan rooms have an outside bathroom. It also has a restaurant.

Hotel Sentral (☎ 21896; Jl Jen Achmed Yani 48; s/d 40,000/50,000Rp, with air-con 75,000/80,000Rp; ☒) This place is simple, clean and has a nice fish pond.

Café Lima Lima (☎ 21769; dishes 4000-9000Rp) and **Kantin Koka** (☎ 23686; dishes 3000-7500Rp) are clean, inexpensive places side by side on Jl Achmed Jen Yani, and attract a few students. In the evening, there are food stalls in the night market on Jl Durian, and various *warung* (food stalls) around the bemo and bus terminals.

Self-caterers should head to **Hardy's Supermarket** (Jl Pramuka; ☒ 8am-8pm), a large grocery and variety store. The market and night market are also good sources for cheap local food and other supplies.

Getting There & Away
BEMO & BUS
Singaraja is the transport hub for the northern coast, with three main bemo/bus terminals. From the main Sukasada terminal,

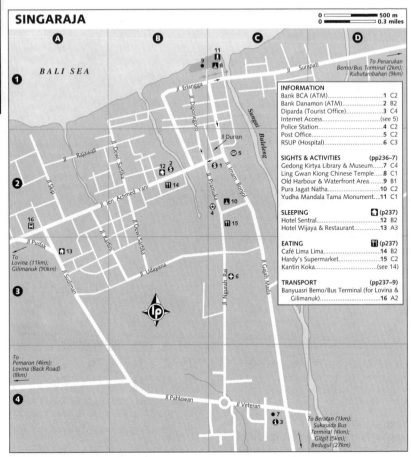

SINGARAJA

0 — 500 m
0 — 0.3 miles

BALI SEA

To Penarukan
Bemo/Bus Terminal (2km);
Kubutambahan (9km)

INFORMATION
Bank BCA (ATM)............................**1** C2
Bank Danamon (ATM)...................**2** B2
Diparda (Tourist Office)...............**3** C4
Internet Access..........................(see 5)
Police Station..............................**4** C2
Post Office...................................**5** C2
RSUP (Hospital)..........................**6** C3

SIGHTS & ACTIVITIES   (pp236–7)
Gedong Kirtya Library & Museum.....**7** C4
Ling Gwan Kiong Chinese Temple.....**8** C1
Old Harbour & Waterfront Area........**9** B1
Pura Jagat Natha............................**10** C2
Yudha Mandala Tama Monument...**11** C1

SLEEPING   (p237)
Hotel Sentral..............................**12** B2
Hotel Wijaya & Restaurant..............**13** A3

EATING   (p237)
Café Lima Lima.............................**14** B2
Hardy's Supermarket.....................**15** C2
Kantin Koka...............................(see 14)

TRANSPORT   (pp237–9)
Banyuasri Bemo/Bus Terminal (for Lovina &
    Gilimanuk)...............................**16** A2

To Penarukan
Bemo/Bus Terminal (2km);
Kubutambahan (9km)

To Lovina (11km);
Gilimanuk (90km)

To Pemaron (4km);
Lovina (Back Road)
(8km)

To Beratan (1km);
Sukasada Bus
Terminal (4km);
Gitgit (5km);
Bedugul (27km)

---

about 3km south of town, minibuses go to Denpasar (Ubung terminal, 11,000Rp) via Bedugul/Pancasari (7000Rp) about every 30 minutes from 6am to 4pm. There is also a tiny bemo stop, next to the *puskesmas* (community health centre) in Sukasada, with services to Gitgit.

The Banyuasri terminal, on the western side of town, has buses heading for Seririt (4000Rp), Gilimanuk (12,000Rp) and Java (see right), and plenty of blue bemos to Lovina (4000Rp).

The Penarukan terminal, 2km east of town, has bemos to Yeh Sanih (5000Rp) and Amlapura (6000Rp) via the coastal road; and also minibuses to Denpasar (Batubulan terminal; 14,000Rp) via Kintamani.

To Java

From Singaraja, several bus companies have overnight services to Surabaya (85,000Rp to 100,000Rp, 11 hours) and Jakarta (150,000Rp, 24 hours) on Java, via Gilimanuk and the public ferry – book at Banyuasri terminal a day before. Many agencies along the western end of Jl Jen Achmed Yani also sell tickets.

TOURIST SHUTTLE BUS

All of the Perama shuttle buses going to Lovina (see p240) from South Bali via Bedugul can drop you off in Singaraja.

Getting Around

Plenty of bemos link the three main bemo/bus terminals, and zip along all main roads in between. The bemos are all well signed and colour-coded, and cost about 2000Rp for a ride anywhere around town. The green Banyuasri–Sukasada bemo goes along Jl Gajah Mada to the tourist office; this bemo, as well as the brown one between Penarukan and Banyuasri terminals, also goes along Jl Jen Achmed Yani.

AROUND SINGARAJA

Interesting sites around Singaraja include some of Bali's best-known temples. See p58 for more information.

Sangsit

A few kilometres northeast of Singaraja, you can see an excellent example of the colourful architectural style of North Bali. Sangsit's **Pura Beji** is a *subak* (village association for rice-growers) temple, dedicated to the goddess Dewi Sri, who looks after irrigated rice fields. The sculptured panels along the front wall set the tone with their Disneyland-like demons and amazing *naga* (mythical snake-like creatures). The inside also has a variety of sculptures covering every available space. It's about 500m off the main road towards the coast.

The **Pura Dalem** shows scenes of punishment in the afterlife, and other humorous, and sometimes erotic, pictures. You'll find it in the rice fields, about 500m northeast of Pura Beji.

Buses and bemos going east from Singaraja's Penarukan terminal will stop at Sangsit.

Jagaraga

It was the capture of the local rajah's stronghold at Jagaraga that marked the arrival of Dutch power on Bali in 1849. The village, which is a few kilometres south of the main road, also has a **Pura Dalem**. The small, interesting temple has delightful sculptured panels along its front wall, both inside and out. On the outer wall look for a vintage car driving sedately past, a steamer at sea and even an aerial dogfight between early aircraft. Jagaraga is also famous for its Legong (classic Balinese dance) troupe, said to be the best in North Bali, but performances are irregular.

Bemos from the Penarukan terminal in Singaraja stop at Jagaraga on the way to Sawan.

Sawan

Several kilometres inland from Jagaraga, Sawan is a centre for the manufacture of *gamelan* (traditional Balinese orchestra) gongs and instruments. You can see them being cast and the intricately carved gamelan frames being made. The strange-looking **Pura Batu Bolong** is also worth a look. Around Sawan, there are cold water springs that are believed to cure all sorts of illnesses.

Regular bemos to Sawan leave from Penarukan terminal in Singaraja.

Kubutambahan

About a kilometre east of the turn-off to Kintamani is **Pura Maduwe Karang** (Temple of the Land Owner). Like Pura Beji at Sangsit, the temple is dedicated to agricultural spirits, but this one looks after non-irrigated land.

This is one of the finest temples in North Bali and is particularly noted for its sculptured panels, including the famous bicycle stone-carved relief that depicts a gentleman riding a bicycle with flowers for wheels. It's on the base of the main plinth in the inner enclosure. The cyclist may be WOJ Nieuwenkamp, a Dutch artist who, in 1904, brought probably the first bicycle to Bali.

The temple is easy to find in the village. Kubutambahan is on the road between Singaraja and Amlapura, and there are regular bemos and buses.

Gitgit

About 11km south of Singaraja, a well-signposted path goes 800m west from the main road to the touristy waterfall of **Air Terjun Gitgit** (adult/child 3300/1600Rp). The path is lined with souvenir stalls, and persistent guides offer their services, which you have no need for at all. The 40m waterfalls are quite pretty, and a great place for a picnic, but far from pristine. You buy a ticket about halfway down the path, and you also pay to park (1000Rp). There are warung along the path to the falls.

About 2km further up the hill, **Gitgit Multi-tier Waterfall** (donation 3000-5000Rp) is about 600m off the western side of the main road, by a small side track then a good walking path, with only a few clusters of souvenir stalls. The path crosses a narrow bridge and follows the river up past several sets of waterfalls, through verdant jungle and with several places to swim – if things haven't dried up during the May to September dry season.

GETTING THERE & AWAY

Regular bemos and minibuses between Denpasar (Ubung terminal) and Singaraja (Sukasada terminal) stop at Gitgit. More regular bemos to Gitgit (3500Rp) leave from outside the *puskesmas* near Sukasada terminal – let the driver know where you want to get off. Gitgit is also a major stop on organised tours of central and North Bali.

LOVINA

☎ 0362

Almost merging into Singaraja to the west, a string of coastal villages – Pemaron, Tukad Mungga, Anturan, Kalibukbuk, Kaliasem and Temukus – collectively known as Lovina, are a popular low-key beach resort. It's still a low-rise development, but hotels and restaurants have spread over the surrounding rice fields.

It's not all that idyllic – the quiet pace expected of the north of Bali isn't evident. The main street, Jl Raya Lovina, is incredibly busy as trucks and vehicles zoom to and from Gilimanuk, and locals are even more aggressive than those in Kuta in their fervour to sell dolphin trips, snorkelling tours and transport. Still, you are able get away from the hassle, especially as visitor numbers plunged after 2002 and the air went out of the tourism balloon. Many spas, restaurants and other services have subsequently closed, but there are still good options available.

Lovina is a convenient base for trips around the north coast or the central mountains. The beaches are made up of washed-out grey and black volcanic sand, and they are mostly clean near the hotel areas, but generally unspectacular. Reefs protect the shore, so the water is usually calm and clear. A highlight is every afternoon, at fishing villages like Anturan, watching *prahu*, traditional outrigger canoes, being prepared for the night's fishing; as sunset reddens the sky, the lights of the fishing boats appear as bright dots across the horizon.

Orientation

The Lovina tourist area stretches over 8km, but the main focus is Kalibukbuk, 10.5km west of Singaraja and often referred to by tourists as Lovina. It's hard to know where one village ends and the next one begins, but signposts along Jl Raya Lovina indicate the location of various hotels and restaurants and make convenient landmarks.

Information

If you are planning a reading holiday in Lovina, come prepared. There's no decent place to buy a book and you can't buy a newspaper either.

EMERGENCY

Police station (Jl Raya Lovina) Near the tourist office.

INTERNET ACCESS

Several Internet places on Jl Bina Ria and elsewhere in Kalibukbuk provide slow Internet access for similar rates.

Spice Cyber (☎ 41305; Jl Bina Ria; per min 200Rp; ☽ 8am-midnight; ☒) The best place for Internet access, and it's air-conditioned.

MEDICAL SERVICES

Lovina Clinic (☎ 41106; Jl Raya Lovina; consultation 200,000Rp; ☽ 24hr) This clinic has English-speaking doctors who can deal with minor ailments. Otherwise ask at your hotel.

MONEY

There are plenty of moneychangers around Lovina, especially in Kalibukbuk. There are ATMs on Jl Bina Ria and at the Jl Raya Lovina intersection

Bank BPD Bali (Jl Raya Lovina) Changes travellers cheques.

POST

The main post office is 1km west of central Kalibukbuk.

Tip Top Postal Agency (Jl Raya Lovina; ☽ 8am-8pm) Postal agencies such as this are common.

TELEPHONE

Most Internet places also offer phone service and *wartels* are found in every concentration of hotels.

TOURIST INFORMATION

Tourist office (☎ 41910; Jl Raya Lovina; ☽ 8am-8pm) Offers brochures of Lovina, and the staff will do their best to answer any questions.

Sights & Activities

BEACHES

A paved beach path runs along the sand in Kalibukbuk. It greatly eases a beach stroll – even if it is popular with scooters.

Otherwise, the best beach areas include the main beach east of the Dolphin Monument as well as the curving stretch a bit west. The former is big for pick-up volleyball games. The cluster of cheap hotels in Anturan also enjoy a good beach. There are many other decent swaths of sand in the area.

DOLPHIN WATCHING

Sunrise boat trips to see dolphins are Lovina's special tourist attraction – so much so that a large concrete crowned **monument** has been erected in honour of the over-touted cetaceans, which is fittingly known by local expats as the 'fish on a stick'. Some days, no dolphins are sighted, but most of the time at least a few surface.

Expect constant hassle from your hotel and touts selling dolphin trips – if you want to go, it's best to buy a ticket the day before. The price is fixed at 30,000Rp per person by the boat owners' cartel and the trips usually run from six to 8am. Promises of 'your money back' if you don't see Flipper only really mean that you'll be offered another ride and get up before dawn yet again.

DIVING

Scuba diving on the local reef is better at lower depths and night diving is particularly recommended. Some of the best dive sites on Bali are accessible from Lovina – particularly Pulau Menjangan in Taman Nasional Bali Barat (p263).

For a two-dive trip, including transport and all equipment, expect to pay about US$35 for a Lovina reef or night dive; and around US$50 to Amed, Tulamben or Pulau Menjangan.

Spice Dive (☎ 41509; www.balispicedive.com) has the best reputation locally and is the only five-star Professional Association of Diving Instructors (PADI) centre in Lovina. It runs four-dive PADI open-water certificate courses for US$250. It is based at the pleasant Café Spice, at the end of the beach path.

SNORKELLING

Generally, the water is clear and some parts of the reef are quite good for snorkelling, though the coral has been damaged by 'bleaching' and, in places, by dynamite fishing. The best place is to the west, a few-hundred metres offshore from Billibo Beach Cottages. A boat trip will cost about 30,000Rp per person for two people for two hours, including equipment. Snorkelling gear costs about 20,000Rp per day.

MASSAGE & SPAS

Lovina Wellness Spa (☎ 0812 377 2046; Jl Ketapang; massage from 70,000Rp; 🕙 10am-7pm) has some traffic noise, but overall it's a pleasant place, where massage rooms feature pebbled baths. Massage techniques on offer include

---

THE DAWN PATROL

At sunrise all along Lovina's beaches boats loudly motor out a few kilometres offshore and begin their hunt for dolphins. Drivers putter around, not knowing which way to turn, going in ever-widening circles, while tourists sit desperately clutching cameras, scanning the waters and breathing in petrol fumes from the crowd of boats. When a dolphin school is finally spotted, the scores of boats open their throttles and charge to surround it. The dolphins stay up long enough to breathe and arc out of the water, and then disappear, and the flotilla recommences its aimless motoring through the water. This scene replays several times through the sunrise hour.

Dolphin 'watching' Lovina-style is on a par with hunting without a spear – dolphins are chased mercilessly through the water, and there is no sense of playfulness or interactivity on their part, just a doggedness to outrun the flotilla. As your boat returns to the shore, you'll be greeted surreally by young boys selling carved dolphins neatly laid on a platter, and the inevitable offers of massage and snorkelling.

If you really want to see dolphins in the wild, as opposed to dolphins intimidated for the purpose of making tourists happy, make contact with local tuna fisherman at the southern end of the Kalibukbuk beach. They leave at 4.30am and use the dolphins to help track the tuna catch. Or, to create minimum interference with the sea life, don't participate at all and sleep in – you are on holiday after all.

NORTH BALI

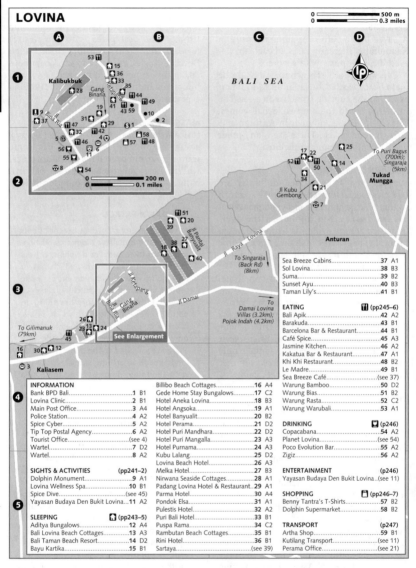

LOVINA

Balinese, Ayurveda, and foot massage, as well as 'rebirthing' (for those who missed the fun the first time).

BULL RACES
The **Yayasan Budaya Den Bukit Lovina** (Lovina Culture Foundation; ☎ 41293; Jl Raya Lovina) organises traditional Sapi Gerumbungan bull races

on Friday at 4pm for 40,000Rp, just west of Kalibukbuk. The races follow the same format as those in West Bali (see p260) and style is actually as important as speed.

Tours
Most local transport touts and some hotels offer tours of local attractions, such as

Beratan, Gitgit, the central mountains area, Air Panas Banjar hot springs and eastern destinations. They can be a good option if your time is limited. A full-day tour with a chartered vehicle and driver will cost between 150,000Rp and 200,000Rp, depending on the season, your choice of destina-tions and your bargaining skills.

Sleeping

Hotels are spread out along Jl Raya Lovina, and on the side roads going off to the beach. There are decent places to stay in every price range and while visitor numbers remain down, bargains are commonplace and many mid-range places are now budget. Also be aware that some places – especially at the extremes of the Lovina area – have suffered such a drop in business since the bombings in 2002 that standards have fallen precipitously.

Singaraja to Anturan is very quiet with a few scattered places to stay. Anturan is largely a backpackers' beach with a mellow charm. There are some nice places grouped from Anturan to Kalibukbuk – which is jammed with all manner of accommodation and services. West of Kalibukbuk the hotel density again diminishes right along with the beach.

BUDGET
Singaraja to Anturan

Kubu Lalang (☎ 42207; http://kubu.balihotelguide .com; r 75,000-170,000Rp) This hotel's name means 'small house of long grass' which fits the bungalows here, designed in traditional rice-barn style. Edged in between rice paddies, each bungalow is different, exotic-ally decorated and has a modern open-air bathroom, some with hot water and tubs. This is a great place for couples to chill in peace. The restaurant is good and features an Austrian cook.

Anturan

A few tiny side tracks and one proper sealed road, Jl Kubu Gembong, lead to this lively little fishing village, busy with swimming locals and moored fishing boats. It's a real travellers' hang-out, courtesy of the proximity of the Perama stop in front of Hotel Perama. It's a long way from Lovina nightlife though – expect to pay around 20,000Rp for transport back to Anturan

from Kalibukbuk after 6pm when the bemos stop operating.

Gede Home Stay Bungalows (☎ 41526; Jl Kubu Gembong; r 35,000-100,000Rp; 🕱) Many readers – including women travelling solo – have praised the friendliness of the staff here, which is no small feat on Bali where competition is tough. Cheap rooms have cold water while better ones have hot water and air-con.

Puspa Rama (☎ 42070; Jl Kubu Gembong; s/d 60,000/70,000Rp) This is one of several cheap places on this street. Rooms have hot water and are set in very lush grounds.

Hotel Puri Mandhara (☎ 41476; s/d 50,000/ 60,000Rp) Near the beach and has clean rooms with cold water set in pleasant grounds.

Hotel Perama (☎ 41161; peramalovina@yahoo.com; Jl Raya Lovina; r 25,000-150,000Rp; 🕱) At the back of the Perama office on the main road, this eponymous hotel is a clean and decent place if you can't be bothered to find a room elsewhere. Cheap rooms share bathrooms while those at the high end have air-con and hot water. It runs a shuttle bus into Kalibukbuk twice daily (5000Rp).

Anturan to Kalibukbuk

Jl Pantai Banyualit has a good selection of hotels, although the beachfront area is not very inspiring.

Suma (☎ 41566; Jl Pantai Banyualit; s/d 40,000/ 60,000Rp; r with hot water & air-con 150,000Rp, dishes 10,000-20,000Rp; 🕱) In a very pretty stone building, Suma has views of the sea from its upstairs rooms. Rooms are mostly basic but fine. There's also a pleasant café.

Sartaya (☎ 42240; Jl Pantai Banyualit; r 50,000Rp, with air-con 80,000Rp; 🕱) Built in traditional Balinese style, Sartaya has clean, decent rooms set in pretty grounds.

Sunset Ayu (☎ /fax 41054; Jl Pantai Banyualit; r 50,000-100,000Rp; 🕱) This small place has a nice atmosphere that makes for a no-fuss visit. More expensive rooms have hot water and air-con.

Kalibukbuk

A little over 10km from Singaraja, the 'centre' of Lovina is the village of Kali-bukbuk, which is good for people who want to do more than just hang out at their hotel and beach. Jl Ketapang is marginally quieter and more pleasant than Jl Bina Ria. There are small *gangs* (alleys or footpaths) off both.

Rini Hotel (☎ /fax 41386; rinihotel@telkom.net; Jl Ketapang; r 70,000-250,000Rp; 🔁 🏊) This super-clean and well-run place has a large saltwater pool. Cheaper rooms are basic but the more expensive ones are huge, with air-con and hot water.

Taman Lily's (☎ 41307; gervanleenen@hotmail.com; Jl Ketapang; s/d 60,000/75,000Rp; 🅿) This has a friendly atmosphere and six good-value rooms on a nice, grassy yard. There's also parking.

Puri Bali Hotel (☎ 41485; www.puribalilovina.com; Jl Ketapang; r 80,000-180,000Rp; 🔁 🏊) The pool area is very attractive and the better rooms, with hot water and air-con, are comfortable.

Pulestis Hotel (☎ 41035; jokoartawan@hotmail.com; Jl Bina Ria; r 70,000-100,000Rp; 🔁 🏊) The 14 rooms here have funky exteriors, clean interiors and pebbled open-air bathrooms – some with hot water. The café overlooks a modern pool and is popular with divers and lost surfers. Management is genial.

Hotel Angsoka (☎ 41841; angsoka@singaraja.wasantara.net.id; Gang Binaria; r 40,000-200,000Rp; 🔁 🏊) There's an amazing range of rooms here, from cold-water basic to large with air-con and hot water. All enjoy the good-sized pool and quiet gardens.

Padang Lovina Hotel (☎ 41302; padanglovina@yahoo.com; Gang Binaria; r from 70,000Rp) The 14 rooms here are large and have hot water. There's a serene garden.

Pondok Elsa (☎ 41186; Gang Binaria; s/d 50,000/60,000Rp, with air-con 80,000/100,000Rp; 🔁) This two-storey heavily ornate building has clean, pleasant rooms.

West of Kalibukbuk

Lovina Beach Hotel (☎ 41005; www.lovinabeachhotel.com; r 70,000-175,000Rp, bungalows 250,000Rp; 🏊) Want a great beachfront location? Come here – although the cheaper rooms are closer to the main road. Clean rooms in heavily detailed Balinese bungalows off Jl Raya Lovina are set in pleasant grounds. Better ones come with hot water and private bungalows are equipped with air-con and sea views.

Billibo Beach Cottages (☎ 41355; Jl Raya Lovina; r 70,000-150,000Rp; 🔁) Located near one of the best spots for snorkelling, the cottages here are clean and comfortable with hot water and good access to the beach.

Hotel Purnama (☎ 41043; Jl Raya Lovina; s/d 30,000/35,000Rp) One of the best deals on this stretch has clean rooms with cold water. The beach is close by.

Hotel Puri Mangalla (☎ 41371; Jl Raya Lovina; r 50,000-75,000Rp, with air-con 100,000Rp; 🔁) You can access the beach from this hotel which has rooms set around a courtyard. Better ones have hot water.

Parma Hotel (☎ 41555; Jl Raya Lovina; r 40,000Rp) Maintenance here is as relaxed as the staff but rooms are clean and reasonably well protected from traffic noise. Rooms that face the sea are great value.

MID-RANGE
Anturan

Bali Taman Beach Resort (☎ 41126; www.indo.com/hotels/bali_taman; Jl Raya Lovina; r US$35-85; 🔁 🏊) Facing the busy road but extending down to the beach, the Bali Taman has 30 rooms that vary greatly. The best ones are bungalows with ocean views. The pool faces the ocean and is surrounded by leafy gardens. Rooms have TV and minibars and some have outdoor showers.

Anturan to Kalibukbuk

Melka Hotel (☎ 41552; melka@singaraja.wasantara.net.id; Jl Pantai Banyualit; r 80,000-300,000Rp; 🔁 🏊) Coming complete with its own animal menagerie (a shark, snakes and birds) and a beer garden, the Melka defines idiosyncratic. There is a range of rooms, from those with cold water and fan to those with air-con, hot water, balconies with views and satellite TV. The German owner has festooned the place with signs offering directions.

Hotel Banyualit (☎ 41789; www.banyualit.com; Jl Pantai Banyualit; r 300,000-700,000Rp, economy r 70,000Rp; 🔁 🏊) Back from the beach, the Banyualit has a lush garden of snaking vines, flowers, statues and a large pool. The 22 rooms offer great choice and better ones come with satellite TV and other amenities. There are also a couple of economy rooms.

Kalibukbuk

Sea Breeze Cabins (☎ 41138; bungalows US$35-50; 🔁 🏊) An excellent choice in the heart of Kalibukbuk, off Jl Bina Ria, the Sea Breeze has lovely bungalows right on the beach, some with sensational views from their verandas. A variety of carved tropical woods are used in each unit. The pool is small but pretty. The restaurant (see p246) is recommended.

Nirwana Seaside Cottages (☎ 41288; nirwana@singaraja.wasantara.net.id; bungalows 100,000-125,000Rp, deluxe r 210,000-300,000Rp; ❄ ⛱) On large and lovely beachfront grounds also off Jl Bina Ria, the Nirwana has a vast beachfront site. All bungalows have some character and hot water, and fan rooms have open-air bathrooms. Those with beach views are a great deal. A new wing has more sedate hotel-style air-con rooms.

Bali Lovina Beach Cottages (☎ 41285; sales@balilovinahotel.com; Jl Ketepang; r US$25-55; ❄ ⛱) This is a very comfortable beachfront hotel and an enjoyable place to stay. The pool is large and bungalows on the beach have deep verandas with good views. There's a pond with big carp and rice paddies across the road.

Bayu Kartika (☎ 41219; www.bayukartikaresort.com; Jl Ketepang; r 80,000-300,000Rp; ❄ ⛱) There is a range of pleasant rooms here. The best ones have air-con and ocean or pool views. The sprawling grounds feature a small creek.

Rambutan Beach Cottages (☎ 41388; www.rambutan.org; Jl Ketepang; s/d 300,000/315,000Rp, deluxe r 450,000/495,000Rp; ❄ ⛱) The creative kids' play area here tells you this is a family-friendly place. The hotel, on a large area of land, features two swimming pools and charming gardens. Rooms, and especially the villas, are tasteful with lashings of Balinese style. There are a few cold-water economy rooms for about 100,000Rp.

West of Kalibukbuk

Aditya Bungalows (☎ 41059; www.indo.com/hotels/aditya; r 300,000-500,000Rp; ❄ ⛱) There are 65 rooms at this big place on the beach. The best ones have views of the ocean and all have a good range of amenities and attractive bathrooms. The large pool is especially nice.

TOP END

Also see Damai Lovina Villas (p247) for another luxury option.

Singaraja to Anturan

Puri Bagus (☎ 21430; www.bagus-discovery.com; villa US$125-175; ❄ ⛱) Well off the main road, Puri Bagus has 40 private villas set on immaculate grounds along a stone beach. The stylish units have large bathrooms with outdoor showers and nice verandas. The pool is large and free-form and the hotel is surrounded by rice paddies. The restaurant

has good seafood dishes and there are sunset cocktail cruises on the resort's sailboat.

Anturan to Kalibukbuk

Hotel Aneka Lovina (☎ 41121; www.anekahotels.com; Jl Raya Lovina; s/d US$61/67, villa US$79/91; ❄ ⛱) Extending all the way to the beach, the Aneka is a pleasant place. The 59 rooms have minibars and modern bathrooms. The grounds are spacious and units are well separated. The large pool area has good views.

Sol Lovina (☎ 41775; www.sollovinabali.com; r US$85-130, villas US$240-360; ❄ ⛱) Off Jl Raya Lovina, the imposing entrance to this place leads to a large beachfront resort with comfortable rooms and good services. Villas come variously with private plunge pools, whirlpools and ocean views. Grounds are verdant with banana trees and other tropical plants.

Eating

Just about every hotel has a café or restaurant. In addition, Kalibukbuk has food carts, warung, cafés and some excellent restaurants. There are two good places in the hills above Lovina (see p247). Many of the places listed here are also good for an end-of-the-day drink.

ANTURAN

Warung Rasta (☎ 41275; Jl Kubu Gembong; dishes 15,000-35,000Rp) As offbeat as the name implies, the menu here features 'vegetarian Rasta food', such as 'spagety cheese'. It has a great chill-out ambience by the waterfront. Views are framed by fishing boats, and fresh fish is grilled right at the front of the restaurant.

Warung Bamboo (dishes 7000-30,000Rp; ⏱ 4am-10pm) A small, open-fronted place, Bamboo fronts a lively section of beach. It serves typical travellers' fare, cheapish beer and has a relaxed feel. To find it, walk east along the beach from the end of Jl Kubu Gembong.

ANTURAN TO KALIBUKBUK

Warung Bias (☎ 411692; Jl Pantai Banyualit; dishes 10,000-40,000Rp; ⏱ noon-9pm) Worth a trip, Bias offers home-made Bavarian and French breads, muffins and cookies, as well as Indian curries, European dishes like wiener schnitzel, pastas and pizzas. It's in a lovely setting surrounded by a carp pond.

KALIBUKBUK

Jasmine Kitchen (☎ 41565; Gang Binaria; dishes 15,000-30,000Rp) Enjoy excellent Thai fare in this elegant two-level restaurant. The menu is long and authentic and the help gracious. While soft jazz plays, try the home-made ice cream for dessert.

Barakuda (Jl Ketepang; dishes 13,000-25,000Rp) Seafood is the speciality here. The prawns in many forms are excellent. On many nights you can get giant lobster for 135,000Rp. Balinese specialities can be ordered the day before.

Barcelona Bar & Restaurant (☎ 41894; Jl Ketepang; dishes 10,000-30,000Rp) This restaurant has a lovely, open-air, shady area out the back. The food is excellent, and includes *sate pelecing* (fish satay with Balinese spices) and *pepesan babi guling* (suckling pig slices wrapped in banana leaf).

Le Madre (☎ 081 755 4399; Jl Ketepang; dishes 15,000-25,000Rp) Surprisingly authentic Italian cuisine is served at open-air tables under frangipani trees. The lovely owners trained at some fine restaurants in Seminyak.

Warung Warubali (☎ 41533; Jl Ketepang; mains 8500-26,500Rp) Right where the road ends at the beach, this is a good place to watch the sun set, which coincides with happy hour. Food is standard travellers' fare.

Kakatua Bar & Restaurant (☎ 41344; Jl Bina Ria; dishes 7000-30,000Rp) A shrieking sulphur-crested cockatoo at the front of the restaurant beckons you in (stay clear if you have a hangover). The menu agglomerates Mexican, Thai, Indian and Balinese (and let's not forget pizza) – all of which is OK.

Sea Breeze Cafe (☎ 41138; dishes 13,000-38,000Rp) Right by the beach off Jl Bina Ria with an un-interrupted outlook, it has a range of Indonesian and Western dishes and good breakfasts. It's another spot for sunset drinks. The cottages here are good too (p244).

Khi Khi Restaurant (☎ 41548; dishes 10,000-135,000Rp) Well off Jl Raya Lovina, this barn of a place is filled with fishy aromas. It specialises in Chinese food and grilled seafood. It's down-at-heel, and you'll find yourself eating among locals.

Bali Apik (☎ 41050; Gang Binaria; dishes 7000-25,000Rp) A classic travellers' hang-out, this low-key bar-restaurant has been spiffed up a bit. Food is good value with large portions of Indonesian and Western classics. It brags about its very cold Bintang.

WEST OF KALIBUKBUK

Cafe Spice (☎ 41509; dishes 24,000-42,000Rp) Part of Spice Dive, this delightful beachside place is right at the western end of the beach path, off Jl Raya Lovina. The walls are covered in artwork and the menu is interesting and good. Besides the dive vibe you can sometimes hear the squeals of local kids learning English at the shop's free school upstairs.

Drinking & Entertainment
BARS & CLUBS

Between 6pm and 8pm many restaurants have 'happy hours' – at such times there's an outbreak of happy-hour war (much to the delight of thirsty travellers) when a large Bintang is only around 10,000Rp. At too many places, you can expect to hear the same tired reggae CDs playing one more time.

Lovina's social scene centres on Jl Bina Ria, which is happy-hour HQ, and has several bar-restaurants.

Poco Evolution Bar (☎ 41535; Jl Bina Ria; dishes 12,000-18,000Rp; ☽ 11am-1am) At various times there are movies shown and cover bands perform at this popular place. There is an Internet area off the bar. Classic travellers' fare is served.

Zigiz (Jl Bina Ria; small/large Bintang 6000/11,000Rp; ☽ 6pm-1am) This small place has walls covered in artwork and live music some nights.

Copacabana (☎ 42265; Jl Raya Lovina; large Bintang 15,000Rp; ☽ 6pm-1am) A big open-air place cranks up the reggae and the country and western to drown out street noise.

Planet Lovina (Jl Raya Lovina; large Bintang 15,000Rp; ☽ 5pm-1am) Next door to Copacabana, Bob Marley meets disco in this large open-air place.

BALINESE DANCE

The **Yayasan Budaya Den Bukit Lovina** (Lovina Culture Foundation; ☎ 41293; Jl Raya Lovina; ☽ 9pm Tue) organises Kecak dances from good local troupes.

Shopping

Shops on the main streets of Kalibukbuk sell a range of souvenirs, sundries and groceries.

Dolphin Supermarket (☎ 42154; Jl Raya Lovina) This has the best selection, but even that is limited.

Benny Tantra's T-Shirts (Jl Raya Lovina) For something different, check out the amusing range of T-shirts and postcards which portray to an uncanny degree the daily life of a tourist in Lovina.

Getting There & Away
BUS & BEMO
To reach Lovina from South Bali by public transport, you'll need to change in Singaraja (see p235). Regular blue bemos go from Singaraja's Banyuasri terminal to Kalibukbuk (about 4000Rp) – you can flag them down anywhere on the main road.

If you are coming by long-distance bus from the west you can ask to be dropped off anywhere along the main road. Long-distance buses depart from Singaraja (p237).

TOURIST SHUTTLE BUS
Perama links Lovina with the south.

Destination	Fare
Candidasa	80,000Rp
Kuta & airport	50,000Rp
Padangbai	80,000Rp
Sanur	50,000Rp
Ubud	50,000Rp

Perama buses stop at its office, in front of **Hotel Perama** (☎ 41161; peramalovina@yahoo.com; Jl Raya Lovina) in Anturan. Passengers are then ferried to other points on the Lovina strip (5000Rp).

Getting Around
The Lovina strip is *very* spread out, but you can easily travel back and forth on bemos (2000Rp).

BICYCLE
Rent bicycles at **Artha Shop** (☎ 41091; Jl Ketepang; per day 20,000Rp). Jl Raya Lovina is flat, but busy. The back road between Kalibukbuk and Singaraja, which runs a kilometre or so inland, is recommended for cyclists.

CAR & MOTORCYCLE
Lovina is an excellent base from which to explore central and North Bali, and rental prices are reasonable, but check rental vehicles very carefully. Approximate rates per day are 35,000Rp for a motorcycle and

80,000Rp for a Suzuki jeep. A chartered vehicle and driver will cost about 170,000Rp per day.

Rentals and charters can be organised through your hotel. **Kutilang Transport** (☎ 28036; Jl Raya Lovina) rents vehicles and arranges for drivers and vehicle charters.

SOUTH OF LOVINA
☎ 0362
In the hills around Lovina there are a couple of interesting places. At the main junction in Kalibukbuk, go south on Jl Damai and follow the road for about 3km.

A boutique hotel that has a fabulous view of the ocean from the hills behind Lovina, **Damai Lovina Villas** (☎ 41008; www.damai.com; villa US$172-190, lunch US$4-10, 5-course dinner US$38; ❄ ☒) has just eight luxury bungalows, all interestingly furnished with beautiful wood and fabrics and antiques. A divine pool seemingly spills onto a landscape of peanut fields, rice paddies and coconut palms. The restaurant, on a raised pavilion fringed by cerise bougainvillea and distant sea views, focuses on beautifully presented gourmet Asian-European nouvelle cuisine using home-grown produce – call for a dinner reservation and free transport.

About 1km on from Damai Lovina Villas on a narrow stretch of road, **Pojok Indah** (☎ 41571; dishes 25,000-60,000Rp; ☽ noon-8pm) has breathtaking views and a tiny menu that specialises in Australian steaks. It's associated with the nearby Bali Fruit Drink Winery, which produces a range of white wines from tropical fruits, such as banana, pineapple and even ginger. Try a glass (27,500Rp) while you watch the sun sink into the Bali Sea.

WEST OF LOVINA
A good road goes west of Lovina, passing several interesting attractions and following an unspoiled coast, where a few resorts and diving centres take advantage of the secluded beaches and coral reefs. The road continues to the Taman Nasional Bali Barat (p261) and the port of Gilimanuk (see p264).

Air Terjun Singsing
About 5km west of Kalibukbuk, a sign points to **Air Terjun Singsing** (Daybreak Waterfall). About 1km from the main road, there is a warung on the left and a

car park on the right. Walk past the warung and along the path for about 200m to the lower falls. The waterfall is not huge, but the pool underneath is ideal for swimming. The water isn't crystal clear, but it's cooler than the sea and very refreshing.

Clamber further up the hill to another waterfall, **Singsing Dua**, which is slightly bigger and has a mud bath, which is supposedly good for the skin. This one also cascades into a deep swimming pool.

The area is pretty and makes a nice day trip from Lovina. The falls are more spectacular in the wet season, and may be just a trickle in the dry season.

Brahma Vihara Arama

Bali's single Buddhist monastery, only vaguely Buddhist in appearance, with colourful decorations, a bright orange roof and statues of Buddha, has very Balinese decorative carvings and door guardians. It's quite a handsome structure in a commanding location, with views down the valley and across the rice fields to the sea. You should wear long pants or a sarong (which can be hired for a small donation; see p38). The monastery doesn't advertise any regular courses or programmes, but visitors are welcome to meditate in special rooms.

The temple is about 3.3km off the main road – take the obvious turn-off in Dencarik. If you don't have your own transport, arrange an *ojek* (motorcycle that carries paying pillion passengers) at the turn-off (6000Rp). The road continues past the monastery, winding further up into the hills to Pedewa, a Bali Aga village.

Air Panas Banjar

☎ 0362

Not far from Brahma Vihara Arama, these **hot springs** (adult/child 3000/1500Rp, parking 500Rp; ☼ 8am-6pm) are beautifully landscaped with lush tropical plants. You can relax here for a few hours and have lunch at the restaurant, or even stay the night.

Eight fierce-faced carved stone *naga* pour water from a natural hot spring into the first bath, which then overflows (via the mouths of five more *naga*), into a second, larger pool. In a third pool, water pours from 3m-high spouts to give you a pummelling massage. The water is slightly sulphurous and pleasantly hot, so you might enjoy it

more in the morning or the evening than in the heat of the day. You must wear a swimsuit and you shouldn't use soap in the pools, but you can do so under an adjacent outdoor shower.

The change rooms and lockers are under the restaurant, on the right-hand side.

In a wonderful setting on a hillside very close to the baths, the rooms at **Pondok Wisata Grya Sari** (☎ 92903; fax 92966; s/d 90,000/120,000Rp, ste 200,000Rp) are clean and have outdoor bathrooms. Treks into the surrounding countryside can be organised from here.

Overlooking the baths, **Restoran Komala Tirta** (dishes 8000-16,000Rp) does good, inexpensive Indonesian food.

It's only about 3km from the monastery to the hot springs if you take the short cut – go down to Banjar Tega, turn left in the centre of the village and follow the small road west, then south to Banjar village. From there it's a short distance uphill before you see the 'Air Panas 1km' sign on the left (on the corner by the police station). From the main road to the hot springs you can take an *ojek*; going back is a 2.4km downhill stroll.

Seririt

Seririt is a junction for roads that run south over the mountains to Pulukan or Antosari, on the way to Denpasar. The road running west along the coast towards Gilimanuk is quite good, with pretty coastal scenery and few tourists. There's a Bank BCA ATM at the Lovina end of Seririt. There are many warung and *rumah makan* (restaurants) in the market area, just north of the bemo stop, and you can find petrol stations on the main road.

Celukanbawang

Celukanbawang is the main cargo port for North Bali, and has a large wharf. Bugis schooners – the magnificent sailing ships that take their name from the seafaring Bugis people of Sulawesi – can sometimes be seen anchoring here.

Pulaki

Pulaki is famous for its many grape vines and for **Pura Pulaki**, a coastal temple that was completely rebuilt in the early 1980s, and is home to a large troop of monkeys.

A few hundred metres east of the temple, a well-signposted 3km paved road leads to

Pura Melanting. This temple is set dramatically in the foothills, and is gloriously devoid of tourists and hawkers. A donation is expected to enter the complex, although you're not permitted in the main worship area.

Pemuteran

☎ 0362

This wonderfully isolated area, with limited facilities, has extensive, untouched coral reefs about 3km offshore, good snorkelling, and is handy for dive sites on Pulau Menjangan to the west.

The area is home to the Reef Seen Turtle Project, run by the Australian-owned **Reef Seen Aquatics** (☎ 92339; www.reefseen.com). Turtle eggs and small turtles purchased from locals are looked after here until they're ready for ocean release. More than 5000 turtles have been released since 1994. You can visit the small hatchery and make a donation of US$5 to sponsor and release a tiny turtle.

Reef Seen also offers diving, boat cruises and horse riding. A PADI introductory dives costs US$49 and dives at Pemuteran/ Pulau Menjangan are US$55/65 for two dives. Sunset and sunrise cruises and glass-bottomed boat trips (150,000Rp per person) are offered. Horse-riding treks pass through the local villages and beaches (290,000Rp for two hours). Simple accommodation (150,000Rp for a room) is available to dive guests and horse riders.

Easy Divers (☎ 94736; joerg@easydivers-bali.com) comes well recommended and offers a worthwhile five-day PADI open-water course for US$350. Dive trips to Tulamben and Menjangan cost US$65.

Pemuteran's hotels all have their own dive operations.

SLEEPING & EATING

Pemuteran is a delightful place to stay with many mid-range and top-end choices. There are several small warung along the main drag, otherwise all the hotels have good restaurants.

Matahari Beach Resort & Spa (☎ 92312; www .matahari-beach-resort.com; r US$169-440; 🔲 🔊) One of Bali's best hotels, the Matahari is an elegant place in an isolated location on the eastern outskirts of Pemuteran. Beautiful and traditionally furnished bungalows are set in attractive gardens, and the pool overlooks the black-sand beach. It offers diving, tennis, windsurfing, mountain bikes, gym and library facilities. The most amazing part of the resort however is the spa, which is like a grand water palace. The central entrance area features a huge lily pond, surrounded by fountain statues, while relief sculptures line the massage-room walls. The spa is open to nonguests, but call first as guests have priority.

Pondok Sari (☎ 94738, 92337; www.pondoksari.com; s/d US$31/36, with air-con US$35/40, dishes 14,000-30,000Rp; 🔲) There are pleasant bungalows here with traditional rooms and lovely flower-filled open-air bathrooms. Snorkelling is possible to the left and right of the beach. The restaurant features Western and Indo classics and *rijstaffel* (Indonesian banquet encompassing a wide variety of dishes) can be ordered two hours beforehand.

Menjangan Resort (☎ 94700; www.menjangan.net; Monsoon Forest Resort r US$200-350, Cliff Villas US$400-950; 🔲 🔊) There are two separate properties here: the Monsoon Forest Resort and Cliff Villas. The former is set in slightly dry forest and features rustic buildings around a pool. The latter has posh stylish rooms perched right above an ocean cove. Service at both is quite good. Activities include a full range of water sports as well as horseback riding. The resort is right at the west end of North Bali.

Taman Selini Beach Bungalows (☎ 94746; r US$60, dishes 18,000-35,000Rp; 🔲 🔊) The first

---

THE AUTHOR'S CHOICE

Taman Sari Bali Cottages (☎ 288096; www .balitamansari.com; bungalows US$35-65, ste US$80-150; 🔲 🔊) The spacious grounds here feature little fountains. Thirty-one rooms are set in gorgeous bungalows which feature intricate carvings and other traditional artwork. Furnishings are very comfortable and you can relax on a rocking chair (best done from one of the rooms with a beach view). Some of the suites are good for families. The pool is close to the long stretch of quiet beach. The restaurant specialises in Thai food. The resort is also involved in an off-shore reef restoration project. Their efforts make for interesting reading.

things you'll see coming from the east are these thatch-roofed bungalows. Rooms have four-poster beds and big outdoor bathrooms, which open onto a small garden area. The restaurant, Caffe Selini, is a picturesque, relaxed spot featuring Indonesian and Greek cuisine.

Jubawa Home Stay (☎ 94745; r 150,000-200,000Rp; 🞨 🖳) Not far from the Matahari, this cheery place is a good budget choice. The best rooms have hot water and air-con and guests have free Internet access. The café serves Balinese and Thai food and there is a long list of cocktails.

West Bali

WEST BALI

Most of the places regularly visited in West Bali, like Pura Tanah Lot or Sangeh, are easy day trips from South Bali or the Kuta region. Further west, there's lots of through traffic going to and from Java, but the area is well off the main tourist trails. There are secluded places to stay, long stretches of deserted black-sand beaches, a few surf spots and countless side tracks to villages that rarely see a tourist.

Pura Tanah Lot easily ranks as the most visited place in West Bali. The temple is remarkably photogenic and an entire industry has grown up to serve the many visitors who flock here. The most satisfying experiences in the region, however, are often those you create for yourself off the beaten track, where bamboo as thick as your leg arcs over the roadway like a green cathedral. In the hills above Tabanan are some of the oldest rice fields on the island; the ancient terraces and irrigation channels are something to behold.

At the most western end of Bali is Taman Nasional Bali Barat, the renowned national park which is home to much of Bali's remaining wilderness. Here you find hundreds of species of bird and other wildlife, including the rare Bali starling. The best way to explore this area is on one of many treks through the park. Offshore, there are a number of excellent diving areas which draw divers from all over the island.

In the latter half of the 19th century, this was an area of warring kingdoms. With the Dutch takeover in the early 20th century, however, the princes' lands were redistributed among the general population. With this bounty of rich agricultural land, the region around Tabanan was cultivated with beautiful rice fields and became one of the wealthiest parts of Bali.

TOP FIVE

- Soaking up superb sunset silhouettes of the serene sea temple of **Pura Rambut Siwi** (p259)
- Viewing the *sawah* (rice field) scenery, especially the picturesque **Tabanan district** (p256)
- Trekking in **Taman Nasional Bali Barat** (p261) and possibly spotting an endangered Bali starling
- Diving at the spectacular **Pulau Menjangan** (p263)
- Visiting small villages, traversing the Bali's back roads and exploring **Pujungan waterfall** (p258)

MICHAEL AW

Diver and school of fish, Lovina (p240)

ANDERS BLOMQVIST

Air Terjun Gitgit (p239)

Fishermen, Lovina Beach (p240)

ANDREW BROWNBILL

Rice terraces, Tabanan (p256)

JERRY ALEXANDER

Nudibranches off Gilimanuk Bay (p264)

TIM RO...

Pura Tanah Lot (p253)

JULIET COOM...

PURA TANAH LOT

☎ 0361

The brilliantly located **Pura Tanah Lot** (adult/child 3300/1800Rp, car park 1500Rp) is possibly the best-known and most photographed temple on Bali. It's an obligatory stop on many tours from South Bali, very commercialised, and especially crowded at sunset. It has all the authenticity of a stage set – even the tower of rock the temple sits upon was artfully reconstructed with Japanese money, as the entire structure was crumbling. Over one-third of the rock you see is artificial.

For the Balinese, Pura Tanah Lot is one of the most important and venerated sea temples. Like Pura Luhur Ulu Watu (p130), at the tip of the southern Bukit Peninsula, and Pura Rambut Siwi (p259) to the west, it is closely associated with the Majapahit priest, Nirartha. It's said that each of the 'sea temples' was intended to be within sight of the next, so they formed a chain along Bali's southwestern coast – from Pura Tanah Lot you can certainly see the cliff-top site of Pura Ulu Watu, and the long sweep of sea shore around to Perancak, near Negara.

Tanah Lot, however, is a well-organised tourist trap. To reach the temple, a walkway runs through a sort of sideshow alley with dozens of souvenir shops down to the sea. To ease the task of making purchases, there is an ATM.

To visit the temple you should pick the correct time – everybody shows up for sunset and the mobs obliterate any spiritual feel the place has. If you visit before noon, crowds are few and the vendors are all but asleep. When you get to the promenade overlooking the temple, walk as far as possible up the hill to the right for great views of the site and along the coast to Kuta.

You can walk over to the temple itself at low tide (but non-Balinese are not allowed to enter), or if you need a pricey drink, walk up the slope to the left and sit at one of the many tables along the cliff top. One other thing to note: local legend has it that if you bring a partner to Tanah Lot before marriage, you will end up as split as the temple. Let that be a warning or an inducement to visit, as you prefer.

Sleeping & Eating

If you want to enjoy the sunset spectacle and also avoid traffic afterwards, there are lodging options near Tanah Lot. There are cheap *warung* (food stalls) around the car park, and more expensive restaurants inside the grounds and on the cliff tops facing the temple.

Dewi Sinta Restaurant & Villa (☎ 812933; dewisinta@denpasar.wasantara.net.id; r US$16-55, dishes 18,000-60,000Rp, buffet lunches 50,000Rp; 🍴 🏊) Off a souvenir-shop *gang* (alley or footpath), not far from the ticket office lies this mid-range hotel. There's a range of rooms, and some look across the pool and beyond to rural views. The restaurant offers buffet lunches and Balinese dance performances some nights.

Le Meridien Nirwana Golf Spa & Resort (☎ 815900; www.lemeridien-bali.com; r from US$150; 🍴 🏊) Occupying a swath of black-sand beach, this large resort has over 270 rooms and an 18-hole golf course. The grounds and pools are especially attractive and have a wonderful view of Tanah Lot, albeit from a disrespectful viewpoint (it's set higher than the temple). The Penguin Club is a well-equipped kids' part of the hotel.

Pondok Wisata Astiti Graha (☎ 812955; r 60,000Rp) About 800m before the car park, this bare-bones place offers basic rooms with views across the farmlands.

Getting There & Away

Coming from South Bali with your own transport, take the coastal road west from Kerobokan, which is north of the Kuta region, and follow the signs or the traffic. From other parts of Bali, turn off the Denpasar–Gilimanuk road near Kediri and follow the signs. To avoid the traffic jams on your journey back, leave very promptly after sunset, or stay for a leisurely dinner and return after dark.

By *bemo* (small pick-up truck), go from Denpasar's Ubung terminal to Tanah Lot (4000Rp) via Kediri. Bemos usually stop running by nightfall, so if you want to see the sunset, you may need to stay overnight at Tanah Lot or charter a vehicle back. Alternatively, take an organised tour from Ubud or South Bali, which may include other sites such as Bedugul, Mengwi and Sangeh.

KAPAL

About 10km north of Denpasar, Kapal is the garden-gnome and temple-curlicue centre

WEST BALI

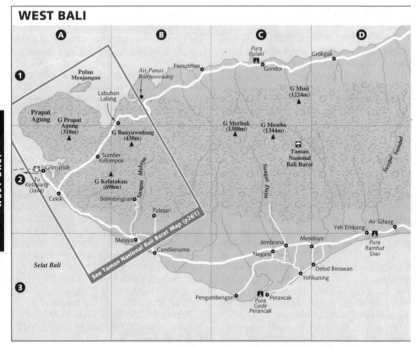

of Bali. If you need a new temple guardian, technicolour deer, roof ornament, planter pot or any of the other countless standard architectural decorations, you've come to shop at the right place.

The most important temple in the area is **Pura Sadat**. It was possibly built in the 12th century, then damaged in an earthquake early in the 20th century and subsequently restored after WWII.

Throughout this part of Bali you will see peanuts and corn growing in rotation with rice. Bananas grow wild along the roads.

PURA TAMAN AYUN

The huge state temple of **Pura Taman Ayun** (adult/child 3300/1800Rp; 8am-6pm), surrounded by a wide, elegant moat, was the main temple of the Mengwi kingdom, which survived until 1891, when it was conquered by the neighbouring kingdoms of Tabanan and Badung. The large, spacious temple was built in 1634 and extensively renovated in 1937. It's a lovely place to wander around, especially before the tour buses arrive.

The first courtyard is a large, open, grassy expanse and the inner courtyard has a multitude of *meru* (multiroofed shrines).

Getting There & Away

Any bemo running between Denpasar (Ubung terminal) and Bedugul or Singaraja can drop you off at the roundabout in Mengwi, where signs indicate the road (250m) to the temple. Pura Taman Ayun is a stop-off on many organised tours from Ubud or southern Bali.

BELAYU

In the small village of Belayu (or Blayu), 3km north of Mengwi, traditional *songket* (silver or gold-threaded cloth) sarongs are intricately woven with gold threads. These are for ceremonial use only and not for everyday wear.

Getting There & Away

Take any bemo or bus between Denpasar (Ubung terminal) and Bedugul or Singaraja, get off at the turn-off to Belayu and walk about 1km west; alternatively bemos go

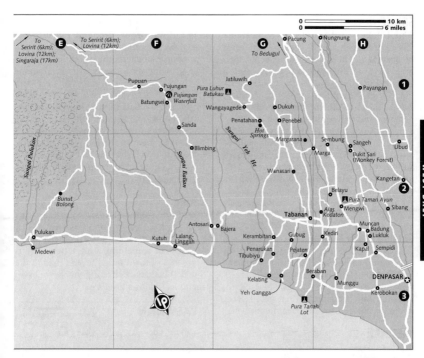

directly from Ubung terminal to Belayu (4000Rp).

MARGA
Between the walls of traditional family compounds, there are some beautifully shaded roads in Marga – but this town wasn't always so peaceful. On 20 November 1946, a much larger and better-armed Dutch force, fighting to regain Bali as a colony after the departure of the Japanese, surrounded a force of 96 independence fighters. The outcome was similar to the *puputan* (fight to the death) of 40 years earlier – Ngurah Rai, who lead the resistance against the Dutch, and every one of his men were killed. There was, however, one important difference – this time the Dutch suffered heavy casualties as well, and this may have helped weaken their resolve to hang onto the rebellious colony.

The independence struggle is commemorated at the **Margarana** (admission 3000Rp; ⏰ 9am-5pm), northwest of Marga village. Tourists seldom visit, but every Balinese schoolchild comes here at least once, and a ceremony is held annually on 20 November. In a large compound stands a 17m-high pillar, and nearby there's a museum, with a few photos, home-made weapons and other artefacts from the conflict. Behind is a smaller compound with 1372 small stone memorials to those who gave their lives for the cause of independence – they're like gravestones in a military cemetery, though bodies are not actually buried here. Each memorial has a symbol indicating the hero's religion, mostly the Hindu swastika, but also Islamic crescent moons and even a few Christian crosses. Look for the memorials to 11 Japanese who stayed on after WWII and fought with the Balinese against the Dutch.

Getting There & Away
Take any bemo between Denpasar and Bedugul, and get off at Marga, about 6km north of Mengwi. To get to the Margarana complex, walk northwestward about 2km through Marga. Even with your own transport it's easy to get lost, so ask directions.

SANGEH

About 20km north of Denpasar, near the village of Sangeh, stands the monkey forest of **Bukit Sari**. There's a rare grove of nutmeg trees in the monkey forest and a temple, Pura Bukit Sari, with an interesting old *Garuda* (mythical man-bird creature) statue. Take note: the monkeys are all about business and will jump on you if you have a pocketful of peanuts and don't dispense them fast enough. The cheeky monkeys have also been known to steal hats, sunglasses and even sandals, from fleeing tourists. This place is definitely touristy, but the forest is cool, green and shady. The souvenir sellers are restricted to certain areas and are easy to avoid.

Getting There & Away

You can reach Sangeh and Bukit Sari on any bemo heading to Plaga from Wangaya terminal in Denpasar (3000Rp). There is also road access from Mengwi and Ubud, but no public transport. Most people visit on an organised tour or drive themselves.

TABANAN

☎ 0361

Tabanan is the capital of the district of the same name. Like many such towns on Bali, it's a large, well-organised place. It is also a renowned centre for dancing and *gamelan* (traditional Balinese orchestra) playing. Mario, the renowned dancer of the pre-war period, hailed from Tabanan. His greatest achievement was to perfect the Kebyar dance and he is also featured in Miguel Covarrubias' classic book, *Island of Bali*.

Information

You'll find ATMs, *wartels* (public telephone office) and Internet access, shops, a hospital, a **police station** (☎ 91210), a market and a post office in Tabanan, but unless you need these services there's no real reason to stop here.

Sights

A *subak* is the village association that deals with water, water rights and irrigation. The **Mandala Mathika Subak** (☎ 810315; Jl Raya Kediri) is quite a large complex devoted to Tabanan's *subak* organisations and incorporates the rather forlorn Subak Museum,

which has displays about the irrigation and cultivation of rice, and the intricate social systems that govern it. The exhibits are poorly labelled and it's really only for rice-growing enthusiasts; this is a shame as there's a good story to tell here and the local waterways are some the most impressive in Bali. If you stumble on one of the poorly paid staffers they may regale you with their efforts to keep it open. It's up a steep road on the left just before you come into town from the east – look out for the sign. Opening hours and visitor service are very casual.

Eating

There are plenty of basic eateries in the town centre.

Taliwang Bersandara (☎ 811412; dishes 7000-16,000Rp) For something a bit better, try this place east of town near the side road to the Subak Museum. It has a good Indonesian menu as well as a grocery.

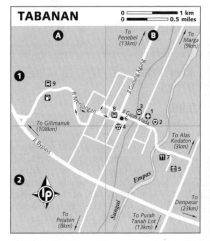

Getting There & Away

All bemos and buses between Denpasar (Ubung terminal) and Gilimanuk stop at the terminal at the western end of Tabanan. The bemo terminal in the town centre only has transport to nearby villages. If you're driving, note that most main streets are one way, with traffic moving in a clockwise direction around the central blocks. There's a bypass south of town if you're heading further west.

SOUTH OF TABANAN

There are not a lot of tourist attractions in the southern part of Tabanan district, but it's easy to access with your own transport. You can reach the main villages by local bemo from Tabanan, especially in the mornings. **Kediri** has Pasar Hewan, one of Bali's busiest cattle markets, and is the terminal for bemos to Pura Tanah Lot. About 10km south of Tabanan is **Pejaten**, a centre for the production of traditional pottery, including elaborate ornamental roof tiles. Porcelain clay objects, which are made purely for decorative use, can be seen in a few workshops in the village.

A little west of Tabanan, a road goes 8km south via Gubug to the secluded coast at **Yeh Gangga**. The next road west from Tabanan turns down to the coast via **Kerambitan**, a village noted for its beautiful old buildings (including two 17th-century palaces); a tradition of *wayang*-style painting; and its own styles of music and dance, especially Tektekan, a ceremonial procession.

South of Kerambitan, you will pass through **Penarukan**, known for its stone- and wood-carvers, and also its dancers. Continue to the coast, where you'll find the beach at **Kelating** wide, black and usually deserted.

About 4km from southern Kerambitan is **Tibubiyu**. For a gorgeous drive through huge bamboo, fruit trees, rice paddies and more, take the scenic road northwest from Kerambitan to the main road.

Sleeping

Bali Wisata Bungalows (☎ 0361-744 3561; www.baliwisatabungalows.com; Yeh Gangga; bungalows 120,000-250,000Rp; ⚅ ⚄) West of Tabanan and on the coast at Yeh Gangga, this stylish accommodation has excellent views in a superb setting on 15km of black-sand beach.

Bibi's Bungalows (☎ 081 2360 4517; Tibubiyu; bungalows 100,000-120,000Rp, dishes 12,000-25,000Rp) To find Bibi's, head straight from Puri Anyar and turn left at the T-intersection. At the huge banyan tree, turn right and follow the road through to Tibubiyu. Bibi's is signposted on the left. It's wonderfully isolated, perfectly tranquil and was remodelled in 2004 which changed the accommodation to rather nice bungalows. There are amazing rice-paddy views with the ocean beyond. There's a small, breezy restaurant for guests only.

Puri Anyar Kerambitan (☎ 0361-812668; wiryana2000@yahoo.com; r 250,000Rp) One of Kerambitan's palaces accepts guest bookings in spacious, traditional accommodation in the lively and welcoming palace compound. The prince lives in the palace and you can watch him at work on paintings. The simple rooms are decorated with carved teak and antiques awaiting restoration. Balinese feasts and dancing can also be arranged. Even if you're not bunking with the prince, the compound makes for a good stop.

NORTH OF TABANAN

The area north of Tabanan is good to travel around with your own transport. There are some strictly B-level attractions; the real appeal here is just driving the back roads.

Another monkey forest, **Alas Kedaton** (adult/child 3300/1800Rp; ⏰ 7.30am-6.30pm) is a stop-off on many organised tours from Ubud and South Bali. Your ticket includes a guide, who may do little more than fend off avaricious monkeys and lead you to a cousin's sarong shop nearby.

In the village of Wanasari, 7km from Tabanan, the **Bali Butterfly Park** (Taman Kupu Kupu Bali; ☎ 0361-814282; adult/child 40,000/20,000Rp; ⏰ 8am-5pm) has 15 species of mostly Indonesian butterflies in a large, slightly shabby, enclosed area. The butterflies are most active in the morning, especially on warm, dry days.

About 9km north of Tabanan the road reaches a fork. The left road goes to Pura Luhur Batukau (see p231), via the **hot springs** at Penatahan.

Sleeping & Eating

Yeh Panas Resort (☎ 0361-262356; espa_yehpanes@telkom.net; r US$60-80, dishes 35,000-38,000Rp; ⚄) Some 13km from Tabanan, by the Sungai Yeh Ho (Yeh Ho River), this resort has a small, cool pool, which nonguests can soak in for US$3. Another has water from the hot springs and costs US$15. Rooms are set around the hillside, overlooking the river, and are well maintained. A pleasant open-air restaurant overlooks the picturesque Sungai Yeh Ho.

LALANG-LINGGAH
☎ 0361

A little to the west of Lalang-Linggah, a road leads to the surf breaks near the mouth of Sungai Balian (Balian River); see p319 for details. The main break, at the river mouth, is sometimes called Soka.

Sleeping & Eating

The Taman Rekreasi Indah Soka further to the west is a group of warung.

Gajah Mina (☎ 081 2381 1630; www.gajahmina resort.com; 1-/2-bedroom ste US$80/120, dishes 25,000-50,000Rp; ❷ ❷) This has eight very private, exquisitely furnished bungalows. All have an outdoor and indoor bathroom, and inviting day lounges on the balcony. There are views of the ocean in the near distance from the pool. The restaurant features an international Asian menu. The turn-off from the main road is near the village market and there is a gate where 1000Rp is collected before you make the very pretty 1km drive.

Sacred River Retreat (☎ 814993; www.sacred-river .com; bungalow US$35-55) Just east of town, Sacred River Retreat is a new-agey place with suitably hippyesque décor and activities that include meditation and yoga. Go for room one with its view over the river valley to the ocean.

ROUTES TO THE NORTH COAST

You can cross between Bali's south and north coasts via **Pupuan**, well west of the two main cross-island routes (via Kintamani and Bedugul). From the Denpasar–Gilimanuk road, one road goes north from **Antosari** and another road goes north from **Pulukan** – the two roads meet at Pupuan then drop down to Seririt, west of Lovina. Both routes are served by public bemo.

The road from Antosari starts through rice paddies, climbs into the spice-growing country via **Sanda** and then descends through the coffee plantations to Pupuan. From Pupuan, if you continue 12km or so towards the north coast you reach Mayong,

where you can turn east to Munduk and on to Tamblingan and Buyan lakes.

The Pulukan–Pupuan road climbs steeply up from the coast providing fine views back down to the sea. The route runs through spice-growing country – you'll see (and smell) spices laid out on mats by the road to dry. At one point, the narrow and winding road actually runs right through **Bunut Bolong** – an enormous tree that forms a complete tunnel (the *bunut* tree is a type of ficus; *bolong* means 'hole').

Further on, the road spirals down to Pupuan through some of Bali's most beautiful rice terraces.

It is worth stopping off for a walk to the magnificent **waterfall** near Pujungan, a few kilometres south of Pupuan.

Sleeping

Sanda Bukit Villas & Restaurant (☎ 082 836 9137; www.sandavillas.com; bungalows 800,000-950,000Rp, dishes 20,000-50,000Rp; ❷ ❷) In the foothills of Gunung Batukau, 8km south of Pupuan at Sanda, this is a picturesque boutique hotel with a large salt-water pool and a relaxed ambience. The restaurant features Western and local cuisine.

Homestay CSB (Pulukan; r 50,000Rp) Only a few kilometres away from the Medewi surf break at Pulukan, this place which is signposted from the highway on the ocean side has only two nice bungalows with rice-paddy views and sea views in the near distance.

Gede Bungalow (☎ 081 2397 6668; Pulukan; r 50,000Rp) Only 100m from the beach, Gede Bungalow has rice-barn style cottages set amidst rice paddies. To reach it, go past Homestay CSB and take the first right. It's the first building on the left.

JEMBRANA COAST

About 34km west of Tabanan you cross into Bali's most sparsely populated district, Jembrana. The main road follows the south coast most of the way to Negara. There's some beautiful scenery, but little tourist development along the way, with the exception of the surf action at Medewi.

Medewi
☎ 0365

Along the main road, a large sign points down the paved road (200m) to the surfing mecca of Pantai Medewi. The beach is a stretch of huge, smooth grey rocks interspersed among round black pebbles. It's a placid place where cattle graze by the beach. Medewi is noted not for its beach but for its *long* left-hand wave – and there is little else here. See p318 for details.

SLEEPING & EATING

For a casual meal, some of the finest fare is served up freshly stir-fried at a cart right by the beach.

Puri Dajuma Cottages (☎ 43955; www.dajuma .com; r US$70-90; ⚡ ⚓) Coming from the east, you won't be able to miss this seaside resort, thanks to its prolific signage. Happily, the 18 large rooms actually live up to the billing. Bathrooms are both inside and out, and its location on a pounding bodysurfing break is dramatic. Medewi Beach is a 2km walk west on the sand.

Medewi Beach Cottages (☎ 40029; r US$15-60, dishes 15,000-35,000Rp; ⚡ ⚓) These cottages have an ordinary two-storey building on the western side of the road with second-rate standard cold-water rooms aimed at surfers, and a more stylish wing on the other side with well-furnished rooms around a pool. The posh side features satellite TV and lush grounds, but security measures have obstructed what should be a good view. The restaurant serves pasta and seafood.

Homestay Gede (☎ 081 2397 6668; s/d 40,000/ 45,000Rp, dishes 4000-9000Rp) An unsignposted place about 20m west of the road behind Medewi Beach Cottages, this is a great little low-key homestay with a beachside warung and *bale* (open-sided pavilion) for lounging. Rooms are basic but suit the 'surfari' hideaway atmosphere.

Mai Malu Restaurant & Guesthouse (☎ 43897; s/d 50,000/70,000Rp, dishes 10,000-35,000Rp) Near the highway on the Medewi side road, Mai Malu is popular with surfers, serving crowd-pleasing pizza, burgers and Indonesian meals in its modern, breezy upstairs eating area. Rooms have cold water and fans.

Pura Rambut Siwi

Picturesquely situated on a cliff top overlooking a long, wide stretch of black-sand beach, this superb temple shaded by flowering frangipani trees is one of the important sea temples of West Bali. Like Pura Tanah Lot (p253) and Pura Ulu Watu (p130), it was established in the 16th century

by the priest Nirartha, who had a good eye for ocean scenery. Legend has it that when Nirartha first came here, he donated some of his hair to the local villagers. The hair is now kept in a box buried in this temple, the name of which means 'Worship of the Hair'. Unlike Tanah Lot, it remains a peaceful place and isn't overrun by hordes of local and international tourists.

The caretaker rents sarongs for 2000Rp (see Temple Etiquette, p38) and is happy to show you around the temple and down to the beach. He then opens the guest book and requests a donation – from 5000Rp to 10,000Rp is a suitable amount, regardless of the much higher amounts attributed to previous visitors.

GETTING THERE & AWAY

The temple is between Air Satang and Yeh Embang, at the end of a 300m side road. You'll find it's well signposted, but look for the turn-off near a cluster of warung on the main road. Any of the regular bemos and buses between Denpasar (Ubung terminal) and Gilimanuk will stop at the turn-off.

NEGARA

☎ 0365

Negara, the district capital, is a prosperous little town, and useful for a pit stop, though there's not much to see. The town springs to life when the famous bull races (p260) are held nearby, in July, August, September and/or October. Most banks change money and have ATMs.

Sleeping & Eating

The main road bypasses the town to the north – you'll need to turn in to the main drag, Jl Ngurah Rai. There are assorted warung in the market area.

Hotel Wira Pada (☎ 41161; Jl Ngurah Rai 107; r with fan/air-con 85,000/125,000Rp; ⚡) The cheap rooms are dark and dreary, while the more expensive ones have air-con. The setting is reasonably pleasant, however, and you can make friends with the talking mynah bird.

Hotel Ana (☎ 41063; Jl Ngurah Rai 75; s/d with share bathroom 20,000/25,000Rp, s/d with bathroom 25,000/30,000Rp) Bare bones, friendly and clean sum it up here.

Depot Natalia (dishes 5000-23,000Rp) At Hotel Wira Pada, the Depot serves standard Indonesian food in clean surroundings.

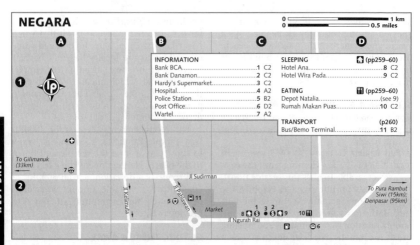

NEGARA

INFORMATION		SLEEPING	🏠 (pp259–60)
Bank BCA..........................1 C2		Hotel Ana.........................8 C2	
Bank Danamon.................2 C2		Hotel Wira Pada................9 C2	
Hardy's Supermarket.........3 C2			
Hospital..........................4 A2		EATING	🍴 (pp259–60)
Police Station...................5 B2		Depot Natalia...................(see 9)	
Post Office.......................6 D2		Rumah Makan Puas.........10 C2	
Wartel...........................7 A2			
		TRANSPORT	(p260)
		Bus/Bemo Terminal..........11 B2	

Rumah Makan Puas (Jl Ngurah Rai) A nice shady spot with good Padang-style food.

Hardy's Supermarket (☎ 40709; Jl Ngurah Rai) Has the best selection of goods in western Bali.

Getting There & Away

Most bemos and minibuses from Denpasar (Ubung terminal) to Gilimanuk drop you in Negara (9000Rp).

AROUND NEGARA

At the southern fringe of Negara, Loloan Timur is largely Bugis community (originally from Sulawesi) that retains 300-year-old traditions. Look for the distinctive houses on stilts, some decorated with wooden fretwork.

To reach **Delod Berawan**, turn off the main Gilimanuk–Denpasar road at Mendoyo and go south to the coast, which has a black-sand beach and irregular surf. You can see bull-race practices Sunday mornings at the nearby football field.

Perancak is the site of Nirartha's arrival on Bali in 1546, commemorated by a small temple, Pura Gede Perancak. Bull races are run at **Taman Wisata Perancak** (☎ 0365-42173), and Balinese buffets are sometimes staged for organised tours from South Bali. If you're travelling independently, give the park a ring before you go out there. In Perancak, ignore the depressing little zoo and go for a walk along the picturesque fishing harbour.

BULL RACES

This part of Bali is famous for the bull races, known as *mekepung*, which culminates in the Bupati Cup in Negara in early August. The racing animals are actually the normally docile water buffalo, which charge down a 2km-long stretch of road or beach pulling tiny chariots. Gaily-clad riders stand or kneel on top of the chariots forcing the bullocks on, sometimes by twisting their tails to make them follow the curve of the makeshift racetrack. The winner, however, is not necessarily first past the post. Style also plays a part and points are awarded for the most elegant runner. Gambling is not legal in Bali, but...

Important races are held during the dry season, from July to October. Occasional races are set up for tourist groups at a park in Perancak on the coast, and minor races and practices are held at several Perancak and other sites on Sunday mornings, including Delod Berawan (see left) and Yeh Embang. Check with your hotel or the **Jembrana Government Tourist Office** (☎ 41210, ext 224) for details.

Once capital of the region, **Jembrana** is the centre of the *gamelan jegog*, a gamelan using huge bamboo instruments that produce a very low-pitched, resonant sound. Performances often feature a number of gamelan groups engaging in musical contest. To see and hear them in action, time your arrival with a local festival, or ask in Negara where you might find a group practising.

BELIMBINGSARI & PALASARI

Christian evangelism on Bali was discouraged by the Dutch, but sporadic missionary activity resulted in a number of converts, many of whom were rejected by their own communities. In 1939 they were encouraged to resettle in Christian communities in the wilds of West Bali.

Belimbingsari was established as a Protestant community, and now has the largest Protestant church on Bali. It's an amazing structure, with features of church architecture rendered in a distinctly Balinese style – in place of a church bell there's a *kulkul* (warning drum) like one in a Hindu temple. The entrance is through an *aling-aling*-style (playfully carved stone) gate, and the attractive carved angels look very Balinese. Go on Sunday to see inside.

Palasari is home to a Catholic community, and their cathedral is also large and impressive (there could be a little competition here). It also shows Balinese touches in the spires, which resemble the *meru* (multiroofed temple) in a Hindu temple, and a façade with the same shape as a temple gate.

These villages are north of the main road, and the best way to see them is with your own transport by doing a loop starting from Melaya, 12km southeast of Cekik. The network of back roads and tracks is very confusing and poorly mapped and signposted, so be prepared to get lost and ask for directions.

CEKIK

At this junction one road continues to Gilimanuk and another heads east towards Lovina. All buses and bemos to and from Gilimanuk pass through Cekik.

Archaeological excavations here during the 1960s yielded the oldest evidence of human life on Bali. Finds include burial mounds with funerary offerings, bronze jewellery, axes, adzes and earthenware vessels from around 1000 BC, give or take a few centuries.

On the southern side of the junction, the pagoda-like structure with a spiral stair-way around the outside is a **War Memorial**. It commemorates the landing of independence

forces on Bali to oppose the Dutch, who were trying to reassert control of Indonesia after WWII.

Cekik is home to the **park headquarters** (☎ 61060; ⏰ 7am-5pm) of the Taman Nasional Bali Barat (West Bali National Park). It displays a topographic model of the park area, and has a little information about plants and wildlife. You can arrange trekking guides and permits here.

There is a free camp ground at the park headquarters. The grounds are not pristine, but the bathroom is clean enough and the toilets decent. A gratuity to the staff is greatly appreciated.

TAMAN NASIONAL BALI BARAT

☎ 0365

The Taman Nasional Bali Barat (West Bali National Park) covers 19,003 hectares of the western tip of Bali. An additional 50,000 hectares are protected in the national park extension, as well as almost 7000 hectares of coral reef and coastal waters. On an island as small and densely populated as Bali, this represents a major commitment

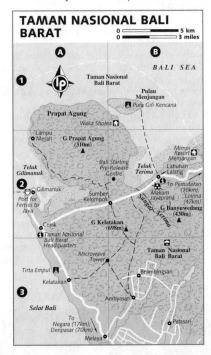

to nature conservation. Although you'll soon see a lot of firewood vendors along the road, who cut down trees and replace them with coffee plants.

The **park headquarters** (☎ 61060; ☿ 7am-5pm) at Cekik displays a topographic model of the park area, and has a little information about plants and wildlife. You can arrange trekking guides and permits here. There is also the small **Labuhan Lalang Visitors Centre** (☿ 8am-3pm) on the northern coast, where boats leave for Pulau Menjangan.

The main roads to Gilimanuk go through the national park, but you don't have to pay an entrance fee just to drive through. If you want to stop and visit any of the sites within the park, you must buy a ticket (2500Rp).

What most strikes many visitors who venture into the park is the symphony of sounds from the myriad of birds and the rustling of the various trees. Just getting off the road a bit on one of the many trails, including those on p263, transports you into the heart of nature.

Sights & Activities
WILDLIFE
Most of the natural vegetation in the park is not tropical rainforest, which requires rain year-round, but coastal savannah, with deciduous trees that become bare in the dry season. The southern slopes receive more regular rainfall, and hence have more tropical vegetation, while the coastal lowlands have extensive mangroves.

There are more than 200 species of plant inhabiting the park. Local fauna includes black monkeys, leaf monkeys and macaques (seen in the afternoon along the main road near Sumber Kelompok); rusa, barking, sambar, Java and mouse deer (*muncak*); and some wild pigs, squirrels, buffalo, iguanas, pythons and green snakes. There were once tigers, but the last confirmed sighting was in 1937 – and that one was shot. The bird life is prolific, with many of Bali's 300 species found here, including the very rare Bali starling.

TREKKING
All trekkers must be accompanied by an authorised guide. It's best to arrive the day before you want to trek, and make inquiries at the park headquarters at Cekik, the visitors' centre at Labuhan Lalang or

---

THE BALI STARLING

Also known as the Bali myna, Rothschild's mynah, or locally as *jalak putih*, the Bali starling is Bali's only endemic bird. It is striking white in colour, with black tips to the wings and tail, and a distinctive bright blue mask. The wild population has been estimated to be as low as a dozen – well below the number needed for sustainable reproduction. Unfortunately the bird is much sought after by collectors and hundreds are in captivity around the world. Given it fetches US$6000 or more on the black market, it shouldn't come as a surprise that the birds are continually poached from the wild.

The internationally supported Bali Starling Project is attempting to rebuild the population by re-introducing captive birds to the wild. At the Bali Starling Pre-Release Centre, formerly caged birds are introduced to the food sources of the natural environment and encouraged to nest in native trees, before being released around Taman Nasional Bali Barat. It's a difficult process, and many attempts have been sadly unsuccessful: birds are often killed by predatory falcons, and have been stolen from the Pre-Release Centre by armed thieves.

It's possible to visit the **Pre-Release Centre** (☿ 8am-3pm). Some 6km off the main road, it looks like an armed encampment even though poachers still attack. Here you can see the striking birds awaiting release and talk to the remarkably dedicated staff. To visit, you must first obtain a permit (100,000Rp) from one of the park offices. It's good for any number of people. The chances of spotting a Bali starling in the wildare extremely low.

---

any hotel in Gilimanuk. Guides may miraculously appear at your hotel within minutes of your arrival, but first make sure they are authorised.

The set rates for guides in the park depend on the size of the group and the length of the trek – with one or two people it's 65,000Rp for one or two hours, 95,000Rp for three or four hours, and 207,000Rp for five to seven hours; with three to five people it's 104,000Rp, 152,000Rp or 310,000Rp.

Transport and food are extra and all the prices are negotiable. Early morning, say 6am, is the best time to start – it's cooler and you're more likely to see some wildlife. The following are some of the more popular treks.

Teluk Terima From a trail west of Labuhan Lalang, hike around the mangroves here. Then partially follow the Sungai Terima into the hills and walk back down to the road along the steps at Makam Jayaprana. You might see grey macaques, deer and black monkeys (allow two to three hours).

Kelatakan Starting at the village, climb to the microwave tower, go down to Ambyasari and get transport back to Cekik (four hours). This takes you through the forested southern sector of the park. From the tower you get a feel for what much of Bali looked like centuries ago.

Gunung Kelatakan From Sumber Kelompok, go up the mountain (698m), then down to the main road near Kelatakan village (six to seven hours). You may be able to get permission from park headquarters to stay overnight in the forest – if you don't have a tent, your guide can make a shelter from branches and leaves which will be an adventure in itself. Clear streams abound in the dense woods.

Prapat Agung From Sumber Kelompok, you can trek around here, via the Bali Starling Pre-Release Centre and Batu Lucin – but only from about June to September, when the sensitive Bali starlings move further inland (allow at least five hours). It's easier and quicker to access the peninsula by chartered boat from Gilimanuk. Here you will see the mangroves and drier savannah landscape.

BOAT TRIPS
The best way to explore the mangroves of Teluk Gilimanuk or the west side of Prapat Agung is by chartering a boat (maximum of two people) for about 100,000Rp per boat per hour. You can arrange this at either of the park offices. A guide will cost another 100,000Rp. This is the ideal way to see bird life, including the kingfisher, the Javanese heron and, very, very rarely, the Bali starling.

DIVING
Teluk Gilimanuk is a shallow bay with marine life quite different from that in other parts of Bali – it's especially interesting for divers with a strong interest in marine biology. The closest and most convenient dive operators are found at Pemuteran (p249) and Lovina (p240).

Pulau Menjangan is one of Bali's best-known dive areas, with a dozen distinct dive sites. Unfortunately, the coral has suffered somewhat from coral bleaching (caused by warm water during the 1998 El Niño event) and the spread of crown-of-thorns starfish. Nevertheless, the diving is excellent – there's lots of tropical fish (including clown fish, parrot fish, sharks and barracuda), soft corals, great visibility (usually), caves and a spectacular drop-off.

PULAU MENJANGAN
This uninhabited island boasts what is thought to be Bali's oldest temple, **Pura Gili Kencana**, dating from the Majapahit period on Java. You can walk around the island in about an hour, but the attractions are mainly underwater. Snorkellers can find some decent spots not far from the jetty – ask the boatman where to go. Dive sites are dotted all around the island, so it's worth discussing the possibilities with the dive master when you arrange the trip.

MAKAM JAYAPRANA
A 20-minute walk up some stone stairs from the southern side of the road, a little west of Labuhan Lalang, will bring you to Jayaprana's grave. There are fine views to the north at the top. Jayaprana, the foster son of a 17th-century king, planned to marry Leyonsari, a beautiful girl of humble origins. The king, however, also fell in love with Leyonsari and had Jayaprana killed. Leyonsari learned the truth of Jayaprana's death in a dream, and killed herself rather than marry the king. This Romeo and Juliet story is a common theme in Balinese folklore, and the grave is regarded as sacred, even though the ill-fated couple were not deities.

AIR PANAS BANYUWEDANG
According to a local brochure, water from these hot-water springs will 'strengthen the endurance of your body against the attack of skin disease'. You can soak in the unappealing little **bath house** (Map p254; adult/child 3300/1800Rp); the hot springs at Banjar, near Lovina, are far, far better.

Sleeping
Mimpi Resort Menjangan (☎ 0362-94497, 0361-701070; www.mimpi.com; r US$95, villas US$195-325; ❄ ⚑) At isolated Banyuwedang, this resort has a large site extending down to a

small, mangrove-fringed, white-sand beach. The grounds are heavily trimmed, while the rooms have stark, simple design, all with open-air bathrooms. Villas have a hot-spring tub and their own private courtyard; some have a pool. The hotel also has a dive school and spa.

Waka Shorea (☎ 0362-94666; www.wakaexperience .com; bungalow US$135, villa US$190; ⬚ 🔲) Isolated in the park, Waka Shorea is a 10-minute boat ride from the hotel's reception area just east of Labuhan Lalang. It's a luxurious boutique resort and the emphasis is on nature, whether through diving, trekking or bird-watching.

Getting There & Away

The national park is too far away for a comfortable day trip from Ubud or southern Bali, though many dive operators do it. It is much more accessible from Lovina or Pemuteran – just get any Gilimanuk-bound bus or bemo to drop you at either the Labuhan Lalang entrance or the park headquarters at Cekik. Alternatively, you can take an organised tour or rent a vehicle.

LABUHAN LALANG

The jetty at this small harbour is the place to catch a boat to Pulau Menjangan in the national park (p263). There's a **visitors centre** (☉ 8am-3pm) here, where you can pay the park entrance fee (2500Rp), several warung and a pleasant beach 200m to the east. Some of the warung rent snorkelling gear (50,000Rp for four hours) and can point out where the best sites are. Parking is 2000Rp for a car and 1000Rp for a motorbike.

Local boat owners have a strict cartel and fixed prices: it costs 250,000Rp for a four-hour trip to Menjangan, and 20,000Rp for every subsequent hour, in a boat holding 10 people (or five scuba divers with equipment). A guide costs an additional 60,000Rp.

To get to Labuhan Lalang, catch a Gilimanuk-bound bus or bemo from Lovina or Pemuteran.

GILIMANUK

☎ 0365

Gilimanuk is the terminus for ferries that shuttle back and forth across the narrow strait to Java.

You can't miss the huge stone quadruped that straddles the road as you enter town (this bizarre edifice comprises four dragons on pedestals, their tails tied together over the middle of the road).

Most travellers to or from Java can get an onward ferry or bus straight away, and won't need to stop in Gilimanuk. The museum is the only attraction – the town is really a place one passes through quickly. It has the closest accommodation to the national park if you want to start a trek early.

Information

There is a Bank BDP Bali (without ATM) on Jl Raya, a post office, a police station and wartels, but not many shops or other services.

Sights

This part of Bali has been occupied for thousands of years. The new **Museum Situs Purbakala Gilimanuk** (☎ 61328; donation 5000Rp; ☉ 8am-4pm Mon-Fri) is centred on a family of skeletons thought to be 4000 years old, which were found locally in 2004. Although the displays are still being developed, you can get an idea of the lives of the truly ancient Balinese.

Sleeping & Eating

Choices here are very thin on the ground. There are plenty of cheap lodgings in Gilimanuk close to the ferry terminal, but are not really worth recommending. There is traffic noise and prayer calls from the mosque to disturb your sleep at any place on Jl Raya.

Assorted cheap-eats options cluster around the market and ferry terminal.

Hotel Sari (☎ 61264; r 50,000Rp, without/with hot water 50,000/100,000Rp, dishes 8000-10,000Rp; ⬚) On the ocean side of Jl Raya and well away from the noise, this is the one place worth recommending. Rooms are clean and decorated with vivid red curtains. The best rooms come with an attached garage in case you want to bed down with your car. It's certainly the most comfortable option for solo female travellers. The upstairs restaurant (open 7pm to 10pm) has Japanese-style cushion seating and good, simple meals. Staff are charming.

Rumah Makan Muslim (Jl Raya; dishes 6000Rp) This is spotlessly clean and inexpensive.

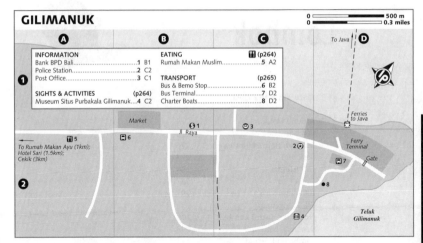

GILIMANUK

INFORMATION	**EATING** (p264)	
Bank BPD Bali.....................**1** B1	Rumah Makan Muslim.....................**5** A2	
Police Station.....................**2** C2		
Post Office.....................**3** C1	**TRANSPORT** (p265)	
	Bus & Bemo Stop.....................**6** B2	
SIGHTS & ACTIVITIES (p264)	Bus Terminal.....................**7** D2	
Museum Situs Purbakala Gilimanuk....**4** C2	Charter Boats.....................**8** D2	

0 ———— 500 m
0 ———— 0.3 miles

To Java

Market

Jl. Raya

To Rumah Makan Ayu (1km);
Hotel Sari (1.5km);
Cekik (3km)

Ferries to Java

Ferry Terminal

Gate

Teluk Gilimanuk

WEST BALI

Getting There & Away

Frequent buses hurtle along the main road between Gilimanuk and Denpasar's Ubung terminal (20,000Rp), or along the north coast road to Singaraja (15,000Rp). It's best to catch a bus, rather than a minibus or bemo, from outside the market, as drivers will probably bump up the fare for tourists, and vehicles are crowded and tend to stop at every place along the way.

Boats to and from Ketapang on Java (adult/child 3500/2500Rp, car and driver 38,000Rp) leave every 30 minutes, 24 hours a day.

Getting Around

At the ferry, bemo and bus terminals, you will be thronged by *ojek* (motorcycle that carries paying pillion passengers) riders, who charge 5000Rp for the short ride to local accommodation. A more leisurely and comfortable option – particularly if you are carrying luggage – are the *dokar* (pony carts).

Lombok

LOMBOK

A steady stream of sun soakers, divers, surfers and trekkers heads to Lombok for the beautiful beaches and underwater sights of the Gili islands, the beach resort town of Senggigi on the west coast, the big breaks of the south coast, and the dramatic summit of Gunung Rinjani. The island also offers a multitude of other attractions where tourists are still a relative novelty – there are pristine and almost untouched beaches in the southwest, stunning mountainous scenery in the east, and handicraft villages dotting the lush central plain.

Less focused on tourism, most of Lombok is much quieter than its more famous neighbour, and has a very different character geographically and culturally. The naturalist Alfred Russel Wallace noted the major differences in the flora and fauna of Bali and Lombok, indicated by his 'Wallace Line'. Lombok's landscape also has sharp contrasts compared with Bali – some parts drip with water, while other pockets are chronically dry.

The indigenous Sasak people make up about 90% of the population. They follow the Islamic religion, but have a culture and language unique to Lombok.

Traditionally a haven for budget travellers where bamboo huts on stilts and *nasi goreng* was the order of the day, certain parts of Lombok now offer the chicest boutique hotels and the finest cuisine from all corners of the globe. Lombok's tourism is developing, yet, it still retains the tranquil and timeless character that has drawn travellers for decades.

LOMBOK

TOP FIVE

- Climbing the challenging and majestic **Gunung Rinjani** (p301), Lombok's highest peak at 3726m

- Enjoying the white sand beaches, clear blue sea, chilled-out atmosphere and nightlife of the **Gili Islands** (p284)

- Exploring the scarcely developed **southwest peninsula** (p276) for its pristine, tranquil beaches – particularly at Gili Nanggu and Gede – and its 'secret' surf spots

- Watching sunsets over the Lombok straits from **Senggigi** (p277), and enjoying the area's sweeping bays, best seen along the coastal road to **Bangsal** (p284)

- Shopping in the handicraft villages around **Tetebatu** (p306) and enjoying the lush scenery and rainforest walks

MATARAM & THE WEST

☎ 0370

Most travellers who visit Lombok spend some time in the west, if only because the airport (Mataram) and the port (Lembar) for ferries to and from Bali are here. It's the most populous part of Lombok, with the largest urban area centred on Mataram, and the biggest tourist resort, the Senggigi beach strip. There are a number of attractive villages around Mataram, as well as some stunning coastal areas on the southwest peninsula.

MATARAM

☎ 0370 / pop 316,000

Lombok's capital, Mataram, is a conglomeration of four separate towns that have merged into one. Ampenan, once the main port of Lombok, has some interesting old buildings and picturesque streets. Mataram is the administrative capital of West Nusa Tenggara (ie Lombok and Sumbawa), with some large and extravagant government buildings; Cakranegara (Cakra) is the main commercial centre, with the best range of budget accommodation and restaurants; and Sweta was the former transport hub (the Mandalika bus terminal at Bertais has replaced it).

Its patchwork of broad avenues makes for a pleasant, open city, and there are some interesting markets and shops, as well as the main banks, travel agencies, and airline offices. Some travellers use Mataram as a base to organise trips elsewhere around the island, but this can be done just as easily from Senggigi. Most head straight to Senggigi or the Gili islands.

Orientation

The four areas of Mataram are spread along one main road that starts as Jl Pabean in Ampenan, quickly becomes Jl Yos Sudarso, then changes to Jl Langko, becomes Mataram around Jl Langko and Jl Pejanggik, and turns into Cakra at Jl Selaparang, which finally travels through Sweta to Bertais. It's a one-way street all the way, running west to east. A parallel one-way road, Jl Tumpang Sari–Jl Panca Usaha–Jl Pancawarga–Jl Caturwarga–Jl Pendidikan, brings traffic back towards the coast.

Information

EMERGENCY

Police station (☎ 631225; Jl Langko, Ampenan) In an emergency, call ☎ 110.

INTERNET ACCESS

Most Internet cafés can be found around the perimeters of Mataram Mall. The cheapest you'll pay for access in Mataram is about 4500Rp per hour.

Warposnet (Jl Sriwijaya 37; ☺ 8am-5pm Mon-Thu & Sat, 8-11am Fri) This is at the main post office.

Yahoo Internet (☎ 627474; ☺ 8am-10pm) At Mataram Mall.

MEDICAL SERVICES

Rumah Sakit Umum Mataram (☎ 622254; Jl Pejanggik 6, Mataram; ☺ 8am-12am special service for tourists) The best hospital on Lombok, it has some English-speaking doctors.

MONEY

Most of the banks are located along the main road through Cakra and behind and inside Mataram Mall. The majority have ATMs, and change cash and travellers cheques. Money-changers (longer hours than the banks) can be found in Ampenan, Mataram Mall and the airport, where there's also an ATM. Mataram or Senggigi are the best places to change money, as rates are terrible elsewhere. Banks BCA, BNI and Bank Mandiri are all on Jl Pejanggik and keep the standard opening hours. There are ATMs situated in the Mataram Mall next to the Hero Supermarket, and a moneychanger on Jl Pabean.

POST

Main post office (Jl Sriwijaya 37, Mataram; ☺ 8am-5pm Mon-Thu & Sat, 8-11am Fri) There's Internet access and poste restante services here.

Sub-post office (Jl Langko, Ampenan; ☺ 8am-5pm Mon-Thu & Sat, 8-11am Fri)

TELEPHONE & FAX

There are *wartel* (public telephone offices) on Jl Pejanggik and at the Selaparang airport.

Telkom office (☎ 633333; Jl Pendidikan 23, Mataram; ☺ 24hr) Offers phone, fax and telegram services. There are several other *wartel* around town.

TOURIST OFFICES

Rinjani Trek Centre Head Office (☎ 641124; www .lomboksumbawa.com; Hotel Lombok Raya, Jl Panca Usaha

Senggigi Beach (p277), Lombok

RICHARD I'ANSON

Harvesting rice at the base of Gunung
Rinjani (p301), Lombok

BERNARD NAPTHINE

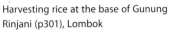

Tetebatu market (p306), Tetebatu

JULIET COOMBE

RICHARD I'ANSON

Fish for sale, Bangsal Harbour (p287)

ANDREW LUBR

Gili Trawangan (p293), Lombok

MICHAEL AW

Underwater seascapes (p285)

LOMBOK

LOMBOK

BALI SEA

Selat Lombok

To Bali

To Bali

0 — 20 km
0 — 12 miles

INDIAN OCEAN

Gili Trawangan
Gili Meno
Gili Air

Pemenang
Bangsal
Teluk Nare
Mangsit
Senggigi
Ampenan
Mataram
Cakranegara
Pantai Senggigi

LOMBOK BARAT (WEST LOMBOK)
Gunung Sabiris (8456m) ▲

See West Lombok Map (p275)

Tanjung
Godang

Akar Akar
Senaru
Kali Putih

Obel Obel
Anyar
Bayan
Salang
Blantung
Protected Forest
Sembalun Lawang
Sembalun Bumbung
Sugian
Sambelia
Labuhan Pandan

Gunung Rinjani (3726m) ▲
Taman Nasional Gunung Rinjani
Danau Segara Anak
Gunung Nangi (2330m) ▲

Labuhan Lombok

Protected Forest
Kali Bangka
Kali Menanga

Sesaot
Suranadi
Taman Narmada
Kediri
Ubung
Bon Jeruk

Sapit
Swela
Pringgabaya

Alkmel
Lenek
Lendang Nangka
Suralaga
Selong
Labuhan Haji

Tanjung Ringgit

Kotaraja
Pringgasela
Pomotong
Sikur
Terara
Sakra
Kenteng
Tanjung Luar
Gili Melayu

Mantang
Kopang
Pancordao
Kali Janapria
Runiak
Jerowaru
Ekas
Kalantan
Gili Saya

Puyung
Praya
Sukarara
Penujak
Penujak
Langko
Mujur
Ganti
Batu Nampar
Teluk Ekas
Awang
Tanjung Aan
Gili Air

LOMBOK TENGAH (CENTRAL LOMBOK)
Sengkol
Rembitan
Sade
Kuta
Mawun
Grupak

Gerung
Lembar
Kali
Gunung Sabiris (716m) ▲
Montongsapah

Mangkung
Kateng
Keling
Selong Blanak
Tamo
Pengantap
Mawi

LOMBOK TIMUR (EAST LOMBOK)
Tetebatu

Gili Nanggu
Taun
Sekotong
Blongas
Sepi

Teluk Terang
Gili Gede
Pelangan
Teluk Mekaki

Desert Point
Bangko Bangko
Labuhan Poh

Gili Lawang
Gili Sulat

Gili Pentangan

Pulau Panjang
Pulau Kalong
Poto Tano

Pulau Nano
Pulau Belang

Selat Alas

PULAU SUMBAWA

Taliwang
Jereweh
Maluk
Teluk Taliwang

11, Mataram; 8am-5pm) If you want some information about climbing Gunung Rinjani before heading to Senaru or Sembalun Lawang – which also have centres – pop in here.

West Lombok Tourist Office (621658; Jl Suprato 20; 7am-2pm Mon-Thu, 7-11am Fri, 7am-12.30pm Sat) Apart from maps and leaflets it's not particularly useful.

West Nusa Tenggara Tourist Office (634800; Jl Singosari 2; 7am-2pm Mon-Thu, 7-11am Fri, 7am-12.30pm Sat) Covering Lombok and Sumbawa, it's more helpful than the West Lombok office.

Sights
PURA SEGARA
This Balinese Hindu sea temple is on the beach about 1km north of Ampenan. It can often be closed, but just inland are remnants of Muslim and Chinese cemeteries which are worth a look if you're visiting the temple. The colourful and intricately decorated Chinese graves line the main road north for a few hundred metres. Many Chinese were killed here as a reaction to the attempted coup in 1965.

MUSEUM NEGERI NUSA TENGGARA BARAT
This modern **museum** (632519; Jl Panji Tilar Negara 6; admission 1500Rp; 8am-2pm Tue-Thu & Sat-Sun, 8-11am Fri) has exhibits on the geology, history and culture of Lombok and Sumbawa. If you intend to buy any antiques or handicrafts, have a look at the *kris* (traditional daggers), *songket* (silver- or gold-threaded cloth), basketware, and masks to give you a starting point for comparison.

MAYURA WATER PALACE
This **palace** (Jl Selaparang; admission 1500Rp incl sash; 8am-5pm) was built in 1744, and was once part of the Balinese kingdom's royal court in Lombok. Its main feature is a large artificial lake, with a *bale kambang* (floating pavilion) in the centre, connected to the shoreline by a raised footpath. This pavilion was used as both a court of justice and a meeting place for the Hindu lords. There are other shrines and fountains in the surrounding park.

The entrance to the walled enclosure of the palace is on the western side, off Jl Selaparang. It's a pleasant retreat now, but in 1894 was the site of bloody battles as Dutch and Balinese forces fought for control of Lombok.

PURA MERU
Directly opposite the water palace is **Pura Meru** (admission by donation; 8am-5pm), the largest Balinese Hindu temple on Lombok. It was built in 1720 under the patronage of the Balinese prince Anak Agung Made Karang of the Singosari kingdom as an attempt to unite all the small kingdoms in Lombok, and as a symbol of the universe, dedicated to the Hindu trinity of Brahma, Vishnu and Shiva.

The outer courtyard has a hall housing the wooden drums that are beaten to call believers to festivals and special ceremonies; the most important is held every June at full moon. The inner courtyard has one large and 33 small shrines, as well as three *meru* (multiroofed shrines): the central *meru*, with 11 tiers, is Shiva's house; the *meru* to the north, with nine tiers, is Vishnu's; and the seven-tiered *meru* to the south is Brahma's. The *meru* are also said to represent the three great mountains – Rinjani, Agung and Bromo.

The caretaker will lend you a sash and sarong if you need one (see Temple Etiquette, p38).

Tours
See p347 for details on boat tours to Komodo Island and the east.

Ideal Tours (633629; fax 636982; Jl Pejanggik 54B, Mataram) Organises an interesting, although pricier, range of tours around Lombok and Sumbawa.

Perama (635928; www.peramatour.com; Jl Pejanggik 66, Mataram; 8am-6pm) Runs a variety of well-priced tours around Lombok, as well as vehicle and driver charters for 350,000Rp per day.

Sleeping
The prices quoted here tend to be the same in high or low season.

BUDGET
Karthika II Hotel (641776; Jl Subak 1, Cakra; r with fan/air-con 55,000Rp/75,000Rp;) Near the Ganesha Inn, this hotel is a step up in comfort. The rooms are squeaky clean and have modern bathrooms. The verandas, with bamboo blinds and surrounded by palms, add a tropical feel.

Nanda Hotel (637032; Jl Jakatawang 1, Cakra; r 35,000Rp) This new addition has 12 well-furnished rooms with large beds, wardrobes and mirrors. The terraces are separated by ikat screens and overlook a small garden.

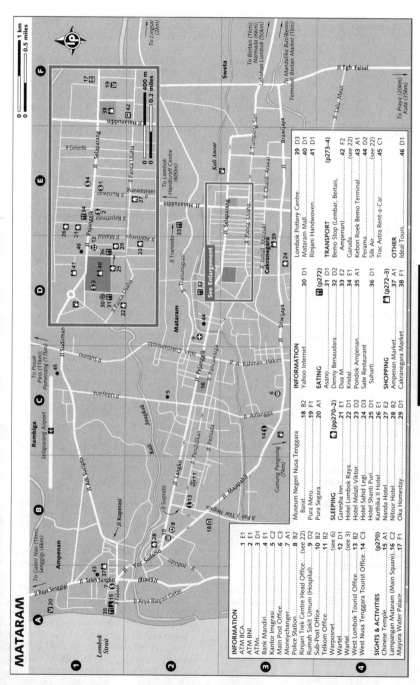

Oka Homestay (☎ 622406; Jl Repatmaja 5, Cakra; s/d 25,000/30,000Rp) This cosy, popular place is run by the friendly and helpful Oka, whose basic rooms are set in a pretty garden complete with Balinese shrine, cats, cockerels and two majestic ravens.

Hotel Melati Viktor (☎ 633830; Jl Abimanyu 1, Cakra; s/d 30,000/35,000, with hot water 75,000/100,000Rp; ⊠) All rooms are smart and sparkling clean, and have tiled floors, cupboards and modern bathrooms. The rooms with cold water and fans are excellent value.

Ganesha Inn (☎ 624878; Jl Subak 1, Cakra; r 30,000-40,000Rp) Just off Cakra's main drag, this mellow place has bright well-maintained rooms with basic Indonesian toilet and bathrooms with cold water.

Hotel Shanti Puri (☎ 632649; Jl Maktal 15, Mataram; r with fan/air-con 50,000/75,000Rp; ⊠) Down a quiet street, these cosy, comfortable rooms have large fans or air-con, good reading lamps and small terraces. A good budget option.

MID-RANGE & TOP END

Hotel Sahid Legi (☎ 636282; sahid@mataram.wasantara.net.id; Jl Sriwijaya 81, Mataram; r 350,000-950,000Rp; ⊠ ⊠) Although further from the centre than Hotel Lombok Raya, Sahid Legi's rooms have more modern furnishings and are better maintained, and there's a more internationally friendly feel. There's a large pool surrounded by lush gardens and expansive lawns.

Nitour Hotel (☎ 623780; fax 625328; Jl Yos Sudarso 4-6, Ampenan; r 200,000-350,000Rp; ⊠) The rooms here have an old-fashioned charm with their finger-dial telephones and standard lamps. All have hot water and air-con but the cheaper rooms need a little TLC. Discounts are readily available if you barter.

Hotel Lombok Raya (☎ 632305; lora@wasantara.net.id; Jl Panca Usaha 11, Mataram; r 380,000-500,000Rp; ⊠ ⊠) A huge rambling place, Lombok Raya is conveniently located and has rooms with all the facilities you'd expect, but they could do with an update. There's a large swimming pool, and the Garuda Indonesia and Silk Air offices are based here.

Eating

Denny Bersaudara (☎ 633619; Jl Pelikan 6, Mataram; dishes 10,000-25,000Rp) Run by the younger brother of the Dua M owner, this restaurant

has an excellent range of Sasak dishes and the environment is airy and light – there's even poetry on the menu!

Dua M (☎ 622914; Jl Transisto 99, Mataram; dishes 12,500-20,000Rp) This is a locals' favourite for Sasak food, such as *ayam goreng Taliwang* (a spicy grilled chicken). A low table facing the garden and pond is the most pleasant spot to sit; the rest is a bit dark.

Kristal (☎ 627564; Jl Pejanggik 22, Cakra; dishes 6000-17,000Rp) This plain but pristine restaurant does reliably good Chinese staples, as well as a selection of seafood dishes.

Aroma (☎ 632585; Jl Palapa 2, Cakra; dishes 7500-35,000Rp) Whirring with fans, this rather dark restaurant is a highly recommended Chinese and seafood place serving succulent treats like fried squid in sweet-and-sour sauce and chilli crab.

Sate Restaurant Suharti (☎ 637958; Jl Maktal 9, Cakra; satay 9000Rp, other dishes 5000-19,000Rp) All sorts of imaginative satay are served up in this bamboo-walled restaurant decorated with wind chimes.

Other recommendations:

Pondok Ampenan (☎ 645027; Jl Pabean; mains 10,000-40,000Rp) Overlooking the 'beach' this place has colonial charm and a diverse menu.

Mataram Mall (Jl Pejanggik; ⏱ 10am-9pm) American fast-food outlets and a good supermarket are here.

Asano (dishes 5000-15,000Rp) You'll find *warung* (food stalls) around the western perimeter of Mataram Mall, including tasty Padang food at this one.

Shopping

Lombok Handicraft Centre (Sayang Sayang) If you don't have time to visit the handicraft villages, visit this centre at Sayang Sayang (north of Cakra), which has a great selection of crafts.

Lombok Pottery Centre (☎ 640351; Jl Sriwijaya 111, Cakra) A vast range from all the pottery centres around the island is on offer here, and the prices are competitive.

Rinjani Handwoven (☎ 633169; Jl Pejanggik 44) One of a few weaving factories in Cakra where you can see dyeing and weaving, and buy ikat or hand-woven *songket* sarongs.

Mataram Mall (Jl Pejanggik; ⏱ 10am-9pm) This massive mall is a good one-stop shop for everything from fashion to electronics.

Galeri Nao (☎ 626835; nao@telkom.net) Unusual in that it recycles local woods and has more contemporary designs, this shop is one of many selling furniture and handicrafts on the road running north from Ampenan to Senggigi.

MARKETS

Located on the south side of Mandalika bus terminal, Bertais Market is the largest and liveliest market in the city. You can find a range of textiles, handicrafts, hardware and produce.

Ampenan Market, by the Kebon Roek *bemo* (small pick-up truck) terminal is a colourful produce market worth a look, and Cakranegara Market, off Jl Hasanuddin, is another good place to find local products.

Getting There & Away

AIR

See p344 for airlines serving Lombok and details on the airport and departure tax.

Garuda Indonesia (☎ 0370-638259; www.garuda -indonesia.com) and **Silk Air** (☎ 0370-628254; www .silkair.com) have offices at Hotel Lombok Raya.

BUS

Mandalika terminal in Bertais is the main bus and bemo terminal for the entire island. It's also the terminal for long-distance buses to Sumbawa, Bali and Java, and is the eastern terminus for local bemos, which shuttle back and forth to Ampenan. The terminal is fairly chaotic, so be sure to keep a level head to avoid the 'help' of the commission-happy touts. Long-distance buses leave from behind the main terminal building; bemos and smaller buses for anywhere on Lombok leave from one of two car parks on either side. Any vehicle without a destination sign on top can usually be chartered. For details of bus services to Java, see p346.

Some distances and current fares for buses and bemos from Mandalika terminal:

Destination	Distance	Price	Duration
Labuhan Lombok	69km	8000Rp	2hr
Lembar	22km	3000Rp	30 min
Praya	27km	3000Rp	30 min
Kuta (via Praya & Sengkol)	54km	3000Rp (+3000Rp)	90 min
Pemenang (for Bangsal)	30km	3000Rp	30 min

Kebon Roek terminal at Ampenan is for bemos to Senggigi and Mandalika. A trip up the coast to Senggigi costs 2000Rp from Ampenan. Some bemos travel between Mandalika and Senggigi, but you'll usually have to change in Ampenan.

TOURIST SHUTTLE BUS

Perama (☎ 635928; www.peramatour.com; Jl Pejanggik 66, Mataram; 8am-6pm) runs convenient shuttle bus/boat services to various destinations in Lombok, Bali and Sumbawa. Tickets can be booked directly or at any travel agency in Lombok or Bali, and include ferry charges.

Getting Around

TO/FROM THE AIRPORT

There's a prepaid **taxi desk** (7.30am-10pm) at the Selaparang airport where dark-blue taxis will take you anywhere in Mataram for 15,000Rp. They cost 30,000Rp to Senggigi, 40,000Rp to Mangsit, 60,000Rp to Bangsal and Lembar, 105,000Rp to Tetebatu, 110,000Rp to Kuta and 175,000Rp to Senaru. If the desk is closed, walk out past the car park to the main road and hail a metered, light-blue Blue Bird or Lombok Taksi. Alternatively, take one of the frequent No 7 bemos which go to the Keban Roek terminal, where you can get bemos to Senggigi for 2000Rp.

BEMO

The areas of Ampenan, Mataram, Cakra and Sweta are very spread out so don't plan to walk from place to place. Yellow bemos shuttle back and forth between the Kebon Roek terminal in Ampenan and the Mandalika terminal. Some make slight detours, but they generally travel along the two main thoroughfares. The fare is a standard 1500Rp, regardless of distance. Outside the market in Cakra, a handy bemo stop has services to Ampenan, Bertais and Lembar. Mandalika and Kebon Roek terminals are good places to charter a bemo.

CAR & MOTORCYCLE

Most hotels can arrange the rental of motorcycles and cars; see p352.

Based near the airport, **Trac Astra Rent-a-Car** (☎ 626363; www.trac.astra.co.id; Jl Adi Sucipto 5, Rembiga Mataram; Kijang with driver per 6hr 385,000Rp, self-drive per day 385,000Rp) has a range of new vehicles.

LOMBOK

TAXI

For an inexpensive metered taxi, call **Lombok Taksi** (☎ 627000).

AROUND MATARAM

East from Mataram there are some gorgeous areas with villages, rice fields, temples and palaces. You can easily visit all the following places in half a day if you have your own transport.

Taman Narmada

Laid out as a miniature replica of the summit of Gunung Rinjani and its crater lake, **Taman Narmada** (Narmada Park; adult/child 2000/1000Rp; ☺ 7am-6pm), in the village of Narmada, was built in 1805 and takes its name from a sacred river in India.

Its temple, Pura Kalasa, is still in use, and the Balinese Pujawali celebration is held here (in November or December) in honour of the god Batara, who dwells on Gunung Rinjani. At the same time, the faithful who have made the trek up the mountain and down to Danau Segara Anak hold a ceremony called *pekelan,* where they throw gold trinkets and objects into the lake.

Apart from the lake, there are also two **swimming pools** (adult/child 2000/1000Rp); don't visit on Sunday when it's very crowded.

Right at the Narmada bemo stop and opposite the entrance to the gardens is the local market, as well as warung.

Frequent bemos from Mandalika will take you to the Narmada market for 2000Rp.

Pura Lingsar

This large temple complex, built in 1714, is the holiest place on Lombok. The temple combines the Balinese Hindu and Wektu Telu religions in one complex. Designed in two separate sections and on different levels, the Hindu temple in the northern section is higher than the Wektu Telu temple in the southern section.

The Wektu Telu temple is noted for its small, enclosed pond devoted to Lord Vishnu. It has a number of holy eels – they can be enticed from their hiding places with hard-boiled eggs, which can be bought from stalls in the temple complex. See Temple Etiquette, p38.

During the annual rain festival at the start of the wet season (between October

and December) the Hindus and Wektu Telu make offerings and pray in their own temples, then come out into the communal compound and pelt each other with *ketupat* (rice wrapped in banana leaves). The ceremony is either to bring the rain, or to give thanks for the rain, depending on the conditions.

To get there, take a bemo from Mandalika to Narmada for around 2000Rp, then catch another to Lingsar for 1500Rp. Ask to be dropped off near the entrance to the temple complex, which is 300m down a well-marked path off the road.

Suranadi

Suranadi is a pleasant little village surrounded by picturesque countryside. It has a temple, a small pocket of forest and a swimming pool, making it a popular spot for locals on weekends.

SIGHTS
Pura Suranadi

This is one of the holiest Hindu temples on Lombok, built around a spring that bubbles icy cold water into pools and a bathing area. Eels and other fish in the pools are sacred, and well fed with hard-boiled eggs. The usual rules for Balinese temple visits apply (see Temple Etiquette, p38).

Hutan Wisata Suranadi

Just opposite the village market, an entrance leads to a small **forest sanctuary** (admission 1000Rp; ☺ 8am-5pm), which is a shady and quiet area for short hikes and good for bird-watching. There's a **Sumatran elephant** (rides through the forest 15/25 min 25,000/50,000Rp) here too.

SLEEPING & EATING

There are a few restaurants along the main road, assorted warung around the car park, and the restaurant in the Surnadi Hotel.

Suranadi Hotel (☎ 633686; r 100,000Rp, 2-/3-bed cottages 150,000/175,000Rp, dishes 8000-20,000Rp; ☒ ☒) Housed in an interesting old Dutch building, this charming hotel is surrounded by rice fields, and has verdant gardens, goldfish ponds, tennis courts and a restaurant. The economy rooms are not much more than cells, but the cottages are clean with air-con and hot water, and some have a small stream bubbling past by them. Non-guests can enjoy the refreshing, spring-fed

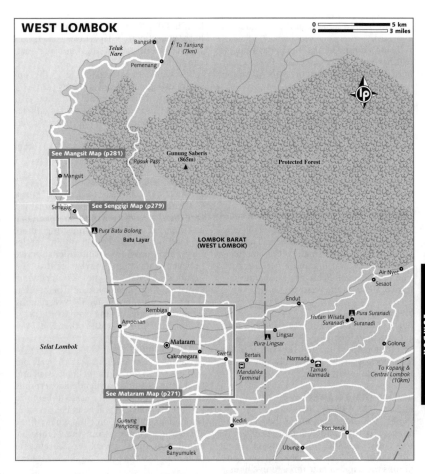

WEST LOMBOK

Teluk Nare
Bangsil
To Tanjung (7km)
Pemenang
See Mangsit Map (p281)
Gunung Saberis (865m)
Pusuk Pass
Protected Forest
Mangsit
See Senggigi Map (p279)
Senggigi
Pura Batu Bolong
Batu Layar
LOMBOK BARAT (WEST LOMBOK)
Air Nyet
Sesaot
Endut
Rembiga
Hutan Wisata Suranadi
Pura Suranadi
Suranadi
Ampenan
Lingsar
Mataram
Pura Lingsar
Golong
Selat Lombok
Cakranegara
Sweta
Bertais
Narmada
Mandalika Terminal
Taman Narmada
To Kopang & Central Lombok (10km)
See Mataram Map (p271)
Gunung Pengsong
Kediri
Bon Jeruk
Banyumulek
Ubung

LOMBOK

pool for 5000Rp, but you must cover up with a T-shirt or such.

Pondok Surya (☎ 0813 3950 6902; r 30,000Rp) Find this place by walking to the end of the car park in front of the Suranadi Hotel and asking for directions – it's through the rice fields – or take the road behind the Suranadi and look for the sign. The four basic rooms next to the Balinese family shrine are on a small hill overlooking a stream and rice fields.

GETTING THERE & AWAY
There are occasional public bemos running between Suranadi and Narmada (1000Rp one way). Failing that, charter one for a negotiable 30,000Rp each way.

Gunung Pengsong
This Balinese temple is 7km south of Mataram, and has great views of rice fields, volcanoes and the sea. The area was used by retreating Japanese soldiers to hide during WWII, and remnants of cannons can be found, as well as plenty of pesky monkeys. Try to get there early in the morning before the clouds envelop Gunung Rinjani.

Once a year, generally in March or April, a buffalo is taken up the steep 100m slope and sacrificed to give thanks for a good harvest. The Desa Bersih festival (p330) also occurs here at harvest time – houses and gardens are cleaned, fences whitewashed, and roads and paths repaired. Once part of a ritual to rid the village of evil spirits, it's now held in honour of the rice goddess Dewi Sri.

There's no set admission charge, but you will have to tip the caretaker. There's very little direct public transport from Mataram; it's best to charter a vehicle.

Banyumulek

This is one of the main pottery centres of Lombok, specialising in decorated pots and pots with a woven fibre covering, as well as more traditional urns and water flasks. It's close to the city, 2km west of the Sweta–Lembar road, which carries frequent bemos.

LEMBAR

Lembar is the main port on Lombok. The ferries to and from Bali dock here. The public ferry terminal is small, with some telephones, a few warung and a parking area. The terminal for Pelni has a separate entrance, 200m to the west.

Sleeping

Tidar (Jl Raya Pelabuhan; s/d 35,000/40,000Rp) If you get stuck in Lembar, this *losmen* (basic accommodation), located 1km north of the ferry port, is clean and friendly, and serves hearty Indonesian meals.

Getting There & Away
PUBLIC FERRY TO/FROM BALI

Public ferries travel nonstop between Padangbai (p188) and Lembar. A one-way trip costs 36,400Rp for motorcycles and 258,700Rp for cars. Depending on conditions the trip can take three to five hours. Boats leave about every 90 minutes and food and drink is sold on board. Unless it's a very

---

MAY I TAKE YOUR BAG, SIR?

Be aware of where your luggage is at all times in Lembar. There have been reports of aggressive 'porters' grabbing bags and then asking for extortionate prices before giving them back. If you are travelling with a shuttle service don't assume that the people who are taking your luggage off the bus are with the shuttle company – they probably aren't. If you allow someone to carry your bags for you, agree on the price beforehand.

---

busy holiday time, you can get tickets at the harbour just before departure. Tickets cost 15,000/9350Rp (adult/child) and the boats run 24 hours a day.

It's worth checking to see if the on-again, off-again **Padangbai Express** (☎ 645974; 55,000Rp), which takes only two hours, is running. Also note that you may still see reference to the Mabua Express, a service which ended years ago.

For details of boat services to other Indonesian islands, see p346.

TOURIST SHUTTLE BUS/BOAT
Perama (☎ 635928; www.peramatour.com; Jl Pejanggik 66, Mataram), and several similar companies, run shuttle buses to and from Padangbai and Lembar harbours, connecting (more or less) with the regular public ferries there. This provides a convenient service between the main tourist centres on Lombok and Bali. Shuttle buses are more expensive than public buses and bemos, but they save considerable hassle by arranging ferry tickets and taking you to the ferry and picking you up at the other end.

Getting Around

For a public bemo into Mataram, walk out of the ferry terminal, up the main road and catch one heading to Mandalika terminal in Bertais (3000Rp). If you get a bemo in the ferry car park, it will be at charter rates (around 40,000Rp). Going to Lembar, there are frequent bemos from the Mandalika terminal or the stop next to Cakranegara market in Mataram.

SOUTHWESTERN PENINSULA

The beautiful beaches and nearby islands around Sekotong are being touted as the next big thing, or the 'new Gilis'.

A road from Lembar goes around the east side of the harbour and then heads south to Sekotong. From there, the road to the south cuts across the peninsula and ends at Sepi on the southern coast. The other road goes westwards and follows the coast through to Bangko Bangko and Desert Point – the famous left-hand surf break. This coast road from Sekotong, which passes Taun and Pelangan, has some fine white-sand beaches, coral, and clear waters. The further you go on this road, however, the rougher it gets and it may become impassable for ordinary cars past Labuhan Poh – you can charter fishing boats instead (see right).

Two groups of picturesque islands off the northern coast of this peninsula are clearly visible from the ferries going to Lembar. Only a few of these islands are inhabited, and most have beautiful, unspoilt white beaches with plenty of palm trees and good snorkelling opportunities (bring your own gear). Gili Nanggu is currently the only island with accommodation – it's great for a romantic day or two.

Further west, Gili Gede is in the second group of islands and the largest of them all. It has a number of traditional villages (where some Bugis settlers make a living from boat building), glorious beaches and clear water for snorkelling.

Hotels in Senggigi, such as Bulan Baru (p281), organise day trips to the beaches or islands here.

Sleeping & Eating
There are places to stay and restaurants along the coast from Sekotong through to Pelangan.

MAINLAND
Bola Bola Paradis (☎ 646645; Jl Raya Bangko-Bangko; r 150,000-250,000Rp; mains 19,000-50,000Rp; ☒) Just west of Pelangan, this hotel has funky octagonal villas with maritime white and blue rooms, or more luxurious bronze and yellow rooms. There's an adjoining restaurant and chic lounge area. Boats can be chartered from here (see right).

Pasir Putih (☎ 6605088; Jl Raja Sekotong Barat; r 250,000Rp; ☒ ☒) On the beach side of the road heading from Sekotong to Taun you'll see a large gate with a metal fish on it. In here are two stylish A-frame thatched cottages with small individual lotus ponds out front, and a swimming pool by the beach next to the restaurant.

Nirvana Roemah Air (☎ 640107; www.lombok andbeyond.com/lombokhotels/nirvana.html; Jl Raya Medang, Sekotong Barat; r US$200-250) Off the coast of Sekotong, these new, smartly decorated villas are set on stilts out in the sea.

Sekotong Indah Beach Cottages (☎ 0818 362 326; r without/with air-con 55,000/85,000Rp; dishes 5000-20,000Rp; ☒) West of Taun, these standard, tiled-floor cottages are rather plain and run-down. They sometimes close in the low

season. The restaurant serves Indo-Chinese food.

Putri Doyang (☎ 0812 3752 459; Jl Raya Pelangangi, Tembowong; s/d 25,000/50,000Rp) Located 2km north of Pelangan, this very basic place has clean rooms and friendly owners.

GILI NANGGU ISLAND
Gili Nanggu Cottages (☎ 623783; lumbung cottages s/d 80,000/100,000Rp, bungalows 200,000/250,000Rp, dishes 15,000-25,000Rp; ☒) The best value rooms are the comfortable two-storey cottages, built in *lumbung* (rice barn) style and set on the best beach. The bungalows are less interesting and back from the beach.

Getting There & Away
You can reach Gili Nanggu and Gili Gede by chartered *prahu* (outrigger fishing boat).

The tiny Tawun harbour in Tuan is the main place for chartering boats. A return trip to Gili Nanggu will cost 120,000Rp with a maximum of six people, and takes 30 minutes. A return trip to Gili Gede from Tawun harbour costs costs 250,000Rp and takes one hour, and a return trip to Gili Ringit costs 250,000Rp and takes one hour and 15 minutes.

There's a public boat to Gili Gede and Gili Ringit from Tembowong which costs 4000Rp return. You'll find it by Putri Doyong losmen, 2km north of Pelangan. Alternatively, you can charter boats here for about 40,000Rp.

Gili Nanggu Cottages (see above) does pick-ups from Lembar (70,000Rp one way), for a maximum of eight people.

You can also charter boats from Bola Bola Paradis (see left) hotel and Bangko Bangko on the mainland to Gili Gede, Gili Ringit and Gili Raja for about 200,000Rp.

SENGGIGI
Occupying a series of sweeping bays, with fine beaches all along the coast, Senggigi is the most developed tourist area in Lombok. It has accommodation to suit all budgets, and attractive beachfront restaurants and bars. It feels rather empty in low season but there are lots of accommodation bargains to be had for those seeking creature comforts. In the busier months it's a buzzing place with some lively nightspots. The sunsets over the Lombok strait are spectacular, and as it gets dark the fishing fleet lines up

offshore, its bright lanterns like a floating village against the night sky.

Senggigi is a good base to explore Lombok as the major attractions in the north, west and central areas are within two hours' drive from the beach resort. The airport is easily accessible and the Gilis are a boat ride away.

Orientation

The Senggigi area has hotels spread along Jl Raya Senggigi. Most of the restaurants, shops and other tourist facilities are concentrated on this road, which begins about 6km north of Ampenan. This coastal road continues north, past Mangsit (where there are more hotels) and Teluk Nare (which is a tiny harbour) to a junction about 1km from Bangsal harbour (the port for the Gili islands).

Information

EMERGENCY

The police station is outside the Art Market. Call ☎ 110 in the event of an emergency.

INTERNET ACCESS

Most Internet cafés on the main strip also double as wartel.

Millennium Internet Café (☎ 693860; per min 400Rp; ☺ 9am-11pm)

Planet Internet (per min 400Rp; ☺ 9am-10pm)

MEDICAL SERVICES

The nearest hospitals are in Mataram.

Senggigi Medical Clinic (☎ 693856) Based at the Senggigi Beach Hotel.

MONEY

Money and travellers cheques can be exchanged at most of the big hotels, but it's better to use one of the moneychangers along Jl Raya Senggigi. There are ATMs outside Senggigi Jaya and Senggigi Abadi supermarkets, as well as one at the entrance to Senggigi Square. BCA and BNI banks are both along Jl Raya Senggigi and keep standard opening hours.

Multigraha moneychanger (☎ 693680; ☺ 9am-9pm) Next to Oleh Oleh gift shop, it has the best rates.

POST

Post office (Jl Raya Senggigi) Poste restante should be addressed to Senggigi, Lombok, 83355.

TELEPHONE

The Telkom office is inconveniently positioned northwest of the main shopping area, but there are other wartel along Jl Raya Senggigi, including one in the Indra Photo processing shop.

Sights & Activities

PURA BATU BOLONG

This **temple** (admission by donation; ☺ 7am-6pm) is on a rocky point that juts into the sea about 2km south of central Senggigi. As a Balinese temple, it's oriented towards Gunung Agung, Bali's holiest mountain. The rock underneath the temple has a natural hole that gives it its name – *batu bolong* (literally, 'rock with hole'). There's a good view of Senggigi from the point, and it's a great place to watch the sun set. See Temple Etiquette, p38.

DIVING

Most dive trips from Senggigi go to sites around the Gili islands, and the following dive operators have centres there too.

Blue Marlin (www.diveindo.com) Main Office (☎ 692003, 693719; Jl Raya Senggigi); Holiday Inn (☎ 693719; Jl Raya Senggigi, Mangsit)

Dive Indonesia (☎ 642289; diveindo_senggigi@iname .com; Jl Raya Senggigi)

Dream Divers (☎ 693738, 692047; www.dreamdivers .com; Jl Raya Senggigi)

SNORKELLING

There's reasonable snorkelling off the point in central Senggigi, in the sheltered bay around the headland, and in front of Windy Cottages, a few kilometres north of the town – be careful of the strong currents. Many hotels and restaurants hire out mask-snorkel-fin sets for about 20,000Rp to 25,000Rp per day.

SURF CHARTERS

Dreamweaver (☎ 0812 3808 607; www.dreamweaver -surf.com; 1 week US$795-895, incl food, drink & transfers) has an air-conditioned surf charter boat that goes to sites in Lombok, Sumbawa and Bali. Its office is really based in Bali, but the boat alternates between being based in Lombok and Bali.

MASSAGE & SPAS

Several hotels have spas, including the Sheraton (p281), the Holiday Inn (p281) and the Senggigi Beach Hotel (p281). Nonguests are welcome to enjoy the facilities also.

TENNIS

The Holiday Inn and Sheraton both have tennis courts (around 60,000Rp/1hr including rackets) available to guests and nonguests.

WATERSLIDE

If you have kids, the waterslide at the **Hotel Graha Senggigi** (☎ 693101; www.indo.com/hotels /graha-senggigi; per day adult/child 27,500/20,000Rp) will keep them happy.

Tours

There are a number of travel agencies offering tours on the main strip. Many hotels

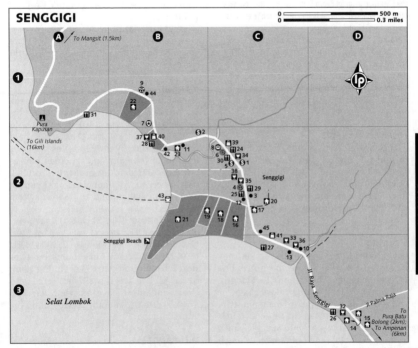

SENGGIGI

0 ─────── 500 m
0 ─────── 0.3 miles

To Mangsit (1.5km)

Pura Kapusan

To Gili Islands (16km)

Senggigi

Senggigi Beach

Selat Lombok

LOMBOK

Jl Raya Senggigi

Jl Palma Raja

To Pura Batu Bolong (2km), To Ampenan (6km)

have their own drivers and can organise tailor-made trips (see p283). Lots of attractions, like the waterfalls in the north or the islands in the southwest, can be seen on day trips.

Recommended agencies:

Anjani (☎ 693587; ✆ 8am-7pm) This agency also runs tours around Lombok with similar prices to Perama.

Bidy Tour (☎ 693333 ext 4005; ✆ 9am-4pm) Based at the Sheraton Senggigi Beach Resort (p281), this company organises an interesting, although pricier, range of tours around Lombok and Sumbawa.

Perama (☎ 693007; www.peramatour.com; 2/3 days 500,000/750,000Rp; ✆ 6am-10pm) A variety of tours around Lombok are offered here, such as a two- or three-day trips around Lombok including Tetebatu, handicraft villages, the 'Perama' Island off the east coast, and Kuta beach. It also offers three-day boat trips from Senggigi to Komodo and Flores (see p347).

Festivals & Events

The Senggigi Festival runs for one week in mid-July and is a great opportunity to see Sasak dance and music. There are stalls offering textiles, pottery and woodcarvings from villages around the island, and daily and nightly performances at the Senggigi Plaza.

Sleeping

If you want to be close to the action, stay in central Senggigi where the hotels line Jl Raya Senggigi. The options in Mangsit, further north, tend to offer more character and style than you'll find on the main strip. Many of the mid-range to top-end hotels here offer free transport into Senggigi and a number of the top-end hotels offer as much as 50% off their published rates in the low season, but ask any time.

BUDGET
Senggigi

Raja's Bungalows (☎ 0812 3770 138; rajas22@yahoo.com; r 60,000Rp) Down a side street, these thatched bungalows set in a flower-filled garden have immaculate rooms with a groovy décor of bright colours and bamboo furniture. The seating areas, filled with cushions and a small library, add to the laid-back atmosphere.

Hotel Elen (☎ 693014; r without/with air-con 40,000/60,000Rp; ✖) Although near the mosque (you'll be woken by calls to prayer of a morning), this budget option is better value

than the cheaper Sonya Homestay. The rooms are clean and bright with shower. Look for the sign by Indra Photo.

Lina Cottages (☎ 693237; r with cold/hot water 75,000/150,000Rp, dishes 10,000-30,000Rp; ✖) Lina's weather-worn air-con rooms are a bit pokey but the larger sea-view rooms are good value. There's an adjoining beachfront Indo-Chinese restaurant. It's also very convenient, as it is the Perama drop-off point.

Sonya Homestay (☎ 693447; s/d 25,000/30,000Rp) Down an alley by the Art Market, this place offers basic rooms with matching no-frills prices.

Mangsit

Santai Beach Inn (Map p281; ☎ 693038; www.santaibeachinn.com; lumbung with separate bathroom 65,000Rp, bungalows with cold water 100,000Rp, with hot water 145,000-160,000Rp, lunch/dinner 12,000/20,000Rp) Set in a lush garden by the beach this place has traditional *lumbung* and spacious bungalows, decorated in an authentic Lombok style. There's a communal eating option in a pleasant pavilion, and an honour system for drinks.

Windy Cottages (Map p281; ☎ 693191; lidya@mataram.wasantara.net.id; cottages with cold/hot water 100,000/140,000Rp, r with hot water 125,000Rp, dishes 12,000-27,000Rp) Windy's has rooms and two-storey bamboo cottages set among palm trees. All are large, well decorated and clean, and most have sea-view terraces. There's also a restaurant serving basic Indonesian fare.

MID-RANGE
Senggigi

Café Wayan (Homestay) (☎ 693098; s/d 100,000/150,000Rp) At the rear of Café Wayan, these four light and airy bungalows are decorated with bamboo furniture and ikat bedspreads. The comfortable verandas look over a blossoming garden. You must ask when you want hot water.

Batu Bolong Cottages (☎ 693065; fax 693198; inland/beachside bungalows 100,000/200,000Rp; ✖) These bungalows are located on both the beach and inland sides of the road. The spacious rooms on the inland side were looking run-down at the time of research, but those with the ocean views are much newer and better value. Most rooms have fridges, hot water and air-con.

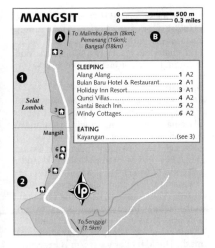

MANGSIT

0 — 500 m
0 — 0.3 miles

To Malimbu Beach (8km);
Pemenang (16km);
Bangsal (18km)

Selat
Lombok

Mangsit

SLEEPING
Alang Alang....................................1 A2
Bulan Baru Hotel & Restaurant..........2 A1
Holiday Inn Resort............................3 A1
Qunci Villas....................................4 A2
Santai Beach Inn.............................5 A2
Windy Cottages...............................6 A2

EATING
Kayangan ....(see 3)

To Senggigi
(1.5km)

Hotel Dharmarie (☎ 693050; www.dharmarievista
.com; garden/sea view 200,000/250,000Rp; ✗) On
the beach, this centrally located place has
smart, spacious, minimalist-style villas with
large French doors opening onto views of
either the sea, or the coconut-tree-studded
lawn. All rooms have air-con and hot water.
Great value.

Mascot Berugaq Elen Cottages (☎ 693365;
garden/sea view 200,000-250,000Rp, dishes 16,000-
25,000Rp; ✗) Next door to Hotel Dharmarie,
Mascot also has large bungalows with good
amenities but the rooms lack character
and the décor is a bit tacky. There's a
restaurant with a varied menu overlooking
the beach.

Mangsit
Bulan Baru (New Moon Hotel; Map p281; ☎ 693786;
http://groups.msn.comlombokbulanbaruhotel; s/d 120,000/
150,000Rp, honeymoon ste 200,000Rp; ✗ ✦) Just
north of Mangsit, this great-value hotel
run by an Australian couple has spacious,
well-furnished rooms that are adorned with
fresh flowers every day, and have minibars,
air-con and hot water. The open-air bathrooms have been painted in different themes,
and the terraces overlook a swimming pool
and a flourishing garden.

TOP END
Senggigi
Senggigi Beach Hotel (☎ 693210; http://senggigi
beach.aerowisata.com; garden r US$80, beach bungalows
US$100-160; ✗ ✦) Located on the headland,
this hotel has sea aspects all around. The
tastefully decorated rooms are set in a lush
garden and have all the mod cons. There's a
Mandara spa, tennis courts and a relatively
small swimming pool.

Pool Villa Club (☎ 693210; www.indo.com/hotels
/poolvillaclub; villas US$380; ✗ ✦) Ideal for
honeymooners, this small cluster of luxury
two-storey villas features huge bedrooms
and lounge and dining areas, all impeccably
decorated in natural colours. There are
sweeping balcony views upstairs, and the
very private downstairs terraces lead directly
into the canal-style pool.

Sheraton Senggigi Beach Resort (☎ 693333;
www.sheraton.com/senggigi; r US$170-999; ✦) This
huge hotel has a labyrinth of corridors
leading to comfortably furnished rooms
with all the facilities you'd expect of a five-
star hotel. There's an elaborate pool with a
slide fashioned in the shape of a head, a spa,
and a children's playground.

Mangsit
Alang Alang (Map p281; ☎ 693518; hotel@alang-alang
-villas.com; r US$90-110, villa low/high season US$250/600,
mains 36,000-72,000Rp; ✗ ✦) One of the most
charming hotels in Senggigi, this place
has gorgeously decorated bungalows
with Lombok-style furniture, and open-
air bathrooms. They are set in a jungly,
winding garden leading to a pool and
restaurant right on the cove beach. There's
also a stunning villa with two bedrooms, a
lounge, kitchen, and private pool.

Qunci Villas (Map p281; ☎ 693800; www.quncivillas
.com; r garden/ocean view US$75/90; ✗ ✦) A
favourite of hip Jakartans and young expats,
this boutique hotel set on Mangsit beach is
all contemporary design, sleek lines, and
luxe Lombok touches. The minimalist-
style rooms are contrasted with open-air
bathrooms filled with foliage, and the small
infinity pool looks out to sea.

Holiday Inn Resort (Map p281; ☎ 693444; www
.bluebirdgroup.com/holiday; r US$80-120, bungalows
US$140-250, apt US$180; ✗ ✦) With Lombok-
style architecture, helpful staff, and a
multitude of facilities, this impressive hotel
stands out. The rooms and bungalows are
well equipped and stylishly decorated. The
canal pool, spa, tennis courts, dive shop
and beach dining (see p282) add to the
attractions. The apartments are great for
families.

Eating

Some restaurants provide free transport for diners, so it might be worth phoning ahead if you are staying a little way out.

For inexpensive eating, try the warung on the hill (past the Sheraton and on the way to Mangsit). The views from here over the bay are stunning, particularly at sunset. For self-caterers, there are two small supermarkets – **Senggigi Abadi** and **Senggigi Jaya**.

South of Senggigi

Café Wayan & Bakery (☎ 693098; dishes 8500-45,000Rp) Run by the same good folk that operate in Bali, the menu here is diverse, but the main draw are the freshly baked breads and cakes, as well as the pasta dishes – the tagliatelle is home-made.

Café Alberto (☎ 693313; dishes 30,000-85,000Rp, lobster 18,000Rp/100gms, pizzas 35,000-46,000Rp) On the beach, this restaurant serves seafood and pizzas after 6pm, as well as Indo-Chinese fare. Occasionally Lombok music and dance performances are held here.

Senggigi

Bumbu (☎ 692236; bumbu_café@yahoo.com; mains 17,000-28,000Rp) One of the most popular restaurants on the main strip, this tiny place serves superb Thai dishes like tasty red, green and yellow curries, as well as other options like seafood platters.

Asmara (☎ 693619; www.asmara-group.com; mains 22,000-75,000Rp) This large and airy two-storey thatched building has a relaxed ambience, and is one of the most well-regarded restaurants in Senggigi. There's a good selection of European food, as well as some Lombok specialities.

Happy Café (☎ 693984; mains 17,500-40,000Rp; ☺ 4pm-1am) This café does grilled fish, steaks and pizza well, and turns into a lively night spot later in the evening (see right).

Papaya Café (☎ 693616; mains 20,000-60,000Rp) Funkily decorated with tribal art, this café specialises in great seafood dishes, as well as Chinese food and the usual Western offerings. Dishes come in small, medium or large portions.

Lotus Restaurant (☎ 693758; mains 21,000-50,000Rp) At the back of the Art Market facing the beach, this colourful restaurant has an international menu that's consistently good. After dinner, pop next door to the popular Office bar (see right) for a drink.

Sate House Suharti (☎ 693148; mains 5000-21,000Rp) Opposite Asmara, this simple restaurant with a few wooden tables and chairs serves tasty Indonesian food, including satay, at inexpensive prices.

Mangsit

Bulan Baru (Map p281; ☎ 693786; mains 24,000-48,000Rp) Just north of Mangsit, this friendly place has a great menu ranging from meaty bangers and creamy mash to delicate fish dishes and well-executed Indonesian favourites. They also offer imported steaks and a selection of wines – well worth the trip.

Kayangan (Map p281; ☎ 693444; mains 40,000-90,000Rp) This romantic beachside restaurant at the Holiday Inn has delicious, and reasonably priced, dishes. Try the rack of lamb with thyme jus or succulent pan-fried salmon with mash. The Mars Bar ice cream is heavenly.

Drinking

Senggigi has really the only nightlife on Lombok, apart from a little on Gili Trawangan. It's pretty low-key apart from Friday and Saturday nights. Early in the evening most people gather at bars like Happy Café or Papaya before moving on to the Marina club for late-night revelling.

Happy Café (☎ 693984) On the main strip, this was the liveliest place at the time of writing. The nightly cover band has bongos and a violin, making it a bit more unusual.

Papaya Café (☎ 693616) Opposite Happy Café, this larger place with a funkier décor also has live bands every night. There's 30% off drinks between 4pm and 8pm.

Office (☎ 693162) Behind the Art Market, this is another popular gathering place. Take advantage of its lovely spot on the beach overlooking colourful boats, and, on Saturdays, the afternoon happy hours until sunset.

Beach Club (☎ 693637; Jl Raya Senggigi) Just south of the main strip, this open, airy place with tables on the beach, a pool table and a pretty fish pond is popular with expats.

Sugar (☎ 0812 3962 206; Senggigi Plaza) This stylish place down a side street in Senggigi Plaza is the nearest you'll get to a gay bar.

Café Berry (☎ 693524; Jl Raya Senggigi) There's a transvestite cabaret here every Saturday night, and the flamboyant owner always keeps things entertaining.

Marina (☎ 693136; Jl Raya Senggigi; admission 10,000Rp; ☺ 4pm-2am) This Hard Rock Café clone serves up American snacks and live music, and has enthusiastic staff. It's the liveliest place after hours on a Friday or Saturday night.

Club Tropicana (☎ 693432; Jl Raya Senggigi; admission 25,000Rp; ☺ 11am-2am) The club in this huge Mediterranean-style building dominating the main street is popular with revellers from Mataram.

Shopping

Although the **Pasar Seni** (Art Market) was partially destroyed by fire in 2002, it's slowly reopening and has some handicraft stalls.

There are souvenir shops along the main strip. The ones selling the most unusual trinkets are **Asmara Shop** (☺ 9am-9.30pm), in front of the restaurant of the same name, and **Pamour Art Gallery** (☺ 8am-7pm), which also has some furniture.

The new shopping mall, **Galleria** (☺ 8am-7pm), is woefully under-occupied.

For a range of furniture and crafts at lower prices than in Senggigi, browse through the shops along the main road to Ampenan.

Getting There & Away
BEMO
Regular bemos travel between the Kebon Roek terminal in Ampenan and Senggigi/ Mangsit for 2000/2500Rp, usually continuing north as far as Pemenang (for Bangsal harbour). There are no bemos direct from Cakra or Mataram. After 6pm, *ojek* (motorcycles that carry paying pillion passengers) can take you from Kebon Roek terminal in Ampenan to Senggigi for 3000Rp. Don't be surprised if you are over-charged a little on any bemo going to or from Senggigi.

SHUTTLE BUS/BOAT
Perama (☎ 693007; www.peramatour.com; ☺ 6am-10pm) has daily bus connections between Senggigi and the main tourist centres on Lombok, such as Mataram (25,000Rp), Tetebatu and Kuta (both 60,000Rp), as well as bus/ferry connections to various destinations in Bali.

Perama has a new boat service going directly from Senggigi beach to Padangbai in Bali, depending on weather conditions. Departing Padangbai at 9am and Senggigi

at 1pm, it takes four hours and costs 100,000Rp. Bus transfers from Padangbai can be bought in conjunction with the boat transfer (10,000Rp to Candidasa, 30,000Rp to Kuta, Sanur, the airport or Ubud), as can boat transfers to the Gilis from Senggigi (50,000Rp). Perama also runs a shuttle service from Senggigi (including the ferry ticket) to Sumbawa Besar, Dompu or Sape.

With its small office beside the Art Market, **Anjani** (☎ 693587; ☺ 8am-7pm) runs similar bus shuttle services to Perama.

To the Gili Islands
Perama operates small boats from Senggigi directly to the Gili islands. The 1½-hour ride costs 50,000Rp, and runs Tuesday to Sunday at 9am and 1pm, and Monday at 3pm. Boats only go if there's a minimum of four people and if the sea conditions are fine. If the boat is not running, Perama operates shuttle buses to Bangsal harbour for 25,000Rp. From there, you have to purchase your own boat ticket to the islands.

On the flip side, Perama isn't allowed to run boats directly from the Gili islands to Senggigi, though it can provide 'through' tickets on this route using a boat to Bangsal and a bus to Senggigi. Inclusive prices are: Gili Air 35,000Rp; Gili Meno 36,000Rp; and Gili Trawangan 37,000Rp.

Bounty Cruises (☎ 643636, 649090; www.bali bountygroup.com) has a limited catamaran service from Teluk Nare harbour – just north of Senggigi – to Gili Meno. Passengers are taken by bus to the harbour from Senggigi. Tickets can be bought at travel agencies.

Blue Marlin (☎ 692003, 693719) and **Dream Divers** (☎ 693738, 692047) also do customer bus and boat transfers from their Senggigi offices (via Teluk Nare) to the Gili islands, and vice versa.

Getting Around
Coming from Ampenan and sometimes going as far as Pemenang, bemos regularly ply up and down Jl Raya Senggigi.

There are plenty of taxis in Senggigi looking for customers. The light-blue Blue Bird or Lombok Taksi are reliable and use their meters. If you do need to call a taxi ring **Lombok Taksi** (☎ 627000). A prepaid taxi from the airport to Senggigi/Mangsit costs 30,000/40,000Rp.

LOMBOK

You can arrange charter vehicles through hotels and travel agencies or negotiate directly with a driver on the street (there are always loads shouting 'transport!').

Bulan Baru (Map p281; ☎ 693786; http://groups.msn .com/lombokbulanbaruhotel) This hotel has excellent English-speaking drivers who know a lot about Sasak culture. They charge from 250,000Rp to 300,000Rp a day depending on the trip.

Cinta Lombok Lestari (CLL; ☎ 693561; fax 693562; ⌚ 9am-4pm) Almost opposite the Sheraton, this is a reputable firm that offers better rates for motorbike and car hire than Trac.

Perama (☎ 693007; www.peramatour.com; ⌚ 6am-10pm) This tour and shuttle bus company charges 350,000Rp a day for car and driver (maximum three people).

Trac Astra Rent-a-Car (☎ 693333 ext 1037; www .trac.astra.co.id; Kijang with driver per 6hr 385,000Rp, self-drive per day 385,000Rp; ⌚ 9am-5pm) Based at the Sheraton (p281), Trac Astra has well-maintained cars, but expect expensive rates.

GILI ISLANDS

☎ 0370

Off the northwest coast of Lombok are three small, coral-fringed islands – Gili Air, Gili Meno and Gili Trawangan. Collectively known as the Gili Islands, and each with its own character, they all have superb, white sandy beaches, clear water, brilliantly coloured fish and accessible snorkelling and diving.

The islands are *the* place to be for young travellers in Lombok, who come for the simple pleasures of sun, scuba diving and socialising. Delightfully free of cars and motorcycles, the only traffic on the Gilis is the tinkling *cidomo* (pony cart with wheels) and the occasional bicycle. Hawkers are around, but even they don't hassle you as much as in other parts of Lombok.

Standard accommodation on the Gilis is usually a plain little bamboo bungalow on stilts, with a thatched roof, a small veranda out the front and a bathroom at the back. Inside, there will be one or two beds with mosquito nets. Smarter options with air-con and swimming pools are popping up on all three islands. The accommodation prices quoted here are high-season prices – early July to mid-September and mid-December to early January – but expect to pay around a third off that in quieter periods.

Information

INTERNET & TELEPHONE

There are wartel and Internet cafés on all three islands. Internet access is around 400Rp per minute but the connections are infuriatingly slow.

MONEY

There are no banks on the Gilis and money-changer exchange rates at the shops and hotels are woeful. Credit-card cash advances are available through many dive operators, although a 7% commission is generally charged. It's better to change money in Mataram or Senggigi or use the ATMs there. Try to bring as many small-denomination notes as possible, as there's often a problem with changing the bigger notes.

Dangers & Annoyances

There are no police on any of the Gilis, so report any theft to the island *kepala desa* (village head), or, if you are on Gili Trawangan, notify Satgas, the community organisation that runs island affairs (you can ask for them at the *kepala desa* office or Manta Dive). Satgas uses its community contacts to resolve problems or track down stolen property with a minimum of fuss. If there's no response, go to a police station on the mainland.

Touts often meet boats as they land, and they can be quick to take your luggage, plus you, to the place of *their* choice. If you want to stay in a particular place, don't let a tout convince you that it's full, expensive or closed, or doesn't exist.

Several foreign women have experienced sexual harassment or even assault by Indonesian and foreign men while on Gili Trawangan. Always try to stay in pairs if walking back to quieter parts of the island.

On the beach, jellyfish are common when strong winds blow from the mainland; be careful, as they can leave a painful rash.

Getting There & Away

It's possible to reach the Gilis using a combination of bus and boat from Mataram and Senggigi, but many travellers coming from Bali end up using the Perama service for the sake of convenience. There's also a luxury catamaran linking Benoa in Bali and Gili Meno.

LOMBOK

DIVING & SNORKELLING IN THE GILI ISLANDS

The Gili Islands are a favourite haunt for divers of all levels, with varied terrain and an abundance of marine life – turtles and seasonal manta rays can be seen at most dive sites. The water depth is 6m to 27m. The visibility for divers and snorkellers is fair to good, and is best in the dry season (June to September). The coral is not what it used to be since El Niño warmed up the waters here, bleaching everything, but there are still good heads below 20m.

Before El Niño, fish bombing and the careless use of anchors resulted in the damage of coral reefs. This has now been stamped out around the Gilis, but unfortunately many visitors are unwittingly causing more damage by standing and walking on the reefs while snorkelling or boating. Perfectly formed corals are easily broken and take years to recover; reef ecology is very sensitive.

The Gili Eco Trust, established as a partnership between dive operators and the local community, is working to preserve the variety of aquatic life and to protect and encourage the regrowth of the reefs. This is being achieved with the introduction of no-fishing zones and a patrol boat checking that banned fishing techniques stay that way. Other projects include improving the waste disposal and recycling facilities of the islands. All divers help fund the trust by paying a one-off fee of 30,000Rp with their first dive.

All dive operators are very professional on the Gilis, and safety standards are as good as anywhere in the world. The Gilis are the most popular place in Indonesia to become a certified diver, as the dive sites are easily accessible and safe (rip currents are rare). A range of Professional Association of Diving Instructors (PADI) courses are on offer, including Introduction to Scuba Diving (US$50; four hours), Open Water (US$275; four days), and Dive Master (US$500; four weeks). Dives cost US$30 for the first dive, US$45 for two, and US$67 for three. Whether you are based on Air, Meno, Trawangan or in Senggigi you'll be diving the same sites around the islands and most operators have adhered to a pricing agreement, so charges are the same all over.

Recommended operators:

- **Blue Marlin Dive Centre** (p288) This sociable and extremely professional lot has the longest-running dive centre on Trawangan (plus centres on Air and Meno and an office in Senggigi). It certifies divers galore, and specialises in technical diving. It also offers a wreck dive of a WWII Japanese patrol boat and live-aboard trips to other Nusa Tenggara islands.

- **Dream Divers** (p288) This German-run outfit with centres on Trawangan and Air (and an office in Senggigi) is popular with organised groups. Apart from running courses and fun dives it also offers diving sites in south Lombok for advanced divers.

- **Manta Dive** (p294) Between them, the instructors in this English company on Trawangan can speak Dutch, German, English, Swedish and French! They have a well-known local guide and do a lot of business in fun dives and PADI open-water courses.

- **Big Bubble** (p294) This smaller and highly regarded operation on Trawangan is run by an English woman who is very involved in the Eco Trust.

- **Dive Indonesia** (p294) On Trawangan (with an office in Senggigi), this Indonesian-run operator is good for fun dives, but instructors are not always available.

- **Villa Ombak Diving Academy** (p294) The newcomer to the scene, this dive academy located in the luxe Hotel Villa Ombak in Trawangan has already gained a good reputation.

- **Reefseekers Dive Centre & Turtle Nursery** (p288) Based in Gili Air, this small diving company also has a centre on Flores. You will learn a lot about marine life when diving with these guys. They are committed to marine conservation and help protect turtles.

For more ideas on diving in this area, check out Lonely Planet's *Diving & Snorkeling Bali & Lombok* by Tim Rock.

LOMBOK

Most boats to the Gilis leave from Bangsal harbour, north of Senggigi, but some private transfers leave from Teluk Nare (see right). Although plans are afoot to improve Bangsal, it's currently a real headache, full of pushy touts, sellers and porters. See Surviving Bangsal (p287).

BUS/BEMO/TAXI TO BANGSAL

From Mandalika terminal (Mataram) there are buses to the main road in Pemenang, from where it's a 1km walk or a 3000Rp *cidomo* ride to Bangsal harbour.

If you take a bemo, taxi or shuttle bus, the vehicle will stop at the bemo stop/parking area, from where it's a 400m walk or a 2000Rp *cidomo* ride to the harbour. From Rembiga (east of the airport) there's a direct bemo to Pemenang (3000Rp). Alternatively, from Kebon Roek terminal in Ampenan take a bemo to Senggigi (2000Rp), then charter a bemo to Pemenang (approx 30,000Rp). A metered taxi from Senggigi to Pemenang is around 40,000Rp.

BOAT

Small local boats with bamboo outriggers ferry people and supplies to the islands from the beach at Bangsal – be ready to wade out with your luggage (anyone who helps with your stuff will expect to be paid). Sometimes the weather can be rough and passengers and luggage can get soaked.

The Koperasi Angkutan Laut (Sea Transport Cooperative) is the boat owners' cartel, which monopolises public transport between Bangsal and the islands. Buy tickets for its public, shuttle or charter boats only at the prominent white building on the beach. Boat fare price lists are given out if asked.

Charters

A chartered boat costs 68,000Rp to Gili Air, 78,000Rp to Gili Meno and 88,000Rp to Gili Trawangan. Boats can be chartered from 8am to 6pm. If the ticket office is closed go

STRONG CURRENTS

Be aware that the waters surrounding the Gilis are subject to strong currents. Do not attempt to swim or snorkel between the islands – travellers have drowned doing so.

directly to the boats and negotiate with the captains. Expect to pay an extra 20,000Rp if you go through a tout.

Public Boats

The one-way fare is 3500Rp to Gili Air, 4000Rp to Gili Meno and 4500Rp to Gili Trawangan. Boats leave when they're full (about 20 people) – it's best to arrive early. Public boats run from 8am to 4pm.

Shuttle Boats

There's a shuttle boat that goes at 4.30pm to Gili Air (11,000Rp), Gili Meno (12,000Rp) and Gili Trawangan (13,000Rp) from Bangsal. From Gili Air (10,000Rp) and Gili Trawangan (12,000Rp) there's a shuttle boat to the mainland, via Gili Meno, at 8.30am every morning.

TOURIST SHUTTLE BUS & BOAT

Perama (☎ 693007; www.peramatour.com; ⓨ 6am-10pm) operates boats from Senggigi directly to the Gili islands or shuttle buses to Bangsal (see p283).

The fast, modern **Bounty Cruises** (☎ 0361 726666 in Bali, ☎ 643636 or 649090 in Lombok; www .balibountygroup.com; one way US$40-45) boats link Benoa in Bali with Gili Meno (the terminus is at Bounty Beach Bungalows). They tend to go only in high season so check schedules, and diving customers are the priority. Tickets can be bought from travel agencies. **Blue Marlin Dive Centre** (☎ 692003, 693719), and **Dream Divers** (☎ 693738, 692047) do boat transfers from the Gili islands to Senggigi and vice versa. **Manta Dive** (☎ 643649) and **Villa Ombak** (☎ 638531, 642336) on Gili Trawangan also offer transfers. All charge around 100,000Rp per person.

Getting Around

BOAT

The Koperasi runs a convenient shuttle-boat service between the islands, so you can stay on one island and explore the others. The schedule does not allow you to visit two other islands in one day. The boats do two runs a day, departing from Gili Air at 8.30am and 3pm and Gili Trawangan at 9.30am and 4pm, both calling at Gili Meno. Prices for one-way tickets are 12,000Rp for the morning boats and 15,000Rp for the afternoon ones.

The Koperasi also offers boat charters between islands from 8am to 6pm. Prices

---

SURVIVING BANGSAL

Bangsal is notorious for rip-offs and hassles, the worst possible introduction to the serenity of the Gili islands. Unfortunately for most backpackers, it's the gateway to Air, Meno and Trawangan.

On the small road to the harbour lined with small restaurants and agencies, touts push extremely overpriced tickets onto visitors, declaring that it's necessary to buy return tickets back to Bangsal (and even Bali) otherwise you'll get stuck on the islands. This is completely untrue – tickets to Bangsal, as well as destinations in Lombok, Bali, Sumbawa and even Flores, are widely available on the islands. Avoid engaging with these touts as it can be difficult to get away from the scene. Quite a few travellers have been shaken by the aggression of some touts.

The best way to deal with it is to walk – or take a *cidomo* (pony cart with wheels) for 2000Rp – straight to the prominent white building on the beach. This is the Koperasi harbour office, where you can buy inexpensive, fixed-price, public boat tickets (as well as shuttle and charter tickets) to the three Gili islands – there are printed price lists available. The harbour office has a waiting area, where they announce when the public boats have enough passengers to depart.

Be aware of porters who may grab bags and ask for crazy prices. If you do need help getting your luggage onto the boat, negotiate with the porter before they pick up your bag – the normal price is 1000Rp to 2000Rp a bag.

It's also worth noting that, despite what sellers might tell you, anything being sold at Bangsal can also be bought in the Gilis, usually at a cheaper price.

Leaving Bangsal is generally easier. If you don't already have transport arranged, head straight down the road to Pemenang, where transport prices are cheaper.

There have been reports from travellers who bought shuttle-service tickets from Bali through to the Gilis and were then pressured into buying return tickets in Mataram by the shuttle company, which maintained they'd be stuck on the islands if they didn't. When readers have bought a return ticket they've often found that the prepaid ticket is invalid on the way back. One way to avoid this is to go with a reputable company like Perama (p280) or just buy a single ticket.

If you get stuck overnight in Bangsal, **Taman Sari Homestay** (☎ 626295; s/d 30,000/50,000Rp) opposite the parking area has basic rooms.

---

start at 80,000Rp for a one-way ticket – check the fixed prices at the Koperasi huts by the harbours on each island.

CIDOMO
Cidomo tend to cluster at the harbour on all three islands; otherwise, hail them as they trot along. They cost a negotiable 5000Rp per person for short trips.

WALKING & CYCLING
The main mode of transport on the islands is walking. A torch (flashlight) is useful at night – they can be bought at local shops for around 25,000Rp.

Cycling around the islands is popular, but sandy tracks make the going tough. Gili Trawangan offers the best possibilities. Bicycles are available to hire from Ozzy's Shop (p288) or Yon's Bookshop (p291) in Gili Air and at the harbour at Trawangan for around 15,000Rp per day.

GILI AIR
Closest to the mainland and with the largest local population (around 1600), Gili Air's coconut grove–filled, flat landscape is juxtaposed with dramatic views of Gunung Rinjani and, on a clear day, Gunung Agung in Bali. The white-sand beaches, clear turquoise water and laid-back atmosphere have been a draw for many a traveller – most end up staying for weeks rather than the intended few days. In recent years new lively bars have made partying an option, but the tranquil, rural character that Gili Air has always been known for is still very much there.

Orientation & Information
It's surprisingly easy to become disoriented on the network of tracks crisscrossing the island and through the village. The simplest option is to follow the coastal path around the island – it's a lovely walk that

LOMBOK

AVOIDING OFFENCE

The Gili islanders are Muslims, and visitors should respect their cultural beliefs. In particular, topless sunbathing is offensive to them – some local children are no longer allowed to go to the beach because tourists there are indecently dressed. Away from the beach it's even more important to dress modestly, especially in the *kampung* (village) where locals live, and in the vicinity of the mosques. Many visitors are insensitive to local customs, and walk around the island in skimpy clothing. The behaviour is so common that you may get the impression that the local people don't mind – they do.

---

takes about an hour. Most accommodation and restaurants are situated on the east coast: head here if you want to do some socialising, but it's best to head west if you want seclusion.

There are beaches around most of the island, but some are not suitable for swimming because they're quite shallow and have sharp coral below. The beach with the largest stretch of sand, and the best place to swim, is in front of Dream Divers on the east coast. The northeast also has good beaches but the ones on the west side are virtually nonexistent.

Boats stop at the southern end of the island, near the jetty. The **Koperasi** (8am-5.30pm) has a hut next to the jetty with the prices marked clearly outside. There's a small **Perama** (☎ 637816) office next to the Gili Indah Hotel.

Make sure you've always got fresh water; refill your water bottle for 2000Rp at Blue Marlin Dive Centre (right), Dream Divers (right), Coconut Cottages (p289) and Ozzy's Shop (below).

INTERNET ACCESS & TELEPHONE
Candung (per min 400Rp; 8am-9pm) There's also a wartel here.
Gili Indah Hotel (☎ 637328; per min 600Rp)
Hotel Gili Air (☎ 634435; www.hotelgiliair.com; per min 830Rp)
Ozzy's Shop (☎ 622179; per min 400Rp; 8am-8pm) Very slow Internet access is available here, as well as a wartel.

MONEY
Although there are moneychangers at Ozzy's Shop, Hotel Gili Air and Gili Indah Hotel, the exchange rates are poor. It's better to change or withdraw money on the mainland.

MEDICAL SERVICES
There's a clinic in the village but the nurse isn't always there.

Activities
SNORKELLING & BOAT TRIPS
The best snorkelling is off the eastern and northern sides of the island – try just north of Dream Divers. Snorkelling gear can be hired from Ozzy's Shop (left) and Yon's Bookshop (p291) for 15,000Rp a day. Ask boatmen or dive centres about currents where you want to snorkel, as sometimes they can be extremely strong.

Ozzy's Shop also operates glass-bottomed boat tours around all three islands between 9.30am and 3pm. Tours cost 40,000Rp per person with a minimum of four, and include snorkelling gear.

DIVING
There's excellent scuba diving within a short boat ride. See Diving & Snorkelling in the Gili Islands on p285 for more information.
Blue Marlin Dive Centre (☎ 634387; www.diveindo.com)
Dream Divers (☎ 634547; www.dreamdivers.com)
Reefseekers Dive Centre & Turtle Nursery (☎ 641008; www.reefseekers.net)

Sleeping
Most places to stay are located along the east coast, with others dotted around the rest of the island. Prices quoted are high-season rates – expect about a third off in low season. Breakfast is included in all of the hotels listed.

BUDGET
Sunrise Cottages & Restaurant (☎ 642370; s 50,000-75,000Rp, d 80,000-100,000Rp) This place has charming two-storey *lumbung*-style bungalows with bathroom and chill-out area (day bed and hammock) on the lower floor, and well-furnished bedrooms on the upper floor. Some rooms are big enough for families.

Abdi Fantastik (☎ 636421; r 75,000-80,000Rp) Facing the beach, these pleasant – rather

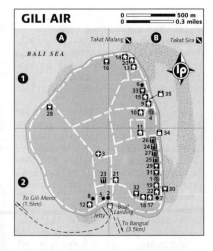

than 'Fantastik' – thatched bungalows come with hammocks. They are run by a friendly family, and have *buruga* (thatched platforms on stilts) on the beach where you can eat your breakfast, and later in the day, their delicious Sasak dishes (p290).

Gili Air Santay (☎ 641022; giliair_santay@yahoo .com; r 50,000-100,000Rp; dishes 8000-35,000Rp) This place offers two types of good-sized bungalows, situated back from the beach. They have a touch more comfort than the usual bamboo huts, with some furniture and modern bathrooms. The balconies face a coconut grove and garden of red hibiscus. The beachfront restaurant is a nice spot to contemplate Gunung Rinjani.

Pino Cottages (☎ 639304; r 60,000-70,000Rp) Situated back from the beach in a rather plain garden, Pino is well-maintained and clean thatched cottages with hammocks.

Gusung Indah (☎ 0812 3789 054; r 100,000Rp) Further north and facing a good stretch of beach, Gusung Indah is good value with its smart wooden bungalows and sizable terraces.

Pondok Sandi (s/d 50,000/100,000Rp) Next door to Gusung Indah and also facing the beach, Pondok Sandi has large bungalows with modern bathrooms.

Other recommendations:

Resota Bungalows (s 30,000-50,000Rp, d 50,000-80,000Rp) Behind the harbour, it has basic rooms with sea views and hammocks.

Nusa Tiga Bungalows (r 40,000-50,000Rp) Basic bamboo bungalows set in a coconut grove, inland from the east coast.

Mawar Cottages (s/d 35,000/40,000Rp) Like Nusa Tiga Bungalows, this place is set in a coconut grove.

Legend Pub & Bungalows (r 40,000-50,000Rp) Home to the island's liveliest 'party' every Wednesday night (☾ 10pm-2am), its bungalows are spot-on for partygoers who don't want to stagger far to bed.

MID-RANGE

Coconut Cottages (☎ 635365; www.coconuts-giliair .com; r 80,000-150,000Rp) With its labyrinth garden filled with hibiscus and frangipani, and its quiet location nestled in a coconut grove, this place has a real sense of retreat, yet it's not far from the most popular bars and restaurants. The four types of cottages available range from comfortable bamboo huts to large, well-equipped bungalows with Lombok styling and hot water. The restaurant up front can be a good social spot (see p290).

Kira Kira (☎ 641021; kirakira@mataram.wasantara .net.id; s 65,000-120,000Rp, d 80,000-130,000Rp, dishes 8000-30,000Rp) Fifty metres inland on the east coast, Kira Kira's stylish cottages have rattan furniture, large ceiling fans, huge beds and hammocks, which overlook a small garden with winding paths. The extra rupiah affords hot water. The **restaurant** (☯ 7am-9pm) offers Japanese dishes like tempura.

Hotel Gili Air (☎ 634435; www.hotelgiliair.com; r US$17, with hot water US$33, with hot water & TV US$43-63; ☒ ☒) The most comfortable option on Gili Air, these smart cottages with open-air bathrooms are set in a neat garden facing a good beach and a swimming pool – the only one on the island. The less-expensive rooms are better value with their sea and pool aspects and larger terraces. Don't pet the hotel's *cidomo* horse – it has bitten guests before.

Gili Indah Hotel (☎ 637328; www.mataram.wasan tara.net.id/gili; s/d 140,000/150,000Rp, with hot water 190,000/200,000Rp; ☒) By the harbour, this hotel features a variety of bungalows with large terraces set in a pleasant garden facing the beach. It's a bit out of the action, which may be a blessing in high season, but it feels very cut off in quiet periods.

Eating

The coast is lined with picturesque, simple, beachfront restaurants with views of either Lombok's Gunung Rinjani or Bali's Gunung Agung (on a clear day), or both if you're lucky. Inexpensive Western, Indonesian and Chinese food is served, as well as fresh fish. Be prepared to wait though – service can be pretty slow.

Munchies (dishes 6000-25,000Rp; ☯ noon-11pm) This great little restaurant with bamboo tables and chairs on the beach does the best curries on the island, as well as overflowing sandwiches and grilled fresh fish.

Abdi Fantastik (☎ 636421; dishes 8000-25,000Rp) This simple place on the beachfront serves the best Sasak food on the island. Try the *ayam gafe* (a chicken dish with a rich coconut and chilli sauce) and *kangkung pelecing* (spicy water spinach – which local lore says is good for insomniacs!).

Hotel Gili Air (☎ 634435; dishes 15,000-54,000Rp) The best pizzas on the island are found here, as well as a good selection of Indonesian dishes, pastas and steaks. Sneak into one of the *buruga* on the beach to watch the sunset,

and order the very cheap beer at **happy hour** (☯ 5.30-6.30pm; large Bintang beer 10,000Rp).

Coconut Cottages (☎ 635365; dishes 8000-24,000Rp, Wed buffet per person 40,000Rp) This hotel restaurant is in a shady garden set back from the beach. There's a fantastic Sasak buffet here every Wednesday night in high season.

Han's Café (dishes 14,000-35,000Rp, pizzas 25,000-35,000Rp; ☯ happy hour 5-8pm) In a picturesque beachside position, this place focuses more on Western dishes – its pizzas are raved about. Being next to the popular Chill Out Bar makes it a lively spot, and the happy hour(s) applies to pizzas as well as drinks.

Gecko Café (☎ 641014; dishes 10,000-25,000Rp Mon-Tue & Thu-Sun, Wed dinner 35,000Rp) Behind the harbour, Dee and Majid's Wednesday night meals – such as shepherd's pie and apple crumble or roast dinners and banoffi pie – are an institution for long-termers. Telephone or drop in the day before to book a place. The rest of the time the café offers mainly Indonesian favourites.

Next door to each other, **Gili Air Simple** (dishes 7000-30,000Rp; ☯ noon-11pm) and **Wiwin Café** (dishes 7000-30,000Rp; ☯ noon-11pm) both display a variety of fresh fish every night, which is served on low tables in beachfront *buruga*.

Drinking

Gili Air doesn't pull people in for its nightlife – head to Trawangan for that. If you do want to have a night out you'll easily find surprisingly lively pockets on this usually tranquil island.

BARS

In the places listed below, drinks cost from around 15,000Rp for a large Bintang beer to 35,000Rp for a cocktail.

Chill Out Bar (☯ 11-2am) At the time of writing, this was the most popular place to gather for drinks. A good selection of spirits and cocktails, as well as the ubiquitous Bintang beer, is served from a simple square bar on the beach, accompanied by mainly ambient music.

Corner Bar (☯ 11-2am) The other hip place of the moment, it has *buruga* on the beach. Consequently, it attracts daytime sunbathers/drinkers with many carrying on into the night.

Gita Gili (☯ 11-2am) Nearby, this friendly bar is set slightly back from the beach.

Star Bar (🕐 3pm-late Thu-Tue) Next to the Blue Marlin Dive Centre, this turns into an animated spot by night and stays open until the last person leaves.

Bargus (🕐 3pm-midnight) This out-of-the-way bar in the west of the island is great for sipping a drink or two and watching the sun set.

PARTIES

Legend Pub (🕐 10pm-2am Wed, happy hour 5-7pm) Located in the north, this has been the one place consistently trying to bring the party to Gili Air, but it only gets going in the summer months. The music is mostly reggae.

Go Go Pub (🕐 10.30pm-2am Sat) Just behind the harbour, this place plays dance music with some live bands in high season (it even has a disco ball!). Again, this only gets going in busy periods.

Shopping

Hany Shop and Oleh Oleh sell sarongs, surfing shorts and dresses. A few small shops dotted along the east coast sell basic supplies like soap, shampoo and torches. **Yon's Bookshop** (🕐 8am-7pm) sells and exchanges books, as does Coconut Cottages (p289) and Hany Shop.

GILI MENO

Gili Meno, the middle island, has the smallest permanent population of around 300. It has the best beaches of the three Gilis, is the quietest island, and has the fewest tourists. Most of the accommodation is on the eastern side, near the widest and most picturesque beach. Inland you'll find scattered houses, coconut plantations and a shallow lake that produces salt in the dry season.

Information

Most places now have electricity running from at least 5pm to 7am. There's also more fresh water available on the island since a water tank has been built.

There are a couple of minimarkets on the island, so you will be able to locate most basic supplies.

INTERNET ACCESS & TELEPHONE

Internet access (per min 750Rp) Internet access and a wartel are available near the boat landing.

MEDICAL SERVICES

Medical Clinic (thegilimenoclinic@hotmail.com) Funded by donations and in conjunction with the Lombok health authority. Near the Taman Burung Bird Park in the village there's a resident nurse, and a doctor who comes in once a week or is on call from Mataram.

MONEY

Money can be exchanged at hotels like Gazebo Meno, Kontiki and Bounty Beach, but rates are much worse than in Senggigi.

TRAVEL AGENCIES

Perama (☎ 632824) There is an agent available at Kontiki Meno bungalows.

Sights & Activities

TAMAN BURUNG

In the centre of the island, this **bird park** (☎ 642321; admission 30,000Rp; 🕐 9am-5pm) has an impressive and well-cared-for collection of colourful, exotic species from Indonesia and Australasia, as well as three kangaroos and a baby Komodo Dragon. The birds are let out of their cages for three hours a day, when they fly around a large expanse covered by a net. There's also accommodation available (p292).

SNORKELLING & DIVING

Snorkelling trips, sometimes in glass-bottomed boats, are advertised along the main strip by the jetty. Expect to pay about 40,000Rp per head, if there are at least five people, including snorkelling gear. There's good snorkelling from Turtle Heaven in the north around to Gili Meno wall in the northwest – gear is available for 15,000Rp per day. Always ask about the state of the currents.

Blue Marlin Dive Centre (☎ 639979; www.diveindo.com) offers fun dives and courses from Discover Scuba to Dive Master.

Sleeping

BUDGET

The basic places are generally more expensive than equivalent lodgings on the other Gilis, and don't usually include breakfast. Prices quoted are high-season rates.

Tao Kombo (☎ 0812 3722 174; tao_kombo@yahoo.com; platforms/bungalows 20,000/80,000Rp) South of the boat landing and down a path going inland, this mellow place has open bamboo platforms (with mattresses, mosquito nets

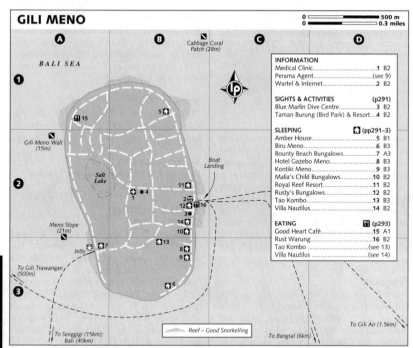

GILI MENO

and safety boxes) to sleep in, as well as beautifully decorated bungalows with open-air bathrooms and terraces. The restaurant and bar are filled with rattan mats and cushions, adding to the lounging vibe.

Rusty's Bungalows (Pondok Wisata; ☎ 642324; s/d 50,000/60,000Rp) At the focus of the tourist activity and just behind the boat dock, these basic, big rooms face a pretty garden.

Malia's Child Bungalows (☎ 622007; www.gilimeno -mallias.com; r 80,000Rp) These standard bamboo bungalows on stilts are located on a top-notch beach.

Kontiki Meno (☎ 632824; r 60,000Rp, with fan/ air-con 90,000/150,000Rp; 🟦) This place has a good selection of clean and well-maintained bungalows, ranging from sea-view rooms with Balinese doors and no fans, to better-furnished, air-con rooms with four-poster beds. The Perama agent is here in high season.

Biru Meno (☎ 0813 3950 623; r 80,000-100,000Rp) Located in a quiet spot just south from the main strip, this charming place has six large, stylish bamboo bungalows with sofas, coloured matt tiles, modern bathrooms and spacious verandas. The bungalows face the sea, and there's also a restaurant.

Other recommendations:

Royal Reef Resort (☎ 642340; r 150,000Rp) To the north of the boat landing, these large and well-furnished bungalows overlook the sea.

Amber House (☎ 643676; amber_house02@hotmail .com; s/d from 30,000/40,000Rp) The best option at the northern part of the island, these bamboo bungalows are set in a flourishing garden and have sea aspects.

MID-RANGE

Taman Burung (Bird Park) Resort (☎ 642321; www .balipvbgroup.com; dm/deluxe r 10,000/300,000Rp; 🟦) With its grand fountain, bar and pool table, the resort feels slightly incongruous in the middle of this quiet island. There's a funky dormitory with three short bunk beds, fan and toilets next door, as well as four smart air-con rooms with large beds and kitchen equipment.

Hotel Gazebo Meno (☎ /fax 635795; r US$45; 🟦 🟦) These bungalows are the most charming on the island. Set among coconut trees, the rooms have a slightly colonial feel with their 1930s prints, tasteful Javanese furniture and chaise lounges. There's a small lounge area and the bedrooms are on a slightly higher level. There's a small saltwater swimming pool.

Bounty Beach Bungalows (☎ 649090; www.bali bountygroup.com; r US$45-78; 🕸 🖭) On the west coast where the Bounty catamaran docks, this hotel has 26 smart, spacious rooms with some Lombok styling. There's a restaurant, a large pool, and ping-pong and pool tables. The hotel is popular with groups, but it feels desolate in low season as there's nothing much else around here.

TOP END

Villa Nautilus (☎ 642143; www.villanautilus.com; r US$75; 🕸) These five well-spaced bungalows make the most of the sea views with their wooden decks complete with sun lounges and windows all around. There's a lounge area and raised bedroom decorated immaculately in dark wood, creams and pale stone. The only quibble is that the shower, down some slippery stairs, is separate from the rest of the bathroom.

Eating & Drinking

The beachfront restaurants near the boat landing are extremely pleasant places to eat, but don't expect *haute cuisine* or snappy service anywhere. All offer Indonesian favourites, pizza, pasta, soups, sandwiches and grilled seafood.

Rust Warung (☎ 642324; mains 6000-28,000Rp) Right on the beach near where the boats dock, these simple *buruga* with low tables are a great spot to have a bite to eat and take in the view of Gunung Rinjani.

Good Heart Café (mains 7500-20,000Rp; 🕑 happy hour 6-8pm) A great place to watch the sunset, Good Heart has a relaxed atmosphere aided by bamboo wind chimes and shells decorating the trees. There are regular BBQs and the bar has a variety of cocktails.

Tao Kombo (☎ 0812 3722 174; mains 9000-24,000Rp) The most popular bar on the island, this laid-back place is run by a Frenchman going by the name of 'Bob'. There are cool tunes, cocktails and beers, and a pool table. The restaurant turns out tasty Italian and Indonesian cuisine, with Sasak specials on busy nights.

Villa Nautilus (☎ 642143; mains 6000-27,000Rp) The hotel's restaurant on the beachfront serves great pizza, sandwiches and fish dishes.

GILI TRAWANGAN

Trawangan is the party island, and feels like a metropolis compared to Gili Air and Meno. In busy times, restaurants and bars are buzzing until the early hours and it can be hard to get a room. Trawangan has the most visitors and widest range of facilities and activities, but there are still plenty of chilled-out spots. It's the largest of the islands – about 3km north to south and 2km east to west – with a local population of about 800, not counting workers from other parts of Indonesia and overseas.

Orientation & Information

Boats pull up on the beach just north of the jetty. South of here are where most of the tourist facilities are – a buzzing line of restaurants, bars, hotels and dive shops. The best beaches are north of the jetty, where you'll find a line of losmen, more intimate bars and restaurants, and a laid-back atmosphere. There are a few places to stay at other points around the coast – they're very quiet and far from most of the action.

EMERGENCY

Ask at Manta Dive for the Satgas and *kepala desa*.

INTERNET ACCESS & TELEPHONE

There are several wartel on the island, including one next to Blue Marlin, one near the Perama office and one in Cyberstream Internet.

NOT WHAT WAS PLANNED

In the early 1990s the land facing the best beaches in the northeast of Trawangan was bought up, and local businesses were aggressively shut down in order to build grandiose golf courses and four-star hotels. The grand plans never happened, halted by local resistance and national crisis, so desolate fields faced some of the best northern beaches. In recent years however, an eclectic collection of funky bars, restaurants, *losmen* (small hotel) and hotels has filled the empty spaces, and this area north of the jetty has become a more relaxed and interesting alternative to the main southern strip – clearly preferable to another empty, upmarket resort.

Borobodur Restaurant & Cybercafé (☎ 634893; per min 400Rp; ⏰ 8am-10pm) Offers extremely slow Internet access.

Cyberstream Internet (per min 400Rp; ⏰ 8am-midnight)

MEDICAL SERVICES
Villa Ombak Clinic (☎ 642336; ⏰ 8am-5pm) This clinic has two doctors and a nurse on hand.

MONEY
Several places will change cash or travellers cheques at a high rate. Most of the dive shops will give cash advances on Visa or MasterCard, but will want a hefty commission of 7% or more.

TRAVEL AGENCIES
Perama (☎ 638514; www.peramatour.com; ⏰ 7am-10pm) The office is a little north of the jetty.

Activities
DIVING
Dive operators on the tourist strip arrange trips and courses – most have attractive pools for introductory dive training. See Diving & Snorkelling in the Gili Islands, p285.

Big Bubble (☎ 625020; www.bigbubblediving.com)
Blue Marlin Dive Centre (☎ 632424; www.dive indo.com)
Dive Indonesia (☎ 642289; diveindo_senggigi@ iname.com)
Dream Divers (☎ 634496; www.dreamdivers.com)
Manta Dive (☎ 643649; www.manta-dive.com)
Villa Ombak Diving Academy (☎ 638531; gilidive@mataram.wasantara.net.id)

BOAT TRIPS & SNORKELLING
Four-hour trips in glass-bottomed boats to snorkelling spots around the Gilis are sold at various shops-cum-travel agencies lining the main strip and north of the harbour, for around 40,000Rp per person, including snorkelling equipment.

The best area for snorkelling is off the northeastern coast. There's coral around most of the island, but much of the reef on the eastern side has been damaged. Beware of strong currents on the eastern side, between Trawangan and Meno. Snorkelling gear can be hired for around 15,000Rp per day from shacks near the boat landing.

WATER SPORTS
North of the jetty, **Fun Ferrari** (☎ 639248, 0812 3756 138; www.thegiliislands.com; watersports per 15 min

incl tuition 150,000Rp; fishing US$50) offers water-skiing, parasailing and wakeboarding from its bright-red speedboat, as well as white-knuckle rides on its motored inflatable. It's all done from Teluk Nare (on the mainland) so as not to disturb the beachfront vibe. If partaking in the energetic sports fishing, expect to catch fish like tuna and barracuda.

HORSE RIDING
With well-looked-after horses from Europe, Australia and Sumba, **Stud** (☎ 639248, 0812 3703 338; www.thegiliislands.com; paddock training 30 min 70,000Rp; 90 min tours 120,000-150,000Rp) has a paddock for riding lessons. It offers a variety of horse-riding tours, including beachfront riding and sunrise and sunset tours. Guides can lead horses if you can't ride. Book at the Fun Ferrari office (left).

Horse riding on local *cidomo*-like horses is available at **Balikana Retreat** (☎ 622386; www.bali kanaretreat.com; per hr 150,000Rp).

WALKING & CYCLING
You can walk around the whole island in a couple of pleasant hours. From the hill in the southwestern corner you'll have fine views of Bali's Gunung Agung, especially at sunset. Sunrise over Gunung Rinjani is also impressive. On the far side of the hill, look for the remains of an old Japanese gun.

There are some good mountain-biking trails around the hill; bikes can be hired for around 15,000Rp a day from where the boats pull up, north of the jetty.

Sleeping
Most bungalows are set back from the beach. For those wanting to stay near the action, there are plenty of places along the main strip, and in the village just behind. The 'up-and-coming' area north of the harbour is less frantic and faces the best beaches. Other options outside of these two areas are very quiet and will cost at least 5000Rp by *cidomo* to reach. Rates quoted are high-season prices. What follows is a small selection of what's available.

BUDGET
Main Strip
Kreatif Satu (☎ 634861; r with fan/air-con 70,000/ 120,000Rp, dishes 10,000-27,000Rp; ▨) Lombok landscapes painted by the owner are used as

dividers between terraces. Rooms are large and clean, but rather characterless.

Danau Hijau Cottages (☎ 638517; r with fan/air-con 60,000/100,000Rp; ✖) Behind Frenchies bar, this place has pale-green brick bungalows with tiled floors and clean rooms.

Pak Majid (r 50,000Rp) Standard concrete bungalows with plain rooms are on offer here; breakfast is not included.

In the Village

Pondok Sederhana (☎ 0813 3860 9964; r 50,000Rp) Run by a house-proud and friendly Balinese lady, the spotless rooms face a neat little garden.

Pondok Lita (r 70,000-90,000Rp) Set around a small courtyard, this modest family-run place has spacious rooms – some have three beds – with bamboo furniture and tiled floors.

Edy Homestay (☎ 0812 3767 514; r 75,000Rp) This homestay offers good-value, spacious rooms with bamboo furniture. The hammocks on the terraces face some greenery.

Losman Eky (☎ 623582; r 50,000Rp) The clean large rooms are uninspiring but inexpensive.

North of the Harbour

Blue Beach Cottages (☎ 623538; bbc@indo.net.18; r with fan/air-con 100,000/150,000Rp; ✖) This great-value place has beds covered in romantic muslin canopies, some nice furnishings, bathrooms with hot water, and minibars. There's a funky two-storey restaurant up front overlooking a lovely beach, and a small Internet café and wartel next door.

Beach Wind Bungalows (☎ 0812 3764 347; s/d 50,000/75,000Rp, bike rental per hr 10,000Rp, snorkelling gear rental per day 13,000Rp) This is a good one-stop shop. The rooms have more furniture than usual and large ceiling fans, there's a book exchange, and bikes and snorkelling gear are available for hire.

Sirwa Homestay (s/d 40,000/45,000Rp, dishes 7000-22,000Rp) This place has big rooms – some have two double beds – with prices to suit those on a strict budget. There's a simple restaurant up front.

Other Areas

Pondok Santai (s/d 50,000/60,000Rp) On the south coast, this is for those who want a more secluded stay.

Sunset Cottages (s/d 50,000/60,000Rp) Further west, this is a great spot for watching sunsets over Bali.

Nusa Tiga (☎ 643249; r 75,000Rp) On the island's quiet northernmost tip, this place has large but uninspiring bungalows.

MID-RANGE
Main Strip

Tir na Nog (☎ 639463; tirnanog@mataram.wasantara .net.id; r without/with air-con US$10/20; ✖) Around the back of this popular Irish bar are 10 huge and elegant rooms. The rooms upstairs have spacious private terraces and all have modern bathrooms and hot water. Try not to stay in rooms one and two on Tuesday nights (party night), as these are nearest to the bar. Otherwise it's very peaceful.

Manta Dive (☎ 643649; www.manta-dive.com; r 150,000-200,000Rp; ✖ 🏊) Behind the dive shop, some funky-looking bungalows with open-air bathrooms and hot water were nearly finished when we visited. Conveniently located just south of the harbour, they're worth checking out.

Blue Marlin (☎ 632424; www.diveindo.com; r US$25; 🏊) Down the side of the dive shop, these simple wooden bungalows are surprisingly well equipped and furnished with wardrobes and desks, hot water and baths, TV and air-con. There's a lovely swimming pool at the front.

In the Village

Martas (☎ 0812 3722 777; martas_trawangan@yahoo .com; s/d/tr 150,000/200,000/250,000Rp; ✖) Some of the most stylish accommodation options on Trawangan, these two-storey bungalows set in a lovely flowering garden are decked out with modern Balinese furniture and calming creams, browns, sandstone and rattan. There are well-designed hot-water bathrooms downstairs, and upstairs, charming air-con bedrooms with A-frame ceilings.

Puri Hondje (r 150,000Rp; ✖) This is a hidden gem at the end of a village lane. Open the Balinese-style entrance and you'll find two rooms overlooking a small fish pond surrounded by bougainvillea and palms, as well as a couple of pretty white ducks. Open-air bathrooms, stone floors, ikat on the walls, comfy rattan furniture, hammocks and wind chimes make this a stylish retreat.

North of the Harbour

Sama Sama Bungalows (☎ 0812 3763 650; sama2x 2001@yahoo.com; r with fan/air-con 150,000/250,000Rp;

LOMBOK

) Behind Pamour Art Gallery are two immaculate rooms (twin or double) that are well furnished and decorated with coconut wood and cream linen. The modern bathrooms have hot water and there's a choice of fan or air-con.

Gitra (☎ 0812 3729 426; s/d 150,000/200,000Rp) Further north, it's easy to miss this place due to its small faded sign. The enormous rooms are a good option if staying long-term (ask for discounts) as they are comfortably decorated with Lombok-style furniture, such as inlaid mother-of-pearl wardrobes, desks and dressing tables, as well as ikat on the wall and rattan mats on the floor.

Balikana Retreat (☎ 622386; www.balikanaretreat .com; d 175,000-450,000, tr 275,000-550,000Rp + 21% tax; 🔀 🥤) In an isolated northern spot, this romantic place has a variety of accommodation options, including garden-view rooms decorated with paint effects, and more traditional loft-style bungalows featuring sunset balcony views. All have hot water and air-con. A swimming pool was being built when we visited.

TOP END

Hotel Villa Ombak (☎ 642336; www.hotelombak .com; r US$95-115 + 21% tax; 🔀 🥤) In a quieter spot but still near the action, the *lumbung*-style rooms and bungalows here all come with air-con, satellite TV, safety boxes and stunning open-air bathrooms. They surround an ocean-view swimming pool and lovely beach. There's also a spa, diving academy and restaurant here. Nonguests can use the pool for 50,000Rp.

Desa Dunia Beda (☎ 641575; www.desaduniabeda .com; US$110 + 21% tax; 🔀 🥤) Out on their own in the northwest of the island, these lovely Javanese Joglo bungalows are perfect for a romantic retreat. They are all decorated with elegant Javanese furniture and natural colours. The huge rooms have large canopied beds, carved wooden screens, sofas and muted batiks, as well as open-air bathrooms. There's also a large rectangular pool overlooking the sea and a smart restaurant.

Villa Almarik (☎ 638520; www.almarik-lombok.com; r US$75-90; 🔀 🥤) Flowering bougainvillea canopies lead to tastefully decorated bungalows with large bathrooms, hot water, air-con, TV and minibars, as well as day beds overlooking the garden. The curvy swimming pool is at the front of the hotel.

Eating

There's a variety of eating options on Trawangan, including warung food, sushi and even Irish stew!

Kiki Nova (dishes 5000Rp) This small warung behind the art market does a wicked *nasi campur* – expect a huge portion of tasty *rendang* (beef or buffalo coconut curry), chicken, tempeh, veg and rice.

Kayangan (☎ 637932; dishes 7500-15,000Rp) Although it looks unimpressive with just a few rather grubby-looking plastic chairs and tables back from the beach, the inexpensive Chinese and Indonesian dishes served here are excellent.

Reccy Living Room (☎ 0812 3690 154; dishes 12,000-23,000Rp) This very friendly place has *buruga* overlooking a lovely beach. Its international menu has been recommended, especially the salads and the lasagne.

Juku Restaurant (☎ 639266; dishes 13,000-55,000Rp) This place has a romantic setting with *buruga* and tables on the beach. Its fish dishes, like the prawn butterfly with sweet pepper sauce, are delicious.

Café Wayan & Bakery (dishes 15,000-35,000Rp) Known for its freshly baked breads and pastries, it also has a wide variety of mains – the lemon-chicken salad is great.

Tir na Nog (☎ 639463; dishes 20,000-35,000Rp) For some serious filling up come to this restaurant at the hotel (p295) for enormous portions of dishes like Irish stew and fish and chips, and puds like apple crumble and cream and banoffi pie. There is a BBQ every night, and some local dishes.

Ryoshi (☎ 639463; dishes 15,000-43,000Rp, set menu vegetarian/fish 55,000/70,000Rp) This always seems to be the first place recommended by Trawangan expats. Its top-quality sushi and sashimi is super fresh and prepared by Indonesians trained by Japanese sushi chefs. On the beachfront, its chunky low tables, red lanterns and cushions make it a bit special.

Other recommendations:

Hotel Villa Ombak (☎ 642336; mains 25,000-60,000Rp) With tables on the beach and around the pool, this highly regarded restaurant has a mix of international and Asian cuisine.

Blue Marlin (☎ 632424; mains 9000-35,000Rp) This popular restaurant alongside the pool has a diverse menu to suit all tastes.

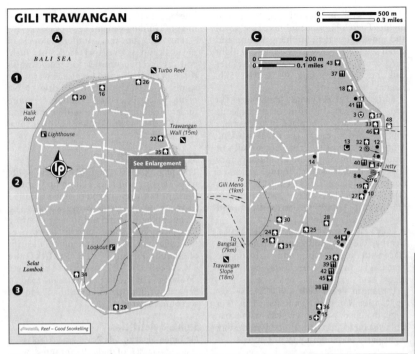

GILI TRAWANGAN

0 — 500 m
0 — 0.3 miles

BALI SEA

Turbo Reef

0 — 200 m
0 — 0.1 miles

Halik Reef

Lighthouse

Trawangan Wall (15m)

See Enlargement

To Gili Meno (1km)

To Bangsal (7km)

Trawangan Slope (18m)

Lookout

Selat Lombok

Jetty

Reef – Good Snorkelling

LOMBOK

Dream Divers (☎ 634496; mains 19,000-36,000Rp) This recommended restaurant has a terrace upstairs and tables surrounding the pool downstairs.

Drinking

Most evenings in Trawangan start with a movie, as many places along the main strip have a film programme and big screens. Tir Na Nog has individual TVs in private *buruga* – you can choose from 550 DVDs.

Trawangan is famous for its rotating parties that go on until 4am. The parties, sometimes with live music, are held at Rudy's Pub (Friday), Dive Indonesia (Saturday), Blue Marlin (Monday), Tir Na Nog (Tuesday), and Trawangan Beach Club (Wednesday). Blue Marlin's on Monday is the most celebrated.

Tir Na Nog (☎ 639463; 🕑 7am-2am Wed-Mon, 7am-4am Tue) Gili Trawangan's barn like Irish presence is the number one nightspot most nights. There's a restaurant here (see p296) and movies to watch, but hang around and you'll see a lively crowd. The Tuesday night party is a bit tongue in cheek with a glitter ball and '60s, '70s and '80s music. 'Silly Sunday' has 25% off spirits.

Horizontal Bar & Lounge (www.horizontalbar .com; ☉ 10am-2am) In front of a gorgeous stretch of beach, this place offers a more sophisticated vibe than the usual drinking spots in Trawangan. Primarily a chill-out lounge, it's decorated in a contemporary style, with luxe scarlet lounges, decked floors, and lots of funky details. It features fantastic cocktails (try the raspberry margarita), tapas, Italian coffees and occasional international DJs.

Rudy's Pub (☉ 8am-4am Fri, 8am-11pm Sat-Thu) Nearby, Rudy's is another popular gathering place with *buruga*, tables and chairs on the beach. The music at its Friday party is a mixed bag.

Trawangan Beach Club (☎ 0812 3744 306; ☉ 10am-4am Wed, 10am-11pm Thu-Tue) This is a huge, thatched, two-storey place with a bar and restaurant up front. Its Wednesday night party plays mainly techno music.

Shopping
The **Pasar Seni (Art Market)** (☉ 8am-6pm) has a postal agent and shops selling clothes, sarongs and some handicrafts. North of the jetty, the **Pamour Art Gallery** (☎ 0812 3766 481; ☉ 9am-9pm) sells interesting knick-knacks from around Indonesia.

There are plenty of small shops selling basic supplies like (expensive) sun cream, mosquito repellent and shampoo.

NORTH & CENTRAL LOMBOK

☎ 0370

The sparsely populated northern part of Lombok is remarkably beautiful, with a variety of landscapes and seascapes, few tourists and even fewer facilities. Public transport is not frequent, nor does it detour from the main road. With a set of wheels, however, you can stop along the way to admire the views, and make side trips to the coast, waterfalls and inland villages.

The major attraction is unquestionably the mighty Gunung Rinjani.

The area on the southern slopes of the volcano is well watered and lush, and offers opportunities for scenic walks through rice fields and jungle. Towards the southern coast the country is drier. Most of the places in central Lombok are more or less traditional Sasak settlements, and several of them are known for their local handicrafts.

SENARU & BATU KOQ
The picturesque village of Senaru is the usual starting point for a climb up Gunung Rinjani, but even if you're not interested in climbing, it is still worth a visit. The accommodation here and in neighbouring Batu Koq has some superb views over the valley to the east and up to the rim of Gunung Rinjani. Visit **Rinjani Trek Centre** (RTC; ☎ 0868 1210 4132; www.lomboksumbawa.com; ☉ 6am-5pm), at the top of the main road in Senaru, for information on Rinjani and the surrounding area.

Sights & Activities
Air Terjun Sindang Gila (admission 2000Rp) is a spectacular set of falls 30 minutes' walk from Senaru. The walk is partly through forest and partly alongside an irrigation canal that follows the contour of the hill, occasionally disappearing into tunnels where the cliffs are too steep.

Another 40 minutes or so further up the hill is **Air Terjun Tiu Kelep**, and a spot where you can go swimming. The track is steep and tough at times, so it's a good idea to take a guide, which will cost you around 10,000Rp.

Tours
There are several community tourism activities around Senaru. These get the villagers involved in the tourism industry and help travellers gain valuable insights into the local way of life. The activities include a visit to the traditional village of **Dusun Senaru** (with a guide 5000Rp), which has an air of antiquity; a **Rice Terraces and Waterfalls Walk** (2hr 30,000Rp), which includes Sindang Gila and some stunning vistas; and the **Senaru Panorama Walk** (4hr 45,000Rp), which is led by female guides and takes in local lifestyles. The last two walks include a free

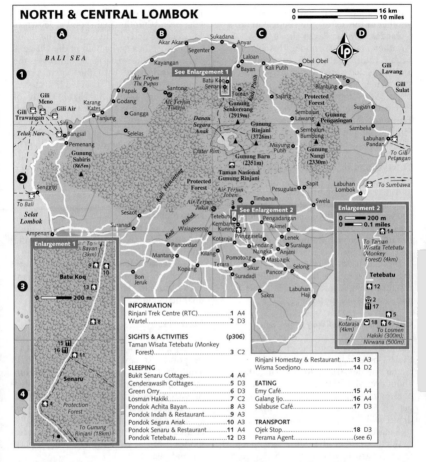

NORTH & CENTRAL LOMBOK

| | | 0 | 16 km |
| | | 0 | 10 miles |

BALI SEA

INFORMATION
Rinjani Trek Centre (RTC)................1 A4
Wartel..2 D3

SIGHTS & ACTIVITIES   (p306)
Taman Wisata Tetebatu (Monkey
   Forest)..3 C2

SLEEPING
Bukit Senaru Cottages......................4 A4
Cenderawasih Cottages....................5 D3
Green Orry...6 D3
Losman Hakiki.....................................7 C2
Pondok Achita Bayan........................8 A3
Pondok Indah & Restaurant.............9 A3
Pondok Segara Anak........................10 A3
Pondok Senaru & Restaurant..........11 A4
Pondok Tetebatu................................12 D3

Rinjani Homestay & Restaurant......13 A3
Wisma Soedjono...............................14 D2

EATING
Emy Café...15 A4
Galang Ijo...16 A4
Salabuse Café....................................17 D3

TRANSPORT
Ojek Stop...18 D3
Perama Agent.............................(see 6)

bemo ride back. Ask for information at the RTC (see p298).

Sleeping & Eating

Losmen are located along the main road through Senaru to Batu Koq and are all of a pretty similar standard with *mandi* (Indonesian 'bath' consisting of a large water tank from which you ladle cold water over yourself), cold water and Indonesian squat toilet. Don't expect fans as the climate is cooler here.

Rinjani Homestay (☎ 0817 5750 889; s/d 25,000/ 35,000Rp; dishes 7000-25,000Rp) The Rinjani foot-hills can be seen from the steps of the open-air bathrooms, and the plain rooms are spotless. The restaurant offers Western

and Indonesian dishes. The owner can be a bit gruff.

Bukit Senaru Cottages (r 40,000Rp) Overlook-ing a garden and with basic facilities, these rooms are well maintained, with pink concrete walls and smart bamboo furniture on the terraces.

Pondok Indah & Restaurant (☎ 639476; s/d 30,000/40,000Rp, dishes 7000-18,000Rp) This is one of the most pleasant places to stay in Senaru. A friendly family runs these spacious and sparkling clean rooms. Rooms and restaurant, with jolly gingham tablecloths, have breathtaking views over the Rinjani foothills.

Pondok Segara Anak (r 30,000Rp) Opposite Pondok Indah, this place has an equally good panorama, and neat and clean rooms. It's another of the better-value budget options.

Pondok Achita Bayan (r 40,000-50,000Rp) Another standout option, this place has bright rooms with high *lumbung* roofs, and some have two verandas – one with spectacular views of Gunung Rinjani, the other with views of the garden. The more expensive rooms have Western toilets. From the back you can see Air Terjun Sindang Gila in the distance.

Pondok Senaru & Restaurant (☎ 622868, 0868 1210 4141; r 60,000-130,000Rp, dishes 9000-19,000Rp) This is the most expensive option in Senaru, mainly due to the rooms' large windows and terraces, which make the most of the sublime Rinjani vistas. The spacious rooms with tiled floors and bamboo walls are comfortable but have no hot water. The restaurant serving Indonesian dishes also takes advantage of the views.

Emy Café (dishes 5000-7500Rp) and **Galang Ijo** (dishes 5000-7500Rp) are the only independent restaurants in Senaru. Both do simple food and some Sasak specials.

Getting There & Away

Catch a bus between 9am and noon from Mandalika bus terminal in Mataram for the 2½-hour ride to Anyar (8000Rp). From Anyar, bemos travel to Senaru (3000Rp) about every 20 minutes until 4pm. If you're coming from, or going to, eastern Lombok, get off at the junction near Bayan (your driver will know it) from where bemos go to Senaru.

Bemo charters after dusk (about 6pm) from Senaru to Mataram or Senggigi will cost in the region of a hefty 300,000Rp.

There's no public transport between Senaru and Sembalun Lawang. *Ojek* can be chartered for 30,000Rp to 40,000Rp, as can bemos for approximately 75,000Rp. If you have bought a trekking package with the RTC or one of the associated cooperatives, then your transport from Sembalun Lawang back to Senaru (or vice versa) should be included.

SEMBALUN LAWANG & SEMBALUN BUMBUNG

☎ 0376

High on the eastern side of Gunung Rinjani is the beautiful Sembalun valley, whose inhabitants descend from the Hindu Javanese. Sembalun Lawang is a satellite village, and the other main point of departure for trekking up Gunung Rinjani. The statue of an enormous garlic bulb in the village is indicative of the area's garlic industry – the village is infused with the potent bulbs' aroma when they are harvested in October.

Sembalun Bumbung, 3km south of Sembalun Lawang just off the main road, is a sprawling and relatively wealthy village. It's often referred to simply as Sembalun; the 'Bumbung' is used to differentiate it from Sembalun Lawang. The latter is the more convenient place to stay for organising treks, although there is one basic homestay in Sembalun Bumbung.

Information

There's a wartel and post office next door to Bale Galeng (p301) in Sembulun Lawang but its opening hours are sporadic.

The **Rinjani Information Centre** (RIC; ◷ 6am-6pm), which is connected with the Rinjani Trek Centre in Senaru, organises treks with qualified guides.

Activities

The Sembalun Wildflower Walk, run by the RIC, is a two-day and one-night trek to Propok in Rinjani's National Park (p302). You'll get sweeping views of Sembalun Lawang and Bumbung, and flower-filled grasslands, and will learn about agricultural activities. It costs 540,000Rp for two people. If there are three of you, it costs 450,000Rp and descends further. The price includes guides, porters, camping equipment, park fee and meals.

The RIC has also helped local women to revive traditional weaving in Sembalun Lawang and some nice products are on sale here. Follow the signs in the centre of the village and visit the weavers in their home workshops.

Sleeping & Eating

Sembalun Lawang is a more expensive place to stay than Senaru or Batoq, but the vistas are more impressive.

Sembalun Nauli (☎ 23029; Sembalun Lawan; r 100,000Rp, dishes 6000-15,000Rp) These two new bungalows surrounded by stunning mountains are just before Sembalun Lawang on the road from Senaru. The rooms are large, clean and nicely furnished, with a small terrace looking up to Rinjani. There's a restaurant and a strawberry patch out front. It's noisy when the generator is running.

Losman Lembah Rinjani (s/d 125,000/150,000Rp, with shared bathroom 50,000/75,000Rp, dishes 8000-14,000Rp) At the garlic statue next to the RIC, turn right down a side road to find this collection of spotlessly clean rooms with good aspects on the volcano. The cheaper rooms have a less advantageous view; the pricier have two terraces and blankets. There's a restaurant on site.

Maria Guesthouse (r with shared bathroom 30,000Rp) Run by a flamboyant owner, these two plain and basic rooms are set in the family house. Breakfast and dinner are included in the price.

Bale Galeng (s/d with shared bathroom 25,000/40,000Rp) A quirky alternative, this place has very simple rooms in *lumbung* cottages with a rambling garden. The owner grows a wide variety of herbs and flowers for the villages' traditional medicines. It's about 1km from the RIC.

Puri Rinyani (r 35,000-50,000Rp) These five basic rooms with Indonesian toilets and mandi are presentable, and currently the only accommodation available in Sembalun Bumbung.

Getting There & Away

You can get to Sembalun Lawang from Mandalika bus terminal two ways; either take a bus to Masbagit (5000Rp) and then change there for another bus to Sembalun Lawang (7000Rp), or take a bus to Aikmel (5000Rp) and change buses there for Sembalun Lawang (7000Rp).

Between Lawang and Bumbung there's a pick-up truck that can be hailed every hour between 7am and 5pm (3000Rp).

There's no public transport between Sembalun Lawang and Senaru. *Ojek* can be chartered for 30,000Rp to 40,000Rp, as can bemos for approximately 75,000Rp. If you have bought a trekking package from the RIC, RTC or another operator (see p302) then free transport to Senaru should be included.

From the Sembalun valley there are occasional bemos to Sapit (7000Rp). The road snakes up a 2000m pass of hairpin bends and spectacular scenery, but it can sometimes be closed due to landslides.

SAPIT
☎ 0376

On the southeastern slopes of Gunung Rinjani, Sapit is a tiny village with views across to Sumbawa and an impressive panorama of Rinjani. You'll see red-brick tobacco-drying buildings dotted about as this is a major tobacco growing area – blocks can be bought in the daily morning market. Sapit is a relaxing place to hang out.

Sights

Between Swela and Sapit, a side road leads to **Taman Lemor** (Lemor Park; admission 1500Rp; ☽ 8am-4pm), where there's a refreshing spring-fed swimming pool, a few pesky monkeys and a rubbish problem at weekends. Further down the road towards Pringgabaya, another side road goes to **Makam Selaparang**, the burial place of ancient Selaparang kings. Neither place is particularly exciting, but it's a good excuse for some trekking.

You can also visit a few hot-water springs and small waterfalls near Sapit. Ask either homestay for directions.

Sleeping

Hati Suci Homestay (☎ 0818 545 655; www.hatisuci.tk; s 30,000-35,000Rp, d 70,000-80,000Rp, dishes 9000-15,000Rp) Set in a labyrinthine garden filled with bougainvillea bushes and marigolds, these neat bungalows with bamboo furniture have amazing views across the rice fields and sea to Sumbawa. The restaurant takes full advantage of these aspects.

Balelangga Bed & Breakfast (☎ 22197; s/d with shared bathroom 30,000/50,000Rp) Nearby, this is a simpler option than Hati Suci. It's sometimes closed in low season (see p13).

Getting There & Away

To reach Sapit, first catch a bus to Pringgabaya, then a bemo to Sapit. Occasional bemos also go to Sapit from the Sembalun valley in the north.

GUNUNG RINJANI

Gunung Rinjani National Park is one of the 43 National Parks of Indonesia. Established in 1997 the 41,330 hectare park has great cultural significance, with the crater-lake being the destination for thousands of Sasak and Balinese pilgrims who place offerings

LOMBOK

in the water, bathe in the hot springs and revere the mountain as a sacred place and abode of deities.

Gunung Rinjani is the highest mountain in Lombok and the second-highest in Indonesia; at 3726m it soars above the island. Its huge crater contains a large, crescent-shaped lake, **Danau Segara Anak** (Child of the Sea), which is about 6km across at its widest point.

Rinjani has a series of *mata air panas* (natural hot springs) known as **Air Kalak**, on the northeastern side of this crater, which are said to have healing powers, particularly for skin diseases. The lake is 600 vertical metres below the crater rim, and in the middle of its curve is the new cone, **Gunung Baru** (or Gunung Barujari), which is only a couple of hundred years old. Rinjani is an active volcano and erupted as recently as 1994, changing the shape of this inner cone and sprinkling ash over much of Lombok.

Both the Balinese and Sasak revere Rinjani. To the Balinese, it is equal to Gunung Agung (p186), a seat of the gods, and many Balinese make an annual pilgrimage here.

In a ceremony called *pekelan*, people throw jewellery into the lake and make offerings to the spirit of the mountain. Some Sasak make several pilgrimages a year – full moon is their favourite time for paying respect to the mountain and curing their ailments by bathing in Air Kalak.

The climb to the crater lake is not to be taken lightly. Don't try it during the wet season (November to March), because the tracks will be slippery and dangerous. Because of this the National Park usually closes the Rinjani trek for the first three months of the year. June to August is the only time you are guaranteed (well, almost) no rain or cloud, but it can still get *very* cold at the summit.

Senaru has the best services for trekkers so most start their treks there. Those who want the fastest summit climb, however, should start from Sembalun Lawang on the eastern side.

Organised Treks

The best and most inexpensive way to organise a trip is to head to either the

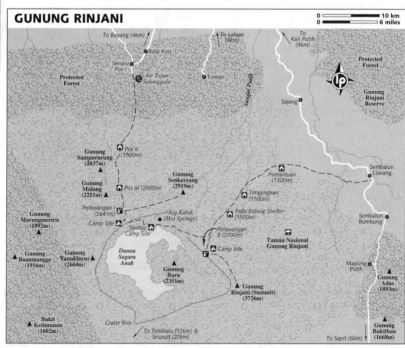

AIRPORT TAXI BILL 3
KARCIS TAXI BANDARA NGURAH RAI

Waiting fee (biaya tunggu)
Empty run (kilometer kosong)
Order fee (biaya pesan)

CHARGE

- Flag fall Rp. 4.000,-
- Per kilometer Rp. 2.000,-

INCLUDING INSURANCE
TERMASUK ASURANSI

If have any complain contact phone 751011 ext. 5566
Bila ada masalah hubungi telp. 751011 ext. 5555

No. A 526177

21 FEB 2020

FOR PASSENGER *(UNTUK PENUMPANG)*

Rinjani Trek Centre (p298) in Senaru or the Rinjani Information Centre (p300) in Sembalun Lawang. Anyone passing through Mataram can first contact the Rinjani Trek Centre's Head Office (p268). Funded by the New Zealand government, the centres have started several community tourism initiatives and have persuaded local trek operators to run a rotation system so that everyone gets a share of the cake. Both local trek organisers and guides have formed associations, making the whole trek business more reliable and secure than it was before – the armed bandits scenarios of 2000 have not been repeated. This also means that whether you decide to book through your losmen in Senaru or Sembalun Lawang, or directly at the RTC or RIC, they offer the same trek packages at the same prices. The Rinjani Trek in Gunung Rinjani National Park won the 2004 World Legacy Award for Destination Stewardship.

A variety of treks are on offer. The most popular is the three-day, two-night trek that takes in the summit, goes from Senaru to Sembalun Lawang and includes food, equipment, guide, porters, park fee and transport back to Senaru. This costs 1,610,000Rp for one, but the price drops to 966,000Rp for two of you and 821,000Rp for three. The most inexpensive package is the two-day, one-night trek to the crater rim, which starts and ends in Senaru. It costs 1,190,000Rp for one, 714,000Rp for two and 606,900Rp for three. The deals are cheaper the more of you there are.

A number of agencies in Mataram, Senggigi and the Gili Islands can organise all-inclusive treks. Prices tend to include everything outlined above, plus transport from the point of origin. For example, **Perama** (☎ 693007; www.peramatour.com; Jl Raya Senggigi, Mataram) has a trekking package that leaves from Mataram, Senggigi or the Gilis, and begins the trek at Sembalun Lawang. RTC official guides are used and there are transport links to pick up and transfer from the end point of the trek (Senaru) to Senggigi, Mataram or Bangsal.

Guides & Porters

If you don't want to do an all-inclusive trekking package with RTC or RIC you can hire guides and porters from them independently. Experienced trekkers can make it from Senaru to the hot springs and back without a guide (the trail is well defined), but you will need a porter – they carry supplies and tend to be familiar with the routes. Failing that, hire a radio for safety (10,000Rp per day). For other treks, especially from the Sembalun Lawang side, always hire a guide.

Make sure the guides and porters you contract are from the centres in Senaru and Sembalun Lawang, as they are licensed for your security. Guides cost 100,000Rp per day and porters cost 80,000Rp. Guides are knowledgeable and informative, but won't carry anything for you, so take at least one porter. You also have to provide food, water and transport for them, and probably cigarettes as well.

Entrance Fee & Equipment

The entrance fee for the Rinjani National Park is 25,000Rp – register and pay at the RTC in Senaru or the RIC in Sembalun Lawang before you start your trek.

There are some crude shelters on the way, but don't rely on them – sleeping bag and tent are essential. RTC charges the following per day: two-/three-person tent 33,000/39,000Rp; sleeping bag 13,000Rp; sleeping mat 7500Rp; cooking gear 30,000Rp; and radio 10,000Rp. You'll also need solid footwear, layers of warm clothing, wet-weather gear and a torch (flashlight), but these can also be hired from the RTC.

Take a stove so you don't need to deplete the limited supply of firewood. Carry all rubbish out with you and make sure others in your party do the same.

Food & Supplies

Trek organisers at RTC and RIC can arrange trekking food or you can take your own. It's better to buy most supplies in Mataram or Senggigi, where it's cheaper and there's more choice, but some provisions are available in Senaru. Take plenty of water and matches.

Left Luggage

Most people organise their treks from Senaru where the facilities are better, as well as starting and finishing their climbs here (either by walking back down or via transport from Sembalun Lawang). Gear can be left at most losmen in Senaru or in

CLIMBING GUNUNG RINJANI

The two most popular ways to climb Gunung Rinjani are a five-day trek (described below) that starts at Senaru (p298) and finishes at Sembalun Lawang (p300), or a strenuous dash from Senaru to the crater rim and back. A guide is essential from the hot springs to Sembalun Lawang, as the path is indistinct (see p303). This trek is outlined on the Gunung Rinjani map (p302). Another good map is the one from the Rinjani Trek Centre – it is large, colour, glossy and easy to understand.

Day 1: Senaru to Pos III (five to six hours)

At the southern end of the village is the Rinjani Trek Centre (Pos I, 601m), where you register and pay the park fee. Just beyond the post the trail forks – continue straight ahead on the right fork. The trail climbs steadily through scrubby farmland for about half an hour to the sign at the entrance to Gunung Rinjani National Park. The wide trail climbs for another 2½ hours until you reach Pos II (1500m), where there's a shelter. Water can be found 100m down the slopes from the trail, but it should be treated or boiled.

Another 1½ hours' steady walk uphill brings you to Pos III (2000m), where there are another two shelters in disrepair. Water is 100m off the trail to the right, but sometimes evaporates in the dry season. Pos III is the usual place to camp at the end of the first day.

Day 2: Pos III to Segara Anak & Hot Springs (four hours)

From Pos III, it takes about 1½ hours to reach the rim, Pelawangan I, at an altitude of 2641m. Set off very early for the stunning sunrise. It's possible to camp at Pelawangan I, but there are drawbacks: level sites are limited, there's no water and it can be very blustery.

It takes about two hours to descend to Danau Segara Anak and around to the hot springs (Aiq Kalak). The first hour is a very steep descent and involves low-grade rock climbing in parts. From the bottom of the crater wall it's an easy 30-minute walk across undulating terrain around the lake's edge. There are several places to camp, but most locals prefer to be near the hot springs to soak their weary bodies and recuperate. There are also some caves nearby which are interesting, but not used for shelter. The nicest camp sites are at the lake's edge, and fresh water can be gathered from a spring near the hot springs. Some hikers spend two nights or even more at the lake, but most who are returning to Senaru from here head back the next day. The climb back up the rim is certainly taxing – allow at least three hours and start early to make it back to Senaru in one day. Allow five hours from the rim down to Senaru. Instead of retracing your steps, the best option is to complete the Rinjani trek by continuing to Sembalun Lawang and arranging transport back to Senaru (see p306).

Day 3: Hot Springs to Pelawangan II (three to four hours)

The trail starts beside the last shelter at the hot springs and heads away from the lake for about 100m before veering right. The trail traverses the northern slope of the crater, and it's an easy one-hour walk along the grassy slopes. It's then a steep and constant climb; from the lake it takes about three hours to reach the crater rim (2639m). At the rim, a sign points the way back to Danau Segara Anak. Water can be found down the slope near the sign. The trail forks here – go straight on to Lawang or continue along the rim to the camp site of Pelawangan II (2700m). It's only about 10 minutes more to the camp site which is on a bare ridge.

Day 4: Pelawangan II to Rinjani Summit (five to six hours return)

Gunung Rinjani stretches in an arc above the camp site at Pelawangan II and looks deceptively close. Start the climb at 3am in order to reach the summit in time for the sunrise and before the clouds roll in.

It takes about 45 minutes to clamber up a steep, slippery and indistinct trail to the ridge that leads to Rinjani. Once on the ridge it's a relatively easy walk uphill. After about an hour heading towards what looks like the peak, the real summit of Rinjani looms behind and towers above you.

The trail then gets steeper and steeper. About 350m before the summit, the scree is composed of loose, fist-sized rocks – it's easier to scramble on all fours. This section can take about an hour. The views from the top are truly magnificent on a clear day. The descent is much easier, but again, take it easy on the scree. In total it takes three hours or more to reach the summit, and two to get back down.

Day 5: Pelawangan II to Sembalun Lawang (five to six hours)

After negotiating the peak it's possible to reach Lawang the same day. After a two-hour descent, it's a long and hot three-hour walk back to the village. Head off early to avoid as much of the heat of the day as possible and make sure you have plenty of water. From the camp site, head back along the ridge-crest trail. A couple of hundred metres past the turn-off to Danau Segara Anak is a signposted right turn leading down a subsidiary ridge to Pada Balong and Sembalun Lawang. Once on the trail, it's easy to follow and takes around two hours to reach the bottom.

At the bottom of the ridge (where you'll find Pada Balong shelter; 1800m) the trail levels out and crosses undulating to flat grassland all the way to Sembalun Lawang. After about an hour you will hit the relatively new Tengengean shelter (1500m); it's then another 30 minutes to Pemantuan shelter (1300m). Early in the season long grass obscures the trail until about 30 minutes beyond Pemantuan. The trail crosses many bridges; at the final bridge, just before it climbs uphill to a lone tree, the trail seems to fork; take the right fork and climb the rise. From here, the trail follows the flank of Rinjani before swinging around to Lawang at the end. A guide is essential for this part of the trip.

Variations

Possible variations to the route described above, are outlined here:

- Compress the last two days into one (racking up a hefty 10 to 11 hours on the trail). On the plus side it's downhill all the way after the hard climb to the summit.
- Retrace your steps to Senaru after climbing to the summit, making a five-day circuit that includes another night at the hot springs.
- Another popular route, because the trail is well defined and (if you're experienced) can be trekked with only a porter, is a three-day trek from Senaru to the hot springs and back. The first night is spent at Pos III and the second at the hot springs. The return to Senaru on the final day takes eight to nine hours.
- For (almost) instant gratification (if you travel light and climb fast) you can reach the crater rim from Senaru in about six hours. You'll gain an altitude of approximately 2040m in 10km. Armed with a torch (flashlight), some moonlight and a guide, set off at midnight to arrive for sunrise. The return takes about four hours.
- If you reach Pelawangan I early in the day, consider a side trip following the crater rim around to the east for about 3km to Gunung Senkereang (2919m). This point overlooks the gap in the rim where the stream from the hot springs flows out of the crater and northeast towards the sea. It's not an easy walk, however, and the track is narrow and very exposed in places – it would take around two hours to get there and back.
- Start trekking from Sembalun Lawang (a guide is essential), from where it takes six or seven hours to get to Pelewangan II. This is a shorter walk to the rim than from Senaru, with only a three-hour trek up the ridge.

the RTC. Both charge around 5000Rp to leave one backpack for three to four days.

Getting There & Away

For transport options from Sembalun Lawang to Senaru see p301. If you've purchased a trekking package, transport back to the point of origin is usually included.

LABUHAN LOMBOK

Labuhan Lombok, also known as Labuhan Kayangan, is the port for ferries and boats to Sumbawa. The town of Labuhan Lombok, 3km from the ferry terminal, is a scruffy place but has great views of Gunung Rinjani.

Sleeping & Eating

Try to arrive early here and avoid staying overnight. The choices on offer are limited and have very basic facilities and shared bathrooms.

Hotel Melati Lima Tiga (s/d 18,000/35,000Rp) On the road to the port, this is the best option, although it's noisy.

Losmen Munawar (r 30,000Rp) and **Losmen Dian Dutaku** (r 25,000Rp) are last resorts.

There are some warung in the town and around the ferry terminal.

Getting There & Away

BUS & BEMO

Frequent buses and bemos travel between Labuhan Lombok and Mandalika terminal in Mataram (two hours, 7500Rp), and also head north from Labuhan Lombok to Anyar. Note that public transport to and from Labuhan Lombok is often marked 'Labuhan Kayangan' or 'Tanjung Kayangan'. Buses and bemos that don't go directly to Labuhan Lombok, but just travel the main road along the east coast, will only drop you off at the port entrance, from where you'll have to catch another bemo to the ferry terminal. Don't walk; it's too far.

FERRY

Sumbawa Ferries travel between Labuhan Lombok and Poto Tano on Sumbawa every hour (adult 10,000Rp; motorcycle 13,500Rp; car 135,000Rp). The trip takes 1½ hours. Coming from Sumbawa, start early so you can reach Labuhan Lombok by 4pm, as public transport is limited after this time.

See p347 for additional details of ferry and bus services between Lombok and Sumbawa.

TETEBATU

☎ 0376

Wonderfully located at the foot of Gunung Rinjani, Tetebatu is a lovely, cool mountain retreat. There are magnificent views across southern Lombok, east to the sea and north to Gunung Rinjani, and it's the perfect place to relax for a few days, hike to the nearby waterfalls or visit the surrounding handicraft villages.

There's a **wartel** (🕐 9am-9pm) next to Salabuse Café.

Sights & Activities

TAMAN WISATA TETEBATU (MONKEY FOREST)

A shady 4km track leading from the main road just north of the mosque heads into this pocket of forest with black monkeys and waterfalls – you will need a guide to find them. Alternatively, you could take an *ojek* from the turn-off.

WATERFALLS

On the southern slopes of Gunung Rinjani National Park there are two waterfalls. Both are accessible only by private transport, or on a lovely 1½-hour walk (one way) through the rice fields from Tetebatu. If walking, even in a group, *be sure* to hire a reputable guide (ask at your losmen).

Locals believe that water from **Air Terjun Jukut** (Jeruk Manis, Air Temer; Map p299; admission 1500Rp) will increase hair growth. The falls are a steep 2km walk from the car park at the end of the road.

To the northeast, **Air Terjun Joben** (Otak Kokok Gading; Map p299; admission 1500Rp) is more of a public swimming pool, so less alluring; locals believe the water here can cure all sorts of ailments.

Sleeping & Eating

Losmen are found on the northern and eastern road from the southern intersection. Nicknamed Waterfall Rd, the eastern road has the funkier options.

Losmen Hakiki (Map p299; r 40,000-70,000Rp, dishes 6000-15,000Rp) The most charming and beautifully located option in Tetebatu, these traditional two-storey *lumbung* are set in the rice fields with great views of Gunung Rinjani. The rooms range from small cottages with outdoor bathrooms to larger ones with a terrace on each floor. All are simply decorated, and there's a restaurant set on stilts in the fields.

Wisma Soedjono (Map p299; ☎ 21309; r 35,000-80,000Rp, dishes 10,000-25,000Rp; ☎) Further north, this colonial-era building has great views, but it was looking neglected when we visited. Accommodation ranges from sparsely furnished rooms to bungalows with hot water and good aspects. There's a large swimming pool but it was extremely dirty when we visited. There's also a restaurant.

Cendrawasih Cottages (Map p299; s/d 30,000/50,000Rp, dishes 5000-20,000Rp) This place has small, two-storey, red-brick cottages overlooking a pretty garden. The octagonal lounge and eating area set on a high platform gives panoramic views of the surrounding area.

Nirwana (Map p299; r 35,000Rp) Walk further up the hill and follow the signposted 200m track to these two charming thatched bungalows set in a lush garden and surrounded by rice fields.

Pondok Tetebatu (Map p299; ☎ 22522; r 40,000Rp, dishes 8000-35,000Rp) This losmen has pristine rooms facing each other and lining a small garden. There's a well-positioned *buruga* for taking in sweeping views of the Rinjani foothills, as well as an adjoining restaurant.

Green Orry (Map p299; Pondok Wisata Lentera Indah; ☎ 22782; r 40,000-70,000Rp, dishes 6000-20,000Rp) The cheaper bamboo bungalows here are run down but the more expensive ones are well furnished, and have modern bathrooms and tiled, clean floors. Rooms overlook each other rather than views. The Perama agent is located here and there's a restaurant serving Western and Indonesian dishes.

Salabuse Café (Map p299; ☎ 081 7573 1143; dishes 6000-17,500Rp; ⏰ 7am-10pm) This good all-rounder serves Western, Indonesian and Sasak meals. It's inexpensive, the setting is pleasant and the owners are friendly; service can be slow, however.

Getting There & Around

Buses go from Mandalika to Pomotong (5000Rp), which is on the main east–west road. From there take a bemo to Kotaraja (1500Rp), then an *ojek* (2500Rp) or *cidomo* (3000Rp) to Tetebatu.

Perama (☎ 22782), at Green Orry Cottages (left), has shuttles to Mataram and Bali that should be booked the day before; there are no shuttles to Kuta in south Lombok.

Bicycles and motorbikes can be rented at Green Orry, as well as other losmen, for 12,000Rp and 40,000Rp per day, respectively.

SOUTH OF TETEBATU

It's best to rent or charter private transport from Tetebatu to visit the craft villages in the area.

The nearest market town to Tetebatu is **Kotaraja**, which is also the transport hub of the area. It's known for its skilled blacksmiths. There's a market on Monday and Wednesday mornings.

Loyok is noted for its fine basketry and **Rungkang** is known for its pottery, made from a local black clay.

Masbagik is quite a large town with a daily morning market, a huge cattle market on Monday afternoon, and an impressive new mosque with elegant minarets. You will find an ATM opposite the mosque. Masbagik Timur, which is 1km east, is a centre for black-clay pottery and ceramic production.

Lendang Nangka is a Sasak village surrounded by picturesque countryside. In and around the village you can see blacksmiths who make knives, hoes and other tools using traditional techniques.

Pringgasela is a centre for traditional weaving on simple looms. The cloth produced here features coloured stripes. You can watch the weavers in action and buy the finished products.

SOUTH LOMBOK

☎ 0370

South Lombok is drier than the rest of the island and more sparsely populated, with fewer roads and limited public transport. Many tourists visit craft villages on day trips from west Lombok, while others want to kick back at Kuta, a much more serene beach area than Kuta on Bali. If you have your own transport you can explore remote villages and sections of coast with stunning scenery, while surfers can charter bemos and boats to visit some excellent surf spots.

PRAYA

This is the main town in the southwest. The bemo terminal, on the northwestern side of town, is the transport hub for the area. ATMs can be found on the main street of Jl Raya Sudirman.

The **Dienda Hayu Hotel** (☎ 654319; Jl Untung Surapati 28; r 40,000-60,000Rp; 🔀) has a choice of cold-water rooms that have seen better days but are still comfortable. On the same street are travel agents offering tours and flight-booking services.

AROUND PRAYA
Sukarara

The main street here is given over to touristy, commercial craft shops, but it's still worth a visit to see the various styles of weaving. **Darnia Setia Artshop** (🕑 7am-6pm) has the widest range of textiles, some coming from further east than Lombok. Be aware that if anyone takes you to one of these shops they will get commission, making the price higher. Even if you bargain hard it will be around 5% to 10%, if not around 20%.

To reach Sukarara, take a bemo to Puyung along the main road. From there, hire a *cidomo* or walk the 2km to Sukarara.

Penujak

Penujak is well known for its traditional *gerabah* pottery made from a local clay with the simplest of techniques. The pots range in size up to 1m high, and there are also various kitchen vessels and decorative figurines. The traditional pottery is a rich terracotta colour and hand burnished.

Penujak is on the main road from Praya to the south coast; any bemo to Sengkol or Kuta will drop you off.

Rembitan & Sade

The area from Sengkol down to Kuta is a centre for traditional Sasak culture. There are regular bemos on this route, especially in the morning.

Rembitan is on a hill just west of the main road. It's a slightly sanitised Sasak village, but still an authentic cluster of thatched houses and *lumbung* surrounded by a wooden fence. On top of the hill is **Masjid Kuno**, an old thatched-roof mosque.

On the road between Rembitan and Sade are shops selling Javanese batik paintings (albeit painted by locals), which rather takes away from the 'traditional Sasak' feel.

A little further south is **Sade**, another traditional, picturesque village that has been extensively renovated. It has informative guides who'll tell you about Sasak houses and village life. Donations are 'requested' by guides at both villages – 2000Rp to 5000Rp is enough.

KUTA

Lombok's Kuta beach (sometimes spelt Kute) is a magnificent stretch of white sand and turquoise sea with rugged hills rising around it. Surfers are attracted here for the surrounding surf, and there are some stunning beaches set in dramatic bays nearby. Despite big plans for five-star resorts, this superb coast is still undeveloped, with far, far fewer facilities than the (in)famous Kuta Beach in Bali. Kuta comes alive during the annual Nyale fishing festival (in February or March; see Nyale Fishing Festival p310) and during the main tourist season (August), but for the rest of the year, it's very quiet.

Information

Several places change money, including Kuta Indah Hotel, the privately run **Tourist Information** (☎ 655269), and Segare Anak Cottages (see p309), which is also a postal agency.

There's a small wartel in town and an Internet café next to Matahari Inn. Internet access is also available at Anda Cottages and Segare Anak Cottages (both 400Rp per minute).

The local market fires up on Sunday and Wednesday.

Perama (☎ 654846), based at Segare Anak Cottages (p309), has one tourist shuttle bus per day to Mataram and Senggigi (both 60,000Rp).

Dangers & Annoyances

Some female readers have reported being hassled and even spied on in Kuta. Take care with guys who hang around budget hotels and check the room for peep-holes.

LOMBOK

KUTA

0 ——————— 1 km
0 ——————— 0.5 miles

INFORMATION	
Internet Café.................................1	B2
Market..2	B2
Perama.....................................(see 14)	
Tourist Information.......................3	B2
Wartel...4	B2

SIGHTS & ACTIVITIES	(p309)
Kuta Reef Surf Shop.....................5	C3

SLEEPING	🏠 (pp309–10)
Anda Cottages...............................6	C3
G'day Inn & Restaurant.................7	B2
Ketapang Bungalows......................8	B2
Kuta Indah Hotel...........................9	B2
Matahari Inn................................10	B2
Melon Homestay...........................11	B2
Novotel Coralia............................12	D3
Rinjani Bungalows........................13	C3
Segare Anak Cottages...................14	C3
Surfers Inn...................................15	C3
Tastura Beach Resort....................16	C3

EATING	🍴 (pp310–11)
Café Lombok Lounge.....................17	B2
Café Riveria.................................18	B2
Empat Ikan.............................(see 12)	
Family Café..................................19	B2
Kafe Chilli..............................(see 12)	
Ocean's Life.................................20	B3
Warung...21	B3

DRINKING	🍸 (p310)
Mascot Pub..................................22	C3

To Sengkol (12.5km);
Praya (25.5km)

To Mawan
(8km);
Selong Blanak
(18km)

Kuta

Teluk Kuta

To Gerupak
(7km)

Pantai Segar

LOMBOK

Activities
SURFING

Plenty of good waves break on the reefs, including 'lefts' and 'rights', in the bay in front of Kuta, and some more on the reefs east of Tanjung Aan. Local boatmen will take you out for around 40,000Rp. About 7km east of Kuta is the fishing village of **Gerupak**, where there are several potential breaks on the reefs at the entrance of Teluk Gerupak (Gerupak Bay). There are plenty of breaks further out, but nearly all need a boat; the current charter rate is a negotiable 200,000Rp per day.

Several shops offer surfboard and boogie-board rentals, as well as repairs and tips. **Kuta Reef Surf Shop** (boogie board/surfboard per day 25,000/30,000Rp; ⏱ 7am-10pm) is one of them.

Sleeping
BUDGET

Melon Homestay (☎ 0817 367 892; angela_grannemann@web.de; r 80,000Rp) By far the best budget option in Kuta, these two apartment-like lodgings are set in a neat two-storey house. They have a large lounge and bedroom decorated with Lombok textiles, a well-equipped kitchen and a modern bathroom. The upstairs apartment has a terrace with a sea view.

Segare Anak Cottages (☎ 654846; segareanakcott@telkom.net.id; bungalow 35,000Rp; r 50,000-100,000Rp; 🖥) Segare Anak offers very basic bungalows, as well as two types of larger, cleaner rooms that overlook a pretty garden. There's a moneychanger, and Internet access (400Rp per minute), and the Perama office is here.

Anda Cottages (☎ 654836; r 40,000-50,000Rp; 🖥) These clean, well-maintained rooms are a good budget choice. Unfortunately, they have monster bathrooms with concrete 'rock' formations. Internet access is available (400Rp per minute), as well as a ping-pong table.

G'Day Inn (☎ 655432; s/d 25,000/40,000Rp, mains 7000-25,000Rp) This smart family-run pad has five clean rooms and a popular café up front.

Ketapang Bungalows (☎ 655194; s/d 30,000/40,000Rp) Near the beach, this place has simple thatched-roof bungalows with a small terrace.

NYALE FISHING FESTIVAL

On the 19th day of the 10th month in the Sasak calendar (generally February or March) thousands of Sasak gather on the beach at Kuta. When night falls, fires are built and young people sit around competing with each other in rhyming couplets called *pantun*. At dawn the next day, the first sea worms of the season are caught as they surface for their reproductive season. After that, it's time for the teenagers to have fun. In a colourful procession, they sail out to sea – in different boats – and chase one another with lots of noise and laughter. This commemorates the legend of a beautiful princess who went out to sea and drowned herself rather than choose between her many admirers – her long hair was transformed into the worm like fish the Sasak call *nyale*. *Nyale* are eaten raw or grilled, and are believed to have aphrodisiac properties. A good catch is a sign that the rice harvest will also be good.

Rinjani Bungalows (☎ 654849; r 30,000-50,000Rp) Next door, this place was having a complete refit when we visited. The majority will be cold-water bungalows.

MID-RANGE

Matahari Inn (☎ 655000; www.matahariinn.com; r 75,000-150,000Rp, with hot water 200,000Rp-550,000Rp; ☒ ☒) This hotel has expansive leafy grounds and a pool. The rooms have Balinese-style furniture and shady balconies. There's free transport to Tanjung Aan, daily updated surfing information, and surfboards to rent (per day 30,000Rp). They do offer massages, but on the day we visited, they weren't that great.

Kutah Indah Hotel (☎ 653781; kutaindah@indonet .id; r US$20-25, with TV & hot water US$40-65; ☒ ☒) This large hotel has decent but characterless rooms around a pool and garden. Prices are very flexible, so aim for half the quoted rates in quiet periods. There's free transport to local beaches and surf spots.

Surfers Inn (☎ 655582; r with fan & cold water 90,000-150,000Rp, with fan & hot water 250,000-400,000Rp; ☒ ☒) This new small hotel on the beachfront looks tacky from the outside with its bright pyramid structures, but the rooms that surround the swimming pool

are well decorated with muted colours, large beds, sofas and minibars.

TOP END

Novotel Coralia (☎ 653333; www.novotel-lombok.com; r without/with terrace US$140/160, villa US$255 + 21% tax; ☒ ☒) This resort has thatched Sasak-style buildings and two swimming pools facing a superb beach and picture-perfect bay. The villas share their own pool and are beautifully decorated with Lombok styling. The rooms are equally well equipped, although the corridors leading to them are dingy. Children are well catered for, and there's a fantastic spa on site.

Tastura Beach Resort (☎ 655540; tastura@mata ram.wasantara.net.id; r US$50-100; ☒ ☒) This brand-new place on the beach road has luxurious bungalows set among neat lawns with a curving pool in the centre. Decorated in green, teak and sandstone, they have lovely open-air bathrooms, but the beds are oddly positioned right in the middle of the room.

Eating & Drinking

There are warung along the esplanade; the food stall on the beach with a sign stipulating 'laundry service' does the best *nasi campur* for 5000Rp.

Family Cafe (☎ 653748; mains 6000-28,000Rp) Ranging from *ayam pelecing* (spicy barbecued chicken) to black-pepper steak, this pleasant spot serves its Sasak and Western dishes on chunky wooden tables set in a garden of bamboo and grasses.

G'Day Inn (☎ 655342; mains 7000-25,000Rp) This place has a good reputation. It offers comfort food for surfers, including Indonesian dishes.

Empat Ikan (mains 65,000-175,000Rp) A bit out of the way at the Novotel Coralia, the beachside location makes this restaurant good for special occasions. It has a small, simple seafood menu.

Kafe Chilli (mains 35,000-135,000Rp) Also at the Novotel Coralia, Kafe Chilli has excellent international choices with an extensive wine list.

Mascot Pub (⊗ 11-2am) This place is little more than a hut in a field, but it provides the only nightlife in Kuta, with live music on Friday and Saturday.

Ocean's Life (☎ 081 7577 0336; mains 9500-30,000Rp), **Cafe Lombok Lounge** (☎ 655542; 7500-30,000Rp) and

Cafe Riveria (mains 7000-23,000Rp), all located on the same street, offer fairly diverse menus including Indo basics and pizza/pasta, as well as fresh seafood.

Getting There & Away

To reach Kuta, catch a bus from Mandalika terminal in Mataram to Praya (2600Rp), then to Sengkol (1500Rp) and finally to Kuta (1500Rp). You'll often have to change buses at these places so many people try and get a direct shuttle bus from Senggigi or the Gili Islands to Kuta. Travel early or you may get stuck and have to charter a vehicle some of the way. Some prefer to make their own way here by rented motorbike or car – make arrangements in Senggigi or Mataram.

Bemos also go east of Kuta to Awang and Tanjung Aan (2500Rp), and west to Selong Blanak (3000Rp).

Getting Around

Ojek congregate around the main intersection as you enter Kuta.

G'Day Inn (p310) rents motorbikes for 35,000Rp a day. The Tourist Information (p308) can arrange motorbike (per day 40,000Rp) and Kijang (per day 175,000Rp) rental. You can charter bemos to nearby beaches and surf spots.

EAST OF KUTA

Quite good roads traverse the coast to the east, passing a series of beautiful bays punctuated by headlands. There's public transport, but it's easier with a motorbike.

Pantai Segar (Segar Beach) is about 2km east around the first headland, within walking distance of the town . An enormous rock another 2km further east offers superb views across the countryside. From Kuta the road goes 5km east to a village called **Tanjung Aan**, where there's a beach with very fine, powdery, white sand. Due to a spate of problems with stealing, there's a security guard keeping an eye on the place – even so, do not bring valuables to the beach. The

> **SECURITY ALERT**
>
> There have been several reports of ambushings and violent muggings in and around Mawi; in particular people being pulled off their motorbikes and attacked. Previously there was a theft problem in Mawan and Selong Blanak but this has improved due to security guards now being in place – even so, do not bring valuables here. In general be careful on the back roads west of Kuta.

road continues another 2km to the fishing village of **Gerupak**, where there's a market on Tuesday. Alternatively, turn northeast just before **Tanjung Aan** and go to **Awang**, a fishing village with a sideline in seaweed harvesting. You could take a boat from Awang across to **Ekas**, or to some of the other not-so-secret surf spots in this bay.

WEST OF KUTA

The road west of Kuta is potholed but passes fine beaches that all have good surf in the right conditions. The road doesn't follow the coast closely, but you'll catch regular and spectacular ocean vistas. You'll need to detour slightly to find the beaches. **Mawan** (parking motorbike/car 4000/2000Rp) is the most impressive with its deep-curved beach and white sand. **Tampa** is similar but a little wilder – you'll need to drive through rice fields on a grassy road and past a tiny village to get there. **Mawi** (parking motorbike/car 4000/2000Rp) is also beautiful, but stealing is common here. **Selong Blanak** is a lovely sandy bay.

From **Pengantap**, the road climbs across a headland to descend to another superb bay; follow this around for about 1km then look out for the turn-off west to **Blongas**, which is a very steep, rough and winding road with breathtaking scenery. There are some good places for surfing and diving – contact Dream Divers in Senggigi (p278) for more details.

Directory

CONTENTS

ACCOMMODATION

All accommodation attracts a combined tax and service ('plus plus') charge of 21%. In the budget places, this is generally included in the price, but check first. Many mid-range (but not all) and top-end places will add it on, which can add substantially to your bill. In this guide, the rates quoted are the peak-season published rates – prices for budget accommodation include tax and service, and prices for mid-range and top-end accommodation exclude tax and service charges unless otherwise stated.

The range of prices used in this book is as follows:

Budget Most rooms cost less than 250,000Rp per night.
Mid-Range Most rooms cost between 250,000Rp and 700,000Rp (around US$75).
Top End Most rooms cost more than 700,000Rp (more than US$75).

The published rate is always negotiable, especially outside the main peak season, and if you are staying for a few days (or longer) at mid-range or top-end places, you should always seek a discount. In the low season, discounts between 30% and 50% are not uncommon in many mid-range and top-end hotels. Note that a high-season surcharge applies in many top-end hotels during holiday periods such as Christmas.

Since 2002, the prices of rooms on Bali have fallen dramatically. Bargains truly

---

PRACTICALITIES

- Current issues of English-language dailies (*Jakarta Post and the International Herald Tribune*) and major news magazines can be found at bookshops and some minimarts in South Bali and Ubud. Don't buy either newspaper at more than cover price from street vendors, who also are the only source for Australian newspapers, which they sell for outrageous prices.

- Pop radio on Bali often has DJs jamming away in English. Short-wave broadcasts, such as Voice of America and the BBC World Service, can be picked up on Bali. Better hotels and some bars have satellite TV with all the international channels.

- Indonesia uses the PAL broadcasting standard, the same as Australia, New Zealand, the UK and most of Europe.

- Electricity is usually 220V to 240V AC in Bali. Wall plugs are the standard European variety – round with two pins. Service is usually reliable although outages occur.

- Indonesia follows the metric system. There is a conversion table for the imperial system on the inside front cover.

abound and you shouldn't have a hard time getting significant discounts off the prices listed in this book.

Camping

The only campground on the whole island is at the headquarters of the Taman Nasional Bali Barat at Cekik in western Bali. It is only useful if you want to trek in the national park, and you will have to bring your own camping and cooking equipment.

Even if you're trekking in the central mountains, or in the national park, you will rarely find use for a tent – there are usually shelters of some sort, and most hikes can be completed in one day anyway.

Hotels

Pretty much every place to stay on Bali and Lombok will arrange tours, car rental and other services. Laundry service is universally available, sometimes for free.

BUDGET HOTELS

The cheapest accommodation on Bali is in small places that are simple, but clean and comfortable. A *losmen* is a small hotel, often family-run, which rarely has more than about 10 rooms; names usually include the word 'losmen', 'homestay' or 'inn'. Losmen are often built in the style of a Balinese home, ie a compound with an outer wall and separate buildings around an inner garden.

There are losmen all over Bali, and they vary widely in standards and price. In a few places you'll find a room for as little as 35,000Rp, but generally they're in the 50,000Rp to 150,000Rp range. Some of the cheap rooms are definitely on the dull and dismal side, but others are attractive, well kept and excellent value for money. A lush garden can be one of the most attractive features, even in very cheap places. The price usually includes a light breakfast, and rooms have an attached bathroom with a shower (cold water only), basin and generally a Western-style toilet and a fan.

Many budget places also resemble hotels and as competition on Bali has heated up, it's not uncommon to find amenities like pools and air-con in budget places with rooms under 250,000Rp. Don't expect great levels of service in any of these places – although smiles abound.

MID-RANGE HOTELS

Mid-range hotels are often constructed in Balinese bungalow style and set on spacious grounds with a pool. In the less expensive mid-range hotels, rooms are priced from about 250,000Rp to 350,000Rp, which includes breakfast and a private bathroom. Mid-range hotels may have a variety of rooms and prices, with the main difference being air-con and hot water versus a fan and cold water. Pools are common.

Upper-mid-range hotels normally give their price in US dollars. Prices range from US$30 to US$75, and should include hot water, air-con, satellite TV and the like. Rooms at the top price end are likely to have a sunken bar in the swimming pool (sometimes unattended, but it looks good on the brochure).

TOP-END HOTELS

Top-end hotels on Bali are world-class. You can find excellent places in Seminyak, Ubud and on the resort strip of Nusa Dua and Tajung Benoa. Exclusive properties can be found around the coast of East Bali and around Pemuteran in North Bali. Service is refined and you can expect décor that seems plucked from the pages of a magazine. Views are superb – whether they are of the ocean or of Bali's lush valleys and rice paddies. At the best places you can expect daily deliveries of fresh fruit and flowers to your room. Bali regularly has several places in surveys of top hotels such as the one done by *Conde Nast Traveller*.

Although top end in this book usually means any place where the average room costs at least US$75, you can multiply that by a factor of five at some of the world-class resorts. Deals for these wonderful places can be found from many sources: the hotel's websites, Internet booking services or as part of holiday packages. It pays to shop around.

Long-term Accommodation

Many villas are available for longer stays. At the minimum they have a kitchen, living room and private garden, and often two or more bedrooms, so they are suitable for a family or a group of friends.

But many villas go far beyond the norm. Some are literally straight out of the pages of *Architectural Digest* and other design magazines and come with pools, views, beaches and more. Often the houses are staffed and you have the services of a cook, driver etc. Some villas are part of developments – common in Seminyak – and may be linked to a hotel, which gives you access to additional services. Others are free-standing homes in rural areas such as the coast around Canggu.

Rates can range anywhere from US$500 for a modest villa to US$4000 per week and beyond for your own tropical estate. There are often deals, especially in the off-season. Also you can save quite a bit by waiting until the last minute, but during the high season the best villas can book up months in advance. The following agencies are among the many on Bali.

Agencies Bali Villas (☎ 0361-241304; www.agencies-bali-villas.com)

Bali Villas (☎ 0361-703060; www.balivillas.com)

Elite Havens (☎ 0361-731074; www.elitehavens.com)

House of Bali (☎ 0361-739541; www.houseofbali.com)

Village Accommodation

In remote villages, you can often find a place to stay by asking the *kepala desa* (village chief or headman) and it will usually be a case of sleeping in a pavilion in a family compound. The price is negotiable, maybe about 25,000Rp per person per night. Your hosts may not even ask for payment, and in these cases you should definitely offer some gifts, like bottled water, sweets or fruit. If they give you a meal, it is even more important to make an offer of payment or gifts. It's a very good idea to take a Balinese friend or guide to help facilitate introductions, and to ensure that you make as few cultural faux pas as possible.

ACTIVITIES

Surfing, diving and snorkelling are major activities on Bali, but there are lots of other activities available too, ranging from adventure activities for tourists seeking a day's diversion to indulge hours spent at massage spas.

Most outdoor activities operators include pick-up from hotels in the southern Bali resorts, and will drop off at the end of the day. The most comprehensive programme is offered by **Bali Adventure Tours** (☎ 0361-721480; www.baliadventuretours.com), which offers a choice of elephant rides, rafting, mountain biking, tandem parachuting, tandem paragliding and helicopter tours.

Other general activities include cruises and boat trips to Nusa Lembongan (p209), snorkelling and fishing trips from most seaside destinations and water sports particularly at Sanur and Tanjung Benoa.

Diving & Snorkelling

With its warm water, extensive coral reefs and abundant marine life, Bali offers excellent diving and snorkelling possibilities. Reliable dive schools and operators all around Bali's coast can train complete beginners or arrange challenging trips that will satisfy the most experienced divers. The best sites can all be accessed in a day trip from the south of Bali, though the more distant ones will involve several hours of travelling time.

Snorkelling gear is available near all the most accessible spots, but if you're keen, it's definitely worthwhile to bring your own, and to check out some of the less visited parts of the coast. For easy access, try the reefs off Nusa Dua, Padangbai, Candidasa, Tulamben, Amed and various points along the northeast coast.

During the wet season storms tend to reduce visibility at times, although Pulau Menjangan and Nusa Penida can still be good. Some coral bleaching occurred during the 1998 El Niño event, with some shallow-water coral on the north and northeast coast being killed, but there are still plenty of fish to see, and most of the coral deeper than 10m is OK.

For a detailed guide to Bali's underwater possibilities, see Lonely Planet's *Diving & Snorkeling Bali & Lombok.*

DIVE COSTS

On a local trip, count on US$40 to US$75 per person for two dives, which includes all equipment. Many operators offer open-water diving certification for US$350 to US$400.

DIVE COURSES

If you're not a qualified diver, and you want to try some scuba diving on Bali, you have three options.

First, nearly all the operators offer an 'introductory', 'orientation' or 'initial' dive for beginners, usually after some classroom training and shallow-water practise. These

RESPONSIBLE DIVING

The popularity of diving is placing immense pressure on many sites. Please consider the following tips when diving and help preserve the ecology and beauty of reefs.

- Do not use anchors on the reef, and take care not to ground boats on coral. Encourage dive operators to use permanent moorings at popular dive sites.

- Avoid touching living marine organisms with your body or dragging equipment across the reef. Polyps can be damaged by even the gentlest contact. Never stand on corals, even if they look solid and robust. If you must hold on to the reef, only touch exposed rock or dead coral.

- Be conscious of your fins. Even without contact, the surge from heavy fin strokes near the reef can damage delicate organisms. When treading water in shallow reef areas, take care not to kick up clouds of sand. Settling sand can easily smother the delicate organisms of the reef.

- Practise and maintain proper buoyancy control. Major damage can be done by divers descending too fast and colliding with the reef. Make sure you are correctly weighted and that your weight belt is positioned so that you stay horizontal. Be aware that buoyancy can change over the period of an extended trip: initially you may breathe harder and need more weight; a few days later you may breathe more easily and need less weight.

- Take great care in underwater caves. Spend as little time within them as possible as your air bubbles may be caught within the roof and thereby leave previously submerged organisms high and dry. Taking turns to inspect the interior of a small cave will lessen the chances of damaging contact.

- Don't buy coral or shell souvenirs. Aside from the ecological damage, taking home marine souvenirs depletes the beauty of a site and spoils the enjoyment of others. The same goes for marine shipwreck sites – respect their integrity.

- Ensure that you take home all your rubbish and any litter you may find as well. Plastics in particular are a serious threat to marine life. Turtles can mistake plastic for jellyfish and eat it.

- Don't feed fish. You may disturb their normal eating habits, encourage aggressive behaviour or feed them food that is detrimental to their health.

- Minimise your disturbance of marine animals. In particular, do not ride on the backs of turtles, as this causes them great anxiety.

courses are reasonably cheap (from around US$60 for one dive), but it is essential to stick to one of the recommended dive operators (see below).

Second, some of the larger hotels and diving agencies offer four- or five-day courses that certify you for basic dives in the location where you do the course. A resort course will give you a better standard of training than just an introductory dive, but it doesn't make you a qualified diver. These courses cost about US$300.

Finally, if you are serious about diving, the best option is to enrol in a full open-water diving course, which gives you an internationally recognised qualification. A four-day open-water course, to Professional Association of Diving Instructors (PADI) standards, with a qualified instructor, manual, dive table and certification, will cost about US$300 to US$400. Experienced

divers can also upgrade their skills with advanced open-water courses in night, wreck and deep diving etc, from around US$200 for a three-day course.

DIVE OPERATORS

Major dive operators in tourist areas can arrange trips to the main dive sites all around the island. But distances can be long, so it's better to stay relatively close to your destination.

Places with good dive shops include Sanur (p122), Padangbai (p189), Candidasa (p194), Amed (p202), Tulamben (p206), Lovina (p241), Pemuteran (p249) and Nusa Lembongan (p209).

DIVE SITES
Bali

Bali's main dive sites include the places listed above with good dive centres. For

SAFETY GUIDELINES FOR DIVING

Before embarking on a scuba diving, skin diving or snorkelling trip, carefully consider the following points to ensure a safe and enjoyable experience:

- Possess a current diving certification card from a recognised scuba diving instructional agency (if scuba diving).
- Be sure you are healthy and feel comfortable diving.
- Obtain reliable information about physical and environmental conditions at the dive site (eg from a reputable local dive operation).
- Be aware of local laws, regulations and etiquette about marine life and the environment.
- Dive only at sites within your realm of experience; if available, engage the services of a competent, professionally trained dive instructor or dive master.
- Be aware that underwater conditions vary significantly from one region, or even site, to another. Seasonal changes can significantly alter any site and dive conditions. These differences influence the way divers dress for a dive and what diving techniques they use.
- Ask about the environmental characteristics that can affect your diving and how local trained divers deal with these considerations.

details see those sections of the book. In addition, Nusa Penida (p213) and Pulau Menjangan (p263) in Taman Nasional Bali Barat (West Bali National Park) are renowned for their diving.

Lombok

There is some very good scuba diving and snorkelling off the Gili Islands (see Diving and Snorkelling in the Gili Islands, p285), though some of the coral has been damaged by dynamite fishing. There are also some good reefs near Senggigi (p278). Quite a few dive operators are based on the Gilis and in Senggigi and many have good reputations.

EQUIPMENT

All the equipment you need is available on Bali, but you may not be able to get exactly what you want in the size you need, and the quality is variable – some operators use equipment right to the end of its service life. Most dive operators on Bali include the cost of equipment in the cost of the dive, but if you have your own equipment (excluding mask, snorkel and fins), you'll receive a discounted rate. Tanks and weight belt – as well as lunch, drinking water, transport, guides and insurance – are generally included in dive trips.

The basic equipment to bring is a mask, snorkel and fins – you know they'll fit and they're not too difficult to carry. At any area with coral and tourists you will be able to rent snorkelling gear for around 20,000Rp per day, but check the condition of the equipment before you take it away.

Also worth bringing if you plan to do a lot of diving is a thin, full-length wetsuit, which is important for protection against stinging animals and coral abrasions. A thicker one (3mm) would be preferable if you plan frequent diving, deep dives or a night dive – the water can be cold, especially deeper down. Some small, easy-to-carry things to bring from home include protective gloves, spare straps, silicone lubricant and extra globes for your torch (flashlight). Most dive operators can rent good-quality regulators (about US$5 per day) and BCVs (aka BCDs; about US$5), but if you bring your own you'll save money, and it's a good idea especially if you're planning to dive in more remote and secluded locations than Bali, where the rental equipment may not be as good.

Golf

There are 18-hole golf courses at Nusa Dua (p133), near Danau Bratan (p230) and Tanah Lot (p253).

Horse Riding

You can ride horses from stables in Kerobokan (p118) and Pemuteran (p249). In Lombok, horse riding is available in Gili Trawangan (p294).

Rafting

Rafting is very popular, usually as a day trip from South Bali or Ubud (Ubud is closest to the best rapids; see p151). Operators pick you up from your hotel, take you to the put-in point, provide all the equipment and guides, and return you to your hotel at the end of the day. The best time is during the wet season (October to March), or just after; by the middle of the dry season (April to September), the best river rapids may just be a dribble.

Most operators use the Sungai Ayung, near Ubud, where there are between 19 and 25 Class II to III rapids (ie exciting but not perilous). During the rare bits of calm water, you can admire the stunning gorges and rice paddies from the boat.

Bring shorts, shirt/T-shirt, sneakers and sunblock. Afterwards, you'll need a full change of clothes and a towel (although this may be supplied for you). The operator should provide plastic bags for cameras and any other item that may be damaged by water. Prices include transport, equipment, insurance and lunch. You can book any trip directly, or you can go through a travel agent or one of the hotels in the tourist centres.

Advertised prices run from around US$40 to US$70, but those with high published rates will often discount. Like scuba diving, however, it is worth paying more for a reputable operator, with reliable equipment and experienced guides.

Spa Treatments

Whether it's a total fix for the mind, body and spirit, or simply the desire for some quick-fix serenity, lots of travellers in Bali are spending hours and days being massaged, scrubbed, perfumed, pampered, bathed and blissed-out. See the boxed text

---

MASSAGE, SCRUB & SOAK

Massage and herbal body scrubs have an important place in Balinese family life. From birth, parents massage their children, and as soon as children are able it's normal for them to reciprocate. Anyone with an ailment receives a specially formulated scrub, and men provide and receive massage as much as women. The Balinese massage techniques of stretching, long strokes, skin rolling and palm and thumb pressure result in a lowering of tension, improved blood flow and circulation, and an all-over feeling of calm.

So what can you expect in a spa? It's basically a three-stage process – the massage, the scrub and the soak. Therapists are often female, although top-end spas may have male therapists. Many massage rooms are also set up with two massage beds, so you can have a massage alongside your partner or friend.

A basic therapeutic massage is a one-hour, top-to-toe, deep-tissue massage to relax the muscles, tone the skin and eliminate stress, while aromatherapy massages feature a choice of essential oils, such as ginger, nutmeg, coconut and sandalwood. Commonly offered massage options include Shiatsu, Thai and Swedish massage and reflexology (concentrating on pressure points of the feet). For something special, the 'four-hands' massage, where two therapists will treat you, is also an option at many spas.

Based on traditional herbal treatments, popular spa options include the *mandi rempah* (spice bath) and the *mandi susu* (milk bath). The *mandi rempah* begins with a massage, followed by a body scrub with a paste made from assorted spices, and ending with a herbal-and-spice hot bath. The *mandi susu* begins with a massage, followed by a herbal scrub and a milk-and-yoghurt body mask. The treatment ends with a soak in a milk bath.

The most popular treatment though, is the Javanese *mandi lulur* body scrub. Based on a centuries-old Javanese palace ritual, the *mandi lulur* takes almost two hours but it feels longer as all sense of time is lost during the deep-tissue massage (ask for strong treatment if you dare). The massage is followed by a full body rub made from a vibrant yellow paste of turmeric, sandalwood and rice powder. This is allowed to dry and then gently rubbed off, exfoliating and polishing the skin. Next, a mixture of yoghurt and honey is smoothed on, to moisturise and feed the skin and restore the perfect pH balance. After a quick rinsing shower, the highlight follows – a long and lovely bath in fragrant essential oils amid pale, floating frangipani petals. Refreshing hot ginger tea is normally served during the calming recovery time following the bath, when you'll feel so good you'll be dreamily planning another two hours of luxurious bliss.

'Massage, Soak & Scrub', p317, about the specifics of Balinese massage.

Every upmarket hotel worth its stars has spa facilities (which are generally open to nonguests) offering health, beauty and relaxation treatments. Day spas are also common in all the tourist centres, particularly Ubud (p151). Kuta (p99) and Seminyak (p113) are also good places for spas.

Surfing

In recent years, the number of surfers on Bali has increased enormously, and good breaks can get very crowded. Many Balinese have taken to surfing, and the grace of traditional dancing is said to influence their style. The surfing competitions on Bali are a major local event. Facilities for surfers have improved, and surf shops in Kuta will sell just about everything you need.

A long-running place, Tubes Surf Bar & Restaurant (p99) is a popular centre for anything to do with surfing – the Tubes tide chart is widely available.

Indo Surf & Lingo (www.indosurf.com.au) by Peter Neely tells surfers where and when to find good waves around Bali and other Indonesian islands. The book also has a language guide with Indonesian translations of useful words. It's available at surf shops in the Kuta region.

Surfing Indonesia by Leonard and Lorca Lueras has about 80 pages on Bali. It has great photos, a comprehensive coverage of the waves, and some good surfing background.

Look for the free newspaper *Magic Wave*, which is distributed around Kuta and has full coverage of the Bali surfing scene.

EQUIPMENT

A small board is usually adequate for the smaller breaks, but a few extra inches on your usual board length won't go astray. For the bigger waves – 8ft and upwards – you will need a gun. For a surfer of average height and build, a board around the 7ft mark is perfect.

You can bring a couple of boards, but if you have more than two or three, customs officials may object, suggesting that you intend to sell them.

To get your boards to Bali in reasonable condition, you need a good board cover.

Bali-bound airlines are used to carrying boards, but fins still get broken. Long hikes with your board are difficult unless you have a board-strap. Take a good pair of running shoes for walking down steep, rocky paths on cliff faces. When you book any long-distance buses, find out if they take surfboards – some don't, or will charge extra. Bring a soft roof-rack to secure your boards to a car or taxi.

There are surfboards and boogie boards for rent at Kuta (p99), with very variable quality and prices.

Wax is available locally, but take your own anyway if you use it – in the tepid water and the hot sun a sticky wax is best. Board repairs and materials are readily available in Kuta, but it's always advisable to have your own, especially if you're going to more remote spots.

To protect your feet take a pair of wetsuit booties or reef boots. A wetsuit vest is also very handy for chilly, windy overcast days, and it also protects your back and chest from sunburn, and from being ground into the reefs. If you are a real tube maniac and will drive into anything no matter what the consequences, you are advised to take a short-sleeved spring-suit. A Lycra swim-shirt or rash vest is good protection against chills and sunburn.

Bring surgical spirit, and cotton buds to put on your cuts each night. Also bring a needle and pointed tweezers to remove sea urchin spines. Adhesive bandages that won't come off in the water are also necessary.

A surfing helmet is a good idea, not just for protection from the reefs, but also to keep the sun off while you wait in the line-up. And it will probably give you better protection in a motorcycle accident than the helmets that come with rented bikes.

SURF TRIPS FROM BALI

Charter boats take groups of surfers for day trips around various local reefs, or for one-week 'surfaris' to great breaks on eastern Java (Grajagan, also known as G-Land), Nusa Lembongan, Lombok and Sumbawa, some of which cannot be reached by land. These are especially popular with those who find that the waves on Bali are too crowded. You'll see them advertised in numerous agents and surf shops in Kuta. Prices start at around 300,000Rp per person per week (seven days/six nights), including food. The most basic boats are converted Indonesian fishing boats with minimal comforts and safety equipment.

Wanasari Wisata (☎ 0361-755588; www.grajagan .com) is one of the most established operators in the area.

Surf Travel Online (0361-750550; www.surftravel online.com) has information on surf camps, boat charters and package deals for surf trips to remote Indonesian locations, as well as Nusa Lembongan.

WHERE TO SURF

The swells come from the Indian Ocean, so the surf is on the southern side of the island and, strangely, on the northwest coast of Nusa Lembongan, where the swell funnels into the strait between there and the Bali coast.

In the dry season (around April to September), the west coast has the best breaks, with the trade winds coming in from the southeast; this is also when Nusa Lembongan works best. In the wet season,

surf the eastern side of the island, from Nusa Dua around to Padangbai. If there's a north wind – or no wind at all – there are also a couple of breaks on the south coast of Bukit Peninsula.

Lombok has some good surfing as well, and the dearth of tourists means that breaks are uncrowded.

Balangan

Go through Pecatu Indah resort and follow the 'alternative' road around to the right to reach the Balangan *warung* (food stall). Balangan (p130) is a fast left over a shallow reef, unsurfable at low tide, good at mid-tide with anything over a 4ft swell; with an 8ft swell, this can be a classic wave.

Balian

There are a few peaks near the mouth of Sungai Balian (Balian River, p258) in western Bali – sea water here is often murky because the river can carry a lot of pollution. Look for the Taman Rekreasi Indah Soka, along the main road, just west of Lalang-Linggah. The best break here is

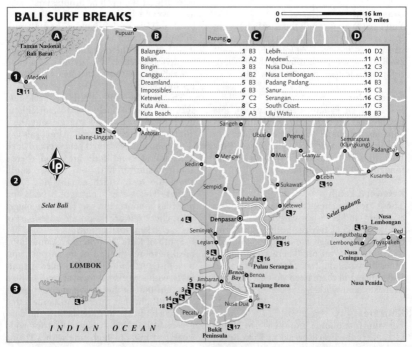

BALI SURF BREAKS

Balangan...........................1 B3	Lebih.............................10 D2
Balian..............................2 A2	Medewi..........................11 A1
Bingin.............................3 B3	Nusa Dua........................12 C3
Canggu............................4 B2	Nusa Lembongan................13 D2
Dreamland........................5 B3	Padang Padang..................14 B3
Impossibles......................6 B3	Sanur.............................15 C3
Ketewel...........................7 C2	Serangan.........................16 C3
Kuta Area.........................8 C3	South Coast......................17 C3
Kuta Beach.......................9 A3	Ulu Watu.........................18 B3

an enjoyable and consistent left-hander that works well at mid- to high tide if there's no wind.

Bingin

North of Padang and accessible by road, this spot (p130) can now get crowded. It's best at mid-tide with a 6ft swell, when it manufactures short but perfect left-hand barrels.

Canggu

North of Kuta-Legian-Seminyak, on the northern extremity of the bay, Canggu (p118) has a nice white beach and a few surfers. The peak breaks over a 'soft' rock ledge – well, it's softer than coral. An optimum size for Canggu is 5ft to 6ft. There's a good right-hander that you can really hook into, which works at full tide, and what the surf writer Peter Neely calls 'a sucky left ledge that tubes like Ulu but without the coral cuts', which works from mid-tide. A drivable track goes right to the beach – get there early, before the crowds and the wind. Echo Beach just west is also a good spot.

Dreamland

You have to go through the abortive Pecatu Indah resort to reach this spot (p130), which can also get crowded. At low tide with a 5ft swell, this solid peak offers a short, sharp right and a longer, more tubular left.

Impossibles

Just north of Padang Padang (p130), this outside reef break has three shifting peaks with fast left-hand tube sections that can join up if the conditions are perfect (low tide, 5ft swell), but don't stay on for too long, or you'll run out of water.

Ketewel & Lebih

These two beaches (p176) are northeast of Sanur, and access is easy from the new coastal road. They're both right-hand beach breaks, which are dodgy at low tide and close out over 6ft. There are probably other breaks along this coast all the way to Padangbai, but there needs to be a big swell to make them work.

Kuta Area

For your first plunge into the warm Indian Ocean, try the beach breaks at Kuta Beach (p98); on full tide go out near the life-saving club at the southern end of the beach road. At low tide, try the tubes around Half-way Kuta (p99), probably the best place on Bali for beginners to practise. Start at the beach breaks if you are a bit rusty. The sand here is fine and packed hard, so it can hurt when you hit it. Treat even these breaks with respect. They provide zippering left and right barrels over shallow banks and can be quite a lot of fun.

Further north, the breaks at Legian Beach (p99) can be pretty powerful, with lefts and rights on the sand bars off Jl Melasti and Jl Padma. At Kuta and Legian you will encounter most of the local Balinese surfers.

Further north again, there are more beach breaks off Seminyak (p113), such as the Oberoi, near the hotel of the same name. The sea here is fickle and can have dangerous rip tides – take a friend.

For more serious stuff, go to the reefs south of the beach breaks, about 1km out to sea. Kuta Reef, a vast stretch of coral, provides a variety of waves. You can paddle out in around 20 minutes, but the easiest way is by outrigger. You will be dropped out there and brought back in for a fee. The main break is a classic left-hander, best at mid- to high tide with a 5ft to 6ft swell, when it peels across the reef and has a beautiful inside tube section; the first part is a good workable wave. Over 7ft it tends to double up and section.

The reef is well suited for backhand surfing. Unfortunately it's not surfable at dead-low tide, but you can get out there not long after the tide turns. The locals can advise you if necessary. It gets very crowded here, but if conditions are good there's another, shorter left, 50m further south along the reef, which usually has fewer surfers. This wave is more of a peak and provides a short, intense ride. On bigger days, check out breaks on the outer part of the reef, 150m further out.

South of Kuta Reef there are some good breaks around the end of the airport runway. Just north is a reef break called Airport Lefts, with a workable wave at mid- to high tide. On the southern side of the runway, Airport Rights has three right-handers that can be a bit fickle, and are shallow and dangerous at low tide – they're best for good surfers at mid- to high tide with a strong swell. Get there by outrigger from Kuta or Jimbaran (p129).

Lombok

Kuta Beach (p309) is an excellent place for surfing with left and right breaks on its turquoise bay. The beaches to the west (p311) and the east (p311) are known for their good waves as well. The Gilis (p284) attract surfers more for their fun reputation than because the waves there are worth mentioning.

Medewi

Further along the south coast of western Bali is a softer left called Medewi (p258) – it's a point break that can give a long ride right into the river mouth. This wave has a big drop, which fills up then runs into a workable inside section. It's worth surfing if you feel like something different, but to catch it you need to get up early, because it gets blown out as the wind picks up. It works best at mid- to high tide with a 6ft swell, but it depends on the direction.

Nusa Dua

During the wet season you should surf on the east side of the island, where there are some very fine reef breaks. The reef off the Nusa Dua (p133) has very consistent swells. The main break is 1km off the beach to the south of Nusa Dua – go past the golf course and look for the whole row of warung and some boats to take you out. There are lefts and rights that work well on a small swell at low to mid-tide. On bigger days, take a longer board and go further out, where powerful peaks offer long-rides, fat tubes and lots of variety. Further north, in front of the Club Med, is a fast, barrelling, right reef break called Sri Lanka, which works best at mid-tide and can handle swells from 6ft to 10ft.

Nusa Lembongan

In the Nusa Penida group, this island (p209) is separated from the southeast coast of Bali by the Selat Badung (Badung Strait).

The strait is very deep and generates huge swells that break over the reefs off the northwest coast of Lembongan. Shipwreck, clearly visible from the beach, is the most popular break, a longish right that gets a good barrel at mid-tide with a 5ft swell.

A bit to the south, Lacerations is a very fast, hollow right breaking over a very shallow reef – hence the name. Still further south is a smaller, more user-friendly left-hander called Playground. Remember that Lembongan is best with an easterly wind, like Kuta and Ulu Watu, so it's dry-season surfing.

Padang Padang

Just Padang for short, this super shallow, left-hand reef break (p130) is just north of Ulu Watu towards Kuta. Again, check this place carefully before venturing out. It's a very demanding break that only works over about 6ft from mid- to high tide – it's a great place to watch from the clifftop.

If you can't surf tubes, backhand or forehand, don't go out: Padang is a tube. After a ledgey take-off, you power along the bottom before pulling up into the barrel. So far so good, now for the tricky part. The last section turns inside out like a washing machine on fast-forward. You have to drive high through this section, all the time while in the tube. Don't worry if you fail to negotiate this trap, plenty of other surfers have been caught too. After this, the wave fills up and you flick off. Not a wave for the faint-hearted and definitely not a wave to surf when there's a crowd.

Sanur

Sanur Reef (p121) has a hollow wave with excellent barrels. It's fickle, and doesn't even start till you get a 6ft swell, but anything over 8ft will be world-class, and anything over 10ft will be brown boardshorts material. There are other reefs further offshore and most of them are surfable.

Hyatt Reef, over 2km from shore, has a shifty right peak that can give a great ride at full tide. Closer in, opposite the Sanur Beach Market, Tanjung Sari gives long left rides at low tide with a big swell, while Tanjung Right can be a very speedy wall on a big swell. The classic right is off the Grand Bali Beach Hotel. A couple of kilometres north, Padang Galak is a beach break at high tide on a small to medium swell, but it can be very dirty.

Serangan

The abortive development at Pulau Serangan entailed huge earthworks at the southern and eastern sides of the island, and this has made the surf here much more consistent, though the landfill looks like a disaster. The new causeway has made the island much more accessible, and a dozen or so warung face the water, where waves break right and left in anything over a 3ft swell (see p126).

South Coast

The extreme south coast (p131), around the end of Bukit Peninsula, can be surfed any time of the year provided there is a northerly wind, or no wind at all – get there very early to avoid onshore winds. The peninsula is fringed with reefs and big swells are produced, but access is a problem. There are a few roads, but the shoreline is all cliff. If you want to explore it, charter a boat on a day with no wind and a small swell.

Nyang Nyang is a right-hand reef break, reached by a steep track down the cliff. Green Ball is another right, which works well on a small to medium swell, ie when it's almost flat everywhere else. Take the road to the Bali Cliffs Resort, fork left just before you get there and take the steps down the cliff. The south coast has few facilities and tricky currents, and it would be a bad place to get into trouble.

Ulu Watu

When Kuta Reef is 5ft to 6ft, Ulu Watu (p130), the most famous surfing break on Bali, will be 6ft to 8ft with bigger sets. Kuta and Legian sit on a huge bay – Ulu Watu is way out on the southern extremity of the bay, and consequently picks up more swell than Kuta. It's about a half-hour journey from downtown Kuta by private transport.

ʻUlu Watu Bay is a great setup for surfers – local boys will wax your board, get drinks for you and carry the board down into the cave, which is the usual access to the wave. There are warung.

Ulu Watu has about seven different breaks. If it's your first trip here, sit for a while in the shade and survey the situation. See where other surfers are sitting in the line-up and watch where they flick off. The Corner is straight in front of you to the right. It's a fast-breaking, hollow left that holds about 6ft. The reef shelf under

this break is extremely shallow, so try to avoid falling headfirst. At high tide, the Peak starts to work. This is good from 5ft to 8ft, with bigger waves occasionally right on the Peak itself. You can take off from this inside part or further down the line. A great wave. At low tide, if the swell isn't huge, go further south to the Racetrack, a whole series of bowls.

At low tide when the swell is bigger, Outside Corner starts operating, further out from the Racetrack. This is a tremendous break and on a good day you can surf one wave for hundreds of metres. The wall here on a 10ft wave jacks up with a big drop and bottom turn, then the bowl section. After this it becomes a big workable face. You can usually get tubed only in the first section. When surfing this break you need a board with length, otherwise you won't be getting down the face of any of the amazing waves.

Another left runs off the cliff that forms the southern flank of the bay. It breaks outside this in bigger swells, and once it's 7ft, a left-hander pitches right out in front of a temple on the southern extremity. Out behind the Peak, when it's big, is a bombora (submerged reef) appropriately called the Bommie. This is another big left-hander and it doesn't start operating until the swell is about 10ft. On a normal 5ft to 8ft day there are also breaks south of the Peak. One is a very fast left, and is also very hollow, usually only ridden by goofy-footers, due to its speed.

Observe where other surfers paddle out and follow them. If you are in doubt, ask someone. It is better having some knowledge than none at all. Climb down into the cave and paddle out from there. When the swell is bigger you will be swept to your right. Don't panic, it is an easy matter to paddle around the white water from down along the cliff. Coming back in you have to aim for the cave. When the swell is bigger, come from the southern side of the cave as the current runs to the north. If you miss the cave, paddle out again and repeat the procedure.

Trekking

Bali is not usually thought of as a trekking destination, but so many people climb Gunung Batur to see the sunrise that it can get crowded up there some mornings (see p220). There are numerous other possibilities for treks in the Batur area, around the volcanoes near Bedugul (p227) and in Taman Nasional Bali Barat in western Bali (p262). The biggest challenge is a climb of the 3142m Gunung Agung (p218).

Bali does not offer remote 'wilderness treks'; it's simply too densely populated. For the most part, you make day trips from the closest village, often leaving before dawn to avoid the clouds that usually blanket the peaks by mid-morning – for most treks, you won't need a tent, sleeping bag or stove. However, waterproof clothing and a sweater are essential for trekking in the Central Mountains.

Trekking is also a good way to explore the backblocks of Bali – you can trek from village to village on small tracks and between the rice paddies. You can easily go on short hikes, without guides, around Tirta Gangga (p200); to splendid villages near Ubud (p152); and around Tamblingan (p230), Buyan and Bratan lakes and Munduk (p231).

Several agencies offer organised walking and trekking trips. See the Ubud chapter (p155), the Central Mountains chapter (p218) and the East Bali chapter (p187).

On Lombok, the Gunung Rinjani area (p301) is superb for trekking.

BUSINESS HOURS

Government office hours on Bali and Lombok are roughly from 8am to 3pm Monday to Thursday and from 8am to noon on Friday, but they are not completely standardised. Postal agencies will often keep longer hours, and the main post offices are often open every day (from about 8am to 2pm Monday to Thursday and 8am to noon Friday; in the larger tourist centres, the main post offices are often open on weekends). Banking hours are generally from 8am to 2pm Monday to Thursday, from 8am to noon Friday and from 8am to about 11am Saturday. The banks enjoy many public holidays.

In this book it is assumed that restaurants and cafés are usually open about 8am to 10pm daily. Shops and services catering to tourists are open from 9am to about 8pm. Where hours vary from these they are noted in the text.

SAFETY GUIDELINES FOR TREKKING

Before embarking on a trekking trip, consider the following points to ensure a safe and enjoyable experience:

- Pay any fees and possess any permits required by local authorities.

- Be sure you are healthy and feel comfortable walking for a sustained period.

- Obtain reliable information about physical and environmental conditions along your intended route (eg from park authorities).

- Be aware of local laws, regulations and etiquette about wildlife and the environment.

- Walk only in regions, and on trails/ tracks, within your realm of experience.

- Be aware that weather conditions and terrain vary significantly from one region, or even from one trail/track, to another. Seasonal changes can significantly alter any trail/track. These differences influence the way walkers dress and the equipment they carry.

- Ask before you set out about the environmental characteristics that can affect your walk and how local, ex-perienced walkers deal with these considerations.

CHILDREN

Travelling with *anak-anak* (children) anywhere requires energy and organisation (see Lonely Planet's *Travel with Children* by Cathy Lanigan), but on Bali the problems are somewhat lessened by the Balinese affection for children. They believe that children come straight from God, and the younger they are, the closer they are to God. To the Balinese, children are considered part of the community and everyone, not just the parents, has a responsibility towards them. If a young child cries, the Balinese get most upset and insist on finding a parent and handing the child over with a reproachful look. Sometimes they despair of uncaring Western parents, and the child will be whisked off to a place where it can be cuddled, cosseted and fed. In tourist areas this is less likely, but it's still common in a more traditional environment. A toddler may even get too much attention!

Children are a social asset when you travel on Bali, and people will display great interest in any Western child they meet. You will have to learn your child's age and sex in Bahasa Indonesia – *bulan* (month), *tahun* (year), *laki-laki* (boy) and *perempuan* (girl). You should also make polite inquiries about the other person's children, present or absent.

Lombok is generally quieter than Bali and the traffic is much less dangerous. People are fond of kids, but less demonstrative about it than the Balinese. The main difference is that services for children are much less developed.

Practicalities
ACCOMMODATION
A hotel with a swimming pool, air-con and a beachfront location is fun for kids and very convenient, and provides a good break for the parents. Sanur, Nusa Dua and Lovina are all good places for kids as the surf is placid and the streets quieter than the Kuta area.

Most places, at whatever price level, have a 'family plan', which means that children up to about 12 years old can share a room with their parents free of charge. The catch is that hotels charge for extra beds. If you need more space, just rent a separate room for the kids.

As noted in the text, many top-end hotels offer special programmes or supervised activities for kids, and where this isn't the case, most hotels can arrange a baby-sitter.

Hotel and restaurant staff are usually very willing to help and improvise, so always ask if you need something for your children. The situation is improving as more young kids come to Bali and more parents make their wishes known.

FOOD
The same rules apply as for adults – kids should drink only clean water and eat only well-cooked food or fruit that you have peeled yourself. If you're travelling with a young baby, breast-feeding is much easier than bottles. For older babies, mashed bananas, eggs, peelable fruit and *bubur* (rice cooked to a mush in chicken stock) are all generally available. In tourist areas, supermarkets sell jars of Western baby food and packaged UHT milk and fruit juice. Bottled drinking water is available everywhere. Bring plastic bowls, plates, cups and spoons for do-it-yourself meals.

SAFETY PRECAUTIONS
The main danger is traffic, so try to stay in less busy areas. If your children can't look after themselves in the water then they must be supervised – don't expect local people to act as life savers.

On Bali, the sorts of facilities, safeguards and services that Western parents regard as basic may not be present. Not many restaurants provide a highchair; many places with great views have nothing to stop your kids falling over the edge and shops often have breakable things at kiddie height.

WHAT TO BRING
Apart from those items mentioned in the Health chapter (p359), bring some infant analgesic, antilice shampoo, a medicine measure and a thermometer.

You can take disposable nappies (diapers) with you, but they're widely available on Bali and to a lesser degree on Lombok.

For small children, bring a folding stroller or pusher, or you will be condemned to having them on your knee constantly, at meals and everywhere else. However, it won't be much use for strolling, as there are few paved footpaths that are wide and smooth enough. A papoose or a backpack carrier is a much easier way to move around with children.

Some equipment, such as snorkelling gear and boogie boards, can be rented easily in the tourist centres. A simple camera, or a couple of the throwaway ones, will help your child feel like a real tourist.

Sights & Activities
Many of the things that adults want to do on Bali will not interest their children. Have days when you do what they want, to offset the times you drag them to shops or temples. Encourage them to learn about the islands so they can understand and enjoy more of what they see.

Water play is always fun – you can often use a hotel pool, even if you're not staying there. Waterbom Park in Tuban (p99) is a big hit with most kids. If your kids can swim a little, they can have a lot of fun with a mask and snorkel. Colourful kites are sold in many shops and market stalls; get some string at a supermarket.

Other activities popular with kids include visiting Taman Burung Bali Bird Park and Rimba Reptil Park near Ubud (p140) and river rafting (p316). The water sports places in Tajung Benoa (p135) are very popular with kids.

CLIMATE CHARTS

Just 8° south of the equator, Bali has a tropical climate – the average temperature hovers around 30°C (86°F) all year. Direct sun feels incredibly hot, especially in the middle of the day. In the wet season, from October to March, the humidity can be very high and oppressive. The almost daily tropical downpours come as a relief, then pass quickly, leaving flooded streets and renewed humidity. The dry season (April to September) is generally sunnier, less humid and, from a weather point of view, the best time to visit, though downpours can occur at any time.

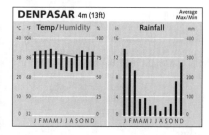

There are marked variations across the island. The coast is hotter, but sea breezes can temper the heat. As you move inland you also move up, so the altitude works to keep things cool – at times it can get chilly up in the highlands, and a warm sweater or light jacket can be a good idea in mountain villages such as Kintamani and Candikuning. The northern slopes of Gunung Batur always seem to be wet and misty, while a few kilometres away, the east coast is nearly always dry and sunny.

COURSES

More and more people find it rewarding to take one of the various courses available on Bali. For an overview of diving courses, see p314.

Arts & Crafts

The Ubud area is the best place for art courses, see p154. A wide range of courses is available, including batik, jewellery making and painting.

Cooking

See p74 for information on Bali cooking courses.

Language

Denpasar (p85) and Ubud (p155) have schools for learning Bahasa Indonesia.

Meditation & Spiritual Interests

For the Balinese, everything on the island is imbued with spiritual significance, and this ambience is an attraction for travellers looking for an alternative holiday experience. Ubud (p155) is a good place to go for spiritual enlightenment.

Music & Dance

Denpasar (p85) and Ubud (p155) have schools for Balinese music and dance.

Surfing

Schools in Kuta (p99) offer beginner surfing courses.

CUSTOMS

Indonesia has the usual list of prohibited imports, including drugs, weapons and anything remotely pornographic. In addition, TV sets, radio receivers, fresh fruit, Chinese medicines and printed matter containing Chinese characters are prohibited.

Each adult can bring in 200 cigarettes (or 50 cigars or 100g of tobacco), a 'reasonable amount' of perfume and 1L of alcohol.

Officially, photographic equipment (both still and video cameras), computers and tape recorders must be declared to customs on entry, and you must take them with you when you leave. In practice, customs officials rarely worry about the usual gear tourists bring into Bali. Surfers with more than two or three boards may be charged a 'fee', and this could apply to other items if the officials suspect that you aim to sell them in Indonesia. If you have nothing to declare, customs clearance is quick and painless.

There is no restriction on foreign currency, but the import or export of

---

TRAVEL ADVISORIES

Government departments charged with foreign affairs maintain websites with travel information and warnings for specific countries and regions. It's a good idea for travellers to check the following websites before a trip in order to confirm local conditions. Once in Bali, travellers can get the very latest information through the local consulate (p329) or from embassies in Jakarta (p329).

- **Australia Department of Foreign Affairs and Trade** (www.dfat.gov.au)
- **Canada Foreign Affairs** (www.voyage.gc.ca)
- **New Zealand Ministry of Foreign Affairs and Trade** (www.mfat.govt.nz/travel)
- **UK Foreign and Commonwealth Office** (www.fco.gov.uk)
- **US Department of State** (www.travel.state.gov)

---

rupiah is limited to 5,000,000Rp. Amounts greater than that must be declared.

Indonesia is a signatory to the Convention on International Trade in Endangered Species (CITES), and as such bans the import and export of products made from endangered species. In particular, it is forbidden to export any product made from green sea turtles or turtleshells. In the interests of conservation, as well as conformity to customs laws, please don't buy turtleshell products. There may also be some ivory artefacts for sale on Bali, and the import and export of these is also banned in most countries.

It's also forbidden to export antiquities, ancient artefacts or other cultural treasures, so if someone tries to sell you an 'ancient' bronze statue, remind them of this law and they may decide it's not so old after all!

DANGERS & ANNOYANCES

It's important to note that compared to many places in the world, Bali is fairly safe. There are some hassles from the avaricious, but many visitors face many more dangers at home.

Following the October 2002 Kuta bombings (see p96) there was an immediate increase in security measures that now seems to be fading away. International hotels often have a vehicle checkpoint but these are generally cursory at best.

Be careful, not paranoid. The likelihood of further attacks is widely thought to be minimal, but on Bali you now need to be aware of the same sort of issues faced in most countries. As for all destinations, you might want to check your government's travel advisories before you depart, and listen to local advice when you arrive.

In addition to the warnings below, see p98 for warnings specific to the Kuta region.

Outside the Mataram/Senggigi area on Lombok, emergency services may be nonexistent, or a long time coming. Don't expect an ambulance to collect injured surfers from the southwest coast. The Gili islands don't have a formal police force.

For information on Bali's notorious dogs, see p67. See p361 for details on international clinics and medical care on Bali.

Begging
You may be approached by the occasional beggar on the streets of Kuta – typically a woman with a young child. Begging has no place in traditional Balinese society, so it's likely that most of the beggars come from elsewhere. (In Ubud, some beggars from the central mountains Bali Aga village of Trunyan walk the streets.)

Drugs
You may be offered dope on the street, particularly in the Kuta region, and tablets purported to be ecstasy are sometimes sold on the street and at some nightclubs, but they could contain just about anything. In all cases, entrapment by police and informers is a real possibility. The authorities take a dim view of recreational drug use, and losmen owners can be quick to turn you in.

Bali's famed *oong* (magic mushrooms) come out during the wet season. They are usually mixed with food, such as an omelette, or in a drink – if a barman offers you an 'umbrella cocktail' you may get more than you bargained for. The mushrooms contain psylocibin, which is a powerful hallucinogen. It may give you a stratospheric high, but it may also result in paranoid or psychotic reactions that can be extremely unpleasant. Mushrooms are most common in low-budget beach resorts like Lovina or Lombok's Gili islands.

Hawkers, Pedlars & Touts

Many visitors regard the persistent attentions of people trying to sell as *the* No 1 annoyance on Bali (and in tourist areas of Lombok). These activities are officially restricted in many areas but hawkers will still work just outside the fence. Elsewhere, especially around many tourist attractions, visitors are frequently, and often constantly, hassled to buy things.

The best way to deal with hawkers is to completely ignore them from the first instance. Eye contact is crucial – don't make any! Even a polite '*tidak*' (no) seems to encourage them. Never ask the price or comment on the quality unless you're interested in buying, or you want to spend half an hour haggling. It may seem very rude to ignore people who smile and greet you so cheerfully, but you might have to be a lot ruder to get rid of a hawker after you've spent a few minutes politely discussing his/her watches, rings and prices. Keep in mind though, that ultimately they're just people trying to make an honest living and if you don't want to buy anything then you are wasting their time trying to be polite.

Scams

Bali has such a relaxed atmosphere, and the people are so friendly, that you may not be on the lookout for scams. It's hard to say when an 'accepted' practice like overcharging becomes an unacceptable rip-off, but be warned that there are some people on Bali (not always Balinese) who will engage in a practised deceit in order to get money from a visitor.

Most Balinese would never perpetrate a rip-off, but it seems that very few would warn a foreigner when one is happening. Be suspicious if you notice that bystanders are uncommunicative and perhaps uneasy, and one guy is doing all the talking.

Here is a rundown of the most common scams.

CAR CON

Friendly locals (often working in pairs) discover a 'serious problem' with your car or motorcycle – it's blowing smoke, leaking oil or petrol, or a wheel is wobbling badly (problems that one of the pair creates while the other distracts you). Coincidentally, he has a brother/cousin/friend nearby who can help, and before you know it they've put some oil in the sump, or changed the wheel, and are demanding an outrageous sum for their trouble. The con relies on creating a sense of urgency, so beware of anyone who tries to rush you into something without mentioning a price.

HARD LUCK STORY

A Balinese guy takes a foreign friend to see 'his' poor village – usually it's not the guy's own village but the friend doesn't know that. The visitor is shocked by the poor circumstances of their Balinese friend, who concocts a hard-luck story about a sick mother who can't pay for an operation, a brother who needs money for his education or an important religious ceremony that his family can't afford. Visitors have been persuaded to hand over large sums of money on such a pretext. A healthy scepticism is your best defence.

EASY MONEY

Friendly locals will convince a visitor that easy money can be made in a card game. They're taken to some obscure place, and do well at first. Then, after a few drinks and a spell of bad luck, they find themselves being escorted to a bank, where they need a large cash advance on their credit card to pay off the debt. Gambling is illegal in Indonesia, so the victim has no legal recourse.

HIGH RATES – NO COMMISSION

In the South Bali area especially, many travellers are ripped off by moneychangers, who use sleight of hand and rigged calculators. The moneychangers who offer the highest rates are usually the ones to look out for. Always count your money at least twice in front of the moneychanger, and don't let him touch the money again after you've finally counted it. Try to change even amounts, eg US$100, which are easier to convert to rupiah, or bring your own pocket calculator.

Swimming

The beaches at Kuta, Legian and Seminyak are subject to heavy surf and strong currents – always swim between the flags. Trained lifeguards operate only at Kuta-Legian, Nusa Dua, Sanur and (sometimes) Senggigi. Most other beaches are protected by coral reefs, so they don't have big waves, but the currents can still be treacherous, especially along the coast running north and west from Seminyak.

Be careful when swimming over coral, and never walk on it at all. It can be very sharp and coral cuts are easily infected. In addition, you are damaging a fragile environment.

Theft

Violent crime is relatively uncommon, but there is some bag-snatching, pickpocketing and theft from losmen rooms and parked cars in the tourist centres. Don't leave anything exposed in a rental vehicle.

Snatchers sometimes work in pairs from a motorcycle; one guy grabs the bag and slashes the strap and the other hits the throttle. Money belts or bum bags worn *outside* the clothes are particularly vulnerable. Always carry money belts inside your clothes; and bags over your neck (not shoulder). Be sure to secure all your money *before* you leave the ATM, bank or moneychanger.

Pickpockets on bemos are also something to be aware of. Somebody may start a conversation to distract you, while an accomplice steals your wallet or purse. Bemos are always tightly packed, and a painting, large parcel, basket or the like can serve as a cover.

Losmen rooms are often not secure. Don't leave valuables in your room. Thieves will often enter through open-air bathrooms, so be sure to fasten the bathroom door. Most hotels offer some form of secure storage, such as in-room safes or central safety deposit boxes for guests – use it.

Many people lose things simply by leaving them on the beach while they go swimming.

On Lombok theft and robbery are more common. Certainly there are hassles in Kuta, east of Kuta and west of Kuta around Mawi (see p311).

Traffic

Apart from the dangers of driving on Bali (see p354), the traffic in most tourist areas is often annoying, and frequently dangerous to pedestrians. Footpaths can be rough, even unusable, so you often have to walk on the road. Never expect traffic to stop because you think you're on a pedestrian crossing.

The traffic is much lighter in Lombok than on Bali, but there is still a danger of traffic accidents.

DISABLED TRAVELLERS

Bali is a difficult destination for those with limited mobility. While some of the airlines flying to Bali have a good reputation for accommodating people with disabilities, the airport is not well set up. Contact the airlines and ask them what arrangements can be made for disembarking and boarding at the airport.

The bemos, minibuses and buses that provide public transport all over the islands are certainly not made for very large, tall or physically disabled people, nor for wheelchairs. The minibuses used by tourist shuttle bus and tour companies are similar. Upmarket hotels often have steps, but lack ramps for wheelchairs, while the cheaper places usually have more accessible bungalows on ground level. Out on the street, the footpaths, where they exist at all, tend to be narrow, uneven, potholed and frequently obstructed.

The only hotels likely to be set up at all for disabled travellers are the big international chains in south Bali and Ubud. If you're keen to see Bali, your best bet is to contact these hotels and ask them what facilities they have for disabled guests. Often this information can be found on the hotel websites.

Bali is an enormously rewarding destination for unsighted people or for those with limited vision. Balinese music is heard everywhere, and the languages are fascinating to listen to. The smells of incense, spices, tropical fruit and flowers pervade the island, and are as exotic as you could wish for. With a sighted companion, most places should be reasonably accessible.

DISCOUNT CARDS

The International Student Identity Card (ISIC) may get you a discount on domestic flights (a maximum age limit of 26 years applies) although deregulation has put a crimp on this. There are virtually no discounts or special deals for senior citizens.

EMBASSIES & CONSULATES
Indonesian Embassies & Consulates
Countries in which Indonesia has diplomatic representation include the following. See the official **Department of Foreign Affairs website** (www.deplu.go.id) for more information.

Australia (☎ 02-6250 8600; www.kbri-canberra.org.au; 8 Darwin Ave, Yarralumla, ACT 2600)

Canada (☎ 613-724 1100; www.indonesia-ottawa.org; 55 Parkdale Ave, Ottawa, Ontario K1Y 1E5)

China (☎ 10-6532-5486; www.indonesianembassy -china.com; San Li Tun Diplomatic Office Building B, Beijing 100600)

East Timor (☎ 670-312 333; Kompleks Pertamina, Pantai Kelapa, Correios Timor Leste, Dili)

France (☎ 01 45 03 07 60; www.amb-indonesie.fr; 47-49 Rue Cortambert 75116, Paris)

Germany (☎ 030-478 070; www.kbri-berlin.de; Lehrterstr 16-17, 10557 Berlin)

Ireland (☎ 020-7499 7661; www.indonesianembassy .org.uk; 38 Grosvenor Sq, London W1X 9AD)

Japan (☎ 03-3441 4201; www.indonesian-embassy .or.jp; 5-2-9 Higashi Gotanda, Shinagawa-ku, Tokyo 141)

Malaysia (☎ 03-242 1354; www.kbrikl.org.my; 233 Jl Tun Razak, 50400 Kuala Lumpur)

Netherlands (☎ 070-310 8100; www.indonesia.nl; Tobias Asserlaan 8, 2517 KC, The Hague)

New Zealand (☎ 04-475 8697; www.indonesian embassy.org.nz; 70 Glen Rd, Kelburn, Wellington 3543)

Papua New Guinea (☎ 675-325 3116; 1+2/410 Kiroki St, Sir John Guise Dr, Waigani, Port Moresby)

Philippines (☎ 02-892 5061; www.kbrimanila.org.ph; 185 Salcedo St, Legaspi Village, Makati, Manila)

Singapore (☎ 6737 7422; www.kbri.org.sg/portal_kbri .htm; 7 Chatsworth Rd, 249761)

Thailand (☎ 022 523 135; www.kbri-bangkok.com; 600-602 Thanon Phetburi, Phyathai, Bangkok 10400)

UK (☎ 020-7499 7661; www.indonesianembassy.org.uk; 38 Grosvenor Sq, London W1X 9AD)

USA (☎ 202-775 5200; www.embassyofindonesia.org; 2020 Massachusetts Ave NW, Washington, DC, 20036)

Embassies & Consulates in Indonesia
Foreign embassies are in Jakarta, the national capital. Most of the foreign representatives on Bali are consular agents (or honorary consuls) who can not offer the same services as a full consulate or embassy. For many nationalities this means a long trek to Jakarta in the event of a lost passport.

BALI
Only Australia and Japan (which together make up nearly half of all visitors) have formal consulates on Bali. The following offices are open from about 8.30am to noon Monday to Friday, and some also open in the afternoon. All telephone area codes are ☎ 0361.

Australia (Map pp82-3; ☎ 235092; Jl Moh Yamin 4, Renon, Denpasar) The Australian consulate has a consular sharing agreement with Canada, and may also be able to help citizens of New Zealand, Ireland and Papua New Guinea. The embassy may be relocated to a more secure location, so confirm location.

France (Map pp120-1; ☎ 285485; Jl Mertasari, Gang II 8, Sanur)

Germany (Map pp120-1; ☎ 288535; Jl Pantai Karang 17, Batujimbar, Sanur)

Japan (Map pp82-3; ☎ 227628; Jl Raya Puputan 170, Renon, Denpasar)

Netherlands (Map pp94-5; ☎ 751517; Jl Raya Kuta 127/Imam Bonjol, Kuta)

Switzerland (Map pp94-5; ☎ 751735; Kuta Galleria, Blok Valet 2, 12, Kuta)

UK (Map pp120-1; ☎ 270601; Cat & Fiddle, Mertasari 2, Sanur)

USA (Map pp82-3; ☎ 233605; Jl Hayam Wuruk 188, Renon, Denpasar)

JAKARTA
Indonesia is a big country, and is important in the Asian region. Most nations have an embassy in Jakarta (telephone area code ☎ 021), including the following.

Australia (☎ 2550 5555; www.austembjak.or.id; Jl HR Rasuna Said, Kav C 15-16, Kuningan)

Canada (☎ 2550 7800; World Trade Centre, 6th fl, Jl Jenderal Sudirman, Kav 29)

France (☎ 314 2807; Jl MH Thamrin 20)

Germany (☎ 390 1750; Jl MH Thamrin 1)

Japan (☎ 324308; Jl Husni Thamrin 24)

Netherlands (☎ 525 1515; Jl HR Rasuna Said, Kav S-3)

New Zealand (☎ 570 9460; BRI II Building, 23rd fl, Jl Jenderal Sudirman, Kav 44-46)

Papua New Guinea (☎ 725 1218; 6th fl, Panin Bank Centre, Jl Jenderal Sudirman 1)

Philippines (☎ 315 0119; Jl Imam Bonjol 6-8)

Singapore (☎ 520 1489; Jl Rasuna Said, Block X/4 Kav 2)

Thailand (☎ 390 4052; Jl Imam Bonjol 74)

UK (☎ 315 6264; www.britain-in-indonesia.or.id; Jl Husni Thamrin 75)

USA (☎ 3435 9000; www.usembassyjakarta.org; Jl Medan Merdeka Selatan 5)

FESTIVALS & EVENTS

Try to obtain a *Calendar of Events* booklet – several versions are published by several levels of government. It lists every temple ceremony and village festival on Bali for the current (Western) year. You can also inquire at tourist offices or at your hotel.

The website www.indo.com/indonesia /events has good information.

Balinese Calendars, Holidays & Festivals

Apart from the usual western calendar, the balinese also use two local calendars.

WUKU CALENDAR

The *wuku* calendar is used to determine festival dates. The calendar uses 10 different types of weeks between one and 10 days long, which all run simultaneously. The intersection of the various weeks determines auspicious days. The seven- and five-day weeks are of particular importance. A full year is made up of 30 individually named seven-day weeks (210 days).

Galungan, which celebrates the death of a legendary tyrant called Mayadenawa, is one of Bali's major festivals. During this 10-day period, held every 210 days, all the gods come down to earth for the festivities. Barong (mythical lion-dog creatures) prance from temple to temple and village to village, and locals rejoice with feasts and visits to families. The celebrations culminate with the Kuningan festival, when the Balinese say thanks and goodbye to the gods.

Every village on Bali will celebrate Galungan and Kuningan in grand style. Forthcoming dates are the following.

Year	Galungan	Kuningan
2005	9 Mar	19 Mar
2005	5 Oct	15 Oct
2006	3 May	13 May
2006	29 Nov	9 Dec
2007	7 Jun	7 Jul

SAKA CALENDAR

The Hindu *saka* (or *caka*) calendar is a lunar cycle that more closely follows the Western calendar in terms of the length of the year. Nyepi (see the boxed text 'Nyepi – the Day of Silence', p331) is the major festival of the *saka* year – it's the last day of the year, ie the day after the new moon of the ninth month. Certain major temples celebrate their festivals by the *saka* calendar.

Bali Events

Bali has a growing list of organised festivals, events which have proven popular with locals and visitors alike.

Bali Art Festival of Buleleng May or June, Singaraja (p237).
Usaba Sambah Festival May or June, Tenganan (p193).
Bali Arts Festival Mid-June to mid-July, Denpasar (p85).
Kuta Karnival Late September and early October, Kuta (p100).
Ubud Writers & Readers Festival October, Ubud (p156).

Lombok Events

Many festivals take place at the start of the rainy season (around October to December) or at harvest time (around April to May). Most of them do not fall on specific days in the Western calendar, including Ramadan, so planning for them is not really possible.

Ramadan, the month of fasting, is the ninth month of the Muslim calendar. During this period, many restaurants are closed, and foreigners eating, drinking (especially alcohol) and smoking in public may attract a very negative reaction.

Other occasions observed on Lombok include the following.

Desa Bersih First Thursday in April – a harvest festival held in honour of Dewi Sri, the rice goddess in the region of Gunung Pengsong.
Nyale Fishing Festival 19th day of the 10th month of the Sasak calendar (generally February or March) – commemorates the legend of a beautiful princess who went out to sea and drowned herself rather than choose between her many admirers – her long hair was transformed into the worm like fish the Sasak call *nyale*.

Temple Festivals

Temple festivals on Bali are quite amazing, and you'll often come across them unexpectedly, even in remote corners of the island. The annual 'temple birthday' is known as an *odalan* and is celebrated once every Balinese year of 210 days. Since most villages have at least three temples, you're assured of at least five or six annual festivals in every village. In addition, there can be special festival days common throughout Bali, festivals for certain important temples and festivals for certain gods. The full moons which fall around the end of September to the beginning of October, or from early to mid-April, are often times for important temple festivals.

The most obvious sign of a temple festival is a long line of women in traditional costume, walking gracefully to the temple with beautifully arranged offerings of food, fruit and flowers piled in huge pyramids which they carry on their heads.

Meanwhile, the various *pemangku* (temple guardians and priests for temple rituals) suggest to the gods that they should come down for a visit. That's what those little thrones are for in the temple shrines – they are symbolic seats for the gods to occupy during festivals. Women dance the stately Pendet, an offering dance for the gods.

All night long there's activity, music and dancing – it's like a country fair, with food, amusements, games, stalls, gambling, noise,

colour and confusion. Finally, as dawn approaches, the entertainment fades away, the *pemangku* suggest to the gods that it's time they made their way back to heaven and the people wind their weary way back home.

When you first arrive, it's well worth asking at a tourist office or your hotel what festivals will be held during your stay. Seeing one will be a highlight of your trip. Foreigners are welcome to watch the festivities and take photographs, but be unobtrusive and dress modestly.

FOOD

You can eat well with locals for under US$1 or have a fabulous meal prepared by a renowned chef for much more on Bali. The constant, however, at any price range is that food is generally very fresh, often quite good and usually much cheaper than you would pay for a similar meal at home. See p70 for details.

NYEPI – THE DAY OF SILENCE

The major festival for the Hindu Balinese is Nyepi, usually falling around the end of March or early April. It celebrates the end of the old year and the start of the new one, according to the *saka* calendar, and usually coincides with the end of the rainy season.

Out with the Old Year...

In the weeks before Nyepi, much work goes into the making of *ogoh-ogoh* – huge monster dolls with menacing fingers and frightening faces – and into the preparation of offerings and rituals that will purify the island in readiness for the new year. The day before Nyepi, Tawur Agung Kesanga, is the 'Day of Great Sacrifices', with ceremonies held at town squares and sports grounds throughout the island. At about 4pm, the villagers, all dressed up in traditional garb, gather in the centre of town, playing music and offering gifts of food and flowers to the *ogoh-ogoh*. Then comes the *ngrupuk* – the great procession where the *ogoh-ogoh* figures are lifted on bamboo poles and carried through the streets, to frighten away all the evil spirits. This is followed by prayers and speeches and then, with flaming torches and bonfires, the *ogoh-ogoh* are burnt, and much revelry ensues. The biggest *ngrupuk* procession is in Denpasar, but any large town will have a pretty impressive parade.

...And in with the New

The day of Nyepi itself officially lasts for 24 hours from sunrise, and is one of complete inactivity, so when the evil spirits descend they decide that Bali is uninhabited and leave the island alone for another year. All human activity stops – all shops, bars and restaurants close, no-one is allowed to leave their home and foreigners must stay in their hotels, and even Bali's international airport is closed down. No fires are permitted and at night all buildings must be blacked out – only emergency services are exempt.

Government offices, banks and many shops close the day before Nyepi, and some shops remain closed the day after. For visitors, Nyepi is a day for catching up on sleep, writing letters or washing. Most hotels with a restaurant will arrange for simple meals to be served for guests.

GAY & LESBIAN TRAVELLERS

Gay travellers on Bali will experience few problems, and many of the island's most influential expatriate artists have been more-or-less openly gay. Physical contact between same-sex couples is quite acceptable and friends of the same sex often hold hands, though this does not indicate homosexuality.

There are many venues where gay men congregate, mostly in Kuta. There's nowhere that's exclusively gay, and nowhere that's even inconspicuously a lesbian scene. Hotels are happy to rent a room with a double bed to any couple. Homosexual behaviour is not illegal, and the age of consent for sexual activity is 16 years. Gay men in Indonesia are referred to as *homo*, or *gay*, and are quite distinct from the female impersonators called *waria*.

Many gays from other parts of the country come to live on Bali, as it is more tolerant, and also because it offers opportunities to meet foreign partners.

Gay prostitutes are mostly from Java, and some have been known to rip off their foreign clients. Gay Balinese men are usually just looking for nothing more than some adventures, though there is an expectation that the (relatively) wealthy foreign guy will pay for meals, drinks, hotels etc.

On Lombok gay and lesbian travellers should definitely refrain from public displays of affection, advice that applies to straight couples as well.

Organisations

Gaya Dewata (☎ 0361-234074; Denpasar) Bali's gay organisation.

Hanafi (see p98) Kuta-based gay-friendly tour operator and guide; good for the lowdown on the local scene.

Utopia Asia (www.utopia-asia.com) Not specific to Bali, but excellent information about the Bali gay scene.

Utopia Tours (www.utopia-tours.com) Organises tours for gay and lesbian travellers.

HOLIDAYS

The following holidays are celebrated throughout Indonesia. Many of these dates change according to the phase of the moon (not by month), and are estimates.

Tahun Baru Masehi (New Year's Day) 1 January
Idul Adha (Muslim festival of sacrifice) February
Muharram (Islamic New Year) February/March
Nyepi (Hindu New Year) March/April
Hari Paskah (Good Friday) April
Ascension of Christ April/May
Hari Waisak (Buddha's birth, enlightenment and death) April/May
Maulud Nabi Mohammed or Hari Natal (Prophet Mohammed's birthday) May
Hari Proklamasi Kemerdekaan (Indonesian Independence Day) 17 August
Isra Miraj Nabi Mohammed (Ascension of the Prophet Mohammed) September
Idul Fitri (End of Ramadan) November/December
Hari Natal (Christmas Day) 25 December

See Festivals & Events (p330) for additional holidays. The Muslim population on Bali observes Islamic festivals and holidays, including Ramadan. Religious and other holidays on Lombok are as follows.

Anniversary of West Lombok April 17 – government holiday.
Ramadan Usually October.
Founding of West Nusa Tenggara December 17 – public holiday.

INSURANCE

Unless you are definitely sure that your health coverage at home will cover you on Bali, you should definitely take out travel insurance – bring a copy of the policy as evidence that you're covered. Get a policy that pays for medical evacuation if necessary.

Some policies specifically exclude 'dangerous activities', which can entail scuba diving, renting a local motorcycle and even trekking. Be aware that a locally acquired motorcycle licence is not valid under some policies.

INTERNET ACCESS

Internet centres are common anywhere there are tourists on Bali. Expect to pay 200Rp to 500Rp per minute for access. Connection speeds are often painfully slow, but broadband access is appearing and excellent Internet places can be found in Kuta (p97), Legian (p97) and Ubud (p147). At these centres you can use a variety of computing services, such as downloading your digital camera or burning CDs. You can also network your laptop.

Many hotels have begun to install Internet centres for their guests. In-room broadband access, however, is limited to the newest of the international hotels, as noted in the individual reviews.

Internet access in Lombok tends to cost 400Rp to 500Rp per minute, although in Mataram it is much cheaper at 4500Rp per hour. However, wherever you go in Lombok Internet access is extremely slow.

LEGAL MATTERS

Gambling is illegal (although it is common, especially at cockfights), as is pornography. The Indonesian government takes the smuggling, using and selling of drugs very, *very* seriously. Once you have been caught, and then put in jail, there is very little that your consulate on Bali (if you have one) can do for you. You may have to wait for up to six months in jail before you even go to trial.

Generally, you are unlikely to have any encounters with the police unless you are driving a rented car or motorcycle (see p354).

Some governments (including the Australian government) have laws making it illegal for their citizens to use child prostitutes or engage in other paedophiliac activities anywhere in the world. There have been recent prosecutions on Bali for foreigners engaged in these activities.

There are police stations in all district capitals. If you have to report a crime or have other business at a police station, expect a lengthy and bureaucratic encounter. You should dress as respectably as possible, bring a fluent Indonesian-speaking friend for interpretation and moral support, arrive early and be very polite.

Police officers frequently expect to receive bribes, either to overlook some crime, misdemeanour or traffic infringement, or to provide a service that they should provide anyway. Generally, it's easiest to pay up – and the sooner you do it and the less fuss you make, the less it will cost. If you're in trouble, contact your consulate as soon as you can – they can't get you out, but they can recommend English-speaking lawyers and may have useful contacts.

LEGAL AGE

The legal age of consent on Bali is 16. The legal age for drinking is 18, but this is not strictly enforced. The driving age is 18.

MAPS

For tourist resorts and towns, the maps in this guidebook are as good as you'll get. If you need a more detailed road map of the island, there are some OK sheet maps available in bookshops in the touristed areas. The following are examples of good maps that are available. There are many more which are old and/or useless.

- Nelles' full-colour *Bali & Lombok* map (1:180,000) is good for topography and roads, although it's not fully up to date and the maps of Kuta, Denpasar and Ubud aren't particularly good.
- Periplus Travel Maps has a decent *Bali* contour map (1:250,000), with a detailed section on southern Bali, plus maps of the main towns areas. However, the labelling and names used for towns are often incomprehensible. The *Lombok & Sumbawa* map is useful.
- The Periplus *Street Atlas Bali* may be more than you need, but it is more accurate than the sheet map.

MONEY

Indonesia's unit of currency is the rupiah (Rp). There are coins worth 50, 100, 500 and 1000Rp. Notes come in denominations of 500Rp (rare), 1000Rp, 5000Rp, 10,000Rp, 20,000Rp, 50,000Rp and 100,000Rp.

Check out the front cover of this book for an idea about current exchange rates of the rupiah. In recent times the currency has been fairly stable against others. Many mid-range hotels and all top-end hotels, along with some tourist attractions and tour companies, list their prices in US dollars, although you can usually pay in rupiah at a poorer exchange rate.

US dollars are the most negotiable currency. British, Canadian, Euro, Japanese and Australian cash and travellers cheques are negotiable at competitive rates in tourist areas, and can be changed in most major towns.

Many travellers now rely mostly on their ATM for cash while on Bali. It is a good idea, however, to carry some backup funds in case your card is lost or the network goes down (usually just for a few hours).

If you're heading into more remote regions carry a good supply of rupiah in small denominations with you.

ATMs

There are ATMs all over Bali. Most accept your ATM card from your account at home and major credit cards for cash advances. The exchange rates for ATM withdrawals are usually quite good, but check to see if your home bank will hit you with an outrageous fee. Most ATMs on Bali allow a maximum withdrawal of 600,000Rp to 1,000,000Rp.

Banks

Major banks have branches in the main tourist centres and provincial capitals. Smaller towns may not have banks at all or have banks that don't exchange currency. Changing money can be time-consuming.

Cash

Changing money on Bali is not difficult in tourist areas. It's easiest to exchange US banknotes, especially US$100 bills. However, make certain that your money is new and recent. Older designs and damaged notes will often be refused.

Rupiah bills of 50,000Rp and larger can be hard to break in remote areas. Always keep lots of small bills for public transport and other services.

Credit Cards

Visa, MasterCard and American Express (Amex) are accepted by most of the larger businesses that cater to tourists. You sign for the amount in rupiah – or dollars – and the bill is converted into your domestic currency. The conversion is at the interbank rate and is usually quite good, though some banks add a foreign exchange transaction fee.

You can also get cash advances on major credit cards at an ATM.

Moneychangers

Exchange rates offered by moneychangers are normally better than the banks, plus they offer quicker service and keep much longer hours. The exchange rates are advertised on boards along the footpaths or on windows outside the shops. It's worth looking around because rates vary a little, but beware of places advertising exceptionally high rates – they may make their profit by shortchanging their customers. These moneychangers are very common in Kuta – see p97 and also p326. In hotels and shopping centres, the rates can be up to 20% less than a street moneychanger.

Tipping

Tipping a set percentage is not expected on Bali, but restaurant workers are poorly paid; if the service is good, it's appropriate to leave 4000Rp or more. Most mid-range hotels and restaurants and all top-end hotels and restaurants add 21% to the bill for tax and service (known as 'plus plus'). This service component is distributed among hotel staff (one hopes), so you needn't tip under these circumstances.

Travellers Cheques

The exchange rates offered for travellers cheques are sometimes a little less than for cash, and small denominations usually get a lower rate, sometimes much lower. Bring travellers cheques in denominations of US$100 or equivalent.

PHOTOGRAPHY & VIDEO

Bali is one of the most photogenic places on Earth, so be prepared.

Cameras

A good variety of film is widely available at reasonable prices – always check the expiry date first. Developing and printing is available in tourist areas; it's very cheap and of good quality. Slide film is generally sent to Jakarta for processing and takes three or four days to develop.

Digital cameras are fast surpassing film. You can buy additional memory cards at photo shops in the major tourist centres, but you're really better off bringing what you need from home.

The best Internet places (see p332) will allow you to download your photos onto their computers for distribution to lucky friends and relatives worldwide or for burning onto a CD for storage. But make certain you understand how to do this before you leave home. It's also a good idea to bring along whatever cable your camera requires. The process is easiest for people who carry their own laptops and use the Internet centre's networks.

Photographing People

Photograph with discretion and manners. It's always polite to ask first, and if they say no, then don't. A gesture, smile and nod are all that is usually necessary.

Restrictions

Military installations are not widespread on Bali, but you should be aware that these are sensitive subjects – if in doubt, ask before you shoot. You are usually welcome to take photos of ceremonies in the villages and temples, but try not to be intrusive. Ask before taking photos inside a temple.

There's one place where you must not take photographs at all – public bathing places. Balinese think of these places as private and do not 'see' one another when they're bathing. To intrude with a camera is very rude voyeurism.

Video

Blank video tapes are available in the main tourist areas. They're not particularly cheap and the range is limited, so consider bringing what you need from home in sealed packages – to avoid a customs search for prohibited material.

POST

Sending postcards and normal-sized letters (ie under 20g) by airmail is cheap, but not really fast. A postcard/letter to the USA costs 5000/10,000Rp (allow 13 days); to Australia costs 7500/15,000Rp (15 days); and to the UK costs 8000/18,000Rp (21 days).

For anything over 20g, the charge is based on weight. Sending large parcels is quite expensive, but at least you can get them properly wrapped and sealed at any post office.

Every substantial town has a *kantor pos* (post office). In tourist centres, there are also postal agencies. They are often open long hours and provide postal services. Many will also wrap and pack parcels.

There are poste restante services at the various post offices around Bali. You're best off having mail sent to you via the post offices at Kuta and Ubud. Mail should be addressed to you with your surname underlined and in capital letters, then 'Kantor Pos', the name of the town, and then 'Bali, Indonesia'. You can also have mail sent to your hotel.

Express companies offer reliable, fast and expensive service.

DHL (☎ 0361-762138)
FedEx (☎ 0361-701727)
TNT (☎ 0361-703519)
UPS (☎ 0361-756148) Has shops near Kuta (p97) and in Ubud (p148).

See p337 for details on shipping large items.

SHOPPING

Many people come to Bali to 'shop 'til they drop', and everyone else will probably end up buying quite a few things anyway. You will find a plethora of shop and stalls anywhere tourists congregate. The growing number of Western-style department stores and shopping centres in Denpasar and the Kuta area sell a large variety of clothing, shoes, leathergoods, sports gear and toys. There's a huge range and prices are mostly very good because of the low value of the rupiah.

The clothing industry has enjoyed spectacular growth from making beachwear for tourists – it now accounts for around half the value of Balinese exports. Furniture is a growth industry, with contemporary furniture and reproduction antiques being popular.

For details of where to buy arts and crafts, see p51.

The best buys on Lombok are handicrafts, such as boxes, basketware, pottery and handwoven textiles.

Ceramics

Nearly all local pottery is made from low-fired terracotta. Most styles are very ornate, even for functional items such as vases, flasks, ashtrays and lamp bases. Pejaten (p257) near Tabanan also has a number of pottery workshops producing small ceramic figures and glazed ornamental roof tiles. For details of where to buy ceramics, see p51.

Clothing

All sorts of clothing is made locally, and sold in hundreds of small shops in all tourist centres, especially the Kuta area and Seminyak. It's mostly pretty casual, but it's not just beachwear – you can get just about anything you want, including tailor-made clothing, and there are many designer shops. Leatherwear is quite cheap and popular.

THE ART OF BARGAINING

Many everyday purchases on Bali require bargaining. This particularly applies to clothing, arts and crafts. Accommodation has a set price, but this is usually negotiable in the low season, or if you are staying at the hotel for several days.

In an everyday bargaining situation the first step is to establish a starting price – it's usually better to ask the seller for their price rather than make an initial offer. It also helps if you have some idea what the item is worth.

Generally, your first price could be anything from one-third to two-thirds of the asking price – assuming that the asking price is not completely over the top. Then, with offer and counteroffer, you move closer to an acceptable price. For example, the seller asks 60,000Rp for the handicraft, you offer 30,000Rp and so on, until eventually you both agree at somewhere around 45,000Rp. If you don't get to an acceptable price you're quite entitled to walk away – the vendor may even call you back with a lower price.

Note that when you name a price, you're committed – you have to buy if your offer is accepted. Remember, bargaining should be an enjoyable part of shopping on Bali, so maintain your sense of humour and keep things in perspective.

Fabrics & Weaving

Gianyar (p176), in eastern Bali, is a major textile centre with a number of factories where you can watch ikat sarongs being woven on a hand-and-foot powered loom. Any market will have a good range of textiles.

The village of Tenganan (p193) uses a double ikat process called *gringsing*, in which both the warp and weft are predyed – this is time-consuming and expensive. Belayu (p254), a small village in southwestern Bali is a centre for *songket* (silver or gold-threaded cloth) weaving. Ubud (p154) is another good place for traditional weaving.

Furniture

Wood furniture is a big industry, though much of it is actually made on Java and sent to Bali for finishing and sale. Tourists are tempted by contemporary designs and reproduction antiques at much lower prices than they'd find at home. Some of the most attractive pieces are tropical-style interior furnishings. Outdoor furniture made from teak, mahogany and other rainforest timbers is often spectacular and better than you'd get at home for 10 times the price.

Harvesting timber for the local furniture industry and furniture manufacturing involves a high local value-added content and probably has a lesser impact on rainforests than large-scale clearing for export of logs and wood chips, which are much more significant causes of deforestation, and generate a lot less local employment.

The best places to look for furniture are the stores/warehouses along Jl Bypass Ngurah Rai in South Bali and in Kuta (p111). Mas (p142), south of Ubud, is also good. Many of these places will offer to make furniture to order, but if you're a one-off buyer on a short visit it's best to stick to items that are in stock, so you can see what you're getting.

Gamelan

If you are interested in seeing gamelan instruments being made, visit the village of Blahbatuh (p142) near Ubud.

In northern Bali, Sawan (p239), a small village southeast of Singaraja, is also a centre for the manufacture of gamelan instruments. Jembrana (p260), in western Bali, makes giant gamelan instruments.

Jewellery

Celuk (p141) has always been the village associated with silversmithing. The large shops that line the road into Celuk have imposing, bus-sized driveways and slick facilities. If you want to see the 'real' Celuk, go about 1km east of the road to visit family workshops. Other silverwork centres include Kamasan (p181), near Semarapura in eastern Bali.

Jewellery can be purchased ready-made or made-to-order – there's a wide range of earrings, bracelets and rings available, some using gemstones, which are imported from all over the world. Different design influences can be detected, from African patterning to the New Age preoccupation with dolphins and healing crystals.

Music & Video

Piracy is a major problem on Bali. CDs and DVDs featuring popular artists and entertainment cost as little as 10,000Rp and are widely sold in tourist areas. Quality is often bad, the format may not work with your system and in general you may just be giving away your money while you also break the law.

Legitimate DVDs are rare but authentic CDs are often sold in the same places offering fakes. They are good value at around 80,000Rp to 90,000Rp. The cost of CDs featuring Balinese and Indonesian artists is generally lower.

Paintings

There are a relatively small number of creative original painters on Bali today, and an enormous number of imitators who produce copies, or near copies, in well-established styles. Many of these imitative works are nevertheless very well-executed and attractive pieces. Originality is not considered as important in Balinese art as it is in the West. A painting is esteemed not for being new and unique but for taking a well-worn and popular idea and making a good reproduction of it. Some renowned artists will simply draw out the design, decide the colours and then employ apprentices to actually apply the paint. This leads to the mass production of similar works that is so characteristic of Balinese art.

Unfortunately, much of the painting today is churned out for the tourist market and much of that market is extremely undiscriminating about what it buys. Thus, the shops are packed full of paintings in the various popular styles – some of them quite good, a few of them really excellent, and many of them uniformly alike and uniformly poor in quality.

Before making a purchase, visit the museums and galleries of Ubud (p149) to see the best of Balinese art and some of the European influences that have shaped it. At the galleries you will get an idea of how to value truly deserving Balinese paintings.

Sculpture

Balinese stone is surprisingly light and it's not at all out of the realms of possibility to bring a friendly stone demon back with you in your airline baggage. A typical temple door guardian weighs around 10kg. The stone, however, is very fragile so packing must be done carefully if you're going to get it home without damage. Some of the Batubulan workshops will pack figures quickly and expertly, often suspending the piece in the middle of a wooden framework and packing around it with shredded paper. There are also many capable packing and forwarding agents, though the shipping costs will almost certainly be more than the cost of the article.

Batubulan, on the main highway from South Bali to Ubud (p140), is a major stone-carving centre. Workshops are found further north along the road in Tegaltamu and Silakarang. Stone figures from 25cm to 2m tall line both sides of the road, and stone carvers can be seen in action in the many workshops here.

Wayang Kulit

Wayang kulit (leather puppets) are made in the village of Puaya (p141) near Sukawati, south of Ubud, and in Peliatan (p168) near Ubud.

Woodcarvings

As with paintings, try to see some of the best-quality woodcarvings in museums and galleries before you consider buying. Again, many standard pieces are produced in the same basic designs, and craft shops are full of them. Even with a basic lizard, hand or fisherman design, some are much better than others. Look for quality first, then look at the price – you may see the same article vary in price by anything from 10% to 1000%!

Apart from the retail mark-up and your bargaining skills, many factors determine costs, including the artist, the type of wood used, the originality of the item and the size. The simplest small carvings start at around 15,000Rp, while many fine pieces can be found for under 100,000Rp, and there's no upper limit.

Ubud (p168) and Mas (p142) are good places to look for woodcarving. For more details of where to buy arts and crafts, see p51.

SOLO TRAVELLERS

Bali (and to a lesser degree Lombok) is a good place for solo travellers. Both locals and other travellers tend to be open and friendly, making it easy to hook up with others while exploring the island.

Most places to stay have accommodation for single travellers for a price at least a little cheaper than pairs. Women travelling alone should refer to the Women Travellers section (p340).

TELEPHONE & FAX

The telecommunications service within Indonesia is provided by Telkom, a government monopoly. All of Indonesia is covered by a domestic satellite telecom-munications network. To call any country direct from Indonesia dial 001 + country code + area code + number, or make a call via the international operator (☎ 101).

The country code for Indonesia is ☎ 62. The area code for Jakarta is ☎ 021 and for Lombok it's ☎ 0370. Bali has six telephone area codes, listed in the relevant chapters of this book. Phone numbers beginning with ☎ 081 or ☎ 082 are mobile phones.

Telkom publishes a good phone book for Bali that includes yellow pages in English. Local directory assistance operators (☎ 108) are very helpful and some of them speak English. If you call directory assistance and have to spell out a name, try to use the Alpha, Bravo, Charlie system of saying the letters.

Calling internationally can easily cost US$1 or more a minute no matter which of the methods you choose to opt for as outlined below.

Some foreign telephone companies issue cards that enable you to make calls from Indonesian phones and have the cost billed to your home phone account. However, the catch is that most public telephones, *wartel* (public telephone offices) and hotels won't allow you to call the toll-free ☎ 008 or ☎ 001 access numbers needed to use these phonecards or other home-billing schemes, and the few hotels and wartels that do permit it charge a particular fee for doing so. See below for more information about the use of phonecards with a magnetic strip.

Mobile Phones

The cellular service in Indonesia is GSM. There are several local providers. If your phone company offers international 'roaming' in Indonesia, you can use your own mobile telephone on Bali – check first with the company to find out how much they charge, text messaging is generally the cheapest mobile option to use).

Alternatively, a mobile telephone (called a handphone in Indonesia) using the GSM system can be used more cheaply if you purchase a prepaid SIM card with a chip that you insert into your phone once you get to Bali. This will cost about 30,000Rp from shops in Kuta and you will have your own local telephone number. Long-distance and international calls from a mobile can be less expensive than through the regular phone system.

Phonecards

The vast majority of public phones use phonecards. The more common ones use the regular *kartu telepo* (phonecard) with a magnetic strip. The newer ones use a *kartu chip*, which has an electronic chip embedded in it. You can buy phonecards in denominations of 5000Rp, 10,000Rp, 25,000Rp, 50,000Rp and 100,000Rp at wartel, moneychangers, post offices and many shops. An international call from a card phone costs about the same per minute as a call from a wartel.

Telephone Offices

A *kantor telekomunikasi* (telecommunications office) is a main telephone office operated by Telkom, usually only found in bigger towns. Wartel are sometimes run by Telkom, but the vast majority are private, and there's a lot of them. You can make local, *inter-lokal* (long-distance) and international calls from any wartel.

The charge for international calls is the same from all parts of Bali, but may be cheaper in Telkom offices than in private ones. In most areas you dial the number yourself, and the cost increases in *pulsa* – a unit of time that varies according to the destination.

The official Telkom price of a one-minute call is about the equivalent of US$1 to most parts of the world. Most wartels, however, will charge higher per-minute rates.

You can sometimes make reverse-charge (collect) calls from a Telkom wartel, though most private ones don't allow it and those that do will charge a set fee. Very few private wartel will let you receive an incoming call.

TIME

Bali, Lombok and the islands of Nusa Tenggara to the east are all on Waktu Indonesian Tengah or WIT (Central Indonesian Standard Time), which is eight hours ahead of Greenwich Mean Time/ Universal Time or two hours behind Australian Eastern Standard Time. Java is another hour behind Bali and Lombok.

Not allowing for variations due to daylight-saving time in foreign countries, when it's noon on Bali and Lombok, it's 11pm the previous day in New York and 8pm in Los Angeles, 4am in London, 5am in Paris and Amsterdam, noon in Perth, 1pm in Tokyo, and 2pm in Sydney and Melbourne. See the World Time Zones map (p368).

'Bali time' is an expression that refers to the Balinese reluctance to be obsessed by punctuality.

TOILETS

You'll still encounter Asian-style toilets in the cheapest losmen around Bali (particularly in the far west). These toilets have two footrests and a hole in the floor – you squat down and aim. In almost every place catering for tourists, Western-style sit-down toilets are the norm. At some tourist attractions on Bali, there are public toilets that cost about 500Rp per visit.

Apart from tourist cafés and restaurants, and mid-range and top-end accommodation, you won't find toilet paper, so bring your own. If there is a bin next to the toilet, it's for toilet paper. Where public toilets exist they are often horrible. Use the refuges above.

TOURIST INFORMATION

The tourist office in Ubud is an excellent source of information on cultural events. Otherwise the tourist offices in this book are largely hit or miss. It helps to have a specific question and don't bother asking about tourist services like tours. Hotels are usually good sources of info.

Some of the best information is found in the many free publications aimed at tourists and expats which are distributed in South Bali and Ubud. These include the following.

Bali Advertiser Newspaper with voluminous ads and comprehensive information; idiosyncratic columnists.

Bali & Beyond Glossy tourist magazine.

Bali Plus Narrow format with comprehensive listings.

Hello Bali Excellent features, good restaurant and entertainment reviews.

What's Up Bali Useful map-based weekly brochure with complete entertainment listings.

The website **Bali Discovery** (www.balidiscovery.com) has a first-rate section with Bali news.

VISAS

The visa situation in Bali seems to be constantly in flux. It is essential that you confirm current formalities before you arrive in Bali. Failure to meet all the entrance requirements can see you on the first flight out.

No matter what type of visa you are going to use, your passport *must* be valid for at least six months from the date of your arrival.

The main visa options for visitors to Bali follow.

Visa Free Citizens of Brunei, Chile, Hong Kong, Macau, Malaysia, Morocco, Peru, Philippines, Singapore, Thailand and Vietnam may receive a 30-day visa for free when they arrive at the airport in Bali. This visa cannot not be extended.

Visa in Advance Citizens of countries not mentioned above must apply for a visa before they arrive in Indonesia. Typically this is a visitors visa, which comes in two flavours: 30- and 60-day. Details vary by country, so you should contact the nearest Indonesian embassy or consulate in order to determine processing fees and time. Note this is the only way people from *any* country can obtain a 60-day visitor visa.

Visa on Arrival Citizens of Argentina, Australia, Brazil, Canada, Denmark, Finland, France, Germany, Hungary, Italy, Japan, New Zealand, Norway, Poland, South Africa, South Korea, Switzerland, United Arab Emirates, UK, US, and Taiwan may apply for a visa when they arrive at the airport in Bali. There is a special lane for this at immigration in the arrivals area. The cost is US$25, collectable on the spot. You can pay by credit card or major currency, which will be converted. This visa is only good for 30 days and cannot be extended. Note that only EU citizens who carry passports issued by the countries listed above can use visa on arrival.

Whichever type of visa you use to enter Bali, you'll be issued with a tourist card that is valid for a 30- or 60-day stay according to your visa (if you have obtained one of the coveted 60-day visas in advance, be sure the immigration official at the airport gives you a 60-day card). Keep the tourist card with your passport, as you'll have to hand it back when you leave the country. Note that some travellers have been fined for overstaying by only a day or so or for losing their tourist card.

Lombok

The vast majority of visitors to Lombok first pass through Bali or another Indonesian city such as Jakarta (where the visa situation is the same as Bali) so they already have tourist cards. There are, however, a few direct flights to Lombok from other countries so in these instances the same visa rules outlined above apply.

Other Requirements

Officially, an onward/return ticket is a requirement for a tourist card (and visitors visa), and visitors are frequently asked to show their ticket on arrival. If you look scruffy or broke, you may also be asked to present evidence of sufficient funds to support yourself during your stay – US$1000 in cash or travellers cheques (or the equivalent in other currencies) should be sufficient. A credit card in lieu of cash

or travellers cheques may not satisfy these requirements, although this is rare.

It's not possible to extend a tourist card, unless there's a medical emergency or you have to answer legal charges. If you want to spend more time in Indonesia you have to leave the country and then re-enter – some long-term foreign residents have been doing this for years. Singapore is the destination of choice for obtaining a new visa.

There are two main *kantor imigrasi* (immigration offices) on Bali. The **Denpasar office** (Map pp82-3; ☎ 0361-227828; ☼ 8am-2pm Mon-Thu, 8am-11am Fri, 8am-noon Sat) is just up the street from the main post office in Renon. The other **immigration office** (☎ 0361-751038) keeps similar hours and is at the airport. There is also an **immigration office** (Map p271; ☎ 632520; Jl Udayana 2; ☼ 7am-2pm Mon-Thu; 7am-11am Fri, 7am-12.30am Sat) in Mataram on Lombok . If you have to apply for changes to your visa, make sure you're neatly dressed, but don't be overly optimistic.

Social & Business Visas

If you have a good reason for staying longer (eg study or family reasons), you can apply for a *sosial/budaya* (social/cultural) visa. You will need an application form from an Indonesian embassy or consulate, and a letter of introduction or promise of sponsorship from a reputable person or school in Indonesia. It's initially valid for three months, but it can be extended for one month at a time at an immigration office within Indonesia for a maximum of six months. There are fees for the application and for extending the visa too.

Kartu Izin Tinggal Terbatas or KITAS (limited-stay visas), valid for one-year periods, are also issued, usually for those who have permission to run a business or to work. In the latter case, a work permit must be obtained first from the Ministry of Manpower and should be arranged by your employer. Those granted limited stay are issued with a KITAS card, often referred to as a KIMS card.

WOMEN TRAVELLERS

Women travelling solo on Bali will get a lot of attention from Balinese guys, but Balinese men are, on the whole, fairly benign. Generally, Bali is safer for women than most areas of the world and, with the usual care, women should feel secure travelling alone.

Some precautions are simply the same for any traveller, but women should take extra care not to find themselves alone on empty beaches, down dark streets or in other situations where help might not be available. Late at night in the tourist centres, solo women should take a taxi, and sit in the back. Note that problems do occur and it is a good idea to practise the same precautions you use at home.

If you are going to stay on Bali for longer than a short holiday, the **Bali International Women's Association** (BIWA; ☎ 0361-285552; www .biwabali.com) can prove essential. BIWA was established by expats to 'foster friendship and mutual understanding' and meets monthly to organise support for local charities. It also works to help members integrate better in local life.

Kuta Cowboys

In tourist areas of Bali (and Lombok), you'll encounter young men who are keen to spend time with visiting women. Commonly called Kuta Cowboys, beach boys, bad boys, guides or gigolos, these guys think they're super cool, with long hair, lean bodies, tight jeans and lots of tattoos. While they don't usually work a straight sex-for-money deal, the visiting woman pays for the meals, drinks and accommodation, and commonly buys the guy presents.

It's not uncommon for them to form long-term relationships, with the guy hopeful of finding a new and better life with his partner in Europe, Japan, Australia or the US. While most of these guys around Bali are genuinely friendly and quite charming, some are predatory con artists who practise elaborate deceits. Many of them now come from outside Bali, and have a long succession of foreign lovers. Be healthily sceptical about what they tell you, particularly if it comes down to them needing money. Always insist on using condoms.

Lombok

Traditionally, women on Lombok are treated with respect, but in the touristy areas, harassment of single foreign women may occur. Would-be guides/boyfriends/gigolos are often persistent in their approaches,

and aggressive when ignored or rejected. Clothes that aren't too revealing are a good idea – beachwear should be reserved for the beach, and the less skin you expose the better. Two or more women together are less likely to experience problems, and women accompanied by a man are unlikely to be harassed. It is better not to walk alone at night.

WORK

Quite a lot of foreigners own businesses on Bali – mostly hotels, restaurants and tour agencies. To do so legally, foreigners need the appropriate work or business visa, which requires sponsorship from an employer, or evidence of a business that brings investment to Indonesia. Many foreigners are engaged in buying and exporting clothing, handicrafts or furniture, and stay for short periods – within the limits of a 30- or 60-day tourist card. It's illegal to work if you've entered Indonesia on a tourist card, and you'll have to leave the country to change your visa status. Even if you do get work, typically teaching English, payment is often in rupiah, which doesn't convert into a lot of foreign currency.

Volunteer & Aid Work
INTERNATIONAL ORGANISATIONS
Anyone seeking long-term paid or volunteer work in Bali may want to contact one of the following agencies.

Australian Volunteers International (www .australianvolunteers.com) Organises professional contracts for Australians.

Global Volunteers (www.globalvolunteers.org) Arranges professional and paid volunteer work for US citizens.

Lisle Fellowship (www.lisleinternational.org) Arranges short community programmes on Bali for any nationality; some fees may apply.

Voluntary Service Overseas (www.vso.org.uk) British overseas volunteer programme accepts qualified volunteers from other countries. Branches in Canada (www.vso canada.org) and the Netherlands (www.vso.nl).

Volunteer Service Abroad (www.vsa.org.nz) Organises professional contracts for New Zealanders.

LOCAL ORGANISATIONS
BIWA (see left) is a useful clearing house for information on local charities. In Ubud, the **Pondok Pecak Library & Learning Centre** (Map pp146-7; ☎ 976194; Monkey Forest Rd; ⏲ 9am-5pm

Mon-Sat, 1-5pm Sun) has information on a number of local charities.

The Bali Cares store (p168) has information on a number of non-profit and volunteer gruops, including the following.

SOS (Sumatran Orangutan Society; www.orangutans-sos .org) An Ubud-based group that works to save endangered species throughout Indonesia.

VIBE (Volunteers & Interns for Balinese Education; www .vibefoundation.org) An Ubud-based group that works to support English-language courses to Bali schools.

Otherwise the following organisations can use funding, material donations and possibly volunteer services.

Yakkum Bali (☎ 0812 399 0701; yakkumbali@yahoo .co.uk) Works at rehabilitation and education of the disabled; needs vocational trainers.

YKIP (Humanitarian Foundation of Mother Earth; ☎ 0361-759544; www.ykip.org) Established after the 2002 bombings, the founders were business people, doctors, officials and volunteers. It organises health and education projects for Bali's poor.

Transport

CONTENTS

GETTING THERE & AWAY

Most international visitors to Bali will arrive by air, either directly or via Jakarta. For island-hoppers, there are frequent ferries between eastern Java and Bali, and between Bali and Lombok, as well as domestic flights between the islands. Lombok is usually visited as a side trip from Bali, by plane or ferry.

Lombok is very accessible by air and sea from the neighbouring islands. The vast majority of travellers arrive from Bali, less than 50km away, while others arrive via Jakarta or island hop from the east via Sumbawa.

ENTERING THE COUNTRY

Arrival procedures at the international airport are fairly painless, although it can take some time for a whole planeload of visitors to clear immigration. At the baggage claim area, porters are keen to help get your luggage to the customs tables and beyond, and they've been known to ask up to US$20 for their services – if you want help with your

---

THINGS CHANGE...

The information in this chapter is particularly vulnerable to change. Check directly with the airline or a travel agent to make sure you understand how a fare (and ticket you may buy) works and be aware of the security requirements for international travel. Shop carefully. The details given in this chapter should be regarded as pointers and are not a substitute for your own careful, up-to-date research.

---

bags, agree on a price beforehand. The formal price is a paltry 2000Rp per piece.

Once through customs, you're out with the tour operators, touts and taxi drivers. The touts will be working hard to convince you to come and stay at some place in the Kuta area. Most have contacts at a few places, and if you're not sure where you intend to stay, they may be worth considering, but you'll likely pay more for accommodation if a tout or a taxi driver takes you there without a reservation.

Passport

Your passport must be valid for six months after your date of arrival in Indonesia. See the visa section (p339) for details on what type of visa you will require.

AIR

Although Jakarta, the national capital, is the gateway airport to Indonesia, there are also many direct international flights to Denpasar. If you fly to Jakarta first, take one of the very frequent domestic flights to Denpasar, or travel overland through Java to Bali.

There are direct flights from Jakarta to Lombok, see below for more details.

Airports & Airlines
BALI AIRPORT
The only airport on Bali, Ngurah Rai Airport (DPS) is just south of Kuta, however it is referred to internationally as Denpasar or on some Internet flight booking sites as Bali.

The **domestic terminal** (☎ 0361-751011) and **international terminal** (☎ 0361-751011) are a few hundred metres apart.

See p356 for information on transport from the airport.

Airlines flying to and from Bali:

Air Asia (airline code AK; ☎ 0361-760116; www.airasia .com; hub Kuala Lumpur)

Air Paradise (airline code AK; ☎ 0361-756666; www .airparadise.com.au; hub Bali)

Australian Airlines (airline code AO; ☎ 0361-288331; www.australianairlines.com.au)

Bouraq (airline code BO; ☎ 0361-766929; www.bouraq .com)

Cathay Pacific Airways (airline code CX; ☎ 0361-766931; www.cathaypacific.com; hub Hong Kong)

Continental Airlines (airline code CO; ☎ 0361-768358; www.continental.com; hubs Newark, Houston)

Eva Air (airline code BR; ☎ 0361-751011; www.evaair .com; hub Taipai)

Garuda Indonesia (airline code GA; ☎ 0361-227824; www.garuda-indonesia.com; hubs Bali, Jakarta)

Japan Airlines (airline code JL; ☎ 0361-757077; www.jal.co.jp; hub Tokyo)

Lion Air (airline code JT; ☎ 0361-763872; www.lion airlines.com)

Malaysia Airlines (airline code MH; ☎ 0361-764995; www.mas.com.my; hub Kuala Lumpur)

Mandala Airlines (airline code RI; ☎ 0361-751011; www.mandalaair.com)

Merpati Airlines (airline code MZ; ☎ 0361-235358; www.merpati.co.id)

Qantas Airways (airline code QF; ☎ 0361-288331; www.qantas.com.au; hubs Sydney, Melbourne)

Singapore Airlines (airline code SQ; ☎ 0361-768388; www.singaporeair.com; hub Singapore)

Thai Airways International (airline code TG; ☎ 0361-288141; www.thaiair.com; hub Bangkok)

Money
The rates offered at the exchange counters at the international and domestic terminals are competitive, and as good as the money-changers in Kuta and the tourist centres. There are several ATMs.

Luggage
The **left-luggage room** (per piece per day 10,000Rp; ☯ 24hr) is in the international terminal, behind the McDonald's near the departures area.

LOMBOK AIRPORT
Lombok's Selaparang Airport (AMI) is just north of Mataram. Its international arrival area has been renovated to accommodate the Visa on Arrival scheme (see p340). The airport has hotel reservations desks, cafés, ATMs, moneychangers and Internet access.

Airlines flying to and from Lombok:

Garuda Indonesia (airline code GA; ☎ 0370-638259; www.garuda-indonesia.com)

Lion Air (airline code JT; ☎ 0370-629111, 0370-692222; www.lionairlines.com)

Merpati Airlines (airline code MZ; ☎ 0370-621111; www.merpati.co.id)

Silk Air (airline code MI; ☎ 0370-628254; www.silkair .com)

Tropical Airstrip (☎ 0370-635472)

Tickets
Deregulation in the Indonesian and the Asian aviation markets means that there are frequent deals to Bali. Airlines such as Malaysia's Air Asia are selling seats cheap. Bali's own Air Paradise and the Qantas off-shoot Australia Airlines are bringing prices down from Australia. Look for more cheap airline start-ups as the big national carriers finally face major competition.

Within Indonesia there are scores of airlines, with the line-up changing daily. But the result is that for trips on popular routes such as Bali to Jakarta frequent deals put the price of a plane ticket in the same class as the bus – with a savings of about 22 hours in transit time.

INTERCONTINENTAL (ROUND-THE-WORLD) TICKETS
Round-the-world (RTW) tickets that include Bali are usually offered by an alliance of several airlines such as **Star Alliance** (www .staralliance.com) and **One World** (www.oneworld .com). These tickets come in many flavours, but most let you visit several continents over a period of time that can be as long as a year. It's also worth investigating Circle Pacific-type tickets which are similar to RTW tickets but limit you to the Pacific region.

These types of tickets can be great deals. Prices for RTW tickets are usually well under US$2000 in economy and under US$5000 in business class. In the latter case, that's cheaper than a simple return fare from many parts of the world.

Besides the websites above, it's worth checking the ads in the Sunday newspaper travel section where you live as local travel

DEPARTURE TAX

The departure tax for all domestic flights from Bali is 20,000Rp, and 100,000Rp for all international flights. Only children under two years of age are exempt; you can pay by credit card. From Lombok the fee is 10,000Rp for domestic flights and 75,000Rp for international flights.

agents often assemble and advertise very good RTW airfares.

Asia

Bali is well connected to Asian cities. There is a regular nonstop service to Bangkok, Hong Kong, Kuala Lumpur, Singapore, Taipai and Tokyo. Lombok is now linked to Singapore. New discount airlines in Asia are targeting Bali for service, including Malaysia's Air Asia. Singapore is a hub, with service by Singapore Airlines, Garuda Indonesia and Australian Airlines.

STA Travel proliferates in Asia, with branches in **Bangkok** (☎ 02-236 0262; www.sta travel.co.th), **Singapore** (☎ 6737 7188; www.statravel .com.sg), **Hong Kong** (☎ 2736 1618; www.statravel.com .hk) and **Japan** (☎ 03 5391 2922; www.statravel.co.jp). Another resource in Japan is **No 1 Travel** (☎ 03 3205 6073; www.no1-travel.com); in Hong Kong try **Four Seas Tours** (☎ 2200 7760; www.fourseastravel .com/english).

Australia

There are several options for service to Bali. The Qantas discount carrier flies from Sydney and Melbourne, the parent carrier flies from Perth and Darwin. Garuda Indonesia serves several major Australian cities on a constantly changing basis. Bali's Air Paradise serves Adelaide, Melbourne, Perth and Sydney.

A well-known agency for discount fares nationwide is **STA Travel** (☎ 1300 733 035; www .statravel.com.au). **Flight Centre** (☎ 133 133; www .flightcentre.com.au) has offices throughout Australia. For online bookings, try www.travel. com.au.

Canada

From Canada you'll change planes at an Asian hub.

Travel Cuts (☎ 800-667-2887; www.travelcuts.com) is Canada's national student travel agency.

For online bookings try www.expedia.ca and www.travelocity.ca.

Continental Europe

None of the major European carriers fly to Bali at present, although if tourism numbers keep increasing they may well again. In the meantime, Singapore is the most likely place to change planes coming from Europe, with Kuala Lumpur and Bangkok also being popular.

FRANCE

Recommended agencies:

Anyway (☎ 08 92 89 38 92; www.anyway.fr)
Lastminute (☎ 08 92 0 50 00; www.lastminute.fr)
Nouvelles Frontières (☎ 08 25 00 07 47; www .nouvelles-frontieres.fr)
OTU Voyages (☎ 08 20 81 78 17; www.otu.fr) This agency specialises in student and youth travellers.
Voyageurs du Monde (☎ 01 40 15 11 15; www.vdm .com)

GERMANY

Recommended agencies:

Expedia (www.expedia.de)
Just Travel (☎ 089 747 3330; www.justtravel.de)
Lastminute (☎ 01805 284 366; www.lastminute.de)
STA Travel (☎ 01805 456 422; www.statravel.de) For travellers under the age of 26.

THE NETHERLANDS

One recommended agency is **Airfair** (☎ 020 620 5121; www.airfair.nl).

New Zealand

Garuda Indonesia has infrequent flights to Auckland which stop in Brisbane. Otherwise you will have to change planes in Australia. Air New Zealand has suspended service on this route.

Both **Flight Centre** (☎ 0800 243 544; www.flight centre.co.nz) and **STA Travel** (☎ 0508 782 872; www .statravel.co.nz) have branches throughout the country. The site www.travel.co.nz is recommended for online bookings.

Other Indonesian Islands

From Bali, Bouraq, Garuda Indonesia, Lion Air, Mandala Airlines and Merpapti Airlines offer domestic service to much of Indonesia. Flights to Lombok, Jakarta and Surabaya are frequent and served by multiple carriers. Flights also go to other major destinations including the eastern islands cities Kupang, Maumere and Waingapu, as well as Yogyakarta on Java.

For tickets, you can compare the airline's websites but if you are already on Bali, then just go down to the domestic terminal at the airport where all the domestic airlines have ticket offices. At times it has the feel of a bazaar as new lower fares are taped up in the windows. You should be able to get a flight to Jakarta for under US$50. This is true to a lesser extent on Lombok.

UK & Ireland
From London, the most direct service is on Singapore Airlines through Singapore. Malaysia Airlines also offers a good connection through Kuala Lumpur but Singapore has multiple flights and connections daily.

Discount air travel is big business in London. Advertisements for many travel agencies appear in the travel pages of the weekend broadsheet newspapers, in *Time Out*, the *Evening Standard* and in the free magazine *TNT*.

Recommended travel agencies include the following:

Bridge the World (☎ 0870 444 7474; www.b-t-w.co.uk)
Flightbookers (☎ 0870 010 7000; www.ebookers.com)
Flight Centre (☎ 0870 890 8099; www.flightcentre.co.uk)
North-South Travel (☎ 01245 608 291; www.northsouthtravel.co.uk) North-South Travel donates part of its profit to projects in the developing world.
Quest Travel (☎ 0870 442 3542; www.questtravel.com)
STA Travel (☎ 0870 160 0599; www.statravel.co.uk) For travellers under the age of 26.
Trailfinders (☎ 0845 05 05 891; www.trailfinders.co.uk)
Travel Bag (☎ 0870 890 1456; www.travelbag.co.uk)

USA
Continental Airlines is the sole American carrier to serve Bali, however it does so as part of its local Pacific service which means you will stop in Hawaii and Guam on your way. Often quicker connections can be had through any of the major Asian cities with nonstop service to Bali (see Asia, p345).

Discount travel agents in the USA are known as consolidators (although you won't see a sign on the door saying 'Consolidator'). San Francisco is the ticket consolidator capital of America, although some good deals can be found in Los Angeles, New York and other big cities.

The following agencies are recommended for online bookings:
Cheap Tickets (www.cheaptickets.com)
Expedia (www.expedia.com) (www.itn.net)
Lowest Fare (www.lowestfare.com)
Orbitz (www.orbitz.com)
STA Travel (www.sta.com) For travellers under the age of 26.
Travelocity (www.travelocity.com)

SEA
You can reach Java, just west of Bali, and Sumbawa, just west of Lombok, via ferries. Through buses can take you all the way to Jakarta. Longer distance boats serve Indonesia's eastern islands.

Java
When visiting Java from Bali and Lombok, some land travel is necessary.

FERRY
Ferries (adult/child 3500/2500Rp, car and driver 38,000Rp; every 30 minutes) run 24 hours, crossing the Bali Strait between Gilimanuk (p265) in western Bali and Ketapang (Java). The actual crossing takes under 30 minutes, but you'll spend longer than this loading, unloading and waiting around. Car rental contracts usually prohibit rental vehicles being taken out of Bali, but it may be possible to take a rented motorcycle across, by arrangement with the owner.

From Ketapang, *bemos* (small pick-up trucks) travel 4km north to the terminal, where buses leave for Baluran, Probolingo (for Gunung Bromo), Surabaya, Yogyakarta and Jakarta. There's a train station near the ferry port, with trains to Probolingo, Surabaya, Yogyakarta and Jakarta. Contact the **Train Information Service** (☎ 0361-227131) for more information.

BUS
To/From Bali
The ferry crossing is included in the services to/from Ubung terminal in Denpasar offered by numerous bus companies. Many of them travel overnight, and they can arrive at an uncomfortably early hour in the morning. It's advisable to buy your ticket at least one day in advance, at travel agents in all the tourist centres or at the Ubung terminal. Note too that fierce air

---

BOAT TRIPS TO KOMODO

Boat trips east from Lombok are really only for the hardiest of adventure travellers – most are basic set-ups, offering minimal comforts and few safety provisions. The main destination is Pulau Komodo, an island near Flores, famous for the giant monitor lizards called Komodo dragons. The usual boat trips include stops at other islands for snorkelling, trekking, sightseeing and beach parties. Some trips finish in Labuanbajo on Flores, and passengers then continue eastwards or find their own way back to Lombok. In these cases, flying back to Bali may be a good idea as the trip can be rough.

Try to get a recent personal endorsement for a particular trip, and find out *exactly* what the cost includes. Prices can be negotiable, depending particularly on the number of passengers and the itinerary, but they are generally inexpensive – from around 450,000Rp per person for a four-day trip. It's worth paying a little more for a less crowded boat and better conditions.

There are several operators, with ticket outlets on Gili Trawangan, Bangsal and in Mataram. Buses generally depart from Mataram and travel to a boat waiting in Labuan Lombok.

Perama (☎ 0370-635928; www.peramatour.com; Jl Pejanggik 66, Mataram; ☽ 8am-6pm) is much more reliable. It offers three-day boat trips to Labuanbajo on Flores (and vice versa), taking in Komodo en route. Prices are 750,000Rp/1,050,000Rp deck/cabin from west to east and 500,000Rp/700,000Rp deck/cabin in the other direction.

---

competition has put tickets to Jakarta and Surabaya in the range of bus prices.

Fares vary between operators, and depend on what sort of comfort you want – it's worth paying extra for a decent seat and aircon. For a comfortable bus ride, typical fares and travel times are Surabaya (65,000Rp, 10 to 12 hours), Yogyakarta (120,000Rp, 16 hours) and Jakarta (180,000Rp, 26 to 30 hours). Some companies travel directly between Java and Singaraja, via Lovina, on the north coast of Bali (see p238). Prices are similar to those from Denpasar, and travel times are a bit shorter.

To/From Lombok

Public buses go daily from Mandalika terminal (p273) to major cities on Java (the price includes the ferry trips). Most buses are comfortable, with air-con and reclining seats. Destinations include Denpasar (80,000Rp, six hours), Surabaya (125,000Rp, 20 hours), Semarang (165,000Rp, 28hr), Yogyakarta (185,000Rp, 30 hours) and Jakarta (270,000Rp, 48 hours).

Sumbawa

Sumbawa Ferries run 24 hours, travelling between Labuhan Lombok (p306) and Poto Tano on Sumbawa every hour (adult 10,000Rp, motorcycle 13,500Rp, car 135,000Rp, 90 minutes). Coming from Sumbawa, start early so you can reach Labuhan Lombok by 4pm, as public transport is limited after this time.

Comfortable long-distance buses go from Mandalika terminal through to the port of Sape on Sumbawa (85,000Rp, 14 hours), from where you can travel onward to Komodo and Flores.

Perama (☎ 693007 in Senggigi, ☎ 635928 in Mataram; www.peramatour.com) serves Sumbawa Besar, Dompu or Sape. Confirm schedules and prices.

Other Indonesian Islands

Services to other islands in Indonesia are often in flux, although Pelni (see below) is reliable. Recently there have been relatively fast ferry services linking Bali with Kupang (West Timor) via Bima (Sumbawa), Maumere (Flores) and Larantuka (Flores). Bali has also been a stop on a boat linking Surabaya (Java) and Maumere via Bima. These services may only operate once a week or less and they may vanish overnight so check with a travel agent or at Benoa Harbour (p127).

PELNI

The national shipping line is **Pelni** (www.pelni .co.id), which schedules large boats on long-distance runs throughout Indonesia.

To/From Bali

Three ships from Pelni stop at Benoa Harbour (see p127) as part of their regular loops throughout Indonesia. *Dobonsolo* with Java, Nusa Tenggara, Maluku and northern Papua; and *Awu* and *Tilongkabila* with Nusa Tenggara and southern Sulawesi. Prices are dependent on the route and the class of travel, and this can range widely in price. The main **Pelni office** (☎ 0361-763063, 0800-107 3564; ☷ 9am-3pm Mon-Fri, 9am-noon Sat) is located at Benoa Harbour, there is also another office in **Tuban** (Map p101; ☎ 0361-720962; 299 Jl Raya Tuban).

To/From Lombok

Currently three Pelni boats stop at Lembar (p276) about once a fortnight. Destinations from Lembar are Bima, Labuanbajo, Makassar, Bau Bau, Surabaya, Larantuka, Kupan, Saumlak, Dobo, Timika and Merauke, but depending on the direction of travel, it may take a long time to get from Lembar to these places. The islands of Bali, Sumbawa and Flores are a journey of approximately four hours, 16 hours and 24 hours respectively. Book tickets at the Ampenan or Lembar **Pelni office** (Ampenan ☎ 681209; Jl Industri; ☷ 9am-3pm Mon-Fri, 9am-noon Sat; Lembar ☎ 681204; ☷ 24hr).

GETTING AROUND

Especially on Bali, the best way to get around is with your own transport whether you drive or you hire a driver. This gives you the flexibility to explore at will and allows you to reach many places that are otherwise inaccessible.

Public transport can be ridiculously cheap but can be cause for very long journeys if you are not sticking to a major route. In addition, some places may be impossible to reach.

There are tourist shuttle buses and these combine economy with convenience. These services, however, were greatly cut back after 2002.

AIR

Garuda Indonesia and Merpati Airlines have several flights daily between Bali and Lombok. The route is competitive and fares hover around about 230,000Rp, although new entrants in the market may offer better deals. See p343 for details on the airlines, airports and departure tax.

BEMO

The main form of public transport on Bali is the *bemo*. A generic term for any vehicle

used as public transport, it's normally a minibus or van with a row of low seats down each side. The word 'bemo' is a contraction of *becak* (bicycle rickshaw) and *mobil* (car). Riding bemos can be part of your Bali adventure or a major nightmare depending on your outlook at the moment in time. Certainly you can expect journeys to be rather lengthy and you find that getting to many places is both time-consuming and inconvenient.

On Lombok, bemos, small buses and even trucks are more interchangeable for transport. The fare information below generally applies. See Buses (p350) for more information about bemos.

See p328 for information on pickpocketing on public bemos.

Fares

Bemos operate on a standard route for a set (but unwritten) fare. Unless you get on at a regular starting point, and get off at a regular finishing point, the fares are likely to be fuzzy. The cost per kilometre is pretty variable, but is cheaper on longer trips. The minimum fare is about 2000Rp. The fares listed in this book were correct at the time of writing and reflect what a tourist should reasonably expect to pay.

Bemos are justly famous for overcharging tourists, and finding out the *harga biasa* ('correct' fare) requires local knowledge and subtlety. The best procedure is to hand over the correct fare as you get off, as the locals do, no questions asked. To find out the correct fare, consult a trusted local before you get on – if you're staying at a cheap *losmen* (basic accommodation), the owner will usually be helpful (at an expensive hotel they'll discourage you from using bemos and offer to charter transport for you). Note what other passengers pay when they get off, bearing in mind that schoolchildren and the driver's friends pay less. If you speak Bahasa Indonesia, you can ask your fellow passengers, but in a dispute they will probably support the bemo jockey.

The whole business of overcharging tourists is a bit of a game; bemo drivers and jockeys are usually good-humoured about it, but some tourists take it very seriously and have unpleasant arguments over a few hundred rupiah. Sometimes you will be charged extra (perhaps double the passenger price) if you have a big bag, as you will be taking up space where otherwise a paying passenger could squeeze in.

Make sure you know where you're going, and accept that the bemo normally won't leave until it's full and will usually take a roundabout route to collect and deliver as many passengers as possible. One way to hurry up a departure, and make yourself instantly popular with other frustrated passengers, is to fork out a few extra thousand rupiah and pay for the one or more fares that you seem to be waiting all day for. If you get into an empty bemo, always make it clear that you do not want to charter it. (The word 'charter' is understood by all drivers.)

Terminals & Routes

Every town has at least one terminal *(terminal bis)* for all forms of public transport. There are often several terminals in larger towns, according to the direction the bus or bemo is heading. For example, Denpasar, the hub of Bali's transport system (see p87) has four main bus/bemo terminals and three minor ones. Terminals can be confusing, but most bemos and buses have signs and, if in doubt, you will be told where to go by a bemo jockey or driver anyway.

To go from one part of Bali to another, it is often necessary to go via one or more of the terminals in Denpasar, or via a terminal in one of the other larger regional towns. For example, to get from Sanur to Ubud by public bemo, you go to the Kereneng terminal in Denpasar, transfer to the Batubulan terminal, and then take a third bemo to Ubud. This is circuitous and time-consuming, so many visitors prefer the tourist shuttle buses (see p350).

BICYCLE

A famous temple carving shows the Dutch artist WOJ Nieuwenkamp pedalling through Bali in 1904. Bali's roads have improved greatly since then, but surprisingly few people tour the island on a *sepeda* (bicycle). Many visitors, however, are using bikes around the towns and for day trips; good quality rental bikes are available, and several companies organise full-day cycle trips in the back country. Mountain bikes are widely available in tourist areas, and their low gear ratios and softer tyres are much better suited to Bali than a 10-speed touring bike.

Some people are put off cycle touring by Bali's tropical heat, heavy traffic, frequent showers and high mountains. But when you're riding on the level or downhill, the breeze really moderates the heat, and once you're out of the congested southern region, and especially on the back roads, traffic is lighter. Frequent roadside food stalls are great for a drink, a snack, or as shelter from a downpour. Multigear mountain bikes make it possible to get up the higher mountains, but with a bit of negotiating and patience, you can get a bemo or minibus to take you and your bike up the steepest sections.

The main advantage of seeing Bali by bicycle is the quality of the experience. By bicycle you can be totally immersed in the environment – you can hear the wind rustling in the rice paddies, the sound of a *gamelan* (traditional Balinese orchestra) practicing, and catch the scent of the flowers. Even at the height of the tourist season, cycle tourers on the back roads experience the friendliness that seems all but lost on the usual tourist circuit.

Lombok is ideal for touring by bicycle, and excellent for mountain bikes. Bikes can be rented in the main tourist centers in Lombok but most of them are pretty rickety – always check breaks, gears etc first.

In the populated areas, the roads are flat and the traffic is less dangerous than on Bali. East of Mataram are several attractions that would make a good day trip from Mataram, or you could go south to Banyumulek via Gunung Pengsong and return (p274).

Some of the coastal roads have hills and curves like a roller coaster – try going north from Mataram, via Senggigi, to Pemenang, and then (if you feel energetic) return via the steep climb over the Pusuk Pass.

You can usually bring your bicycle with you by air, but may have to pay a fee or pay for excess baggage. You may have to box the bike, take the pedals off and/or turn the handlebars sideways. Some airlines will provide a bike box for a small charge – contact the airline in advance to make arrangements.

Hire

There are plenty of bicycles for rent in the tourist areas, but many of them are in poor condition (check to see if all the nuts are securely tightened, especially those attached to the seat, the wheel nuts, the brake linkage cables and the brake rims, which tend to loosen with vibration). The best place to rent a good quality mountain bike is in Ubud. Generally prices range from 20,000Rp to 30,000Rp per day.

Touring
See Roads (p354) for more information, and make sure your bike is equipped for these conditions.

Even the smallest village has some semblance of a bike shop – a flat tyre should cost about 4000Rp to fix. Denpasar has a number of shops selling spare parts and complete bicycles – check at the many shopping centres (p87).

BOAT
Public ferries (adult/child 15,000/9350Rp;) travel nonstop between Padangbai (p191) on Bali and Lembar (p276) on Lombok. Motorcycles cost 36,400Rp and cars cost 258,700Rp – go through the weighbridge at the west corner of the car park. Depending on conditions the trip can take three to five hours. Boats run 24 hours and leave about every 90 minutes; food and drink is sold on board.

Anyone who carries your luggage on or off the ferries at both ports will expect to be paid, so agree on the price first or carry your own stuff. Also, watch out for scams where the porter may try to sell you a ticket you've already bought. Lembar is worse for this.

It's worth checking to see if the on-again, off-again Padangbai Express (55,000Rp; two hours) is running. Also note that you may still see reference to the Mabua Express, a service which ended years ago.

Perama (Padangbai ☎ 0363-41419; Café Dona, Jl Pelabuhan; ☒ 7am-8pm; Senggigi ☎ 0370-693007; ☒ 6am-10pm) has a 40-passenger boat that takes four hours to travel from Padangbai to Senggigi (100,00Rp depart 9am, return 1pm), where you can get another boat to the Gilis (50,000Rp). Snacks are sold on board.

Bounty Cruises (☎ 0361-726666 in Bali, ☎ 0370-643636 in Lombok; www.balibountygroup.com) offers a sporadic service on its fast, modern boat linking Benoa Harbour on Bali with Gili Meno (p283) off Lombok (one way US$40 to $45, two hours).

BUS
Distances on Bali and Lombok are relatively short so you won't have cause to ride many large buses unless you are transferring between islands or going from one side to another.

Public Bus
BALI
Larger minibuses and full-size buses ply the longer routes, particularly between Denpasar and Singaraja, and on to Gilimanuk along the northern coastal route. They operate out of the same terminals as the bemos. Buses are faster than bemos because they do not make as many stops along the way. A bus is also often slightly cheaper than a bemo if you take it for the full trip (eg Singaraja to Denpasar), but it is more expensive if you want to get off halfway, as only a set fare is available.

LOMBOK
Buses and bemos of various sizes are the cheapest and most common way of getting around Lombok. On rough roads in remote areas, trucks may be used as public transport. Mandalika is the main bus terminal for all of Lombok; see p306. The terminal was formerly at Sweta, and some buses still have 'Sweta' written on them, but to add to confusion the terminal is also referred to as Mandalika or Bertais. There are also regional terminals at Praya and Pancor (near Selong). You may have to go via one or more of these transport hubs to get from one part of Lombok to another.

Public transport fares are fixed by the provincial government, and displayed on a noticeboard outside the terminal office of Mandalika terminal. You may have to pay more if you have a large bag or surfboard.

Tourist Shuttle Bus
Tourist shuttle buses travel between the main tourist centres on Bali and connect to destinations on Lombok. Shuttle buses are quicker, more comfortable and more convenient than public transport, and though more expensive, they are very popular with budget and mid-range travellers. If you're with a group of three or more people (or sometimes even two), it will probably be cheaper to charter a vehicle, however.

The network of these buses was sharply reduced after 2002. **Perama** (www.peramatour .com) is the main operator. It also has offices or agents in Kuta (p111), Sanur (p126), Ubud (p169), Lovina (p247), Padangbai (p191) and Candidasa (p198). At least one bus a day links these tourist centres with more frequent services to the airport. There are also services to Kitimani and along the east coast from Lovina to/from Candidasa via Amed by demand.

Fares are reasonable (for example Kuta to Lovina is 50,000Rp). Be sure to book your trip at least a day ahead in order to confirm schedules. It is also important to understand where Perama buses will pick you up and drop you off as you may need to pay an extra 5000Rp to get to/from your hotel.

Note that shuttle buses often do not provide a direct service – those from Kuta to Candidasa may stop en route at Sanur, Ubud and Padangbai, and maybe other towns on request.

Perama also operates on Lombok. Currently, this service only links Mataram (p273) with Kuta, Senggigi (p308), Bangsal (p293) and Tetebatu (p307) – so you can't travel from Kuta to Bangsal without changing in Mataram, but you can normally connect on the same day. From Senggigi, there are also shuttle boats to the Gili Islands (p286).

CAR & MOTORCYCLE
Driving Licence
If you plan to drive a car, you *must* have an International Driving Permit (IDP). It's easy to obtain one from your national motoring organisation if you have a normal driving licence. Bring your home licence as well – it's supposed to be carried in conjunction with the IDP.

MOTORCYCLE LICENCE
If you also have a motorcycle licence at home, get your IDP endorsed for motorcycles too.

If you have an IDP endorsed for motorcycles you will have no problems. If not, you should obtain a local licence, which is valid for one month on Bali only. It's not worth getting a motorcycle licence for a day or two – rent or charter a car or minibus instead.

ROAD DISTANCES (KM)

	Amed	Bangli	Bedugul	Candidasa	Denpasar	Gilimanuk	Kintamani	Kuta	Lovina	Negara	Nusa Dua	Padangbai	Sanur	Semarapura	Singaraja	Tirtagangga	Ubud
Amed	---																
Bangli	59	---															
Bedugul	144	97	---														
Candidasa	32	52	88	---													
Denpasar	98	47	78	72	---												
Gilimanuk	238	181	148	206	134	---											
Kintamani	108	20	89	71	67	135	---										
Kuta	114	57	57	82	10	144	77	---									
Lovina	89	86	41	139	89	79	70	99	---								
Negara	202	135	115	167	95	33	104	107	---								
Nusa Dua	122	81	102	96	24	158	91	14	113	109	---						
Padangbai	45	39	75	13	59	219	58	69	126	154	83	---					
Sanur	105	40	85	79	7	141	78	15	96	102	22	78	---				
Semarapura	37	26	61	27	47	181	46	57	112	124	71	14	52	---			
Singaraja	78	75	30	128	78	90	59	88	11	118	92	115	85	105	---		
Tirtagangga	14	65	101	13	84	212	85	95	112	179	108	26	91	44	142	---	
Ubud	68	29	35	54	23	157	29	33	40	120	47	41	30	29	95	67	---

TRANSPORT

The person renting the bike may not check your licence or IDP, and the cop who stops you may be happy with a nonendorsed IDP or bribe. You might get away without a motorcycle endorsement, but you *must* have an IDP. Officially there's a 2,000,000Rp fine for riding without a proper licence, and the motorcycle can be impounded – unofficially, the cop may expect a substantial 'on-the-spot' payment. And if you have an accident without a proper licence, your insurance company might refuse coverage.

To get a local motorcycle licence, go independently (or have the rental agency/owner take you) to the **Denpasar Police Office** (Map pp82-3; ☎ 424346; Jl Pattimura) for a Temporary Permit, which is valid for 30 days, and will cost 100,000Rp. Take along your passport, three passport photos and your IDP. Remember to dress appropriately.

Fuel & Spare Parts

Bensin (petrol) is sold by the government-owned Pertamina company, and currently costs a dirt-cheap 2000Rp per litre. Bali has numerous petrol stations but there are gaps in their coverage notably along the east coast north of Amlapura and in the mountains. In that case, look for the little roadside fuel shops that fill your tank from a plastic container with a funnel for a similar price per litre. Petrol pumps usually have a meter, which records the litres and a table that shows how much to pay for various amounts. Make sure to check that the pump is reset to zero before the attendant starts to put petrol in your vehicle, and check the total amount that goes in before the pump is reset for the next customer.

Tyre repair services can be found in almost every town.

Hire

Very few agencies on Bali will allow you to take their rental cars or motorcycles to Lombok – the regular vehicle insurance is not valid outside Bali.

See Insurance (p353) for details or rental insurance.

CAR

Renting a car can open up Bali for exploration and can also leave you counting the

minutes until you return it. See Road Conditions on p354 for details of the at times harrowing driving conditions on Bali.

By far the most popular rental vehicle is the small Suzuki jeep – they're compact, have good ground clearance and the low gear ratio is well suited to exploring Bali's back roads, although the bench seats at the back are uncomfortable on a long trip. The main alternative is the larger Toyota Kijang, which seats six but is still economical and lightweight. Automatic transmission is uncommon in rental cars.

Rental and travel agencies at all tourist centres advertise cars for rent. A Suzuki jeep costs about 80,000Rp per day, with unlimited kilometres and very limited insurance – maybe less per day for longer rentals. A Toyota Kijang costs from around 120,000Rp per day. These costs will vary considerably according to demand, the condition of the vehicle, length of hire and your bargaining talents. It's common for extra days to cost much less than the first day.

There's no reason to book rental cars in advance over the Internet or with a tour package, and it will almost certainly cost more than arranging it locally. Shop around for a good deal, and check the car carefully before you sign up – it's unusual to find a car that has everything working. Don't wait until you really need the horn, wipers, lights, spare tyre or registration papers before you find that they're not there. Rental cars usually have to be returned to the place from where they are rented – you can't do a one-way rental, but some operators will let you leave a car at the airport.

Big international rental operators have a presence and are worth investigating if you're not travelling on a budget – vehicle quality and condition will likely be of high standard. Typical rates run well more than US$60 per day with another US$30 per day for a driver.

Avis (☎ 0361-282635; www.avis.com)
Hertz (☎ 0361-286967; www.hertz.com)

On Lombok, look to the tourist centres for car rental agencies. Hotels are usually a good source of options. Prices and conditions are similar, but due to low volumes may run somewhat higher at times.

TRANSPORT

MOTORCYCLE

Motorcycles are a popular way of getting around Bali, especially with Balinese, who ride pillion on a *sepeda motor* (motorcycle) almost from birth. Motorcycling is just as convenient and flexible as driving and the environmental impact and the cost are much less.

Motorcycles are ideal for Lombok's tiny, rough roads, which may be difficult or impassable by car. Once you get out of the main centres there's not much traffic, apart from people, dogs and water buffalo – watch out for the numerous potholes.

But think carefully before renting a motorcycle. It is dangerous and every year a number of visitors go home in a wheelchair, or in a box – Bali and Lombok are no places to learn to ride a motorcycle.

Motorcycles for rent on Bali and Lombok are almost all between 90cc and 200cc, with 100cc the usual size. You really don't need anything bigger, as the distances are short and the roads are rarely suitable for travelling fast.

Rental charges vary with the motorcycle and the period of rental – bigger, newer motorcycles cost more, while longer rental periods attract lower rates. A new-ish 125cc Honda in good condition might cost 30,000Rp to 35,000Rp a day, but for a week or more you might get the same motorcycle for as little as 25,000Rp per day. This should include minimal insurance for the motorcycle (probably with a US$100 excess), but not for any other person or property.

Individual owners rent out the majority of motorcycles. Generally it's travel agencies, restaurants, losmen or shops with a sign advertising 'motorcycle for rent'. On Bali, the Kuta region is the easiest and cheapest place to rent a motorcycle, but you'll have no trouble finding one anywhere tourists regularly visit including on Lombok.

See Insurance (right) for details on rental insurance.

Riding Considerations

Check the motorcycle over before riding off – some are in very bad condition. You must carry the motorcycle's registration papers with you while riding. Make sure the agency/owner gives them to you before you ride off.

Helmets are compulsory and this requirement is enforced in tourist areas, but less so in the countryside. You can even be stopped for not having the chin-strap fastened – a favourite of policemen on the lookout for some extra cash. The standard helmets you get with rental bikes are pretty lightweight. If you value your skull, bring a solid helmet from home (but don't leave it lying around because it'll get pinched).

Despite the tropical climate, it's still wise to dress properly for motorcycling. Thongs, shorts and a T-shirt are not going to protect your skin from being ground off as you slide along the pavement. As well as protection against a spill, be prepared for the weather. It can get pretty cold on a cloudy day in the mountains. Coming over the top of Gunung Batur you might wish you were wearing gloves. And when it rains on Bali, it really rains. A poncho is handy, but it's best to get off the road and sit out the storm.

Insurance

Rental agencies and owners usually insist that the vehicle itself is insured, and minimal insurance should be included in the basic rental deal – often with an excess of as much as US$100 for a motorcycle and US$500 for a car (ie the customer pays the first US$100/500 of any claim). The more formal motorcycle and car rental agencies may offer additional insurance to reduce the level of the excess, and cover damage to other people or their property, ie 'third-party' or 'liability' cover.

Especially with cars, the owner's main concern is insuring the vehicle. In some cases, a policy might cover the car for 30 million Rp, but provide for only 10 million Rp third-party cover. Your travel insurance may provide some additional protection, although liability for motor accidents is specifically excluded from many policies. The third-party cover might seem inadequate, but if you do cause damage or injury, it's usually enough for your consulate to get you out of jail.

A private owner renting a motorcycle may not offer any insurance at all. See the text above for a discussion of insurance issues you should consider.

Ensure that your personal travel insurance covers injuries incurred while motorcycling. Some policies specifically exclude coverage for motorcycle riding, or have special conditions.

Road Conditions

The traffic can be horrendous around south Bali, Denpasar and from Batubulan to Ubud, and is usually quite heavy as far as Padangbai to the east and Tabanan to the west. Finding your way around the main tourist sites can be a challenge, as roads are only sometimes signposted and maps are often out of date. Off the main routes, roads can be rough, but they are usually surfaced – there are few dirt roads on Bali. Driving is most difficult in the large towns, where streets are congested, traffic can be awful, and one-way streets are infuriating.

Roads in Lombok are often very rough.

Road Hazards

Avoid driving at night or at dusk. Many bicycles, carts and horse-drawn vehicles do not have proper lights, and street lighting is limited. Motorcycling at dusk offers the unique sensation of numerous insects, large and small, hitting your face at 60km/h.

POLICE

Police will stop drivers on some very slender pretexts, and it's fair to say that they're not motivated by a desire to enhance road safety. If a cop sees your front wheel half an inch over the faded line at a stop sign, if the chin-strap of your helmet isn't fastened, or if you don't observe one of the ever-changing and poorly signposted one-way traffic restrictions, you may be waved down. They also do spot checks of licences and vehicle registrations, especially before major holiday periods.

The cop will ask to see your licence and the vehicle's registration papers, and he will also tell you what a serious offence you've committed. He may start talking about court appearances, heavy fines and long delays. Stay cool and don't argue. Don't offer him a bribe. Eventually he'll suggest that you can pay him some amount of money to deal with the matter. If it's a very large amount, tell him politely that you don't have that much. These matters can be settled for something between 40,000Rp and 60,000Rp; although it will be more like 100,000Rp if you don't have an IDP or if you argue. Always make sure you have the correct papers, and don't have too much visible cash in your wallet. If things deteriorate, ask for the cop's name and talk about contacting your consulate.

Road Rules

Visiting drivers commonly complain about crazy Balinese drivers, but often it's because the visitors don't understand the local conventions of road use. The following rules are very useful.

- Watch your front – it's your responsibility to avoid anything that gets in front of your vehicle. A car, motorcycle or anything else pulling out in front of you, in effect, has the right of way. Often drivers won't even look to see what's coming when they turn left at a junction – they listen for the horn.
- Use your horn to warn anything in front that you're there, especially if you're about to overtake.
- Drive on the left side of the road, although it's often a case of driving on whatever side of the road is available, after avoiding the roadworks, livestock and other vehicles.

CHARTERING A VEHICLE & DRIVER

An excellent way to travel anywhere around Bali is by chartered vehicle. It literally allows you to leave the driving and inherent frustrations to others. If you are part of a group it can make sound economic sense as well.

It's easy to arrange a charter: just listen for one of the frequent offers of 'transport?' in the streets around the tourist centres; approach a driver yourself; or ask at your hotel. Many car rental places will also supply a driver as well.

Chartering a vehicle costs about 100,000Rp to 200,000Rp – although this depends greatly on the distance and, more importantly, your negotiating skills. If you are planning to start early, finish late and cover an awful lot of territory, then you will have to pay more. Although a driver may reasonably ask for an advance for petrol, never pay the full fare until you have returned. For day trips, you will be expected to buy meals for the driver (*nasi campur* – steamed rice topped with a little bit of everything – and water is the standard), particularly if you stop to eat yourself. Tipping for a job well done is expected.

Drivers that hang around tourist spots and upmarket hotels will tend to over-charge and are rarely interested in negotiating or bargaining. Beware of tactics like claiming you must hire the vehicle for a minimum of five hours, or assertions that your destination is 'very far' or that 'the roads are very rough'. Agree clearly on a route beforehand.

You can sometimes arrange to charter an entire bemo for your trip at a bemo terminal. The cost is about the same as for chatering a vehicle and you will enjoy the adventure of a bemo without the crowds – or chickens.

DOKAR & CIDOMO

The small *dokar* (pony cart) still provides local transport in some remote areas, and even in areas of Denpasar, but they're extremely slow and are not particularly cheap. Prices start at 2000Rp per person for a short trip, but are very negotiable, depending on demand, number of passengers, nearby competition, and your bargaining skills. The tourist price can be high if the driver thinks the tourist will pay big-time for the novelty value.

The pony cart used on Lombok is known as a *cidomo* – a contraction of *cika* (a traditional handcart), *dokar* (Balinese word for a pony cart) and *mobil* (because car wheels and tyres are used). They are often brightly coloured and the horses decorated with coloured tassels and jingling bells. A typical *cidomo* has a narrow bench seat on either side. The ponies appear to some visitors to be heavily laden and harshly treated, but they are usually looked after reasonably well, if only because the owners depend on them for their livelihood. *Cidomos* are a very popular form of transport in many parts of Lombok, and often go to places that bemos don't, won't or can't.

Fares are not set by the government. The price will always depend on demand, the number of passengers, the destination and your negotiating skills – maybe 2000Rp to 4000Rp per passenger for a short trip.

HITCHING

You can hitchhike on Bali, but it's not a very useful option for getting around, as public transport is so cheap and frequent and private vehicles are often full.

TO/FROM BALI AIRPORT

From the official counters, just outside the international and domestic terminals at Ngurah Rai Airport, the cost of prepaid airport taxis costs the following. Buy your voucher and you are good to go. Ignore any pleas from independent operators who will try to charge more.

Destination	Fare
Candidasa	199,000Rp
Denpasar	40,000Rp
Denpasar (Ubung terminal)	50,000Rp
Tuban	20,000Rp
Kuta Beach	25,000Rp
Legian	30,000Rp
Nusa Dua	55,000Rp
Sanur	55,000Rp
Seminyak	35,000Rp
Tanjung Benoa	60,000Rp
Ubud	115,000Rp

You can only share a prepaid airport taxi if all passengers are going to the same place; they won't allow passengers to be dropped off along the way.

If you walk across the airport car park, northeast to Jl Raya Tuban, taxis may stop and take you to your destination for the metered rate, which might be cheaper than a prepaid airport taxi.

Using a metered taxi *to* the airport should cost much less than the prepaid taxi rates.

Bear in mind, also, that hitching is never entirely safe in any country and we don't recommend it. Travellers who decide to hitch should understand that they are taking a small but potentially serious risk. People who do choose to hitch will be safer if they travel in pairs and let someone know where they plan to go.

LOCAL TRANSPORT
Ojek

Around some major towns, and along roads where bemos rarely or never venture, transport may be provided by an *ojek* (a motorcycle that takes a paying pillion passenger). However, with increased vehicle ownership in Bali, *ojek* are becoming increasingly less common. They're OK on quiet country roads, but a high-risk option in the big towns. The fare is negotiable, but about 5000Rp for 5km is fairly standard.

Taxi

BALI

Metered taxis are common in South Bali, Denpasar and Ubud. They are essential for getting around Kuta and Seminyak, where you can easily flag one down. Elsewhere, they're often a lot less hassle than haggling with bemo jockeys and charter drivers.

The usual rate for a taxi is 4000Rp flag fall and 1500Rp per kilometre, but the rate is higher in the evening. If you phone for a taxi, the minimum charge is 8000Rp. Any driver that claims meter problems or which won't use it should be avoided.

The most reputable taxi agency is **Bali Taxi** (☎ 0361-701111), which uses distinctive blue vehicles with the words 'Bluebird Group' over the windshield. Drivers speak reasonable English and use the meter at all times. There's even a number to call with complaints (☎ 0361-701621).

After Bali Taxi, standards decline rapidly. Some are acceptable, although you may have a hassle getting the driver to use the meter after dark. Others may claim that their meters are often 'broken' or nonexistent, and negotiated fees can be over the odds (all the more reason to tip Bali Taxi about 10%).

Taxis can be annoying with their constant honking to attract patrons. And men, especially single men, will find that some taxi drivers may promote a 'complete massage' at a 'spa'. Drivers will enthusiastically pantomime some of the activities that this entails. At the very least, insist that they keep their hands on the wheel.

LOMBOK

There are plenty of bemos and taxis around Mataram and Senggigi. In Lombok, the Blue Bird or **Lombok Taksi** (☎ 0370-627000) always use the meter without you having to ask (they are easier than Bali cab drivers in that way); but even so just check they have turned it on. The only place where you would need to negotiate a taxi fare is if you get in a taxi at Bangsal harbour (but not on the main road in Pemenang). See Surviving Bangsal, p287, for more details.

TOURS

Many travellers end up taking one or two organised tours because it can be such a quick and convenient way to visit a few places, especially where public transport is limited (eg Pura Besakih) or nonexistent (eg Ulu Watu after sunset). All sorts of tours are available from the tourist centres – the posh hotels can arrange expensive day tours for their guests, while tour companies along the main streets in the tourist centres advertise cheaper trips for those on a budget.

There is an extraordinarily wide range of prices for basically the same sort of tour. The cheaper ones may have less comfortable vehicles, less-qualified guides and be less organised, but the savings can be considerable. Higher priced tours may include a buffet lunch, an English-speaking guide and air-conditioning, but generally a higher price is no guarantee of higher quality. Some tours make long stops at craft shops, so you can buy things and the tour company can earn commissions for the tour operator. Tours are typically in an eight- to 12-seat minibus, which picks you up and drops you off at your hotel.

Tours can be booked at the desk of any large hotel, but these will be much more expensive than a similar tour booked at a travel agency with the price in rupiah. If you can get together a group of four or more, most tour agencies will arrange a tour to suit you; or you can easily create your own tour by chartering a vehicle.

Day Tours

The following are the usual tours sold around Bali. They are available from most hotels and shops selling services to tourists. Typically you will be picked up in the morning and along with other travellers at nearby hotels. You may then go to a central area where you are redistributed to the minibus doing *your* tour. Typically the operations are quite well organised.

Prices can range from 20,000Rp to 100,000Rp even if standards seem similar, so it pays to shop around.

Bedugul Tour Includes Sangeh or Alas Kedaton, Mengwi, Jatiluwih, Candikuning and sunset at Tanah Lot.

Besakih Tour Includes craft shops at Celuk, Mas and Batuan, Gianyar, Semarapura (Klungkung), Pura Besakih, and return via Bukit Jambal.

Denpasar Tour Takes in the arts centre, markets, museum and perhaps a temple or two.

East Bali Tour Includes the usual craft shops, Semarapura (Klungkung), Kusamba, Goa Lawah, Candidasa and Tenganan.

Kintamani–Gunung Batur Tour Takes in the craft shops at Celuk, Mas and Batuan, a dance at Batubulan, Tampaksiring and views of Gunung Batur. Alternatively, the tour may go to Goa Gajah, Pejeng, Tampaksiring and Kintamani.

Singaraja–Lovina Tour Goes to Mengwi, Bedugul, Gitgit, Singaraja, Lovina, Banjar and Pupuan.

Sunset Tour Includes Mengwi, Marga, Alas Kedaton and the sunset at Tanah Lot.

Other Tours

Some agencies, including **Suta Tours** (☎ 0361-465249; www.sutatour.com), arrange trips to see cremation ceremonies and special temple festivals, for around US$15. It may seem in poor taste to advertise for paying visits to a cremation, but good tour companies are sensitive about these occasions, and will ensure that their participants dress and behave appropriately. **Ubud Tourist Information** (Yaysan Bina Wisata; Map pp146-7; ☎ 973285; Jl Raya Ubud; ☒ 8am-8pm) organises simple yet effective cultural tours, especially around special religious events.

Lombok

Some companies organise day tours around Lombok from Bali, which cost US$100 or more and involve tearing through Senggigi and a few villages by minibus. A longer tour, with more time for sightseeing and relaxing, will be more expensive but more satisfying.

For a list of tours originating in Lombok, see p279.

TRANSPORT

Health Dr Trish Batchelor

CONTENTS

Treatment for minor injuries and common traveller's health problems is easily accessed on Bali and to a lesser degree on Lombok (see p360). But be aware that for serious conditions, you will need to leave the islands.

Travellers tend to worry about contracting infectious diseases when in the tropics, but infections are a rare cause of serious illness or death in travellers. Pre-existing medical conditions such as heart disease, and accidental injury (especially traffic accidents), account for most life-threatening problems. Becoming ill in some way, however, is relatively common. Fortunately most common illnesses can either be prevented with some common-sense behaviour or be treated easily with a well-stocked traveller's medical kit.

The following advice is a general guide only and does not replace the advice of a doctor trained in travel medicine.

BEFORE YOU GO

Pack medications in their original, clearly labelled, containers. A signed and dated letter from your physician describing your medical conditions and medications, including generic names, is also a good idea. If carrying syringes or needles, be sure to have a physician's letter documenting their medical necessity. If you have a heart condition ensure you bring a copy of your electrocardiogram taken just prior to travelling.

If you happen to take any regular medication bring double your needs in case of loss or theft. In most Southeast Asian countries, excluding Singapore, you can buy many medications over the counter without a doctor's prescription, but it can be difficult to find some of the newer drugs, particularly the latest antidepressant drugs, blood pressure medications and contraceptive pills.

INSURANCE

Even if you are fit and healthy, don't travel without health insurance – accidents do happen. Declare any existing medical conditions you have – the insurance company will check if your problem is pre-existing and will not cover you if it is undeclared. You may require extra cover for adventure activities such as rock climbing. If your health insurance doesn't cover you for medical expenses abroad, consider getting extra insurance – check Lonely Planet's **subwwway** (www.lonelyplanet.com) for more information. If you're uninsured, emergency evacuation is expensive – bills of over US$100,000 are not uncommon.

Find out in advance if your insurance plan will make payments directly to providers or reimburse you later for overseas health expenditures. (In many countries doctors expect payment in cash.) Some policies offer lower and higher medical-expense options; the higher ones are chiefly for countries that have extremely high medical costs, such as the USA. You may prefer a policy that pays doctors or hospitals directly rather than you having to pay on the spot and claim later. If you have to claim later, make sure you keep all documentation. Some policies ask you to call back (reverse charges) to a centre in your home country where an immediate assessment of your problem is made.

RECOMMENDED VACCINATIONS

Specialised travel-medicine clinics are your best source of information; they stock all available vaccines and will be able to give specific recommendations for you and your trip. The doctors will take into account factors such as past vaccination history, the length of your trip, activities you may be undertaking and underlying medical conditions, such as pregnancy.

Most vaccines don't produce immunity until at least two weeks after they're given, so visit a doctor four to eight weeks before departure. Ask your doctor for an International Certificate of Vaccination (otherwise known as the yellow booklet), which will list all the vaccinations you've received.

The World Health Organization recommends the following vaccinations for travellers to Southeast Asia:

Adult diphtheria and tetanus Single booster recommended if none in the previous 10 years. Side effects include sore arm and fever.

Hepatitis A Provides almost 100% protection for up to a year, a booster after 12 months provides at least another 20 years protection. Mild side effects such as headache and sore arm occur in 5% to 10% of people.

Hepatitis B Now considered routine for most travellers. Given as three shots over six months. A rapid schedule is also available, as is a combined vaccination with Hepatitis A. Side effects are mild and uncommon, usually headache and sore arm. Lifetime protection occurs in 95% of people.

Measles, mumps and rubella (MMR) Two doses of MMR required unless you have had the diseases. Occasionally a rash and flu-like illness can develop a week after receiving the vaccine. Many young adults require a booster.

Polio In 2002, no countries in Southeast Asia reported cases of polio. Only one booster required as an adult for lifetime protection. Inactivated polio vaccine is safe during pregnancy.

Typhoid Recommended unless your trip is less than a week and only to developed cities. The vaccine offers around 70% protection, lasts for two to three years and comes as a single shot. Tablets are also available, however the injection is usually recommended as it has fewer side effects. Sore arm and fever may occur.

Varicella If you haven't had chickenpox, discuss this vaccination with your doctor.

These immunisations are recommended for long-term travellers (more than one month) or those at special risk:

Japanese B Encephalitis Three injections in all. Booster recommended after two years. Sore arm and headache are the most common side effects. Rarely an allergic reaction comprising hives and swelling can occur up to 10 days after any of the three doses.

Meningitis Single injection. There are two types of vaccination: the quadrivalent vaccine gives two to three years protection; meningitis group C vaccine gives around 10 years protection. Recommended for long-term backpackers aged under 25.

Rabies Three injections in all. A booster after one year will then provide 10 years protection. Side effects are rare – occasionally headache and sore arm.

Tuberculosis (TB) A complex issue. Adult long-term travellers are usually recommended to have a TB skin test before and after travel, rather than vaccination. Only one vaccine given in a lifetime.

REQUIRED VACCINATIONS

The only vaccine required by international regulations is yellow fever. Proof of vaccination will only be required if you have visited a country in the yellow-fever zone within the six days prior to entering Southeast Asia. If you are travelling to Southeast Asia from Africa or South America you should check to see if you require proof of vaccination.

MEDICAL CHECKLIST

Recommended items for a personal medical kit:

- antifungal cream (eg clotrimazole)
- antibacterial cream (eg muciprocin)
- antibiotic for skin infections (eg amoxicillin/clavulanate or cephalexin)
- antibiotics for diarrhoea include norfloxacin or ciprofloxacin; for bacterial diarrhoea azithromycin; for giardiasis or amoebic dysentery tinidazole
- antihistamine – there are many options (eg cetirizine for daytime and promethazine for night)
- antiseptic (eg Betadine)
- antispasmodic for stomach cramps (eg buscopan)
- contraceptives
- decongestant (eg pseudoephedrine)
- DEET-based insect repellent
- diarrhoea treatment – consider an oral rehydration solution (eg Gastrolyte), diarrhoea 'stopper' (eg loperamide) and antinausea medication (eg prochlorperazine)
- first-aid items such as scissors, Elastoplasts, bandages, gauze, thermometer (but not mercury), sterile needles and syringes, safety pins and tweezers

- ibuprofen or another anti-inflammatory
- indigestion medication (eg Quick Eze or Mylanta)
- laxative (eg Coloxyl)
- migraine medication – take your personal medicine
- paracetamol
- steroid cream for allergic/itchy rashes (eg 1% to 2% hydrocortisone)
- sunscreen and hat
- throat lozenges
- thrush (vaginal yeast infection) treatment (eg clotrimazole pessaries or diflucan tablet)
- Ural or equivalent if you're prone to urine infections

INTERNET RESOURCES
There is a wealth of travel health advice on the Internet. For further information, **LonelyPlanet.com** (www.lonelyplanet.com) is a good place to start. The **World Health Organization** (WHO; www.who.int/ith/) publishes a superb book called *International Travel & Health*, which is revised annually and is available online at no cost. Another website of general interest is **MD Travel Health** (www.mdtravelhealth .com), which provides complete travel health recommendations for every country and is updated daily. The **Centers for Disease Control and Prevention** (CDC; www.cdc.gov) website also has good general information.

FURTHER READING
Lonely Planet's *Healthy Travel – Asia & India* is a handy pocket-sized book that is packed with useful information including pretrip planning, emergency first aid, immunisation and disease information and what to do if you get sick on the road. Other recommended references include *Traveller's Health* by Dr Richard Dawood and *Travelling Well* by Dr Deborah Mills – check out the website (www.travellingwell.com.au).

IN TRANSIT

DEEP VEIN THROMBOSIS (DVT)
Deep vein thrombosis (DVT) occurs when blood clots form in the legs during plane flights, chiefly because of prolonged immobility. The longer the flight, the greater the risk. Though most blood clots are reabsorbed uneventfully, some may break off

and travel through the blood vessels to the lungs, where they may cause life-threatening complications.

The chief symptom of DVT is swelling or pain of the foot, ankle, or calf, usually but not always on just one side. When a blood clot travels to the lungs, it may cause chest pain and difficulty in breathing. Travellers with any of these symptoms should immediately seek medical attention.

To prevent the development of DVT on long flights you should walk about the cabin, perform isometric compressions of the leg muscles (ie contract the leg muscles while sitting), drink plenty of fluids, and avoid alcohol and tobacco.

JET LAG & MOTION SICKNESS
Jet lag is common when crossing more than five time zones; it results in insomnia, fatigue, malaise or nausea. To avoid jet lag try drinking plenty of fluids (nonalcoholic) and eating light meals. Upon arrival, seek exposure to natural sunlight and readjust your schedule (for meals, sleep etc) as soon as possible.

Antihistamines such as dimenhydrinate (Dramamine) and meclizine (Antivert, Bonine) are usually the first choice for treating motion sickness. Their main side effect is drowsiness. A herbal alternative is ginger, which works like a charm for some people.

IN BALI & LOMBOK

AVAILABILITY & COST OF HEALTH CARE
Bali's best public hospitals are in Denpasar and Singaraja. In the first instance, foreigners would be best served in one of two

private clinics that cater mainly to tourists and expats.

BIMC (Map p93; ☎ 761263; www.bimcbali.com; Jl Ngurah Rai 100X; ⏱ 24hr) is on the bypass road just east of Kuta near the Bali Galleria and easily accessible from most of southern Bali. It's a modern Australian-run clinic that can do tests, hotel visits and arrange medical evacuation. It has an Indonesian doctor always on duty and other staff drawn from English-speaking countries. A basic consultation costs 540,000Rp.

International SOS (Map p93; ☎ 710505; www.sos-bali.com; Jl Ngurah Rai 505X; ⏱ 24hr) is near BIMC and offers similar services at similar prices. It too has English-speaking Indonesian doctors in the office who are linked to physicians in Australia and Japan.

At both these places you should confirm that your health and/or travel insurance will cover you. In cases where your medical condition is considered serious you may well be evacuated by air ambulance to top-flight hospitals in Jakarta or Singapore. Here's where proper insurance is vital as these flights can cost more than US$10,000.

In Kuta, Nusa Dua and Ubud there are also locally owned clinics catering to tourists and just about any hotel can put you in touch with an English-speaking doctor.

In more remote areas, facilities are basic; generally a small public hospital, doctor's surgery or *puskesmas* (community health care centre). Specialist facilities for neurosurgery and heart surgery are nonexistent, and the range of available drugs (including painkillers) is limited. Travel insurance policies often have an emergency assistance phone number, which might be able to recommend a doctor or clinic, or use its contacts to find one in a remote area.

Health care is not free on Bali, and you will get more prompt attention if you can pay cash up-front for treatment, drugs, surgical equipment, drinking water, food and so on. Try to get receipts and paperwork so you can claim it all later on your travel insurance.

In government-run clinics and hospitals, services such as meals, washing and clean clothing are normally provided by the patient's family. If you are unfortunate enough to be on your own in a Bali hospital, contact your consulate – you need help.

The best hospital in Lombok is in Mataram, and there are more basic ones in Praya and Selong. There are pharmacies in the main towns and tourist centres, but the choice of medicines is limited.

Self-treatment may be appropriate if your problem is minor (eg traveller's diarrhoea), you are carrying the appropriate medication and you cannot attend a recommended clinic. If you think you may have a serious disease, especially malaria, do not waste time – travel to the nearest quality facility to receive attention. It is always better to be assessed by a doctor than to rely on self-treatment.

Outside of tourist centres, buying medication over the counter is not recommended, as fake medications and poorly stored or out-of-date drugs are common. Check with a large international hotel for a recommendation of a good local pharmacy.

INFECTIOUS DISEASES
Dengue Fever
This mosquito-borne disease is becomingly increasingly problematic throughout Southeast Asia, especially in the cities. As there is no vaccine available it can only be prevented by avoiding mosquito bites. The mosquito that carries dengue bites day and night, so use insect avoidance measures at all times. Symptoms include high fever, severe headache and body ache (dengue was previously known as 'breakbone fever'). Some people develop a rash and experience diarrhoea. The southern islands of Thailand are particularly high risk. There is no specific treatment, just rest and paracetamol – do not take aspirin as it increases the likelihood of haemorrhaging. See a doctor to be diagnosed and monitored.

Hepatitis A
A problem throughout the region, this food- and waterborne virus infects the liver, causing jaundice (yellow skin and eyes), nausea and lethargy. There is no specific treatment for hepatitis A, you just need to allow time for the liver to heal. All travellers to Southeast Asia should be vaccinated against hepatitis A.

Hepatitis B
The only sexually transmitted disease that can be prevented by vaccination, hepatitis

B is spread by body fluids, including sexual contact. In some parts of Southeast Asia up to 20% of the population are carriers of hepatitis B, and usually are unaware of this. The long-term consequences can include liver cancer and cirrhosis.

Hepatitis E

Hepatitis E is transmitted through contaminated food and water and has similar symptoms to hepatitis A, but is far less common. It is a severe problem in pregnant women and can result in the death of both mother and baby. There is currently no vaccine, and prevention is by following safe eating and drinking guidelines.

HIV

HIV is a major problem in many Asian countries, and Bali has one of the highest rates of HIV infection in Indonesia. Official HIV figures in Indonesia are unrealistically low and it's believed the incidence of the disease will increase significantly unless hospital procedures are improved and safe sex is promoted. The main risk for most travellers is sexual contact with locals, prostitutes and other travellers – in Indonesia the spread of HIV is primarily through heterosexual activity.

The risk of sexual transmission of the HIV virus can be dramatically reduced by the use of a *kondom* (condom). These are available from supermarkets, street stalls and drugstores in tourist areas, and from the *apotik* (pharmacy) in almost any town (from about 1500Rp to 3000Rp each – it's worth getting the more expensive brands).

Japanese B Encephalitis

While a rare disease in travellers, at least 50,000 locals are infected each year. This viral disease is transmitted by mosquitoes. Most cases occur in rural areas and vaccination is recommended for travellers spending more than one month outside of cities. There is no treatment, and one-third of infected people will die while another third will suffer permanent brain damage. Highest risk areas include Vietnam, Thailand and Indonesia.

Malaria

The risk of contracting malaria on Bali is extremely low, but Lombok is viewed as a malaria risk area. During and just after the wet season (October to March), there is a very low risk of malaria in northern Bali, and a slightly higher risk in far western Bali, particularly in and around Gilimanuk. So, if you are staying in budget accommodation anywhere outside of southern Bali, or trekking in northern or western Bali during, or just after, the rainy season, you should consider taking antimalarial drugs and seek medical advice about this. However, it is not currently considered necessary to take antimalarial drugs if you are sticking to the tourist centres in southern Bali, regardless of the season – but confirm this with your doctor prior to departure.

If you are going to Lombok, or further afield in Indonesia, you should take preventative measures, even though significant progress has been made in reducing the number of mosquitoes on Lombok, and therefore the risk of malaria and other insect-borne diseases. The risk is greatest in the wet months and in remote areas. The very serious *Plasmodium falciparum* strain causes cerebral malaria and may be resistant to many drugs.

For such a serious and potentially deadly disease, there is an enormous amount of misinformation concerning malaria. You must get expert advice as to whether your trip actually puts you at risk. Many parts of Southeast Asia, particularly city and resort areas, have minimal to no risk of malaria, and the risk of side effects from the tablets may outweigh the risk of getting the disease. For most rural areas, however, the risk of contracting the disease far outweighs the risk of any tablet side effects. Remember that malaria can be fatal. Before you travel, seek medical advice on the right medication and dosage for you.

Malaria is caused by a parasite transmitted by the bite of an infected mosquito. The most important symptom of malaria is fever, but general symptoms such as headache, diarrhoea, cough, or chills may also occur. Diagnosis can only be made by taking a blood sample.

Two strategies should be combined to prevent malaria – mosquito avoidance, and antimalarial medications. Most people who catch malaria are taking inadequate or no antimalarial medication.

Travellers are advised to prevent mosquito bites by taking these steps:

- Use a DEET-containing insect repellent on exposed skin. Wash this off at night, as long as you are sleeping under a mosquito net. Natural repellents such as Citronella can be effective, but must be applied more frequently than products containing DEET.
- Sleep under a mosquito net impregnated with Permethrin.
- Choose accommodation with screens and fans (if not air-conditioned).
- Impregnate clothing with Permethrin in high-risk areas.
- Wear long sleeves and trousers in light colours.
- Use mosquito coils.
- Spray your room with insect repellent before going out for your evening meal.

There are a variety of medications available:

Artesunate Derivatives of Artesunate are not suitable as a preventive medication. They are useful treatments under medical supervision.

Chloroquine and Paludrine The effectiveness of this combination is now limited in most of Southeast Asia. Common side effects include nausea (40% of people) and mouth ulcers. Generally not recommended.

Doxycycline This daily tablet is a broad-spectrum antibiotic that has the added benefit of helping to prevent a variety of tropical diseases, including leptospirosis, tick-borne disease, typhus and meliodosis. The potential side effects include photosensitivity (a tendency to sunburn), thrush in women, indigestion, heartburn, nausea and interference with the contraceptive pill. More serious side effects include ulceration of the oesophagus – you can help prevent this by taking your tablet with a meal and a large glass of water, and never lying down within half an hour of taking it. Must be taken for four weeks after leaving the risk area.

Lariam (Mefloquine) Lariam has received much bad press, some of it justified, some not. This weekly tablet suits many people. Serious side effects are rare but include depression, anxiety, psychosis and having fits. Anyone with a history of depression, anxiety, other psychological disorder, or epilepsy should not take Lariam. It is considered safe in the second and third trimesters of pregnancy. It is around 90% effective in most parts of Southeast Asia, but there is significant resistance in parts of northern Thailand, Laos and Cambodia. Tablets must be taken for four weeks after leaving the risk area.

Malarone This new drug is a combination of Atovaquone and Proguanil. Side effects are uncommon and mild, most commonly nausea and headache. It is the best tablet for scuba divers and for those on short trips to high-risk areas. It must be taken for one week after leaving the risk area.

A final option is to take no preventive medication but to have a supply of emergency medication should you develop the symptoms of malaria. This is less than ideal, and you'll need to get to a good medical facility within 24 hours of developing a fever. If you choose this option the most effective and safest treatment is Malarone (four tablets once daily for three days). Other options include Mefloquine and Quinine but the side effects of these drugs at treatment doses make them less desirable. Fansidar is no longer recommended.

Rabies

Still a common problem in most parts of Southeast Asia. This uniformly fatal disease is spread by the bite or lick of an infected animal – most commonly a dog or monkey. You should seek medical advice immediately after any animal bite and commence post-exposure treatment. Having pre-travel vaccination means the post-bite treatment is greatly simplified. If an animal bites you, gently wash the wound with soap and water, and apply an iodine-based antiseptic. If you are not pre-vaccinated you will need to receive rabies immunoglobulin as soon as possible.

STDs

Sexually transmitted diseases most common in Southeast Asia include herpes, warts, syphilis, gonorrhoea and chlamydia. People carrying these diseases often have no signs of infection. Condoms will prevent gonorrhoea and chlamydia but not warts or herpes. If after a sexual encounter you develop any rash, lumps, discharge or pain when passing urine seek immediate medical attention. If you have been sexually active during your travels have an STD check on your return home.

Tuberculosis

While rare in travellers, medical and aid workers, and long-term travellers who have significant contact with the local population should take precautions. Vaccination is usually only given to children under the age of five, but adults at risk are recommended

HEALTH

pre- and post-travel TB testing. The main symptoms are fever, cough, weight loss, night sweats and tiredness.

Typhoid

This serious bacterial infection is also spread via food and water. It gives a high and slowly progressive fever, headache and may be accompanied by a dry cough and stomach pain. It is diagnosed by blood tests and treated with antibiotics. Vaccination is recommended for all travellers spending more than a week in Southeast Asia, or travelling outside of the major cities. Be aware that vaccination is not 100% effective so you must still be careful with what you eat and drink.

Typhus

Murine typhus is spread by the bite of a flea whereas scrub typhus is spread via a mite. These diseases are rare in travellers. Symptoms include fever, muscle pains and a rash. You can avoid these diseases by following general insect-avoidance measures. Doxycycline will also prevent them.

TRAVELLER'S DIARRHOEA

Traveller's diarrhoea is by far the most common problem affecting travellers – between 30% and 50% of people will suffer from it within two weeks of starting their trip. In over 80% of cases, traveller's diarrhoea is caused by bacteria (there are numerous potential culprits), and therefore responds promptly to treatment with antibiotics. Treatment with antibiotics will depend on your situation – how sick you are, how quickly you need to get better, where you are etc.

Traveller's diarrhoea is defined as the passage of more than three watery bowel-actions within 24 hours, plus at least one other symptom such as fever, cramps, nausea, vomiting or feeling generally unwell.

Treatment consists of staying well-hydrated; rehydration solutions like Gastro-lyte are the best for this. Antibiotics such as Norfloxacin, Ciprofloxacin or Azithromycin will kill the bacteria quickly.

Loperamide is just a 'stopper' and doesn't get to the cause of the problem. It can be helpful, for example if you have to go on a long bus ride. Don't take Loperamide if you have a fever, or blood in your stools.

Seek medical attention quickly if you do not respond to an appropriate antibiotic.

Amoebic Dysentery

Amoebic dysentery is very rare in travellers but is often misdiagnosed by poor quality labs in Southeast Asia. Symptoms are similar to bacterial diarrhoea, ie fever, bloody diarrhoea and generally feeling unwell. You should always seek reliable medical care if you have blood in your diarrhoea. Treatment involves two drugs; Tinidazole or Metroniadzole to kill the parasite in your gut and then a second drug to kill the cysts. If left untreated complications such as liver or gut abscesses can occur.

Giardiasis

Giardia lamblia is a parasite that is relatively common in travellers. Symptoms include nausea, bloating, excess gas, fatigue and intermittent diarrhoea. 'Eggy' burps are often attributed solely to giardiasis, but work in Nepal has shown that they are not specific to this infection. The parasite will eventually go away if left untreated but this can take months. The treatment of choice is Tinidazole, with Metronidazole being a second-line option.

ENVIRONMENTAL HAZARDS
Diving

Divers and surfers should seek specialised advice before they travel to ensure their medical kit contains treatment for coral cuts and tropical ear infections, as well as the standard problems. Divers should ensure their insurance covers them for decompression illness – get specialised dive insurance through an organisation such as **Divers Alert Network** (DAN; www.danseap.org). Have a dive medical before you leave your home country – there are certain medical conditions that are incompatible with diving and economic considerations may override health considerations for some dive operators in Southeast Asia.

Food

Eating in restaurants is the biggest risk factor for contracting traveller's diarrhoea. Ways to avoid it include eating only freshly cooked food, avoiding shellfish and food that has been sitting around in buffets. Peel all fruit, cook vegetables, and soak salads

---

DRINKING WATER

- Never drink tap water.

- Bottled water is generally safe – check the seal is intact at purchase.

- Avoid ice.

- Avoid fresh juices – they may have been watered down.

- Boiling water is the most efficient method of purifying it.

- The best chemical purifier is iodine. It should not be used by pregnant women or those people who suffer with thyroid problems.

- Water filters should also filter out viruses. Ensure your filter has a chemical barrier such as iodine and a small pore size, eg less than four microns.

---

in iodine water for at least 20 minutes. Eat in busy restaurants with a high turnover of customers.

Heat

Many parts of Southeast Asia are hot and humid throughout the year. For most people it takes at least two weeks to adapt to the hot climate. Swelling of the feet and ankles is common, as are muscle cramps caused by excessive sweating. Prevent these by avoiding dehydration and excessive activity in the heat. Take it easy when you first arrive. Don't eat salt tablets (they aggravate the gut) but drinking rehydration solution or eating salty food helps. Treat cramps by stopping activity, resting, rehydrating with double-strength rehydration solution and gently stretching.

Dehydration is the main contributor to heat exhaustion. Symptoms include feeling weak, headache, irritability, nausea or vomiting, sweaty skin, a fast, weak pulse and a normal or slightly elevated body temperature. Treatment involves getting out of the heat and/or sun, fanning the victim and applying cool wet cloths to the skin, laying the victim flat with their legs raised and rehydrating with water containing one-quarter of a teaspoon of salt per litre. Recovery is usually rapid and it is common to feel weak for some days afterwards.

Heat stroke is a serious medical emergency. Symptoms come on suddenly and include weakness, nausea, a hot dry body with a body temperature of over 41°C, dizziness, confusion, loss of coordination, fits and eventually collapse and loss of consciousness. Seek medical help and commence cooling by getting the person out of the heat, removing their clothes, fanning them and applying cool wet cloths or ice to their body, especially to the groin and armpits.

Prickly heat is a common skin rash in the tropics, caused by sweat being trapped under the skin. The result is an itchy rash of tiny lumps. Treat by moving out of the heat and into an air-conditioned area for a few hours and by having cool showers. Creams and ointments clog the skin so they should be avoided. Locally bought prickly-heat powder can be helpful.

Tropical fatigue is common in long-term expats based in the tropics. It's rarely due to disease and is caused by the climate, inadequate mental rest, excessive alcohol intake and the demands of daily work in a different culture.

Insect Bites & Stings

Bedbugs don't carry disease but their bites are very itchy. They live in the cracks of furniture and walls and then migrate to the bed at night to feed on you. You can treat the itch with an antihistamine. Lice inhabit various parts of your body but most commonly your head and pubic area. Transmission is via close contact with an infected person. They can be difficult to treat and you may need numerous applications of an antilice shampoo such as Permethrin. Pubic lice are usually contracted from sexual contact.

Ticks are contracted after walking in rural areas. Ticks are commonly found behind the ears, on the belly and in armpits. If you have had a tick bite and experience symptoms such as a rash at the site of the bite or elsewhere, fever, or muscle aches you should see a doctor. Doxycycline prevents tick-borne diseases.

Leeches are found in humid rainforest areas. They do not transmit any disease but their bites are often intensely itchy for weeks afterwards and can easily become infected. Apply an iodine-based antiseptic to any leech bite to help prevent infection.

Bee and wasp stings mainly cause problems for people who are allergic to them. Anyone with a serious bee or wasp allergy should carry an injection of adrenaline (eg an Epipen) for emergency treatment. For others pain is the main problem – apply ice to the sting and take painkillers.

Most jellyfish in Southeast Asian waters are not dangerous, just irritating. Some jellyfish, including the Portuguese man-of-war, occur on the north coast of Bali, especially in July and August, and also between the Gili islands and Lombok. The sting is extremely painful but rarely fatal. First aid for jellyfish stings involves pouring vinegar onto the affected area to neutralise the poison. Do not rub sand or water onto the stings. Take painkillers, and anyone who feels ill in any way after being stung should seek medical advice. Take local advice if there are dangerous jellyfish around and keep out of the water.

Parasites

Numerous parasites are common in local populations in Southeast Asia; however, most of these are rare in travellers. The two rules to follow if you wish to avoid parasitic infections are to wear shoes and to avoid eating raw food, especially fish, pork and vegetables. A number of parasites are transmitted via the skin by walking barefoot including strongyloides, hookworm and cutaneous larva migrans.

Skin Problems

Fungal rashes are common in humid climates. There are two common fungal rashes that affect travellers. The first occurs in moist areas that get less air such as the groin, armpits and between the toes. It starts as a red patch that slowly spreads and is usually itchy. Treatment involves keeping the skin dry, avoiding chafing and using an antifungal cream such as Clotrimazole or Lamisil. *Tinea versicolor* is also common – this fungus causes small, light-coloured patches, most commonly on the back, chest and shoulders. Consult a doctor.

Cuts and scratches become easily infected in humid climates. Take meticulous care of any cuts and scratches to prevent complications such as abscesses. Immediately wash all wounds in clean water and apply antiseptic. If you develop signs of infection (increasing pain and redness) see a doctor. Divers and surfers should be particularly careful with coral cuts as they become easily infected.

Snakes

Southeast Asia is home to many species of both poisonous and harmless snakes. Although you are unlikely to run into snakes on Bali or Lombok (you may come across the black-and-white stripy sea snakes in Lombok), assume all snakes are poisonous and never touch one.

Sunburn

Even on a cloudy day sunburn can occur rapidly. Always use a strong sunscreen (at least factor 30), making sure to reapply after a swim, and always wear a wide-brimmed hat and sunglasses outdoors. Avoid lying in the sun during the hottest part of the day (10am to 2pm). If you become sunburnt stay out of the sun until you have recovered, apply cool compresses and take painkillers for the discomfort. One per cent hydrocortisone cream applied twice daily is also helpful.

WOMEN'S HEALTH

Pregnant women should receive specialised advice before travelling. The ideal time to travel is in the second trimester (between 16 and 28 weeks), when the risk of pregnancy-related problems are at their lowest and pregnant women generally feel at their best. During the first trimester there is a risk of miscarriage and in the third trimester complications such as premature labour and high blood pressure are possible. It's wise to travel with a companion. Always carry a list of quality medical facilities available at your destination and ensure you continue your standard antenatal care at these facilities. Avoid rural travel in areas with poor transportation and medical facilities. Most of all, ensure travel insurance covers all pregnancy-related possibilities, including premature labour.

Malaria is a high-risk disease in pregnancy. WHO recommends that pregnant women do not travel to areas with Chloroquine-resistant malaria. None of the more effective antimalarial drugs are completely safe in pregnancy.

Traveller's diarrhoea can quickly lead to dehydration and result in inadequate blood flow to the placenta. Many of the drugs used to treat various diarrhoea bugs are not recommended in pregnancy. Azithromycin is considered safe.

In the tourist areas of Bali, supplies of sanitary products and brands that are familiar are readily available. In Lombok the major brand sanitary towels are not a problem to get hold of and are reasonably priced. Tampons, however, are like gold dust, they are hard to find and super expensive! Try and bring you own from home or stock up on them in Hero supermarket in Mataram or in the supermarkets in Senggigi. Tampax and Lillets are available.

Birth-control options may be limited so bring adequate supplies of your own form of contraception.

Heat, humidity and antibiotics can all contribute to thrush. Treatment is with antifungal creams and pessaries such as Clotrimazole. A practical alternative is a single tablet of Fluconazole (Diflucan). Urinary tract infections can be precipitated by dehydration or long bus journeys without toilet stops; bring suitable antibiotics.

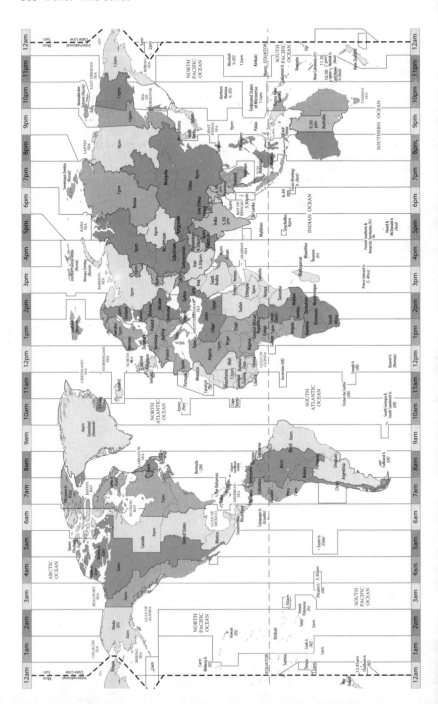

Language

CONTENTS

WHO SPEAKS WHAT WHERE?
Bali

The indigenous language, Bahasa Bali, has various forms based on traditional caste distinctions. The average traveller needn't worry about learning Balinese, but it can be fun to learn a few words. For practical purposes, it probably makes better sense to concentrate your efforts on learning Bahasa Indonesia.

Bahasa Indonesia is the national language, used in the education system and for all legal and administrative purposes. It's becoming more and more widely used, partly because of its official language status and partly because it serves as a lingua franca (a linking language), allowing the many non-Balinese now living and working on Bali to communicate – and avoid the intricacies of the caste system inherent in Bahasa Bali.

A good phrasebook is a wise investment. Lonely Planet's *Indonesian Phrasebook* is a handy, pocket-sized introduction to the language. The *Bali Pocket Dictionary* can be found at a few bookshops on Bali. It lists grammar and vocabulary in English, Indonesian, and low, polite and high Balinese.

English is common in the tourist areas, and is usually spoken very well. Many Balinese in the tourist industry also have a smattering (or more) of German, Japanese, French and/or Italian. A few older people speak Dutch and are often keen to practise it, but if you want to travel in remote areas, and communicate with people who aren't in the tourist business, it's a good idea to learn some Bahasa Indonesia.

Lombok

Most people on Lombok speak their own indigenous language (Sasak) and Bahasa Indonesia, which they are taught at school and use as their formal and official mode of communication. Apart from those working in the tourist industry, few people on Lombok speak English, and this includes police and other officials. English is becoming more widely spoken, but is still rare outside the main towns and tourist centres.

BAHASA BALI

The national language of Indonesia, Bahasa Indonesia, is widely used on Bali, but it isn't Balinese. Balinese, or Bahasa Bali, is another language entirely. It has a completely different vocabulary and grammar, and the rules governing its use are much more complex. It's a difficult language for a foreigner to come to grips with. Firstly, it isn't a written language, so there's no definitive guide to its grammar or vocabulary, and there is considerable variation in usage from one part of the island to another. Bahasa Bali isn't taught in schools either, and dictionaries and grammars that do exist are attempts to document current or historical usage, rather than set down rules for correct syntax or pronunciation.

Balinese is greatly complicated by its caste influences. In effect, different vocabularies and grammatical structures are used, depending on the relative social position of the speaker, the person being spoken to and the person being spoken about. Even traditional usage has always been somewhat arbitrary, because of the intricacies of the caste system.

LANGUAGE

The various forms of the language (or languages) and their respective uses are categorised as follows:

- **Basa Lumrah** (also called Biasa or Ketah) is used when talking to people of the same caste or level, and between friends and family. It is an old language of mixed origin, with words drawn from Malayan, Polynesian and Australasian sources.
- **Basa Sor** (also called Rendah) is used when talking with people of a lower caste, or to people who are non-caste.
- **Basa Alus** is used among educated people, and is derived from the Hindu-Javanese court languages of the 10th century.
- **Basa Madia** (also called Midah), a mixture of Basa Lumrah and Basa Alus, is used as a polite language for speaking to or about strangers, or people to whom one wishes to show respect.
- **Basa Singgih**, virtually a separate language, is used to address persons of high caste, particularly in formal and religious contexts. Even the Balinese are not always fluent in this language. It is based on the ancient Hindu Kawi language, and can be written using a script that resembles Sanskrit, as seen in the *lontar* (palm) books where it's inscribed on strips of leaf (see Lontar Books on p45). Written Basa Singgih is also seen on the signs that welcome you to, and farewell you from, most villages on Bali.

The different vocabularies only exist for about 1000 basic words, mostly relating to people and their actions. Other words (in fact, an increasing proportion of the modern vocabulary), are the same regardless of relative caste levels.

Usage is also changing with the decline of the traditional caste system and modern tendencies towards democratisation and social equality. It is now common practice to describe the language in terms of only three forms:

- **Low Balinese** (Ia), equivalent to Basa Lumrah, is used between friends and family, and also when speaking with persons of equal or lower caste, or about oneself.
- **Polite Balinese** (Ipun), the equivalent of Basa Madia, is used for speaking to superiors or strangers, and is becoming more widespread as a sort of common language that isn't so closely linked to caste.
- **High Balinese** (Ida), a mixture of Basa Alus and Basa Singgih, is used to indicate respect for the person being addressed or the person being spoken about.

The polite and high forms of the language frequently use the same word, while the low form often uses the same word as Bahasa Indonesia. The polite form, Basa Madia or Midah, is being used as a more egalitarian language, often combined with Bahasa Indonesia to avoid the risk of embarrassment in case the correct caste distinctions aren't made.

So how does one Balinese know at which level to address another? Initially, a conversation between two strangers would commence in the high language. At some point the question of caste would be asked and then the level adjusted accordingly. Among friends, however, a conversation is likely to be carried on in low Balinese, no matter what the caste of the speakers may be.

Bahasa Bali uses very few greetings and civilities on an everyday basis. There are no equivalents for 'please' and 'thank you'. Nor is there a usage that translates as 'good morning' or 'good evening', although the low Balinese *kenken kebara?* (how are you?/how's it going?) is sometimes used. More common is *lunga kija?*, which literally means 'where are you going?' (in low, polite and high Balinese).

BAHASA INDONESIA

Like most languages, Indonesian has a simplified colloquial form and a more developed literary form. It's among the easiest of all spoken languages to learn – there are no tenses, plurals or genders and, even better, it's easy to pronounce.

Apart from ease of learning, there's another very good reason for trying to pick up at least a handful of Indonesian words and phrases: few people are as delighted with visitors learning their language as Indonesians. They won't criticise you if you mangle your pronunciation or tangle your grammar and they make you feel like you're an expert even if you only know a dozen or so words. Bargaining also seems a whole lot easier and more natural when you do it in their language.

Written Indonesian can be idiosyncratic, however, and there are often inconsistent spellings of place names. Compound names are written as one word or two, eg Airsanih or Air Sanih, Padangbai or Padang Bai. Words starting with 'Ker' sometimes lose the 'e', as in Kerobokan/Krobokan.

In addition, some Dutch variant spellings remain in common use. These tend to occur in business names, with 'tj' instead of the modern **c** (as in Tjampuhan/Campuan), and 'oe' instead of the **u** (as in Soekarno/ Sukarno).

PRONUNCIATION

Most letters have a pronunciation more or less the same as their English counterparts. Nearly all the syllables carry equal emphasis, but a good approximation is to stress the second to last syllable. The main exception to the rule is the unstressed **e** in words such as *besar* (big), pronounced 'be-sarr'.

a	as in 'father'
e	as in 'bet' when unstressed, although sometimes it's hardly pronounced at all, as in the greeting *selamat*, which sounds like 'slamat' if said quickly. When stressed, **e** is like the 'a' in 'may', as in *becak* (rickshaw), pronounced 'baycha'. There's no set rule as to when **e** is stressed or unstressed.
i	as in 'unique'
o	as in 'hot'
u	as in 'put'
ai	as in 'Thai'
au	as the 'ow' in 'cow'
ua	as 'w' when at the start of a word, eg *uang* (money), pronounced 'wong'
c	as the 'ch' in 'chair'
g	as in 'get'
ng	as the 'ng' in 'sing'
ngg	as the 'ng' in 'anger'
j	as in 'jet'
r	slightly rolled
h	a little stronger than the 'h' in 'her'; almost silent at the end of a word
k	like English 'k', except at the end of a word when it's like a closing of the throat with no sound released, eg *tidak* (no/not), pronounced 'tee-da'
ny	as the 'ny' in canyon

ACCOMMODATION

I'm looking for a ...	*Saya mencari ...*
campground	*tempat kemah*
guesthouse	*rumah yang disewakan*
hotel	*hotel*
youth hostel	*losmen pemuda*

MAKING A RESERVATION

(for written and phone inquiries)

I'd like to book ...	*Saya mau pesan ...*
in the name of ...	*atas nama ...*
date	*tanggal*
from ... (date)	*dari ...*
to ... (date)	*sampai ...*
credit card	*kartu kredit*
number	*nomor*
expiry date	*masa berlakunya sampai*
Please confirm availability and price.	*Tolong dikonfirmasi mengenai ketersediaan kamar dan harga.*

Where is a cheap hotel?
Hotel yang murah di mana?
What is the address?
Alamatnya di mana?
Could you write it down, please?
Anda bisa tolong tuliskan?
Do you have any rooms available?
Ada kamar kosong?

How much is it ... ?	*Berapa harganya ... ?*
per day	*sehari*
per person	*seorang*
one night	*satu malam*
one person	*satu orang*
room	*kamar*
bathroom	*kamar mandi*
I'd like a ...	*Saya cari ...*
bed	*tempat tidur*
single room	*kamar untuk seorang*
double bedroom	*tempat tidur besar satu kamar*
room with two beds	*kamar dengan dua tempat tidur*
room with a bathroom	*kamar dengan kamar mandi*
I'd like to share a dorm.	*Saya mau satu tempat tidur di asrama.*

Is breakfast included?	*Apakah harganya termasuk makan pagi/sarapan?*
May I see it?	*Boleh saya lihat?*
Where is the bathroom?	*Kamar mandi di mana?*
Where is the toilet?	*Kamar kecil di mana?*
I'm/we're leaving today.	*Saya/Kami berangkat hari ini.*

CONVERSATION & ESSENTIALS
Addressing People

Pronouns, particularly 'you', are rarely used in Indonesian. When speaking to an older man (or anyone old enough to be a father), it's common to call them *bapak* (father) or simply *pak*. Similarly, an older woman is *ibu* (mother) or simply *bu*. *Tuan* is a respectful term for a man, like 'sir'. *Nyonya* is the equivalent for a married woman, and *nona* for an unmarried woman. *Anda* is the egalitarian form designed to overcome the plethora of words for the second person.

To indicate negation, *tidak* is used with verbs, adjectives and adverbs; *bukan* with nouns and pronouns.

Welcome.	*Selamat datang.*
Good morning.	*Selamat pagi.* (before 11am)
Good day.	*Selamat siang.* (noon to 2pm)
Good day.	*Selamat sore.* (3pm to 6pm)
Good evening.	*Selamat malam.* (after dark)
Good night.	*Selamat tidur.* (to someone going to bed)
Goodbye.	*Selamat tinggal.* (to person staying)
Goodbye.	*Selamat jalan.* (to person leaving)
Yes.	*Ya.*
No. (not)	*Tidak.*
No. (negative)	*Bukan.*
Maybe.	*Mungkin.*
Please.	*Tolong.* (asking for help)
Please.	*Silahkan.* (giving permission)
Thank you (very much).	*Terima kasih (banyak).*
You're welcome.	*Kembali.*
Sorry.	*Maaf.*
Excuse me.	*Permisi.*
Just a minute.	*Tunggu sebentar*
How are you?	*Apa kabar?*
I'm fine.	*Kabar baik.*
What's your name?	*Siapa nama Anda?*
My name is ...	*Nama saya ...*
Are you married?	*Sudah kawin?*
Not yet.	*Belum.*

How old are you?	*Berapa umur Anda?*
I'm ... years old.	*Umur saya ... tahun.*
Where are you from?	*Anda dari mana?*
I'm from ...	*Saya dari ...*
I like ...	*Saya suka ...*
I don't like ...	*Saya tidak suka ...*
Good.	*Bagus.*
Good, fine, OK.	*Baik.*

DIRECTIONS

Where is ...?	*Di mana ...?*
How many kilometres?	*Berapa kilometer?*
Which way?	*Ke mana?*
Go straight ahead.	*Jalan terus.*
Turn left/right.	*Belok kiri/kanan.*
Stop!	*Berhenti!*
at the corner	*di sudut*
at the traffic lights	*di lampu merah*
here/there/over there	*di sini/situ/sana*
behind	*di belakang*
in front of	*di depan*
opposite	*di seberang*
far (from)	*jauh (dari)*
near (to)	*dekat (dengan)*
north	*utara*
south	*selatan*
east	*timur*
west	*barat*
beach	*pantai*
island	*pulau*
lake	*danau*
main square	*alun-alun*
market	*pasar*
sea	*laut*

SIGNS	
Masuk	Entrance
Keluar	Exit
Informasi	Information
Buka	Open
Tutup	Closed
Dilarang	Prohibited
Ada Kamar Kosong	Rooms Available
Penuh (Tidak Ada Kamar Kosong)	Full (No Vacancies)
Polisi	Police
Kamar Kecil/Toilet	Toilets/WC
Pria	Men
Wanitai	Women

LANGUAGE

EMERGENCIES

Help!	Tolong saya!
There's been an accident!	Ada kecelakaan!
I'm lost.	Saya tersesat.
Leave me alone!	Jangan ganggu saya!
Call ...!	Panggil ...!
a doctor	dokter
the police	polisi

HEALTH

| I'm ill. | Saya sakit. |
| It hurts here. | Sakitnya di sini. |

I'm ...	Saya sakit
asthmatic	asma
diabetic	kencing manis
epileptic	epilepsi

I'm allergic to ...	Saya alergi
antibiotics	antibiotik
aspirin	aspirin
penicillin	penisilin
bees	tawon/kumbang
nuts	kacang

antiseptic	penangkal infeksi/antiseptik
condoms	kondom
contraceptive	kontrasepsi
diarrhoea	mencret/diare
medicine	obat
nausea	mual
sunblock cream	sunscreen/tabir surya/sunblock
tampons	tampon

LANGUAGE DIFFICULTIES

I (don't) understand.
   Saya (tidak) mengerti.
Do you speak English?
   Bisa berbicara Bahasa Inggris?
Does anyone here speak English?
   Ada yang bisa berbicara Bahasa Inggris di sini?
How do you say ... in Indonesian?
   Bagaimana mengatakan ... dalam Bahasa Indonesia?
What does ... mean?
   Apa artinya ...?
I can only speak a little (Indonesian).
   Saya hanya bisa berbicara (Bahasa Indonesia) sedikit.
Please write that down.
   Tolong tuliskan kata itu.
Can you show me (on the map)?
   Anda bisa tolong tunjukkan pada saya (di peta)?

NUMBERS

1	satu
2	dua
3	tiga
4	empat
5	lima
6	enam
7	tujuh
8	delapan
9	sembilan
10	sepuluh

A half is *setengah*, which is pronounced 'stenger', eg *stenger kilo* (half a kilo). 'Approximately' is *kira-kira*. After the numbers one to 10, the 'teens' are *belas*, the 'tens' are *puluh*, the 'hundreds' are *ratus*, the 'thousands' are *ribu* and 'millions' are *juta* – but as a prefix *satu* (one) becomes *se-*, eg *seratus* (one hundred). Thus:

11	sebelas
12	duabelas
13	tigabelas
20	dua puluh
21	dua puluh satu
25	dua puluh lima
30	tiga puluh
99	sembilan puluh sembilan
100	seratus
150	seratus limapuluh
200	dua ratus
888	delapan ratus delapan puluh delapan
1000	seribu

PAPERWORK

name	nama
nationality	kebangsaan
date of birth	tanggal kelahiran
place of birth	tempat kelahiran
sex/gender	jenis kelamin
passport	paspor
visa	visa

QUESTION WORDS

Who?	Siapa?
What?	Apa?
What is it?	Apa itu?
When?	Kapan?
Where?	Di mana?
Which?	Yang mana?
Why?	Kenapa?
How?	Bagaimana?

LANGUAGE

SHOPPING & SERVICES

What is this?	*Apa ini?*
How much is it?	*Berapa (harganya)?*
I'd like to buy ...	*Saya mau beli ...*
I don't like it.	*Saya tidak suka.*
May I look at it?	*Boleh saya lihat?*
I'm just looking.	*Saya lihat-lihat saja.*
I'll take it.	*Saya beli.*

this/that	*ini/itu*
big	*besar*
small	*kecil*
more	*lebih*
less	*kurang*
bigger	*lebih besar*
smaller	*lebih keci*
expensive	*mahal*
another/one more	*satu lagi*

Do you accept ...?	*Bisa bayar pakai ...?*
credit cards	*kartu kredit*
travellers cheques	*cek perjalanan*

What time does it open/close?	*Jam berapa buka/tutup?*
May I take photos?	*Boleh saya potret?*

I'm looking for a/the ...	*Saya cari ...*
bank	*bank*
church	*gereja*
city centre	*pusat kota*
... embassy	*kedutaan*
food stall	*warung*
hospital	*rumah sakit*
market	*pasar*
museum	*museum*
police	*kantor polisi*
post office	*kantor pos*
public phone	*telepon umum*
public toilet	*WC ('way say') umum*
restaurant	*rumah makan*
telephone centre	*wartel*
tourist office	*kantor pariwisata*

TIME & DATES

What time is it?	*Jam berapa sekarang?*
When?	*Kapan?*
What time?	*Jam berapa?*
7 o'clock	*jam tujuh*
How many hours?	*Berapa jam?*
five hours	*lima jam*
in the morning	*pagi*
in the afternoon	*siang*

in the evening	*malam*
today	*hari ini*
tomorrow	*besok*
yesterday	*kemarin*
hour	*jam*
day	*hari*
week	*minggu*
month	*bulan*
year	*tahun*

Monday	*hari Senin*
Tuesday	*hari Selasa*
Wednesday	*hari Rabu*
Thursday	*hari Kamis*
Friday	*hari Jumat*
Saturday	*hari Sabtu*
Sunday	*hari Minggu*

January	*Januari*
February	*Februari*
March	*Maret*
April	*April*
May	*Mei*
June	*Juni*
July	*Juli*
August	*Agustus*
September	*September*
October	*Oktober*
November	*Nopember*
December	*Desember*

TRANSPORT
Public Transport

What time does the ... leave/arrive?	*Jam berapa ... berangkat/datang?*
boat/ship	*kapal*
bus	*bis*
plane	*kapal terbang*

I'd like a ... ticket.	*Saya mau tiket ...*
one-way	*sekali jalan*
return	*pulang pergi*
1st class	*kelas satu*
2nd class	*kelas dua*

I want to go to ...	*Saya mau ke ...*
The train has been delayed/cancelled.	*Kereta terlambat/dibatalkan.*

the first	*pertama*
the last	*terakhir*
ticket	*karcis*
ticket office	*loket*
timetable	*jadwal*

Private Transport

Where can I hire a ...?	*Di mana saya bisa sewa ...?*
I'd like to hire a ...	*Saya mau sewa ...*
bicycle	*sepeda*
car	*mobil*
4WD	*gardan ganda*
motorbike	*sepeda motor*

ROAD SIGNS

Beri Jalan	Give Way
Bahaya	Danger
Dilarang Parkir	No Parking
Jalan Memutar	Detour
Masuk	Entry
Dilarang Mendahului	No Overtaking
Kurangi Kecepatan	Slow Down
Dilarang Masuk	No Entry
Satu Arah	One Way
Keluar	Exit
Kosongkan	Keep Clear

Is this the road to ...?	*Apakah jalan ini ke ...*
Where's a service station?	*Di mana pompa bensin?*
Please fill it up.	*Tolong isi sampai penuh.*
I'd like ... litres.	*Minta ... liter bensin.*
diesel	*disel*
leaded petrol	*bensin bertimbal*
unleaded petrol	*bensin tanpa timbal*
I need a mechanic.	*Saya perlu montir.*

The car has broken down at ...	*Mobil mogok di...*
The motorbike won't start.	*Motor tidak bisa jalan.*
I have a flat tyre.	*Ban saya kempes.*
I've run out of petrol.	*Saya kehabisan bensin.*
I had an accident.	*Saya mengalami kecelakaan.*
(How long) Can I park here?	*(Berapa lama) Saya boleh parkir di sini?*
Where do I pay?	*Saya membayar di mana?*

TRAVEL WITH CHILDREN

Is there a/an ...?	*Ada .....?*
I need a ...	*Saya perlu....*
baby change room	*tempat ganti popok kamar*
car baby seat	*kursi anak untuk di mobil*
child-minding service	*tempat penitipan anak*
children's menu	*menu untuk anak-anak*
disposable nappies/diapers	*popok sekali pakai*
formula	*susu kaleng*
(English-speaking) babysitter	*suster yang bisa berbicara Bahasa Inggris*
highchair	*kursi anak*
potty	*pispot*
stroller	*kereta anak/dorongan anak*

Are children allowed?	
Boleh bawa anak-anak?	

Also available from Lonely Planet:
Indonesian Phrasebook

LANGUAGE

Glossary

For food and drink terms, see Eat Your Words on p75.

adat – tradition, customs and manners
aling aling – gateway backed by a small wall
alus – identifiable goodies in an *arja* drama
anak-anak – children
angker – evil power
angklung – portable form of the *gamelan*
anjing – *dogs*
apotik – *pharmacy*
arja – refined operatic form of Balinese theatre/a dance-drama, comparable to Western opera
Arjuna – a hero of the *Mahabharata* epic and a popular temple gate guardian image

bahasa – language; Bahasa Indonesia is the national language of Indonesia
bale – an open-sided pavilion with a steeply pitched thatched roof
bale banjar – communal meeting place of a *banjar*; a house for meetings and *gamelan* practice
bale gede – reception room or guesthouse in the home of a wealthy Balinese
bale kambang – floating pavilion; a building surrounded by a moat
bale tani – family house; see also *serambi*
balian – see *dukun*
banjar – local division of a village consisting of all the married adult males
banyan – a type of ficus tree, often considered holy; see *waringin*
bapak – father; also a polite form of address to any older man; also *pak*
Barong – mythical lion-dog creature
Barong Landung – literally 'tall *Barong*'
Barong Tengkok – portable *gamelan* used for wedding processions and circumcision ceremonies on Lombok
baten tegeh – decorated pyramids of fruit, rice cakes and flowers
batik – process of colouring fabric by coating part of the cloth with wax, then dyeing it and melting the wax out; the waxed part is not coloured, and repeated waxing and dyeing builds up a pattern
batu bolong – rock with a hole
Bedaulu, Dalem – legendary last ruler of the Pejeng dynasty
bejak – bicycle rickshaw, no longer used on Bali or Lombok
belalu – quick-growing light wood
bemo – popular local transport on Bali and Lombok, traditionally a small pick-up truck with a bench seat down each side in the back; small minibuses are now also commonly used
bensin – petrol (gasoline)
beruga – communal meeting hall on Bali; open-sided pavilion on Lombok
bhur – world of demons
bhwah – world of humans
Bima Suarga – a hero of the *Mahabharata* epic
bioskop – cinema
bokor – artisans, who produce the silver bowls used in traditional ceremonies
Brahma – the creator, one of the trinity of Hindu gods
Brahmana – the caste of priests and highest of the Balinese castes; although all priests are Brahmanas, not all Brahmanas are priests
bu – shortened form of *ibu* (mother)
bukit – hill; also the name of the southern peninsula of Bali
bulau – month
bupati – government official in charge of a *kabupaten*
buruga – thatched platforms on stilts

cabang – large tanks with water stored for the dry season
camat – government official in charge of a *kecamatan*
candi – shrine, originally of Javanese design; also known as *prasada*
candi bentar – gateway entrance to a temple
caste – hereditary classes into which Hindu society is divided. There are four castes:three branches of the 'nobility' (*Brahmana*, *Ksatriyasa* and *Wesia*), and the common people (*Sudra*)
cendrawasih – birds of paradise
cengceng – cymbals
cidomo – pony cart with car wheels on Lombok
cucuk – gold headpieces

dalang – puppet master and storyteller in a *wayang kulit* performance
danau – lake
dangdut – pop music
desa – village
dewa – deity or supernatural spirit
dewi – goddess
Dewi Danau – goddess of the lakes
Dewi Sri – goddess of rice
dokar – pony cart; known as a *cidomo* on Lombok
dukun – 'witch doctor'; faith healer and herbal doctor
Durga – goddess of death and destruction, and consort of shiva
dusun – local divisions of a village

Dwarpala – guardian figure who keeps evil spirits at bay in temples

endek – elegant fabric, like *songket*, but the weft threads are predyed

Gajah Mada – famous Majapahit prime minister who defeated the last great king of Bali and extended Majapahit power over the island
Galungan – great Balinese festival, an annual event in the 210-day Balinese *wuku* calendar
gamelan – traditional Balinese orchestra, with mostly percussion instruments like large xylophones and gongs. Also called a *gong*
Ganesha – Shiva's elephant-headed son
gang – alley or footpath
gangsa – xylophone-like instrument
Garuda – mythical man-bird creature, the vehicle of Vishnu, a modern symbol of Indonesia and the name of the national airline
gendang beleq – like the Oncer dance; a war dance
gedong – shrine
gendong – street vendors who sell *jamu,* said to be a cure-all tonic
gili – small island (Lombok)
goa – cave; also spelt *gua*
gong gede – large orchestra; traditional form of the gamelan with 35 to 40 musicians
gong kebyar – is the modern, popular form of a *gonge gede*, and has up to 25 instruments
gringsing – rare double ikat woven cloth
gua – cave; also spelt *goa*
gunung – mountain
gunung api – volcano
gusti – polite title for members of the *Wesia* caste

Hanuman – monkey god who plays a major part in the *Ramayana*
harga biasa – standard price
harga turis – inflated price for tourists
homestay – small, family-run *losmen*

ibu – mother; also polite form of address to any older woman
Ida Bagus – honourable title for a male *Brahmana*
iders-iders – long painted scrolls used as temple decorations
ikat – cloth where a pattern is produced by dyeing the individual threads before weaving; see also *gringsing*
Indra – king of the gods

jalak putih – local name for Bali starling
jalan – road or street; abbreviated to *Jl*
jalan jalan – to walk around
jamu – a cure-all tonic; see also *gendong*

Jepun – frangipani trees
jidur – large cylindrical drums played throughout Lombok
Jimny – small jeep-like Suzuki vehicle; the usual type of rental car
Jl – *jalan*; road or street
jukung – see *prahu*

kabupaten – administrative districts (known as regencies during Dutch rule)
kahyangan jagat – directional temples
kain – a length of material wrapped tightly around the hips and waist, over a sarong
kain poleng – black-and-white chequered cloth
kaja – in the direction of the mountains; see also *kelod*
kaja–kangin – corner of the courtyard
kaki lima – food carts
kala – demonic face often seen over temple gateways
kamben – a length of *songket* wrapped around the chest at formal occasions
kampung – village or neighbourhood
kangin – sunrise
kantor – office
kantor imigrasi – immigration office
kantor pos – post office
Kawi – classical Javanese, the language of poetry
kebyar – a type of dance
Kecak – traditional Balinese dance, which tells a tale from the Ramayana about Prince Rama and Princess Siwi
kecamatan – subdistrict
kelod – opposite of *kaja;* the direction away from the mountains and towards the sea
kelurahan – local government area
kemban – woman's breast-cloth
kempli – gong
kendang – drums
kepala desa – village head
kepeng – old Chinese coins with a hole in the centre
kori agung – gateway to the second courtyard in a temple
kota – city
kras – identified baddies in an *arja* drama
kris – traditional dagger
Ksatriyasa – second Balinese caste
kuah – sunset side
kulkul – hollow tree-trunk drum used to sound a warning or call meetings

labuhan – harbour; also called *pelabuhan*
laki-laki – boy
lamak – long woven palm-leaf strips used as decorations in festivals and celebrations
lambung – long black sarongs worn by *Sasak* women; see also *sabuk*
langse – rectangular decorative hangings used in palaces or temples

Legong – classic Balinese dance

legong – young girls who perform the Legong

leyak – evil spirit that can assume fantastic forms by the use of black magic

lingam – phallic symbol of the Hindu god Shiva

lontar – specially prepared palm leaves

losmen – small Balinese hotel, often family-run

lukisan antic – antique paintings

lulur – body mask

lumbung – rice barn with a round roof; an architectural symbol of Lombok

madia – the body

Mahabharata – one of the great Hindu holy books, the epic poem tells of the battle between the Pandavas and the Korawas

Majapahit – last great Hindu dynasty on Java

makan Padang – Padang food

mandi – Indonesian 'bath' consisting of a large water tank from which you ladle cold water over yourself

manusa yadnya – ceremonies which mark the various stages of Balinese life from before birth to after cremation

mapadik – marriage by request, as opposed to *ngrorod*

mata air panas – natural hot springs

meditasi – swimming and sunbathing

mekepung – traditional water buffalo races

meru – multiroofed shrines in Balinese temples; the name comes from the Hindu holy mountain Mahameru

mobil – car

moksa – freedom from earthly desires

muncak – mouse deer

naga – mythical snake-like creature

ngrorod – marriage by elopement; see also *mapadik*

ngrupuk – great procession where *ogoh-ogoh* figures are used to ward of evil spirits

nista – the legs

nusa – island; also called *pulau*

Nusa Tenggara Barat (NTB) – West Nusa Tenggara; a province of Indonesia comprising the islands of Lombok and Sumbawa

nyale – worm-like fish caught off Kuta Beach, Lombok

Nyepi – major annual festival in the Hindu *saka* calendar, this is a day of complete stillness after a night of chasing out evil spirits

odalan – Balinese 'temple birthday' festival held in every temple annually (according to the *wuku* calendar, ie once every 210 days)

ogoh-ogoh – huge monster dolls used in the *Nyepi* festival

ojek – motorcycle that carries paying pillion passengers

oong – Bali's famed magic mushrooms

padi – growing rice plant

padmasana – temple shrine resembling a vacant chair; a throne for the supreme god Sanghyang Widhi in the manifestation of Siwa Raditya

pak – father; shortened form of *bapak*

palinggihs – temple shrines consisting of a simple little throne

pal ungan – shallow trough

panca dewata – centre and four cardinal points in a temple

pande – blacksmiths; they are treated somewhat like a caste in their own right

pantai – beach

pantun – ancient Malay poetical verse in rhyming couplets

paras – a soft, grey volcanic stone used in stone-carving

pasar – market

pasar malam – night market

pedanda – high priest

pekelan – ceremony where gold trinkets and objects throw into the lake

pelabuhan – harbour; also called *labuhan*

Pelni – the national shipping line

pemangku – temple guardians and priests for temple rituals

penjor – long bamboo pole with decorated end, arched over the road or pathway during festivals or ceremonies

perbekel – government official in charge of a *desa*

perempuan – girl

pesmangku – priest for temple rituals

pitra yadna – cremation

plus plus – a combined tax and service charge of 21% added by mid-range and top-end accommodation and restaurants

prada – cloth highlighted in gold and/or silver

prahu – traditional Indonesian boat with outriggers

prasada – shrine; see also *candi*

prasasti – *inscribed copper plates*

pria – man; male

propinsi – province; Indonesia has 27 propinsi; Bali is a propinsi, Lombok and its neighbouring island of Sumbawa comprise propinsi Nusa Tenggara Barat

puasa – to fast, or a fast

pulau – island; also called *nusa*

puputan – warrior's fight to the death; an honourable but suicidal option when faced with an unbeatable enemy

pura – temple

pura dalem – temple of the dead

pura desa – temple of the village for everyday functions

pura puseh – temple of the village founders or fathers, honouring the village's origins

pura subak – temple of the rice growers' association

puri – palace

puskesmas – community health centre

rajah – lord or prince

Ramadan – Muslim month of fasting

Ramayana – one of the great Hindu holy books, from which stories form the keystone of many Balinese dances and tales

Rangda – widow-witch who represents evil in Balinese theatre and dance

rebab – bowed lute

RRI – Radio Republik Indonesia; Indonesia's national radio broadcaster

RSU or RSUP – Rumah Sakit Umum or Rumah Sakit Umum Propinsi; a public hospital or provincial public hospital

rumah makan – restaurant; literally 'eating place'

sabuk – 4m-long scarf that holds the *lambung* in place

sadkahyangan – most sacred temples or 'world sanctuaries'

saka – Balinese calendar which is based on the lunar cycle; see also *wuku*

sampian – palm leaf decoration

Sasak – native of Lombok; also the language

sawah – individual rice field; see also *subak*

selandong – traditional scarf

selat – strait

sepeda – bicycle

sepeda motor – motorcycle

serambi – open veranda on a *bale tani,* the traditional Lombok family house

Shiva – the creator and destroyer; one of the three great Hindu gods

sinetron – soap operas

songket – silver- or gold-threaded cloth, hand-woven using a floating weft technique

subak – village association that organises rice terraces and shares out water for irrigation

stupas – domes for housing Buddha relics

Sudra – common caste to which the majority of Balinese belong

sungai – river

swah – world of gods

tahun – year

taksu – divine interpreter for the gods

tambulilingan – bumblebees

tanjung – cape or point

tektekan – ceremonial procession

teluk – gulf or bay

tiing – bamboo

tirta – water

toya – water

transmigrasi – government program of transmigration

trimurti – Hindu trinity

triwangsa – caste divided into three people (*Brahmana, Ksatriyasa* and *Wesia*)

trompong – drums

TU – Telepon Umum; a public telephone

tugu – lord of the ground

tukang prada – group of artisans who make temple umbrellas

tukang wadah – group of artisans who make cremation towers

undagi – designer of a building, usually an architect-priest

utama – the head

Vishnu – the preserver; one of the three great Hindu gods

wanita – woman; female

wantilan – large *bale* pavilion used for meetings, performances and cockfights

waria – female impersonator, transvestite or transgendered; combination of the words *wanita* and *pria*; see also *banci*

waringin – banyan tree; large shady tree with drooping branches, which root to produce new trees

warnet – *warung* Internet

wartel – public telephone office; contraction of *warung telekomunikasi*

warung – food stall

wayang kulit – leather puppet used in shadow puppet plays

wayang wong – masked drama playing scenes from the *Ramayana*

Wektu Telu – religion peculiar to Lombok, which originated in Bayan and combines many tenets of Islam and aspects of other faiths

Wesia – military caste and most numerous of the Balinese noble castes

WIB – Waktu Indonesia Barat; West Indonesia Time

wihara – monastery

WIT – Waktu Indonesia Tengah; Central Indonesia Time

wuku – Balinese calendar made up of 10 different weeks, between one and 10 days long, all running concurrently; see also *saka*

yeh – water; also river

yoni – female symbol of the Hindu god Shiva

Behind the Scenes

THIS BOOK

This is the 10th edition of Bali & Lombok. Tony Wheeler first covered the islands as part of his pioneering *Southeast Asia on a shoestring* in the mid-1970s. He then expanded and improved the coverage, with Mary Coverton, to create the first edition of Bali & Lombok in 1984. Alan Samagalski updated both Bali and Lombok for the 3rd edition and James Lyon assisted him for the 4th. James covered both the islands for the 5th and 6th editions. The 7th edition was updated by Paul Greenway, and James returned to update the 8th edition. Kate Daly updated the 9th edition, Bali. For this edition Ryan Ver Berkmoes (coordinating author) investigated the beaches, bars and spas of Bali (a tough job, but he was up for it), and Lisa Steer-Guérard explored the road a bit less travelled – Lombok.

Jocelyn Harewood wrote the Culture chapter, Dr Trish Batchelor wrote the Health chapter, Patrick Witton co-wrote the Food & Drink chapter and Philip Goad wrote the Contemporary Hotel Design boxed text in the Architecture chapter.

The following people contributed material and expertise to previous editions of this book: Michael Slovsky (arts and crafts), Kirk Wilcox (surfing) and Tony Wheeler (luxury hotels).

THANKS from the Authors

Ryan Ver Berkmoes I dedicate this book to Maria Donohoe, who taught me much about life and friendship. I'll miss her always.

While researching the book, I was ably assisted by Hanafi, who didn't drive me mad but drove me every other place and also explained the meaning of monkey business to me. Jeremy Allan was one of my better discoveries; before, during and after many Bintangs. Kerry and Milton Turner set a table that was a home away from home and Ove Sandstrom showed me a place I want to make my home. Many others who were generous with their time include John Hardy, Milo, Janet de Neefe, Mark Mickleford, Robbie Drexhage and the whole crew at the Vilarisi. Sara Marley first insisted I go to Bali more than 10 years ago and she was spot on.

I am indebted to the many excellent LP authors who preceded me to Bali and gave me such a solid foundation: Tony Wheeler, James Lyon, Paul Greenway, Kate Daly et al. At LP, the irrepressible Virginia Maxwell and Mary Neighbour got me going on the project. Marg Toohey proved to be a dream commissioning editor when events beyond Bali almost proved my undoing. Thanks to her for her professionalism, understanding and support. And thanks to the many others in-house who rallied to the cause then and now.

Finally thanks to Erin Corrigan for giving me a reason to find myself and find my way home.

Lisa Steer-Guérard Thanks to Barbara Lucas-Higgs at Bulan Baru for all her invaluable help and knowledge about Lombok; also Hassan for his skilful driving, guiding and interesting info on all things Sasak. Gratitude to Mal Clarbrough and Asmuni at NZAID-Rinjani Trek for their volcano expertise; as well as Marcus Stevens at Manta Dive in Trawangan for his map and top tips. To BJ, Guy Somers and Nadine McQueen at Fun Ferrari for

---

THE LONELY PLANET STORY

The story begins with a classic travel adventure: Tony and Maureen Wheeler's 1972 journey across Europe and Asia to Australia. There was no useful information about the overland trail then, so Tony and Maureen published the first Lonely Planet guidebook to meet a growing need.

From a kitchen table, Lonely Planet has grown to become the largest independent travel publisher in the world, with offices in Melbourne (Australia), Oakland (USA) and London (UK).

Today Lonely Planet guidebooks cover the globe. There is an ever-growing list of books and information in a variety of media. Some things haven't changed. The main aim is still to make it possible for adventurous travellers to get out there – to explore and better understand the world.

At Lonely Planet we believe travellers can make a positive contribution to the countries they visit – if they respect their host communities and spend their money wisely.

making the Gilis special; and Gilles Guérard for our Indonesian history. At LP, thanks to Marg Toohey for being such a star.

CREDITS

This title was commissioned and developed in Lonely Planet's Melbourne office by Marg Toohey. Cartography for this guide was developed by Corrine Waddell.

Coordinating the production for Lonely Planet were Damien Demaj (cartography), Kristin Guthrie (cover design), Quentin Frayne (language), and Andrew Weatherill and Charles Rawlings-Way (project management), with assistance from Marion Byass (cartography) and Wayne Murphy (back cover map).

Coordinating the production for Palmer Higgs Pty Ltd were Celia Purdey and Danielle De Maio (editorial), Sandra Goodes (layout design), William Ainger (photo researcher) and Selina Brendish (project management) and John Simkin (indexer), with assistance from Simon Longstaff (editorial production support).

THANKS from Lonely Planet
Many thanks to the travellers who used the last edition and wrote to us with helpful hints, useful advice and interesting anecdotes:

A Shinji Aikawa, Erik Albrecht, Gyllyan Anderson, Lisa Antoine, Chris Aubin, Mel Auston **B** Anne Barker, Silke Baron, John Barrett, Georgina Benison, Pamela Berghegen, Carol Betera, Robert Black, Wil te Boekhorst, Maarten Boersema, Jorma Bosch, Bruce Briscoe, Lynda Brown, Mark & Cielito Brownbridge **C** Brenna Callinan, Melissa Cambage, Kirsty Cambridge, Stephanie Carr, Jon Casey, HC Champion, Terry Chester, Marjo Chorus, Gerald Chung, Rosalyn Clare, Jim Cogan, Jonathan Copeland, Janet Croft, Hugh Cropp, Carlos da Cruz **D** Stuart Davie, Caroline Dawes, Arno De Jong, Paris Der-Krikorian, Graham Down, Pip Duncan, Angela Dunlop, Frank Dux **E** Jennifer Evans **F** Bill Faries, Steven Faulkner, Irene Finder, Carlos Flores Ramirez, Rosemary Forgan, Laurence Fougeras **G** Jenny Gardham, Jacques van Gelder, Lia Genovese, Erick Gilbert, Bob Giles, Tracey Goodwin, Jen Graf, Sharon Greenspan, Aziz Grieve, Nicolas Guyot **H** Rachel Kyoko Habgood, Clare Harris, Christina Hautzinger, Amelia Hawkins, Tracey Helman, Ingrid Hendrickx, Sophia Heng, Jo Holden, Eelko Hooijmaaijers, Aziza Horsham, Jerry Hoss, Caitlin Hu, Ingrid & Niklaus Hufenus, Jim Hulme, Alain Huvenne **I** Frank Igelhorst, Stephen Ireland **J** Kelly Janz, Philip Johnson, Pam Johnston, Brian Jones, Wally Jones,

SEND US YOUR FEEDBACK

We love to hear from travellers – your comments keep us on our toes and help make our books better. Our well-travelled team reads every word on what you loved or loathed about this book. Although we cannot reply individually to postal submissions, we always guarantee that your feedback goes straight to the appropriate authors, in time for the next edition. Each person who sends us information is thanked in the next edition – and the most useful submissions are rewarded with a free book.

To send us your updates – and find out about LP events, newsletters and travel news – visit our award-winning website: **www.lonelyplanet.com**.

Note: We may edit, reproduce and incorporate your comments in Lonely Planet products such as guidebooks, websites and digital products, so let us know if you don't want your comments reproduced or your name acknowledged. For a copy of our privacy policy visit www.lonelyplanet.com/privacy.

Francesca Joyce, Barbara Jung **K** Collette Kilty, James & Kasia Kilvington, Neile King, Sonja de Koning, Eric Kloor, Paul Kuck **L** Marie-Therese Le Roux, Jeanette Lebney, Michael Ledwidge, Mark Lee, Raymond Lim, Alena Liskova, Lorraine Lohan, Mun Kwong Loke, Harro Lotsy, Jerry Low **M** Laurent Maerschalk, Vladimir Marhefka, Daniel Martin, Cristina Mascolo, Errol Matena, Maree Matena, Jess Matthews, Grace Meadow, Alison Merridew, Allan Miles, Tetje Modersohn, David Moodie, Kathy Morf, Simon Mudge **N** Marc Neyt, Akane Nishimura **O** Dan Oberthier, Doug Odell **P** Hayley Patterson, Ian Patterson, Hadleigh Pedler, Sylvie Peron **R** Elin Ranum, Preethy Rao-Patel, Luisa & Felix Rayner, Viveka Ribbing, Kevin Richards, András Rohonyi, Stella van Room, Lado Rot **S** Geoffrey Saft, Lily Santoso, Ruth Schellenberg, Walter Schellenberg, Nicole Schlaegel, Johanna M Seipp, Fabienne Seydoux, Jerry Sharman, John Smilgin, Casey Smith, Petra Soder, Lucas Stalman, Dean Stephens, Joan Stokes, Louise Sullivan **T** Sami Takieddine, Tom & Donna Tate, Tutunt Tene, Mark Terry, Debbie Thurston, Rick Tjeerds, Grant Turnbull **V** Jarno Verboom, Bastiaan Vernier, Naylene Vuurens **W** Lizzie Warrener, Wendelin Weishaupt, Jay Weissman, David Welch, Frans van der Werf, Terry Williams, Matthew Willis, Danielle Wolbers, Robert & Leigh Wunce

Index

INDEX

INDEX

INDEX

INDEX

(handwritten notes)

10 = 6.93
100 = 69.31
1,000 = 693.17
10,000 = 6,931.70
100,000 SGD = 69,317

10 = 3.12
100 = 31.17
1,000 = 311.74
10,000 = 3,117.44
100,000 MYR = 31,174.41

1,000 = 12¢
10,000 = $1.17
100,000 = $11.72
1M IDR = $117 Cdn

MAP LEGEND

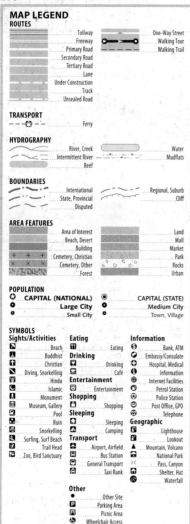

ROUTES

Tollway
Freeway
Primary Road
Secondary Road
Tertiary Road
Lane
Under Construction
Track
Unsealed Road

One-Way Street
Walking Tour
Walking Trail

TRANSPORT

Ferry

HYDROGRAPHY

River, Creek
Intermittent River
Reef

Water
Mudflats

BOUNDARIES

International
State, Provincial
Disputed

Regional, Suburb
Cliff

AREA FEATURES

Area of Interest
Beach, Desert
Building
Cemetery, Christian
Cemetery, Other
Forest

Land
Mall
Market
Park
Rocks
Urban

POPULATION

CAPITAL (NATIONAL)
Large City
Small City

CAPITAL (STATE)
Medium City
Town, Village

SYMBOLS

Sights/Activities
Beach
Buddhist
Christian
Diving, Snorkelling
Hindu
Islamic
Monument
Museum, Gallery
Pool
Ruin
Snorkelling
Surfing, Surf Beach
Trail Head
Zoo, Bird Sanctuary

Eating
Eating

Drinking
Drinking
Café

Entertainment
Entertainment

Shopping
Shopping

Sleeping
Sleeping
Camping

Transport
Airport, Airfield
Bus Station
General Transport
Taxi Rank

Other
Other Site
Parking Area
Picnic Area
Wheelchair Access

Information
Bank, ATM
Embassy/Consulate
Hospital, Medical
Information
Internet Facilities
Petrol Station
Police Station
Post Office, GPO
Telephone

Geographic
Lighthouse
Lookout
Mountain, Volcano
National Park
Pass, Canyon
Shelter, Hut
Waterfall

LONELY PLANET OFFICES

Australia
Head Office
Locked Bag 1, Footscray, Victoria 3011
☎ 03 8379 8000, fax 03 8379 8111
talk2us@lonelyplanet.com.au

USA
150 Linden St, Oakland, CA 94607
☎ 510 893 8555, toll free 800 275 8555
fax 510 893 8572, info@lonelyplanet.com

UK
72–82 Rosebery Ave,
Clerkenwell, London EC1R 4RW
☎ 020 7841 9000, fax 020 7841 9001
go@lonelyplanet.co.uk

Published by Lonely Planet Publications Pty Ltd
ABN 36 005 607 983